Lecture Notes in Artificial Intelligence 4133

Edited by J. G. Carbonell and J. Siekmann

Subseries of Lecture Notes in Computer Science

T0223678

Jonathan Gratch   Michael Young
Ruth Aylett   Daniel Ballin
Patrick Olivier (Eds.)

Intelligent Virtual Agents

6th International Conference, IVA 2006
Marina Del Rey, CA, USA, August 21-23, 2006
Proceedings

 Springer

Series Editors

Jaime G. Carbonell, Carnegie Mellon University, Pittsburgh, PA, USA
Jörg Siekmann, University of Saarland, Saarbrücken, Germany

Volume Editors

Jonathan Gratch
University of Southern California, Institute for Creative Technologies
13274 Fiji Way, Marina del Rey, CA, USA
E-mail: gratch@ict.usc.edu

Michael Young
North Carolina State University, Department of Computer Science
Box 8206, Raleigh, NC, 27695-8206, USA
E-mail: young@csc.ncsu.edu

Ruth Aylett
Heriot-Watt University, School of Maths and Computer Science
Edinburgh, E14 4AS, UK
E-mail: ruth@macs.hw.ac.uk

Daniel Ballin
British Telecom, Adastral Park, Ipswich IP5 3RE, UK
E-mail: daniel.ballin@bt.com

Patrick Olivier
University of Newcastle Upon Tyne, Information Research Institute
Newcastle upon Tyne NE1 7RU, UK
E-mail: p.l.olivier@newcastle.ac.uk

Library of Congress Control Number: 2006930617

CR Subject Classification (1998): I.2.11, I.2, H.5, H.4, K.3

LNCS Sublibrary: SL 7 – Artificial Intelligence

ISSN   0302-9743
ISBN-10   3-540-37593-7 Springer Berlin Heidelberg New York
ISBN-13   978-3-540-37593-7 Springer Berlin Heidelberg New York

Springer is a part of Springer Science+Business Media

springer.com

© Springer-Verlag Berlin Heidelberg 2006

Typesetting: Camera-ready by author, data conversion by Scientific Publishing Services, Chennai, India
Printed on acid-free paper   SPIN: 11821830   06/3142   5 4 3 2 1 0

Preface

The origin of the Intelligent Virtual Agents conference dates from a successful workshop on Intelligent Virtual Environments held in Brighton, UK at the 13th European Conference on Artificial Intelligence (ECAI'98). This workshop was followed by a second one held in Salford in Manchester, UK in 1999. Subsequent events took place in Madrid, Spain in 2001, Isree, Germany in 2003 and Kos, Greece in 2005. Starting in 2006, Intelligent Virtual Agents moved from being a biennial to an annual event and became a full fledged international conference, hosted in California.

This volume contains the proceedings of the 6th International Conference on Intelligent Virtual Agents, IVA 2006, held in Marina del Rey, California, USA from August 21–23. For the second year in a row, IVA also hosted the Gathering of Animated Lifelike Agents (GALA 2006), an annual festival to showcase the latest animated lifelike agents created by university students and academic or industrial research groups. IVA 2006 received 73 submissions from Europe, the Americas and Asia. The papers published here are the 24 full papers and 11 short papers presented at the conference, as well as one-page descriptions of posters and the featured invited talks by Brian Parkinson of Oxford University, Rod Humble of Electronic Arts, and Michael Mateas of the University of California, Santa Cruz and Andrew Stern of Procedural Arts.

We would like to thank a number of people who contributed to the success of this conference. First of all, we thank the authors for their high-quality work and their willingness to share their ideas. We thank the Program Committee, consisting of the editors and other distinguished researchers who worked hard to review the submissions and to select the best of them for presentation. A special thanks goes to the Local Organizing Committee and the student volunteers – Cornelis Versloot, Mark terMaat and Judith Siegel – for their efficient work on preparing and running the event. We would like to thank the University of Southern California's Institute for Creative Technologies for their overwhelming support, our sponsors for their financial support, and last but not least, we thank all those who attended the conference.

We invite readers to enjoy the papers in this book and look forward to the next Intelligent Virtual Agents conference.

June 2006

Jonathan Gratch
Michael Young
Ruth Aylett
Daniel Ballin
Patrick Olivier

Organization

Conference Chairs

Jonathan Gratch, University of Southern California, USA
Michael Young, North Carolina State University, USA
Ruth Aylett, Heriot-Watt University, UK
Daniel Ballin, Chief Technology Office, BT Group
Patrick Olivier, University of Newcastle Upon Tyne, UK

Local Organizing Committee

Jonathan Gratch, (Local Co-chair)
Michael Young (Conference Co-chair)
Patrick Kenny, University of Southern California
Mark Riedl, University of Southern California
Hyeok-Soo Kim, University of Southern California
Wenji Mao, University of Southern California
Anya Okhmatovskaia, University of Southern California
Byung-Chull (Leo) Bae, North Carolina State University

Invited Speakers

Brian Parkinson, Oxford University
Rob Humble, Electronic Arts
Michael Mateas, University of California, Santa Cruz
Andrew Stern, Procedural Arts

Program Committee

Jan Albeck
Elisabeth André
Norman Badler
Jeremy Bailenson
Joanna Bryson
Lola Cañamero
Justine Cassell
Marc Cavazza

Kerstin Dautenhahn
Angélica de Antonio
Fiorella de Rosis
Patrick Doyle
Patrick Gebhard
Marco Gillies
Randy Hill
Katherine Isbister

Mitsuru Ishizuka
Ido Iurgel
Martin Klesen
Stefan Kopp
Brigitte Krenn
John Laird
Jina Lee
James Lester
Craig Lindley
Brian Loyall
Steve Maddock
Suresh Manandhar
Andrew Marriot
Wenji Mao
Stacy Marsella
Alexander Nareyek
Anton Nijholt
Anya Okhmatovskaia
Ana Paiva

Catherine Pelachaud
Paolo Petta
John Pickering
Tony Polichroniadis
Helmut Prendinger
Stephen Read
Matthias Rehm
Mark Riedl
Daniela Romano
Zsófia Ruttkay
Mei Si
Matthew Stone
Demetri Terzopoulos
Daniel Thalmann
Kris Thórisson
David Traum
Hannes Vilhjálmsson
Spyros Vosinakis

Sponsoring Institutions

University of Southern California's Institute for Creative Technologies
The HUMAINE Network
Boston Dynamics, Inc.
Soar Technology, Inc.
Electronic Arts

Held in Cooperation with

The American Association of Artificial Intelligence (AAAI)
The European Association for Computer Graphics (EG)
The Association for Computing Machinery (ACM)
Special Interest Group on Artificial Intelligence (SIGART)
Special Interest Group on Computer Graphics (SIGGRAPH)
Special Interest Group on Computer-Human Interaction (SIGCHI)

Table of Contents

Embodied Conversational Agents

Characteristics of Nonverbal Behavior

Behavior Representation Languages

Generation of Nonverbal Behavior with Speech

IVAs in Serious Games

Cognition and Emotion I

Cognition and Emotion II

Applications of IVAs

Invited Talks

Posters

Why Fat Interface Characters Are Better e-Health Advisors

H.C. van Vugt, E.A. Konijn, J.F. Hoorn, and J. Veldhuis

Vrije Universiteit, Amsterdam

Abstract. In an experimental setting, we investigated whether body shape similarity between user and interface character affected involvement with, distance towards, as well as intentions to use the character in an e-health context. Users interacted with an interface character with the same (similar) or with a different (dissimilar) body shape as their own. Furthermore, the character's body shape was negatively valenced (heavier than ideal) or positively valenced (same as ideal). In contrast to what one might expect from stereotype research, users perceived non-ideal (fatter) characters as more credible and trustworthy than ideal (slim) characters. Especially users similar in body shape to a non-ideal character felt the least distant towards fatter characters. These users also preferred to *use* relatively fat characters over slim characters. Considering the increasing amount of overweight people in society, it seems most effective to design interface characters with bodies fatter than in current e-health applications, which often feature slim characters.

1 Introduction

Media such as the Internet can be used as powerful tools for health promotion and disease prevention [1; 2]. Interface characters may help to achieve these goals. Interface characters may significantly improve health care systems [3] by enriching the interfaces of e-health systems, and boost the use of such systems. A reason might be that they are likely to elicit social responses [cf. 4], such as trust, believability and involvement, especially when they display emotional communicative behaviors [5; 6; 7]. Some argue that users may even have the illusion of interacting with a human trainer or advisor, rather than just a tool [e.g., 8]. Indeed, research has shown that interface characters can be used effectively as virtual exercise trainers [5; 6], or diet advisors [8]. Hence, it is important to understand what factors contribute to involvement with and the willingness to use such characters in an e-health system.

In the present study, we are particularly interested in the effects of *similarity* between user and interface character on involvement and intentions to use the interface character system in an e-health context. In real life, similar others are often preferred over dissimilar others [9; 10; 11]. Apparently, people feel attracted to or comfortable with the similarity they perceive in others, which supports involvement. Hence, similarity is a core concept in involvement theory. Research has shown that people may compare themselves to interface characters as well, on dimensions such as gender [12; 13], face [14], ethnicity [15], and personality [16]. The overall pattern in these studies was that people preferred and had more positive attitudes towards interface characters that were

J. Gratch et al. (Eds.): IVA 2006, LNAI 4133, pp. 1–13, 2006.

similar to themselves. Similarity attracts. Users of e-health interface character systems may thus perceive similarities between their own bodies and those on screen, which may alter their involvement with and intentions to use the interface character system.

Although previous research suggests that similarity attracts, the effects of similarity are likely to be more complex. Research in interpersonal communication has shown that when similarity is paired with negative characteristics, such as unattractiveness or evidence of mental disturbance, people do *not* prefer similar, but dissimilar others [e.g., 16; 17]. Similarity to the *ideal* self is not only an important predictor of liking, but sometimes even more important than similarity to the current self [18; 19; 10]. This refers to 'wish identification' and 'role modeling' [cf. 1]. Although similarity to the ideal self seems influential, it is a relatively untouched research object in an interface character context [an exception is the work of Dryer, 16]. Therefore, this study addresses not only similarity to the current self, but also similarity to the ideal self. In the following sections, we will describe how the present study looks into the effects of ideal and non-ideal, similar and dissimilar interface characters in an e-health context.

2   Our Study

The comparison dimensions we focus on in our study is *body shape*, as this dimension allows us to study not only similarity effects but also the effects of ideal and non-ideal features. We refer to ideal body shapes as *positively valenced* body shapes and non-ideal body shapes as *negatively valenced* body shapes [cf. Frijda, 20].

In Western society, body shapes that are slim are perceived as ideal, that is, they are positively valenced. Slim and slender figures are consistently rated as more beautiful than heavier ones and are overrepresented in the media. In addition, fat people are generally attributed more negative characteristics such as laziness, sloppiness, and stupidity than slim people [e.g., 21]. The slim body ideal stirs the desirability of attaining a slim figure, which is especially true amongst women [22]. At present, 40 percent of the adult population in the Netherlands is overweight and 10 percent obese [23]. For children and adolescents, the situation is alarming as well: the percentage of overweight children doubled since the 1980's and accounts for approximately 12 percent [23]. All in all, we can conclude society is fattening up. Because of the current slim body ideal, fat people may perceive their body shape as non-ideal, or negatively valenced. In contrast, slim users may perceive their body shape as ideal, or positively valenced. Our study will provide an answer to the question whether fat users respond differently to equally fat interface characters (similar but negatively valenced) than to thin interface characters (dissimilar, but positively valenced). And, whether slim users respond differently to equally slim interface characters (similar and positively valenced) than to fat interface characters (dissimilar and negatively valenced). This may affect how interface characters should be designed as virtual exercise trainers or health advisors.

Based on the similarity-attracts paradigm, fat users are expected to be more involved with a fat interface character than with a thin interface character. However, when a fat user interacts with a fat interface character, the user may not simply be affected by body shape similarity. The similar feature may be perceived of as negative, or non-ideal, which may interfere with the similarity effect. In other words, when similarity is negatively valenced, it may not increase but decrease involvement. Furthermore, when a fat user interacts with a slim interface character, more involvement may be evoked, as the slim body shape is perceived of as an ideal, positive feature of dissimilarity (cf. wish identification). In other words, when dissimilarity is positively valenced, it may not decrease but increase involvement. Indeed, in another context Novak and Lemer [17] found that positively valenced dissimilarity may be preferred over negatively valenced similarity.

Furthermore, Taylor and Mettee [cf. 24] found that similar others are evaluated more positively in case of a positive (personality) feature than dissimilar others having the same (personality) feature. Hence, ideal similar others are preferred over ideal dissimilar others. In addition, similar others are evaluated more negatively in case of a negative (personality) feature than dissimilar others having the same (personality) feature. Hence, non-ideal similar others are disfavored over non-ideal dissimilar others. In sum, ideal similar others were preferred over ideal dissimilar others, and non-ideal similar others were disfavored over non-ideal dissimilar others. Thus, the valence of a feature (negative/positive) seems to interact with similarity in explaining liking. Previous research has shown that involvement with and liking a character are highly re-

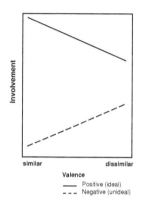

Fig. 1. Hypothesized (interaction) effects of similarity and valence on user involvement with an interface character

lated [25; 26]. Therefore, in line with the results of Taylor and Mettee, we hypothesize that similarity and valence interact in explaining user involvement with an interface character, as depicted in Figure 1. Our hypothesis runs as follows:

Hypothesis 1. Similarity and valence interact in explaining user involvement. People are more involved with positively valenced similar others, than with positively valenced dissimilar others. People are less involved with negatively valenced similar others, than with negatively valenced dissimilar others.

Because the *use* of technology is an important end-goal in human-computer interaction, we also study the effects of similarity on intentions to use the interface character, expanding on existing similarity research which mostly focused on the effects of (dis)similarity on attraction and liking. Traditional human-computer interaction literature argues that system use mainly depends on the usefulness and usability of the system [27]. More recent literature, however, suggests that the appearance of a system also affects system use [e.g., 28]. Whether similarity between user and interface character affects system use, resembling interpersonal communication, is unclear and, to our knowledge, not yet studied. Do fat users prefer to use slim virtual trainers, for example, because the slim body of the trainer motivates them to lose weight, or do they prefer to use equally fat virtual trainers, with whom they can identify? Therefore, we pose the following research questions:

Research questions. 1. Does similarity between a user and an interface character affect the user's intentions to use the interface character? 2. Does valence (positive or negative features) affect intentions to use the interface character? And, 3. which is the best predictor of use intentions?

Important to the present study is also that involvement and use intentions may be moderated by several other user perceptions [26; 29]. Users do not only perceive (dis)similarity, but they also perceive characters in terms of aesthetics (e.g., is the character attractive), ethics (e.g., is the character trustworthy and credible), realism (e.g., is the character fantasy-like or realistic) and affordances (e.g., is the character skillful). Such perceptions may be related to similarity. For example, users may perceive a similar character as more beautiful than a dissimilar character, especially when the dissimilar character is negatively valenced (e.g., fat). Similarity may thus boost aesthetic judgments, hence altering the level of involvement. In addition, stereotype research suggests a greater activation of negative traits upon exposure to fat than upon exposure to thin characters [cf. 'what is beautiful is good', 30], especially female ones [e.g., 31]. As a range of perceptions may influence users' involvement with and intentions to use an interface character, it is insightful to study them in coalition with similarity effects.

3   Method

3.1   Participants and Design

Participants in our experiment were 80 university students (24 males and 56 females; mean age = 23, SD = 7.8), with body mass index ratings (mean = 22 kg/m^2, SD = 3.8) categorized as normal according to the classification of the World Health Organization. They were paid 2.50 Euro for their participation.

A 2 (similarity: similar versus dissimilar) x 2 (valence: positive versus negative) factorial design was used to test our hypotheses (see Table 1). Assignment of participants to experimental conditions was slightly unbalanced because the 'similar and ideal' condition was created after data-collection. This condition existed of those participants that had indicated the *same* figure to represent their current and ideal body shape (see section 3.2).

Table 1. Similarity and valence conditions in the experiment

	Similar to current self	Dissimilar to current self
Positively valenced feature	similar and ideal (n = 17)	dissimilar but ideal (n = 14)
Negatively valenced feature	similar but non-ideal (n = 18)	dissimilar and non-ideal (n = 27)

Note 1. Positively valenced = ideal; Negatively valenced = non-ideal

The first dependent variable was user involvement. The second dependent variable was user distance. Involvement and distance are distinct experiences that do not comprise two ends of a single dimension; both can be experienced at the same time [25; 26; 32]. The third dependent variable was intentions to use the interface character. Last, we measured perceived aesthetics, realism, ethics, and affordances to study the effects of similarity and valence on these perceptions, and their effects on the dependents (see section 3.4).

3.2 Materials

An online, colored, and modernized version of the Figural Rating Scale [33, see Figure 2][1] was used to measure current, ideal, and non-ideal body shapes. Male participants were shown the male version (upper row) and female participants were shown the female version (lower row). The Figural Rating Scale is considered to be a reliable measure that is highly related to the Body Mass Index [33; 34; 35].

Fig. 2. Modernized version of the Figural Rating Scale

One of these figures was used as the interface character with which the participant would interact in the e-health context (see section 3.3). Both the interface character and the participant always had the same gender, as gender may influence similarity perceptions [e.g., 12; 13]. The interface character was called René (male) or Renée (female) and was positioned centrally on the screen and enlarged to occupy a large part of the computer screen (see Figure 3). René(e) had four different poses and the text was positioned right next to him/her.

Fig. 3. Screenshots of the René(e) software

3.3 Procedure

Participants were seated individually, in front of a computer in one of the cubicles in a research lab at the Free University in Amsterdam. The participants were welcomed by the computer and told that their data would be processed anonymously. Then, they were asked to enter their gender, age, weight, and length. After that, they were asked to rate

---

[1] Reprinted from [33] with permission.

their current-self (what figure do you look like best), their ideal-self (what figure do you want to look like), and their non-ideal-self (what figure do you not want to look like) on three Figural Rating Scales. These were subsequently asked on separate Web pages, ordered randomly to prevent order effects. Each time, participants had to push on the 'next' button to proceed to the next question. The computer did not allow unanswered questions.

Then, an interface character appeared on the screen. Approximately 1/3 of the participants saw an interface character that was equal to their current-self, 1/3 to their ideal self, and 1/3 to their non-ideal self. At the first page, the interface character asked for the participant's name, then introduced itself as either René (male) or Renée (female), and welcomed the participant. In the following pages, personal information was gathered and René(e) asked participants their opinion or knowledge on several health-related issues using closed-answered questions, sometimes preceded by small introductory texts For example, 'Three quarters of the Internet users, about 9 million people, search for information on health issues on the Internet. Do you search the Internet for health information?', or, 'How important is your health to you?'. At the end, René(e) told that 'Soon, you can ask me questions on the Internet about a healthy lifestyle! For example, do you eat healthy?' We used questions, as opposed to solely plain text, to ensure a relatively lively interaction between interface character and participant, and to get more insight into their (un)healthy behaviors (these results will be addressed elsewhere). After the interaction, that took about 6 minutes, the participant was asked to complete the user perception questionnaire, presented on several subsequent Web pages. After completing the questionnaire, participants were debriefed and dismissed.

3.4   Measurements

All measurements were taken by means of a questionnaire containing Likert-type scales. Each item was followed by a 6 point rating scale, ranging from 1 (do not agree at all), 2 (do not agree), 3 (barely agree), 4 (agree a little), 5 (agree), to 6 (fully agree). Items were presented in random order. For the present study, we used shortened versions of reliable scales used in previous experiments [26; 29]. Where necessary, items were adjusted to the purpose of the present study, the specific material, and the language use of the target group of participants (university students).

Reliability analyses ($N = 80$) were performed on each set of items concerning separate scales. Selection criteria were 1) an optimal contribution to Cronbach's alpha by showing little or no increase in the alpha level when the item was deleted, 2) a minimal inter-item correlation of .30, and 3) a minimum of 2 items per scale. Further, we checked whether items were normally distributed. Items that failed on one or more of these criteria were not included in the measurement scales used in subsequent analyses.

Similarity. We checked for the similarity manipulations by means of a *perceived similarity* scale. Tversky [36] showed that similarity is psychologically asymmetrical, which means that similarity ratings may depend on the referent. If the interface character is used as referent (I look like René) similarity ratings may be different than when the participant is used as referent (René looks like me). Therefore, our perceived similarity scale used items with different referents.[2] To avoid directing the participant in an affirmative answering mode [see 37], half of the similarity items were indicative and the other half counter-indicative (reverse-coded). The scale was reliable with a Cronbach's alpha of .93.

Valence. We also measured to what extent René(e) looked like the participant's *ideal* or not, using 2 items ('Do you want to look like me?'; 'Do you want to look differently than me?'). These *valence* items correlated significantly ($r = .68$).

Dependent measures. Involvement and distance were measured using 3 items each, based on [25]: Involvement ('Do you feel good about me?'; 'Do you feel involved with me'; 'Do you think it is pleasant to deal with me?', Cronbach's alpha = .72) and Distance ('Do you feel negatively about me?'; 'Do you feel distance between us?'; 'Do you think it is annoying to deal with me?'. Cronbach's alpha = .81). Use Intention, based on [26], was measured using 2 indicative ('Do you want to see me more often on the Internet?'; 'Do you want more information from me in the future?') and 3 counter-indicative ('Do you want to get rid of me'; 'Would you rather avoid me?'; 'Would you rather remove me from the screen?') items, Cronbach's alpha = .88.

Additional measures. In addition, we measured several other user perceptions[3]: perceived aesthetics (2 items, $r = .71$), perceived realism (2 items, $r = .64$), perceived affordances (5 items, Cronbach's alpha = .70), and perceived ethics (3 items, 1 item was left out of the scale because Cronbach's alpha increased substantially when the item was deleted. The remaining items, concerning trustworthiness and credibility, correlated significantly with $r = .62$). Finally, questions asked for personal information about the participants: the participant's gender, age, weight, length, computer experience, ethnicity, education, and body shape satisfaction.

4   Results

Preliminary analyses. For each item, outliers were replaced by the mean of the remaining values. Further, four participants had outliers on five or more items of various scales. These participants were regarded as unreliable and were disregarded in subsequent analyses.

We assessed the effectiveness of our manipulations of similarity (similar versus dissimilar body shape) and valence (ideal versus non-ideal body shape) by performing a MANOVA with perceived similarity and perceived valence as dependents. The tests of between-subject effects revealed a significant effect of the similarity conditions on similarity perceptions in accordance with our intentions ($F(1, 72) = 14.15$; $p < .001$, partial $\eta^2 = .16$; similar to current body shape $M = 3.1$, $SD = .87$; dissimilar to current body shape $M = 2.2$, $SD = .96$). Furthermore, there was a significant effect of the valence conditions on valence perceptions (ideal-non-ideal) into the right direction ($F(1, 72) = 18.79$, $p < .001$, partial $\eta^2 = .21$; ideal body shape $M = 3.2$, $SD = .89$; non-ideal body shape $M = 2.2$, $SD = 1.0$). These effects thus supported our manipulation aims.

---

[2] In the first set of items, the participant was the referent (e.g., 'Do you think I am like you?'). In the second set, the interface character was the referent (e.g., 'Do you think you are like me?'). In the third set, there was no explicit referent (e.g., 'Do you think we resemble each other?').

[3] Only scales relevant to the present paper are presented.

Table 2. The effects of similarity, valence, perceived aesthetics, ethics, realism, and affordances on involvement, distance and use intentions

Source	Dependents	df	F	partial η^2	p
Main effects					
Similarity (Between-Ss factor)	multivariate	(3,58)	.54	.03	.659
Valence (Between-Ss factor)	multivariate	(3,58)	.32	.02	.809
Affordances	multivariate	(3,58)	.60	.03	.621
Aesthetics	multivariate	(3,58)	1.47	.07	.232
Ethics	multivariate	(3,58)	4.30	.18	.008*
	involvement	(1, 60)	10.45	.15	.002*
	distance	(1, 60)	2.90	.05	.094
	use intentions	(1, 60)	8.47	.12	.005*
Realism	multivariate	(3,58)	2.45	.11	.073
	involvement	(1, 60)	4.80	.07	.032*
	distance	(1, 60)	5.52	.08	.022*
	use intentions	(1, 60)	2.05	.03	.157
2-way interactions					
Similarity*Ethics	multivariate	(3,58)	3.22	.14	.029*
	involvement	(1, 60)	1.09	.02	.301
	distance	(1, 60)	9.46	.14	.003*
	use intentions	(1, 60)	5.08	.08	.028*
Valence*Ethics	multivariate	(3,58)	2.80	.13	.048*
	involvement	(1, 60)	.74	.01	.394
	distance	(1, 60)	4.29	.07	.043*
	use intentions	(1, 60)	2.66	.04	.108

Note 2. A MANOVA was performed that revealed both multivariate and univariate effects. Only if the multivariate test showed (marginally) significant results (indicated by *), the univariate effects are given to distinguish between effects on involvement, distance, and use intentions. In addition, only those 2-way interaction effects are shown that were significant.

Main analyses. To test the hypothesis and inspect the research question, a MANOVA was conducted with similarity (similar versus dissimilar) and valence (positive versus negative) as the between-subject factors. The dependent variables were use intentions, involvement, and distance. In addition, perceived aesthetics, ethics, realism and affordances were included as covariates. The multivariate test showed no main effects of the factor similarity and valence, nor of perceived affordances and aesthetics on the dependents (see Table 2). Yet, a main effect was found of perceived ethics and perceived realism on the dependents. In addition, 2-way interaction effects were found of similarity and ethics, and of valence and ethics on the dependents.

Univariate tests confirmed the obtained multivariate results. More specifically, we found a significant main effect of perceived realism on involvement and distance. The more participants perceived the interface character as realistic, the more involvement and the less distance was evoked. In addition, univariate tests showed a significant effect of perceived ethics on involvement and use intentions. The more participants perceived the interface character as ethically good (that is, trustworthy and credible) the more they felt involved with the character, and the more they wanted to use the character.

Furthermore, the 2-way interaction effects showed that the influence of perceived ethics on distance and on use intentions (see Figure 4) was *stronger* for similar than for dissimilar characters. Low perceptions of ethics evoked more distance in the similar than in the dissimilar condition. High perceptions of ethics evoked less distance in the similar than in the dissimilar condition. In addition, the influence of perceived ethics on involvement was stronger for negatively valenced (fat) than positively valenced (slim) characters. In general, low perceptions of ethics evoked more distance in the negatively valenced than in the positively valenced condition. High perceptions of ethics evoked less distance in the negatively valenced than in the positively valenced condition.

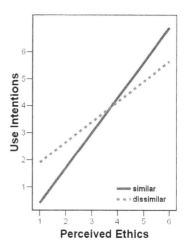

Fig. 4. The effect of perceived ethics on use intentions in the similar and dissimilar conditions

Further analyses showed that negatively valenced (fat) characters were perceived as more realistic than positively valenced (slim) characters (negative: $M = 3.9$, $SD = 1.2$; positive: $M = 3.3$, $SD = .95$; $F(1,76) = 4.48$, p $<.038$, partial $\eta^2 = .06$). They were also perceived as ethically better than positively valenced characters (negative: $M = 3.7$, $SD = .89$); positive: $M = 3.2$, $SD = .77$; $F(1,76) = 5.44$, p $<.023$, partial $\eta^2 = .07$).

5   Conclusion and Discussion

The expected effects of similarity and valence on user responses remained absent. Interestingly, however, perceived ethics (trustworthiness and credibility) was most decisive for user responses. Negatively valenced (fat) interface characters were perceived of as *better* (trustworthy and credible) and more realistic than the positively valenced (slim) interface characters, even though slim interface characters were perceived of as more 'ideal' in terms of body shape. As a result, users felt most involved with, and least distant to the fat characters. They also wanted to use these fat characters more than slim ones. Characters perceived as highly trustworthy and credible led to less distance and evoked stronger use intentions in users similar to the character than to users dissimilar to the character (and vice versa). Last, use intentions were strongest when users were similar in body shape to a non-ideal character.

Yet, an important target group of e-health systems is the increasing number of overweight people. In such systems, virtual health advisors often have an ideal thin body shape, probably set as an example as something to strive for. However, the results of the present study suggest that potential users of such e-health systems would be better off with more similar advisors in terms of their body shape, that is, fatter ones. The slim characters in the present study were perceived as less trustworthy and less credible. Therefore, the use of fatter characters will probably increase the trust that users have in the interface characters. As a result, user distance towards the advisor will decrease and users will probably tend to use the advisor more often. This is precisely what e-health systems designers strive for. It should be noted, however, that the present study examined the *intention* to use the advisor but did not assess participant's actual efforts to use the character again. Although intentions to use and actual use are highly related [27], future research should also include measures of actual use.

The appearance of the interface character in terms of perceived realism further contributed to user's involvement and distance. That is, the more real the users perceived the character, the more users felt involved with the interface character, and the less users felt distant to the interface character. This is in line with the vast amount of literature that points at the advantages of realistic interface characters above unrealistic ones [e.g., 25]. However, that *fat* characters were perceived as more trustworthy and credible than slim characters is inconsistent with stereotype theory. Stereotype theory predicts that more negative traits are assigned to fat than to slim others [e.g., 21]. Apparently, stereotype theory does not hold in all contexts. In specific contexts, like in our study, specific features may counteract stereotype theory. For example, if relevant to a particular context (here health), people may attribute more positive traits (trust, credibility) to the anti-stereotype (here the fatter) interface character than to the stereotype (slim) interface character. Perhaps, users expect a better understanding for health problems from a fat than from a slim e-health advisor. You believe an advisor who tells you that being fat is no fun better when the advisor is fat himself - s/he knows what s/he is talking about. The slim, athletic gym instructor who jumps around telling you that being fat is no fun can be easily dismissed - what does s/he know?

Thus, the present study showed that trust in online health advice is influenced by the look and feel of the character on the Web site. In a similar vein, [38; 39] showed that visual Web site design affects user's trust, next to the quality of information, the branding of the site, the presence of trusted logos, and personalization of the advice to the individual. Persuasion studies [40] showed that both attractiveness, credibility and trustworthiness affect the persuasiveness of messages. The present study further suggests that in e-health advice systems, attractiveness is less important than credibility and trustworthiness (i.e. perceived ethics). This is consistent with previous research on media characters, in which perceived ethics was also the best predictor of engagement with the character [25].

There is a large variation in e-health Web sites, and online advice may take different forms [38]. Therefore, further studies should investigate to which extent the found effect may hold within various contexts. For example, we expect that trust will contribute to user responses (e.g., engagement, use intentions) in online advice systems (e.g., on health, travel, online transactions) and in different e-health systems [c.f. 38]. However, with respect to systems used for entertainment purposes, trust might be less important. Effects of similarity between interface character and user as well as effects of the attractiveness of the interface character might be more decisive for engagement [cf. 26] and/or use intentions in an entertainment context.

In our study, similarity merely raised null effects. Null findings might have many reasons. A plausible reason for the null effect of similarity might be that participants in our sample showed little variance in perceived similarity. Perceived similarity ratings showed that participants felt more *dis*similar than similar in all conditions, although perceptions of similarity differed significantly between the conditions. Other research did find similarity effects on other dimensions such as facial similarity [e.g. 14] and personality similarity [e.g. 16]. As various studies show the complexity of user responses to interface characters [29; 26], it is of value in future similarity studies to measure a range of user perceptions regarding the interface character in order to better understand user responses to interface characters.

Finally, most participants in the present study had a normal to thin posture, and only a few were overweight whereas none were obese. In that sense, the sample was not a representative reflection of the Dutch society (counting approximately 40% overweight). In our next study, we plan to address more overweight participants by playing the online version of the René(e) software on a popular Web site with a more general audience. Participants will be drawn from the visitors of the Web site. We will then retest and refine our hypotheses. The results of future studies may reveal more unexpected implications for the design of persuasive interface character systems in the e-health domain, just like the present study did.

Acknowledgments

We are grateful to the Faculty of Social Sciences and the Faculty of Sciences, Vrije Universiteit in Amsterdam, who granted a 4-year research track (VUBIS) to the first author. We would like to thank Erik Kruithof for implementing the René(e) software.

Bibliography

[1] Bandura, A.: Social cognitive theory of mass communication. Media Psychology **3**(3) (2001) 265–299
[2] Morris, A.M., Katzman, D.K.: The impact of the media on eating disorders in children and adolescents. Paediatrics and Child Health **8**(5) (2003) 287–289
[3] Prendinger, H., Ishizuka, M.: What affective computing and life-like character technology can do for tele-home health care. Online Workshop Proceedings on HCI and Homecare: Connecting Families and Clinicians, in conjunction with CHI-04 (2004)
[4] Louwerse, M.M., Graesser, A.C., Lu, S., Mitchell, H.H.: Social cues in animated conversational agents. Applied Cognitive Psychology **19**(6) (2005) 693–704
[5] Bickmore, T., Gruber, A., Picard, R.W.: Establishing the computer-patient working alliance in automated health behavior change interventions. Patient Educational Counseling **59**(1) (2005) 21–30
[6] Bickmore, T., Caruso, L., Clough-Gorr, K., Heeren, T.: 'its just like you talk to a friend'. relational agents for older adults. Interacting with Computers (in press)
[7] Bates, J.: The role of emotion in believable agents. Communications of the ACM **37**(7) (1994) 122–125
[8] De Rosis, F., Novielli, N., Carofiglio, V., Cavalluzzi, A., De Carolis, B.: User modeling and adaptation in health promotion dialogs with an animated character. Journal of Biomedical Informatics (in press)
[9] Byrne, D.: The attraction paradigm. Academic (1971)

[10] Klohnen, E.C., Luo, S.: Interpersonal attraction and personality: what is attractive–self similarity, ideal similarity, complementarity or attachment security? Journal of Social and Personality Psychology **85**(4) (2003) 709–722

[11] Cialdini, R.B.: Influence: Science and practice. 4th edn. Harper Collins (2001)

[12] Nowak, K.L., Rauh, C.: The influence of the avatar on online perceptions of anthropomorphism, androgyny, credibility, homophily, and attraction. Journal of Computer-Mediated Communication **11**(1) (2005) article 8

[13] Guadagno, R.E., Blascovich, J., Bailenson, J.N., McCall, C.: Virtual humans and persuasion: the effects of agency and behavioural realism (2006) To appear in media psychology.

[14] Bailenson, J.N., Beall, A.C., Blascovich, J., Raimundo, M., Weisbuch, M.: Intelligent agents who wear your face: Users' reactions to the virtual self. In: Proceedings of IVA '01, Springer-Verlag (2001) 86–99

[15] Nass, C., Moon, Y.: Machines and mindlessness: Social responses to computers. Journal of social issues **56**(1) (2000) 81–103

[16] Dryer, D.C.: Getting personal with computers: How to design personalities for agents. Applied Artificial Intelligence **13**(3) (1999) 273–295

[17] Novak, D.W., Lemer, M.: Rejection as a consequence of perceived similarity. Journal of Personality and Social Psychology **9**(1) (1968) 147–152

[18] Wetzel, C.G., Insko, C.A.: The similarity-attraction relationship: Is there an ideal one? Journal of Experimental Social Psychology **18**(9) (1982) 253276

[19] LaPrelle, J., Hoyle, R.H., Insko, C.A., Bernthal, P.: Interpersonal attraction and descriptions of the traits of others: Ideal similarity, self similarity, and liking. Journal of Research in Personality **24** (1990) 216-240

[20] Frijda, N.: The laws of emotion. American Psychologist **43**(5) (1988) 349–58

[21] Puhl, R., Brownell, K.: Bias, discrimination and obesity. Obesity Research **9** (2001) 788805

[22] Baumann, E.: The mass media's role in causing eating disorders: Complex interdependencies instead of direct media effects (2005) ICA'05, New York.

[23] Visscher, T.L., Kromhout, D., Seidell, J.C.: Long-term and recent time trends in the prevalence of obesity among Dutch men and women. International Journal of Obesity and Related Metabolic Disorders **26**(9) (2002) 1218–1224

[24] Taylor, S.E., Mettee, D.R.: When similarity breeds contempt. Journal of Personality and Social Psychology **20**(1) (1971) 75–81

[25] Konijn, E.A., Hoorn, J.F.: Some like it bad. Testing a model for perceiving and experiencing fictional characters. Media Psychology **7**(2) (2005) 107–144

[26] Van Vugt, H.C., Hoorn, J.F., Konijn, E.A., De Bie Dimitriadou, A.: Affective affordances: Improving interface character engagement through interaction. International Journal of Human-Computer Studies (in press)

[27] Davis, F.D.: Perceived usefulness, perceived ease of use, and user acceptance of information technology. MIS Quarterly **13**(3) (1989) 319–339

[28] Norman, D.A.: Emotional design. Why we love (or hate) everyday things. Basic Books, New York (2004

[29] Van Vugt, H.C., Hoorn, J.F., Konijn, E.A., Keur, I., Eliëns, A.: Realism is not all! User engagement with task-related interface characters. Interacting with Computers (in press)

[30] Dion, K., Berscheid, E., Walster, E.: What is beautiful is good. Journal of Personality and Social Psychology **24**(3) (1972) 285–290

[31] Bessenoff, G.R., Sherman, J.W.: Automatic and controlled components of prejudice toward fat people: Evaluation versus stereotype activation. Social Cognition **18** (2000) 329–353

[32] Konijn, E.A., Bushman, B.J.: World leaders as movie characters? Perceptions of J.W. Bush, T. Blair, O. bin Laden, and S. Hussein. Media Psychology (in press)

[33] Stunkard, A.J., Sorenson, T., Schlusinger, F.: Use of the Danish adoption register for the study of obesity and thinness. In S.S. Kety, L.P. Rowland, R.S., Matthysse, S., eds.: The Genetics of Neurological and Psychiatric Disorders, New York, Raven Press (1983) 115–120

[34] Fingeret, M.C., Gleaves, D.H., Pearson, C.A.: On the methodology of body image assessment: the use of figural rating scales to evaluate body dissatisfaction and the ideal body standards of women. Body Image **1** (2004) 207–212

[35] Bulik, C.M., Wade, T.D., Heath, A.C., Martin, N.G., Stunkard, A.J., Eaves, L.J.: Relating body mass index to figural stimuli: population-based normative data for Caucasian. International Journal of Obesity **25**(10) (2001) 1517–1524

[36] Tversky, A.: Features of similarity. Psychological Review **84**(4) (1977) 327–352

[37] Dillman, D.A.: Mail and Internet surveys: The tailored design method. 2th edn. John Wiley and Sons, New York (2000)

[38] Sillence, E., Briggs, P., Harris, P., Fishwick, L.: A framework for understanding trust factors in Web-based health advice. International Journal of Human-Computer Studies **64** (2006) 697–713

[39] Nielsen, J.: Trust or bust: communicating trustworthiness in Web Design Alert-box available online at: http://www.useit.com/alertbox/990307.html

[40] Perloff, R.M.: The dynamics of persuasion: Communication and Attitudes in the 21st Century. 2th edn. Lawrence Erlbaum Associates, Mahwah, New Jersey (2003)

Virtual Rapport

Jonathan Gratch[1], Anna Okhmatovskaia[1], Francois Lamothe[2], Stacy Marsella[1],
Mathieu Morales[2], R.J. van der Werf[3], and Louis-Philippe Morency[4]

[1] University of Southern California
[2] Ecole Spéciale Militaire de St-Cyr
[3] University of Twente
[4] Massachusetts institute of technology

Abstract. Effective face-to-face conversations are highly interactive. Participants respond to each other, engaging in nonconscious behavioral mimicry and backchanneling feedback. Such behaviors produce a subjective sense of rapport and are correlated with effective communication, greater liking and trust, and greater influence between participants. Creating rapport requires a tight sense-act loop that has been traditionally lacking in embodied conversational agents. Here we describe a system, based on psycholinguistic theory, designed to create a sense of rapport between a human speaker and virtual human listener. We provide empirical evidence that it increases speaker fluency and engagement.

1 Introduction

Conversations vary widely in terms of their quality. Sometimes we, er, um... We seem tongue tied. We stutter, pause and repeat our words. Other times, we feel in sync with our conversational partner and words flow without effort. Disfluency is typically a sign of cognitive load and can arise from a number of sources including the complexity of the subject matter or emotions arising from the social setting. One apparent influence on interactional fluency is the nonverbal behavior produced by participants (Chartrand and Bargh 1999). Fluent interactions typically involve nonverbal behavioral synchrony between the interactants. People mirror each other's postures and interject feedback such as nods or interjections (uh-huh) at just the right moment. In such situations, participants report feelings of rapport, like each other better, and are more likely to be persuaded by each other's assertions. Such findings have encouraged the development of embodied conversational agents that can reproduce such social influences.

When it comes to conversational gestures, most virtual human research has focused on half of the interactional equation. Systems emphasize the importance of nonverbal behavior in speech *production*. Only a few systems can interject meaningful nonverbal feedback *during* another's speech and when feedback exists at all, it typically occurs at utterance boundaries (eg.,Tosa 1993). Only a small number of systems have attempted to provide within-utterance listening feedback, and these methods usually rely on simple acoustic cues. For example, REA will execute a head nod or paraverbal (e.g. say "mm-hum") if the user pauses in mid-utterance (Cassell, Bickmore et al.

J. Gratch et al. (Eds.): IVA 2006, LNAI 4133, pp. 14 – 27, 2006.
© Springer-Verlag Berlin Heidelberg 2006

Table 1. Listening Agent Mapping

Lowering of pitch • head nod
Raised loudness → head nod
Speech disfluency → posture/gaze shift
Speaker shifts posture → mimic
Speaker gazes away → mimic
Speaker nods or shakes → mimic

1999). Although there is considerable research showing the benefit of such feedback on human to human interaction, few studies have investigated their impact on human to virtual human rapport (cf. Cassell and Thórisson 1999; Bailenson and Yee 2005).

At last year's IVA conference we presented a Listening Agent that would try to create a sense of rapport simply by tying listening feedback to shallow features of a speaker's voice and bodily movements (Maatman, Gratch et al. 2005). Such an approach is clearly simpler than attempts to tie such feedback to a deep model of coordinated activity (Nakano, Reinstein et al. 2003; Heylen 2005). Here we present evidence that it can also be effective in positively influencing the quantity and quality of human speech.

2 Rapport Agent

The RAPPORT AGENT described here is an evolution of the LISTENING AGENT presented at IVA05 (Maatman, Gratch et al. 2005). The LISTENING AGENT was a simple approach to produce within-utterance listening behaviors based on real-time analysis of a speaker's voice, head motion, and body posture. The system was inspired by psycho-linguistic findings that feelings of rapport are correlated with simple contingent behaviors between speaker and listener, including behavioral mimicry (Chartrand and Bargh 1999) and backchannel continuers (Yngve 1970). The LISTENING AGENT used a head-mounted motion tracker and signal processing of the speech signal to drive the listening mapping displayed in Table 1.

The system was directed at passing our proposed "Duncan Test," inspired by the work of Sue Duncan on studying rapport (Welji and Duncan 2004). Following the standard setup adopted by Duncan and McNeill, we suggest having a human partici-pant watch a short cartoon and then describe it to a listening agent. To pass the test, the interaction between speaker and the agent should exhibit the same correlations between nonverbal behaviors, self and other reports of rapport, and social outcomes such as liking, persuasion and conversational fluency.

Preliminary evaluations suggested the LISTENING AGENT was viable for such a task, but also revealed limitations that we addressed in the creation of the RAPPORT AGENT:

- Contextual constraints on listening behavior: As the LISTENING AGENT employed a direct (i.e., stateless) mapping between detected features and responses, it couldn't account for important contextual features. For example, it might detect a "Speaker Gaze-Left" event, but could not condition its response on the state of the speaker (e.g., the speaker is silent), the state of the LISTENING AGENT (e.g., the agent is looking away), or other arbitrary features (e.g., the speaker's gender).

Table 2. Rapport Agent detected speaker features

Motion Features		Vocal Features	
Gestures	nod, shake	Intensity	silent, normal, loud
Head roll	upright, lean left, lean right	Range	wide, narrow
Gaze	straight, up, down, left, right	Other	backchannel opportunity

- Temporal constraints on listening behavior: the LISTENING AGENT had no notion of time, which, when coupled with lack of state, limited its ability to control the temporal dynamics of the listening behavior. For example, there was no easy way to constrain the number of behaviors produced within some interval of time.
- Variability of behavioral responses: the LISTENING AGENT enforced a 1-1 mapping between detected events and agent responses. This led to considerable repetition in the elicited behaviors and conveyed the sense that one was speaking to a robot.
- Portability: the LISTENING AGENT was restricted to a specialized room with a ceiling-mounted motion tracking system and a large screen to display the agent's graphical body. This hampered our ability to perform user testing in this heavily-utilized space and limited our ability to share the system with other colleagues.
- Feature detection: preliminary testing revealed shortcomings in the feature detectors. For example, the detection of speaker nods and shakes worked well for recognizing enacted (typically exaggerated) behavior but proved less reliable in recognizing more naturally elicited behavior. Further, head motions produced during speech introduced audio artifacts that influenced the detection of audio features.

These concerns led to a redesign of many of the LISTENING AGENT components. The resulting RAPPORT AGENT has an open modular architecture that facilitates the incorporation of different feature detectors and animation systems, and has an easily authored mapping between features and behavior. The behavior mapping language incorporates contextual features, probabilistic responses, and some control over the temporal dynamics of behavior. To address the issue of portability, we moved to a vision-based tracker and changed the setting from a standing interaction with a life-sized character to a seated interaction with a life-sized image of a character's head displayed on a computer monitor. Finally, we updated the original feature-detection algorithms and broadened the repertoire of recognized features. Here we give a high-level overview of the new architecture. Details can be found at (Lamothe and Morales 2006; van der Werf 2006). Figure 1 illustrates the basic outlines of the RAPPORT AGENT architecture.

Feature Detection

To produce listening behaviors, the RAPPORT AGENT first collects and analyzes the speaker's upper-body movements and voice to detect the features listed in Table 2.

For detecting features from the participants' movements, we focus on the motion of the speakers head. Watson, developed by Louis-Phillipe Morency, is an image-based tracking library that uses stereo images to track the participants' head position and orientation (Morency, Sidner et al. 2005). Watson also incorporates learned motion classifiers that detect head nods and shakes from a vector of head velocities. Other features are derived from the position and orientation of participant's head (filtered to

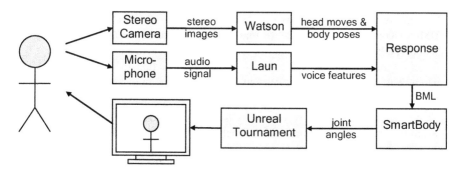

Fig. 1. Rapport Agent architecture

reduce the impact of noise). For example, from the head position, given the participant is seated in a fixed chair, we can infer the posture of the spine.

Acoustic features are derived from properties of the pitch and intensity of the speech signal (the RAPPORT AGENT ignores the semantic content of the speaker's speech), using a signal processing package, LAUN, developed by Mathieu Morales. Speaker pitch is approximated with the cepstrum of the speech signal (Oppenheim and Schafer 2004) and processed every 20ms. Audio artifacts introduced by the motion of the Speaker's head are minimized by filtering low frequency noise. Speech intensity is derived from amplitude of the signal.

We split speech feature detections into two families: the "instant" are derived in real-time, and the "delayed" detections that can be analyzed at the end of the "sentences" featuring them. Instant features include silent/normal/loud speech (derived from signal intensity) and backchannel opportunity points (derived using the approach of Ward and Tsukahara 2000). In addition, we make a crude attempt to separate utterances based on silences and attempt to detect some features that hold across the utterance including pitch-range (positive affect is often associated with wider pitch-range).

Behavior Mapping

Recognized speaker features are mapped into listening behaviors through a set of authorable mapping rules. The language is based on five primitives.

- Each participant in the interaction is described by an *agent*. Agents consist of a set actions, states, animations and reactions. For the discussion that follows, we will assume two agents: the agent that represents the human speaker and the agent that represent the RAPPORT AGENT listener.
- *Actions* represent discrete behavioral events that can be generated by an agent. These can consist of the detectable features of human behavior (Table 2) or arbitrary behavior outputs of the RAPPORT AGENT.
- *States* describe characteristics of an agent that can persist over time. Typically, states are asserted as consequences of actions (e.g., after detecting LeanLeft, the speaker is in the state of LeaningLeft). States can be constrained logically (e.g., the speaker cannot be simultaneously speaking and silent) and temporally (e.g., to ensure an agent stays in some state for some period of time).

- *Animations* are physical behaviors described in the Behavior Markup Language (BML) (Kopp, Krenn et al. 2006) that can be associated with agent actions. For example, a backchannel continuer might be associated with a nod animation.
- *Reactions* map from an action in one agent to an action in another agent. The mapping is conditional on the current state of one or more agents and can map, probabilistically, to one of a set of other actions.

Typically, reactions map actions of the speaker to (re)actions by the RAPPORT AGENT. For example, if LAUN detects a backchannel opportunity point in the speaker, this could cause the RAPPORT AGENT to react with a Nod with probability 0.6 or GazeUp with probability 0.2, assuming the RAPPORT AGENT is in the state of GazingForward. The framework, however, can support more general settings. For example, one could define mapping rules for multiparty settings (e.g., multiple speakers or multiple listening agents). Alternatively, one could transform the behavior of a human listener into some, perhaps altered animated behavior (c.f., Bailenson, Beall et al. 2004).

Animation
RAPPORT AGENT animation commands are passed to the SmartBody animation system (Kallmann and Marsella 2005). This is a virtual human animation system designed to seamlessly blend animations and procedural behaviors. These animations are rendered in the Unreal Tournament™ game engine and displayed to the Speaker.

3 Evaluation

While RAPPORT AGENT described above could be integrated into a wide variety of embodied conversational agent applications, there are a number of questions that need to be addressed first to ensure the suitability of such integration:

- Does the system correctly detect features of the speaker's behavior, such as head nods, shakes, pauses in speech, etc.?
- How well do behavior mapping rules approximate the behavior of human listeners?
- Is the agent's behavior judged to be natural when it is performed?
- Do listening behaviors of the agent have the predicted influence on the human speaker's behavior and perceptions?

Our preliminary analysis suggests that feature detection is reasonably accurate and we are currently collecting data on human face-to-face communication to address the second question. The study presented here focuses on the last two questions and attempts to replicate certain well-known findings in social psychology about the effects of listener's feedback in face-to-face communication. In this study we try to demonstrate that nonverbal behavior displayed by the RAPPORT AGENT contributes to its perceived believability, positively affects the speaker's motivation and speech fluency, and can induce subjective feelings of rapport in human participants.

Hypotheses
People are more willing to communicate when their conversational partners display interest and may be quite frustrated when such feedback is absent. Several studies have demonstrated increased speaker engagement when listeners provide feedback

such as nods and mimicry, whether the interaction is between humans or between humans and synthetic agents. For example, Tatar (1997) has demonstrated that speakers talking about life experiences told shorter stories and reported that they were less engaged when the listener was distracted and, thus, provided less feedback. In a GrandChair project (Smith 2000), elderly people were found to tell longer stories to a virtual child agent that displayed active listening behavior.

Based on these findings we can hypothesize that human subjects would be more engaged in interaction with a responsive agent that displays positive listening behaviors, as opposed to no or inappropriate feedback. While this claim is very straightforward, it is less obvious how to measure the degree of speaker's engagement. Different studies have looked at self-reports, the amount of gesticulation, facial expression, posture, gazing behavior, speech production. In this study we focus on duration of interaction, arguing that engaged speakers would tend to speak more.

It is important to point out that the relation between the amount and type of listener's feedback on one hand and speech quantity on the other hand is complex. Contrary to Smith (2000) and Tatar (1997), some studies found that that speakers produced fewer utterances when provided with feedback, which was explained by arguing the feedback reduced ambiguity and promoted greater communicative efficiency (Krauss, Garlock et al. 1977; Cassell and Thórisson 1999). One may notice, however, that these two groups of studies have utilized rather different types of communicative tasks in their experiments. Both the speaker goals and the function of listener's feedback can vary considerably depending on the context of the task. In tasks where the primary goal is to convey information (e.g., Krauss, Garlock et al. 1977) or when faced with time pressure, one might expect feedback to promote efficient communication and thus reduced speech quantity. Listener's feedback under these conditions can indicate comprehension and allow the speaker to compact their speech and avoid repetitions. The story-telling tasks typically have different emphasis: the speaker is either explicitly or implicitly encouraged to speak more and provide more details. Listener's feedback in this case may serve as positive reinforcement and motivate the speaker to continue interaction.

The task used in current study (retelling a funny cartoon) most likely belongs to the second category. We could thus assume that longer interaction with the system reflects the subject's engagement and motivation, rather than inefficiency.

H1: People will interact with a responsive listener longer than an unresponsive one.

As the effects of listener's feedback on speech quantity can be quite complex, it is important to also look at speech quality. Studies show that in the absence of such feedback or when the feedback is incoherent, the speakers become disrupted, and their speech – less structured (Kraut, Lewis et al. 1982; Bavelas, Coates et al. 2000).

One possible explanation for this effect is that listening feedback provided in a timely fashion reduces cognitive load on the speaker. Sources of this load can vary depending on the task and social setting, but they all produce uncertainty that the speaker constantly needs to resolve (e.g. Did this person understand me? Does he/she agree with what I am saying? etc.). Following this explanation it can be expected that incoherent or inappropriate feedback can be even more disruptive than the absence of feedback.

In this study we focus on one particular aspect of speech quality – fluency. Improved speech fluency is a prominent characteristic of rapport interactions, and we expect to achieve similar positive effect of non-verbal feedback provided by the RAP-PORT AGENT on the speaker's quality of speech in our study.

H2: People will speak more fluently when interacting with a responsive agent.

Thus far we have focused on objective characteristics of interactions that involve social rapport. However in addition, participants of such interactions typically experience subjective feelings of rapport, which are available via self-report. People point out that they felt a connection with each other – that they "clicked". We hope to supplement our other findings by this self-reported sense of rapport.

H3: When interacting with a responsive agent people will indicate feelings of rapport in verbal self-reports.

Experimental Setup
In evaluating the system we adapt the "McNeill lab" paradigm (McNeill 1992) for studying gesture research. In this research, one participant, the Speaker, has previously observed some incident, and describes it to another participant, the Listener. Here, we replace the Listener with the RAPPORT AGENT system.

People can be socially influenced by a virtual character whether or not they believe it represents a real person (Nass and Reeves 1996) although there can be important differences depending on how the situation is framed. In this study, we use a cover story to make the subjects believe that they interact with a real human. The participants are told that the study evaluates an advanced telecommunication device, specifically a computer program that accurately captures all movements of one person and displays them on the screen (using an Avatar) to another person. According to the cover story, we were interested in comparing this new device to a more traditional telecommunication medium such as video camera, which is why one of the participants was sited in front of the monitor displaying a video image, while the other saw a life-size head of an avatar (see Figure 2).

Fig. 2. Experimental setup

The subjects were randomly assigned to one of two conditions labeled respectively "responsive" and "unresponsive". In a *responsive condition* the Avatar was controlled by the RAPPORT AGENT, as described earlier. The Avatar therefore displayed a range of nonverbal behaviors intended to provide positive feedback to the speaker and to create an impression of active listening.

In an *unresponsive condition* the Avatar's behavior was controlled by a pre-recorded random script and was independent of the Speaker's or Listener's behavior. The script was built from the same set of animations as those used in responsive condition, excluding head nods and shakes. Thus, the Avatar's behavioral repertoire was limited to head turns and posture shifts.

Procedure

Each subject participated in an experiment twice: once in a role of a Speaker and once as a Listener. The order was selected randomly.

While the Listener waited outside of the room, the Speaker watched a short segment of Sylvester and Tweety cartoon, after which s/he was instructed to describe the segment to the Listener. The participants were told that they would be judged based on the Listener's story comprehension. The Speaker was encouraged to describe the story in as much detail as possible. In order to prevent the Listener from speaking back we have emphasized the distinct roles assigned to participants, but did not explicitly prohibit the Listener from talking. No time constraints were introduced.

After describing the cartoon (during which time the Speaker was sitting in front of the Avatar), the Speaker was asked to fill out a short questionnaire collecting the subject's feedback about his experience with the system. Then the participants switched their roles and the procedure was repeated. A different cartoon from the same series and of similar length was used for the second round.

At the end of the experiment, both participants were debriefed. The experimenter collected some informal qualitative feedback on their experience with the system, probed for suspicion and finally revealed the goals of the study and experimental manipulations.

Dependent Variables

The collected data can be grouped into 3 major categories:

1. *Duration of interaction.* To measure the duration of interaction, we record the total time it takes the subject to tell the story. To obtain a measure independent of individual differences in speech rate, we count the number of words in the subject's story. We also differentiate between total word count and the number of "meaningful" (lexical and functional) words. For the later, speech disfluencies, such as pause fillers and stutters are excluded.
2. *Speech fluency.* To assess the speaker's fluency we use two groups of measures: speech rate and the amount of speech disfluencies (Alibali, Heath et al. 2001). For speech rate we distinguish between overall speech rate (all words per second) and fluent speech rate (lexical and functional words per second). To measure the amount of disfluencies, we use disfluency rate (disfluencis per second) and disfluency frequency (a ratio of the number of disfluencies to total word count).
3. *Self-reported measures of rapport.* Included in this category are several items of the questionnaire (see Figure 3). The questionnaire includes both forced choice and free format open-ended questions. The later were used as a source of qualitative data.

The research hypotheses can be now operationalized in terms of dependent variables:

H1a: Total time to tell the story will be higher in responsive condition.

H1b: The recorded stories will be longer in responsive condition in terms of both total word count and the number of lexical and functional words

H2a: Overall and fluent speech rate will be higher in responsive condition

H2b: The disfluency rate and disfluency frequency will be higher in an unresponsive condition

H3a: The subjects in responsive condition will be more likely to report a sense of rapport on the questionnaire.

Subjects

The participants were 30 volunteers from among employees of USC's Institute for Creative Technologies. Two subjects were excluded from analysis due to an unforeseen interruption of experimental procedure. The final sample size was 28: 16 in a responsive and 12 in an unresponsive condition.

Results

Because of a relatively small sample size used for this study, we have refrained from making assumptions regarding data distribution, and used non-parametric statistics to evaluate the differences between two groups of subjects: Mann-Whitney U – for scale variables (length of interaction, speech fluency), and Chi-square – for nominal data (forced-choice questionnaire items). $p < .05$ was used as a criterion.

Table 3 summarizes the data on duration of interaction and speech fluency. Consistent with H1a and H1b, the subjects in responsive condition talked significantly longer both in terms of overall time and word count. An increase in word count was associated with the higher number of lexical and functional words, while the total number of filled pauses and other speech disfluencies remained the same.

Consistent with H2b, the disfluency rate was significantly higher in unresponsive condition. The same is true for the disfluency frequency. Contrary to H2a, the subjects in unresponsive condition tended to speak faster, not slower. This finding, however, is non-significant for both the overall speech rate and fluent speech rate.

Table 3. Duration of interaction and fluency of speech

var	Responsive[a]	Unresponsive[a]	Mann-Whitney U	Sig.[b]
total time	188.68	98.50	30.0	0.001*
N words	432	300	44.0	0.015*
N words - disfluencies	411	288	39.0	0.007*
Speech rate	2.55	2.77	57.5	0.074
Fluent speech rate	2.42	2.60	66.5	0.174
Disfluency rate	0.13	0.21	28.5	0.001*
Frequency of disfl.	0.05	0.08	48.0	0.026*

[a] – median used as a measure of central tendency   * – $p < .05$

[b] – 2-tailed criterion

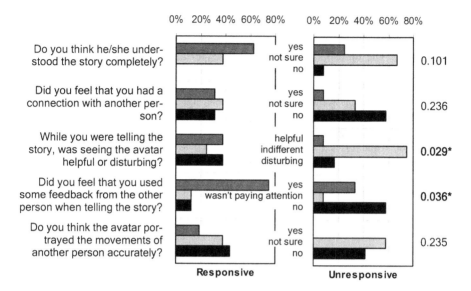

Fig. 3. Summary of subjects' responses to selected questions

Self-report data is presented in Figure 3. Several trends are worth mentioning:

- Subjects in the responsive condition were more likely to feel that they had a connection with their conversational partner, and to form an impression that the listener understood them. They also reported that they used the listener's feedback when they were telling the story.
- Most subjects did not consider the avatar to be an accurate representation of a real listener; those few who did – all belonged to the responsive condition.
- Opinions on the helpfulness of the avatar were markedly different across the conditions. The subjects in responsive condition found the avatar to be either helpful or disturbing. In unresponsive condition 75% of the speakers had indifferent attitude.

Not all of the differences in self-reported measures reached statistical significance, and thus additional data may be needed to support these findings.

Discussion

The results obtained for the duration of interaction (word count and time) fully support our predictions, and are also consistent with some findings mentioned earlier (Smith 2000). The subjects spent more time talking to a responsive agent, and produced longer stories. What is important to note here is that there were significantly more "meaningful" words in these stories, suggesting that the increase in quantity of speech was not associated with a decreased quality.

We believe that this finding can be explained in terms of the subjects' willingness to interact with the listener (represented by an avatar in our experiment). The nonverbal behavior generated by the RAPPORT AGENT was intended to create an impression of an engaged and attentive listener and encourage the speaker. During the debriefing procedure after the experiment two subjects in the unresponsive condition (tested in different sessions) pointed out that they intentionally kept their stories short because the listener seemed to be uninterested. This observation brings to light an important consideration in the design of embodied conversational agents: human observers tend to interpret not only the nonverbal clues displayed by the agent, but the absence of clues as well. The unresponsive agent in our experiment differed from a responsive one only by the absence of head nods, and randomized timing of posture and gaze shifts, so there weren't any specific behaviors that conveyed lack of interest or boredom. And yet, at least some subjects saw these signs in the agent's behavior. This suggests that one must carefully model the nonverbal behavior in embodied agents, since not only inappropriate behaviors, but sometimes just the lack of behaviors can produce undesirable effects in human observers depending on the context.

There is also evidence that human speakers were more engaged in conversation with a responsive agent, which is based on observations we made during the experiment. Several subjects in a responsive condition responded verbally to the feedback provided by the agent. In particular they could say "yes" and nod after the agent nodded. Or they could ask "Did you get it so far?", and then continue only after the agent nodded. This was not observed in an unresponsive condition. Since the experiment was built as a one-way communication, and such spontaneous interactions were actually discouraged by an instruction, they indicate a potential power of the system in producing social effects. These observations require further elaboration and formal experimental verification. Additional data on speaker's engagement may be obtained from analyzing gaze and gesturing behavior, which we plan to do in future studies.

We do not rule out additional explanations of these results. For instance, it is possible that speakers in the responsive condition remember the cartoon better and, thus, provide more details. This explanation does not exclude the one we presented before, and the next logical step for further research would be to find out what the weights of different factors underlying increased speech quantity are.

Our hypothesis regarding speech fluency was only partially supported: there was support for the amount of disfluencies (H2b), but not for speech rate (H2a). This suggests that speech rate may have a more complex relationship with conversational fluency than we believed. Indeed, speaking quickly does not necessarily mean speaking fluently. Particularly, in our study an increase in speech rate in the unresponsive condition was mainly due to more frequent inclusion of pause fillers, indicating that the subjects in this condition talked fast but with many disfluencies.

It is important to keep in mind that speech rate can be affected by a number of factors, in particular emotional. It is possible that the subjects in the unresponsive condition spoke faster because they felt uncomfortable and were trying to complete the task as quickly as possible. It was previously shown that synthetic agents can elicit anxiety in human users (Rickenberg and Reeves 2000) and, particularly, that unresponsive virtual audience produces greater anxiety in the speaker (Pertaub, Slater et al. 2001). Our results for the unresponsive condition are consistent with these findings.

As our experiment was not designed to control for social anxiety, presented explanations would need to be tested in further studies. In general, the problem of how social anxiety mediates the effects of listener's feedback on the speaker and how it interacts with rapport has not been yet investigated.

The results on self-reported feelings of rapport did not reach statistical significance, however the observed trends are consistent with our predictions. Increasing the sample size and using more fine-grained scales (compared to just "yes/no/unsure") may help obtain more conclusive results.

One particular finding derived from self-report data deserves attention: indifferent attitude towards the agent in unresponsive condition and either positive, or negative, and sometimes ambivalent – in responsive condition. The subjects seemed to ignore the agent when his behavior was unresponsive, but apparently could not do it when he was "actively listening". Several subjects in responsive condition admitted afterwards that they felt distracted by the agent and tried not to look at him to better concentrate on the story. This finding does not quite agree with the results on speech fluency and with our expectations for the responsive behavior to be helpful to the speaker. The question is: why such distraction occurs and what one can do to minimize it?

People appear to be more sensitive to some feedback – head nods and shakes – than to other components of listening behavior. As Chiu et. al. (1995) point out, it is hard for the speakers to ignore listener's feedback when it is relevant for the speech they are planning. Head nods and shakes typically appear to be of high relevance. When they are delivered at exactly the right moments, this improves interactional fluency. However if not perfectly timed, the head nods (and especially head shakes) are more disruptive than helpful. One obvious way to address this problem in RAPPORT AGENT is to make the head nod animation more subtle. At a deeper level, further work on improving feature detection and behavioral mapping rules is needed to ensure the agent's nonverbal feedback is in sync with the speaker's behavior.

We shall admit that overall self-reported measures of rapport and ratings of believability were lower than desired. Only about 30% of the subjects in responsive condition reported that they felt a connection with their conversational partner, and less than 20% considered the avatar to be an accurate representation of a real listener.

In order to find out what were the reasons for such results, we analyzed some qualitative data. In addition to answering formal yes/no questions, the subjects shared their comments on what difficulties they encountered when interacting with an agent, and what the reasons for his unnatural behavior were. The following factors seem to contribute to the subjects' overall impression of the agent and their experience of rapport:

- The Avatar did not display facial expressions, and many of the subjects felt that they were missing a significant part of the feedback the real listener was providing.
- The participants in responsive condition noticed imperfections in the animations: head nods seemed to be exaggerated and sometimes jerky, transitions between animations were not always smooth.
- Several subjects explicitly mentioned that some head nods were not properly timed.

These current limitations of the system will be addressed in our future work.

We have demonstrated that the RAPPORT AGENT exerts certain effects on the human speaker. However in order to further improve the system we need to know what it is about generated listening behavior that is responsible for these effects. Could the same results be achieved by manipulating the overall amount of movement displayed by the agent, or type of movement is important? Is it the mere occurrence of certain behaviors, or their timing that matters? How the results would change if the subjects believed they were talking to a computer and not to another human? We have already performed some additional analysis and are planning to gather more data to address these questions.

4 Conclusions

Presented in the current work is an Agent that aims at creating a sense of rapport in human speaker simply by tying nonverbal listening feedback to shallow features of a speaker's voice and bodily movements. This sense of rapport is believed to facilitate communication and to contribute to positive impression formation and trust between conversational partners.

We have conducted an empirical study, in which we attempted to replicate some of the known effects of rapport in human-to-virtual human communication. The results of this first round of system evaluation largely support our hypotheses. The RAPPORT AGENT was demonstrated to be effective in positively influencing the quality of their speech, their motivation and overall impression of communication. Noteworthy, the agent succeeded in achieving this effect without having a slightest idea of what the speakers were talking about.

The results also suggest how the system can be improved to further increase user satisfaction and subjectively perceived sense of rapport.

Acknowledgements

We would like to thank Susan Duncan, Jeremy Bailenson, Kris Thórisson, and Nigel Ward for very helpful feedback on this draft. Jillian Gerten provided crucial help in transcribing and analyzing subject dialogues. This work was sponsored by the U.S. Army Research, Development, and Engineering Command (RDECOM), and the content does not necessarily reflect the position or the policy of the Government, and no official endorsement should be inferred.

References

Alibali, M. W., D. C. Heath, et al. (2001). "Effects of visibility between speaker and listener on gesture production: some gestures are meant to be seen." Journal of Memory and Language 44: 169-188.
Bailenson, J., A. Beall, et al. (2004). "Transformed Social Interaction: Decoupling Representation from Behavior and Form in Collaborative Virtual Environments." PRESENCE: Teleoperators and Virtual Environments 13(4): 428-441.
Bailenson, J. N. and N. Yee (2005). "Digital Chameleons: Automatic assimilation of nonverbal gestures in immersive virtual environments." Psychological Science 16: 814-819.
Bavelas, J. B., L. Coates, et al. (2000). "Listeners as Co-narrators." Jurnal of Personality and Social Psychology 79(6): 941-952.
Cassell, J., T. Bickmore, et al. (1999). "Embodiment in Conversational Interfaces: Rea." Conference on Human Factors in Computing Systems, Pittsburgh, PA.
Cassell, J. and K. R. Thórisson (1999). "The Power of a Nod and a Glance: Envelope vs. Emotional Feedback in Animated Conversational Agents." International Journal of Applied Artificial Intelligence 13(4-5): 519-538.
Chartrand, T. L. and J. A. Bargh (1999). "The Chameleon Effect: The Perception-Behavior Link and Social Interaction." Journal of Personality and Social Psychology 76(6): 893-910.

Chiu, C., Y. Hong, et al. (1995). Gaze direction and fluency in conversational speech: Unpublished manuscript.

Heylen, D. (2005). "Challenges Ahead. Head Movements and other social acts in conversation." *AISB*, Hertfordshire, UK.

Kallmann, M. and S. Marsella (2005). "Hierarchical Motion Controllers for Real-Time Autonomous Virtual Humans." *5th International Working Conference on Intelligent Virtual Agents*, Kos, Greece, Springer.

Kopp, S., B. Krenn, et al. (2006). "Towards a common framework for multimodal generation in ECAs: The behavior markup language." *Intelligent Virtual Agents*, Marina del Rey, CA.

Krauss, R. M., C. M. Garlock, et al. (1977). "The Role of Audible and Visible Back-Channel Responses in Interpersonal Communication." Journal of Personality and Social Psychology **35**: 523-529.

Kraut, R. K., S. H. Lewis, et al. (1982). "Listener Responsiveness and the Coordination of Conversation." Journal of Personality and Social Psychology: 718-731.

Lamothe, F. and M. Morales (2006). Response Behavior. Marina del Rey, CA, University of Southern California: Technical Report ICT TR 01.2006.

Maatman, M., J. Gratch, et al. (2005). "Natural Behavior of a Listening Agent." *5th International Working Conference on Intelligent VirtualAgents*, Kos, Greece.

McNeill, D. (1992). Hand and mind: What gestures reveal about thought. Chicago, IL, The University of Chicago Press.

Morency, L.-P., C. Sidner, et al. (2005). "Contextual Recognition of Head Gestures." *7th International Conference on Multimodal Interactions*, Toronto, Italy.

Nakano, Y., G. Reinstein, et al. (2003). "Towards a Model of Face-to-Face Grounding." *Meeting of the Association for Computational Linguistics*, Sapporo, Japan.

Nass, C. and B. Reeves (1996). The Media Equation, Cambridge University Press.

Oppenheim, A. V. and R. W. Schafer (2004). From Frequency to Quefrency: A History of the Cepstrum. IEEE Signal Processing Magazine. **September:** 95-106.

Pertaub, D.-P., M. Slater, et al. (2001). "An Experiment on Public Speaking Anxiety in Response to Three Different Types of Virtual Audience." Presence: Teleoperators and Virtual Environments **11**(1): 68-78.

Rickenberg, R. and B. Reeves (2000). "The effects of animated characters on anxiety, task performance, and evaluations of user interfaces,." *SIGCHI conference on Human factors in computing systems*, The Hague, The Netherlands.

Smith, J. (2000). GrandChair: Conversational Collection of Family Stories. Cambridge, MA, Media Lab, MIT.

Tatar, D. (1997). Social and personal consequences of a preoccupied listener. Department of Psychology. Stanford, CA, Stanford University: Unpublished doctoral dissertation.

Tosa, N. (1993). "Neurobaby." ACM SIGGRAPH: 212-213.

van der Werf, R. (2006). Creating Rapport with Virtual Humans. Marina del Rey, CA, University of Southern California: Technical Report ICT TR 02.2006.

Ward, N. and W. Tsukahara (2000). "Prosodic features which cue back-channel responses in English and Japanese." Journal of Pragmatics **23**: 1177-1207.

Welji, H. and S. Duncan (2004). "Characteristics of face-to-face interactions, with and without rapport: Friends vs. strangers." *Symposium on Cognitive Processing Effects of 'Social Resonance' in Interaction, 26th Annual Meeting of the Cognitive Science Society*.

Yngve, V. H. (1970). "On getting a word in edgewise." *Sixth regional Meeting of the Chicago Linguistic Society*.

Imitation Learning and Response Facilitation in Embodied Agents

Stefan Kopp and Olaf Graeser

Artificial Intelligence Group, University of Bielefeld
P.O.Box 100131, D-33501 Bielefeld, Germany
{skopp, ograeser}@techfak.uni-bielefeld.de

Abstract. Imitation is supposedly a fundamental mechanism for humans to learn new actions and to gain knowledge about another's intentions. The basis of this behavior seems to be a direct influencing of the motor system by the perceptual system, affording fast, selective enhancement of a motor response already in the repertoire (*response facilitation*) as well as learning and delayed reproduction of new actions (*true imitation*). In this paper, we present an approach to attain these capabilities in virtual embodied agents. Building upon a computational motor control model, our approach connects visual representations of observed hand and arm movements to graph-based representations of motor commands. Forward and inverse models are employed to allow for both fast mimicking responses as well as imitation learning.

1 Introduction

Human children and adults effortlessly mimic and imitate others. They do so in a variety of situations and different types of imitative behavior can be distinguished [6]. *Stimulus enhancement* refers to the increased probability to act upon an object, on which another individual has acted in a similar way before. *Response facilitation* is the selective enhancement of a motor response already in the repertoire simply by seeing a conspecific performing an action. Finally, *(true) imitation* refers to the case in which an action that has not been part of the own repertoire before is learnt by observing others and can be reproduced with a possible time delay. One can observe all of these kinds of behavior already in human infants [12]. Yet, the question why we imitate each other so often is hard to answer. Many rationales or purposes have been put forward, among them the acquisition of new behaviors, the realization and signaling of the fact that another one is like me [11], or the mutual alignment and convergence in social interactions [13]. In addition, imitative behaviors such as mimicking gestures were suspected to gain knowledge about the intentions of conversational partners [4].

One central mechanism that seems to underlie imitative behavior is the selective influencing of the motor system by the perceptual system. These links open the possibility to equate an observed action with one's own actions through an implicit form of simulating them in the motor system. With the finding of 'mirror regions' with neurons that respond to both self-generated actions and the actions of others [8],

J. Gratch et al. (Eds.): IVA 2006, LNAI 4133, pp. 28–41, 2006.

research in neuroscience has started to discover properties of our brain that may provide explanation for this. Motor areas seem to start to selectively *resonate* as soon as an appropriate visual stimulus is present. This provides functionally equivalent representations of both planned actions and observed actions. The motor system may thus play a central role not only in controlling bodily actions, but also in understanding behaviors of others, reaching into higher cognitive levels of operation and of social interaction and embodied communication [14].

The motivation of this work originates from the question whether it is possible (and helpful) to endow virtual humanoid agents with this ability, namely, to exploit their own motor system for understanding or adapting to other embodied agents in social interaction–including human users. In other words: can an embodied agent utilize his knowledge about the own body, the motor actions he is capable of with this body, and the utility of these actions for pursuing goals, to arrive at a better and faster understanding of the goals, needs, or affective states behind an interlocutor's bodily actions?

In this paper we address two important questions that must be answered prior to this: How can an agent be enabled to pick up and adapt to a human-like repertoire of motor behavior from observing others, and how can such a repertoire and its automatic activation be coupled to perceptual processes? In terms of imitative behavior we thus try to model capabilities of response facilitation and true imitation in embodied agents. As a side effect, making embodied agents capable of true imitation promises to provide a new means of building up natural behavior lexicons, namely, by interactively teaching agents how to employ their own motor resources for demonstrated behaviors. This exceeds the usual use of motion capture techniques to collect low-level animation data that must be mapped onto the agent's body and edited every time to fit particular context conditions.

We start with discussing related work in the next section. In Sect. 3, we describe the computational model of motor control for hand-arm movements in animated humanoid agents that we start out from. To study the modeling of imitative behavior we employ a scenario with two virtual humanoid agents, *Max* and *Moritz*. Moritz acts as the demonstrator and can perform arbitrary movements by executing predefined keyframe animations, whereas Max takes on the role of the learner and imitator. Sect. 4 presents our approach to connect the agent's perceptual representation with his motor representations via forward and inverse models in order to enable imitation. Examples of the imitation learning as well as fast mimicking responses that are possible with this model are given in Sect. 5.

2 Related Work

A number of researchers have addressed the imitation learning of movements by artificial systems. Billard et al. [2] developed a biologically inspired, connectionist architecture that simulates mirror neurons as link between visual and motor representations. The model employs a hierarchy of neural networks to remodel the primates brain's visuo-motor pathways. In this sense, it includes a temporal cortex for movement recognition, a pre-motor cortex for activity transfer into primary motor nodes, and a cerebellum for sequences of movements. Learning of motor sequences is achieved by Hebbian update of the connections between these components. In a more recent approach, Billard et al. [3] propose a model to probabilistically learn the relevant features for imitation of an object manipulation task. The resulting strategies range from simply reproducing a goal (i.e. hitting the object) to reproducing the exact movement, the generation of which includes calculating and interpolating target points by means of inverse kinematics or by Hidden Markov Models representing a sequence of joint angles. Other computational studies of motor control suggest explicit internal models that predict the sensory consequences of a motor command (called *forward models* as they model the causal relationship between actions and their consequences) and that are employed to functionally implement *inverse models* (mapping from sensor stimulus onto efferent motor signals). For example, Amit & Mataric [1] use motor primitives both to detect and execute movements. This architecture combines base primitives that encode forward models for classes of movements and, additionally, serve as an inverse model able to determine parameters of an observed instance of that movement type. During demonstration, such parameters are passed on to higher levels for learning specific instances of a movement and even complex, composite movement sequences using Hidden Markov Models. Wolpert et al. [15] proposed the MOSAIC architecture of paired forward and inverse models (predictors and controllers, respectively). The idea is that the brain simultaneously runs multiple forward models to predict the consequences of motor behaviors in order to determine the dynamics of the body when interacting with objects. The MOSAIC model is able to learn a set of predictors that cover best experienced behaviors, and it ensures that the corresponding controllers are used in the right context. Applied for imitation, this model tries to predict the next state of the demonstrator's body (positions of limbs or joint angles). By comparing the predictions with the demonstrator's next state, the controller with the smallest prediction error is activated to mimic the seen movement.

Demiris & Hayes [7] distinguish between passive and active imitation. In the former, the imitator runs a ``perceive-recognize-reproduce'' cycle and the motor systems are involved only during the ``reproduce'' phase; in the latter, the imitator's motor systems are actively involved in perception, again, by comparing predictions of the available forward models with the observed movement. If none of the forward model matches, significant postures will be extracted via passive imitation to form a new behavior that is then added to the imitator's repertoire.

Most recently, Buchsbaum & Blumberg [5] have presented a graph-based approach for motor planning and a hierarchical action-trigger-model to account for the meaning of movements. Nodes in their graph represent poses, movements are transitions between them, with special nodes for predefined rest postures. After the complete observation of a movement the imitator tries to map an observed movement onto a path through the pose graph. That is, this model does not account for response facilitation, i.e. imitation in overlap with the demonstration. The meaning of a movement is inferred by connecting every action (e.g. eating) in the pose graph to a trigger (e.g. being hungry) referring to a goal. The goals and their triggers are organized in a hierarchical fashion and may be directed towards an optional object (e.g. grasping is a sub-goal of eating and is transitive, i.e. directed to an object). This representation allows for infering from an observed action to the goal structure behind it or to properties of the object acted upon.

In our approach (see Sect. 4), we have combined and extended aspects from several of the models discussed here, notably, active and passive imitation, coupled forward and inverse models, and graph-based representations.

3 Computational Motor Control

In previous work we have developed an incremental model for the realization of multimodal utterances in embodied conversational agents [9]. A part of this model is a component for the on-the-fly creation of coverbal gestures animations, which tries to achieve a high degree of control and flexibility w.r.t. shape and time properties, while at the same time ensuring naturalness of the movement. A special motor planner accomplishes this task. It receives a set of timed morphological features of a gesture, e.g. hand shapes or arm movement specifications, and seeks a solution to drive the kinematic skeleton of the humanoid agent properly. To this end, a functional-anatomical decomposition of motor control is adopted. Specialized motor planning modules for the hands, the wrists, the arms, as well as the neck and the eyes instantiate *local motor programs* (LMPs) that autonomously control submovements, i.e. movements within a limited set of degrees of freedom (DOF) and over a designated period of time (see right part of Fig. 1). To combine the LMPs for a motor planning modules with a representation of control signals for the target submovement (left part of Fig. 1). When activating itself at execution time, every LMP turns this representation into a kinematic controller for the corresponding submovement.

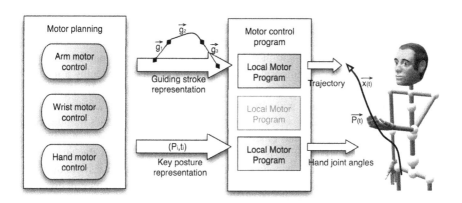

Fig. 1. Overview of the motor control and representation model

Since human arm movement exhibits external kinematic regularities, and since gestures often must reproduce external form features, arm movement trajectories are created directly in working space, as opposed to planning and controlling them in joint angles or torques. Our approach to forming wrist trajectories relies on well-known observations on complex arm movements [11]. Motor control for such trajectories is incrementally exerted so as to successive segments are performed more or less "ballistically". Due to skeleton structure and muscle dynamics, each segment is more or less straight or curvilinear (either C- or S-shaped), stays within a fixed movement plane, exhibits a symmetrical bell-shaped velocity profile, a quasi-linear relation between amplitude and peak velocity, and an approximate logarithmic relation between its extent and its duration. The segmentation corresponds to the points of maximum curvature or change of the movement plane, at which movement speed usually drops. Relying on these assumptions, both path and kinematics of an arm movement can be defined locally at these break points and in terms of a small set of control parameters. Consequently, in our model, the motor command representation for arm movement consists of a sequence of linear or curvilinear *guiding strokes*, which are concatenated to form the desired trajectory. Each guiding stroke bridges from one break point to the next by stating the target position, the time to get there, the basic shape of the trajectory, the moment of maximum velocity, and a velocity gain factor for movement at the end point. For curvilinear guiding strokes, the normal vector of the movement plane as well as the overall form (left/right C, left/right S) must be defined. In addition, the form of the curvilinear segment can be specified by the degree of curvature (from nearly straight to semicircle), the roundness (from nearly rectangular to nearly triangular), and the skewness (flattened toward the beginning or the end).

During motor planning, an LMP is created with such a sequence of guiding strokes. At execution time, this LMP continually estimates how long a hypothetical preparatory movement from the current hand location to the required start position of the first guiding stroke would take and decides whether it's time to activate itself. Once activated, the LMP forms a trajectory by (1) inserting a first preparatory guiding stroke, (2) checking for collisions with the torso and inserting, if necessary, circumventing guiding strokes, (3) setting up all position constraints, (4) estimating the velocities at interior segmentation points, and (5) calculating a parametric spline curve that satisfies the spatio-temporal gesture features, while reproducing a naturally segmented velocity profile (for details see [9]). In result, the LMP possesses a controller that defines for each point in time the target position of the wrist in space. The MCP then solves inverse kinematics for the 7 DOF arm. The arm's redundancy is interpreted as swivel angle of the elbow about the shoulder-wrist axis and is either controlled by a dedicated LMP or is heuristically determined from the target wrist position, the longitudinal axis of the hand, a tendency to minimize wrist bending, and damping for low arm elevations. The solution arm configuration is calculated by selecting, for the 3-DOF shoulder and wrist joint, an Euler angle set that satisfies the twist limits at current joint altitude and elevation. Finally, other LMPs that directly affect joint angles influence the posture by overriding the respective set of angles. For example, as illustrated in Fig. 1, a LMP for hand-internal movement may have been created from a sequence of key hand postures along with parameters specifying the movement dynamics along the transitions and, after completing itself, directly sets the joint angles of the fingers.

4 Imitation Learning and Response Facilitation

The motor control model described in the previous section provides two levels of representation of a movement: First, the overt movement can be represented in terms of the wrist trajectory through space, the wrist orientation vectors, and the hand configurations. These features are directly accessible to visual observation and can be considered a *perceptual representation* of an observed movement. Secondly, when producing a movement, the agent needs to construct a structured *motor representation*. It consists of a sequence of motor commands that determine how the self-organizing, peripheral motor resources in the body (the LMPs) will be producing movement, and with which degree of control or autonomy. As described above, each motor commands lays down the initiation of a ballistically executed movement segment corresponding to a motor "impulse". Depending on the motor systems involved, a movement segment representation can be a guiding stroke that encapsulates control parameters for arm movement through space (goal position or configuration), for wrist movement (target orientation), or for hand-internal movement (target postures), each possibly along with a parameter for the manner of execution (time of maximum velocity).

Since the agent plans and stores actions in terms of the more abstract and more efficient motor representation, the first step in utilizing motor resources for perceptual and understanding processes is to realize the mapping from perceptual representations to motor representations, also allowing him to imitate the observed action. Most models assume a repertoire of motor actions on the observer's part. In result, the mapping problem becomes one of selecting and activating the right action from this set, and we want this property from our model too. That is, if the agent disposes of a motor command for a movement *similar* to the observed one, the model should provide fast facilitation of an imitative response. If the sighted action is not in the agent's repertoire, however, the model should also account for ways to learn new motor representations, thus allowing to continually extend the agent's motor repertoire through learning by (true) imitation.

We approach this problem in a scenario where two virtual humanoid agents, *Max* and *Moritz*, are facing each other. Moritz acts as a demonstrator and can execute arbitrary animations, whereas Max takes on the role of the learner and imitator. That is, although he is equipped with general motor capabilities as to how a motor representation can be executed (see Sect. 3), Max has no knowledge about how to command his motor system, and hence how to control movements of his body in order to carry out certain actions. The goal, here, is to enable Max to acquire this knowledge just by watching Moritz making some movements.

4.1 Architectural Pre-requisites

Max is based upon a cognitive architecture that comprises a virtual view sensor for simulating his field of view, an ultra-short term sensory buffer for compensating sensor drop outs, and a perception component. The perception manages a perceptual memory by adding, modifying, and removing *percepts* as a result of virtual sensory stimulations. It can further apply simple and fast pattern detectors that can turn newly arisen constellations of percepts (e.g. a brown bushy region atop of a skin-colored elliptical region) into more complex percepts (e.g. Moritz's head). When Max first sees Moritz, his perception recognizes Moritz's hands, wrists, and elbows and asserts percepts that contain the positions of the corresponding perceived body parts. All positions are coded in a body-centered frame of reference and are updated every time step. For simplicity, the hand percepts comprise information about the configurations of Moritz's finger joints, i.e. we do not employ an inverse hand model yet.

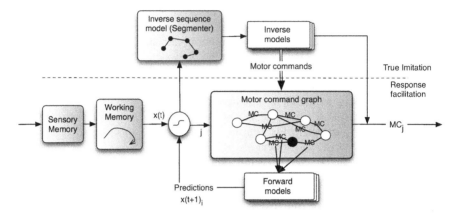

Fig. 2. The proposed model to map perceptual representations (in the working memory) to motor representations for imitative repsonse. A motor command graph is used to context-sensitively create forward models that make predictions about the ongoing movement. The motor command that is predicting correctly and best (MC$_j$) is selected for execution. Via a more indirect route, inverse models are employed for imitation learning of new motor commands.

Our imitation model is shown in Fig. 2. A sensory memory of fixed size is always updated with the most recent percepts; older entries are deleted while new entries are added. This memory holds data for about only a tenth of a second and it is used to detect the onsets and ends of an observed movement. A visual working memory continually stores positions and directions of the wrist movement as well as the finger joint angles for the part of the movement that is currently under consideration. These perceptual representations are mapped onto motor representations, as described in the following sections.

4.2 Motor Command Graph

Building upon Buchsbaum & Blumberg's approach [5] we employ a graph-based representation of movement. However, we extend it in twofold ways: First, we use a graph for representing not direct movement, but the motor commands that lead from one configuration of the motor system to another. We hence use the term *motor command graph* (see Fig. 2). Secondly, we employ multiple graphs at once in order to account for the possibly concurrent execution of submovements in different motor subsystems within a complex hand-arm-motion. Currently, we apply four motor command graphs for movement of the left and the right wrist and hands, respectively. Nodes in these graphs correspond to static motor system states, e.g. positions of the wrists in a body-centered frame of reference, or configurations of joint angles of one hand. At each point in time, the agent is either at a certain state (henceforth, the *active* node) or on a movement that bridges between two states. Special *hub-nodes* in the graphs (cf. [5]) serve as representations of typical start states, positions and configurations in which a complete movement normally starts and ends[1]. The edges between nodes represent single motor commands that the agent thinks can be applied in a certain state. For instance, edges in the wrist position graphs are guiding strokes that define single movement segments. Note that there can be multiple edges with the same start and end nodes, but for different movements in-between. Edges in the hand graphs represent parametric transition functions that define the duration and velocity profile of a movement from one hand configuration (start node) into another (end node).

4.3 Imitation Learning

In our imitation model, motor learning occurs whenever a demonstrated movement is new to Max, i.e., when no edge coming off the currently active state in the motor command graph can predict the incoming visual perceptions. If Max observes a completed but unknown movement, a two-stage inverse model is employed to construct appropriate motor commands from the percepts stored in the working memory. The first inverse model accomplishes segmentation, i.e. it is an inverse model of the sequencing of motor commands; the second one is an inverse model mapping single perceptual segments to candidate motor commands that may be used to produce them.

Arm movement is perceptually represented as wrist trajectory, given as a sequence of movement vectors calculated from each two successive sample positions. Each vector thus gives the direction of movement at that point in time as well as the speed (length of the vector divided by the time needed for this movement sample). Segmentation of arm movement is carried out based on both movement speed and direction. For segmentation based on *speed*, the velocity profile is searched for local minima that fall below a threshold relative to their neighboring maxima, i.e. they represent significant drops of movement speed. These points are taken as break points since two distinct guiding strokes will be needed to reproduce the observed velocity profile. Note that a minima with a considerably high speed compared to its surroundings would rather hint to a curved, yet single movement segment.

For the segmentation based on movement *direction* a divisive clustering method is employed. In the first step, all movement vectors are normalized to a length of one and are collapsed into one cluster. The average element of this cluster, the vector pointing into the gross movement direction, is then compared with every element of this cluster. If at least one element is significantly different, i.e. pointing into a significantly other direction, a new cluster with the direction of the most different element as average value is created. In that case, all clusters are cleared, except from their average values, and the movement vectors will again be distributed among the clusters based on their similarity with the average values. This procedure is iterated for every cluster until all elements in each cluster resemble the respective average value up to a certain threshold. Finally, after clustering, the affiliation of the movement vectors in working memory to a cluster is checked. A break point is set if two succeeding movement

---

[1] Note that the usage of hub-nodes presupposes that the imitator has recognized a structural congruency with the demonstrator, and that both can be in coincident bodily states.

vectors fall into different clusters, i.e. a significant change in movement direction compared to the overall curvature of the trajectory has been detected.

After segmentation, an inverse model is applied to each segment in order to calculate the parameters needed to produce it by a guiding stroke. To this end, the equations for trajectory formation (see [9]) are applied in inverse direction. A new edge is formed from the resultant guiding stroke and added to the arm motor command graph, leading from the currently active node to a newly inserted node that corresponds to the end state of this segment. After adding the new edge and the new node to the graph, the new motor command is executed to move the imitator's wrist into the new position, whose corresponding node now becomes the active node.

Likewise, if Max observes a completed, unknown finger movement by the demonstrator, the movement will be segmented both, at angular velocity minima and according to a clustering of movement directions, to detect the start, end, and via postures of the sighted hand movements. These configurations are used as key postures to create a new edge in the hand motor command graph, leading away from the currently active node into a new node corresponding to the new hand configuration. Upon adding the new edge and the new node to the movement graph, the according movement is executed and the new node becomes active.

The overall imitation process is illustrated as pseudo-code algorithm in Fig. 3. The described imitation learning occurs in the top part, whenever no motor command is available that could predict what is being observed. This process of learning new

```
do {
        edges ← motor commands that can predict the observed movement
        --- imitation learning ---
        if (no egde found) {
                segment after velocity profile and by clustering direction vectors
                for each segment {
                        motor command ← apply inverse model (segment)
                        create and insert new egde and end node to graph
                }
                execute newly learned motor command sequence
                active node ← final node of sequence
        }
        --- response facilitation ---
        else if (one edge predicts correctly and best) {
                execute motor command of the selected edge
                while (demonstration ongoing and imitative movement correct {
                        keep on executing motor command
                }
                if (imitation deviates from demonstration) {
                        stop imitative movement
                        exclude edge from future predictions of this segment
                        return to last correct motor state node
                        active node ← last correct motor state node
                }
                else      active node ← end node of executed motor command
        }
} while (true)
```

Fig. 3. The imitation process in pseudo-code

motor commands, and adding new edges and nodes to the motor command graph, respectively, is iterated as long as the demonstrator performs a movement. Complex movements are that way translated into sequences of motor commands that are stored in the graph representation as paths spanning several edges and nodes. Parts of the movement that are known already are readily incorporated into the newly learned motor command sequence.

4.4 Response Facilitation

The motor command graph constructed in this way can serve as basis for identifying, imitating, and even predicting the action of other's. In our approach, just like in previous work by others, forward models are employed to selectively activate motor knowledge of the agent that can successfully explain a demonstrated behavior (see Fig. 2). However, in our approach, these forward models are created dependent on the motor context, instead of testing all behaviors in the repertoire every time.

As illustrated in Fig. 3, this process facilitates immediate imitative responses, when active motor representations are continuously being executed and compared to the demonstration. If the demonstrator performs a movement, Max stores the movement directions in his working memory and compares all edges leading away from the current node instantaneously to the observation. That is, forward models of all motor commands that seem applicable are being computed in parallel to derive predictions of the possible future courses of movement. These predictions are compared to the observed movement. Every motor command that causes a prediction error below a certain threshold is considered a possible candidate to explain and reproduce the observed movement. If there is more than one candidate, this observation, prediction, and comparison cycle will go on until only one edge with a low prediction error prevails. This is the winning edge, which is used to construct a motor program to reproduce the observed movement. That is, Max starts to imitate Moritz immediately, possibly well before the demonstration has ended (active imitation or response facilitation). Note that, if the demonstrated movement is in principle familiar to Max but now performed with a different speed, the predictions of the corresponding forward model (or edge) will not be correct. That is, movements with different execution speeds would be learned as separate edges by the algorithm in Fig. 3. One solution to this problem is to map the length of the movement seen so far onto the trajectory predicted by a forward model, yielding the time parameter at which the corresponding motor command (with the speed demonstrated at first) would have produced a movement of the same length. Form this, the speed difference can be calculated and used to re-parameterize the motor command.

While imitating, Max continually compares his movements with the observed ones. Since Max reproduces behavior with his very own motor control and body, the imitation may well differ from the demonstrated one. In our current approach, we take an imitation to be successful as long as it meets with a sufficient degree of accuracy the "movement goals" as far as captured by the motor representations, i.e. target positions/configurations and wrist trajectories. Demonstrations of, in this sense, successfully imitated movement segments are removed from the working memory. If, however, a difference between the observed and self-performed movements becomes too big, the execution of the movement will be interrupted and the imitator returns into the last node at which accordance with the demonstrated movement was found.

Since the chosen edge from this node on was not the right but the best fitting one, the perceived movement is new. In this case, the last part of the observed movement as stored in the imitator's working memory will be subjected to the inverse model for segmenting in order to learn and impart new edges to the motor command graphs.

5   Example

To demonstrate our model, let us consider a sequence of three successive imitation games between Max and Moritz. The following figures show snapshots of the virtual scene (Max is to the right) and illustrate how the motor command graph is being constructed and processed. In the beginning (1), Max and Moritz are standing face-to-face and in relaxed poses. Max is in his hub node (black circle; active node indicated by the arrowhead) and is assuming this posture corresponds to Moritz's current pose. Moritz starts demonstrating a left arm movement (2). Max observes the movement up to its end and then applies his inverse models to segment it (here, it consists of a single guiding stroke) and to derive a corresponding motor command that gets added as new edge to the graph (dashed arrow).

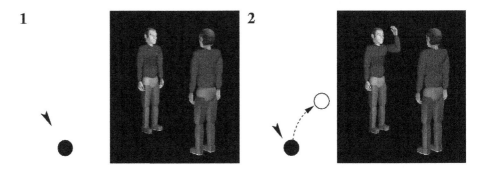

Performing a true imitation, Max carries out the newly acquired motor command and arrives in the new motor system state (3). Moritz moves his arm back to rest, observed by Max who learns a motor command for this movement segment as new edge leading back to the hub state (4), and can then move his arm accordingly.

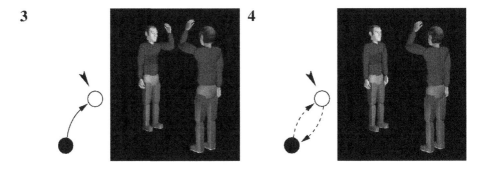

Moritz then starts to demonstrate another movement, starting out in the same direction as the previous one. Max tests whether any of his motor commands (only one at this time) matches (5) and finds that the previously learnt command successfully predicts the movement up to now. This facilitates an immediate imitation (6), until the error becomes so large as to rule out the motor command. Max thus stops his imitation.

Returning to the last correct node, Max employs his inverse models to learn the new motor command and adds a corresponding new node and edge to the graph (7). He then imitates this new movement and arrives in a new active motor system state (8).

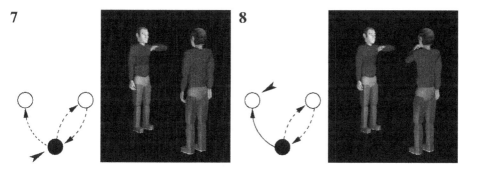

Seeing Moritz returning to the rest pose, Max learns the motor command for this movement too (9), and a new demonstration by Moritz starts (10). This time, Max finds two possible candidate edges to explain the observed movement.

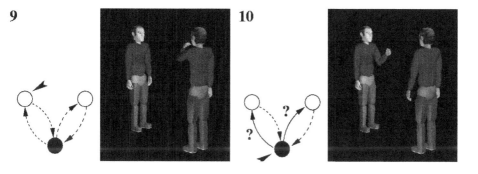

Max thus remains in the current motor state (here, the hub node) until one of the candidates fails to predict the observed movement. At this time (11), the identification of a motor command triggers an immediate imitation (response facilitation), leading into a motor state that Max assumes identical to Moritz's (12).

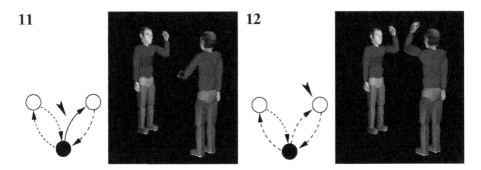

6   Conclusion

In this paper, we have presented work towards embodied agents that dispose of rich motor control representations to control their body for goal-directed actions, and that can employ these motor resources also for understanding and predicting the behavior of other, structurally congruent individuals. We have described an imitation model that enables our agents to map from perceptual representations to motor representations, possibly finding its outlet in immediate mimicking, and to learn an unknown motor behavior through (true) imitation.

A lot of work remains to be done. For one thing, our agents learn and perform any movement that they perceive and are able to process using their inverse and forward models of motor control. Yet, it would be more plausible to let an agent run through a stage of "body babbling", in which he can create a sense of his own body and its motor capabilities. We can now also imagine replacing the virtual demonstrator Moritz by a human demonstrator, using a tracking system for detecting the positions of the wrists and using data gloves for perceptions of the finger configurations. What needs to be done then is, among other things, an adjustment of the arm length and the body height to transform body-centric wrist positions of the demonstrator into according target wrist positions for the imitator. Finally, our model right now pertains to „meaningless" imitation. A movement is being reproduced based on own motor capabilities, but without reconstructing and attaching meaning to it, in the sense of actions that are fulfilling a specific goal. The work by Buchsbaum & Blumberg (2005) has pointed into possible directions to tackle this problem. It may also be a venue for addressing the open problem of *complex* (true) imitation, i.e. learning and imitating sequences or hierarchies of motor action by employing structured symbolic representations—an approach we have previously used for imitating iconic gestures [10]. With these steps, for which a lot of work that remains to be done cannot even be foreseen at this point, we may eventually arrive at humanoid agents that are capable of modeling the similarities and differences between the own and others' internal states, as they arise out of and make their way into our bodies.

References

1. R. Amit, M.J. Mataric (2002). Learning Movement Sequences from Demonstration. Int. Conf. on Development and Learning, 302-306
2. A. Billard, M.J.Mataric (2001). Learning human arm movements by imitation: evaluation of a biologically inspired connectionist architecture. Robotics & Autonomous systems 37(2-3): 145-160
3. A. Billard, Y. Epars, S. Calinon, S. Schaal, G. Cheng (2004). Discovering optimal imitation strategies. Robotics & Autonomous Systems: 47(2-3): 69-77
4. Blakemore, S.-J., & Decety, J. (2001). From the perception of action to the understanding of intention. *Nature Reviews Neuroscience, 2*, 561–567.
5. D. Buchsbaum & B.Blumberg (2005). Imitation as a First Step to Social Learning in Synthetic Characters: A Graph-based Approach, ACM Symp. on Computer Animation, 9-18
6. Byrne, R.W. (1995). The thinking ape. Evolutionary origins of intelligence. Oxford University Press.
7. Y. Demiris, Gillian Hayes (2002). Imitation as a dual-route process featuring predictive and learning components: a biologically-plausible computational model. In: Imitation in Animals and Artifacts, Chapter 13, MIT Press.
8. Iacoboni, M., Woods, R. P., Brass, M., Bekkering, H., Mazziotta, J. C., & Rizzolatti, G. (1999). Cortical mechanisms of human imitation. Science, 286 (5449), 2526–2528.
9. S. Kopp, I. Wachsmuth (2004). Synthesizing multimodal utterances for conversational agents, Computer Animation & Virtual Worlds, 15(1): 39-52
10. S. Kopp, T. Sowa, I. Wachsmuth (2004). Imitation games with an artificial agents: From mimicking to understanding shape-related iconic gestures. In Camurri, Volpe (eds.): Gesture-Based Communication in Human-Computer Interaction, 436-447, Berlin: Springer-Verlag
11. Latash M.L. (1993) Control of Human Movement. Human Kinetics: Urbana, IL.
12. Meltzoff, A. N. (2005). Imitation and other minds: The "Like Me" hypothesis. In S. Hurley & N. Chater (Eds.), Perspectives on imitation (pp. 55-77). MIT Press.
13. Rizzolatti, G., Fogassi, L., & Gallese, V. (2001). Neurophysiological mechanisms underlying the understanding and imitation of action. *Nat. Rev. Neurosc., 2*, 661–670.
14. Wallbott, H.G. (1995). Congruence, contagion, and motor-mimicry: Mutualities in nonverbal exchange. In I. Markova, C. Graumann, & K. Foppa (Eds.), Mutualities in dialogue. Cambridge University Press.
15. Wachsmuth, I. & Knoblich, G. (2005). Embodied communication in humans and machines - a research agenda. Artificial Intelligence Review 24(3-4): 517-522.
16. D.M. Wolpert, K. Doya, M. Kawato (2003). A unifying computational framework for motor control and social interaction, Philos Trans R Soc Lond B Biol Sci. 358(1431): 593-602

Robust Recognition of Emotion from Speech

Mohammed E. Hoque[1], Mohammed Yeasin[1], and Max M. Louwerse[2]

[1] Department of Electrical and Computer Engineering / Institute for Intelligent Systems
[2] Department of Psychology / Institute for Intelligent Systems
The University of Memphis
Memphis, TN 38152 USA
{mhoque, myeasin, mlouwerse}@memphis.edu

Abstract. This paper presents robust recognition of a subset of emotions by animated agents from salient spoken words. To develop and evaluate the model for each emotion from the chosen subset, both the prosodic and acoustic features were used to extract the intonational patterns and correlates of emotion from speech samples. The computed features were projected using a combination of linear projection techniques for compact and clustered representation of features. The projected features were used to build models of emotions using a set of classifiers organized in hierarchical fashion. The performances of the models were obtained using number of classifiers from the WEKA machine learning toolbox. Empirical analysis indicated that the lexical information computed from both the prosodic and acoustic features at word level yielded robust classification of emotions.

Keywords: emotion recognition, prosody, speech, machine learning.

1 Introduction

Animated conversational agents allow for natural multimodal human-computer interaction and have shown to be effective in various intelligent systems, including intelligent tutoring systems [1, 2]. Agents used in intelligent tutoring are designed to articulate difficult concepts in a well paced, adaptive and responsive atmosphere based on the learners' affective and cognitive states. Expert educators, both human and artificial, are expected to identify the cognitive states of mind of the learners' and take appropriate pedagogical actions [3]. Because of the realization that monitoring cognitive states in the student through the student's verbal feedback alone is not enough, research that focuses on monitoring of other modalities like speech has become more common [4, 5]. There is no doubt that high accuracy recognition of cognitive states and emotions relies on multiple modalities, rather than one specific modality. For instance, when a speaker is surprised, this emotion can be expressed through language (syntax), facial expressions (eyebrows moving up), through gestures (showing palms of both hands), through eye gaze (making continued eye contact with dialogue partner) as well as through speech (intonational contours). Moreover, in addition to multiple modalities being responsible for the recognition of emotions and

J. Gratch et al. (Eds.): IVA 2006, LNAI 4133, pp. 42–53, 2006.

cognitive states, the interaction of modalities is of importance, because one modality can compensate the absence of another. Because of the current state of human-computer interaction, the modalities animated conversational agents can use for their response to a dialogue partner are speech and language.

Despite the fact that we know linguistic modalities (e.g. dialog move, intonation, pause) and paralinguistic modalities (e.g. facial expressions, eye gaze, gestures) interact in communication, the exact nature of this interaction remains unclear [6]. There are two primary reasons why an insight in the interaction of modalities in the communicative process is beneficial.

First, from a psychological point of view it helps us understand how communicative processes take shape in the minds of dialog participants. Under what psychological conditions are different channels aligned? Does a channel add information to the communicative process or does it merely co-occur with other channels? Research in psychology has shed light on the interaction of modalities, for instance comparing eye gaze [7, 8], gestures [9-11] and facial expressions [12] but many questions regarding multiple – i.e., more than pairs of – channels and their alignment remain unanswered.

Second, insight in multimodal communication is beneficial from a computational point of view, for instance in the development of animated conversational agents [13]. The naturalness of the human-computer interaction can be maximized by the use of animated conversational agents, because of the availability of both linguistic (semantics, syntax) and paralinguistic (pragmatic, sociological) features. These animated agents have anthropomorphic, automated, talking heads with facial features and gestures that are coordinated with text-to-speech-engines [14-16]). Examples of these agents are Baldi [17], COSMO [18], STEVE [19], Herman the Bug [18] and AutoTutor [20]. Though the naturalness of these agents is progressively changing, there is room for improvement. Current agents for instance incessantly stare at the dialog partner, use limited facial features rather randomly, or produce bursts of unpaused speech. Both psycholinguistics and computational linguistics would thus benefit from answers to questions regarding the interaction of multimodal channels.

There is a growing interest in robust recognition of emotion from speech by researchers from various interdisciplinary areas. Examples of specific domains are affective interface [3] and call center environments [21]. In recent work by Dellaert *et al.* [22] accuracies in the range of 60% -65% were reported in distinguishing patterns among sadness, anger, happiness, and fear in the general domain of Human-Computer Interaction (HCI). The results were obtained using a cross-validation approach by fusing three classifiers: the maximum likelihood Bayes classification, kernel regression, and the *k*-nearest neighbor (k-NN) methods using the pitch contour features. For a call center environment Lee *et al.* [23] distinguish between two emotions: positive and negative, using linear discrimination, k-NN classifiers, and support vector machines achieving a maximum accuracy rate of 75%.

Paeschke [24] used a real-time emotion recognizer with neural networks adopted for call center applications and reported 77% classification accuracy in two emotions: agitation and calmness. Several studies showed how "quality features" (based on formant analysis) are used in addition to "prosody features", (particularly pitch and energy) to improve the classification of multiple emotions [25], [26]. This technique is known to exploit emotional dimensions other than prosody. Yu *et al.* [27] used SVMs, binary classifiers, to detect one emotion versus the rest. On four distinct emotions such as anger, happiness, sadness, and neutral, they achieved an accuracy of 73%.

Robust recognition of emotion expressed in speech requires a thorough understanding of the lexical aspects of speech [21]. Lee *et al.* hypothesized that a group of positive and negative words were related to different emotions. The occurrences of such predefined words were used to infer the emotional reaction of a caller using a probabilistic framework. Lee *et al.* argued that there a one-to-one correspondence may be assumed between a word and a positive or negative emotion.

Though this may be true for some words that have a semantic bias, more commonly a word does not have such a bias and can convey different emotions by the use of different intonational patterns. For example, the frequently used discourse marker "okay", is often used to express affirmation (S1 "Ready?" S2 "Okay"), but can also be used to express delight (S1 "So and that's how the procedure works" S2 "Okay!"), confidence (S1 "You're ready for the jump?" "Okay"), or confusion (S1 "You just multiply by the divider" S2 "Okay…?") [28]. The meaning of these different uses of "okay" may be guessed by their context, but to a large extent their

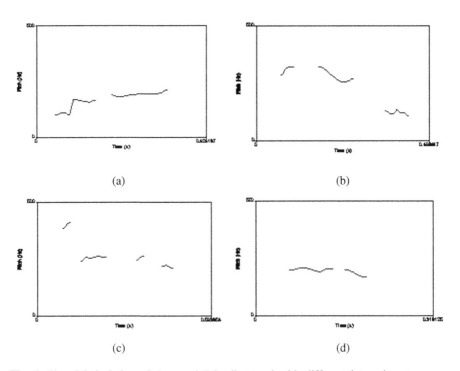

(a)   (b)

(c)   (d)

Fig. 1. Pictorial depiction of the word "okay" uttered with different intonations to express different emotions. The pitch contour of various emotions: (a) confusion, (b) flow, (c) delight and (d) neutral are plotted to highlight the differences manifested at lexical level by various emotions.

emotional value only becomes clear in the intonational patterns used to express the word. Figure 1 shows that despite the fact that a word like "okay" is the same, the intonational patterns are very different depending on the emotions. We therefore predict that lexical information extracted from combined prosodic and acoustic features that correspond to intonational pattern of "salient words" will yield robust recognition of emotion from speech, providing a framework for signal level analysis of speech for emotion.

To test this hypothesis, a small database of audio samples representing various emotions was used. Based on the domain knowledge, preprocessing of audio samples is performed to extract the salient words and selected word-level utterances were used to compute features such as fundamental frequency (F0), energy, rhythm, pause and duration. The computed features were projected and then, fused in a feature level framework to build models for various emotions.

2 Proposed Approach

The proposed approach consists of five major components (see Figure 2): (i) collection of suitable data sets for training and testing, (ii) extraction of feature, (iii) projection of feature to lower dimensional space, (iv) learning the models using machine learning techniques and (v) evaluation of models. This paper thereby presents a holistic approach in robust recognition of emotion from speech.

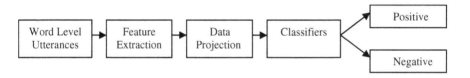

Fig. 2. The high level description of the overall emotion recognition process

First, a suitable database is captured for building and evaluating the models. Second, intonational patterns from spoken "salient words" are extracted with a combination of prosodic and acoustic features. Third, the extracted features are projected onto the lower dimensional space using combined Principle Component Analysis (PCA) [29] and Linear Discriminant Analysis (LDA) for a compact and clustered representation of computed features. Fourth, a set of machine learning techniques from the WEKA [30] toolbox are used to learn the models from the training samples. Finally, testing samples are used to evaluate the performance of the models. We describe the details of various components of robust recognition of emotion from speech below.

2.1 Database and Preparation

Collecting large databases of natural and unbiased emotion is challenging. One needs a representative data set to infer various emotions from speech using machine learning technique to establish the hypothesis and to obtain meaningful results. The performance of a classifier that can distinguish different emotional patterns ultimately depends on the completeness of the training and testing samples and how similar these samples are to real-world data.

The data captured to perform experiments can be categorized into three methods depending on how they are captured. The first method employs actors to utter various or similar sentences in various feigned emotional patterns. The second method utilizes a system that interacts with a human subject and draws him/her to an emotional point and records the response. The third approach is to extract real-life human utterances, which express various natural emotions.

The main drawback of having actors expressing emotional utterance is that the utterances are acted out independently from one another typically in a laboratory setting. These data may converge very well, but may not be suitable for real-life human-computer interaction settings. On the other hand, setting up an experiment where individuals interact with computers or other individuals is expensive and time consuming for testing out classifiers. In the study reported here, emotional utterances were clipped from movies. Though it is true that emotions are still "acted out", the discourse context and the absence of a lab setting makes it more natural than the first method. Utterances were taken from three movies: "Fahrenheit 911", "Bowling for Columbine" and "Before Sunset". "Fahrenheit 911" and "Bowling for Columbine" are political documentaries containing real interviews with many cases of positive and negative emotions. "Before Sunset" is a chatty romantic movie with delightful, frustrating and confusing expressions with minimal background music. Fifteen utterances were selected from these movies covering four classes of emotions: confusion/uncertain, delight, flow (confident, encouragement), and frustration [3, [4, 5]. Selected utterances were stand-alone expressions in conversations that had an ambiguous meaning, dependent on the context (e.g. "Great", "Yes", "Yeah", "No", "Ok", "Good", "Right", "Really", "What", "God"). Three graduate students listened to the audio clips without specific instructions as to what intonational patterns to listen to and successfully distinguished between the positive and negative emotions 65% of the time. A hierarchical classifier was designed to first distinguish between positive (delight and flow) and negative (confusion and frustration) emotions. The same set of classifiers were applied again on positive and negative emotions

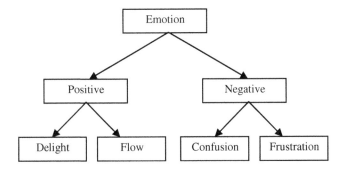

Fig. 3. The design of the hierarchical binary classifiers

separately to differentiate between delight and flow under positive emotions, and confusion and frustration under negative emotions as shown in Figure 3.

2.2 Emotion Models Using Lexical Information

To compute the lexical information from spoken salient words, 22 acoustic and prosodic features related to segmental and suprasegmental information, which are believed to be correlates of emotion, were calculated. Computed features were utterance level statistics related to fundamental frequency (F0) [31-33]. Other features were related to duration, intensity, and formants. In particular, the following features were computed for developing the models.

1. **Pitch:** Minimum, maximum, mean, standard deviation, absolute value, quantile, ratio between voiced and unvoiced frames.
2. **Duration:** ε_{time} ε_{height}
3. **Intensity:** Minimum, maximum, mean, standard deviation, quantile.
4. **Formant:** First formant, second formant, third formant, fourth formant, fifth formant, second formant / first formant, third formant / first formant
5. **Rhythm:** Speaking rate.

The speech processing software Praat [34] was used to calculate the features in batch mode. ε_{time}, ε_{height} features, which are part of duration, are prominent measures.

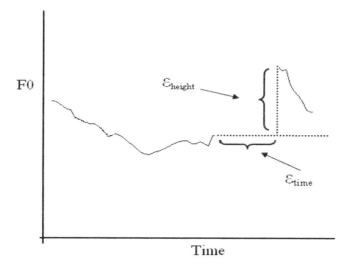

Fig. 4. Measures of F0 for computing parameters ($\varepsilon time$, $\varepsilon height$) which corresponds to rising and lowering of intonational

ε_{height} and ε_{time} features are related to phenomenon when fundamental frequency breaks down in word levels. ε_{time} refers to the pause time between two disjoint segments of F0 (often referred as Pitch), whereas ε_{height} refers to the vertical distance between the segments symbolizing voice breaks as shown in Figure 4. Inclusion of *height* and *time* accounts for possible low or high pitch accents. The frequency shift between the segments was selected rather than absolute measures to take into account the discourse [35].

The first model fed the raw 22 features directly into the classifier. The second and the third model applied PCA on the raw features and took the first 15 (F15) and 20 (F20) eigenvectors respectively to de-correlate the base features. In the fourth model, LDA is directly used on the raw features to project them directly onto lower dimension. The fifth model consisted of the combination of PCA (F15) and LDA. A 10-fold cross validation technique was used whereby the training data was randomly split into ten sets, 9 of which were used in training and the 10th for validations. Then iteratively another nine were picked.

Table 1. The list of classifiers used to validate the robustness of the algorithm using weka toolbox

Types of Classifiers				
Rules	**Trees**	**Meta**	**Functions**	**Bayes**
Part	RandomForrest	AdaBoostM1	Logistic	Naïve Bayes
NNge	J48	Bagging	Multi-layer Perceptron	Naïve Bayes Simple
Ridor	Logistic Model Tree	Classification via Regression	RBF Network	Naïve Bayes Updateable
-	-	LogitBoost	Simple Logistics	-
-	-	Multi Class Classifier	SMO	-
-	-	Ordinal Class Classifier	-	-
-	-	Threshold Selector	-	-

2.3 Results and Discussion

Results showed that the combination of data projection techniques such as PCA and LDA yielded better performance as opposed to using raw features or using LDA or PCA alone (Table 2). An average of 83.33% accuracy was achieved using the combination of PCA and LDA. On the other hand, features like PCA (F15), PCA (F20) and LDA resulted in accuracy rates of respectively 50.79%, 57.1%, 61%, and 52.01% on average. The performance of combining PCA and LDA is higher than PCA or LDA itself mainly because PCA de-correlates the data, whereas LDA projects the data onto lower dimension. Therefore, the combination of PCA and LDA is expected to work better.

When the same models were applied to positive emotions and negative emotions separately even more impressive results emerged (Table 3). The performance of the diverse set of classifiers to recognize negative emotions is better than the performance to recognize positive emotions. One potential explanation for this is that negative emotions may deviate more from the standard than positive emotions. In other words, positive emotions may in general less likely be recognized as an emotion, because they map onto the default. Negative emotions on the other hand deviate from that default, thereby facilitating recognition, both in humans and computers.

Table 2. Summary of classification results for 21 selected classifiers

Category	Classifiers	Accuracy (%)				
		Features (a)	PCA (b)		LDA (c)	PCA+LDA (d)
			F15 (b1)	F20 (b2)		
Rules	Part	50	66.67	66.67	47.61	83.33
	NNge	33.33	33.33	38.09	38.09	83.33
	Ridor	66.67	83.33	100	47.20	66.67
Trees	Random Forrest	50	50	50	66.67	83.33
	J48	50	66.67	66.67	47.61	83.33
	Logistic Model Tree	33.33	47.61	83.33	66.67	71.67
Meta	AdaBoostM1	61.90	71.42	71.42	42.85	61.90
	Bagging	33.33	66.67	83.33	42.85	66.67
	Classification via Regression	50	66.67	66.67	47.61	83.33
	Logit Boost	50	50	61.90	52.38	83.33
	Multi Class Classifier	50	42.85	52.38	57.14	83.33
	Ordinal Class Classifier	50	66.67	66.67	47.62	83.33
	Threshold Selector	50	66.67	66.67	61.90	100
Functions	Logistic	50	42.85	57.38	57.14	83.33
	Multi-layer Perceptron	50	57.14	52.38	50	83.33
	RBF Network	33.33	66.67	52.38	38.09	83.33
	Simple Logistics	33.33	47.61	83.33	66.67	66.67
	SMO	71.42	57.14	61.90	52.38	71.42
Bayes	Naïve Bayes	66.67	50	33.33	52.38	66.67
	Naïve Bayes Simple	66.67	50	33.33	57.14	66.67
	Naïve Bayes Updateable	66.67	50	33.33	52.38	66.67

Note. (a) raw features are used into classifiers, (b1) using the first 15 (f15) eigenvectors of PCA into the classifiers, (b2) using the first 20 (f20) eigenvectors of PCA into the classifiers. (c) using LDA to project the data into lower dimension and then use them into the classifiers. (d) combination of both PCA and LDA to not only de-correlate the data redundant feature space, but also to project them into lower dimension and then use them into the classifiers.

Table 3. Summary of classification results for 21 classifiers on positive and negative emotions

Category	Classifiers	Accuracy (%)	
		Delight + Flow	Confusion + Frustration
Rules	Part	72.72	100
	NNge	80	100
	Ridor	66.67	100
Trees	RandomForrest	63.63	66.67
	J48	72.72	100
	LMT	72.72	100
Meta	AdaBoostM1	54.44	100
	Bagging	63.64	66.67
	Classification via Regression	72.72	100
	LogitBoost	63.64	100
	Multi Class Classifier	72.72	100
	Ordinal Class Classifier	72.72	100
	Threshold Selector	83.33	100
Functions	Logistic	72.72	100
	Multi-layer Perceptron	66.67	100
	RBF Network	66.67	100
	Simple Logistics	72.72	100
	SMO	72.72	100
Bayes	Naïve Bayes	72.72	100
	Naïve Bayes Simple	72.72	100
	Native Bayes Updateable	72.72	100

Note. Results with the combination of PCA + LDA were only recorded as they comparatively produce better results as shown in Table 2.

It needs to be noted that the results presented in Table 2 and 3 are satisfactory but very similar. The most likely explanation for this result is the limited dataset that does not provide the variability that can be found in larger sets of spoken discourse. Indeed, additional data collection needs to be conducted in order to provide a larger sample set for training and testing.

The total classifiers used can be broken into five categories. Rule based classifiers produce rules for classification from the training data and then apply them on the testing set. Tree based classifiers produce classification trees as their outputs. Function-based classifiers, on the other hand, represent the well-known support vector machine, neural network, linear regression types of classifiers. Meta classifiers combine several classifiers, e.g. Vote or enhance a single classifier, e.g. bagging. Bayes group consists of simple probabilistic classifiers. From Tables 2 & 3, it is evident that, with the exception of Bayes, all the classifiers perform similarly in this particular problem domain. It can be easily explained that due to the limited database, probabilistic based classifiers such as Bayes did not perform equally well compared to the other classifiers. In the second phase of this study with more challenging map-task data, similar performances across a variety of classifiers would be unlikely. This may provide a better conclusive result about a set of optimum classifiers for this given problem.

3 Conclusions

Robust autonomous recognition of emotion is gaining attention due to the widespread applications into various domains, including those with animated conversational agents. Automated recognizing emotion with high accuracy still remains an elusive goal due to the lack of complete understanding and agreement of emotion in human minds. The study presented in this paper achieved an average of 83.33% success rate of defining positive and negative emotion using a varied set of classifiers confined to learning environment. Lexical and prosodic features were used on word level emotional utterances to improve the performance of the emotion recognition system. Our results indicate that using a proper set of projection techniques on word level lexical and prosodic features yields an accuracy rate of 80 to 100%. It is worth noting that the datasets were tested by three graduate students who were able to classify the emotions into correct bins 65% of the time. This supports our hypothesis that word level prosodic and lexical features provide useful clues about positive and negative emotions. This hypothesis also enables us to have a framework for signal level analysis.

Obviously, there is a risk involved in clipping arbitrary words from a conversation, which may be ineffective at various cases as some words may convey more in context only. Therefore, our goal for the immediate future is to look at meaningful words in a sequence while introducing context in our analysis as well. A research project that investigates multimodal communication (prosody, dialog structure, eye gaze and facial expressions) in Map Task scenarios will thereby generate the needed data [5, 6]. In the second phase of this project the results of the data analysis will allow us to develop an animated conversational agent that uses the right intonational contours in the right contexts, expressing the right emotions.

Visual information modifies the perception of speech [17], while combinations of visual and audio information provide robust performance when modalities are captured in noisy environment [36]. Therefore, in order for an animated conversational agent to be successful in learning environments, it is imperative that the agent should be able to fuse the audio and video data to reach a decision regarding the emotional states of the learners. Therefore, our future efforts will include fusion of video and audio data in a signal level framework to boost the performance of our existing emotion recognition system.

Acknowledgements

This research was partially supported by grant NSF-IIS-0416128 awarded to the third author. Any opinions, findings, and conclusions or recommendations expressed in this material are those of the authors and do not necessarily reflect the views of the funding institution.

References

[1]   A. C. Graesser, K. VanLehn, C. Rose, P. Jordan, and D. Harter, "Intelligent tutoring systems with conversational dialogue.," *AI Magazine*, vol. 22, pp. 39-51, 2001.

[2]   M. M. Louwerse, A. C. Graesser, S. Lu, and H. H. Mitchell, "Social cues in animated conversational agents," *Applied Cognitive Psychology*, vol. 19, pp. 1-12, 2005.

[3]   B. Kort, R. Reilly, and R. W. Picard, "An Affective Model of Interplay Between Emotions and Learning: Reengineering Educational Pedagogy-Building a Learning Companion.," presented at In Proceedings of International Conference on Advanced Learning Technologies (ICALT 2001), Madison, Wisconsin, August 2001.

[4]   S. K. D'Mello, S. D. Craig, A. Witherspoon, J. Sullins, B. McDaniel, B. Gholson, and A. C. Graesser, "The relationship between affective states and dialog patterns during interactions with AutoTutor," presented at Proceedings of the World Conference on E-learning in Corporate, Government, Health Care, and Higher Education, Chesapeake, VA, 2005.

[5]   M. Louwerse, P. Jeuniaux, M. Hoque, J. Wu, and G. Lewis, "Multimodal Communication in Computer-Mediated Map Task Scenarios," presented at The 28th Annual Conference of the Cognitive Science Society, Vancouver, Canada, July 2006.

[6]   M. M. Louwerse, E. G. Bard, M. Steedman, X. Hu, and A. C. Graesser, "Tracking multimodal communication in humans and agents," Institute for Intelligent Systems, University of Memphis, Memphis, TN., 2004.

[7]   M. Argyle and M. Cook, *Gaze and Mutual Gaze*, 1976.

[8]   G. Doherty-Sneddon, A. H. Anderson, C. O'Malley, S. Langton, S. Garrod, and V. Bruce, "Face-to-face and video-mediated communication: A comparison of dialogue structure and task performance," *Journal of Experimental Psychology-Applied*, vol. 3(2), pp. 105-125, 1997.

[9]   S. Goldin-Meadow and M. A. Singer, "From children's hands to adults' ears: Gesture's role in teaching and learning.," *Developmental Psychology*, pp. 509-520, 2003.

[10] M. M. Louwerse and A. Bangerter, "Focusing attention with deictic gestures and linguistic expressions," presented at Proceedings of the Cognitive Science Society, 2005.

[11] D. McNeill, " Hand and mind: What gestures reveal about thought.," 1992.

[12] P. Ekman, "About brows: emotional and conversational signals.," *Human Ethology*, pp. 169-248, 1979.

[13] M. M. Louwerse, A. C. Graesser, S. Lu, and H. H. Mitchell, "Social cues in animated conversational agents," *Applied Cognitive Psychology*, vol. 19, pp. 1-12, 2004.

[14] J. Cassell and K. Thorisson, "The Power of a Nod and a Glance: Envelope vs. Emotional Feedback in Animated Conversational Agents.," *Journal of Applied Artifical Intelligence*, vol. 13 (3), pp. 519-538, 1999.

[15] M. M. Cohen and D. W. Massaro, "Development and Experimentation with Synthetic Visible Speech Behavioral Research Methods and Instrumentation," vol. 26, pp. 260-265, 1994.

[16] R. Picard, "Affective Computing," 1997.

[17] D. W. Massaro, "Illusions and Issues in Bimodal SpeechPerception.," presented at Proceedings of Auditory Visual Speech Perception '98., Terrigal-Sydney Australia, December, 1998.

[18] J. Lester, B. B. Stone, and G. Stelling, "Lifelike Pedagogical Agents for Mixed-Initiative Problem Solving in Constructivist Learning Environments.," *User Modeling and User-Adapted Interaction*, vol. 9, pp. 1-44, 1999.

[19] J. Rickel and W. L. Johnson, "Animated agents for procedural training in virtual reality: Perception, cognition, and motor control.," *In Applied Artificial Intelligence*, vol. 13, pp. 343--382, 1999.

[20] N. Person, A. Graesser, L. Bautista, E. M. and, and TRG, "Evaluating student learning gains in two versions of AutoTutor," Artificial Intelligence in Education: AI-ED in the Wired and Wireless Future, J. Moore, C. Redfield, and W. Johnson, Eds., pp. 286--293, 2001.

[21] C. Lee and S. Narayanan, "Toward detecting emotions in spoken dialogs," *IEEE transaction on speech and audio processing*, vol. 13, 2005.

[22] F. Dellaert, T. Polzin, and A. Waibel, "Recognizing Emotion in Speech," presented at Proceedings of the ICSLP, 1996.

[23] C. Lee, S. Narayanan, and R. Pieraccini, "Classifying Emotions in Human-Machine Spoken Dialogs," presented at Proc. of International Conference on Multimedia and Expo, Lausanne, Switzerland, August 2002.

[24] A. Paeschke and W. F. Sendlmeier, "Prosodic Characteristics of Emotional Speech: Measurements of Fundamental Frequency Movements," presented at Proceedings of theISCA-Workshop on Speech and Emotion, 2000.

[25] R. Tato, R. Santos, R. Kompe, and J. M. Pardo, "Emotional Space Improves Emotion Recognition," presented at Proc. Of ICSLP-2002, Denver, Colorado, September 2002.

[26] S. Yacoub, S. Simske, X. Lin, and J. Burns, "Recognition of Emotions in Interactive Voice Response Systems," presented at The Eurospeech 2003, 8th European Conference on Speech Communication and Technology, Geneva, Switzerland, 1-4 September 2003.

[27] F. Yu, E. Chang, Y. Q. Xu, and H. Y. Shum, "Emotion Detection From Speech To Enrich Multimedia Content," presented at the Second IEEE Pacific-Rim Conference on Multimedia, Beijing, China, October 24-26, 2001.

[28] M. M. Louwerse and H. H. Mitchell, "Towards a taxonomy of a set of discourse markers in dialog: A theoretical and computational linguistic account.," *Discourse Processes*, pp. 199-239, 2003.

[29] R. Duda, P. Hart, and D. Stork, *Pattern Classification*, 2nd ed. New York: Wiley, 2001.

[30] I. H. Witten and E. Frank, *Data Mining: Practical machine learning tools and techniques*, 2nd ed. San Francisco: Morgan Kaufmann, 2005.

[31] C. E. Williams and K. N. Stevens, "Emotions and speech:Some acoustical correlates," *JASA*, vol. 52, pp. 1238-1250, 1972.

[32] R. Banse and K. R. Scherer, "Acoustic profiles in vocal emotion expression," *J. Personality and Social Psychology*, vol. 70, pp. 614–636, 1996.

[33] S. Mozziconacci, "The expression of emotion considered in the framework of an intonational model," *Proc. ISCA Wrksp. Speech and Emotion*, pp. 45-52, 2000.

[34] P. Boersma and D. Weenink, " Praat: doing phonetics by computer," Version 4.4.16 ed, 2006.

[35] S. Kettebekov, M. Yeasin, and R. Sharma, "Prosody-based Audio Visual co-analysis for co-verbal gesture recognition," *IEEE transaction on Multimedia*, vol. 7, pp. 234-242, 2005.

[36] M. Pantic and L. J. M. Rothkrantz, "Toward an affect-sensitive multimodal human-computer interaction.," *Proceedings of the IEEE*, vol. 91, pp. 1370 – 1390, Sept. 2003.

Affect Detection from Human-Computer Dialogue with an Intelligent Tutoring System

Sidney D'Mello[1] and Art Graesser[2]

[1] Department of Computer Science, The University of Memphis
Memphis, TN, 38152, USA
sdmello@memphis.edu
[2] Department of Psychology, The University of Memphis
Memphis, TN, 38152, USA
a-graesser@memphis.edu

Abstract. We investigated the possibility of detecting affect from natural language dialogue in an attempt to endow an intelligent tutoring system, AutoTutor, with the ability to incorporate the learner's affect into its pedagogical strategies. Training and validation data were collected in a study in which college students completed a learning session with AutoTutor and subsequently affective states of the learner were identified by the learner, a peer, and two trained judges. We analyzed each of these 4 data sets with the judges' affect decisions, along with several dialogue features that were mined from AutoTutor's log files. Multiple regression analyses confirmed that dialogue features could significantly predict particular affective states (boredom, confusion, flow, and frustration). A variety of standard classifiers were applied to the dialogue features in order to assess the accuracy of discriminating between the individual affective states compared with the baseline state of neutral.

1 Introduction

An emerging trend in the development of intelligent virtual agents (IVAs) has involved the modeling of the user's affective states, with the long-term goal of delivering a more engaging, adaptive, naturalistic experience [1, 2]. Over the last few years, a particular class of IVAs, namely intelligent tutoring systems (ITSs) with animated pedagogical agents [3-5], have been designed to assist learners in the active construction of knowledge, particularly at deeper levels of comprehension. Most of these systems provide one-on-one tutoring, which is known to be a powerful method of promoting knowledge construction [6], whereas others assist individual learners with a cast of animated agents that perform different functions [4, 7].

While ITSs have typically focused on the learner's cognitive states they can be endowed with the ability to recognize, assess, and react to a learner's affective state [8-11]. There is some evidence that an affect sensitive ITS would have a positive impact on learning. For example, Kim [12] conducted a study that demonstrated that the interest and self-efficacy of a learner significantly increased when the learner was

J. Gratch et al. (Eds.): IVA 2006, LNAI 4133,, pp. 54–67, 2006.

accompanied by a pedagogical agent acting as a virtual learning companion sensitive to the learner's affect. Linnerenbrink and Pintrich [13] reported that the posttest scores of physics understanding decreased as a function of negative affect during learning. Craig et al. [14] reported that increased levels of boredom were negatively correlated with learning of computer literacy, whereas levels of confusion and the state of flow (being absorbed in the learning process, [15]) were positively correlated with learning in an AutoTutor learning environment. AutoTutor is an intelligent tutoring system that helps learners construct explanations by interacting with them in natural language and helping them use simulation environments [9, 16]. The focus of this paper is on the transformation of AutoTutor into an affect-sensitive intelligent tutoring system [17, 18].

Much of the work in affect detection involves the use of bodily sensors that monitor facial expressions [19], gross body language [20], acoustic-prosodic vocal features [21-24], and physiological measures such as heart rate monitors, electromyography, skin conductance, etc. [25, 26]. This paper investigates a less frequently explored channel, namely human-computer natural language dialogue. There have been some investigations of emotions in human-human dialogues [21, 27] and human-computer dialogues [22], but the literature on automated affect detection is sparse. The use of dialogue to detect affect in learning environments is a reasonable information source to explore, as opposed to bodily sensors, because dialogue information is abundant in virtually all conversations and is inexpensive to collect.

Perhaps the most relevant work investigating dialogue and emotions has been conducted on the program ITSPOKE [23]. ITSPOKE integrates a spoken language component into the Why2-Atlas tutoring system [28]. The spoken student dialogue turns were analyzed on the basis of lexical and acoustic features, with codings of negative, neutral or positive affect. The algorithms were able to reach high levels of accuracy in detecting affect [22].   Another interesting use of natural language dialogue for affect detection is provided by Carberry, Lambert, and Schroeder [29] who developed an algorithm to recognize doubt by examining linguistic and contextual features in conjunction with world knowledge. The major difference between these research efforts and our approach is that we are concerned with a larger set of affective states (boredom, confusion, delight, flow, frustration, neutral, and surprise) as well as a novel set of dialogue features as will be elaborated below.

We begin this paper by describing the various information channels that are tracked during interactions with AutoTutor and are stored in its text log files. Next we describe a study used to systematically gather affect judgments (from four raters) and dialogue patterns while participants interacted with AutoTutor. The data collected in this study served as training and testing data for the machine learning algorithms, with the affect judgments of each judge representing the ground truth from his or her perspective. Statistical analyses assessed which of the affective states could be predicted from the dialogue features. A variety of machine learning algorithms were then applied to the features selected by the statistical methods in an attempt to assess the reliability in automatically detecting the learner's affect from AutoTutor's dialogue. We conclude by addressing limitations of this research and presenting options to alleviate some of the known problems.

2   AutoTutor's Mixed-Initiative Dialogue

The Tutoring Research Group (TRG) at the University of Memphis developed AutoTutor, a fully automated computer tutor that simulates human tutors and holds conversations with students in natural language [9, 30]. AutoTutor attempts to comprehend the students' natural language contributions and then responds to the students' verbal input with adaptive dialogue moves similar to human tutors. AutoTutor helps students learn by presenting challenging problems (or questions) from a curriculum script and engaging in a mixed-initiative dialogue while the learner constructs an answer.

AutoTutor provides *feedback* on what the student types in (positive, neutral, or negative feedback), *pumps* the student for more information ("What else?"), *prompts* the student to fill in missing words, gives *hints*, fills in missing information with *assertions,* identifies and corrects *misconceptions* and erroneous ideas, *answers* the student's questions, and *summarizes* topics. A full answer to a question is eventually constructed during this dialogue, which normally takes between 30 and 100 turns between the student and tutor for one particular problem or main question.

AutoTutor's knowledge about the topic being tutored (computer literacy in this study) is represented by Latent Semantic Analysis (LSA) [31] and a curriculum script on the material. LSA is a statistical technique that measures the conceptual similarity of two text sources. LSA computes a geometric cosine (ranging from -1 to 1) that represents the conceptual similarity between the two text sources.

A session with AutoTutor is comprised of a set of subtopics (main questions) that cover specific areas of the main topics (hardware, internet, and operating systems). Each subtopic has an associated set of expectations, potential dialogue moves to elicit expectations (e.g., hints, prompts, assertions), misconceptions, corrections of misconceptions, and other slots in the curriculum script that need not be addressed here. The expectations are ideally covered by a series of turns in AutoTutor's conversation with the student in an attempt to construct an answer to the current main question (subtopic). When an acceptable answer with the appropriate details is gleaned from the student's responses, AutoTutor moves on to the next subtopic. At the end of each student turn, AutoTutor maintains a log file that captures the student's response, a variety of assessments of the response, the feedback provided, and the tutor's next move.

As an example, the exchange below is one of the shorter tutorial dialogues between a college student and AutoTutor. This student was an above average student in the computer literacy class.

1. AUTOTUTOR: When you turn on the computer, how is the operating system first activated and loaded into RAM? [this is the *main question*]
2. STUDENT: When the computer is turned on a file is automatically booted up.
3. AUTOTUTOR: Anything else?   [this is a *pump* for more information]
4. STUDENT: This file contains the operating system.
5. AUTOTUTOR: What about storage?   [this is a *hint*]
6. STUDENT: The operating system is then read into RAM and activated.

7. AUTOTUTOR: Right. The CPU executes instructions in ROM, which helps the operating system to start.   [after giving *positive feedback*, there is an *assertion*]
8. STUDENT: After being read from ROM the OS is activated.
9. AUTOTUTOR: Right. Let's review what we've just gone over. The operating system must first be stored on the hard disk. When you turn on the computer, the CPU executes instructions stored in ROM. These instructions help boot the operating system. The operating system is then loaded from the hard disk into RAM. [after *positive feedback* comes a *summary*]

We now briefly describe the relevant information channels that are available in AutoTutor's log files of the interaction history. The information can broadly be divided into five categories: temporal information, response verbosity, answer quality assessments, tutor directness, and the tutor's feedback.

2.1 Temporal Information

The temporal information can be viewed as a combination of global and local temporal markers that span the period of interaction. The *subtopic number* indicates the number of main questions answered. It provides a global measure of sequential position within the entire tutorial session. For example, for a one-hour session covering three subtopics, the third subtopic would indicate that the student is approximately in the 40-60 minute time span. The *turn* on the other hand, provides a local measure of the number of student contributions to the current question (subtopic). Finally, the student response time is the elapsed time (in milliseconds rounded to seconds) between the verbal presentation of the question by AutoTutor and the student submitting an answer.

2.2 Response Verbosity

The verbosity of the student's dialogue contributions is measured by the *number of characters* in the student's response. A qualitative classification of the student's contributions is provided by AutoTutor's Speech Act Classification system [32]. While the system classifies a response into a number of categories, those of interest to this research involved *frozen expressions* (e.g., I don't know, What did you say?) (coded as -1) and topic related *contributions* (scored as a 1).

2.3 Answer Quality

AutoTutor relies on LSA as its primary computation of the quality of student contributions in student turns. The primary measure of answer quality for a given turn is the *local good score,* which measures the student's contribution for that turn on the basis of its similarity to good answers (expectations). Therefore, a high local good score reflects progress in answering the main question. A secondary measure of answer quality is the *global good score* which involves the same assessments as the local parameters, with the exception that the text used for the LSA match is an aggregation of all of the student's turns (1 through N) for a given subtopic. With this scheme, a student's past contributions to a subtopic (main question) are considered in AutoTutor's assessment of the student's current state. Additionally, a *delta local good score* and a *delta global good score*, measures changes in the local good and global good scores respectively. These measure the changes in student answer quality.

2.4 Tutor Directness

At the end of each student turn, AutoTutor incorporates the various LSA assessments when choosing its next pedagogically appropriate dialogue move. When AutoTutor tries to get a single expectation (E) covered (e.g., The hard disc is a storage medium), this goal is posted and is achieved by AutoTutor presenting a series of different dialogue moves across turns until the expectation E is expressed. It first gives a *pump* (What else?), then a *hint* (What about the hard disk?), then a *prompt* for specific information (i.e., an important word, The hard disk is a medium of what?), and then simply *asserts* the information (The hard disc is a medium for storage). After all of the expectations for the problem are covered a *summary* is provided by AutoTutor. Given this mechanism of encouraging the student to cover the expectations, the dialogue moves chosen can be ordered on a *directness* scale (ranging from -1 to 1) on the basis of the amount of information AutoTutor supplies to the learner. The ordering is *pump* < *hint* < *prompt* < *assertion* < *summary*. A pump conveys the minimum amount of information (on the part of AutoTutor) whereas a summary conveys the most amount of explicit information.

2.5 Tutor Feedback

AutoTutor's short *feedback* (positive, neutral positive, neutral, neutral negative, negative) is manifested in its verbal content, intonation, and a host of other non-verbal conversational cues. Examples of positive and negative feedback terms include "good job", "correct" and "wrong", "no" respectively. Similar to the directness scale constructed above, AutoTutor's feedback was mapped onto a scale ranging from -1 (negative feedback) to 1 (positive feedback).

3   Empirical Data Collection

The training and testing of the emotion classifier needs a gold standard for comparison. The appropriate gold standard is undoubtedly debatable, but there needs to be some plausible foundation for establishing ground truth, even though any gold standard proposed is open to challenge. One preliminary step in this process is to examine how reliable humans are at classification of emotions. We investigated three potential measures of ground truth for emotion detection: the participants, novice judges, and trained judges.

We conducted a study which consisted of 28 participants interacting with AutoTutor for 32 minutes on one of three randomly assigned topics in computer literacy: hardware, internet, or operating systems. During the interaction process a video of the participant's face and a video of the screen were recorded. The judging process was initiated by synchronizing the video streams from the screen and the face and displaying to the judge. Judges were instructed to make judgments on what affective states were present in 20-second intervals at which the video automatically paused (freeze-framed). They were also instructed to indicate any affective states that were present in between the 20-second stops.

Four sets of emotion judgments were made for the observed affective states of each participant's AutoTutor session. For the self judgments, the participant watched his or her own session with AutoTutor immediately after having interacted with AutoTutor. Second, for the peer judgments, participants returned approximately a week later to watch and judge another participant's session on the same topic in computer literacy. Finally, two additional judges (called trained judges), who had been trained on how to detect facial action units according to Paul Ekman's Facial Action Coding System (FACS) [33], judged all of the sessions separately. The trained judges also had considerable interaction experience with AutoTutor. Hence, their emotion judgments were based on contextual dialog information as well as the FACS system.

A list of the affective states and definitions was provided for all judges. The states were boredom, confusion, flow, frustration, delight, neutral and surprise. The selection of emotions was based on previous studies of AutoTutor [14, 34] that collected observational data (i.e., trained judges observing learners) and *emote aloud* protocols while college students learned with AutoTutor.

Interjudge reliability was computed using Cohen's kappa for all possible pairs of judges: self, peer, trained judge1, and trained judge2. Cohen's kappa measures the proportion of agreements between two judges with correction for baserate levels and random guessing. There were 6 possible pairs altogether. The kappa's were reported in Graesser et al. [18]: self-peer (.08), self-judge1 (.14), self-judge2 (.16), peer-judge1 (.14), peer-judge2 (.18), and judge1-judge2 (.36). These kappa scores revealed that the trained judges had the highest agreement, the self-peer pair had lowest agreement, and the other pairs of judges were in between. It should be noted, however, that the kappa scores increase substantially when we focus on observations in which the learner declares they have an emotion, as opposed to points when they are essentially neutral. The kappa scores are on par with data reported by other researchers who have assessed identification of emotions by humans [22, 24]. More details on the collection of data in this study and follow up analyses are reported in Graesser el al. [18].

4   Results and Discussion

It is essential to have real-time automatic affect detection in order to achieve the larger goal of extending AutoTutor into an affect-sensitive ITS. Therefore, we applied several standard classification techniques in an attempt to detect the learner's affect from the various conversation features manifested through an interaction with AutoTutor.

The AutoTutor log files were mined to obtain information from the various dialogue channels described above. Four data sets, corresponding to each of the four judge's emotion judgments, were obtained by extracting the set of emotion judgments for each participant (according to the judge in question) and the set of dialogue features for each turn that were associated with the emotion. More specifically, the emotion judgment that immediately followed a dialogue move (within a 15 second interval) was bound to that dialogue move. This allowed us to obtain four sets of labeled dialogue data, each containing 1300 records, aggregated across the 28 participants.

4.1 Statistical Analyses

Multiple regression analyses were conducted to determine the extent to which the seven affective states of interest could be predicted from the various dialogue features. For each of the four data sets (self, peer, trained judge1, trained judge2), seven multiple regression analyses were performed, one for each of the affective states, yielding 28 models in all. The dependent variable for each multiple regression analysis was an affective state and the independent variables were the set of dialogue features.

The multiple regression analyses for the emotion data obtained from the trained judge ratings yielded statistically significant models for the affective states of boredom (F_{self} = 5.90, R^2_{adj} = .184; F_{peer} = 8.12, R^2_{adj} = .211; F_{judge1} = 7.92, R^2_{adj} = .132; F_{judge2} = 12.30, R^2_{adj} = .140), confusion (F_{self} = 7.21, R^2_{adj} = .175; F_{peer} = 1.88, R^2_{adj} = .108; F_{judge1} = 2.37, R^2_{adj} = .075; F_{judge2} = 13.73, R^2_{adj} = .125), flow (F_{judge1} = 14.01, R^2_{adj} = .201; F_{judge2} = 12.21, R^2_{adj} = .139), frustration (F_{self} = 5.75, R^2_{adj} = .188; F_{peer} = 4.53, R^2_{adj} = .106; F_{judge1} = 10.09, R^2_{adj} = .094; F_{judge2} = 6.44, R^2_{adj} = .094) and neutral (F_{self} = 3.03, R^2_{adj} = .335; F_{peer} = 2.93, R^2_{adj} = .291; F_{judge1} = 2.19, R^2_{adj} = .026; F_{judge2} = 4.20, R^2_{adj} = .090); all models were significant at the $p < .05$ level and df_1 = 11, df_2 = 1261. For the novice judges (self and peer), statistically significant models

Table 1. Significant predictors for the multiple regression models for emotions in each data set

Dialogue Features	Boredom				Confusion				Flow				Frustration				Neutral			
	SF	PR	J1	J2	SF	PR	J1	J2	SF	PR	J1	J2	SF	PR	J1	J2	SF	PR	J1	J2
Subtopic Number	+	+	+	+	-	-	-	-			-	-	+						-	-
Turn Number	+	+	+	+	-						-						-			
Response Time					+						+				-					-
No. Characters					-		-	-			+	+								
Global Good											-				-	-				
Delta Global Good																				
Local Good	-						-				+				+	+				
Delta Local Good																	-			
Speech Act	-				-		-	-									+			+
Directness			+	+			-	-												
Feedback								-			+	+	-		-	-	+	+	+	+

SF: Self Judgements, PR: Peer Judgements, J1: Trained Judge1, J2: Trained Judge2
+ or - indicates that the feature is a positive or negative predictor in the multiple regression model, with a signifcance level of p < .05.

were discovered for boredom, confusion, frustration, and neutral, but not for flow. The multiple regression analyses failed to converge on significant models for the affective states of delight and surprise, indicating that these affective states cannot be predicted from the dialogue features. The signs (+, -) of the statistically significant standardized coefficients in the multiple regression analyses are presented in Table 1.

A number of generalizations can be gleaned from Table 1 regarding the relationship between dialogue and affective states. If one considers the significant predictors in which the data from at least two judges agreed, a number of relationships surface. In particular, boredom occurs later in the session (high subtopic number), after multiple attempts to answer the main question (high turn number), and when there are more direct dialogue moves (high directness). Alternatively, confusion occurs earlier in the session (low subtopic number), with slower responses (long response time), shorter responses (less characters), with frozen expressions (negatively coded speech acts), and when the tutor is less direct in providing information. The analyses indicated that flow occurs earlier on in the session (low subtopic numbers), involves longer responses (more characters), and is accompanied by positive feedback from the tutor. Frustration was prevalent with good answers towards the immediate question (high local good score), but poor answers towards the broader topic (low global good score), and negative tutor feedback.

4.2 Machine Learning Experiments

The machine learning experiments focused on these significant predictors of the affective states, thereby reducing the number of features used to train and test the classifiers. In addition to potentially increasing classification accuracy by eliminating unrelated features, this feature selection procedure also offers significant computational advantages in terms of execution time, a crucial requirement for real time computation.

The Waikato Environment for Knowledge Analysis [35] was used to comparatively evaluate the performance of various standard classification techniques in an attempt to detect affect from dialogue. The classification algorithms tested were a Naïve Bayesian classifier, a multilayer perceptron (neural network using back propagation for training), a nearest neighbor classifier, C4.5 decision trees, an additive logistic boosting classifier with a decision stump as the base learner, and support vector machines.

The classification process proceeded in two phases. In the first stage we grouped the four affective states of interest (boredom, confusion, flow, frustration) together and assessed the reliabilities of the various classification algorithms to discriminate among each affective state. In the second phase of the classification analyses, we were interested in the accuracies of detecting each of the four affective states from the base state of neutral.

4.2.1 Discriminating Between Boredom, Confusion, Flow, and Frustration

The first set of classification experiments involved evaluating the classifiers on the four data sets (one for each judge's ratings) in discriminating between boredom, confusion, flow, and frustration. To establish a uniform baseline (a chance value of 25%), we randomly sampled an equal number of observations from each affective state category. This process was repeated for 100 iterations and the reported reliability statistics were averaged across these 100 iterations. Each randomly sampled data set was evaluated on the 6 classification algorithms using k-fold cross-validation (k = 10). The dialogue features that were significant predictors of the multiple regression models listed in Table 1 were used for classification. The classification accuracies are presented in Table 2.

Table 2. Comparison of various classification techniques to detect learner's affect

Classification Algorithm	Self		Peer		Judge 1		Judge 2	
	Acc	Kap	Acc	Kap	Acc	Kap	Acc	Kap
Additive Logistic Regression	35.0	.134	36.1	.147	47.0	.293	47.1	.295
Multilayer Perceptron	34.8	.130	34.7	.130	45.9	.278	45.2	.269
Naïve Bayes	35.3	.137	35.7	.142	45.9	.279	46.2	.282
Nearest Neighbor	28.7	.050	31.7	.089	40.7	.209	40.8	.210
C4.5 Decision Tree	31.1	.081	33.9	.119	42.0	.226	40.6	.208
Support Vector Machines	35.8	.144	36.9	.159	49.1	.321	48.4	.312

Acc: Classification accuracy (%), Kap: Cohen's Kappa. Baseline rate (chance) is 25%.

The various classification algorithms were moderately successful in detecting affect, with the highest performance being 49.1%, a 96.4% improvement over the baseline. This was obtained from the affective judgments of trained judge1, which had a kappa score of .321 and was comparable to inter-judge reliability scores achieved by actual human coders. For example, Litman and Forbes-Riley [22] report kappa scores of around .4 in detecting positive, negative, and neutral affect. Shafran, Riley, and Mohri [24] report kappa scores ranging from .32 to .42 in coding affect. Additionally, this kappa value is on par with the kappa scores reported earlier ([18]) for the trained judges (kappa = .36).

The classification accuracies on the data based on the two trained judge's ratings were on par and quantitatively higher than the accuracies in detecting affect based on the emotion ratings of the self and the peer. This trend is similar to that observed in the human judgments of emotions reported in Graesser et al. [18].

In order to assess class level accuracies, Table 3 lists the precision, recall, and F-measure scores obtained for the four affective states. The precision for class C is the proportion of samples that truly belong to class C among all the samples that were classified as class C. The recall score (sensitivity or true positive rate) provides a measure of the accuracy of the learning scheme in detecting a particular class. The F-measure provides a single metric of performance by combining the precision and recall. Since support vector machines constituted the most successful classifier the precision, recall, and F-measure scores presented in Table 3 are restricted to those obtained with this classifier.

Table 3. Detailed accuracies of the support vector machine classifier for each data set

Affective States	Self			Peer			Judge 1			Judge 2		
	PR	RC	FM	PR	RC	FM	PR	RC	FM	PR	RC	FM
Boredom	.40	.25	.31	.43	.30	.35	.51	.34	.40	.42	.24	.30
Confusion	.39	.33	.36	.33	.12	.17	.45	.29	.35	.52	.37	.42
Flow	.36	.27	.31	.37	.36	.36	.58	.59	.59	.56	.58	.56
Frustration	.33	.58	.42	.36	.70	.47	.45	.74	.56	.46	.76	.57

PR: Precision, RC: Recall, FM: F-Measure

When the same evaluation procedures were conducted on the affect data of the novice judges (self and peer), the F-measure indicated that the classifier was more successful in detecting frustration than the other three affective states. If one considers data from the self reports alone, classification accuracies for boredom and flow are identical and lower than that of confusion. The same trend is observed on the data from the peer judgments, with the exception that the F-measure for confusion was relatively low (.17). For the data collected from the trained judges' identification of emotions, classification accuracies for frustration and flow were similar and quantitatively higher than those for boredom and confusion. On the basis of these results, we conclude that support vector machines offer reasonable accuracies in automatically discriminating between frustration, boredom, confusion and flow.

4.2.2 Discriminating Between the Affective States and Neutral

Another important requirement for an emotion classifier is the ability to detect individual affective states from a baseline state of neutral. Therefore, additional analyses were conducted that assessed the reliability in detecting each of the four affective states (boredom, confusion, flow, and frustration) when compared to the neutral state. These analyses were conducted on each of the four data sets (self, peer, trained judge1, trained judge2). The classification procedures were similar to the random selection procedure described above. Table 4 presents overall classification accuracies and Kappa scores for the classifier that yielded the best performance in detecting each of the four affective states from neutral.

Table 4. Classification accuracies in individually detecting boredom, confusion, flow, and frustration from neutral

Affective States	Self		Peer		Judge 1		Judge 2	
	Acc	Kap	Acc	Kap	Acc	Kap	Acc	Kap
Boredom	61.3	.226	60.3	.206	62.5	.251	60.8	.216
Confusion	59.3	.187	58.1	.162	59.4	.188	61.0	.221
Flow	50.2	.003	53.5	.070	65.9	.319	63.8	.277
Frustration	62.1	.241	64.6	.292	71.8	.435	73.3	.466

Acc: Classification accuracy (%), Kap: Cohen's Kappa. Baseline rate (chance) is 50%.

The reliabilities of the various classification algorithms in discriminating each of the four affective states from neutral followed a similar trend when the four affective states were considered together (Table 3), with the highest accuracies achieved in detecting frustration from neutral. Classification accuracies for the detection of boredom and confusion were moderate and comparable across the data sets provided by each of the four judges. The classifiers, when operating on the data set consisting of the trained judges' emotion ratings, were quite successful in discriminating between flow and the baseline state of neutral. However, classifiers trained on emotion judgments of the novice judges failed to detect flow from neutral, with classification accuracies hovering around the chance rate.

5 Conclusion

Emotion measurement is a field resonating with murky, noisy, and incomplete data compounded with individual differences in experiencing and expressing emotions. On the basis of the natural language dialogue features alone, our results indicate that the standard classifiers were moderately successful in discriminating the affective states of boredom, confusion, flow, and frustration from each other, as well as from the base line state of neutral. A comparison of the accuracies obtained from the four human judges (self, peer, and 2 trained judges) revealed that classification models constructed on the basis of the trained judges' emotion judgments consistently outperformed those of the novice judges. This trend is consistent with the inter-judge reliability results reported by Graesser et al. [18], thus offering convergent validity for the phenomenon that trained judges are better than untrained peers in detecting emotions. However, it is still not firmly established whether the trained judges or the self judgments are closer to the ground truth.

The reliability of the standard classifiers in detecting affect from dialogues validates any future efforts in pursuing more sophisticated classification techniques. For example, biologically motivated classifiers, based on the dynamic behaviors of neural populations involved in the olfaction processes of rabbits, have been experimenttally validated as powerful pattern classifiers for difficult, non-linearly separable, classification problems [36]. Other options to boost the accuracy of AutoTutor in modeling learner affect involve the use of bodily sensors that track facial features, posture patterns, and speech contours [17].

One of the known limitations of the data analyses presented in this paper is that each emotion judgment was analyzed only in the context of the immediately preceding turns of the student and tutor. Perhaps classification accuracies could be boosted by incorporating a broader scope of contextual information, including patterns of conversation that evolve over a series of turns leading up to an emotional experience. Future efforts will be directed towards the analysis of conversation features across a larger temporal resolution and number of turns.

The dialogue channels were unable to detect the affective states of delight and surprise. Perhaps these affective states are simply not manifested through AutoTutor's conversation features and their detection would require more sophisticated sensors. Delight and surprise are affective states that are generally expressed though animated facial features, so it may be possible to detect these states by means of the Facial Action Coding System; particular facial actions are known to be correlated with happiness (similar to delight) and surprise [33].

We conclude by speculating on the generalizability of the discovered relationships between the conversational cues and affective states. Although the features of dialogue we analyzed were specific to AutoTutor, a similar set of features would presumably be expected in any intelligent tutoring system, particularly in those that advocate deeper learning. The lower level features specific to AutoTutor (local good score, global good score, directness, etc.) can be generalized to generic categories of dialogue features, such as temporal assessments, response verbosity, student ability, tutor directness, and tutor feedback. We predict that these broad categories will replicate across most intelligent tutoring systems.

Acknowledgements

We would like to acknowledge our colleagues from the Emotive Computing Group <http://emotion.autotutor.org> at the University of Memphis including Patrick Chipman, Scotty Craig, Stan Franklin, Barry Gholson, Brandon King, Bethany McDaniel, Jeremiah Sullins, Kristy Tapp, and Amy Witherspoon for their valuable contributions to this research. We also thank our partners at the Affective Computing Research Group at MIT <http://affect.media.mit.edu>.

This research was supported by the National Science Foundation (REC 0106965 and ITR 0325428) and the DoD Multidisciplinary University Research Initiative administered by ONR under grant N00014-00-1-0600. Any opinions, findings and conclusions or recommendations expressed in this paper are those of the authors and do not necessarily reflect the views of NSF, DoD, or ONR.

References

1. Morgado, L. and Gaspar, G.: Emotion in Intelligent Virtual Agents: The Flow Model of Emotion. Lecture Notes in Computer Science, Vol. 2792. (2003) 31-38
2. Picard, R.W.: Affective Computing. MIT Press, Cambridge (1997)
3. Graesser, A., VanLehn, K., Rosé, C., Jordan, P., Harter, D.: Intelligent Tutoring Systems with Conversational Dialogue. AI Magazine, Vol. 22. (2001) 39-51
4. Gratch, J., Rickel, J., Andre, E., Cassell, J., Petajan, E., Badler, N.: Creating Interactive Virtual Humans: Some Assembly Required. IEEE Intelligent Systems, Vol. 17. (2002) 54-63
5. Johnson, L.: Pedagogical Agent Research at CARTE. AI Magazine, Vol. 22. (2001) 85-94
6. Cohen, P.A., Kulik, J.A., Kulik, C.C.: Educational Outcomes of Tutoring: A Metaanalysis of Findings. American Educational Research Journal, Vol. 19. (1982) 237-248
7. McNamara, D.S., Levinstein, I.B., Boonthum, C.: iSTART: Interactive Strategy Trainer for Active Reading and Thinking. Behavioral Research Methods, Instruments, and Computers, Vol. 36. (2004) 222-233
8. Guhe, M., Gray, W.D., Schoelles, M.J., Ji, Q.: Towards an Affective Cognitive Architecture. In: Poster Session Presented at the Cognitive Science Conference. (2004)

66   S. D'Mello and A. Graesser

9. Graesser, A.C., Chipman, P., Haynes, B., Olney, A.: AutoTutor: An Intelligent Tutoring System with Mixed-initiative Dialogue. IEEE Transactions in Education, Vol. 48. (2005) 612-618

10. Lepper, M.R. and Chabay, R.W.: Socializing the Intelligent Tutor: Bringing Empathy to Computer Tutors. In: In Learning Issues for Intelligent Tutoring Systems. (1988) 242-257

11. Lepper, M.R. and Woolverton, M.: The Wisdom of Practice: Lessons Learned from the Study of Highly Effective Tutors. In: Improving Academic Achievement: Impact of Psychological Factors on Education. (2002) 135-158

12. Kim, Y.: Empathetic Virtual Peers Enhanced Learner Interest and Self-efficacy. Workshop on Motivation and Affect in Educational Software. In: 12th International Conference on Artificial Intelligence in Education. (2005)

13. Linnenbrink, E.A. and Pintrich, P.R.: The Role of Motivational Beliefs in Conceptual Change. In: Reconsidering Conceptual Change: Issues in Theory and Practice. (2002) 115-135.

14. Craig, S.D., Graesser, A.C., Sullins, J., Gholson, B.: Affect and Learning: An Exploratory Look into the Role of Affect in Learning. Journal of Educational Media, Vol. 29. (2004) 241-250

15. Csikszentmihalyi, M.: Flow: The Psychology of Optimal Experience. Harper-Row, New York (1990)

16. Graesser, A.C., Person, N., Harter, D., Tutoring Research Group.: Teaching Tactics and Dialogue in AutoTutor. International Journal of Artificial Intelligence in Education, Vol. 12. (2001) 257-279

17. D'Mello, S.K., Craig, S.D., Gholson, B., Franklin, S., Picard, R., Graesser, A.C.: Integrating Affect Sensors in an Intelligent Tutoring System. in Affective Interactions: The Computer in the Affective Loop In: Workshop at 2005 International Conference on Intelligent User Interfaces. (2005) 7-13

18. Graesser A.C., McDaniel, B., Chipman, P., Witherspoon, A., D'Mello, S., Gholson, B.: Detection of Emotions During Learning with AutoTutor. In: 28th Annual Conference of the Cognitive Science Society, CogSci2006. In Press

19. Cohn, J.F. and Kanade, T.: Use of Automated Facial Image Analysis for Measurement of Emotion Expression. In: Coan, J.A., and Allen, J.B. (eds.): The Handbook of Emotion Elicitation and Assessment. Oxford University Press Series in Affective Science, New York Oxford. In Press

20. Mota, S. and Picard, R.W.: Automated Posture Analysis for Detecting Learner's Interest Level. In: Workshop on Computer Vision and Pattern Recognition for Human-Computer Interaction, CVPR HCI. (2003)

21. Forbes-Riley, K. and Litman, D.: Predicting Emotion in Spoken Dialogue from Multiple Knowledge Sources. In: Proceedings of the Human Language Technology Conference: 4th Meeting of the North American Chapter of the Association for Computational Linguistics, HLT/NAACL. (2004)

22. Litman, D.J. and Forbes-Riley, K.: Predicting Student Emotions in Computer-Human Tutoring Dialogues. In: Proceedings of the 42nd Annual Meeting of the Association for Computational Linguistics. (2004) 352-359

23. Litman, D.J. and Silliman, S.: ITSPOKE: An Intelligent Tutoring Spoken Dialogue System. In: Proceedings of the Human Language Technology Conference: 3rd Meeting of the North American Chapter of the Association of Computational Linguistics. (2004) 52-54

24. Shafran, I., Riley, M., Mohri, M.: Voice Signatures. In: Proc. IEEE Automatic Speech Recognition and Understanding Workshop. (2003)

25. Nakasone, A., Prendinger, H., Ishizuka, M.: Emotion Recognition from Electromyography and Skin Conductance. In: Fifth International Workshop on Biosignal Interpretation. (2005) 219-222
26. Rani, P., Sarkar, N., Smith, C.A.: An affect-sensitive Human-Robot Cooperation: Theory and Experiments In: Proceedings of the IEEE Conference on Robotics and Automation. (2003) 2382-2387
27. Alm, C.O. and Sproat, R.: Perceptions of Emotions in Expressive Storytelling. In: InterSpeech (2005) 533-536
28. VanLehn, K., Jordan, P., Rosé, C.P., Bhembe, D., Bottner, M., Gaydos, A., et al.: The Architecture of Why2-atlas: A Coach for Qualitative Physics Essay Writing. In: Proceedings of the Sixth International Conference on Intelligent Tutoring (2002) 403-449
29. Carberry, S., Schroeder, L., Lambert, L.: Toward Recognizing and Conveying an Attitude of Doubt via Natural Language. Applied Artificial Intelligence, Vol. 16. (2002) 495-517
30. Graesser, A., Wiemer-Hastings, K., Wiemer-Hastings, P., Kreuz, R., Tutoring Research Group.: AutoTutor: A Simulation of a Human Tutor. Journal of Cognitive Systems Research, Vol. 1 (1999) 35-51
31. Landauer, T.K. and Dumais, S.T.: A Solution to Plato's Problem: The Latent Semantic Analysis Theory of Acquisition, Induction, and Representation of Knowledge. Psychological Review, Vol. 104. (1997) 211-240
32. Olney, A., Louwerse, M., Mathews, E., Marineau, J., Hite-Mitchell, H., Graesser, A.: Utterance Classification in AutoTutor. In: Proceedings of the HLT-NAACL 03 Workshop on Building Educational Applications using Natural Language Processing. (2003) 1-8.
33. Ekman, P. and Friesen, W.V.: The Facial Action Coding System: A Technique for the Measurement of Facial Movement. Consulting Psychologists Press, Palo Alto (1978)
34. D'Mello, S.K., Craig, S.D., Sullins, J., raesser, A.C.: Predicting Affective States through an Emote-Aloud Procedure from AutoTutor's Mixed-Initiative Dialogue. International Journal of Artificial Intelligence in Education, Vol. 16. (2006) 3-28
35. Witten, I.H. and Frank E.: Data Mining: Practical Machine Learning Tools and Techniques. 3rd edn. Morgan Kaufmann, San Francisco (2005)
36. Kozma, R. and Freeman, W.J.: Chaotic Resonance: Methods and Applications for Robust Classification of Noisy and Variable Patterns. International Journal of Bifurcation and Chaos, Vol. 11 (2001) 1607-1629

Exploitation in Affect Detection in Improvisational E-Drama

Li Zhang, John A. Barnden, Robert J. Hendley, and Alan M. Wallington

School of Computer Science, University of Birmingham, Birmingham, B15 2TT, UK
l.zhang@cs.bham.ac.uk

Abstract. We report progress on adding affect-detection to a program for virtual dramatic improvisation, monitored by a human director. To aid the director, we have partially implemented emotion detection. within users' text input. The affect-detection module has been used to help develop an automated virtual actor. The work involves basic research into how affect is conveyed through metaphor and contributes to the conference themes such as building improvisational intelligent virtual agents for interactive narrative environments.

Keywords: E-drama, affect detection, intelligent virtual actor and metaphor.

1 Introduction

Improvised drama and role-play is widely used in education, training, counselling and conflict resolution and researchers are exploring frameworks for e-drama, in which virtual characters (avatars) on computer displays interact under the partial or total control of human users (e.g.[1]). Our research stemmed from an existing system, *edrama*, created by Hi8us Midlands Ltd and used variously in schools for e.g. creative writing. Many students welcome the anonymity of *edrama*. One main aspect of our project is the addition of types of intelligent automation.

In the *edrama* system, up to five virtual characters are controlled on a virtual stage by human users ("actors"), with characters' (textual) "speeches" typed by the actors operating the characters. A director is also involved in a session. A graphical interface on each actor's and director's terminal shows the stage and characters. Speeches are shown as text bubbles. Actors choose their characters clothes and bodily appearance.

Currently, cartoon figures against backdrops of real-life photographic images are used. However, we are bringing in animated gesturing avatars and 3D computer-generated settings using technology from an industrial partners, BT. Actors and the human director work through software clients connecting with the server. Clients communicate using XML stream messages via the server, which is usually remote from the terminals, which may themselves be remote from each other. Terminal-server communication is over the Internet using standard browsers.

The actors are given a loose scenario around which to improvise, but are at liberty to be creative. One scenario we have used is school-bullying where a schoolgirl Lisa is being bullied by her classmate Mayid. There are also roles for two friends and a teacher. Within these parameters, actors must improvise interesting interchanges.

J. Gratch et al. (Eds.): IVA 2006, LNAI 4133, pp. 68–79, 2006.

The human director has a number of roles. S/he must constantly monitor the unfolding drama and the actors' interactions, or lack of them, in order to check whether they are keeping to the general spirit of the scenario. If this is not happening, the director may then intervene. For example, a director may intervene when the emotions expressed or discussed by characters are not as expected (or are not leading consistently in a new interesting direction). The director may also feel the need to intervene if one character is not getting involved, or is dominating the improvisation.

Intervention can take a number of forms. The director can send messages to actors. However, another important means of directorial intervention is for the director to introduce and control a 'bit-part' character. This character will not have a major role in the drama, but might, for example, try to interact with a character who is not participating much in the drama or who is being ignored by the other characters. Alternatively, it might make comments intended to 'stir up' the emotions of those involved, or, by intervening, diffuse any inappropriate exchange developing.

Clearly, all this places a heavy burden on the director. In particular, playing the role of the bit-part character and interacting with other characters whilst keeping interventions limited so as to maintain the main improvisatory drama amongst the actors, makes it difficult to fully monitor the behaviour of all the other actors and send appropriate messages to them should they stray off topic or exhibit inappropriate emotions. The difficulty is particularly acute if the directors are novices, such as teachers trying to use e-drama in their lessons.

One major research aim is accordingly to automate some directorial functions, either to take some of the burden away from a human director, or to provide a fully automated (though necessarily very restricted) director. With a fully-automated director, even if highly restricted in what it can do, little or no human supervision might be required for at least minimally adequate improvisations, and *edrama* could, for example, be added to websites about certain topics allowing visitors to engage in on-line role-play germane to the topic.

However, our main current work is on assisting a human director by providing fully-automated control of a bit-part character (though we are also working on automating limited types of director-to-actor message-sending to allow the human director to concentrate on the more difficult aspects of the task). For this reason, we have created an automated actor, EMMA (emotion, metaphor and affect), which operates a bit-part character (e.g. an acquaintance of the main character), and is under the control of an affect-detection module. The module tries to identify affect in other characters' speeches, allowing the EMMA character to make responses that will hopefully stimulate the improvisation. Within affect we include: basic and complex *emotions* such as anger and embarrassment respectively; *meta-emotions* such as desiring to overcome anxiety; *moods* such as hostility; and *value judgements* (of goodness, importance, etc.). Although merely detecting affect is limited compared to extracting the full meaning of characters' utterances, we have found that in many cases this is sufficient for the purposes of stimulating the improvisation.

Also, even limited types of affect detection are useful. EMMA may not detect all types of affect under all ways it can be expressed or implied, nor do it with a high degree of reliability, but the spirit of the project is to see how far we can get with practical processing techniques, while at the same time investigating theoretically the nature of, and potential computational ways of dealing with, forms of affective expression that are too difficult to handle in a usable implemented system.

Much research has been done on creating affective virtual characters in interactive systems. Picard's work [2] makes great contributions to building affective virtual characters. Also, emotion theories, particularly that of Ortony, Clore and Collins [3] (OCC), have been used widely therein. Prendinger and Ishizuka [4] used the OCC model to reason about emotions and to produce believable emotional expressions. Wiltschko's *eDrama Front Desk* [5] is an online emotional natural language dialogue simulator with a virtual reception interface for pedagogical purposes. Mehdi et al. [6] combined the widely accepted five-factor model of personality [7], mood and OCC in generating emotional behaviour for a fireman training application. Gratch and Marsella [8] presented an integrated model of appraisal and coping, in order to reason about emotions and to provide emotional responses, facial expressions and potential social intelligence for virtual agents. Egges, Kshirsagar and Magnenat-Thalmann [9] have provided virtual characters with conversational emotional responsiveness. Elliott, Rickel and Lester [10] demonstrated tutoring systems that reason about users' emotions. There is much other work in a similar vein.

There has been only a limited amount of work directly comparable to our own, especially given our concentration on improvisation and open-ended language. However, *Facade* [11] included shallow natural language processing for characters' open-ended utterances, but the detection of major emotions, rudeness and value judgements is not mentioned. Zhe and Boucouvalas [12] demonstrated an emotion extraction module embedded in an Internet chatting environment (see also [13]). It uses a part-of-speech tagger and a syntactic chunker to detect the emotional words and to analyse emotion intensity for the first person (e.g. 'I' or 'we'). Unfortunately the emotion detection focuses only on emotional adjectives, and does not address deep issues such as figurative expression of emotion. Also, the concentration purely on first-person emotions is narrow. We might also mention work on general linguistic clues that could be used in practice for affect detection (e.g. [14]).

Our work is distinctive in several respects. Our interest is not just in (a) the first-person, positive expression of affect case: the affective states or attitudes that a virtual character X implies that it itself has (or had or will have, etc.), but also in (b) affect that the character X implies it lacks, (c) affect that X implies that other characters have or lack, and (d) questions, commands, injunctions, etc. concerning affect. We aim also for the software to cope partially with the important case of communication of affect via metaphor [15, 16], and to push forward the theoretical study of such language, as part of our research on metaphor generally (see, e.g., [17]).

Our project does not involve using or developing deep, scientific models of how emotional states, etc., function in cognition. Instead, the deep questions investigated are on linguistic matters such as the metaphorical expression of affect. In studying how ordinary people understand and talk about affect in ordinary life, what is of prime importance is their *common-sense* views of how affect works, irrespective of scientific accuracy of those views. Metaphor is strongly involved in such views.

It should also be appreciated that this paper does not address the emotional, etc. states of the *actors* (or director, or any audience). Our focus is on the affect that the actors make their characters express or mention. While an actor may work him/herself up into, or be put into, a state similar to or affected by those in his/her own characters' speeches or those of other characters, such interesting effects, which go to the heart of the dramatic experience, are beyond the scope of this paper, and so is the possibility of using information one might be able to get about actors' own affective states as a hint about the affective states of their characters or vice-versa.

2 Our Current Affect Detection

Various characterizations of emotion are used in emotion theories. The OCC model uses emotion labels (anger, etc.) and intensity, while Watson and Tellegen [18] use positivity and negativity of affect as the major dimensions. Currently, we use an evaluation dimension (negative-positive), affect labels, and intensity. Affect labels plus intensity are used when strong text clues signalling affect are detected, while the evaluation dimension plus intensity is used when only weak text clues are detected. Moreover, our analysis is based on the transcripts of previous e-drama sessions. Since even a person's interpretations of affect can be very unreliable, our approach combines various weak relevant affect indicators into a stronger and more reliable source of information for affect detection. Now we summarize our affect detection based on multiple streams of information.

2.1 Pre-processing Modules

The language in the speeches created in e-drama sessions severely challenges existing language-analysis tools if accurate semantic information is sought even in the limited domain of restricted affect-detection. The language includes misspellings, ungrammaticality, abbreviations (often as in text messaging), slang, use of upper case and special punctuation (such as repeated exclamation marks) for affective emphasis, repetition of letters or words for emphasis, and open-ended interjective and onomatopoeic elements such as "hm" and "grrrr". In the examples we have studied, which so far involve teenage children improvising around topics such as school bullying, the genre is similar to Internet chat.

To deal with the misspellings, abbreviations, letter repetitions, interjections and onomatopoeia, several types of pre-processing occur before actual detection of affect.

A lookup table deals with abbreviations (e.g. 'im (I am)' and 'c u (see you)'). Most abbreviations used in Internet chat rooms and textese can be so handled. We also deal with abbreviations such as numbers embedded within words, e.g., "l8r" for later using the lookup table. We handle the ambiguity of, say, "2" (to, too, two) in textese (e.g. "I'm 2 hungry 2 walk"), by using two simple rules that consider the POS tags of immediately surrounding words. In evaluations using examples in previous transcripts we have obtained 85.7% accuracy, which is adequate currently.

Letter repetition comes in two flavours: repetition added to ordinary words (e.g. 'yesss', 'seee'); and repetition added to interjections or onomatopoeic elements (e.g. 'grrrr', 'agggghhh'). The iconic use of written word length here (corresponding roughly to imagined sound length) normally implies strong affective states in the characters' input. Usefully, adding letters does not greatly change the pronunciation. We have a small dictionary containing base forms of interjections (e.g. 'grr') and some ordinary words that often have letters repeated in e-drama. Then the Metaphone spelling-correction algorithm [20], which is based on pronunciation, works with the dictionary to locate the base forms of words with letter repetitions. We also aim to develop a detector of onomatopoeic elements that does not rely on particular base forms. We must stress that added letter-repetition is not simply eliminated, but the fact of its occurrence is recorded for the purposes of affect-detection.

Finally, the Levenshtein distance algorithm [21] with a contemporary English dictionary deals with spelling mistakes in users' input. Having described the necessary pre-processing, we turn to the core detection of affect in users' input.

2.2 Affect Detection by Pattern Matching

In an initial stage, we based affect detection purely on textual pattern-matching rules that looked for simple grammatical patterns or templates partially involving lists of specific alternative words. This continues to be a core aspect of our system but we have now added robust parsing using Rasp [19] and some semantic analysis.

In textual pattern-matching, particular keywords, phrases and fragmented sentences are found, but also certain partial sentence structures are extracted. This procedure possesses the robustness and flexibility to accept many ungrammatical fragmented sentences and to deal with the varied positions of sought-after phraseology. However, it lacks other types of generality and can be fooled when the phrases are suitably embedded as subcomponents of other grammatical structures. For example, if the input is "I doubt she's really angry", rules looking for anger in a simple way will fail to provide the expected results. Below we indicate our path beyond these limitations.

The transcripts analysed to inspire our initial knowledge base and pattern-matching rules had independently been produced earlier from Hi8us' *edrama* improvisations. The actors were school children aged from 8 to 12. We have also worked on another, distinctly different scenario - Crohn's disease, based on a TV programme about this disease by Maverick Television Ltd. (another of our industrial partners). One interesting feature in this scenario is meta-emotion (emotion about emotion) and cognition about emotion, because of the need for people to cope with emotions about their illnesses. The rule sets created for one scenario have a useful degree of applicability to other scenarios, though there will be a few changes in the related knowledge database according to EMMA's different roles in specific scenarios.

A rule-based Java framework called Jess [22] is used to implement the pattern-matching rules in EMMA. When Mayid says "Lisa, you Pizza Face! You smell", EMMA detects that he is insulting Lisa. Patterns such as 'you smell' have been used for rule implementation. The rules conjecture the character's emotions, evaluation dimension (negative or positive), politeness (rude or polite) and what response EMMA should make. Here is one simple pseudo-code example rule.

```
(defrule example_rule
?fact <-(any string containing 'get out')
=>
(obtain emotion and response from knowledge database)
```

When a character says "Lisa, get out of here" and EMMA responds, this example rule will be fired. EMMA infers the affective quality from the utterance (*angry and rude* in this case) and obtains the appropriate response from the knowledge database.

Multiple exclamation marks and the capitalisation of whole words are frequently employed to express emphasis in e-drama sessions. If these are detected in a character's utterance, then the emotion intensity is deemed to be comparatively high (and emotion is suggested even in the absence of other indicators).

A reasonably good indicator that an inner state is being described is the use of 'I' (see also Craggs and Wood [14]), especially in combination with the present or future tense. In the school-bullying scenario, when 'I' is followed by a future-tense verb the affective state 'threatening' is normally being expressed; and the utterance is usually the shortened version of an implied conditional, e.g., "I'll scream [if you stay here]." When 'I' is followed by a present-tense verb, other emotional states tend to be expressed, e.g. "I want my mum" (fear) and "I hate you" (dislike). Further analysis of first-person, present-tense cases is described in section 2.4.

2.3 Processing of Imperatives

A useful signal of strong emotions is the imperative mood, especially when used without softeners such as 'please' or 'would you'. We deal with some common imperative phrases such as "shut up" and "mind your own business" directly. They often indicate strong negative emotions. But the phenomenon is more general.

Detecting imperatives accurately is by itself an example of the non-trivial problems we face. To go beyond the limitations of the text matching we have done, we have also used syntactic outputs from the Rasp parser and semantic information in the form of the semantic profiles for the 1,000 most frequently used English words [23] to deal with certain types of imperatives. This helps us to deal with some of the difficulties.

The Rasp parser recognises some types of imperatives directly. Unfortunately, the grammar of the 2002 version that we have used does not deal properly with certain imperatives (John Carroll, p.c). This means that examples like "you shut up", "Matt don't be so blunt", "please leave me alone" and "don't you call me a dog", are not recognized as imperatives, but as declaratives or interrogatives. Hence, extra analysis is needed to detect imperatives, by additional processing applied to the possibly-incorrect syntactic trees Rasp produces. This includes consideration of the nature of the sentence subject, the form of the verb used and whether negation is present. We mention one case of special interest, involving semantic and pragmatic processing.

When a sentence involves a subject and a verb for which there is no difference at all between the base form and the past tense form, then an imperative/declarative ambiguity arises (e.g. "Lisa hit me"). An important special case of this ambiguity is when the object of the verb is 'me'. In order to solve the ambiguity, we have adopted the evaluation value of the verb from Heise's compilation of semantic differential profiles [23]. In these profiles, Heise listed values of evaluation, activation, potency, distance from neutrality, etc. for the 1,000 most frequently used English words. In the evaluation dimension, positive values imply goodness. Because normally people tend to use 'a negative verb + me' to complain about an unfair fact, if the evaluation value of the verb is negative, then the sentence is probably not an imperative but a statement sentence (e.g "Mayid hurt me"). Otherwise, other factors implying imperative are checked in this sentence, such as exclamation marks and capitalizations. If these factors occur, then the input is probably an imperative. Otherwise, the conversation logs are checked to see if there is any question sentence directed toward this speaker recently. If there is, then the input is conjectured to be declarative.

2.4 Using WordNet for a First Person Case

As we mentioned earlier, the first-person with a present-tense verb tends to express an affective state in the speaker. We have used the Rasp parser to detect such a sentence. We are exploiting WordNet [24] synsets to broaden the average of the existing pattern-matching rules to allow rough synonyms of the verbs in the rules to lead to a similar affect, and the analysis of synsets is refined by using Heise's [23] semantic profiles. For example, if the user's input is "I enjoy the movie very much", we use WordNet to obtain the synonyms of the verb 'enjoy' (possibly from different synsets). The set of synonyms is refined by using semantic profiles from Heise's dictionary and we obtain rough synonyms 'love' and 'like'. Then we use 'love' to replace the verb 'enjoy', and send the newly built sentence "I love the movie very much" to the pattern-matching rules in order to obtain the speaker's affective state and EMMA's response. If we cannot successfully obtain such information, we will build another input sentence using the other synonym 'like' and send the sentence "I like the movie very much" to the pattern-matching rules. In general, using Wordnet provides us with the benefit of making our affect detection approach more generalized.

2.5 Responding Regimes

EMMA normally responds, on average, to every Nth speech by another character, where N is a changeable parameter (currently usually set to 3). However, it also responds when EMMA's character's name is mentioned, and makes no response if nothing useful is detected in the utterance. The one-in-N average is achieved by sampling a random variable every time another character says something, although in the future, we plan to have N dynamically adjustable according to how confident EMMA is about what it discerns in the utterance at hand. The random response is chosen from several stored response candidates that are suitable for the affective quality discerned in the utterance being responding to. For example,

> <Another character> Don't mess with me. Don't forget it!
> <EMMA character> Hey, tone down your language a bit.

In addition, EMMA may take part of the user's input string as a sub-component of its response. Because the pre-processing module, reported in section 2.1, replaces the abbreviations and misspellings with 'translations' of the original, this helps obscure the fact that part of EMMA's response is only a reflection. For example,

> <Another character> I'm ur (*your*) best m8 (*mate*).
> <EMMA character> Why are you my best mate?

On the other hand, we purposely put abbreviations and other phenomena used in Internet chat rooms in responses in order to make EMMA 'behave' like a school kid.

For example,

<Another character> You get lost!
<EMMA character> Hey, coool it folks. (notice the lengthening of 'cool')
<Another character> He didn't do it.
<EMMA character> No1 believes you, m8. (where 'no1' stands for 'no one')

The reader should bear in mind that EMMA's responses are not aimed at engaging with the detailed meaning of the utterance, but simply to stimulate the improvisation in a way that is somewhat sensitive to affect being expressed or mentioned. Furthermore, in order to make the EMMA character's responses push the improvisation forward, the character will not only ask scenario related questions to the main characters, but also introduce new topics closely related to the scenario in the improvisation. In a recent user-testing debrief session, secondary school students mentioned that the human bit-part character did not stay in character and said pointless things, while in another session one student, who played a main character, believed that the EMMA character was the only one that stuck to scenario related topics. The directors reported that, even when a main character was silent and the director did not intervene very much, the EMMA character led the improvisation on the right track by raising new topics other characters were concerned about.

3   Affect Via Metaphor

Metaphor is relevant to affect detection for two reasons. It is often used to convey affect and it partly underlies folk theories of affect and emotion. For example, folk theories often talk about, and appear to conceive of, anger as if it were a heated fluid possibly exerting a strong pressure on its containing body. This motivates a wide range of metaphorical expressions both conventional such as "he was boiling with anger and about to blow his top" and more creative variants such as "the temperature in the office was getting higher and this had nothing to do with where the thermostat was set" (modified, slightly from a Google™ search). Passion, or lack of, is also often described in terms of heat and the latter example could in certain contexts be so used.

So far, examples of actors reflecting or commenting on the nature of their or others emotions have been infrequent in the e-drama transcripts, although we might expect to find more examples as more students participate in the Crohn's disease scenario. However, such metaphorically motivated folk models often directly motivate the terminology used to convey affect, as in utterances such as "you leave me cold", which conveys lack of interest or disdain. This use of metaphor to motivate folk models of emotions and, as a consequence, certain forms of direct expression of emotion has been extensively studied in linguistics, [15], [16].

Less recognised is the fact that metaphor frequently conveys emotion more indirectly. Here the metaphor does not describe some aspect of an emotional state, but something else. Crucially, however, it also conveys a negative or positive value judgement which is carried over to what is being described and this attitude hints at the emotion. For example to say of someone's room that "it is a cess-pit" allows the negative evaluation of 'cess-pit' to be transferred to 'the room' and we might assume an emotion of disgust. In our transcripts we find examples such as "smelly attitude" and "you buy your clothes at the rag market" (which we take to be not literally true). Animal insults such as "you pig" frequently take this form, although many are now highly conventionalised. Our analysis of e-drama transcripts shows that this type of metaphor is much more common than the direct use.

It should be apparent that even though conventional metaphorical phraseology may well be listed in specialised lexicons, approaches to metaphor and affect which rely upon a form of lexical look-up to determine the meaning of utterances are likely to miss both the creative variants and extensions of standard metaphors and also the quite general carrying over of affectual evaluations from the literal meaning of an utterance to the intended metaphorical meaning.

At the time of writing (May/June 2006) EMMA incorporates little in the way of metaphor handling. However, certain aspects will be incorporated shortly, since they involve extensions of existing capabilities. Our intended approach is partly to look for stock metaphorical phraseology and straightforward variants of it, which is the most common form of metaphor in most forms of discourse, including edrama. We also plan to employ a simple version of the more open-ended, reasoning-based techniques described in the ATT-Meta project on metaphor processing ([17] [25] [26]).

As a first step, it should be noted that insults and swear words are often metaphorical. We are currently investigating specialised insult dictionaries and the machine-readable version of the OALD, which indicates slang.

Calling someone an animal of any sort often conveys affect, but it can be insulting or affectionate. The young of an animal is often used affectionately, and the same is true of diminutive (e.g., 'piglet') and nursery forms (e.g., 'moo cow'), even when the adult form is usually used as an insult. Thus calling someone 'a cat' or 'catty' differs from describing them as kittenish. Likewise, "you pup" differs from "you dog". We are constructing a dictionary of specific animals used in slang and as insults, but for animals not listed we can use WordNet and electronic dictionaries to determine whether or not it is the young or mature form of the animal that is being used.

We have already noted that in metaphor the affect associated with a source term by default carries across to the target. EMMA already consults Heise's compilation of semantic differential profiles for the evaluation value of the verb. We will extend the determination of the evaluation value to all parts of speech.

Having the means to determine the emotion conveyed by a metaphor is most useful when metaphor can be spotted reliably. There are a number of means of doing this for some metaphors. Thus, idioms are often metaphorical [27] and we can use an existing idiom dictionary, adding to it as necessary. Unfortunately, as is often noted, idioms often show a degree of variation, either by adding modifiers, e.g., 'shut your **big fat** mouth' or by using synonyms of standard lexis, e.g., '**constructing** castles in the air' instead of 'building castles in the air'. This variability will pose a challenge if one is looking for fixed expressions. However, if the idiom dictionary is treated as providing base forms, with for example the nouns being treated as the heads of noun-phrases, then the Rasp parser can be used to determine the noun phrase and the modifiers of the head noun, and likewise with verbs, verb-phrases, etc. Indeed, this approach can be extended beyond highly fixed expressions to other cases of metaphor, since as [28] has noted metaphors tend to display a much greater degree of fixedness compared to non-metaphors, whilst not being as fixed as what are conventionally called idioms.

There are other ways of detecting metaphors. Metaphoricity signals ([29] [30]) such as: *so to speak, sort of, almost* may signal metaphor use. Semantic restriction violations as in "my car **drinks** petrol," often indicate, metaphor ([31] [32] [33]), although not all metaphors violate semantic restrictions. To determine whether semantic restrictions are being violated, domain information from ontologies/thesauri such as WordNet could be used and/or statistical techniques as used by Mason ([33]).

Finally note, physical size is often used metaphorically to emphasise evaluations (e.g. "you big bully") [34], although challengingly the bigness may be literal.

4   User Testing

We conducted a two-day pilot user test with 39 secondary school students in May 2005, to try out and refine a testing methodology and with the primary aim of measuring the extent to which having EMMA as opposed to a human play a character affects levels of enjoyment, sense of engagement, etc. Fig. 1 shows a screen shot. We concealed the fact that EMMA was involved in some sessions in order to have a fair test of the difference that is made. We obtained surprisingly good results. Having a minor bit-part character called "Dave" played by EMMA made no statistically significant difference to measures of user engagement and enjoyment, or indeed to user perceptions of the worth of the contributions made by the character "Dave". Users did comment in debriefing sessions on some utterances of Dave's, so it was not that there was a lack of effect simply because users did not notice Dave at all. Also, the frequencies of human "Dave" and EMMA "Dave" being responded to during the improvisation (sentences of Dave's causing a response divided by all sentences said by "Dave") are both roughly around 30%, again suggesting that users notice Dave. Additionally, the frequency of response to other side-characters was roughly the same – "Matthew": around 30% and "Elise": around 35%.

Furthermore, it surprised us that no user appeared to realize that sometimes Dave was computer-controlled. We stress, however, that it is not an aim of our work to ensure that human actors do not realize this. More extensive, user testing at several

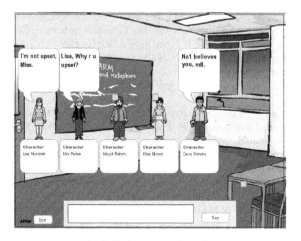

Fig. 1. E-drama user interface

Birmingham secondary schools is being conducted at the time of writing this paper, now that we have tried out and somewhat modified the methodology.

5 Conclusion and Ongoing Work

We have implemented a limited degree of affect-detection in an automated bit-part character in an e-drama application, and fielded the character successfully in pilot user-testing. Although there is a considerable distance to go in terms of the practical affect-detection we plan to implement, the already implemented detection causes reasonably appropriate contributions by the automated character. We later intend to use affect-detection in a module for automatically generating director messages to actors. Aside from affect-sensitive directorial messages, we also intend to implement facilities for automatically generating director messages (or at least hints to the human director) when a particular character is not participating for long periods or when a character appears to be hogging the stage. In general, our work contributes to the issue of what types of automation should be included in the interactive narrative environments and how detecting affect in language can contribute to the development of believable synthetic AI characters, which contribute to the drama improvisation. Moreover, the development of affect detection provides a good test-bed for the accompanying deeper research into how affect is conveyed linguistically.

Acknowledgments. This work is supported by grants RES-328-25-0009 from the ESRC under the ESRC/EPSRC/DTI "PACCIT" programme and grant EP/C538943/1 from the EPSRC. We are grateful to our industrial partners on this grant-Hi8us Midlands Ltd, Maverick Television Ltd and BT-and to our colleagues W.H. Edmondson, S.R. Glasbey, M.G. Lee, Rachel Pilkington and Z. Wen.

References

1. Machado, I., Prada, R. and Paiva, A. 2000. Bringing Drama into a Virtual Stage, In *Proceedings of ACM Conference on Collaborative Virtual Environments*, ACM Press.
2. Picard, R.W. 2000. *Affective Computing*. The MIT Press. Cambridge MA.
3. Ortony, A., Clore, G.L. & Collins, A. 1988. *The Cognitive Structure of Emotions*. C.U.P.
4. Prendinger, H. & Ishizuka, M. 2001. Simulating Affective Communication with Animated Agents. In *Proceedings of Eighth IFIP TC.13 Conference on Human-Computer Interaction*, Tokyo, Japan, pp.182-189.
5. Wiltschko, W. R. 2003. Emotion Dialogue Simulator. eDrama learning, Inc. eDrama Front Desk.
6. Mehdi, E. J., Nico P., Julie D. & Bernard P. 2004. Modeling Character Emotion in an Interactive Virtual Environment. In *Proceedings of AISB 2004 Symposium: Motion, Emotion and Cognition*. Leeds, UK.
7. McCrae, R.R. and John, O.P. 1992. An Introduction to the Five Factor Model and Its Application. *Journal of Personality*, 60, pp.175-215.
8. Gratch, J. & Marsella, S. 2004. A Domain-Independent Framework for Modeling Emotion. *Journal of Cognitive Systems Research*. Vol 5, Issue 4, pp.269-306.
9. Egges, A., Kshirsagar, S. & Magnenat-Thalmann, N. 2003. A Model for Personality and Emotion Simulation, In *Proceedings of Knowledge-Based Intelligent Information & Engineering Systems (KES2003)*, Lecture Notes in AI. Springer-Verlag: Berlin.

10. Elliott, C., Rickel, J. & Lester, J. 1997. Integrating Affective Computing into Animated Tutoring Agents. In *Proceedings of IJCAI'97 Workshop on Intelligent Interface Agents.*
11. Mateas, M. 2002. Ph.D. Thesis. Interactive Drama, Art and Artificial Intelligence. School of Computer Science, Carnegie Mellon University.
12. Zhe, X. & Boucouvalas, A. C. 2002. Text-to-Emotion Engine for Real Time Internet Communication. In *Proceedings of International Symposium on Communication Systems, Networks and DSPs,* Staffordshire University, UK, pp.164-168.
13. Boucouvalas, A. C. 2002. Real Time Text-to-Emotion Engine for Expressive Internet Communications. In *Being There: Concepts, Effects and Measurement of User Presence in Synthetic Environments.* G. Riva, F. Davide and W. IJsselsteijn (eds.) pp.305-318.
14. Craggs, R. & Wood. M. 2004. A Two Dimensional Annotation Scheme for Emotion in Dialogue. In *Proceedings of AAAI Spring Symposium: Exploring Attitude and Affect in Text.*
15. Fussell, S. & Moss, M. 1998. Figurative Language in Emotional Communication. In S. R. Fussell and R. J. Kreuz (Eds.), *Social and Cognitive Approaches to Interpersonal Communication.* Lawrence Erlbaum. pp.113-142.
16. Kövecses, Z. 1998. Are There Any Emotion-Specific Metaphors? In *Speaking of Emotions: Conceptualization and Expression.* Athanasiadou, A. and Tabakowska, E. (eds.), Berlin and New York: Mouton de Gruyter, pp.127-151.
17. Barnden, J.A., Glasbey, S.R., Lee, M.G. & Wallington, A.M. 2004. Varieties and Directions of Inter-domain Influence in Metaphor. *Metaphor and Symbol,* 19(1), pp.1-30.
18. Watson, D. and Tellegen, A. 1985. Toward a Consensual Structure of Mood. *Psychological Bulletin,* 98, pp.219-235.
19. Briscoe, E. and J. Carroll. 2002. Robust Accurate Statistical Annotation of General Text. In *Proceedings of the 3rd International Conference on Language Resources and Evaluation,* Las Palmas, Gran Canaria. pp.1499-1504.
20. Metaphone Algorithm. http://aspell.net/metaphone/.
21. Levenshtein Distance Algorithm http://www.merriampark.com/ld.htm.
22. Jess, 2004. The Rule Engine for Java Platform. Http://herzberg.ca.sandia.gov/jess/.
23. Heise, D. R. 1965. Semantic Differential Profiles for 1,000 Most Frequent English Words. *Psychological Monographs.* 79, pp.1-31.
24. WordNet, A Lexical Database for the English Language. Version 2.1 Cognitive Science Laboratory. Princeton University.
25. Wallington, A.M., Barnden, J.A., Glasbey, S.R. & Lee, M.G. 2006. Metaphorical reasoning with an economical set of mappings. *Delta, 22:1,* pp 147-171.
26. Barnden, J.A. Forthcoming. Metaphor, Semantic Preferences and Context-sensitivity. Invited chapter for a Festschrifft volume. Kluwer.
27. Moon, R 1988. *Fixed idioms and expressions in English.* Clarendon Press: Oxford, U.K.
28. Deignan, A. 2005. *Metaphor and corpus Linguistics.* John Benjamins.
29. Goatly, A. 1997. *The language of metaphors.* Routledge London and New York
30. Wallington A.M., Barnden, J.A., Barnden, M.A., Ferguson, F.J. & Glasbey, S.R. 2003. Metaphoricity Signals: A Corpus-Based Investigation. Technical Report CSRP-03-5, School of Computer Science, The University of Birmingham, U.K.
31. Wilks, Y., 1978. Making preferences more active. *Artificial Intelligence,* 10, pp. 75- 97
32. Fass, D. 1997. *Processing metaphor and metonymy.* Greenwich, Connecticut: Ablex.
33. Mason, Z.J. 2004.CorMet: a computational, corpus-based conventional metaphor extraction system. *Computational Linguistics 30:1.* pp. 23-44.
34. Sharoff, S. 2005. How to Handle Lexical Semantics in SFL: a Corpus Study of Purposes for Using Size Adjectives. *Systemic Linguistics and Corpus.* London: Continuum.

An Exploration of Delsarte's Structural Acting System

Stacy C. Marsella[1], Sharon Marie Carnicke[2], Jonathan Gratch[3],
Anna Okhmatovskaia[3], and Albert Rizzo[3]

[1] Information Sciences Institute
[2] School of Theatre
[3] Institute for Creative Technology
University of Southern California
marsella@isi.edu

Abstract. The designers of virtual agents often draw on a large research literature in psychology, linguistics and human ethology to design embodied agents that can interact with people. In this paper, we consider a structural acting system developed by Francois Delsarte as a possible resource in designing the nonverbal behavior of embodied agents. Using human subjects, we evaluate one component of the system, *Delsarte's Cube*, that addresses the meaning of differing attitudes of the hand in gestures.

Keywords: Virtual Human, Nonverbal Behavior, Acting Technique, Delsarte.

1 Introduction

At a recent forum on emotion at the Swiss National Exchange, Leonard Pitt, an expert in mime and the use of masks, performed in front of an audience of assembled emotion researchers. He donned masks with fixed facial expressions and then proceeded to explore how alterations of posture and gesture could manipulate our impression of the emotional/attitudinal state of his character and override the emotion expressed by the mask. The performance served to demonstrate poignantly the panoply of behaviors that convey personality and emotion. Although it was not the performer's intent, it also demonstrated that designers of virtual humans have a long way to go in creating such expressivity in their behavioral models and animations.

Designers of virtual humans have been very effective in mining the large literature in psychology that has studied such phenomena. Of notable distinction is the work of Ekman & Friesen (1978), along with their collaborators, on the facial action coding system (FACS) that breaks down facial expression into action units. FACS has provided a systematic, exacting basis for emotion researchers to study and catalog the expressive capabilities of the face and its role in human interaction. Not surprisingly, the FACS has also helped to spur significant advances in the facial expressions of ECAs (Embodied Conversational Agent, also known as a virtual human). The systematic coding approach provided by FACS allows for the decomposition and enumeration of the space of all possible facial expressions (though all are not anatomically possible). For example, armed with such descriptions, the designer of an

J. Gratch et al. (Eds.): IVA 2006, LNAI 4133, pp. 80–92, 2006.
© Springer-Verlag Berlin Heidelberg 2006

ECA can build a head that covers that space as well as explore manipulations of the compositions and dynamics of action units.

There has also been extensive work on posture (e.g., Mehrabian, 1969; Walbott, 1998), gesture (Kendon, 2004; McNeill, 1992), gaze (Argyle & Cook, 1976), etc. Unfortunately, this work has typically not matched the systematic level of analysis that the facial expression research has achieved. In particular, the psychological research in these areas has provided far less guidance in the cataloging of the space of all possible head movements or how to exploit and understand the dynamic manner of such movements.

Augmenting the psychological work, there are also a variety of other resources that virtual human researchers can draw upon from the performance arts that augment the psychological literature. Such resources include acting technique, choreography and rhetorical gesture. For example, structural acting systems propose that certain behaviors and the manner in which they are performed convey particular meanings, for example, the work of Laban (see Newlove, 1999) and Delsarte (see Zorn, 1968). This work has in fact informed virtual human research (Noma et al. 2000; Costa et al, 2000; Neff & Fiume, 2004). On the other hand, some acting theories are not directly relevant to our work. For example, Stanislavsky's acting technique (Stanislavski, 1989) informs the performer to put herself in the mental and emotional state of her role and the appropriate physical performance will then naturally follow. This clearly is less relevant to virtual human work, since our virtual humans don't come equipped with a model that maps between internal state and behavior. Indeed it is this mapping that we seek to create.

The analysis technique of Delsarte is particularly intriguing for virtual human researchers. This technique systematically and extensively describes how emotions, attitude and personality are conveyed in dynamic body postures and gestures. Delsarte's work is based on his extensive observations of human behavior across a range of ecologically varied settings. Unfortunately, the description of the technique is often couched in a language and terminology from the 1800s that strikes a 21st century reader as perhaps quaint and metaphysical. More importantly, Delsarte's observations have not been empirically confirmed.

It is in this context that we have been exploring Delsarte's work and asking very basic questions. Are the interpretations that people derive from Delsarte's catalog of movements consistent with Delsarte's analysis or at least reliable across observers? In this paper, we begin to address these questions with some preliminary human experiments targeting what Delsarte describes as *attitudes of the hand*. The results of this pilot study suggest that Delsarte's work deserves some closer scrutiny. For the reader who is not familiar with the Delsarte technique, we will present a brief primer on its relevant features prior to the description of our method and the presentation of results.

2 Acting Methods and Delsarte

Acting operates simultaneously on two levels. The opaque level pertains to the body and voice of the actor; we generally associate this level with the skills and virtuosity of the acting craft. The transparent level pertains to the stories and emotions revealed, as conveyed through the actor's body and voice. In short, the audience looks at the opaque body of the actor in order to see through that body a character.

Contemporary actors usually work from the transparent level and assume that their trained bodies and voices will automatically follow. They generally do not think about their bodies when they perform. Expressivity will come as a natural consequence of establishing the proper internal state. If actors are trained in the Stanislavsky System, they begin by asking a simple question. What would I do, if I were in the circumstances of my character? If actors are trained in the American Method, they ask themselves a slightly different question. What is it in my own life that makes that makes me feel the way my character must feel in this scene? In both cases, the contemporary actor places himself or herself imaginatively in the fictional world of the character and then behaves as that world dictates (see Carnicke, 1998, for a comparison of the two approaches).

Unfortunately, contemporary acting practice does not help much in developing a computer model for encoding emotionally realistic physical gestures in virtual characters. Virtual humans do not come equipped with internal mappings from internal cognitive and emotional states to behavior that can be expected to motivate their movements. As Hooks writes [2000], "Actors create emotion – largely internally – in the present moment, while animators describe internal emotion through the external movement of their characters." Moreover, the goals of the virtual human designer, to describe movement, to break it down into its multiple components--spatial shapes, temporal rhythms, force and direction, and to collect data about the encoding and decoding of emotion through the body are arguably antithetical to the artistic work of the contemporary actor. The contemporary actor allows whatever happens in the moment to occur without intellectually judging it or analyzing it.

In order to address our goals we decided to go back to the past for ways to think about acting—to the time when actors worked more consciously with the opaque level of performance. We thus returned to the techniques of gestural or structural acting.

2.1 Introduction to Delsarte

Francois Delsarte lived from 1811 to 1871, a French singer who had lost his voice because of poor teaching practices. He began to study the relationships between physical behavior, emotion, and language in order to formulate scientific principles of expression. Over many years, he diligently observed the expressive postures and gestures of living people across all walks of life as well as corpses in the Paris morgue, developing a broad model of how emotion, body, and language interact.

Delsarte became the most significant acting teacher in Europe and one of his students, Steele MacKaye, became the leading force in American actor training. MacKaye studied with Delsarte in Paris in 1869, became his assistant in 1870, and founded the first professional acting school in the United States in 1884. Thus, Delsarte provided the predominant form of actor training in the United States until 1923 when Stanislavsky first brought the Moscow Art Theater to the United States.

Delsarte saw that movement involves a "semiotics" (Delsarte's own term)—a sign system that can be "read" by observers. Thus, the body encodes meaning which the viewer can decode. He recognized that physical "signs" come from various sources-- some gestures are ours alone and express our individuality; some are social or cultural conventions, like waving "hello"; and some may be biologically connected to our emotional reactions (from Delsarte's Rhetoric, e.g. see Zorn, 1968).

The complexity of Delsarte's system is both daunting and a potential advantage. It specifies a vast range of potential gestures and postures by working through a series of principles that defines a space of variations across head orientations, stances, hand shapes, leg positions and arm orientations as well as the meanings they convey. Further, Delsarte argues how the zones of the body and space around the body tend to be associated with differing intellectual, emotional and physical interpretations.

In other words, Delsarte's system provides an enumeration of behaviors potentially both in terms of orientations and movements through space. For example, consider head movement. We know from linguistic studies (e.g., McClave, 2000) that a head shake or sweep may signify inclusivity ("everyone"), a tilt upward that averts gaze can signify an effort to think or regulate cognitive load (Argyle & Cook, 1978) and ethologists tell us that a tilt to the side can signify flirting behavior. Pieced together, these studies can greatly assist in the design of virtual humans. However, it is piecemeal. Delsarte, on the other hand, lays out all possible head tilts and what they could signify. Similarly, consider gestures. Delsarte suggests that the orientation of the gesture in space, the shape of the hand and fingers, the starting and ending location of its movement all impacts what the gesture signifies. Overall, this provides a considerable amount of raw material for designing virtual humans.

Other more recent physically based actor training systems (such as that of Laban) reduce the number of distinct movements that actors are expected to study. As Hecht observes (1971), physical training systems for the actor that come after Delsarte get progressively simpler. For the actor, they seem more manageable, hence more useful. But as a consequence are also limiting for our purpose.

The specifics of Delsarte's system are too extensive to cover in any detail. We therefore confine ourselves to a few brief comments about his work.

2.2 Attitudes of the Hand

In describing attitudes of the hand, Delsarte talks of an imaginary cube in front of the speaker. Consider grasping it from each possible surface—use two hands to contain the outer surfaces; push a hand outward against its inner surface; bring a hand upward to its lower surface; explore every possible way of grasping and containing this cube. Each gesture has a different connotation.

Experts on Delsarte differ in the details of what these various positions of the hand signify. There are several sources that describe the cube (e.g., Delaumosne in Zorn, 1968; Shawn, 1963). The basic intuitions of the cube seem on target to us. To address some of the discrepancies across interpretations of Delsarte's teaching, we synthesized the various approaches into the following hypotheses of how they would be interpreted: (The one marked with a plus is a hand posture suggested by the authors.)

- Palm of Hand on face of cube farthest away from body => to limit
- Palm of Hand on interior of face nearest body ⇒to possess +
- Palm of Hand on face of cube nearest body ⇒to stop
- Palm of Hand on side surface of cube ⇒to possess, include
- Palm of Hand on interior side surface of cube ⇒to reject, remove
- Palm of Hand on top surface of cube ⇒to control
- Palm of Hand on bottom surface of cube ⇒to support

2.3 The Three Orders of Movement

Delsarte moves beyond the static systems of gestural actor training that were used in the 17th and 18th centuries by paying close attention to the dynamics of motion. In particular, we became particularly interested in three types of motion that Delsarte identifies:

Oppositions
Any two parts of the body moving in opposite directions simultaneously suggest expressive force, strength, physical or emotional power. For example, a rejecting motion of arm and hand is strengthened by an opposite motion of head and torso. (This brings to mind Newton's Third Law: For every action, there is an equal and opposite reaction.)

Parallelisms
Any two parts of the body moving in parallel directions simultaneously suggest deliberateness, planning, intentionality. An example of this would be arms moving downward in parallel in a beat gesture.

Successions
"Any movement passing through the body which moves each part [of the body in turn] (in a fluid wave-like motion)" (Shawn, 1963). True successions move from the face, through the torsos and into the arms and legs and suggest sincerity and normality. Reverse successions work backwards from the limbs into the face and suggest falsity and insincerity.

3 Evaluation

Delsarte's system appears at times to be full of interesting insights and at other times mired in metaphysics and a performance culture that is less relevant to the scientific study of modern gesture or acting. It is in the hope to extract the insights and validate them that we have begun to experiment with Delsarte-based behaviors. As the focus of our first experiment, we selected Delsarte's idea of the imaginary cube as describing a space of hand attitudes, in part because it resonates with observations on how gestures often manipulate imaginary objects (McNeill, 1992).

Stimuli

The stimuli we constructed were animations of a virtual character that involved the hands moving from a rest pose (arms at the side of the body) to a position on an imaginary cube and then returning to the rest pose.

The animations were crafted with an un-textured body that moved the hand to a position on an imaginary cube. Linear interpolation was used wherever possible, relying largely on simple interpolation between a few poses as opposed to hand-crafting a rich animation. This was done deliberately to avoid inferences from the appearance or physical manner of the animations. The internal cube face animations were designed so that it appears as if the hand was moving through the cube from the opposite face. Figures 2a and 2b depict the position of the hands on the imaginary cube. As can be seen, in some of the interior face stimuli the position of hand is more consistent with having pushed the "cube" as opposed to resting the hand on the interior face. The animations used in this experiment can be found on the web: http://www.isi.edu/~marsella/experiment/. Note that subjects got no other context to guide their interpretations -- the animations are silent, there is no text, sound or dialog. We chose to use animations, instead of stills, because human gestures have motion, but one can imagine a similar experiment using stills.

Hypothesis

Table 1 lists the relationship between faces of the cube, animation files and predictions. Note that we explored a superset of the faces described in writings about Delsarte's cube. As noted earlier, the authors included an animation of the hand moving to the nearest internal face that we predicted would be read as a statement about possession. We also included 3 additional cases of the hand pushing through the cube: the farthest-interior face, the bottom-interior face and the top-interior face. Our predictions for these three additional animations were that they would be the same as the corresponding animation that did not push though the cube. These additional predictions are marked by a plus sign. Also, Delsarte only discusses a single hand, whereas we also explored two handed variants. A 2-handed animation was not done for the side internal face since the hands would have crossed. Our predictions for the two-handed animations are that they would coincide to the single-handed case.

Procedure

We presented these stimuli to subjects, broken into two groups. One group was shown animations that used only one hand and the other group was shown the gestures using both hands moving to positions on the cube. The order of presentation of animations was randomized. There were 28 subjects in the one-hand condition and 22 subjects in the two-handed condition. Subjects were recruited using Craig's List (a web-based job market).

Table 1. Relation between Cube Faces, Animations and Predictions

Face in relation to body	One Hand	Two Hand	Prediction
Farthest, exterior	FarExt	2FarExt	Limit
Nearest, interior	NearInt	2NearInt	Possess +
Nearest, exterior	NearExt	2NearExt	Stop
Farthest, interior	FarInt	2FarInt	Stop +
Side, exterior	SideExt	2SideExt	Possess
Side, interior	SideInt	None	Reject
Top, exterior	TopExt	2TopExt	Control
Bottom, interior	BotInt	2BotInt	Control +
Bottom, exterior	BotExt	2BotExt	Support
Top, interior	TopInt	2TopInt	Support +

To begin the experiment, subjects sat down at a computer interface that provided the following instructions:

> You will see videos of an animated character. Each video will show the character performing a gesture while interacting with someone off-camera.
>
> After each video, you will be asked to choose one phrase that best describes what the gesture conveys.

After each animation, they were then provided a forced choice questionnaire. See Table 2. The authors broke the interpretation of "Stop" into two variants, Stop you and Stop it. Similarly, "Reject" was broken into two variants of Reject It and Reject

He appears to be expressing:

○ Possession: "It's mine"

○ Support: "I am going to support it"

○ Control: "I am going to control it"

○ Limit: "I am going to limit it"

○ Stop: "I am going to stop you"

○ Stop: "I am going to stop it"

○ Reject: "I reject it"

○ Reject: "I reject your idea"

Click submit after making a selection:

(Submit)

Fig. 1. Questionnaire

your Idea. This was done to explore the assumption that some motions may have different referents, either an abstract idea or the listener.

Results

Figures 2a and 2b show frequency distribution plots of subjects' preferred interpretations. Predicted responses are indicated with grey arrows. The white arrows are used to indicate our added predictions. In the case of Stop and Reject, where a prediction was broken into two variants, two arrows identify the predictions.

With the exception of SideExt these distributions are highly unlikely to be obtained by chance (Chi-square test for all 8 categories being equal, $p< 0.05$). This result is, however, not informative enough, since we were mainly interested in the proportions of subjects' responses on predicted categories and did not make any assumptions regarding the distributions of responses on other categories.

For this reason we have performed another series of tests to find out if the proportions of subjects' responses for individual categories were higher than the chance level. For each animation we have aggregated the data into 2 groups: predicted and un-predicted, and used Chi-square statistic to test if the proportions for predicted groups were above chance level. The predicted group contained either a single category or, in the case of Stop and Reject, two categories. We defined chance level as 0.125 (1 out of 8) for a single category, and 0.25 (2 out of 8) for the cases where 2 categories were combined together. The results are presented in Table 2 (left half).

Table 2. Proportions of subjects' responses for selected categories

	Predicted category	Prop.	Sig.	Most frequent category	Prop.	Sig.
FarExt	Limit	0.071	0.029	Possess	0.393	0.000*
NearInt	Possess	**0.714**	**0.000***	Possess	0.714	0.000*
NearExt	Stop (comb.)	**0.929**	**0.000***	Stop (comb.)	0.929	0.000*
FarInt	Stop (comb.)	**0.929**	**0.000***	Stop (comb.)	0.929	0.000*
SideExt	Possess	0.036	0.009	Limit	0.321	0.002*
SideInt	Reject (comb.)	**0.607**	**0.000***	Reject (comb.)	0.607	0.000*
TopExt	Control	0.179	0.383	Limit	0.500	0.000*
BotInt	Control	0.071	0.029	Reject (comb.)	0.464	0.009*
BotExt	Support	**0.607**	**0.000***	Support	0.607	0.000*
TopInt	Support	**0.607**	**0.000***	Support	0.607	0.000*
2FarExt	Limit	0.000	-	Possess	0.714	0.000*
2NearInt	Possess	**0.667**	**0.000***	Possess	0.667	0.000*
2NearExt	Stop (comb.)	**0.905**	**0.000***	Stop (comb.)	0.905	0.000*
2FarInt	Stop (comb.)	**0.810**	**0.000***	Stop (comb.)	0.810	0.000*
2SideExt	Possess	0.048	0.032	Limit	0.333	0.004*
2TopExt	Control	0.238	0.900	Limit	0.476	0.000*
2BotInt	Control	0.048	0.032	Stop (comb.)	0.381	0.166
2BotExt	Support	**0.619**	**0.000***	Support	0.619	0.000*
2TopInt	Support	**0.810**	**0.000***	Support	0.810	0.000*

Observed proportions that were significantly higher than the chance level ($p < 0.05$) are in bold and marked with asterisks.

As one can see from the table, 11 out of 19 predictions are supported by our data. Note, however, that in several of the other cases the proportions for predicted categories were actually lower than the chance level (shown in italic) – sometimes predicted category happened to be the least frequently selected by the subjects. In those cases, where predicted category was not the most frequent one, we have repeated the same analysis using the actual most frequent category instead of predicted. The results are presented in the right half of Table 2, and with a single exception, the subjects' preferences appear to be well above chance level.

The plots and the results of statistical analysis reveal considerable consistency in people's responses with clearly preferred responses. Moreover, the predicted response is generally the preferred category.

When the hand(s) end in a position where the palms face the virtual human (FarExt, 2FarExt, NearInt and 2NearInt), possession is the preferred interpretation. In the case of NearInt and 2NearInt, this was predicted. Given the similar movement and ending position for all 4 of these gestures, it is not surprising that the preferred response for FarExt and 2FarExt are also possession, even though it was not predicted.

When the palm faces away from the virtual human, on the face of the cube closest to it (NearExt and 2NearExt), there is a strong preference for a "stop" interpretation, as predicted. In the case of NearExt, there is a strong preference for "stop you" over other interpretations. In the case of 2NearExt, the responses are largely split between "stop you" and "stop it". (But as noted above, the Chi-square analysis aggregated these two responses).

Table 3. Comparison of distributions for 1 vs. 2 handed animations

Face in relation to body	Compared animations	Chi-Square	Sig.
Farthest, exterior	FarExt – 2FarExt	6.175	.186
Nearest, interior	NearInt – 2NearInt	3.576	.612
Nearest, exterior	NearExt – 2NearExt	4.578	.469
Farthest, interior	FarInt – 2FarInt	7.389	.193
Side, exterior	SideExt – 2SideExt	8.033	.330
Top, exterior	TopExt – 2TopExt	4.594	.467
Bottom, interior	BotInt – 2BotInt	3.833	.699
Bottom, exterior	BotExt – 2BotExt	3.233	.664
Top, interior	TopInt – 2TopInt	7.486	.187

A similar "stop" response is shown when the hand moves forward through the cube - the FarInt and 2FarInt animations. Although here the responses are somewhat more spread over stop you and stop it, aggregated analysis shows a significant difference with the chance distribution.

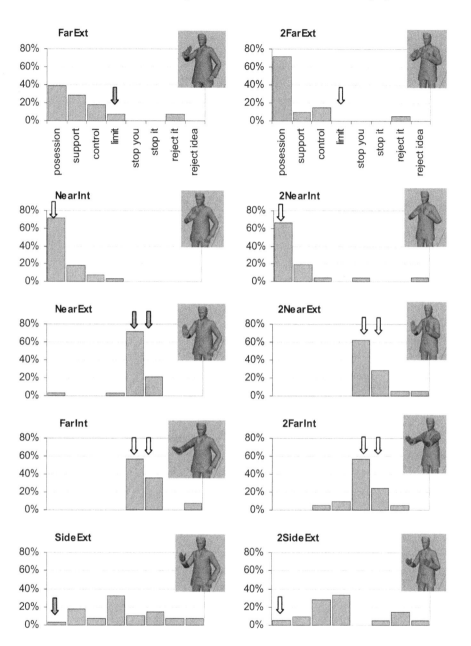

Fig. 2a. Frequency distributions of subjects' interpretations

When the hand is on the side of cube, there is more spread in the responses. SideExt, specifically, is the only animation where the differences between all responses are not significant. We discuss possible explanations in the discussion section. For 2SideExt, they are above chance level, but the most popular response ("limit") is not significantly different from the others.

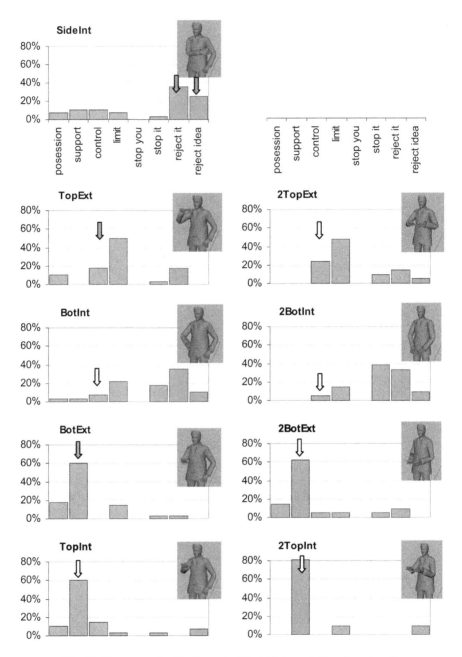

Fig. 2b. Frequency distributions of subjects' interpretations (*continued*)

In SideInt, the hand moving through the cube sideways, there is a strong preference for a combined "reject" interpretation (aggregating reject it and reject you), as predicted. TopExt's preferred response is limit. The predicted response, however, control, is closely related conceptually. In the case of the hands on the bottom of the cube with palms up, BotExt and 2BotExt, there is a strong preference for a support interpretation, as predicted. Finally, a similar, but even more prominent response is seen in the case where the hands move up through the cube, TopInt and 2TopInt.

Finally, comparison between 1-handed and corresponding 2-handed animations shows that their response distributions are very similar. The results of a Chi-square test are presented in Table 3: the differences within each pair of animations are non-significant (at $p < 0.05$).

Discussion

The results reveal considerable consistency in the subject's interpretations. Further the results are generally consistent with predictions. The results are particularly surprising given the minimal context the subjects were presented – they simply got these movements to interpret without other context or dialog. This suggests that Delsarte's cube may provide useful insight in how a virtual human's gestures can use physical space to convey meaning. And going beyond the cube, the current results suggest that perhaps the larger body of Delsarte's work is deserving of closer attention.

In the particular experiments reported here, there is room for improvement. We chose to use animations instead of static poses of the hand resting on the cube faces. Obviously, movement conveys considerable meaning that can easily override the pose. This may in fact explain some of the results that were not consistent with Delsarte's predictions. It will be informative to repeat the study with different motions to the pose. Further, animations whose responses revealed far less consistency may be due to the fact that the categories used in this experiment were synthesized by trying to find an intersection across the writings of several Delsarte experts. As a consequence, this synthesis ended up restricting the number of categories and more importantly the richness of the category descriptions. The fact that some animations did not have a strongly preferred interpretation may be an artifact of there being too few categories and limiting the possible interpretations. It may be informative and more useful to just use the categories as described by a single expert or alternatively to take a union of the interpretations across experts.

Of course, consistent interpretation, free of any specific interactional context or dialog, is a strong test for nonverbal behavior which, by itself, is often ambiguous. In fact, as long as an observer decodes the behavior appropriately in an interactional context that is well defined, the behavior has potential utility for a virtual human designer. There also is the issue of evaluating how natural the gestures appear to the subjects, an issue that is distinct from but may correlate to a degree with consistency of interpretation. Finally, the animations used a single rotation of the hand with respect to the cube face and a single hand shape, and manipulation of these factors may influence the interpretation, as Delsarte argues.

6   Conclusion

The design of virtual humans is an interdisciplinary task. As a community, we all draw heavily on research in artificial intelligence, psychology, human ethology and linguistics, to name a few fields. We have also drawn on insight from the arts, including narrative theory, animation, dance, theatre and film. The preliminary work reported here attempts to go beyond just drawing insights from the arts. The knowledge and aesthetics acquired by the performance arts can provide a more systematic basis for the design of our virtual humans. We believe this to be a common goal shared by many in the virtual human community and see this work in the context of trying to help achieve that goal.

Acknowledgements

This work was sponsored by the U.S. Army Research, Development, and Engineering Command (RDECOM), and the content does not necessarily reflect the position or the policy of the Government, and no official endorsement should be inferred. We also would like to thank Wendy Treynor and Mei Si for their comments and help.

References

1. Argyle, M. & Cook, M. Gaze and Mutual Gaze. Cambridge University Press, Cambridge, (1976).
2. Carnicke, S.M., Stanislavsky in Focus. New York: Harwood/Routledge, (1998).
3. Costa, M. Zhao, L., Chi, D., & Badler, N. The EMOTE model for effort and shape. In Proceedings of SIGGRAPH 2000, (2000).
4. Ekman, P.; Friesen, WV 1978. Facial Action Coding System (FACS). Palo Alto: Consulting Psychologists Press (1978).
5. Hecht, P.A. Kinetic Techniques for the Actor. Ph.D. Thesis, Wayne State University. (1971).
6. Hooks, E. Acting for Animators. Portsmouth, NH: Heinemann, (2000)
7. Kendon, A. *Gesture: Visible Action as Utterance*. Cambridge: Cambridge University Press (2004).
8. McClave, E.Z. Linguistic functions of head movements in the context of speech. *Journal of Pragmatics 37*, 7: 855-878 (2000).
9. McNeill, D Hand and mind: What gestures reveal about thought. Chicago: The University of Chicago Press (1992).
10. Mehrabian, A. Significance of posture and position in the communication of attitude and status relationships. *Psychological Bulletin,* 71, pp. 359-372 (1969)
11. Neff, M. & Fiume, E., Artistically based computer generation of expressive motion. Proceedings of the AISB 2004 Symposium on Language, Speech and Gesture for Expressive Characters, pp. 29–39 (2004).
12. Newlove, J. Laban for Actors and Dancers, Routledge, New York (1999).
13. Noma, T., Zhao, L. & Badler, N. Design of a Virtual human Presenter.. Computer Graphics and Applications. Vol. 20(4), pp 79-85, (2000).
14. Shawn, T. *Every Little Movement*. Dance Horizons, NY, NY, (1963).
15. Stanislavski, C. An Actor Prepares. Routledge, NY, NY (1989).
16. Walbott, H. Bodily expression of emotion. European Journal of Social Psychology, vol. 28, pp. 879-896, (1998).
17. Zorn, J.W. (ed.): The Essential Delsarte. Scarecrow press, Metuchen, NJ (1968).

Perception of Blended Emotions: From Video Corpus to Expressive Agent

Stéphanie Buisine[1], Sarkis Abrilian[2], Radoslaw Niewiadomski[3,4],
Jean-Claude Martin[2], Laurence Devillers[2], and Catherine Pelachaud[3]

[1] LCPI-ENSAM, 151 bd de l'Hôpital,75013 Paris, France
stephanie.buisine@paris.ensam.fr
[2] LIMSI-CNRS, BP 133, 91403 Orsay Cedex, France
{sarkis, martin, devil}@limsi.fr
[3] LINC, IUT of Montreuil, Univ. Paris 8, 140 rue Nouvelle France,
93100 Montreuil, France
c.pelachaud@iut.univ-paris8.fr, radek@dipmat.unipg.it
[4] Department of Mathematics and Computer Science, University of Perugia, Italy

Abstract. Real life emotions are often blended and involve several simultaneous superposed or masked emotions. This paper reports on a study on the perception of multimodal emotional behaviors in Embodied Conversational
Agents. This experimental study aims at evaluating if people detect properly the
signs of emotions in different modalities (speech, facial expressions, gestures)
when they appear to be superposed or masked. We compared the perception of
emotional behaviors annotated in a corpus of TV interviews and replayed by an
expressive agent at different levels of abstraction. The results provide insights
on the use of such protocols for studying the effect of various models and
modalities on the perception of complex emotions.

1 Introduction

Affective behaviors in Embodied Conversational Agents (ECAs) can be quite useful
for experimental studies on the perception of multimodal emotional behaviors as one
can turn on/off a given signal or even a given modality. Real life emotions are often
complex and involve several simultaneous emotions [15, 17, 33]. They may occur
either as the quick succession of different emotions, the superposition of emotions,
the masking of one emotion by another one, the suppression of an emotion or the
overacting of an emotion. We refer to blend of emotions to denote these phenomena.
These blends produce "multiple simultaneous facial expressions" [30].

Depending on the type of blending, the resulting facial expressions are not identical. A masked emotion may leak over the displayed emotion [17]; while superposition
of two emotions will be shown by different facial features (one emotion being shown
on the upper face while another one on the lower face) [17]. Distinguishing these
various types of blends of emotions in ECA systems is relevant as perceptual studies
have shown that people are able to recognize facial expression of felt emotion [14, 37]
as well as fake emotion [16] from real life as well as on ECAs [27]. Moreover, in a
study on deceiving agent, Rhem and André [29] found that the users were able to

J. Gratch et al. (Eds.): IVA 2006, LNAI 4133, pp. 93 – 106, 2006.
© Springer-Verlag Berlin Heidelberg 2006

differentiate when the agent was displaying expressions of felt emotion or expression of fake emotion.

Video corpora of TV interviews enable to explore how people behave during such blended emotions not only by their facial expression but also by their gestures or their speech [11]. Yet, these corpora call for means of validating subjective manual annotations of emotion. Few researchers have used ECAs for validating such manual annotations by testing how people perceive the replay of annotated behaviors by an agent. Ten Ham et al. [34] compared the perception of a video of a human guide vs. an agent using the same speech and similar non-verbal behaviors during a route description task but they did not consider emotion. Becker et al. [5] conducted a study to evaluate the affective feedback of an agent in a card game. They found that the absence of negative emotions from the agent was evaluated as stress-inducing whereas the display of empathic feedback supported the acceptance of the agent as a co-equal opponent.

Aiming at understanding if facial features or regions play identical roles in emotion recognition, researchers performed various perceptual tasks or studied psychological facial activity [4, 7, 8, 20]. They found that positive emotions are mainly perceived from the expression of the lower face (e.g. smile) while negative emotion from the upper face (e.g. frown). One can conclude that reliable features for positive emotion, that is features that convey the strongest characteristics of a positive emotion, are in the lower face. On the other hand, the most reliable features for negative emotion are in the upper face.

Based on these findings we have developed a computational model for facial expressions of blend of emotions. It composes facial expressions from those of single emotions using fuzzy logic rules [26]. Very few models of blended emotions have been developed so far for ECAs. The interpolation between facial parameters of given expressions is commonly used to compute the new expression [3, 12, 27, 31].

This paper reports on an experimental study aiming at evaluating if people detect properly the signs of different emotions in multiple modalities (speech, facial expressions, gestures) when they appear to be superposed or masked. It compares the perception of emotional behaviors in videos of TV interviews with similar behaviors replayed by an expressive agent. The facial expressions of the agent are defined using one of two approaches, namely the computational model of blend of emotions (hereafter called "facial blending replay"), or the annotation of the facial expressions from the video ("multiple levels replay"). We are also interested in evaluating possible differences between visual only vs. audio-visual perception as well as possible gender differences. We aim to test if findings reported in [18, 21] can be replicated here, that is if women tend to be better at recognizing facial expressions of emotions.

Section 2 summarizes our previous work and describes how to replay multimodal emotional behavior from manual annotations. The replay integrates models of expressive behaviors and blended facial expressions. Section 3 describes the protocol. The results are presented and discussed in sections 4 and 5. We conclude in section 6 on the use of such protocols for studying the effect of various models and modalities on the perception of blends of emotions.

2 Annotating and Replaying Multimodal Emotional Behaviors

In order to study multimodal behaviors during real-life emotions, we have collected a corpus of emotionally rich TV interviews [10]. Several levels of annotation were manually coded using Anvil [23]: some information regard the whole video (called the "global level"); while some other information are related to emotional segments (the "local level"); at the lowest level, there is detailed time-based annotation of multimodal behaviors. Three expert coders defined the borders of the emotionally consistent segments of the clip and labeled each resulting segment with one or two labels. The annotation of multimodal behavior includes gesture expressivity since it was observed to be involved in the perception of emotion [24].

Besides, we have created an ECA system, Greta, that incorporates communicative conversational and emotional qualities [28]. Our model of expressivity is based on studies by researchers such as [19, 35, 36]. We describe expressivity by a set of 6 dimensions: Spatial extent, Temporal extent, Power, Fluidity, Repetition and Overall activity [22]. The Greta system takes as input a text tagged with communicative functions described with APML labels [9] as well as values for the expressivity dimensions that characterize the manner of execution of the agent's behaviors. The system parses the input text and selects which behaviors to perform. Gestures and other nonverbal behaviors (facial expressions and gaze behaviors) are synchronized with speech. The system looks for the emphasis word. It aligns the facial expressions and the stroke of a gesture with this word. Then it computes when the preparation phase of the gesture is as well as if a gesture is hold, co-articulates to the next one, if time between consecutive gestures allows it, or returns to the rest position.

We have defined two corpus-based approaches to design different Greta animations based on the video annotations [26]. The "multiple levels replay" approach involves the level of annotation of emotions, and the low-level annotations of multimodal behaviors (such as the gesture expressivity for assigning values to the expressivity parameters of the ECA, and the manual annotation of facial expressions) [25]. The "facial blending replay" approach is identical to the "multiple levels replay" approach except for facial expressions: it uses a computational model for generating facial expressions of blend of emotions [25]. More details are provided below on how these two approaches have been used in our perceptual study.

3 Experimental Protocol

3.1 Protocol Description

The goals of our experiment are to 1) test if subjects perceive a combination of emotions in the replays as in the original videos, and 2) compare the two approaches for replaying blended emotions. We have selected two different video clips of TV interviews for this study, each featuring a different type of blend.

The 1st clip (video #3, 3rd segment) features a woman reacting to a recent trial in which her father and her brother were kept in jail. As revealed by the manual annotation of this video by 3 expert coders, her behavior is perceived as a superposition of anger and despair. This is confirmed by the annotation by 40 coders with various levels of expertise [2]. This emotional behavior is perceived in speech and in several visual modalities (gaze, head movements, torso movements and gestures).

The 2nd clip (video #41) features a woman pretending to be positive after having received the negative election results of her political party, thus masking her disappointment by a smile. Such a video has been annotated as a combination of negative labels (disappointment, sadness, anger) and positive labels (pleased, serenity). The annotation of multimodal behaviors reveals that, for this segment, her lips show a smile but a tense smile that is with pressed lips.

With respect to the contextual cues provided by the audio and the visual channels that might influence the subjects' perception of emotion, both channels provide information on the location (outdoor for video #3, indoor room with other people in video #41). Video #3 features both head and hands movements. Video #41 features only the face in close-up (the hands are not visible). The politician seen in video #41 is not a major figure.

40 subjects (23 males, 17 females), age between 19 and 36 (average 24) had to compare the original videos and the different Greta animations. 33 subjects were students in computer science, 7 were researchers, teachers or engineers. The experiment included two conditions: first without audio, and then with audio. In each condition, the subjects played the original video and four different animations. Two animations were specified with data from the literature on basic emotions in facial expressions [14] and body movements [35]. The two other animations were generated with the two approaches mentioned above for replaying annotated behaviors.

Thus, for the superposition example of emotion in clip #3, four animations were designed: 1) Anger, 2) Despair, 3) multiple levels replay, and 4) facial blending replay. For the facial blending replay, the values assigned to the gesture expressivity parameters were computed from the multiple levels replay (e.g. from the manual annotation of perceived expressivity of hand gestures).

Similarly, for the masking of emotion example in clip #41, the four animations were: 1) Joy, 2) Disappointment, 3) multiple levels replay, and 4) facial blending replay.

Subjects had to assign a value between 1 (high similarity with the video) and 4 (low similarity) to each animation (Fig. 1). The order of presentation of the superposition and masking example, and the location on the graphical interface of the corresponding animations in the audio and no audio conditions were counterbalanced across subjects. Subjects could assign the same similarity value to several animations.

After each condition, subjects had to answer a questionnaire. They had to report on their confidence when assigning similarity values. They could select between 5 confidence scores: 1) I clearly perceived differences between the 4 animations and I easily compared them to the video (4-point confidence score), 2) I perceived some differences that enabled me to do my evaluation (3-point), 3) I perceived some differences but had difficulties to compare the animations with the video (2-point), 4) I perceived few differences between the animations and had a lot of difficulties to evaluate them (1-point), 5) I did not perceive any differences between the animations (0-point).

In the questionnaire, subjects also had to annotate the emotions that they perceived in the animation they ranked as the most similar to the original video. They could select one or several emotion labels from the same list of 18 emotional labels that had been used for the annotation of the videos in a previous experiment [2].

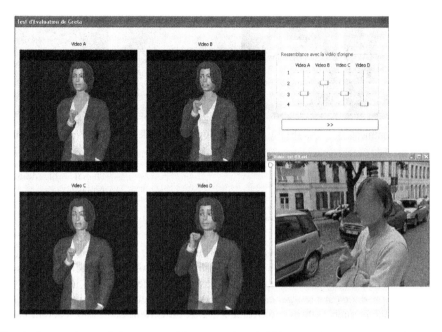

Fig. 1. Screen dump of the superposition example ; 4 different animations and 4 sliders for selecting a similarity value for each animation ; the original video #3 (non blurred during the test) is displayed separately ; the video and the animations feature the facial expressions and the hand gestures ; the masking example is similar to this display but focuses on the face in the video #41 and in the corresponding ECA animations

3.2   Using "Multiple Levels" and "Facial Blending" Replays in the Study

As we explained above, the "multiple levels replay" and the "facial blending replay" differ only by the computation of facial expressions [26]. In this section, we explain how they were used for the perception study.

Our computational model of facial expressions arising from blends of emotions is used in the "facial blending replay". It is based on a face partition approach. Any facial expression is divided into *n* areas. Each *area* represents a unique facial part like brows or lips. The model computes the complex facial expressions of emotions and distinguishes between different types of blending (e.g., superposition and masking). The complex facial expressions are created by composing the face areas of the two source expressions. Different types of blending are implemented with different sets of fuzzy rules for the computation of the complex facial expression. The fuzzy rules are based on Ekman's research on blends of emotions [17].

Figure 2 shows the agent displaying the masked expression of disappointment (computed as similar to sadness) and fake joy. The images a) and b) display the expressions of disappointment and joy, respectively. Image d) shows the masking expression computed by the "facial blending replay". We can notice that the absence of orbicularis oculi activity as indicator of unfelt joy[13] is visible on both images (c) and (d), the annotated video and the corresponding Greta simulation.

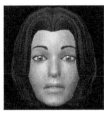   

(a) disappointment   (b) joy   (c) original video   (d)   masking   of
disappointment   by
joy computed in the
"facial   blending"
replay

Fig. 2. Disappointment masked by joy

In this example, single emotions (disapointment (a) and joy (b)) are defined in the system using Ekman's research. In the "facial blending replay", the facial expression is computed using the blending model for masking. In the "multiple levels replay", the facial expressions are not generated from system predefined information. Instead, facial parameters such as brows movements, gaze direction, or mouth tension, have been specified out of the manual annotations of the original video. A correspondance table between the manual annotations and MPEG-4 Facial Animation specifications has been defined in this purpose.

With respect to the audio channel, in order to avoid a bias due to speech synthesis quality in the evaluation of similarity between the ECA animations and the original video, we used in the animations the real speech from the original video.

4 Results

4.1 Superposition of Emotions

We computed the number of times each animation was ranked as the closest to the video. In the no audio condition, Anger is perceived as the closest animation by 61% of the subjects (multiple levels replay 20%, facial blending 9%, Despair 9%). In the audio condition, Anger is perceived as the closest animation by 33% of the subjects (multiple levels replay 26%, facial blending 24%, Despair 17%). The perception of superposed emotions in the 1st clip was also examined using an analysis of variance with Audio output (no audio, audio) and Animation (multiple levels replay, facial blending replay, anger, despair) as within-subjects factors. Gender of subjects (male, female) was included as between-subjects factor. Rankings of animations were converted into similarity scores (the first rank became a 3-point score of similarity; the fourth rank became a 0-point score). The main effect of Animation proved to be significant ($F(1/114)=15.86$; $p<0.001$, see Fig. 3). The similarity score for the Anger animation is significantly higher than the multiple levels replay ($t(39)=3.05$; $p=0.004$); the multiple levels and facial blending replays are not significantly different from one another ($t(39)=1.65$; NS); and the similarity score of the Despair animation tends to be lower than the facial blending replay (t(39)=1.83; p=0.076). The Audio * Animation interaction appeared significant (F(1/114)=5.98; p=0.001, see Fig. 4): this interaction shows that the Animation effect is highly significant in the no-audio condition (F(3/114)=24.11; p<0.001) whereas it is only marginal in the audio condition (F(2/114)=2.42; p=0.087).

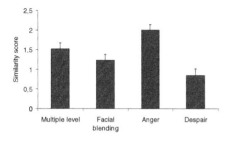 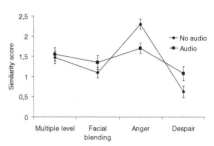

Fig. 3. Similarity scores of the 4 animations with the superposition example

Fig. 4. Similarity scores of the 4 animations as a function of the condition

The Gender * Animation interaction is also significant (F(3/114)=3.61; p=0.016, see Fig. 5). Female subjects gave significantly lower similarity scores to the facial blending replay than male subjects (t(38)=2.70; p=0.010). The similarity scores of the 3 other animations are not significantly different between male and female subjects.

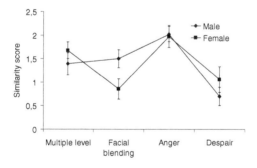

Fig. 5. Similarity scores of the 4 animations as a function of subjects' gender

The overall confidence score reported by subjects in the questionnaire as associated to the ranking of the animations amounts to 2.8/4. There is no main effect of Audio on this variable (F(1/38)=0.45; NS) but the main effect of Gender tends to be significant (F(1/38)=3.82; p=0.058). Female subjects had higher confidence scores (3.1/4) than male subjects (2.6/4).

In the questionnaire, the subjects also had to characterize the animation that they had ranked as the closest to the original video, each subject being allowed to choose more than one label. In the no-audio condition, 82.5% of subjects perceived anger, whereas only 12.5% perceived despair. In the audio condition, the main emotion perceived by subjects was sadness (85% of subjects). Anger was perceived by 67.5% of subjects and despair by 42.5% of subjects. For the no audio condition, only 6 subjects (15%) selected a single label (4 of them for the Anger animation). For the audio condition, only 3 subjects (7,5%) did select a single label (each time the "Despair" label for the animation was selected). Table 1 summarizes the perception of superposed vs. single emotions using macro-classes categories (Anger, Sadness). These results show that, even though the animation perceived as the closest to the original video was the "Anger" animation, subjects nevertheless perceived it as a combination of several emotions.

Table 1. Percentages of subjects who perceived each macro-class of emotion in the animation that they had ranked as the closest to the original video of superposed emotions

	Anger + Sadness	Anger but not Sadness	Sadness but not Anger	Neither Anger nor Sadness	Total
No audio	52,5 %	40 %	0 %	7,5 %	100 %
Audio	85 %	0 %	12,5 %	2,5 %	100 %

4.2 Masking of Emotions

Regarding the masking emotion example, in the no audio condition, Joy was perceived as the closest animation by 40% of the subjects (facial blending 33%, multiple levels replay 20%, Disappointment 7%). In the audio condition, facial blending was perceived as the closest animation by 38% of the subjects (multiple levels replay 27%, Joy 24%, Disappointment 11%).

The perception of masked emotion was also studied by means of an analysis of variance with Audio output (no audio, audio), Animation (multiple levels replay, facial blending replay, Joy, Disappointment) as within-subjects factors and Gender (male, female) as between-subjects factor. The main effect of Animation was the only one that proved significant ($F(1/114)=18.07$; $p<0.001$, see Fig. 6). The similarity score of the facial blending replay is significantly higher than the multiple levels replay ($t(39)=2.05$; $p=0.047$) but not significantly different from Joy ($t(39)=1.36$; NS). The difference between Joy and the multiple levels replay is not significant either ($t(39)=0.83$; NS). However, the similarity score of the Disappointment animation is significantly lower than the multiple levels replay ($t(39)=4.77$; $p<0.001$).

The overall confidence score of subjects for the ranking of these animations is 2.5/4. The analysis showed no main effect of Audio ($F(1/38)=0.21$; NS) nor Gender ($F(1/38)=0.12$; NS) on this variable. In the no audio condition, 35% of subjects rated Disappointment with the label Embarrassment. Joy and Pleased were perceived by 15% and 32.5% of subjects respectively. Disappointment was mentioned by only 5% of subjects. In the audio condition, Worry and Sadness were the most perceived emotions (47.5% and 35% respectively). Joy and Pleased represented only 5% and 7.5%. Positive emotions (e.g. Pleased, Serenity, Joy) represented 32% of labels in the no

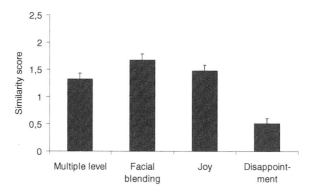

Fig. 6. Similarity scores of the four animations with the original video in the masking example

audio condition and 13% in the audio condition. Negative emotions (e.g. Embarrassment, Doubt, Sadness) represented 43% of labels in the no audio condition and 81% in the audio condition. Only 4 subjects selected a single label in the no audio condition and only 3 subjects in the audio condition. Moreover, some subjects (11 in the no audio condition, 9 in the audio condition) used both positive and negative labels to describe the animations. Table 2 summarizes this perception of mixed vs. single emotions using macro-classes categories.

Table 2. Percentages of subjects who perceived each macro-class of emotion in the animation that they had ranked as the closest to the original video of masked emotions

	Joy + Sadness	Joy but not Sadness	Sadness but not Joy	Neither Joy nor Sadness	Total
No audio	7,5 %	10 %	57,5 %	25 %	100 %
Audio	12,5 %	40 %	30 %	17,5 %	100 %

4.3 Effects of the Complex Emotion Models

We conducted an analysis of variance on the 2 examples of blend of emotions (superposition and masking), the 2 conditions (no audio, audio), our 2 approaches of generation (multiple levels replay and facial blending replay), and subjects' gender. The results show no main effect of approach ($F(1/38)=0.01$; NS), i.e. no overall significant difference between the multiple levels replay and the facial blending replay.

5 Discussion

The 1st goal of this study was to test whether subjects perceive a combination of emotions in our ECA animations. Our results show that subjects tend to perceive one emotion as being predominant: in the superposition example, subjects ordered what we have called "basic Anger" first; in the disappointment masked by joy, basic Joy and facial blending replay were rated similarly. However, this result is partially contradicted when analyzing the result from the labeling task where most subjects associated several emotion labels to the animation they considered as being the most similar to the video. The macro-classes of emotion that they selected are consistent with previous annotations of the videos with 3 expert coders (and 40 coders for the superposition example [2]). In the animations of single emotions that we designed for the superposition example, subjects perceived a secondary emotion, possibly through non-verbal or verbal cues brought by our method of copying the original video. This reveals that these animations, designed to display single emotions, feature instead a relative complexity of emotions.

Besides, our experimental protocol enabled to compare two conditions, audio and no audio. The 4 animations corresponding to the superposition example were better discriminated in the no audio condition; the addition of verbal cues had the effect to lower down the differences between the animations. Moreover, users chose a larger set of emotions to label the animations in the audio condition. In the superposition animations, subjects better perceived the sadness / despair dimension in the audio condition. We may thus infer that, in this particular sequence, anger was primarily displayed by nonverbal behaviors whereas despair was mostly expressed by the verbal stream.

In the disappointment-masked-by-joy example, subjects perceived negative emotions better in the audio condition. This suggests that the person in this video sequence controlled her nonverbal behavior (positive emotions perceived in the mute condition) better than her verbal behaviors (negative cues perceived in the audio condition). This strong effect of verbal behavior may be due to the fact that we used the original voice and not a synthesized voice. This perception of valence of emotion is reported in Table 3. It is compatible with previous studies on the whole corpus in which 2 coders annotated the videos in 3 conditions (Audio only, Video only, Audio and video) [1]. We had observed a high level of quantitative agreement over the whole corpus for the 3 conditions for "Anger". The coders agreed on the "Pain" label for the "Audio only" and "Audio and video" conditions but not for the "Video only" condition, which could be explained by the fact that acoustic cues show well this emotion.

Table 3. Valence of labels assigned to the animations perceived as being closest to the videos

	Positive only	Negative only	Pos. / Neg. conflict	Neutral
Superposition no audio	2,5%	95%	2,5%	0%
Superposition with audio	0%	100%	0%	0%
Masking no audio	32,5%	30%	35%	2,5%
Masking with audio	7,5%	52,5%	37,5%	2,5%

The second goal of this study was to evaluate our two approaches for replaying blends of emotions (multiple levels replay and facial blending replay). Our global analysis (Section 4.3) showed that none of the two approaches was consistently preferred. We may first mention that the two replay approaches share some common features which may partly explain why it was not so easy to discriminate between

them: they were elaborated on the basis of the same annotations and they both included some behaviors automatically generated by the Greta system. However, we
can notice that the facial blending replay was significantly better ranked than the
multiple levels replay in the masking example. Conversely in the superposition example, the two types of replay did not differ significantly except for female subjects who
gave higher similarity scores to the multiple levels replay.

These results suggest that the facial blending replay was more appropriate in the
masking example and the multiple levels replay in the superposition example. These
results alone are not sufficient to understand this interaction. It could be due to the
nature of complex emotions (superposition, masking), or to the particular emotions
tested here (anger / despair, disappointment / joy), or to the modalities available (with
or without hand gesture). For example, the size of the face is not the same in our superposition and in the masking examples.

Finally, in the superposition example, male and female subjects judged differently
the animation generated by facial blending replay. Further data would be necessary to
interpret this effect: for example we could ask subjects to annotate precisely these
animations (not only label them, but also annotate the animation of different parts of
the face), and examine whether there are gender differences when performing this
task. Male and female subjects also gave different confidence scores to their ranking
in the superposition example: female subjects were more confident in their answers.
Such a result is consistent with classical view that female subjects have better abilities
to decode nonverbal cues [18, 21].

6 Conclusions and Future Work

We compared the perception of emotional behaviors annotated in a corpus of TV
interviews replayed by an expressive agent at different levels of abstraction.
One drawback of our corpus approach based on spontaneous behaviors collected
during TV interviews is that it is quite difficult to collect enough data to train statistical models. That is the reason why we use instead an exploratory approach with
selected illustrative cases of different complex emotions (e.g. superposition and masking) for validating our representations.

Thus, future work is needed to validate our copy-synthesis approach (annotation of
emotion and expressivity, computation of signs of blended emotions, animation by an
ECA). Anyhow, the results we reported show that both replay approaches might be of
interest for different types of blend of emotions. We also intend to improve the design
of our "basic" emotion animations and the method of comparing them with our replay
approaches. We will involve complementary videos with respect to the combination
of types of blending and modalities. We plan to adapt our copy-synthesis approach so
that two different individual emotions that are combined can be assigned different
weights. The computational model of the agent expressivity also needs to be improved to better simulate expressive arm movements as well as to better match behaviors observed in such videos (e.g. movement of the torso, separate specifications of
expressivity for different body parts). We will use information that we have collected
on subjects' personality using the EPI (Eysenck Personality Inventory) questionnaire
since introversion / extraversion has been observed to have an impact on the perception of multimodal behaviors displayed by ECAs [6]. Further testing of the influence

of visual and audio channels should also be investigated (e.g. use of synthetic speech, or filtered audio rendering the speech content unintelligible with minimal effect on prosody and voice quality [32]).

We believe that such experimental studies will enable to identify the parts of expressions that are most critical to the perception and display of real-life multimodal emotions.

Acknowledgements

This work was partly funded by the FP6 IST HUMAINE Network of Excellence (http://emotion-research.net). We are very grateful to Maurizio Mancini for his help.

References

1. Abrilian, S., Devillers, L., Buisine, S., Martin, J.-C.: EmoTV1: Annotation of Real-life Emotions for the Specification of Multimodal Affective Interfaces. 11th Int. Conf. Human-Computer Interaction (HCII'2005) (2005) Las Vegas, Nevada, USA
2. Abrilian, S., Devillers, L., Martin, J.-C.: Annotation of Emotions in Real-Life Video Interviews: Variability between Coders. 5th Int. Conf. Language Resources and Evaluation (LREC'2006) (2006) Genoa, Italy
3. Albrecht, I., Schröder, M., Haber, J., Seidel, H.-P.: Mixed feelings: Expression of non-basic emotions in a muscle-based talking head. Special issue of Journal of Virtual Reality on "Language, Speech & Gesture" 8 4 (2005)
4. Bassili, J. N.: Emotion recognition: the role of facial movement and the relative importance of upper and lower areas of the face. Jour. Pers. Soc. Psychol. 37 11 (1979)
5. Becker, C., Prendinger, H., Ishizuka, M., Wachsmuth, I.: Evaluating Affective Feedback of the 3D Agent Max in a Competitive Cards Game. 1st International Conference on Affective Computing & Intelligent Interaction (ACII'2005) (2005) Beijing, China 466-473
6. Buisine, S. Conception et Évaluation d'Agents Conversationnels Multimodaux Bidirectionnels. PhD Thesis. Doctorat de Psychologie Cognitive - Ergonomie, Paris V. 8 avril 2005. Direction J.-C. Martin & J.-C. Sperandio. 2005. http://stephanie.buisine.free.fr/
7. Cacioppo, J. T., Petty, R. P., Losch, M. E., Kim, H. S.: Electromyographic activity over facial muscle regions can differentiate the valence and intensity of affective reactions. Journal of Personality and Social Psychology 50 (1986)
8. Constantini, E., Pianesi, F., Prete, M.: Recognizing Emotions in Human and Synthetic Faces: The Role of the Upper and Lower Parts of the Face. Intelligent User Interfaces (IUI'05) (2005) San Diego, CA, USA 20-27
9. De Carolis, B., Pelachaud, C., Poggi, I., Steedman, M.: APML, a Markup Language for Believable Behavior Generation. Life-like characters. Tools, affective functions and applications. Springer (2004)
10. Devillers, L., Abrilian, S., Martin, J.-C.: Representing real life emotions in audiovisual data with non basic emotional patterns and context features. 1st Int. Conf. Affective Computing and Intelligent Interaction (ACII'2005) (2005) Beijing, China 519-526
11. Douglas-Cowie, E., Devillers, L., Martin, J.-C., Cowie, R., Savvidou, S., Abrilian, S., Cox, C.: Multimodal Databases of Everyday Emotion: Facing up to Complexity. 9th European Conf. Speech Communication and Technology (Interspeech'2005) (2005) Lisbon, Portugal 813-816

12. Duy Bui, T. Creating Emotions And Facial Expressions For Embodied Agents. PhD Thesis. University of Twente. 2004.
13. Ekman, P.: Darwin, Deception, and Facial Expression. Annals of the New York Academy of Sciences 1000 (2003)
14. Ekman, P.: Emotion in the human face. Cambridge University Press (1982)
15. Ekman, P.: The Face Revealed. Weidenfeld & Nicolson London (2003)
16. Ekman, P., Friesen, W.: Felt, false, miserable smiles. Journal of Nonverbal Behavior 6 4 (1982)
17. Ekman, P., Friesen, W. V.: Unmasking the face. A guide to recognizing emotions from facial clues. Prentice-Hall Inc., Englewood Cliffs, N.J. (1975)
18. Feldman, R. S., Philippot, P., Custrini, R. J.: Social competence and nonverbal behavior. Fundamentals of Nonverbal Behavior. Cambridge University Press (1991)
19. Gallaher, P.: Individual differences in nonverbal behavior: Dimensions of style. Journal of Personality and Social Psychology 63 (1992)
20. Gouta, K., Miyamoto, M.: Emotion recognition, facial components associated with various emotions. Shinrigaku Kenkyu 71 3 (2000)
21. Hall, J. A., Matsumoto, D.: Gender differences in judgments of multiple emotions from facial expressions. Emotion 4 2 (2004)
22. Hartmann, B., Mancini, M., Pelachaud, C.: Implementing Expressive Gesture Synthesis for Embodied Conversational Agents. Gesture Workshop (GW'2005) (2005) Vannes, France
23. Kipp, M.: Gesture Generation by Imitation. From Human Behavior to Computer Character Animation. Boca Raton, Dissertation.com Florida (2004)
24. Martin, J.-C., Abrilian, S., Devillers, L.: Annotating Multimodal Behaviors Occurring during Non Basic Emotions. 1st Int. Conf. Affective Computing and Intelligent Interaction (ACII'2005) (2005) Beijing, China 550-557
25. Martin, J.-C., Abrilian, S., Devillers, L., Lamolle, M., Mancini, M., Pelachaud, C.: Levels of Representation in the Annotation of Emotion for the Specification of Expressivity in ECAs. 5th International Working Conference On Intelligent Virtual Agents (IVA'2005) (2005) Kos, Greece 405-417
26. Martin, J.-C., Niewiadomski, R., Devillers, L., Buisine, S., Pelachaud, C.: Multimodal Complex Emotions: Gesture Expressivity And Blended Facial Expressions. Special issue of the Journal of Humanoid Robotics. Eds: C. Pelachaud, L. Canamero. (to appear)
27. Pandzic, I. S., Forchheimer, R.: MPEG-4 Facial Animation. The Standard, Implementation and Applications. John Wiley & Sons, LTD (2002)
28. Pelachaud, C.: Multimodal expressive embodied conversational agent. ACM Multimedia, Brave New Topics session (2005) Singapore 683 - 689
29. Rehm, M., André, E.: Catch Me If You Can - Exploring Lying Agents in Social Settings. Int. Conf. Autonomous Agents and Multiagent Systems (AAMAS'2005) (2005) 937-944
30. Richmond, V. P., Croskey, J. C.: Non Verbal Behavior in Interpersonal relations. Allyn & Bacon Inc. (1999)
31. Ruttkay, Z., Noot, H., ten Hagen, P.: Emotion Disc and Emotion Squares: tools to explore the facial expression face. Computer Graphics Forum 22 1 (2003)
32. Savvidou, S., Cowie, R., Douglas-Cowie, E.: Contributions of Visual and Auditory Channels to Detection of Emotion. British Psychological Society Annual Conference (NI Branch) (2001) Cavan, Republic of Ireland
33. Scherer, K. R.: Analyzing Emotion Blends. Proceedings of the Xth Conference of the International Society for Research on Emotions (1998) Würzburg, Germany 142-148

34. ten Ham, R., Theune, M., Heuvelman, A., Verleur, R.: Judging Laura: Perceived Qualities of a Mediated Human Versus an Embodied Agent. 5th International Working Conference On Intelligent Virtual Agents (IVA'2005) (2005) Kos, Greece 381-393
35. Wallbott, H. G.: Bodily expression of emotion. European Journal of Social Psychology 28 (1998)
36. Wallbott, H. G., Scherer, K. R.: Cues and Channels in Emotion Recognition. Journal of Personality and Social Psychology 51 4 (1986)
37. Wiggers, M.: Jugments of facial expressions of emotion predicted from facial behavior. Journal of Nonverbal Behavior 7 2 (1982)

Perceiving Visual Emotions with Speech

Zhigang Deng[1], Jeremy Bailenson[2], J.P. Lewis[3], and Ulrich Neumann[4]

[1] Department of Computer Science, University of Houston, Houston, TX
deng@zhigang.org
[2] Department of Communication, Stanford University, CA
[3] Computer Graphics Lab, Stanford University, CA
[4] Department of Computer Science, University of Southern California,
Los Angeles, CA

Abstract. Embodied Conversational Agents (ECAs) with realistic faces are becoming an intrinsic part of many graphics systems employed in HCI applications. A fundamental issue is how people visually perceive the affect of a speaking agent. In this paper we present the first study evaluating the relation between objective and subjective visual perception of emotion as displayed on a speaking human face, using both full video and sparse point-rendered representations of the face. We found that objective machine learning analysis of facial marker motion data is correlated with evaluations made by experimental subjects, and in particular, the lower face region provides insightful emotion clues for visual emotion perception. We also found that affect is captured in the abstract point-rendered representation.

1 Introduction

Embodied Conversational Agents (ECAs) [2, 9, 20, 21, 28, 29, 36, 39] are important to graphics and HCI communities. ECAs with emotional behavior models have been proposed as a natural interface between humans and machine systems. The realism of facial displays of ECAs is one of the more difficult hurdles to overcome, both for designers and researchers who evaluate the effectiveness of the ECAs.

However, despite this growing area of research, there currently is not a systematic methodology to validate and understand how we humans visually perceive the affect of a conversational agent. As ECAs become more and more prevalent in HCI systems, understanding the usability of them as well as the significance of different face representations is clearly a priority. In this work, we aim to answer the following questions:

- Are the results from objective analysis of facial marker motion and subjective evaluation of recorded face video clips consistent?
- Does abstract point-rendered facial animation provide cues for visual emotion perception? And is it a useful representation for ECAs?
- Which emotion pairs are easily confused when people perceive emotions from visual talking faces?

J. Gratch et al. (Eds.): IVA 2006, LNAI 4133, pp. 107–120, 2006.
© Springer-Verlag Berlin Heidelberg 2006

To answer the above questions, we investigated the problem of 'visual perception of emotion in speech' using a multifaceted and comparative approach. An actress with markers on her face was directed to recite specified sentences with four basic emotions (neutral, happiness, anger, and sadness). A facial motion capture system captured the 3D motions of the facial markers, while a video camera simultaneously also recorded her face. We analyzed these captured objective motion data using Quadratic Discriminant Analysis (QDA) [22], and conducted subjective evaluation experiments on both the recorded face video clip and a unique rendering of just the facial markers themselves (termed the point-rendered representation in this work). We conducted the above analysis and experiments on different face regions (whole face, the upper face, the lower face). Finally, we did a comparative analysis on the objective/subjective results and considered the implications of our findings.

To our knowledge, this work is the first to investigate the consistency among objective facial marker motion, subjective evaluations of real talking face videos, and abstract point-rendered faces. By combining the objective captured motion analysis and two types of subjective evaluations, we obtain a comprehensive and multifaceted view on the problem of visual emotion perception with speech. Furthermore, we believe that using an abstract rendering of the emotions (i.e., the markers without the face) should provide insight into the ways in which people learn emotions from faces rendered from a finite set of control points. The goal of the current paper is not to learn new theoretical aspects of how people emote, but alternatively to begin to provide a methodological framework for interpreting emotions—whether those emotions are generated by physical faces, digital avatars from real-time tracked humans, or from embodied agents that use algorithms to create emotions.

The remainder of this paper is organized as follows: Section 2 reviews previous work connected emotion perception from human faces. Section 3 describes data capture and the experiment design. Section 4 describes of the analyses of the objective motion capture data. Section 5 describes the subjective evaluation that includes two subjective studies—one in which people attempted to judge emotions from the video of the actress, and one in which they attempted to perceive emotions from a rendering of just the markers themselves without the face. Section 6 gives an in-depth analysis of both the subjective and objective results and their correlations. Finally, Section 7 concludes this work and discusses implications of the results.

2 Background and Related Work

In the computer graphics and computer vision communities, extensive computer facial animation research has been done since Parke's seminal work [33]. Examples of these advances can be seen in work generating realistic speech animation [27, 34, 11, 6, 5, 16, 19, 24] and expressive facial animation [14, 15, 35, 8, 2, 31, 10, 4, 17, 26]. For example, the Facial Action Coding Systems (FACS) proposed by Ekman and Friesen

[17] is a widely used system to represent various human expressions by combining basic facial action units. Essa and Pentland [18] extended FACS to encode the temporal and spatial information by modeling the dynamics of facial expressions, for the purpose of analysis and recognition of facial expressions. The work of [37,38] demonstrated the success of using eigen-faces for the characterization of human faces and face recognition.

In the HCI community, researchers have conducted quite a few experiments to evaluate the effects of using ECAs as a human/machine interface. Walker et al. [25] investigated the benefits of synthetic talking faces in the context of a questionnaire study and found that talking faces made subjects spent more time, made fewer mistakes and gave more comments. Nass et al. [30] compared performance differences when people interacted with their own face or alternatively someone else's face, and found that subjects showed more positive responses when seeing their own faces. Panzdic et al. [32] evaluated and compared the performance of different synthetic talking faces for interactive services. The work of [1, 23] assesses the emotional recognizability of synthetic faces based on the FACS [17], in terms of subjective recognition rates.

Fig. 1. The left panel illustrates the marker layout used in the objective data analysis. Markers above the solid curve represent markers in the upper face region, and markers above the solid curve are for the lower face region. The middle panel is a snapshot of the record video. The right panel illustrates the used motion capture system.

Instead of only using recorded expression sequences without utterances [1, 23], Costantini et al. [12] comparatively evaluated two MPEG-4 synthetic faces (motion capture based and script-based) that spoke with emotions. Two synthetic FAP-based talking faces were evaluated under both conditions, including cross-face comparisons, and comparisons with a human actor. The results indicated that motion-capture based synthetic faces generated more natural results than script based faces. Bassili [3] investigated the role of different facial regions for emotion perception tasks only with subjective experiments. He found that the importance of a region of the face differed depending on the emotion. Costantini et al. [13] not only looked at emotion recognition rates, but also analyzed recognition errors.

3 Data Capture and Experiment Design

A motion capture system was used to capture accurate 3D facial marker motions of a single actress with markers on her face (Figure 1). She was directed to recite three specified sentences four times, and each time a different emotion (from a total of four: neutral, anger, sadness, and happiness) was expressed naturally, without exaggeration. The three sentences are: *"You're truly impossible!"*, *"How do you think you're going to catch up now?"*, and *"So the sock struck your head and injured your pride?"* The motion capture system tracked and recovered 3D motion of every marker at a 120Hz sampling frequency. At the same time, an off-the-shelf video camera recorded her face. We collected data from a single actress (as opposed to getting a larger sample of faces) because our interest was in comparing methodologies of emotion validation, as opposed to discovering universal emotional patterns across people.

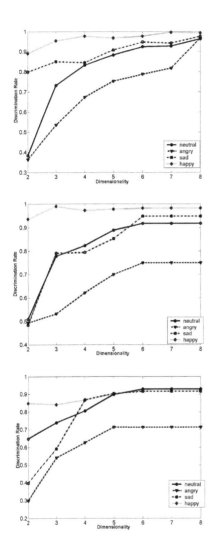

We analyzed the data in both objective and subjective ways. Objectively, we examined results from a discriminant analysis of the recorded expressive facial motion data and distributions of that data in a high dimensional motion space. We performed subjective evaluations by running experiments in which subjects identified and rated various types of stimuli based on the recorded video footage and recorded 3D marker motion without the video behind it. Audio was removed from both stimuli, and the various emotions were played in a random order for experimental subjects.

Fig. 2. The plotting of correct discrimination rate VS reduced dimensionality. The top is for WHOLE-FACE, the middle is for UPPER-FACE, and the bottom is for LOWER-FACE.

4 Objective Motion Discrimination

After the facial motion data were captured, we preprocessed the motion data by aligning motion frames with a chosen reference frame. The alignment included translation (anchoring a nose marker to be the center of each frame) and head motion removal using a statistical shape-analysis method [7]. Hence, all motion frames were located in a uniform coordinate system.

The aligned expressive facial motion data were processed to generate three groups: whole face motion data (WHOLE-FACE), upper face motion data (UPPER-FACE), and lower face motion data (LOWER-FACE). Each of the above three groups has 12 motion capture sequences: 3 sentences*4 expressions = 12. Each frame of UPPER-FACE is composed of only the motions of the markers in the upper face region (the red markers in the left panel in Figure 1), and each frame of LOWER-FACE is for the motions of the markers in the lower face region (the blue markers in the left panel in Figure 1). For each group, Principal Component Analysis (PCA) was applied to reduce original high dimensional motion vectors (concatenating 3D motions of markers in one frame into one vector) into low dimensional vectors.

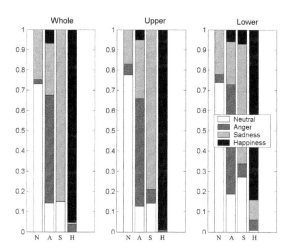

Fig. 3. Plot of emotion confusion matrices of objective data analysis. Here N denotes "Neutral", A denotes "Anger", S denotes "Sadness", and H denotes "Happiness". The left is for the whole face, the middle for the upper face region, and the right for the lower face region.

To observe how these four expressive motions were further discriminated while the reduced dimensionality was varied, a Quadratic Discrimination Analysis (QDA) method [22] was used to discriminate expressive motion. As illustrated in Figure 2, there is a big jump in discrimination rate when the dimensionality is increased from two to three. In all three cases (*WHOLE-FACE, UPPER-FACE* and *LOWER-FACE*), happiness was the easiest emotion to classify and anger was the most difficult one.

Fig. 4. Three versions are used in the subjective evaluation

Based on the above QDA results, we calculated emotion confusion matrices that represent how expressive motions were confused with each other. Figure 3 and Table 1 show the confusion matrices (the reduced dimensionality is 3). In all three cases (the whole face, the upper face and the lower face) anger was easily misidentified as sadness, and sadness and neutral were easily confused with each other. Bold numbers in Table 1 highlight these easily confused visual emotion pairs.

Table 1. Emotion confusion matrices of QDA objective data analysis. Bold numbers highlight these easily confused visual emotion pairs.

	Whole Face				Upper Face				Lower Face			
	N	A	S	H	N	A	S	H	N	A	S	H
N	0.732	0.020	**0.248**	0	0.777	0.053	**0.170**	0	0.739	0.041	**0.220**	0
A	0.142	0.535	**0.256**	0.067	0.128	0.532	**0.290**	0.050	0.188	0.541	**0.211**	0.060
S	**0.149**	0.001	0.850	0	**0.142**	0.068	0.790	0	**0.272**	0.065	0.592	0.071
H	0	0.038	0.008	0.954	0	0.011	0	0.989	0.008	0.053	0.098	0.841

Fig. 5. Illustrations of three versions of rendered point motion snapshots (whole face points, upper face points, and lower face points)

5   Subjective Experiment Evaluations

In this section, we used two types of video clips: video clips (*video faces*) directly recorded during the capture session, and 3D point motion clips (*point-rendered faces*) made by simply rendering captured markers' 3D motion. For the ordinary video clips, we first removed audio. Then, for each video clip, we made three versions: a video clip only showing the upper face region (*UPPER-VIDEO*), a video clip only showing the lower face region (*LOWER-VIDEO*), and one showing the full face (*WHOLE-*

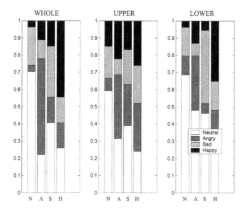

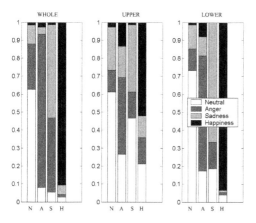

Fig. 6. The illustration of the confusion matrices of face regions for different emotions in the POINT REGION EXPERIMENT (top) and the VIDEO REGION EXPERIMENT (bottom)

VIDEO). The partitioning scheme of a face is illustrated in Figure 4. These black masks were superimposed by video editing tools. The subjective evaluation of these video clips is referred to as the *video region experiment*. For the clips based on only the markers, we directly plotted marker motion using Matlab to generate point-motion clips (Figure 5). As in other conditions, there was no audio. Then we made three versions of point-motion video by only showing motion of specified markers: a motion clip only showing the upper face markers (*UPPER-POINT*), a motion clip only showing the lower face markers (*LOWER-POINT*), and the one showing the full face markers (*WHOLE-POINT*). The subjective evaluation of point motion clips is referred to as the *point region experiment*.

A subjective evaluation experiment was set up in a university classroom. A projector was used to project the video onto a large screen. The experiment was composed of several sub-experiments: video region experiment (including UPPER-VIDEO, LOWER-VIDEO, and WHOLE-VIDEO), and point

Table 2. Emotion confusion matrices of the *video region experiment*

	Whole Face				Upper Face				Lower Face			
	N	A	S	H	N	A	S	H	N	A	S	H
N	**0.627**	0.253	0.107	0.013	**0.613**	0.120	0.240	0.027	**0.733**	0.121	0.133	0.013
A	0.080	**0.853**	0.040	0.027	0.267	**0.427**	0.173	0.133	0.173	**0.640**	0.107	0.080
S	0.053	0.413	**0.521**	0.013	0.467	0.147	**0.373**	0.013	0.186	0.147	**0.667**	0
H	0.027	0.013	0.053	**0.907**	0.213	0.147	0.120	**0.520**	0.041	0.013	0.013	**0.933**

Table 3. Emotion confusion matrices of the POINT REGION EXPERIMENT

	Whole Face				Upper Face				Lower Face			
	N	A	S	H	N	A	S	H	N	A	S	H
N	**0.704**	0.037	0.222	0.037	**0.593**	0.074	0.185	0.148	**0.685**	0.111	0.167	0.037
A	0.222	**0.556**	0.111	0.111	0.315	**0.370**	0.093	0.222	0.481	**0.315**	0.074	0.130
S	0.407	0.148	**0.296**	0.149	0.389	0.241	**0.204**	0.166	0.463	0.056	**0.425**	0.056
H	0.259	0.148	0.148	**0.445**	0.241	0.279	0.222	**0.259**	0.296	0.185	0.167	**0.352**

region experiment (including UPPER-POINT, LOWER-POINT, and WHOLE-POINT). Within each sub-experiment, corresponding clips were randomly played to a total of 25 subjects. The same group of subjects participated in all of the above experiments. The 25 subjects were undergraduate student volunteers who were majoring in various disciplines such as engineering and psychology, and fourteen were female. In each experimental session, a group of participants saw each emotion clip once, and attempted to determine its perceived emotion from four possible options (neutral, anger, sadness and happiness). At the same time, he/she filled in a confidence level for this choice on a scale from 1 to 5 (1 meant "random guess" and 5 meant "very sure"). They could choose the same response option as often as they wanted.

We plotted emotion recognition rate versus facial regions to see what the associations were between visual emotion perceptions and upper or lower facial regions when the audio was removed. Figure 6 and Table 2-3 illustrate the confusion matrices for the point region experiment and for the video region experiment. As we can see from Fig. 6, for neutral, sadness and anger, the point region and video region results were consistent in some places. Since the point motion clips did not provide as much information as the videos, the perception rate on point motion clips was lower than that of corresponding video clips (bold

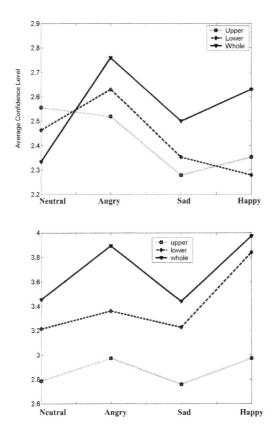

Fig. 7. The plotting of average confidence level vs emotion types in the POINT REGION EXPERIMENT (top) and the VIDEO REGION EXPERIMENT (bottom). As we can see from the figure, their patterns are similar.

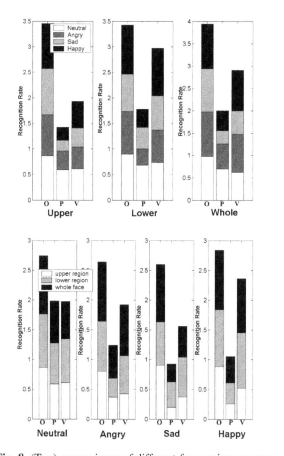

numbers in Table 2-3). However, emotion recognition and confusion patterns (Figure 6) were similar across the two different experiments, indicating that subjects were in fact inferring meaningful emotional cues from the limited information provided by the point clouds.

Both the point region experiment and video region experiment (Figure 6) again confirmed that sadness and neutral were easily confused. It is interesting to notice that happiness was the most easily recognized emotion in the video clips, but was more difficult to recognize from the point motion clips.

Figure 7 illustrates the average confidence level in the video region experiment (right) and the average confidence level in the point region experiment (left). For all emotions, in both the video and point region experiments, generally the average confidence level of the whole face was higher than that

Fig. 8. (Top) comparisons of different face regions on emotional perception. (Bottom) emotion perception rate depended on emotion type. Here O = QDA mocap data objective analysis, P = point region experiment, and V = video region experiment.

of the lower face region, and the average confidence level for the lower face region was higher than the upper face region. As we can see from Figure 7, the point region experiment results share generally similar patterns to the video region experiment.

6   Comparative Analysis

Figure 8 compares the importance of different facial regions in terms of three experimental conditions (motion capture data objective analysis, point region experiment, and video region experiment). As we can see from Figure 8, generally, the mocap objective analysis approach recognizes emotions best, except for the neutral expression. Most likely, subjects put "neutral" as their default choice when unsure, and this caused the high recognition rate for neutral in the point and video region experiments.

The right panel of Figure 8 illustrates that recognition rates depend on the emotion, with happiness and anger being more recognizable than sadness, while the neutral emotion achieves the highest perception accuracy.

Table 4. Difference matrices obtained by subtracting emotion confusion matrices of the *video region experiment* from that of *QDA objective motion analysis*. Significant differences are highlighted with bold.

	Whole Face				Upper Face				Lower Face			
	N	A	S	H	N	A	S	H	N	A	S	H
N	0.105	**-0.23**	**0.141**	-0.01	0.164	-0.07	-0.07	-0.03	0.006	-0.08	0.087	-0.01
A	0.062	**-0.32**	**0.216**	0.040	-0.14	0.105	0.117	-0.08	0.015	0.099	0.104	-0.02
S	0.096	**-0.41**	**0.329**	-0.01	**-0.33**	-0.08	**0.417**	-0.01	0.086	-0.08	-0.08	0.071
H	-0.03	0.025	-0.05	0.047	**-0.21**	-0.14	-0.12	**0.469**	-0.03	0.040	0.085	-0.09

Table 5. Difference matrices obtained by subtracting emotion confusion matrices of the *point region experiment* from that of *video region experiment*. Significant differences are highlighted with bold.

	Whole Face				Upper Face				Lower Face			
	N	A	S	H	N	A	S	H	N	A	S	H
N	-0.08	**0.216**	-0.12	-0.02	0.02	0.046	0.05	-0.12	0.048	0.01	-0.03	-0.02
A	-0.14	**0.297**	-0.07	-0.08	-0.05	0.057	0.08	-0.08	**-0.30**	**0.325**	0.033	-0.05
S	**-0.35**	**0.265**	**0.225**	-0.14	0.078	-0.09	**0.169**	-0.15	**-0.27**	0.091	**0.242**	-0.05
H	**-0.23**	-0.14	-0.09	**0.462**	-0.03	-0.13	-0.10	**0.261**	**-0.25**	-0.17	-0.15	**0.581**

We further investigate the differences between the previous confusion matrices (Table 1-3) generated by three different evaluation approaches. Table 4 shows difference matrices by subtracting the emotion confusion matrices of the video region experiment from that of QDA objective motion analysis. Several significant differences in its whole face section are due to the visual confusions between sad and angry emotions. In the upper face section, QDA objective motion analysis did a much better job than the video region experiment in discriminating sadness and happiness from the upper face motion. Given that there are relatively small amounts of motion in the upper face when humans are making sad or happy speech, experimental subjects often visually misjudged it as neutral. In the lower face section, we were surprised to see a high consistency between QDA objective data analysis and the video region experiment. It suggests that experimental subjects indeed received insightful emotion clues from the lower face region, as such, their emotion confusion matrices were well matched.

Table 5 shows the difference matrices between the point region experiment and video region experiment. Since the abstract point-rendered faces provided less spatial information and less face details than the video faces, we expected the point region experiment to result in a lower recognition rate than the video region experiment. Highlighted differences in the whole face section of Table 5 confirmed our assumption. The upper face section of Table 5, consistent with that of Table 4, shows that subjects had more problems correctly differentiating sadness and happiness from the upper face region alone. Also, except for errors mistaking emotions for neutral, the lower face section of Table 5 shows that emotion confusion matrices of the lower face region of the point-rendering faces had a similar confusion pattern to video faces. It again confirms that the lower face region (abstract point-rendering representation or real video faces) does provide insightful emotion clues for visual emotion perception (confusion) patterns that are consistent with QDA objective facial motion analysis (Table 4).

7 Discussion and Conclusions

In this paper, we investigated how people perceive visual emotions with speech. This work is the first to evaluate the consistency among objective facial motion data analysis, subjective perception of faces in video, and subjective perception of abstract point-rendered faces. We found that the objective discrimination results of motion capture data are highly correlated with those of subjective evaluation experiments. In particular, the lower face region (across multiple representations in rendering) provides insightful clues for visual emotion perception. We also found that anger was easily visually perceived as sadness, and sadness and neutral were difficult to visually discriminate.

In comparison with previous literature [3, 13], the findings of this study are consistent on some points; for instance, our study verifies the importance of the lower face region for most of the emotions [3] and pairs of angry-sad and neutral-sad are easily confused [13]. Our new findings of this work include the fact that the lower face region incorporates important clues for visual emotion perception, because it can generate similar emotion confusion matrices (patterns) among its different face representations. This finding can be further exploited to evaluate expressive embodied conversational agents.

We are aware that the four basic emotions (neutral, anger, sadness, and happiness) studied in this work are not enough to cover comprehensive ECAs, e.g., fear, interest, and disgust were not covered in this work. In future work we plan on examining a wider array of emotions. Furthermore, a major limitation of the current work is that we only studied a single actress when generating the emotions. In order to fully generalize our findings, we plan on replicating this work with a number of actors/actresses. However, the purpose of the current work was to validate a number of methodologies, and given our limited stimulus set, we found excellent convergence in our methods.

There are many questions that remain open. As described in the section on objective motion analysis section, the emotion visual-confusion matrices of the objective analysis are highly consistent with the subjective evaluation experiments. This observation indicates that the objective emotion visual-confusion matrices (especially the lower face region) could be used as a useful benchmark to evaluate synthetic expressive facial animation. For example, for a synthetic expressive speech animation, the same QDA [22] can be applied to the 3D motion dataset (Figure 1) on the animated face. If the new generated objective visual-emotion confusion matrices are close to the ones illustrated in Figure 3 and Table 1, (Measurement could be the Absolute Expressive Performance (AEP) and the Relative Expressive Performance (REP) [1].), then it could suggest that the synthetic expressive animated face sequence is close to a real human. In sum, the current work provides the beginnings of establishing a system of methodologies to evaluate emotions generated by digital ECAs.

Acknowledgements

Special thanks go to Joy Nash and Murtaza Bulut for capturing motion data, and Kimy Tran, Stephanie Parker, and Erica Murphey for helping with the subjective evaluation experiments.

References

1. Ahlberg, J., Pandzic, I.S., and You, L: Evaluating MPEG-4 Facial Animation Players, *MPEG-4 Facial Animation: the standard, implementation and applications*, Pandzic, I.S. and Forchhimer, R. (eds.), 2002, 287-291.
2. Andre, E., Rist, M., and Muller, J: Guiding the User through Dynamically Generated Hypermedia Presentations with a Life-like Character, *IUI '98, pp.* 21-28.
3. Bassili, J.N: Emotion Recognition: The Role of Facial Movement and the Relative Importance of Upper and Lower Areas of the Face, *Journal of the Personality and Social Psychology*, 1979(37), 2049-2058.
4. Blanz, V., Basso, C., Poggio, T., and Vetter, T: Reanimating Faces in Images and Video, *Computer Graphics Forum*, 22(3), 2003
5. Brand, M: Voice Puppetry, *Proc. of ACM SIGGRAPH 1999*, ACM Press, pp. 21-28.
6. Bregler, C., Covell, M., and Slaney, M: Video Rewrite: Driving Visual Speech with Audio, *Proc. of ACM SIGGRAPH'97*, ACM Press, pp.353-360.
7. Busso, C., Deng, Z., Neumann, U., and Narayanan, S: Natural Head Motion Synthesis Driven by Acoustic Prosody Features, *the Journal of Computer Animation and Virtual Worlds*, 16(3-4), July 2005, pp.283-290.
8. Cassell, J., Pelachaud, C., Badler, N., Steedman, M., Achorn, B., Becket, T., Douville, B., Prevost, S., and Stone, M: Animated Conversation: Rule-Based Generation of Facial Expression, Gesture and Spoken intonation for Multiple Conversational Agents, *Proc. of ACM SIGGRAPH'94*, ACM Press, 413-420.
9. Cassell, J., Sullivan, J., Prevost, S., and Churchill, E: Embodied Conversational Agents, MIT Press, 2000.
10. Chuang, E.S., Deshpande, H., and Bregler, C: Facial Expression Space Learning, *Proc. of Pacific Graphics'02*, 2002, 68-76.
11. Cohen, M.M., and Massaro, D.W: Modeling Coarticulation in Synthetic Visual Speech, Magnenat-Thalmann, N., Thalmann, D. (Editors), *Models and Techniques in Computer Animation*, Springer Verlag, 1993, 139-156.
12. Costantini, E., Pianesi, F., and Cosi, P: Evaluation of Synthetic Faces: Human Recognition of Emotional Facial Displays, *Affective Dialogue Systems*, Dybkiaer, L. Minker, W. and Heisterkamp, P. (eds.), 2004.
13. Costantini, E., Pianesi, F., Prete, M: Recognising emotions in human and synthetic faces: the role of the upper and lower parts of the face, *Proc. of IUI'05*, ACM Press (2005), 20-27.

14. Deng, Z., Neumann, U., Lewis, J.P., Kim, T.Y., Bulut, M., and Narayanan, S: Expressive Facial Animation Synthesis by Learning Speech Co-Articulation and Expression Space, *IEEE Transaction on Visualization and Computer Graphics*, 12(6), Nov/Dec, 2006.

15. Deng, Z., Bulut, M., Neumann, U., and Narayanan, S: Automatic Dynamic Expression Synthesis for Speech Animation, *Proc. of IEEE Computer Animation and Social Agents 2004*, July 2004, pp. 267-274.

16. Deng, Z., Lewis, J.P., and Neumann, U: Synthesizing Speech Animation by Learning Compact Speech Co-Articulation Models, *Proc. of Computer Graphics International 2005*, June 2005, pp. 19-25.

17. Ekman, P., Friesen, W.V: Unmasking the Face: A Guide to Recognizing Emotions from Facial Clues, Prentice-Hall, 1975

18. Essa, I. A. and Pentland, A.P: Coding, Analysis, Interpretation, and Recognition of Facial Expressions, *IEEE Transaction on Pattern Analysis and Machine Intelligence*, 19(7), 1997, 757-763

19. Ezzat, T., Geiger, G., and Poggio, T: Trainable Videorealistic Speech Animation, *ACM Trans. Graph.*, 21(3), 2002, 388-398.

20. Gratch, J. and Marsella, S: Evaluating a Computational Model of Emotion, *Journal of Autonomous Agents and Multiagent Systems*, 11(1), pp. 23-43.

21. Gratch, J., Rickel, J., Andre, E., Badler, N., Cassell, J., and Petajan, E: Creating Interactive Virtual Humans: Some Assembly Required, *IEEE Intelligent Systems*, July/August 2002, pp. 54-63.

22. Hastie, T., Ribshirani, R., and Friedman, J: The Elements of Statistical Learning: Data Mining, Inference, and Prediction, Springer-Verlag, 2001.

23. Katsyri, J., Klucharev, V., Frydrych, M., Sams, M: Identification of Synthetic and Natural Emotional Facial Expressions, *Proc. of AVSP'2003*, 2003, 239-244.

24. Kshirsagar, S., and Thalmann, N.M: Visyllable Based Speech Animation, *Computer Graphics Forum*, 22(3), 2003.

25. Walker, J. H., Sproull, L., and Subramani, R: Using a human face in an interface, *Proc. of CHI'94*, ACM Press (1994), 85-91.

26. Lee, Y., Terzopoulos, D., and Waters, K: Realistic modeling for facial animation, *Proc. of ACM SIGGRAPH'95*, ACM Press (1995), 55-62.

27. Lewis, J.P: Automated lip-sync: Background and techniques, *J. of Visualization and Computer Animation*, 1991, 118-122.

28. Lewis, J.P., Purcell, P.: Soft Machine: A Personable Interface, *Proc. of Graphics Interface 84*, pp. 223-226.

29. Marsella, S. and Gratch, J: Modeling the Interplay of Plans and Emotions in Multi-Agent Simulations, *Proc. of the Cognitive Science Society*, 2001.

30. Nass, C., Kim, E.Y., and Lee, E.J: When My Face is the Interface: An Experimental Comparison of Interacting with One's Own Face or Someone Else's Face, *Proc. of CHI'98*, ACM Press (1998), 148-154.

31. Noh, J.Y., and Neumann, U: Expression Cloning, *Proc. of ACM SIGGRAPH'01*, ACM Press (2001), 277-288.

32. Pandzic, I.S., Ostermann, J., and Millen, D: User evaluation: synthetic talking faces for interactive services, *The Visual Computer*, 1999(15), 330-340.

33. Parke, F: Computer Generated Animation of Faces, *Proc. ACM Nat'l Conf.* ACM Press (1972), 451-457.

34. Pelachaud, C., Badler, N., and Steedman, M: Linguistic Issues in Facial Animation, *Proc. of Computer Animation'91*, 1991.

35. Pelachaud, C., Badler, N. and Steedman, M: Generating Facial Expressions for Speech, *Cognitive Science*, 20(1), 1994, 1-46.
36. Rist, M., Andre, E., and Muller, J: Adding animated presentation agents to the interface. *IUI '97: Proc. of Intelligent user interfaces*, ACM Press (1997), 79-86.
37. Sirovich, L. and Kirby, M: Low-dimensional procedure for the characterization of human faces, *J. Opt. Soc. Am. A*, 4(3), 1987 March, 519-524
38. Turk, M. A. and Pentland, A.P: Face Recognition Using Eigenfaces, *IEEE CVPR 91*, 586-591.
39. Uttkay, Z., Doorman, C., and Noot, H: Evaluating ECAs - What and How? *Proc. of the AAMAS02 Workshop on Embodied Conversational Agents*, 2002.

Dealing with Out of Domain Questions in Virtual Characters

Ronakkumar Patel, Anton Leuski, and David Traum

Institute for Creative Technologies
University of Southern California
Marina del Rey, CA 90292, USA
{patelr, leuski, traum}@ict.usc.edu

Abstract. We consider the problem of designing virtual characters that support speech-based interactions in a limited domain. Previously we have shown that classification can be an effective and robust tool for selecting appropriate in-domain responses. In this paper, we consider the problem of dealing with out-of-domain user questions. We introduce a taxonomy of out-of-domain response types. We consider three classification architectures for selecting the most appropriate out-of-domain responses. We evaluate these architectures and show that they significantly improve the quality of the response selection making the user's interaction with the virtual character more natural and engaging.

1 Introduction

Previous work has shown that limited domain virtual humans that use spoken interaction can be quite successful in terms of delivering quality answers to in-domain questions [2,3]. Question-answering characters can serve a number of purposes, including entertainment, training, and education. For a question-answering character, a key point is to give human-like responses to questions when no answer is available. The character should act like a person who either does not know or does not want to reveal the answer: recognizing explicitly that something is "off-topic" and giving a response indicating this recognition is better than providing an inappropriate in-domain answer. While a character could be constructed to always reply with something generic like "I don't know", this can lead to repetitive behavior that breaks a sense of immersion. Having a set of such answers allows the character to seem more engaging, by producing some variety in his responses. Thus we have constructed a set of off-topic responses for our characters to choose from.

We have found, however, that not all off-topic responses are equally satisfactory as replies to each of a range of off-topic questions. In this paper we explore whether the general category "off-topic" can be broken down into appropriate sub-categories to achieve higher performance. We use the SGT Blackwell character [2,3], as a testbed for this exploration, and create a taxonomy of types of off-topic areas, a set of replies for the SGT Blackwell character for each area. We further evaluate performance of several classification-based architectures that

J. Gratch et al. (Eds.): IVA 2006, LNAI 4133, pp. 121–131, 2006.

use the off-topic taxonomy, as to how satisfactory the answers are. The results show that the best architecture significantly out-performs the baseline character, – which does not use the taxonomy, – on both on-topic and off-topic questions.

In the next section we give an overview of the SGT Blackwell character and the baseline question-understanding/response. In Section 3 we discuss a taxonomy of off-topic response classes, which we hope can reduce the number of inappropriate off-topic responses. In Section 4 we describe three different classification-based architectures, which are intended to improve the baseline classifier, using the off-topic taxonomy. In Section 5, we present the results of evaluating the three architectures with respect to the quality of answers given. Finally, in Section 6 we summarize our results and outline some directions for future work.

Fig. 1. SGT Blackwell

2   The Baseline SGT Blackwell System

SGT Blackwell, shown in Figure 1, is a life-sized character projected on a transparent screen. He is meant to answer questions from a user acting as a reporter interviewing him about his role in the Army and the technology at the Institute for Creative Technology that created him. A user talks to SGT Blackwell using a head mounted microphone. For speech recognition, we use a hybrid limited domain/general language model [4], built using the SONIC system [5]. A classifier [3] then analyzes the text output and selects the highest scoring answer. The answers are pre-recorded audio clips linked with animation, which are played through the game engine to show SGT Blackwell providing the response. SGT Blackwell's responses include spoken lines ranging from one word to a couple paragraphs. There are 55 content answers with domain information. When SGT Blackwell detects a question that cannot be answered with one of the content (on-topic) answers, he picks a random answer from a pool of 17 off-topic answers.

The classifier is based on statistical language modeling techniques used in cross-lingual information retrieval. It represents a text string with a language model – a probability distribution over the words in the string. The classifier views both questions and answers as samples from two different "languages" the language of questions and the language of answers. Given an input question from the user, the classifier calculates the language model of the most likely answer for the question, – it uses the training data as a dictionary to "translate" the question into an answer, – then it compares that model to the language model of individual answers, and selects the best matching response. We showed that this technique outperforms traditional text classification approaches such as support-vector machines for tasks that have a large number of response classes [3].

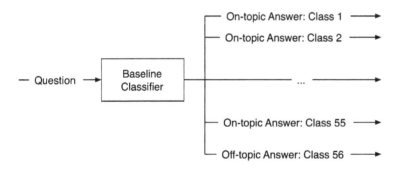

Fig. 2. Baseline classifier architecture

In order to train the classifier, we have created a training corpus of questions linked to either one of the 55 content classes or the "off-topic" class. Questions and answers were created using a multi-stage process, including scripted initial questions, manual paraphrases, and collected questions from a Wizard of Oz study, in which naive users were allowed to ask whatever they wanted, after a brief description of the intended domain. We also used human coders to link questions to appropriate answers using the question-answer quality ranking scheme suggested by Gandhe and his colleagues [6], described in Section 5. The baseline training set included 1572 questions linked to the 56 answer classes.

Figure 2 shows the design of the question-response part of the initial system, which serves as the baseline for our study. It has one classifier, which can deliver on-topic or off-topic answers based the input question. This design assumes that all off-topic answers are equally appropriate to any off-topic question, so we put them into one class. Thus we have 56 response classes for the baseline, 55 for on-topic and 1 for off-topic answers.

This architecture works well at providing the correct answer when the question is in-domain, and recognizing when a question is out of domain [3], however, the answers for out of domain questions are still often far from satisfactory. We noticed that sometimes one out of domain answer works very well for the question while the answer (randomly) selected by the system did not work so well. Some examples of these kinds of problems are shown in Table 1. Column 1 shows some of out of domain questions asked by users. Column 2 shows the answers SGT Blackwell actually provided, while the third column shows other answers that were available in the off-topic set that our human raters preferred.

Table 1. Improvement in selection of off-topic answers

Question	Randomly Selected	Human Selected
What color are my eyes?	I am not liberty to discuss that	You might want to put that one to a real human.
How is the weather?	I can tell you but I'd have to kill you	I would like to know that too.
Have you got any medals?	I would like to know that too.	No
Where are you going next?	Yes	You'll have to talk to the PAO on that one.

3   Taxonomy of Out-of-Domain Response Classes

In order to achieve better conversation with a virtual character, we tried to group the off-topic responses into coherent classes for which the same (set of) answers would apply. First, there is a set of questions which can not be understood as coherent, whether because of speech recognition errors or not enough in-vocabulary words. For these, the character can simply state that he did not hear or understand. Next, there is a simple class of yes-no questions, yielding classes for positive and negative responses. Of the remaining questions, we can make a distinction between those that are really out of the domain vs. those that are appropriately in the domain, but the character's knowledge base does not have an appropriate answer. For those off-topic questions that are in-domain, we can further distinguish between whether it would be legitimate for the character to not know the answer, refuse to tell the answer, or defer the answer to someone else. Of the latter category we also distinguish between specifically asking another domain entity, or a generic "real human". Putting these distinctions together, we end up with the 8 classes shown in Table 2. This table shows the eight classes, along with a brief definition and an example of a question answer pair.

Table 2. Taxonomy of out-of-domain response classes with their meaning

Classes	Meaning and Example
Don't Understand	A question that does not make any sense and/or is very hard to interpret.
	All the region. *Stop mumbling. Just kidding. I didn't get that.*
Out of Domain	A question that asks something that is not about the topic(s) the character is prepared to talk about
	Where is the bathroom? *I don't have that information*
Unknown	A question that concerns the domain, but for which the character does not have an appropriate answer.
	What does AO mean? *I would like to know that too*
Restriction	A question that the character can legitimately refuse to answer.
	Who do you think of new *I'm not at liberty to discuss.* *army uniform?*
Pass	A question that could be better answered by some other domain entity rather than character.
	When will you become Ma- *You'll have to talk to the* *jor?* *PAO on that one.*
Leave to human	A question about specific human characteristics rather than about the domain.
	How much do you weigh? *You might want to put that one to a real human.*
Negative	A question that can be answered with a negative answer.
	Do you have wife? *No*
Positive	A question that can be answered with a positive answer.
	Do you like the army? *Yes*

Table 3 shows the complete set of answers for each of these classes for the initial SGT Blackwell character. Since he represents a soldier, his answers are framed in the way a soldier might put them. Things he doesn't want to talk about can be characterized as classified information. He also refers to AO "area of operations", and PAO "Public Affairs Officer" as ways of characterizing the limits of what he can talk about.

We had three annotators use the above descriptions and examples to categorize off-topic responses into one of the off-topic classes. After removing duplicate and redundant questions, we end up with collection of 1000 on-topic questions and 300 off-topic questions.

Table 3. Response classes and their pool of answers

Classes	Response
Don't Understand	Sorry, I can't hear you.
	I can't understand you.
	Stop mumbling. Just kidding. I didn't get that.
Out of Domain	I don't have that information.
	Sorry. That's outside my AO.
Unknown	I can tell you.....but I would have to kill you (smirks).
	I would like to know that too.
Restriction	That's classified.
	I am not authorized to comment on that.
	No comment.
	I'm not at liberty to discuss.
Pass	You'll have to talk to the PAO on that one.
Leave to Human	You might want to put that one to a real human.
Negative	No.
	Negative, sir.
Positive	Yes.
	Roger.

4 Using the Off-Topic Classes to Improve Classification and Answers

Depending on the way we want to mix or separate the on-topic and off-topic classes, there are several different ways that we could use the data to perform classification and answer selection. These methods use different combinations of different classifiers to achieve the desired effect. We built four classifiers, as described in Table 4 and four classifier architectures, as shown in Figures 2, 3, 4, and 5.

Table 4. Classifier descriptions

Name	Description
Baseline	The classifier used for the original SGT Blackwell character, with 55 on-topic classes and one off-topic class
Binary	A binary classifier, which determines only whether a question was on-topic or off-topic
Off-topic	A classifier that assumes its input is off-topic and classifies to one of the 8 off-topic classes
On-topic	A classifier that assumes its input is on-topic and classifies to one of the 55 on-topic classes
Combined	A classifier that treats on-topic and off-topic classes the same, and classifies to one of 63 classes (55 on-topic and 8 off-topic)

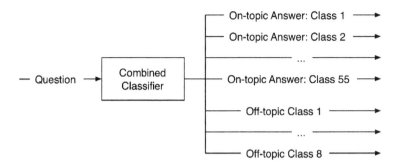

Fig. 3. Architecture 1 with one classifier

The simplest modified architecture is shown in Figure 3 – this is parallel to the baseline architecture shown in Figure 2, although re-trained with new data including more classes. For this classifier we used all 1300 training question-answer pairs.

Since off-topic and on-topic classes are very different, both in the size of the classes and the specificity of the answer, it also seemed prudent to experiment with other classification architectures and methods for distinguishing on-topic from off-topic questions. Our second architecture, shown in Figure 4, includes two classifiers, the baseline, including one off-topic class and 55 on-topic classes (trained on all 1300 training examples), as well as the off-topic classifier (trained on the 300 off-topic examples). This architecture is most directly comparable to the baseline architecture, since only the method of treating off-topic responses has changed.

Finally, we separate the decision problem of "on-topic" vs "off-topic" from the classification within those general categories using the architecture shown in Figure 5. Here we have a two pass-classification procedure, first using the binary

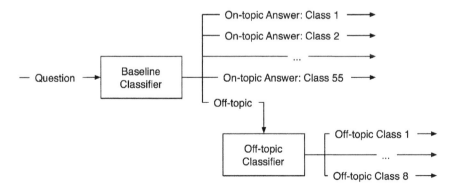

Fig. 4. Architecture 2 with two classifiers

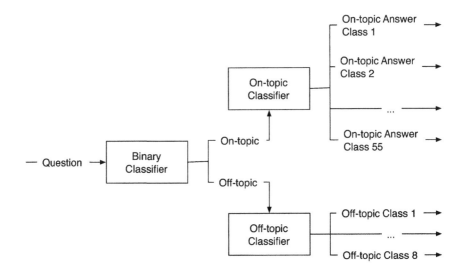

Fig. 5. Architecture 3 with three classifiers

classifier (trained on all 1300 examples), and then dispatching to either the on-topic classifier (55 classes, trained on 1000 on-topic examples) or the off-topic classifier (8 classes, trained on 300 off-topic examples).

5   Evaluation

We evaluated performance of these architectures in order to address the following questions:

1. Is it really helpful to divide off-topic answers into different disjoint classes?
2. If so, which architecture is best among the proposed three?

To answer these questions, we performed a study parallel to the original SGT Blackwell evaluation of the baseline system [2,3]. Our test set had 150 questions, none of which was included in training set. Out of 150 questions 100 were on-topic and 50 were off-topic. This ratio of 1/3 off-topic questions and 2/3 on-topic questions for the test set, was derived from our previous data [3]. The same 150 questions were classified by our baseline architecture shown in Figure 2 as well as the new classifier architectures in Figures 3, 4, and 5. This resulted in 150 question-answer pairs for each architecture.

Three human raters were asked to judge the appropriateness of all Q-A sets, using the 1-6 scale [6], shown in Table 5. We evaluated the agreement between raters by computing Cronbach's alpha score, which measures consistency in the data [1]. The alpha score is 0.885 for baseline, 0.849 for first, 0.781 for second and 0.835 for third architecture respectively, which indicate high consistency among the raters.

Table 5. Appropriateness coding scheme

Grade	Description
1	Response is not related in any way the question
2	Response contains some discussion of people or objects mentioned in the question, but do not really address the question itself.
3	Response partially addresses the question, but little or no coherence between the question and response.
4	Response does mostly address the question, but with major problems in the coherence between question and response; seems like the response is really addressing a different question than the one asked.
5	Response does address the question, but the transition is somewhat awkward.
6	Response answers the question in a perfectly fluent manner.

Table 6. Average appropriateness score for all architectures

	Architecture			
	Baseline	1	2	3
Avg. Score	3.92	3.89	4.16	4.63
Avg. Score (On-topic)	4.58	4.44	4.65	5.14
Ave. Score (Off-topic)	2.59	2.77	3.17	3.62

The average appropriateness scores for all four architectures is displayed in Table 6. The first row shows the overall average for all 150 examples (100 on-topic and 50 off-topic questions). The differences in the scores are statistically significant according to pair-wise t-test with the cutoff set to 5% except for the difference between the baseline and Architecture 1 with one classifier. We can see a marked improvement for Architecture 3, and a slighter improvement for Architecture 2. Looking more closely, the next rows break out the scores for on and off-topic questions. Architecture 3 with 3 classifiers outperforms the baseline on both on-topic and off-topic responses. While all three architectures outperform the baseline on off-topic responses, we can see that Architecture 1 slightly under-performs for on-topic answers (presumably because they are more likely to be confused with the individual off-topic classes than the overall "off-topic" category), and is not to be preferred. We can thus conclude that the off-topic categories are indeed useful, but we must be careful in how we use them in a classifier. Architecture 3 with three classifiers dominates the other three, and is thus preferred, at least for this data set.

Table 7 shows how often the classification architectures confuse on-topic from off-topic questions. For the baseline architecture and Architecture 2, an off-topic label means the question was assigned to the off-topic class, while an on-topic label means that one of the other classes was chosen by the baseline classifier. For Architecture 1 an on-topic label means that one of the on-topic classes was

Table 7. On and off-topic mis-classification

	Architecture			
	Baseline	1	2	3
On label as Off	0.05	0.03	0.05	0.03
Off label as On	0.07	0.09	0.07	0.13

chosen, while an off-topic label means that one of the eight off-topic classes was chosen. Finally, for Architecture 3, the label comes from the results of the binary classifier. The first row in Table 7 displays the ration of total classifications in which the system produces an off-topic answer to an on-topic question. The second row displays the ratio of total classifications in which an on-topic answer was given for an off-topic question. Interestingly, even though Architecture 3 has higher response scores, it has a higher error rate at the binary classification task than the others, which indicates a hybrid architecture might perform even better.

6   Conclusion and Future Work

In this paper we examined the issue of how to improve the performance of a limited-domain question-answering character in the case where the character is given an out of domain question. After some analysis of the types of problems that arise, we constructed a taxonomy of 8 types of off-topic questions and answers. After annotating our data with these classes, we experimented with different classification architectures, and evaluated the performance of these architectures, showing significant improvement in the answers for the three classifier architecture over the baseline system.

While these results are encouraging, there is still much room for more improvement. First, we should probably be a bit more systematic about the definitions and examples for each of these classes. Second, it is unclear to what extent our results would generalize over other data sets and different characters. Finally, it may be the case that other types of classifiers might be appropriate for some of the more specialized tasks.

Acknowledgments

This work has been sponsored by the U.S. Army Research, Development, and Engineering Command (RDECOM). Statements and opinions expressed do not necessarily reflect the position or the policy of the United States Government, and no official endorsement should be inferred. The authors would like to thank Jillian Gerten, Ashish Vaswani, Brandon Kennedy and Jaimin Vaidya for useful discussions and their expertise as human coders in mapping of questions and answers set.

References

1. Chronbach, L. J.: Coefficient alpha and the internal structure of tests. *Psychometrika*, 16, (1951) 297–333.
2. Leuski, A., Pair, J., Traum, D., McNerney, P.J., Georgiou, P., Patel, R.: How to talk to a hologram. In Edmonds, E., Riecken, D., Paris, C.L., Sidner, C.L., eds.: Proceedings of the 11th international conference on Intelligent user interfaces (IUI'06), Sydney, Australia, ACM Press New York, NY, USA (2006) 360–362
3. Leuski, A., Patel, R., Traum, D., Kennedy, B.: Building effective question answering characters. In: Proceedings of the 7th SIGdial Workshop on Discourse and Dialogue. (2006)
4. Sethy, A., Georgiou, P., Narayanan, S.: Building topic specific language models from webdata using competitive models. In: Proceedings of EUROSPEECH, Lisbon, Portugal (2005)
5. Pellom, B.: Sonic: The University of Colorado continuous speech recognizer. Technical Report TR-CSLR-2001-01, University of Colorado, Boulder, CO (2001)
6. Gandhe, S., Gordon, A.S., Traum, D.: Improving question-answering with linking dialogues. In: Proceedings of the 11th international conference on Intelligent user interfaces (IUI'06), New York, NY, USA, ACM Press (2006) 369–371

MIKI: A Speech Enabled Intelligent Kiosk

Lee McCauley and Sidney D'Mello

Department of Computer Science, The University of Memphis
Memphis, TN 38152, USA
{mccauley, sdmello}@memphis.edu

Abstract. We introduce MIKI, a three-dimensional, directory assistance-type digital persona displayed on a prominently-positioned 50 inch plasma unit housed at the FedEx Institute of Technology at the University of Memphis. MIKI, which stands for Memphis Intelligent Kiosk Initiative, guides students, faculty and visitors through the Institute's maze of classrooms, labs, lecture halls and offices through graphically-rich, multidimensional, interactive, touch and voice sensitive digital content. MIKI differs from other intelligent kiosk systems by its advanced natural language understanding capabilities that provide it with the ability to answer informal verbal queries without the need for rigorous phraseology. This paper describes, in general, the design, implementation, and observations of visitor reactions to the Intelligent Kiosk.

1 Introduction

As we find ourselves at the height of the information age the need for user-friendly, naturalistic, and intuitive information systems becomes paramount. Stephandis et al. have predicted that public information systems, terminals, and information appliances will be increasingly used in a variety of domains [1]. Of particular interest in the field of intelligent information systems and virtual agents are information kiosks. These are a special variant of information appliances that are usually deployed in public locations such as transportation hubs, malls, businesses, etc. In addition to the basic issues that accompany the design of typical information systems such as information retrieval, multi-modal communication, and interface design these systems pose some novel and interesting concerns. Cassell et al., point out that kiosk systems differ from traditional systems in that they should stand out so that they are noticed by visitors, their functions should be self-evident, no user training should be required, and they should be able to recover from user errors [2].

One of the information kiosks that demonstrated a significant improvement over earlier systems is the MINNELLI system [3]. MINNELLI facilitates interactions with bank customers primarily by the use of short animated cartoons to present information on bank services. However, the MINNELLI system requires basic user training which reduces its applicability in most public sites. Another successful kiosk with a broader scope than the MINELLI system is the MACK system [2]. MACK is an embodied conversational kiosk that provides information on residents and directions to locations at a research site. It integrates multiple input sources that include speech, gesture, and pressure. The system also exhibits a degree of spatial intelligence by utilizing its awareness of its location and the layout of the building to reference physical locations

J. Gratch et al. (Eds.): IVA 2006, LNAI 4133, pp. 132 – 144, 2006.
© Springer-Verlag Berlin Heidelberg 2006

when it provides directions [4]. The August spoken dialog system is also kiosk based and helps users find their way around Stockholm, Germany using an on-screen street map. August is designed to elicit a conversation from the user and facilitates the study of such interactions [5, 6].

This paper describes the design, implementation, and initial user reactions of one such intelligent kiosk system called MIKI: The Memphis Intelligent Kiosk Initiative. The system is deployed on a plasma screen at the FedEx Institute of Technology, a building that houses a community of interdisciplinary researchers, at the University of Memphis. As a person approaches the display, MIKI greets them, introduces itself, and offers to be of assistance. The individual can then verbally ask a question related to any of the following topics: (1) events at the FedEx Institute of Technology, (2) research groups housed at the Institute, (3) directions to rooms within the building, (4) people involved in research at the Institute. In answer to the visitor's question, the kiosk responds in a number of different ways. The response might include a verbal answer along with 3-D animations, video presentations, images, or additional audio. Along with the prototype kiosk (Figure 1), tools were created that allow for the maintenance and timely update of information presented by the kiosk.

Fig. 1. MIKI: The Memphis Intelligent Kiosk Initiative

MIKI shares several similarities to the MACK system in that both systems use multiple input channels and that they both provide information on people and groups and directions to locations at a research site [2, 4]. However, the MACK system relies on rule based grammars alone for speech input. This greatly restricts the scope of questions with which a user can query the system. MIKI is equipped with a standard grammar as well as a statistical based natural language understanding mechanism that reduces the need for rigorous phraseology in the information requests a user presents to the system. We identify this facet of the Intelligent Kiosk as the paramount factor that distinguishes it from other such systems.

The intelligent kiosk, itself, is a collection of different technologies that are all integrated and work seamlessly together. Among these different technologies is video processing for face detection, a digital avatar, speaker-independent speech recognition, an advanced graphical user interface (GUI), an array microphone for noise cancellation, a database system, a dynamic question answering system, and a cutting-edge touch panel technology for large displays. We proceed by describing the primary components of the system followed by some of the technical challenges encountered. We then present some anecdotal accounts of humans interacting with the system and provide details on some usability studies that are underway.

2 Primary Components

There are several components that comprise the Intelligent Kiosk. A general layout of the major software elements is presented in Figure 2.

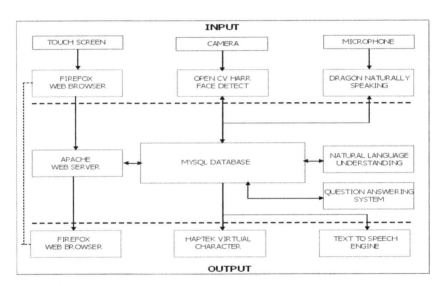

Fig. 2. Major software components of the intelligent kiosk

2.1 The Hardware

The Intelligent Kiosk resides in the lobby of the FedEx Institute of technology on a small wall facing the main entrance. The location was chosen for its optimal visibility to outside visitors. As a visitor enters the building, they see a 50 inch display surrounded by custom-made cabinet. The 50 inch Panasonic® display has been augmented with a touch panel overlay provided by Smart Technologies®. Mounted above the display is a small, FireWire web cam. Just below the display is a somewhat larger Acoustic Magic® array microphone. Both the camera and the array microphone are angled for optimal function for someone standing between 1 and 3 feet in front of the display. Inside the lower part of the cabinet are two Dell® workstations, an Ethernet hub, a KVM switch, and a wireless keyboard and mouse. The two systems are basically identical with 3.2 GHz CPUs, 128 MB AGP video cards, and 2 GB of memory. Both are running windows XP as their operating system. Figure 3 depicts the major hardware components of the Intelligent Kiosk.

Fig. 3. Major hardware components of the intelligent kiosk

2.2 Speech Recognition

For seamless verbal interaction with visitors seeking information a speaker independent speech recognition system was required. We decided to use the commercial available product Dragon NaturallySpeaking developed by Nuance® although it was not designed for speaker independence. This decision was motivated by the fact that we were in the possession of working software to interface with this speech recognition engine through CloudGarden's JSAPI implementation. Therefore, even though we looked into a few other speaker independent speech recognition engines, such as CMU Sphinx, we decided that we would stick with Dragon NaturallySpeaking version 8 primarily due to time constraints. By carefully restricting the language model for speech recognition we were able to simulate a reasonable quality of speaker independent recognition (more details provided below).

2.3 Natural Language Understanding

The natural language understanding module has one responsibility, to provide an analysis of the user's utterance in order to determine what action or actions need to be taken. When a system is employed in a limited domain such as the Intelligent Kiosk and has only a limited number of choices of what to say or do next, it need only classify a visitor's utterance rather than completely comprehend every word. MIKI uses two different NLU technologies that include simple keyword matching and a classification technique based on Latent Semantic Analysis [7, 8]. LSA is a statistical technique that measures the conceptual similarity of two text sources. LSA computes a geometric cosine (ranging from -1 to 1) that represents the conceptual similarity between the two text sources.

Classification approaches to NLU include statistical [e.g.,9, 10], information retrieval [e.g.,11, 12] and connectionist approaches [e.g.,13]. Notable among these approaches are those that are based on word co-occurrence patterns such as LSA [7, 8] and HAL [14]. LSA is an attractive approach because it can be trained on untagged texts and is a simple extension to keyword based techniques.

In general, methods such as LSA, involve the analysis of a large corpus of text in order to create a semantic representation of each word. We then use these semantic representations to categorize incoming utterances as one of the existing grammar rules. There has been research conducted on the application of this type of corpus analysis to speech recognition, although it is generally assumed that the language models produced would replace or modify those in existing speech recognition engines [15, 16]. A simplified version of the algorithm used for natural language understanding in conjunction with LSA for verbal input is presented in Figure 4. More details on the algorithm and preliminary performance analyses on semantic, feature, and gibberish instances on queries relating to appointments in the Microsoft™ Outlook's Calendar program can be found in [17] and [18].

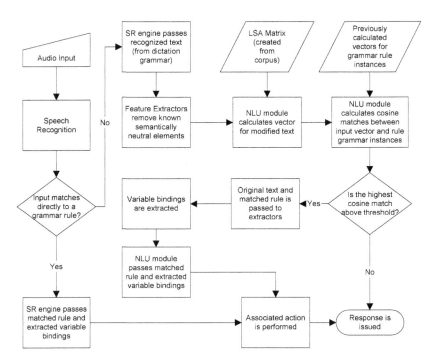

Fig. 4. Algorithm for natural language understanding

2.4 People Tracking

Rather than relying on sophisticated trackers, such as the Kalman Filter [19], a rather simple tracker that relied on face detection was used. The general object detection algorithm consisting of a cascade of boosted classifiers proposed by Viola and Jones [20] was used to detect faces on the basis of Harr-like features. SharperCV, a C# wrapper for the Intel® OpenCV library [21], was used for all video processing. This use of the face detection algorithm provides the ability to not only recognize when someone is approaching the kiosk, but also to count the number of individuals that interacted with the system as opposed to those that walked by. The tracker was based on the assumption that with a large frame rate (30 frames per second) the change in the location of a face from one frame to the next is rather minute. Therefore, a face in the current frame was assigned to the nearest face (based on Euclidian distance) among all the faces in the previous frame as long as the distance was not greater than some predefined maximum threshold.

2.5 Graphical Interface

The graphical interface is a combination of two technologies: a standard web-based front end that is the primary interface and a secondary animated character.

2.5.1 Primary Interface

The primary way that individuals can interact with the kiosk is through a web-based front end. It uses a combination of PHP, HTML, and Flash. The PHP and HTML are used to render dynamic pages based on the data stored in the database. The visual transitions between screens as well as direction animations are provided via several Flash scripts. Of particular interest are the animations for directions to various locations in the building. They were generated using the original CAD files of the building. When a user asks for directions to a given room that flash file is loaded. A small ball is illuminated where the user currently is and is then moved along the path that will get that person to their destination. As the floating ball changes floors, that floor becomes visible and the others fade away. In addition to the animation, the directions are also spoken through the avatar and provided in text below the animation.

2.5.2 The Avatar

The animated avatar was created using Haptek's® PeoplePutty software and displayed with the Haptek Player. The programmatic interface through an ActiveX control is fairly straightforward and creates a realistic animated character. The player is free for distribution and has a small footprint both in respect to memory and CPU resources. Using the PeoplePutty software, we were able to create two avatars based on the two students that also provide the voice for their characters. The result is two characters, one male and one female, that look and sound surprisingly like their human models. Despite the fact that the system has a fully functional text-to-speech (TTS) system as shown in Figure 2, it was noted that most of the vocal interaction from the agent would be known a priori. As this suggests, all of the vocal output produced by the avatar was prerecorded by the human models. These recordings were then processed using a Haptek tool that tags the recordings with mouth movements.

When these recordings are played back through the animated character, the mouth animations of the character match the spoken utterances.

2.6 Question Answering

Question answering was accomplished through a combination of mechanisms but primarily involves a naïve use of the database to disambiguate between a number of possible questions being asked. First, each possible type of response is described through an XML file. Because the vocal interaction with the kiosk is intended to be completely open-ended, it is not possible to define each and every question that might be posed to the system. Therefore, each type of response defined in the XML file is defined primarily by what screen services that response requires. For example, all questions regarding general information about an individual will be answered by displaying a detailed personnel page that is dynamically generated based on information from the database. A single element in the XML file describes how to recognize and respond to all inquiries of this type. Each response element then provides the following types of information: (1) the frame name (screen), (2) a key field in the database, (3) a template for an SQL command, (4) text features (as extracted by the speech recognition and/or NLU module) used to match this response to a question, (5) follow-up question types used to disambiguate between several possible answers, (6) a template for a textual response assuming a positive answer was located, and (7) a template for a textual response assuming a positive answer could not be located. With the current system using prerecorded vocal responses, items 6 and 7 above are not used.

The first two items, the frame name and the key field, are used to communicate with the graphical front end. The frame name informs the GUI what screen to display while the ID field contains specific information about which record to display on that screen. For example, a visitor might say, "can you tell me about John Doe?" The speech recognition/NLU system categorizes this utterance as a request for specific information about John Doe. The question answering system picks this up, matches the question and information provided to a specific response type, and updates a query tracking object with the information provided. It and then binds the variables in the SQL template for that response and runs the database query. Assuming that only one record comes back matching that query, the value in the key field is extracted and a message is sent to the GUI that includes the frame name and the value of the key field for that person's record. The GUI then handles displaying the information on the appropriate screen as well as issuing any messages for actions through the animated avatar.

A distinction should be made between this method and the widely used Artificial Intelligence Mark-up Language (AIML) [22]. Many "chatbots" have been created using AIML as the question-to-answer connection engine. This method essentially maps the text of a question to an appropriate response. What makes this system powerful is its ability to decide between multiple possible answers based on the closeness of the match. MIKI, on the other hand, uses the results of the database search to dictate the final response. As a side note, AIML has been integrated into MIKI as a way of dealing with questions that are not part of the primary database that deals only with information about the FedEx Institute of Technology.

3 Technical Challenges

The following section describes the challenges faced during the implementation of the Intelligent Kiosk. Solutions are also presented although some components are still under refinement now that the system is in place.

3.1 Component Communication

The various pieces of the kiosk communicate through the database. A table in the database, called the "messages" table, holds all information that is being transmitted between components. The table holds some basic information about each message such as an auto-incremented identifier, the sender, the recipient, the message tag (e.g., LOAD, SPEAK), text data (e.g., a recognized utterance), binary data (e.g., a Hashtable mapping features to values, *first-name=John*), and a timestamp. Any number of components can access the messages table and effectively react to the messages. All they need to know is the tag or tags in which they are interested. This is similar to a shared memory framework.

Using a database as the focus of a communication scheme between components has several advantages. For example, a simple ontology can be used to address senders and information types. This allows the system to be implemented quickly without confusion even among a dispersed group of developers. Adding new resources simply involves a name assignment and the definition of new message tags. Even so, this technique is not significantly different from a standard blackboard model. A central component polls the database on a regular basis and messages are distributed to the appropriate modules. Instead of using specific techniques, such as Galaxy Communicator [23] or other similar systems, it was decided that maximum interoperability would be gained through the use of a method that was common to all of the disparate languages. Even the web-based front end could easily make use of an industry standard database. However, this does pose a problem in that the web component has to poll the database independently. As long as the table of messages remains small, this is a minor issue. When the table becomes large, agent and interface response becomes slow. For this reason, daily maintenance is performed on the database that backs up the table of messages into an archive and erases old messages.

The communication scheme is persistent-asynchronous in nature. Message persistence is provided by the messages table in the database. The system is asynchronous because components read and write messages on their own schedules independent of other components. This communication scheme alleviates several problems associated with distributed components. The only thing that each component needs to have a connection to is the database. This is a very simple and well tested procedure that is not specific to a particular language. For instance, the graphical front end is a combination of PHP code running some Macromedia Flash displayed in a Mozilla Firefox web browser. The PHP code has no problems sending or receiving messages from other components to tell it to change screens or display a particular frame. Much of the "back-end" code is written in Java while the virtual agent control software and the tracker is written in C#. Each choice of language for a given component was made based on what core functions were most important and which language supported those functions best. Getting these very different components to talk to each other using some other method like CORBA or SOAP would have been problematic at best and would not have provided any benefit over the database solution. Finally, the database solution already incorporates speed optimizations for the transfer, storage, and logging of data. Logging of the system's internal workings is a simple matter of backing up the messages table.

The use of a database as the medium for sending and delivering messages between components is the central idea that makes the rest of the distributed framework almost trivial. Once the database was in place as the message delivery system, all the components were able to use any method they chose to access from that database. Each component was then designed as a stand-alone process. In addition to the fact that any component could then be run on any accessible computer, this also facilitated easy testing of components in pseudo-isolation. Testing code manually created messages in the database and then read the resulting messages entered by the component being tested to determine if the test passed or failed.

For the Java and C# components, a generic API to facilitate communication with the database was created to allow for easy implementation of various components. The API contained data structures and algorithms to ensure optimal transparency related to the encoding and decoding of messages to and from the database. Such a system could be said to have scale-up problems if the number of separate components were to become excessively large, but for the foreseeable future of less than one hundred separate modules this system should not have a noticeable degradation in performance.

3.2 Speaker Independent Speech Recognition

The commercially available software package Dragon NaturallySpeaking from Nuance® was used for speech recognition. Unfortunately, Dragon NaturallySpeaking was designed for non-speaker independent use. The major motivation for the use of this recognizer over more viable options such as CMU Sphinx was the existence of legacy software using Dragon and a JSAPI implementation from CloudGarden. In order to achieve an acceptable degree of speaker independence we used an untrained speaker profile and replaced the default language model with a much smaller model that consisted of common words that would likely be used in the kiosk domain. To this we added the names of individuals, groups, and some events associated with the FedEx Institute. In other words, the content of the kiosk was used as the majority of the words that the speech recognizer would handle. Additionally, the process of updating the language model was automated by periodically dumping relevant tables (e.g., groups, events, etc) from the database and utilizing the language building tool available as part of the Dragon NaturallySpeaking software suite. Therefore, as people, groups, and events are added, deleted, and modified, the language model is guaranteed to stay consistent.

This method of utilizing a very restrictive language model worked better than was originally expected, but is still unsatisfactory from a performance perspective. Studies are currently under way to determine how well this method performs compared to other methods and recognizers. It is our expectation that we will discover that this method only performs at around 60% accuracy, but that is purely speculation. Ultimately, we are sure that another method or recognition system will be used with better success.

3.3 Session Maintenance

One important issue is how and when to start, end, and maintain a session. We would like the kiosk to proactively initiate interaction whenever a person is looking at the screen. The vision component identifies and tracks faces. Based on the size of the face, an approximate distance from the kiosk can be determined. If the face is within about 4 feet of the kiosk, then it is assumed that the person is within the range of interaction. This is used to open a session if one is not currently open, or maintain a currently open session. Voice input and touching of the screen also triggers an opening or maintaining of a session. Finally, sessions are kept open for a few seconds (currently 30 seconds) even if no face is visible and no other input is received. We have found that this works pretty well. It does not close a session prematurely or keep open a session beyond a reasonable length of time.

4 The Human Component

The purpose of the Intelligent Kiosk is, of course, human interaction. Studies are currently being conducted to determine the general usability of the kiosk along with the number of visitors that choose to use the kiosk compared to the human staffed information pavilion. An unobtrusive, non-reactive, observational study that counts the number of people who approach and use the kiosk as well records details of their interactions is underway. On the basis of the schedule of events at the Institute we determined two days on which we would conduct the observations. These include a typical "slow" day when little or no outside visitation would be expected and a typical "busy" day. The qualitative studies are currently underway, therefore, what follows is anecdotal evidence based on informal observation.

4.1 Visitors' Reactions

The types of interactions that we have observed have been somewhat different than what we expected. First, many of the visitors that have heard a description of the kiosk assume that it will engage them in some form of conversation. Consequently, the first words often spoken to the kiosk are, "hello" or "hey there." Since this was not part of the kiosk's repertoire, the visitors are left not sure what to do next. Other casual users, those that just see the system for the first time and approach it, most often just stand in front of it and do not seem to be sure whether they are allowed to touch it and unaware that they can speak to it. This has revealed one of the primary limitations of the kiosk in its current form, namely that there are not enough cues provided to the casual observer as to what the kiosk is and how to interact with it. This is especially acute when the kiosk is in screen-saver mode. During these times the system is displaying a video about the FedEx Institute and does not look that much different from any of the other plasma screens in the building.

When the kiosk is not in screen-saver mode, the virtual agent has a distinct look that draws some attention. We believe that it is the very presence of this human-like face that causes some people to try to converse naturally with the kiosk. On one occasion, a visitor walking past paused long enough to look at the agent and wave. Needless to say, the kiosk did not wave back.

4.2 The Casual Hacker

One other class of visitor to the kiosk seems to think that it is there duty to show us where the system can be hacked. During the implementation of the kiosk, we did not devote any serious effort to designing security measures for the physically present miscreant. We did put in place several layers of digital security. Nevertheless, we have had several attempts by individuals standing in front of the kiosk to "break" it. The system is running on Windows XP primarily through an Internet browser. This means that we get all of the drawbacks of these two technologies even though we have some advantages. First, the keyboard is locked in a cabinet with the two computers and is not accessible without a key. Second, the only mouse input is through the touch panel meaning that there is no right-mouse-click. Third, the browser is in "kiosk mode" meaning that it is completely full screen without any menus or other parts of the screen visible.

Unfortunately, any bug in the code that causes an error may also cause the program bar or the desktop to become visible. Once this happens, there is almost nothing that a casual hacker can't do to the kiosk. We have had around five such incidents but we have not had any truly destructive hackers. So far, they have been content simply to surf the web or play solitaire. In response, we have added an additional browser window open in kiosk mode behind the kiosk's main window. This means that if the kiosk has an error that causes it to close some module, the user does not have access to the desktop. Instead, another window takes over that does not have any active areas. The numbers of incidents have significantly decreased since this method was put in place. We realize that these measures are not likely to stop a truly knowledgeable and determined hacker, but they have been sufficient up to this point.

5 Future Directions

The current version of the intelligent kiosk serves as a useful prototype for usability analyses and as a test bed for general issues involving speech recognition in noisy environments, natural language understanding from speech, and question answering from incomplete queries. The software which is an amalgamation of Java, C#, C++, HTML, and PHP is modular and extendable with minimal component interaction thus yielding very low coupling and high cohesion. Since each component executes as a separate resource (or process) components can be migrated to additional hardware on the fly. This opens up an interesting research forum for issues related to dynamic resource allocation and recovery from partial failure.

The Intelligent Kiosk is still under development from a number of different directions. The internal workings are being updated to increase the speech recognition accuracy and cosmetic changes are being made to the interface in order to increase user interaction and satisfaction with their experience. From the perspective of speech interaction, a different speech recognition engine will be installed that is specifically designed for speaker-independent recognition.

We are also, as previously stated, in the process of conducting several qualitative and quantitative tests on the kiosk. In addition to determining its general usability, we will also be testing the users' satisfaction with the experience, ease of use, and the implications of using an avatar. Along these same lines, we are interested in how people's reactions and perceptions of the kiosk change with a different gender, voice, and race of the avatar.

Finally, additional installations are being pursued. These might include retail stores, local corporate office buildings, or healthcare institutions. Based on current experience, we would expect these installations could be implemented within three months primarily due to artistic customization.

Acknowledgements

This project was funded by FedEx Institute of Technology Innovation Grants. In addition, many people have contributed to the creation of the Intelligent Kiosk. We would like to acknowledge James Markham from the Intelligent Environments Research Lab (IE-Lab) and Lucas Charles, Austin Hunter, Loel Kim, Kristin Mudd, Susan Popham, and Michael Schmidt from the Center for Multimedia Arts (CMA) at the University of Memphis. We would also like to acknowledge Scansoft for donating the Dragon NaturallySpeaking v8.0 SDK and Smart Technologies Inc. for providing us with an Actalyst touch screen panel at no cost.

References

[1] C. Stephanidis, G. Salvendy, D. Akoumianakis, N. Bevan, J. Brewer, P. L. Emiliani, A. Galetsas, S. Haataja, I. Iakovidis, J. Jacko, P. Jenkins, A. Karshmer, P. Korn, A. Marcus, H. Murphy, C. Stary, G. Vanderheiden, G. Weber, and J. Ziegler, "Toward an Information Society for All: An International R&D Agenda," *International Journal of Human-Computer Interaction*, vol. 10, pp. 107-134, 1998.

[2] J. Cassell, T. Stocky, T. Bickmore, Y. Gao, Y. Nakano, K. Ryokai, D. Tversky, C. Vaucelle, and H. Vilhjálmsson, "MACK: Media lab Autonomous Conversational Kiosk," presented at Imagina '02, Monte Carlo, 2002.

[3] P. Steiger and B. A. Suter, "MINELLI - Experiences with an Interactive Information Kiosk for Casual Users," presented at UBILAB '94, Zurich, 1994.

[4] T. Stocky and J. Cassell, "Reality: Spatial Intelligence in Intuitive User Interfaces," presented at Intelligent User Interfaces, San Francisco, CA, 2002.

[5] J. Gustafson, N. Lindberg, and M. Lundeberg, "The August spoken dialogue system," presented at Eurospeech '99, 1999.

[6] J. Gustafson, M. Lundeberg, and J. Liljencrants, "Experiences from the development of August - a multimodal spoken dialogue system," presented at IDS, 1999.

[7] S. T. Dumais, "Latent semantic indexing (LSI) and TREC-2," in *National Institute of Standards and Technology Text Retrieval Conference*, D. Harman, Ed.: NIST, 1994.

[8] T. K. Landaur and S. T. Dumais, "A solution to Plato's problem: The Latent Semantic Analysis theory of the acquisition, induction, and representation of knowledge," *Psychological Review*, vol. 104, pp. 211-240, 1997.

[9] E. Charniak, *Statistical Language Analysis*. Cambridge, MA: Cambridge University Press, 1993.

[10] A. Sanker and A. Gorin, "Adaptive language acquisition in a multi-sensory device," *IEEE Transactions on Systems, Man and Cybernetics*, 1993.

[11] A. C. Graesser, P. Wiemer-Hastings, K. Wiemer-Hastings, D. Harter, N. Person, and T. R. Group, "Using Latent Semantic Analysis to evaluate the contributions of students in AutoTutor," *Interactive Learning Environments*, vol. 8, pp. 149-169, 2000.

[12] P. Wiemer-Hastings, K. Wiemer-Hastings, and A. C. Graesser, "Improving an intelligent tutor's comprehension of students with Latent Semantic Analysis," in *Proceedings of Artificial Intelligence in Education '99*. Amsterdam: IOS Press, 1999, pp. 535-542.

[13] R. Miikkulainen, "Subsymbolic case-role analysis of sentences with embedded clauses," *Cognitive Science*, vol. 20, pp. 47-74, 1996.

[14] C. Burgess, K. Livesay, and K. Lund, "Explorations in Context Space: Words, Sentences, Discourse," *Discourse Processes*, vol. 25, pp. 211-257, 1998.

[15] Y. Gotoh and S. Renals, "Topic-based mixture language modeling," in *Natural Language Engineering 6*, 2000.

[16] V. Siivola, "Language modeling based on neural clustering of words," presented at IDIAP-Com 02, Martigny, Switzerland, 2000.

[17] L. McCauley, S. D'Mello, and S. Daily, "Understanding Without Formality: augmenting speech recognition to understand informal verbal commands," presented at ACM Southeast Conference (ACMSE '05), Kennesaw, GA, 2005.

[18] S. D'Mello, L. McCauley, and J. Markham, "A Mechanism for Human - Robot Interaction through Informal Voice Commands," presented at IEEE International Workshop on Robot and Human Interactive Communication (RO-MAN), Nashville, TN, 2005.

[19] R. E. Kalman, "A New Approach to Linear Filtering and Prediction Problems," *Transaction of the ASME-Journal of Basic Engineering*, pp. 35-45, 1960.

[20] P. Viola and M. Jones, "Rapid object detection using a boosted cascade of simple features," presented at CVPR, 2001.

[21] "The Intel Open Source Computer Vision Library," vol. 2006: Intel Corp., 2006.

[22] R. J. Wallace, "The Elements of AIML Style," in *ALICE A. I. Foundation*, 2003.

[23] "Galaxy Communicator," The MITRE Corporation, 2006.

Architecture of a Framework
for Generic Assisting Conversational Agents

Jean-Paul Sansonnet, David Leray, and Jean-Claude Martin

LIMSI-CNRS BP 133 F-91403 Orsay Cedex, France
{jps, leray, martin}@limsi.fr

Abstract. In this paper, we focus on the notion of Assisting Conversational Agents (ACA) that are embodied agents dedicated to the function of assistance for novice users of software components and/or web services. We discuss the main requirements of such agents and we emphasize the *genericity issue* arising in the dialogical part of such architectures. This prompts us to propose a mediator-based framework, using a dynamic symbolic representation of the runtime of the assisted components. Then we define three strategies for the development of the mediators that are validated by the implementation of experiences taken in various situations.

1 Introduction

1.1 The Need for Assisted Components and Services

For a few years, the problematics of the Embodied Conversational Agents (ECA) [1,2] stressed on the 'embodiment' feature of the interactive virtual characters and significant progress was made in terms of software architectures [3,4] of course but more especially in terms of: realism [5], dynamicity [6], multimodal expressivity [7], etc. This made it possible to develop, to a certain extent, the credibility of these tools. But their use is however still restrained to auxiliary and/or optional functions in the applications and services because their credibility is not yet sufficient so that designers take any risks of irritation or even of rejection on behalf of the users.

At the same time, one notes a strong and fast evolution in the sociology of the users of computer applications: whereas the initial users were expert users, the current users are *inexperienced beginners* (we will say further 'novice users') who are confronted with a field that they do not grasp but that they are committed to use within their professional or family life: if one considers only the field of the Internet, ordinary users are very numerous (near one billion individuals are connected), and the applications and services are expanding continuously. What complicates even more the problem, is that the use of information and services is more and more *sporadic*: to hold a ticket will be done today on a website and tomorrow on another; to buy a particular product will be made on a specific website, browsed only once by the user... In this new context, current static, instruction manual based, help systems cannot satisfy the requirements of reactivity and dynamicity when confronted to novice users in a situation of failure.

J. Gratch et al. (Eds.): IVA 2006, LNAI 4133, pp. 145 – 156, 2006.

1.2 Assisting Agents

These new needs prompt the revival of the particular issue of the Assisting Agents fully dedicated to the semantic mediation between individuals and computer systems [8]. When a beginner is in a situation of failure in front of an unknown application, the Assisting Agent must carry out three major functions:

The Dialogical Agent: provides the function of *comprehension* [9]: it must be able to grasp the problem of the user. Though it was shown that if individuals prefer to command machines by means of direct GUI interactions (Graphical User Interface), as soon as "things go wrong" natural language becomes the first mode of expression of the user's distress. It is necessary first that the help system should be provided with a textual input (optionally an oral input) making it possible for the user to enter help requests and it is also necessary that the agent should be able to analyze them, with appropriate NLP tools (Natural Language Processing) [10,11,12], in order to transform the natural requests into formal ones.

The Rational Agent: provides the function of *competence* [13,14]: In order to be able to handle the formal help requests, the system must be provided with a dynamic symbolic representation ('at runtime') of the structure and of the operation of the software component that it is intended to assist and it must be able to carry out heuristic reasoning (in the sense of the Common Sense Reasoning community [15,16]) upon this representation in order to answer the users' requests such that the user judges the agent competent.

The Embodied Agent: provides the function of *presence* [17,18]: The expression of the assistance via an anthropomorphic entity restores the trust of the user by the feeling of a 'benevolent presence'. Once regarded as very optional when assistance is given to expert users, this function proves to be crucial in the case of ordinary users and even has proven to be effective (see for example the 'persona effect' of Lester [19] or even the conventional 'chatterbot effect' [20]).

In this paper we discuss the general principles of a framework dedicated to the development of Assisting Conversational Agents (ACA) based on the requirements associated to the three above mentioned functions: dialogism, rationality and embodiment. In section 2, we define the general architecture of our framework and we point out the *genericity issue* at stake. This prompts us to choose a mediator-based solution with three basic strategies. In section 3 we expose the implementation of concrete examples based on the proposed strategies.

2 Architecture Issues

2.1 Organization of the Framework

The general organization of the framework replicates the three main functions of an ACA as shown in figure 1.

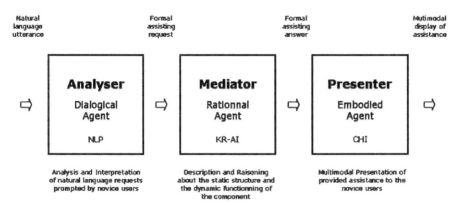

Fig. 1. The framework is based on the conventional sequence of help systems: formalization of the user's request; resolution of the request; presentation of the assistance. The main difference is that the resolution of the request is not achieved directly over the component but over its symbolic representation (called the mediator) which evolves dynamically with its current status.

The framework architecture is composed of three main tools, each one dealing with a specific domain of competence: a) the analyzer is supposed to translate the user natural language request into a formal one, thus dealing with the Natural Language Processing (NLP) community b) the mediator is a *dynamic* symbolic representation of the structure and the functioning of the actual component, on which the rational agent has to resolve the formal request, thus dealing with the Knowledge Representation (KR) and Artificial Intelligence (AI) community c) finally, the presenter has to return the reaction of the agent using multiple modalities as studied in the Computer Human Interaction (CHI) community.

2.2 The Genericity Issue

The three domains of competence involved here point out immediately the multidisciplinary issue that developers of dialogical assisting systems have to beat. Indeed we know that the design of dialog systems can claim already great achievements [10,11,12] but they require huge efforts in terms of NLP expertise, human and implementation time, and they result in complex architectures which are specialized to a given application and cannot be so easily reused.

This is a major drawback for the ACA problematics, because we need to develop assisting systems at the same rate as the development of the new components (that is faster and faster) and at a cost ideally lower than the cost of the component itself (even if we claim that assistance should not be considered optional but on the contrary a first class citizen in the development of applications and services for the public). This issue has been stated by J. Allen since 2001 [9] when he declared that the *genericity of dialogue systems* would be the key to their success in the future. Ideally, a generic dialogue system can be defined as a framework that is not designed for a particular application but a) can be 'plugged' to various applications and b) with minimal linguistic knowledge and minimal adaptation effort for the applications' developers.

These considerations prompted us to propose a two main principles for the handling of the genericity issue in our framework:

P1: A Mediator Based Architecture. The assisting tools do not deal with the application itself but with its symbolic representation. The idea is that developers of software components should need very little NLP competence (ideally none). Developpers need only filling the mediator model in a formal form. Once the model of the component is filled in the mediator (even with a gross model that can be refined incrementally) the ACA is operational and can interact with users: the quality of its assisting service is proportional to the accuracy of the dynamic symbolic representation of the component. We are fully aware that the statement that developers should know little if any NLP sounds like "wishful thinking" but a) we have to do *something* about the genericity problem and discuss solution even considered as ideal b) we don't claim that we have fully implemented this principle; just that it has inspired our architecture.

P2: A 'Gradual Semantic' Approach to the Representation. Then, *depending on the degree of precision the developer wants to provide (or is able to provide) the rational agent with* this representation can be a) variable from rough to accurate in terms of the representing structure and b) variable from static to very dynamic in terms of the synchronization of the status of the variables between the component and the mediator. Actually, in our framework, even if an empty model is provided, the ACA still can work, in a simple "chatbot" mode, because it can handle canonical aspects of conversation (*e.g.* saying *Hello* or *Goodbye*, …) independantly from any application

2.3 Three Mediator Strategies

In this paper, we are mainly concerned with the mediator architecture so we will not discuss the important issue of request handling as stated in principle P2 (see section 3.2 for a quick insight and for more see [21,22]). So our problem can be roughly summarized by two questions:

a) How can we easily develop mediator models for an application? In the following, we propose three strategies for developing mediators ranging from the simplest to the more advanced. They are then experimented in section 3;
b) What is the mediator-based architecture's real impact on the genericity issue? This question will be discussed in section 4 according to the experiences detailed in section 3.

The three mediator-based strategies proposed are as follows:

Post-creation Stitching. The first strategy is dealing with the issue of legacy software, corresponding to the situation where an assistant has to be built for an already existing software component. In this case, the model of the component has to be designed as a separate software entity and we have to face two problems:

— *Post-creation*: The developer of the component must describe the structure and the dynamics of the component in the mediator. This can be viewed as another programming phase, even if it is simpler;

— *Stitching*: At runtime, the variables of the mediator must be synchronized (quite like files can be synchronized between two computers) with their counterparts in the component's runtime. This is achieved by manually installing a "stitching" between the mediator and the component events (see Figure 2).

We have implemented this strategy in our framework. Three examples, corresponding to three variants, are experienced in section 3.1.

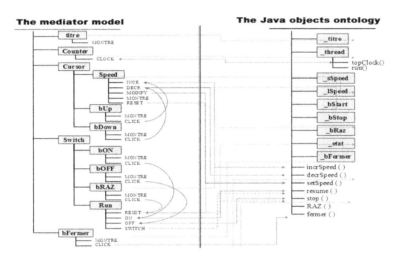

Fig. 2. The stitching diagram, designed for the component "counter" exhibited in figure 3 and detailed in table 1. This figure intends just to give a clue about the fact that developing even a simple model, for an already existing component, can result in *complex interaction maps*.

Model to Component Design. Model ↔ Component stitching is a cumbersome process that can only be achieved manually by competent programmers. In the second strategy we consider the situation where *new* components are to be developed. Hence we can take advantage of more advanced software techniques that are emerging such as the Model Driven Architectures (MDA) [23] where the actual code of the component is automatically generated from a meta model. In this strategy, the programmer designs the component only once, in the mediator modeling language. Then the framework generates a) a symbolic representation for the mediator which is dedicated to the assistance introspection tools and b) the actual runtime of the component. Moreover, this makes it possible to generate the stitching model ↔ component along with the code.

In the current state of work, we cannot generate a complete symbolic model from the meta model because this would say that we can automatically generate symbolic models of computation for any arbitrary software program which remains an open question. Therefore, we have restrained ourselves to a subpart of the components that is both tractable and interesting from the point of view of user-system interaction: its Graphical User Interface (GUI), together with the internal variables that the GUI controls directly (*e.g.* for a `checkbox` its Boolean status, for a `textfield` its string, for a `button` the name of the function that it triggers, …).

We have implemented the GUI part of this strategy in our framework using Mathematica 5.1 as a support for a) the symbolic model b) the NLP handling and c) the automatic generation of Java Swing GUIs. An example is experienced in section 3.2, together with a brief overview of the NLP process involved.

Model to Multi-environment Design. While we have to go deeper into the question of modeling software programs, it appears interesting to make use of our existing meta model approach to deploy components no only for stand alone application (*e.g.* Java-based applications) but also for web-based applications and services which are spreading out very rapidly and which concern mostly novice users. This is the reason why we are currently developing an extension of our framework for website assisting agents which is experienced in section 3.3.

3   Implementation of the Mediator Strategies

3.1   Stitching of Java Applets

The first validation of the mediator strategies has been carried out by developing mediator models for several Java applets, while making use of the stitching technique.

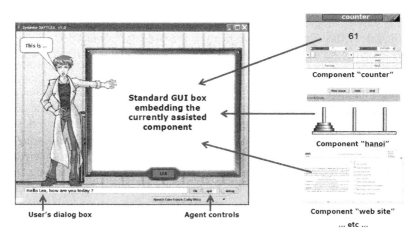

Fig. 3. The assisting framework of the LEA agent. It can embed in the main frame various Java applets. On the right, are the Java GUI of the three examples detailed in the table 1.

Once the symbolic model has been built manually, the applets are embedded into the assisting framework as shown in figure 3.

We implemented <u>three</u> applets (one can see them respectively in the right part of figure 3. from top to bottom) which belong to <u>three</u> different application domains and which were processed according to <u>three</u> different approaches. This has lead to the cross-exploration of a large range of situations, as described in table 1.

Table 1. Cross-exploration of three approaches to Java applet stitching

Component	Domain	Approach
Coco: a simple counter	A Java component provided with autonomous processes (threads). The counting process is controlled by an on/off switch and a cursor for speed.	The mediator and the Java applet are designed and coded at the same time. The mediator reflects exactly the Java objects contained in the application.
Hanoi: a well known game	A Java component functioning in a strictly modal way: if the user does not interact, it does not occur anything.	The Java applet is coded in an independent context then modelled *a posteriori*. The code of the Java applet is filtered in an automatic way in order to be able to send events to the model and to receive orders from the mediator.
AMI: an active web site	The application is a data base displayed as a web service. The user navigates within the base/the site and can update it dialogically.	Here the Java component is limited to the role of display function for the web pages. The site is managed completely in the mediator.

3.2 Generating Swing-Based GUIs from a Symbolic Model

The second mediator strategy is dealing with the automatic generation of the components' code (or part of the code) from its *a priori* description in the symbolic meta model. With regard to arbitrary components, this problem is not yet considered fully tractable; so we made a first attempt in that direction while restricting ourselves to the dialogisation of the GUI part of the components (that is, we model the widgets and the variables that they control – not the inner application functions that remain atomic to the rational agent). The figure 4 shows the developing framework, with the assisting agent answering questions about the structure and the functioning of a simple "Dice game" while being capable of deictic gestures towards the widgets of the GUI.

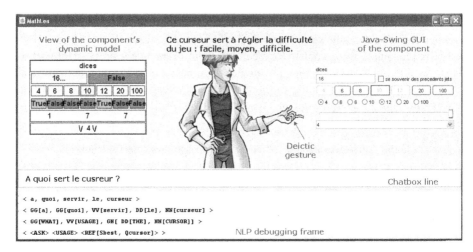

Fig. 4. Screenshot of the developing framework of the "model to component" strategy. On the right is the Java Swing GUI of some "Dice game". It was willingly built to be not intuitive at all so that users are driven to ask questions about it in the chatbox line. Below the chatbox line, there is a debugging frame showing the main phases of the NLP processing of the request (the request "*A quoi sert le cusreur*" is detailed in table 2). On the left, there is a second debugging frame displaying the dynamic status of the symbolic model of the GUI on the right.

The dialogical agent analyzes the utterances of the users in several successive phases summarized (top-down) in the table 2 where CAPITALIZED words are internal semantic markers:

Table 2. Phases of the semantic analysis of assisting requests prompted by the users

Phase sequence	Example
Input utterance	« *à quoi sert le cusreur ? stp* » (what's the use of the cusror please ?)
Possible orthographical or abbreviations correction	" *cusreur* " → " *curseur* " "stp" → "s'il te plait"
Lemmatization	{/a/, /quoi/, /servir/, /le/, /curseur/, /QUEST/, /PLEASE/}
Part of Speech (POS) labelling	{GG[/a/], GG[/quoi/], VV[/servir/], DD[/le/], NN [/curseur/], /QUEST/, /PLEASE/}
Lexical semantic classification of the lemmas	{AT[GG[/a/]], WHAT[GG[/quoi/]], USAGE[VV[/servir/]], DD[/le/], $WIDGET_{CURSOR}$[NN [/curseur/]], /QUEST/, $SPEECHACT_{PLEASE}$[/PLEASE/]}
Global Semantic extraction of the three mains parts of a typical request	SPEECHACT <ASK> PREDICATE <USAGE> ARGUMENT <REF[Sbest, Qcursor]> Sbest=selector THE

The global semantic analysis phase seeks to extract the three main components which appear in formal help requests, according to the following general request format:

$$< < \text{SPEECHACT} >, < \text{PREDICATE} >, < \text{ARGUMENT,}^* > >$$

Speech Act (SA): is the general category of the request, along with [24]. Several SA ontologies have been proposed in dialog systems; here we use a simplified version dedicated to request handling (not dialog handling). In the example, we have: < **ASK** >

Predicate: is an action or a propositional verb or even an attribute. For the sentence given as an example it is the attribute: < **USAGE** >

Argument*.. : zero, one or more Associative Referential Expressions [25], making it possible to locate, via their perceptual properties (indeed *not* their internal programming identifier), the entities involved in the predicate. For the utterance given as an example we will have: **REF[Qcursor]**. It is a reference to any instance, within the application, for which the **Qcursor** predicate takes the value **True**. This referential expression is quite simple but one can find more complex expressions. From the formal request hence obtained, < **<ASK>**, **<USAGE>**, **<REF[Qcursor]>** > > the rational agent must locate, at least, one instance of WIDGET$_{CURSOR}$ in the mediator representation. Then, supposing, as it is the case here, that there is one and only one instance of this kind, it must consult the instance's HELP attribute and produce a multimodal answer. The multimodal answer is expressed through the character-linked modalities and also by optional programmed actions on the model which are in turn mirrored on the application; again, optional deictic gestures by the character can be accompanied by redundant enlightenments of the widgets referred to by the assistant.

3.3 Towards Website Assisting Agents

The third strategy has to do with the idea of automatically generating from a single symbolic description of a component both a stand-alone version (say in Java) and a web version (say in DHTML JavaScript). As the stand-alone deployment has been discussed in the previous section we are concerned here by the web deployment: basically this requires a web server-based architecture with actives pages which is currently implemented. A JavaScript based client version is also accessible to the public at [26] where basic examples of agents interacting both with users and DOM based components are demonstrated.

The figure 5 shows a screenshot of the WebLea site with the four available cartoon-like characters based on the LEA technology developed by Jean-Claude Martin at LIMSI-CNRS [27] in the IST-NICE project [28]. The WebLea agents are dynamically sizable and interchangeable. They can move over and within the pages of a given dialogized website. They can react to natural language users' requests by a) displaying answers in a speech balloon b) displaying popup information c) pointing exactly at the DOM objects of the page d) activating JavaScript programs.

Fig. 5. On the WebLea site [26], one can see and control the LEA agents, displayed on both Mozilla-Firefox and Internet-Explorer navigators. An online "movie" editor for creating animations is available together with a "rule" editor (based on JavaScript RegExpr) for scripting the reactions of the agents to users' questions. The animations are defined in a compact symbolic format and interpreted at the client level making it possible to have a great number of them without bandwidth problems.

The LEA technology is quite simple, being based on animated GIFs body parts, as compared with the state of the art 3D realistic agents of the IVA community (like REA[2], GRETA [17], MAX [3,29], … or even virtual reality systems [30]) but LEA agents can be easily displayed on web pages and they can still express quite a large range of cartoon-like expressions and gestures; this is largely sufficient for *our purpose* which focuses mainly a) on the genericity of our framework so that assisting agents can be easily deployed and b) on the their reasoning capabilities over the components meaning that fine expression of emotions is optional at that stage.

4   Discussion

In this paper, we have first tried to propose the notion of Assisting Conversational Agent (ACA) inheriting its problematics on one side from Human-Machine Dialogue and Reasoning and on the other side from Embodied Conversational Agents. We have claimed that, with the explosion of new components and services and with the explosion of novice users there is a real need for new assisting tools and that ACA can be a user-friendly solution. The second point that we make is that this will not come so candidly: J. Allen and others have discussed the large cost involved in existing dialogue systems and placed the issue of genericity at the core of their actual spreading out. When ACA are concerned, genericity is even more crucial; this is the reason why we proposed a mediator-based architecture where request handling works on a model not directly on the application, making it possible a) to disconnect – to some extent – the NLP world and the programming world and b) to propose a 'gradual semantic' approach of the assistance where the agent can be ranged from a 'daft' chatbot to a 'smart' companion according to the accuracy of the mediator representation.

In section 2, we could not present extensively the internal features of our framework so we focused on the principles and the strategies that we have attempted. In section 3, we developed the presentation of the some implementations of these strategies. According with our experience we can state the three following points:

- The first strategy was implemented in various situations: three applets, belonging to three different domains, processed according to three different approaches. This has proved that, at least for small software components, stitching is tractable and that 'smart' assisting agents can be deployed quite rapidly. However, the third application (an active dialogically editable website) proved to be difficult to maintain in the end, prompting us to the second strategy.

- The second strategy is the most promising for the ACA future. Besides the open question of the full introspectability of arbitrary application code, there is another mental obstacle: conventional programmers consider that dynamic symbolic models are mere gadget applications, "too slow and not professional" but this situation could change with the maturity of web-based scripting (like wikis, active technology,…).

- The third strategy is indeed just an extension of the second one. Our experience with the WebLea site and its good acceptability encourages us to develop our framework in that direction so as to propose webpage assisting agents that are easy to develop and easy to install.

References

1. Cassell, J., Sullivan, J., Prevost, S., Churchill, E., Embodied Conversational Agents, MIT Press. 0-262-03278-3, 2000
2. Cassell J., Bickmore T., Billinghurst M., Campbell L., Chang K., Vilhjálmsson H., Yan H., Embodiment in conversational interfaces: Rea, Proceedings of the SIGCHI conference on Human factors in computing systems: the CHI is the limit, p.520-527, Pittsburgh, 1999
3. Kopp S., Wachsmuth I., Model-based Animation of Coverbal Gesture. Proceedings of Computer Animation (pp. 252-257), IEEE Press, Los Alamitos, CA, 2002
4. Cosi P., Drioli C., Tesser F., Tisato G., INTERFACE toolkit: a new tool for building IVAs, Intelligent Virtual Agents Conference (IVA'05), KOS Greece, 2005
5. McGee D. R, Cohen P. R., Creating tangible interfaces by augmenting physical objects with multimodal language, Proceedings of the 6th international conference on Intelligent user interfaces, p.113-119, Santa Fe CA, 2001
6. Martin A., O'Hare G. M. P., Duffy B. R, Schoen B., Bradley J. F., Maintaining the Identity of Dynamically Embodied Agents, Intelligent Virtual Agents Conference (IVA'05), KOS Greece, 2005

7. Thorisson, K.R., Koons, D. B., Bolt, R. A., Multi-Modal Natural Dialogue. In: Bauersfeld, Penny, Bennett, John, Lynch, Gene (ed.): Proceedings of the ACM CHI 92 Human Factors in Computing Systems Conference, p.653-654, Monterey, 1992

8. Maes P., Agents that reduce workload and information overload, Communications of the ACM, 37(7), 1994

9. Allen J.F., Byron D.K., Dzikosvska M.O., Fergusson G., Galescu L., and Stent A., Towards conversational Human-Computer Interaction, AI magazine, 2001

10. Fergusson G., Allen J., TRAINS-95: Towards a mixed initiative planning assistant. Proc. Conference on Artificial Intelligence and planning systems AIPS-96 Edinburg, 1996

11. Fergusson G., Allen J., TRIPS: an intelligent problem-solving assistant. In Proc of the fifteenth National Conference on Artificial Intelligence AAAI-98, Madison WI, 1998

12. Wahlster W., Reithinger N., Blocher A., SMARTKOM: multimodal communication with a life-like character. In Proc Eurospeech 2001, Aalborg Denmark, 2001

13. Wooldridge M., Reasoning about Rational Agents. MIT Press, 2000

14. Rao A. S., Georgeff M. P., Modeling rational agents within a BDI architecture. In KR'91, pages 473–484, San Mateo, CA, USA, 1991

15. McCarthy J., Hayes P. J., Some philosophical problems from the standpoint of artificial intelligence. In B. Meltzer and D. Michie, editors, Machine Intelligence, volume Volume 4, pages 463–502. Edinburgh University Press, 1969. Reprinted in 1990.

16. Pearl J., Reasoning With Cause and Effect. In Proc. IJCAI'99, pages 1437–1449, 1999.

17. Pélachaud C., Some considerations about embodied agents, Proc. of the Workshop on "Achieving Human-Like Behavior in Interactive Animated Agents", in The Fourth International Conference on Autonomous Agents, Barcelona, 2000

18. Buisine, S., Abrilian, S., Martin, J.-C., Evaluation of Individual Multimodal Behavior of 2D Embodied Agents in Presentation Tasks. Proceedings of the Workshop Embodied Conversational Agents, 2003

19. Lester et al. The Persona Effect: Affective impact of Animated Pedagogical Agents. CHI'97, 1997

20. Laven S., The Chatterbot webpage of Simon Laven: http://www.simonlaven.com/

21. InterViews Project url: http://www.limsi.fr/Individu/jps/interviews/

22. DAFT project url: http://www.limsi.fr/Individu/jps/research/daft/

23. Blanc X, Bouzitouna S., Gervais M-P, A Critical Analysis of MDA Standards through an Implementation : the ModFact Tool, First European Workshop on Model Driven Architecture with Emphasis on Industrial Applications, 2004

24. Searle J. R., Speech acts. Cambridge University Press, 1969

25. Byron D. K, Allen J. F., What's a Reference Resolution Module to do? Redefining the Role of Reference in Language Understanding Systems, Proc. DAARC2002, 2002

26. WebLea site url: http://www.limsi.fr/~jps/online/weblea/leaexamples/leawebsite/index.html

27. Abrillian S., Martin J-C., Buisine S., Algorithms for controlling cooperation between output modalities in 2D embodied conversational agents. ICMI'03, 2003

28. NICE Project url: http://www.niceproject.com/

29. Kopp S., Wachsmuth I., Synthesizing Multimodal Utterances for Conversational Agents. The Journal of Computer Animation and Virtual Worlds, 15(1), 2004.

30. Traum D., Swartout W., Marsella S., Gratch J., Fight, Flight, or Negotiate: Believable Strategies for Conversing under Crisis to be presented at 5th International Working Conference on Intelligent Virtual Agents, September 2005.

A Comprehensive Context Model for Multi-party Interactions with Virtual Characters

Norbert Pfleger and Markus Löckelt

DFKI GmbH, Stuhlsatzenhausweg 3, 66123 Saarbrücken, Germany
{pfleger, loeckelt}@dfki.de
http://www.dfki.de/~pfleger

Abstract. Contextual information plays a crucial role in nearly every conversational setting. When people engage in conversations they rely on what has previously been uttered or done in various ways. Some non-verbal actions are ambiguous when viewed on their own. However, when viewed in their context of use their meaning is obvious. Autonomous virtual characters that perceive and react to events in conversations just like humans do also need a comprehensive representation of this contextual information. In this paper we describe the design and implementation of a comprehensive context model for virtual characters.

1 Introduction

Contextual information influences the understanding and generation of communicational behavior (e. g., [Bunt, 2000]) and it is widely acknowledged that any multimodal dialogue system that deals with more or less natural input must incorporate contextual information. The goal of the work described here is to develop a generic and comprehensive context model that supports the integration of perceived monomodal events into a multimodal representation, the resolution of referring expressions, and the generation of reactive and deliberative actions. Besides the classical linguistic context provided by a discourse history, we have identified sets of physical and conversational context factors that a multimodal dialogue system aiming at real conversational interaction needs to incorporate. Using this extended notion of context, we aim at processing both natural non-verbal and verbal behavior in dyadic as well as multi-party conversations.

We start with describing the VirtualHuman system for which this context model is being developed. Then we outline the key aspect of this model in Sec. 3 and give a brief overview of how we implemented this model for VirtualHuman.

2 The VirtualHuman System

The research reported here has been conducted as part of the VirtualHuman project (see http://www.virtual-human.org/). Our current demonstration system uses multiple virtual characters to enact a story-line for two human users, who can interact with the virtual characters. The system covers different

J. Gratch et al. (Eds.): IVA 2006, LNAI 4133, pp. 157–168, 2006.
© Springer-Verlag Berlin Heidelberg 2006

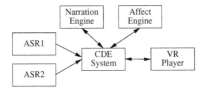

Fig. 1. The architecture of the VirtualHuman system

areas of virtual agent modeling in separate modules. The modules communicate using a blackboard architecture (see Fig. 1).

A dedicated automatic speech recognition (ASR) module is provided for each user to do speech recognition. The *narration engine* module controls the high-level flow of the story by means of *story goals* for each individual character. Depending on the way a goal succeeds or fails, the story can take a different course to match the needs of storytelling. The characters have a representation of affective state which is computed by the *affect engine*. The changes in the world effected by the interaction are rendered by the *VR player*, a real-time 3D player. The CDE system processes the input from the users and the narration engine to generate output for the player.

2.1 The Conversational Dialogue Engines

We use a set of *Conversational Dialogue Engines* (CDEs) where each CDE represents and manages the actions of an individual participant in the scenario. Such a participant may be a virtual character or the representation of a human player. Each CDE acts autonomously in a multi-agent system. Intra-CDE communication is in a uniform format that uses objects that are instances of a dialogue ontology that models all concepts and entities relevant for the system.

Any number of CDEs can be created and removed dynamically by the narration engine during the system run. There are *Character-CDEs* for the former, and *User-CDEs* for the latter type of participant, as depicted in Fig. 2. User-CDEs must interpret the input from ASRs and mouse interactions (delivered from the player) to the internal, ontology-based representation of the system in terms of atomic dialogue acts, while character CDEs must generate a behavior consisting of appropriate steps to realize the story goals, and react to the contributions of users and other characters.

In a Character-CDE, the Fusion and Discourse engine (FADE) takes care to resolve references and maintain the dialog history, while the action manager module is responsible for planning, executing and monitoring character actions with respect to the story goals.

The action manager receives dialog acts from FADE that are enriched (e.g., referring expressions are replaced by their referents) and normalized with respect to the internal representation (e.g., spatial references are in a canonical format). The action manager then uses a combination of planning and dialogue games to devise an appropriate course of action. This allows a highly flexible interaction

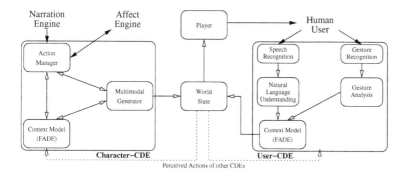

Fig. 2. Abstract architecture of Character- and User-CDEs

since the characters are independent of each other. They can at any time take the initiative in the interaction (however, if some other character is speaking, they must get the floor first). Social conventions in dialogue, such as the obligation to answer a question by another participant, are ensured by the rules of the dialogue games which the characters try to obey. Actions also generate affective events (e. g., a negative event in case of an insult), which are sent to the affect engine. The affect engine uses these events to dynamically compute the emotional state of the characters and informs the action manager about it, which will in turn influence later actions by the affected characters.

The process of action planning was described in detail in [Löckelt, 2005]. It also takes into account the current emotional state of the character, determined by updates from the affect engine; in turn, actions can also be accompanied by emotional events that are sent to the affect engine. FADE will also enrich spoken utterances with accompanying gestures depending on the semantical content, e. g., a pointing gesture may go along with an utterance. The characters will also gaze towards the addressee of an utterance.

2.2   The Scenario of the VirtualHuman Demonstrator

Our current scenario comprises a game show about football (soccer) composed of two stages. The game starts with a football quiz for two human users, a virtual moderator, and two virtual experts. The users are standing in front of a 3D projection of the environment, behind microphone/trackball setups. They are not represented as avatars in the presentation, but can be located relative to the virtual environment because they are at fixed positions. The moderator shows the human contestants short video clips of past football games which are stopped just before the outcome of the scene is revealed, e. g., a player attempts to shoot when the video stops. The contestants then have to judge what happens next or can ask the virtual experts for their opinion. After three video scenes, the moderator gives a final evaluation and declares the winner of this first game phase.

The winner then proceeds to stage two, where she is challenged to put together a lineup for a German national football team with the help of the moderator

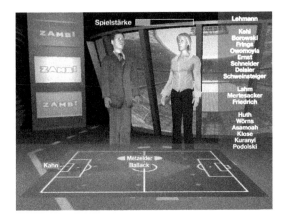

Fig. 3. The graphical representation of the second game stage. The virtual characters are standing in a 3D scenario around the lineup representation showing the player names on a football field.

and one expert (see Fig. 3). From this phase comes an example dialogue that we will use to motivate our work (translated from the German original):

(1) Moderator: *Ok, let's get started.*
(2) User: *Put* [characters gaze at user] *Oliver Kahn up as keeper.*
(3) Expert Herzog: [nods] *That's an excellent move!*
(4) Moderator: [nods] *Great, Kahn as keeper.*
(5) User: *Miss* [characters gaze at user] *Herzog, give me a hint!*
(6) Expert Herzog: [smiles] *I would definitely put Ballack into the central midfield.*
(7) User: *Ok,* [characters gaze at user] *let's do that.*
(8) Expert Herzog: [smiles] (nods) *You won't regret this move.*
(9) Moderator: (nods) *Great, Ballack as central midfielder.*
(10) User: ... [hesitates]
(11) Moderator: [encouraging gesture] *Don't be shy!*
(12) User: *Hhm,* [characters gaze at user] *put Metzelder to Ballack's left.* [. . .]

There are several interesting aspects in this example dialogue. However, we want to focus on those aspects that can only be processed with access to contextual information. Utterance (7) of the user, which is a discourse deictic reference, requires knowledge about what the expert said in the previous turn. Thus, the moderator must integrate this old information with the current utterance of the user. Another example is turn (12) where the user produces a spatial reference to an object in the virtual environment. Here, the receiver must be able to interpret the current organization of the virtual environment in order to be able to determine what location is denoted by '*Ballack's left*'. How these phenomena are processed is discussed in Sec. 4.

Another aspect where contextual information is required is the gazing behavior displayed by the characters (which was not mentioned in the example dialogue for the sake of clarity). Gaze behavior is in multi-party situations frequently used to support the turn-taking process. However, in order to display appropriate gaze behavior, a character must be aware of its own role and the role of the other participants at that moment. The gazes are directed by specifying the 3D position of the dialogue partners (slightly above the microphone position in case of the users).

3   A Comprehensive Context Model for Virtual Characters

Based on the notion of *local context factors* discussed in [Bunt, 2000] we differentiate between five categories of contextual factors that need to be represented in order to be able to deal with the full range of context phenomena:

physical context — objects that are present in the scene and that might serve as potential referents

perceptual context — general events or actions conducted by the other participants; projected/expected actions of the participants

conversational context — current status of the conversation with respect to floor management; current conversational roles of the participants (speaker, hearer, overhearer, eavesdropper)

social context — social roles of the participants

linguistic context — discourse history; including unique representations of referents and a belief system

Important for our approach is the distinction between *interactional* and *propositional* information in contributions (cf. [Cassell et al., 1999]) which require different processing strategies. Interactional information contributes to the structural organization of the conversation as it regulates the exchange of turns, helps to avoid overlapping speech, is used to provide backchannel feedback and supports the identification of the intended addressees of a contribution. Propositional information contributes to the actual content of interaction and needs to be handled in a completely different way.

Based on this distinction we differentiate between two types of context representations that a virtual character in a conversation needs to maintain. The first is the *immediate conversational context* representing the current physical and perceptual context. This immediate turn context serves as a temporal storage for perceived monomodal events that need to be interpreted in their context of use (this approach is derived from [Pfleger, 2004]). The second type is a long-term discourse history representing previous contributions of the participants. This discourse history is used to resolve referring expressions by means of referents derived from accompanying gestures or introduced in the previous discourse.

While interactional nonverbal behavior (such as head nods, gazing, beat gestures) is incorporated into the representation of the immediate turn context, pointing gestures and iconic gestures are incorporated into a discourse model. These latter gestures are typically resolved by a multimodal fusion component, but in our approach they are treated equally to spoken referring expressions.

3.1   The Immediate Conversational Context

The immediate conversational context comprises aspects of the physical context, perceptual context, conversational context, and social context from the perspective of an individual participant of an interaction. The structure of the conversational context is centered around the physical context, the individual participants and their current actions. It also comprises a representation of the conversational roles of the individual characters.

This conversational context also builds the basis for any reactive behavior of the system. All perceived monomodal and so far uninterpreted events are categorized and integrated into this context model. This permits direct reactions to events that are of particular impact for the participant this context representations stands for. If, for example, someone else starts to speak, this is immediately registered in the conversational context which in turn can prevent our participant from unintentionally interrupting the current speaker or even trigger reactive feedback.

Representing Dialogue Participants. The main purpose of the representation of the dialogue participants is to support the generation and interpretation of turn-taking behavior and the identification of the intended addressees. The membership in communal groups, expertise and the social status of a participant also contribute to the processing and generation of dialogue contributions even though in a less direct way than the aforementioned aspects. This information can be used to select appropriate and adapted referring expressions and phrases. Moreover, the perceived emotional state of a participant has also some impact on the interpretation of an utterance (e. g., irony, sarcasm).

The representation of a participant comprises the following aspects:

Name: The participant's first name and last name.
Sex: The participant's sex (i. e., *male* or *female*).
Nonverbal behavior: The currently active nonverbal behavior of that participant.
Position: The participant's position in the scene (i. e., the top-level physical environment).
Emotional state: The perceived emotional state of that participant (if available).
Communal groups: Assumed membership in communal groups (if available).
Expertise: Assumed expertise of the participant (if available).
Social status: Assumed social status of the participant (if available).

Modeling the Conversational Status of the Participants. The conversational status is used to model the current conversational roles of the individual participants. This information is not only useful for the identification of the intended addressee(s) of a contribution, but also for the realization of the character's own contributions. If a character wants to say something, it needs to determine first whether the floor is available. If someone else is holding the floor, the character may decide to display an appropriate turn-request signal.

Current speaker: The current speaker (empty, if the floor is available, i.e. nobody is claiming the speaking turn).
Current addressees: The current addressees.
Current bystanders: The overhearers that are perceived by the speaker and the others as present [Clark, 1996].
Current eavedroppers: The overhearers that are listening without the speaker being aware of it [Clark, 1996].
Previous speaker: The participant that had the previous turn
Previous addressees: The participants that were addressed within the previous turn.

Modeling the Physical Environment. The representation of the physical environment is organized as follows: Each object located in the scene is represented by means of a data structure called *AbsolutePosition*. This AbsolutePosition is represented in our ontology but for now it is sufficient to think of a typed feature structure [Carpenter, 1992] that comprises a set of features. The most important features of this structure are:

Feature *ontologicalInstance*—this feature contains the ontological instance representing the object that is described by an AbsolutePosition.
Feature *coordinates*—this is an optional feature, if the perception components are able to provide two-dimensional or three-dimensional coordinates describing the location of the object with respect to a fixed coordinate system, this slot will contain that information.
Feature *orientation*—this feature describes the current orientation of the object, valid values are: *north, east, south, west*
Feature *northOf*—this feature contains a link to the AbsolutePosition of its northern neighbor (can be empty if there isn't any northern neighbor)
Feature *eastOf*—...

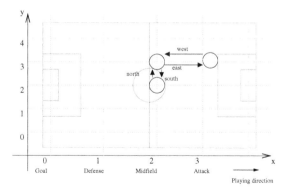

Fig. 4. Example configuration of the physical environment describing the football-field with three players placed on it

This means, each AbsolutePosition that represents an object in the scene also represents the spatial relations the object currently fulfills with respect to the organization of the scene from an absolute point of view (using viewpoint neutral descriptions). See Fig. 4 for an example configuration of the physical environment. Moreover, a physical environment can again contain other physical environments. As in our scenario, the physical environment describing the studio contains a closed physical environment that describes the virtual football field where the line-up is displayed.

3.2   The Discourse Context Model

The discourse context model is used to maintain (i) a sequential representation of the discourse contributions of the individual participants and (ii) an ordered representation of the focused entities introduced into the discourse, the *local focus*. The local focus consists only of those objects that were introduced into the discourse by either spoken utterances or were referenced to by gestures. The model itself is organized in three layers (based on the ideas of [LuperFoy, 1991]): (i) a *Modality Layer* representing the surface realizations of objects, (ii) a *Discourse Object Layer* representing unique objects, collections, or events that were introduced into the discourse and (iii) a *Belief Layer* where the agent's own knowledge (or *beliefs*) and assumptions about the other participants' knowledge are represented. The modality layer consists of three classes of objects reflecting the modality by which the corresponding discourse object was referenced: (i) *linguistic actions*—comprising information like lexical information, number, gender, case and realization time, (ii) *nonverbal actions*—comprising the type of nonverbal action and its start and end time, and (iii) *visual events*—comprising the type of event.

4   Applying the Context Model

A great deal of the context model discussed in the previous section has been implemented in the FADE component of the current version of the VirtualHuman system. FADE consists of two processing layers (see Fig. 5): (i) a production rule system (called PATE; *a Production rule system Based on Typed Feature Structures*) that is responsible for the reactive interpretation of perceived monomodal events, and (ii) a discourse modeler (called DiM) that is responsible for maintaining a coherent representation of the ongoing discourse and for the resolution of referring and elliptical expressions (see [Pfleger et al., 2003]).

Making sense of perceived monomodal events consists of two aspects: (i) interpreting interactional signals in order to trigger appropriate reactions, and (ii) the integration of monomodal contributions that contribute to the propositional content of the turn. The Perception Module distinguishes the incoming monomodal events respectively and updates the immediate turn context and the DiM. Key to our approach is that all processing instructions necessary to interpret the interactional events can be expressed through production rules. The remaining integration task is handled by the discourse modeling subcomponent.

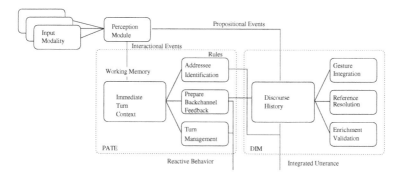

Fig. 5. A schematic overview of FADE and its basic functionality

In the following we will give a short overview of how the general processing strategies for the context dependent phenomena mentioned in Sec. 2.2 are realized.

4.1 Understanding and Generating Turn-Taking Signals

It is crucial for a participant of a multi-party interaction to understand turn-taking signals displayed by the other participants, as well as to display appropriate signals for the other participants. Moreover, timing has a great impact on the naturalness of this behavior. A backchannel feedback that is realized only a little too late might interrupt or at least confuse the current speaker and cause a temporary break-down of the turn-taking system.

For the current version of the VirtualHuman system we focused on the reactive generation of gaze behavior. A participant that perceives, for example, the onset of a verbal contribution of another character usually (but not always) reacts by gazing at the speaker. This is realized by means of a set of specialized production rules of FADE. If appropriate, FADE directly sends a request to the multimodal generator without consulting the dialog manager. The speaker also displays gaze behavior, however, with slightly different intentions. Speakers, in turn, gaze alternately at the participants who they want to address.

4.2 Resolving Discourse Deictic References

The resolution of discourse deictic references requires a comprehensive representation of the ongoing dialogue since not every reference refers to its immediate predecessor. The discourse deictic reference in turn (7) of the example dialogue in Sec. 2.2 is resolved by the characters as follows: First, they access their sequential dialogue history and try to retrieve the last contribution of the character Herzog. Then they need to integrate the proposal of Herzog with the actual utterance of the user.

4.3 Resolving Spatial References

Resolving spatial references depends on the point of view the speaker takes to encode the referring expression. This point of view is called the *frame of reference*

[Levinson, 2003]. The frame of reference a speaker takes directly influences the selection of a particular referring expression, e. g., everything that is on my left is on the right of someone standing in front of me. [Levinson, 2003] distinguishes three main frames of reference: *intrinsic*, *relative* and *absolute*. When using an intrinsic frame of reference, the speaker takes the point of view of the relatum (i. e., the object that is used to locate the target object). In a relative frame of reference, the speaker takes an outside perspective (e. g., his own point of view, or that of someone else). Within an absolute frame of reference, everything is located with respect to the geographic north. While the latter frame of reference is always unambiguous the former two might introduce some ambiguities that need to be resolved.

The resolution of referring expressions involves the following aspects: (i) an up-to-date representation of the physical environment, (ii) knowledge of the currently active type of frame of reference and (iii) a mapping function that converts spatial references to locations or objects in the scene.

In oder to resolve spatial references, FADE first determines the currently activated physical environment and its corresponding active frame of reference and then maps the referring expression to an absolute location. If, for example, the user commands the system to *"Put Metzelder to Ballack's left"*, the system first searches for the current position of the player *Ballack* in the physical environment. Then it retrieves the orientation of that player and maps the referring expression to one of the absolute identifiers. At this point we assume a currently active frame of reference of type *intrinsic*, otherwise the system would need to determine the orientation of the speaker and then compute the mapping. In any case, the mapping function takes the referring expression (*left-of*) and the orientation of the relatum (*eastern*) which would result in an off-set of 1. This means, we need to go *one* neighbor feature further to get the correct neighbor given the orientation. Normally (i. e., if the player would be oriented to the north), left-of would be mapped to the western neighbor, however, in our case we need to go one neighbor further which is the northern neighbor. If the player faces westwards, the mapping function would return an off-set of 3 which means left-of is now the southern neighbor.

5   Conclusion and Future Work

We presented a comprehensive context model for multi-party interactions. We showed how this model is applied in the VirtualHuman system and discussed how three examples of context dependent phenomena are processed within this framework.

Future Work. Even though conversations are organized in turns, this does not mean that only a single participant can speak at the same time. In fact, conversations are characterized by a great amount of overlapping speech without violating the turn-taking protocol. Mostly, this is feedback provided by the listeners/addressees to inform the speaker about their current understanding of the ongoing turn–this is called *backchannel feedback* [Yngve, 1970]. Backchannels can be expressed through both verbal (e.g., *"yes"*, *"ok"*, *"hmm"* etc.) and nonverbal behavior (e.g., head nods, facial expressions, etc.). As [Knapp and Hall, 2002] highlights, those responses can affect the type and amount of information given by the speaker. Another interesting observation is that speakers seem to implicitly request backchannel feedback from their audience as they organize their contributions in so called *installments*—each one separated by a short pause inviting the hearers to give some feedback [Clark and Brennan, 1991].

Currently, the characters display only gaze behavior while someone else is speaking, for the next (and final) version of our system we want to add real backchannel feedback. We plan to add a small component that is able to identify short pauses in the speech signal of the user. The virtual characters in turn will use this information to generate appropriate backchannel feedback (e.g., slight head nods, facial expressions, etc.) depending on their current affective state and their understanding of the conversational state. Moreover, we also plan to extend the backchannel feedback of the characters when another character is speaking.

For the final version of the VirtualHuman system it is planned to integrate an infrared camera based 3D gesture recognition component. This component will be able to detect the location of the user so that the gaze behavior of the characters can be improved but it will also be able to detect some hand and gaze gestures which could be used to improve the turn-taking behavior.

We recently started a formal evaluation of the current system. In this evaluation, naïve subjects are asked to play the game as described in section 2.2 with just as little information as possible. At the end of the experiment, the subjects are asked to fill in a questionnaire with which we hope to get a clearer picture of whether the characters are accepted as a convincing dialogue partner.

All contributions of the subjects are recorded on video for later examination (e.g., we want to annotate the actions of at least some of the participants with the Anvil tool (see [Kipp, 2001])). Given this transcription of the interactions, we plan to update and extend the language models of the ASRs and the corresponding natural language parsers.

Acknowledgements

This research is funded by the German Ministry of Research and Technology (BMBF) under grant 01 IMB 01A. The responsibility lies with the authors.

References

[Bunt, 2000] Bunt, H. (2000). Dialogue pragmatics and context specification. In Bunt, H. and Black, W., editors, *Abduction, Belief and Context in Dialogue*, volume 1 of *Natural Language Processing*, pages 81–150. John Benjamins, Amsterdam.

[Carpenter, 1992] Carpenter, B. (1992). *The logic of typed feature structures*. Cambridge University Press, Cambridge, England.

[Cassell et al., 1999] Cassell, J., Torres, O., and Prevost, S. (1999). Turn Taking vs. Discourse Structure: How Best to Model Multimodal Conversation. In Wilks, Y., editor, *Machine Conversations*, pages 143–154. Kluwer, The Hague.

[Clark, 1996] Clark, H. H. (1996). *Using language*. The Press Syndicate of the University of Cambridge.

[Clark and Brennan, 1991] Clark, H. H. and Brennan, S. E. (1991). Grounding in Communication. In Resnick, L. B., Levine, J., and Teasley, S. D., editors, *Perspectives on Socially Shared Cognition*. American Psychological Association.

[Kipp, 2001] Kipp, M. (2001). Anvil - A Generic Annotation Tool for Multimodal Dialogue. In *Proceedings of the 7th European Conference on Speech Communication and Technology (Eurospeech)*, pages 1367–1370, Aalborg.

[Knapp and Hall, 2002] Knapp, M. L. and Hall, J. A. (2002). *Nonverbal Communication in Human Interaction*. Wadsworth Publishing - ITP.

[Levinson, 2003] Levinson, S. C. (2003). *Space in Language and Cognition*. Press Syndicate of the University of Cambridge.

[Löckelt, 2005] Löckelt, M. (2005). Action Planning for Virtual Human Performances. In *Proceedings of the International Conference on Virtual Storytelling*, Strasbourg, France.

[LuperFoy, 1991] LuperFoy, S. (1991). *Discourse Pegs: A Computational Analysis of Context-Dependent Referring Expressions*. PhD thesis, University of Texas at Austin.

[Pfleger, 2004] Pfleger, N. (2004). Context Based Multimodal Fusion. In *Proceedings of the Sixth International Conference on Multimodal Interfaces (ICMI'04)*, pages 265–272, State College, PA.

[Pfleger et al., 2003] Pfleger, N., Engel, R., and Alexandersson, J. (2003). Robust Multimodal Discourse. In *Proceedings of Diabruck: 7th Workshop on the Semantics and Pragmatics of Dialogue*, pages 107–114, Wallerfangen, Germany.

[Yngve, 1970] Yngve, V. H. (1970). On getting a word in edgewise. In *Papers from the Sixth Regional Meeting*, pages 567–577. Chicago Linguistics Society.

"What Would You Like to Talk About?" An Evaluation of Social Conversations with a Virtual Receptionist

Sabarish Babu, Stephen Schmugge, Tiffany Barnes, and Larry F. Hodges

Department of Computer Science,
University of North Carolina at Charlotte,
4201 University City Blvd,
Charlotte, N.C. - 28262, USA
{sbabu, sjschmug, tbarnes2, lfhodges}@uncc.edu

Abstract. We describe an empirical study of Marve, a virtual receptionist located at the entrance of our research laboratory. Marve engages with lab members and visitors in natural face-to-face communication, takes and delivers messages, tells knock-knock jokes, conducts natural small talk on movies, and discusses the weather. In this research, we investigate the relative popularity of Marve's social conversational capabilities and his role-specific messaging tasks, as well as his perceived social characteristics. Results indicate that users are interested in interacting with Marve, use social conversational conventions with Marve, and perceive and describe him as a social entity.

1 Introduction

Research has demonstrated that Virtual Human Interface Agents are effective in interacting with users and playing an active role in carrying out tasks. However, when deployed in ever present social settings, will users engage the Virtual Human Interface Agent in social conversations, and will users perceive as well as treat the Interface Agent as a social conversational partner?

In several studies, Reeves and Nass have shown that humans often interact with computers as they do with other people, according to social rules and stereotypes with respect to psychosocial phenomena such as personality, politeness, and in-group favoritism [3]. In interpersonal relations, conversation helps people establish and maintain social relationships and accomplish tasks [4]. Anecdotal evidence suggests that people commonly use social conversation such as small talk to help ease the way into conversation [5], help establish common ground [4], and build solidarity or trust [6]. Computer agents that use social dialogue, such as humor and small talk, to affect social relationships are more effective in performing tasks, and are viewed as more likable, competent, and cooperative than those that do not [7]. These conversational elements may help to increase engagement and task performance by improving credibility and positive affect with users.

Several studies demonstrate that virtual humans can influence people through social influence, in mood [8, 9], behavior [8, 9], and task performance (through social

J. Gratch et al. (Eds.): IVA 2006, LNAI 4133, pp. 169–180, 2006.
© Springer-Verlag Berlin Heidelberg 2006

inhibition/facilitation) [10]. Virtual humans also influence communication: people are more inclined to use natural language when interacting with an interface agent, than when interacting with a text-or audio- based system [11]. People also tend to adapt to an agent's voice when interacting with an embodied conversational agent [12], and take the social role of a virtual character into account [17]. However, there are few studies on the social conversational aspects of a virtual human interface agent deployed in an ever-present social setting. With this research, we investigate what social and conversational factors might influence engagement, acceptance of the interface agent's role, and the success of task performance in a public social setting.

Marve was originally built as a prototype embodied agent using our Virtual Human Interface Framework (VHIF), as described in [18]. VHIF combines speech, graphics, voice recognition, and vision technologies with an extensible discourse model. In our previous work, Marve was designed and built as a virtual receptionist with the ability to interact with visitors and lab members to take and deliver messages [18]. Even with his limited capabilities, we noticed that people treated Marve as a social entity, and were inspired to study how additional conversational capabilities might influence people to interact further with Marve, as in Figure 1.

Fig. 1. A user interacting with Marve

In this study, Marve's conversational capabilities featured a subset of context independent social conversation such as entertaining task (telling knock-knock jokes), small talk (talking about current movies), and a social informative task (discussions on the current weather). His role specific goal oriented task was message taking and delivery. We conducted an 18-day study of Marve's interactions, to evaluate:

1. How often did passersby stop and interact with Marve?
2. What was the relative frequency of task-oriented versus social conversation?
3. How successful was Marve in engaging users in both types of conversation?
4. What was the preferred topic of social dialogue (current movies, knock-knock jokes, or the day's weather)?
5. To what extent was Marve perceived and treated as a human-like conversation partner?

2 Related Work

Embodied conversational agents have been in existence for quite some time, and have been built for specific place-related or context-related tasks that use either text input or natural language for dialogue with users. In 1998 researchers at MIT built Gandalf, a communicative humanoid agent to guide planetary exploration [13]. Gandalf's behavior rules for face-to-face conduct are derived from psychology literature on human-human interaction. Rea, built in 2000 at MIT, is a virtual real estate agent [1]. Rea is capable of understanding speech and gesture and is capable of planning multimodal utterances from propositional abstract representations. Rea also keeps a model of interpersonal distance with the user, and uses small talk to reduce interpersonal distance if she notices a lack of closeness with the users [7]. MACK, a project at MIT, gives directions to visitors of the MIT Media Lab based on a repository of user queries and system responses [14]. Valerie from CMU is a virtual receptionist who gives directions based on pre-defined templates [15]. Valerie is displayed on a flat-screen monitor and users interact with her using keyboard input. Raij et. al. examined perceived similarities and differences in experiencing an interpersonal scenario with a real and virtual patient [20]. They found lower ratings on participants' rapport with the virtual patient, and conversational flow, which was attributed to the limited expressiveness of the virtual patient.

The virtual H. C. Andersen system uses spoken and gesture cues to interact with children and educate them about the life and work of H. C. Andersen [16]. The H. C. Andersen system was a virtual museum guide that used fairy tale templates and context specific dialogues templates to interact with users. Max is a virtual museum guide, uses text to interact with children at the HNF museum, a public computer museum in Paderborn, Germany [17]. Max's deliberative component uses domain knowledge and gathers data from users' interruptions in a user model in learning to provide appropriate responses. Analysis of user's dialogue with Max revealed that users constantly engaged Max in a variety of unexpected social conversations such as greetings, farewell, insults, and small talk. Anecdotal observations from research mentioned above provide evidence that an extensive usability study of conversational effects of a virtual human interface agent is needed to investigate social factors that include user's engagement, satisfaction, success, and human-like perceptions of a continuously deployed virtual human interface agent in an interactive social setting.

3 Brief Overview of User's Conversations with Marve

Marve greets all passers-by, and when a user stops to interact, Marve interacts naturally through speech and vision-based gaze tracking. During conversation, Marve first uses his face recognition component to determine if the user is a friend (a user Marve is trained to recognize) or a stranger (an unknown person). Marve then greets his friends with another, more personalized greeting, and delivers any messages that friend may have. If the user is a stranger, Marve asks for his or her name and records it, suggesting that the user should stop by more often (to become a friend).

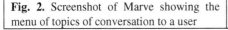

Fig. 2. Screenshot of Marve showing the menu of topics of conversation to a user	**Fig. 3.** Screenshot of Marve telling a knock-knock joke and gesturing a knock to the user

Then Marve asks the user, "What would you like to talk about?" and indicates the topics available through speech and keywords as in Figure 2. If users wish to leave a message with Marve for another user, Marve guides them in conversation through the sequence of interaction necessary to accomplish the task of message taking and delivery. This interaction is described in our previous work on Marve's framework [18]. If a user wishes to engage Marve in a knock-knock joke, then Marve tells them a knock-knock joke (Fig. 3). Marve keeps track of which jokes he has told a particular user so that he does not repeat the same joke to a friend. If a user wishes to discuss the day's weather with Marve, Marve tells the friend about the current weather in interactive conversation and also informs them about the weather update for the next 24 hours. If a user wishes to engage Marve in small-talk on current movies, Marve converses with the user about three current movies with the friend. He uses attributes such as names of the movies, actors, genre, and rating of the movie in small-talk with users. Marve also keeps track of which movies he has talked about with a particular user so that he does not repeat the same topic of conversation with the user. While not interacting with users, Marve mines the web hourly to update his knowledge base for current movies, knock-knock jokes, and, most importantly, the day's weather.

4 Evaluation of Users' Interactions with Marve

In our previous research, we used Marve to evaluate functional aspects of the Virtual Human Interface Framework, including quantitative measures of speed, task performance, and the adaptive ability to recognize new users [18]. In this study, we focus on social interactions with Marve, including types of dialogue preferred by users, percentage of passersby who stop and interact with Marve, Marve's ability to maintain personalized conversation, Marve's ability to understand user's speech accurately, and how quickly the virtual human interface agent responds to the user (responsiveness).

We also measure user perceptions of Marve's human-like characteristics, including appearance, behavior, voice, personality, facial expressions, and gestures. This study was conducted over a period of two and a half weeks (May 3-20, 2005) of Marve's deployment as a virtual receptionist at the primary entrance to the Future Computing Lab at the University of North Carolina at Charlotte. Marve's "friends" were requested to stop by and interact with Marve at least once a day. Objective measures were based on time-stamped log files that were recorded from Marve's dialogue with friends and strangers. Time-stamped images of passers-by and users recognized by Marve's visual perceptual component were also logged. Subjective measures were based on a 23-point survey completed by Marve's users at the end of the study.

4.1 Quantitative Log File Analysis

In this section, we discuss the results from analyzing the log files of interactions with Marve. Table 1 shows the number of times each user (friend or stranger) was in Marve's interaction area during the test period and how many of those times a user stopped to interact with Marve. Table 2 shows the topics chosen by Marve's friends during each interaction.

1. How often did users interact with Marve?
A total of 1,713 times friends and strangers were in Marve's interaction area (i.e., walking in or out of the door by Marve's display). 432 of the 1,713 times (28.74%, S.D. 12.9) the user stopped and interacted with Marve. During the course of the study, the mean number of times each individual user was in Marve's interaction area was 107 (S.D. 76.99), and the average number of times a user stopped to converse with Marve was 27 (S.D. 17.02). The large standard deviations reflect the fact that user interactions with Marve varied significantly by user. For example, some users such as Bonnie, our building custodian, interacted with Marve 53% of the time that she was in Marve's interaction area, while Caroline, a PhD student, interacted only 16.43% of the time.

2. Did Marve engage users in Social Conversations?
Marve's design featured four types of social conversational tasks based on his social role, a useful task (Message taking/delivery), a socially interactive entertaining task (Knock-knock jokes), small talk (based on movies), or providing useful information (discussions on current weather). We wanted to see if the dialogues with the virtual human interface agent bear some resemblance to human-human dialogues, i.e. if Marve is perceived and treated as a human-like conversation partner.

Data from first-time interactions between Marve and his friends showed that 6 out of 15 users preferred to talk about the weather, 5 wanted to hear a joke, 3 left and received messages, and one talked about the movies. This suggests that, when presented with a novel social interface, users were initially inclined to engage Marve in human-like small talk and humor rather than leave and receive messages.

When examining all the interactions with Marve, the data revealed that Marve's friends preferred hearing knock-knock jokes 42% of the time, talking about the weather 20% of the time, talking about movies 18% of the time, and leaving and receiving messages 20% of the time (Table 2). From the data above, Marve engaged his friends in context independent social human-like conversations (small talk elements and entertaining jokes) 80% of the time. Strangers requested Marve to tell a knock-knock joke 50% of the time, discussed the weather 31.2% of the time, and talked about movies and left messages equally 9.4% of the time. Strangers, who can leave but not receive messages, still interacted with Marve for his social dialogue capabilities and most often asked to hear knock-knock jokes.

Table 1. The percentage of times passers-by stop to interact with Marve

Users	Number of times the user passed by Marve	Number of times the user interacted with Marve	Percentage of passbys resulting in an interaction with Marve
Adeel	43	23	53.48%
Amy	266	39	14.66%
Bonnie	90	48	53.33%
Caroline	85	14	16.47%
Cathy	162	42	25.92%
Dong	69	20	23.20%
Jonathan	20	10	50.00%
Larry	107	34	31.77%
Min	40	6	17.50%
Raj	153	23	15.03%
Sab	181	38	21.00%
Steve	210	60	28.57%
Ted	78	25	32.05%
Tiffany	20	5	25.00%
Zack	7	2	28.75%
Strangers	182	42	23.07%
Total	1713	431	
Mean	107.06	26.93	28.74%
SD	76.99	17.02	12.90%

Table 2. Topic choice frequencies for each friend of Marve

Friends	Movies	Jokes	Weather	Messages	Total Interactions
Adeel	10	5	5	3	23
Amy	13	14	8	4	39
Bonnie	6	17	4	21	48
Caroline	0	2	4	8	14
Cathy	4	23	6	9	42
Dong	3	4	9	4	20
Jonathan	1	6	2	1	10
Larry	7	15	7	5	34
Min	2	0	3	1	6
Raj	5	12	4	2	23
Sab	5	16	5	12	38
Steve	11	32	13	4	60
Ted	4	15	5	1	25
Tiffany	1	2	1	1	5
Zack	0	1	1	0	2
Mean	4.8	10.93	5.13	5.06	25.93
S.D.	4.02	9.18	3.18	5.57	17.20
Total	72	164	77	76	389
Percentage of times the topic was chosen	18.00%	42%	20.00%	20.00%	

4.2 Analysis of Surveys from Friends Who Interacted with Marve

At the end of the study period, we surveyed Marve's friends (known users) to understand how his conversational capabilities and other characteristics affected his usability and perceived humanity. The survey, given in Table 3, asks users about the accuracy of speech and face recognition, how they perceived Marve's human-like characteristics, and how engaging and responsive they felt Marve to be. Out of 15 participants, we received 13 completed surveys. The results from our surveys are summarized in the following sections:

a. Marve's Multimodal Input

Most users (12 out of 13) reported that Marve was able to recognize them accurately and consistently by name and was able to carry out personalized conversations effectively. Based on users' feedback on speech recognition accuracy Marve had difficulty recognizing users' speech utterances approximately 17% of the time (S.D. 12.06). One user commented that she had to repeat her commands and phrases to Marve twice about 80% of the time in order for Marve to recognize her commands. We observed that speech recognition difficulties were most common among users with accents or a high pitch of voice. One user mentioned that over time he tried to speak like Marve (entrainment), and then Marve was able to recognize his speech better.

Table 3. User survey, administered to friends at the end of the study

1. Was Marve able to recognize you consistently?
2. What percentage of the time did Marve have trouble understanding what you said?
3. Did you encounter anything pleasing or difficult when interacting with Marve, if so what were they?
4. What aspects of Marve's appearance did you like the most?
5. What aspects of Marve's appearance did you like the least?
6. What aspects of Marve's behavior did you like the most?
7. What aspects of Marve's behavior did you like the least?
8. What aspects of Marve's voice did you like the most?
9. What aspects of Marve's voice did you like the least?
10. What aspects of Marve's personality did you like the most?
11. What aspects of Marve's personality did you like the least?
12. What aspects of Marve's facial expressions and gestures did you like the most?
13. What aspects of Marve's facial expressions and gestures did you like the least?
14. What aspects of Marve's tasks did you like the most?
15. What aspects of Marve's tasks did you like the least?
16. What aspects of Marve were most interesting for you?
17. What aspects of Marve were least interesting for you?
18. On a scale of 1-10, with 10 being very responsive and 1 being lest responsive, please rate Marve's responsiveness?
19. On a scale of 1-10, with 10 being very engaging and 1 being least engaging, please rate Marve's ability to engage you in conversation?
20. What was your favorite topic of conversation with Marve?
21. Why was it your favorite topic of conversation with Marve?
22. Any suggestions for Marve?
23. Other Comments:

---

b. Positive and Negative Affect

In response to questions (3, 6, 7, 10, 11, 16, and 17) on positive and negative affect of users' interactions with Marve, some users (2 out of 13) commented that they found Marve's suggestions on movies *pleasing* and *interested* them in further conversations with Marve. Some users (4 out of 13) suggested that his polite greetings and good bye were pleasing. One user wrote that, *his final words at the end of a conversation (for example: "Good Luck with everything!")* were *pleasing* and *fun*. Some users (3 out of 13) reported that his smiles and positive facial expressions were pleasing as well. Two participants mentioned that they were *excited* to receive messages and acknowledgments personally delivered by Marve. Two users stated that they found Marve's *accurate* weather forecasts on an hourly basis most *interesting and useful* and found him to be a reliable source for *timely weather information on the go*. However, a group of users (4 out of 13) commented that the occasional inability of Marve to provide them with feedback when their spoken utterance was not recognized by the speech recognition component was sometimes "annoying" and "frustrating". A total of 13 positive comments, compared with only 4 negative comments, indicates that overall, users perceived Marve in a positive light.

c. Human-Like Appearance
In response to questions (4, 5, 8, 9, 12, 13, 16, and 17) regarding the appearance of the virtual human interface agent, a group of the responses (6 out of 13) indicated that users *liked* Marve's facial expressions, including *lip and eye movements*. One user commented that she liked Marve's eyebrow movements and said they were *effective in communicating emotion* and *seemed real*. Some users (2 out of 13) claimed that his expressions and gestures seemed *slightly unnatural* or *a little robotic*. Two users remarked that Marve was *pleasant to talk to due to his realistic expressions* and two users liked the familiarity of the UNC-Charlotte logo on his shirt.

d. Marve's Personality and Behavior
In response to questions (6, 7, 10, 11, 16, and 17) regarding the behavior and personality of the virtual human interface agent, most users (9 out of 13) responded that they liked Marve's *polite social human-like behaviors* such as his *expressions, congenial smiles,* and *hand waving when greeting and saying goodbye*. Three users mentioned that his human-like greetings were *engaging and polite*. Four users mentioned that his *courteous* feedback such as, *Sorry, I misunderstood* when Marve's speech recognition component failed to recognize a user's speech input accurately, was *kind, respectful,* and *nice*. Two users mentioned that they liked the fact that Marve, *suggests things for you to talk about*, and *doesn't just start talking about something that you might not be interested in*. One user mentioned that she liked the fact that the nods conveyed understanding in a *quick* and *direct* way.

Many users (8 out of 13) found Marve's habit of presenting the list of topics after each interaction somewhat *repetitive, irritating,* and *predictable*. Two users commented that the inability to interrupt Marve during the discourse to provide a response immediately was *somewhat cumbersome at times*. Three users commented that they liked Marve's ability to maintain gaze in conversation with his human interlocutor, and that it made Marve seem *real, focused, attentive, believable,* and *human-like*. One user commented that Marve *talked too much*, and that he should *respond more*.

These comments suggest that Marve's interactions can be improved with a few simple techniques, such as allowing interruptions, and not presenting the topics for conversation to Marve's frequent visitors.

e. Self-reported Topics of Dialogue Users Enjoyed in Social Conversations with Marve
When asked about the type of social conversational topic users found most satisfying in interacting with Marve (questions 14, 15, 20, and 21), four users reported that they liked the useful task of messaging the most as it was *highly interactive* and *collaborative* with the virtual human. Four users reported that they liked the knock-knock jokes the most, since they were *entertaining, different each time,* and *engaging*. Three users reported that they liked to talk about movies, since it was *very entertaining*, and *fun*. One user said that Marve helped her plan her weekend activity

with his *good suggestions* on movies to watch. Two users liked talking with Marve about the weather, and reported that Marve's weather forecasts were *reliable, accurate, very useful,* and *easy to get as he is always there.* They further reported that Marve was engaging because his *valuable up-to-the-minute weather forecasts* made them to *stop-by more often to chat with Marve about the weather.* One user disagreed and said that the small-talk based on the weather *was informative, but not as much interactive* and hence didn't find it as *engaging as other conversation topics.* Two users mentioned that the conversation about movies was the least interesting as it was *too informative and not enough interactive.* In general, most users expressed a strong preference for one or more of Marve's social conversational topics, although the preference varied from user to user.

f. Overall Perceived Responsiveness and Engagement

It is important that Marve responds to users immediately and provides feedback in an appropriate manner. We requested users to rate how responsive they perceived Marve to be (question 18) on a scale of 1 to 10 (1 = least responsive, 10 = most responsive). Users also rated how engaging they perceived Marve to be (question 19) on a scale of 1 to 10 (1 = least engaging, 10 = most engaging). We also wanted to measure overall how well Marve engages users in conversations, and how effective Marve is in promoting interactions and carrying out conversations. The mean rating of perceived responsiveness of Marve was 7.85 (S.D. 0.88), and the mean rating of perceived engagement of Marve in conversation with users was 7.74 (S.D. 1.47). Overall, most users found Marve both engaging in social conversations and responsive to feedback.

g. Bonnie

Marve is deployed as a virtual receptionist at a research lab. As a result most of our users are people with above average computer usage. However, one unexpected user, with almost no computer usage background, started to interact with Marve and gradually became his friend over a number of visits. Bonnie, our building custodian, began talking to Marve on her visits to the lab. We believe Marve's interactions with Bonnie provide us with insights on the impact of a 3D Virtual Human Interface on users with little to no computer experience.

On average Bonnie interacted with Marve more often than most of the other users. Fifty-three percent of the times (90 pass-bys, 48 interactions) she passed by Marve Bonnie stopped and interacted with him. Bonnie enjoyed leaving messages with Marve for others in the lab the most (43.75% of the time), and Marve also engaged Bonnie in a knock-knock joke 35.4% of the time. Log files indicate that she introduced Marve to several of her friends at 13 different occasions over the course of the study. In her response to the usability survey, she describes him using human-like concepts such as *pleasant, very respectful,* and *kind.* Bonnie's favorite characteristic of Marve was his greeting, and wrote *how nice, he starts out by saying hi, you look nice today.* In response to questions relating to his personality, she mentioned that she likes *the smiles and facial expressions (especially when saying a joke), and the way he looks at me straight when talking to me.* Apart from leaving and receiving messages, Bonnie also liked *hearing jokes and playing along with Marve on knock-knock jokes.* In response to how engaging she felt Marve was, she commented that Marve *holds your attention and became a part of my daily work* and reported *you look forward to seeing him, he has nice things to say.*

4.3 Anecdotal Results

In order to see if Marve was treated as a human-like conversation partner we also collected and analyzed observations of conversations between users and Marve. These observations revealed to us that users often reciprocate when Marve greets them. Users often respond to his greetings by saying "Hi, Marve", or often say "Goodbye Marve" before disengaging in conversations with him. Users also wave at him when saying hello or saying goodbye. Our observations also revealed that users often comment back at Marve by saying "Thank you" when Marve performs an act that users appreciate, such as providing acknowledgements of messages delivered or giving a forecast for the next day. Hence, our observation suggests that people often use human-like strategies such as greetings, farewell, and "commonplace phrases" in conversations with Marve.

4.4 Lessons Learned from the Usability Study

The following bullets summarize lessons learned regarding the social conversation affects of Marve:

- Although users were requested to interact with Marve only once a day for 18 days, on average each user interacted with Marve 27 times, and stopped to interact more than a fourth of the time he passed by. These data suggest that a socially situated greeting and interacting virtual human interface agent was successful in engaging in conversations with his human interlocutors.
- Apart from interacting with Marve for his role specific capabilities such as message taking/delivery and announcements, users also perceived and treated him as a human-like conversation partner and interacted with Marve significantly in social conversations such as small-talk based on movies, discussions on the weather, and telling knock-knock jokes, Marve was able to engage his friends in social conversations 80% of the time.
- Our research also suggests that entertaining conversations (such as the use of humor) initiated by the virtual human interface agent in a social setting may play a major role in the ability to engage users in social conversations with the virtual human. 50% of the human-like social conversations between users and Marve were on knock-knock jokes. Hence, Marve was able to effectively engage known as well as unknown users to play along in a knock-knock joke.
- Marve's ability to provide useful information such as his up-to-the-hour report on the weather and his forecasts for the next 24 hours, although not as interactive as the other topics of conversation, was very popular with his friends. Thus, when provided with the ability to provide useful information such as the weather update upon request, the virtual human does engage users in conversation in those informative types of dialogues as well. Based on the usability surveys, users who preferred to gain information from Marve, perceived him as *trustworthy*, *accurate*, and a *reliable* entity.
- Judging by the responses gathered from the surveys, a significant majority of users show high levels of attributions of sociality to Marve, by describing him as *polite*, *kind*, *respectful*, *courteous*, *focused*, *attentive*, *sincere* etc. All of these descriptions are attributes used to describe and evaluate a real person, suggesting that when presented with a virtual human interface, users are inclined to employ social factors that are used in interpersonal interactions in human-virtual human interactions.

5 Conclusion and Future Work

We have described a study on the social conversational behaviors of a continuously deployed real-time virtual human interface agent in a social setting interacting with real users. Marve's cognitive and behavioral capabilities include a variety of different context independent conversational capabilities to mimic human social dialogue including discussions about current weather, small talk on current movies and humor (telling knock-knock jokes) in an interactive social setting (virtual receptionist), along with his role specific capacities (message taking/delivery). We performed a study to determine if users would engage Marve in social conversations and in our efforts we looked at a narrow subset of social conversational behaviors which included social dialogue in addition to role-specific task oriented behavior of taking and delivering messages. Results of our study suggest that the virtual human interface agent was able to engage users in social conversations in informative, entertaining or context independent human-like social dialogue a significant amount of the time. Judging from the surveys, the majority of users enjoyed social conversations with Marve, and perceived Marve as a human-like conversational partner. Anecdotal evidence also indicates that users tend to treat Marve as a human-like conversational partner. Although our surveys evaluate a wide range of human-like social attributes and characteristics, based on the results we intend to explore some of these factors such as personality, positive and negative affect, in greater depth in further studies.

Our findings suggest that people will use virtual human interfaces and are comfortable using human-like communication protocols with them, such as greetings, goodbyes, small talk elements, and obtaining information through conversation. As found in other studies, Marve's users perceive and react to the virtual human as they might with a real person. Data from one non-technical user of Marve yields highly promising evidence that non-technical audiences may benefit greatly in engagement, satisfaction, enjoyment, and user-friendliness of virtual human interfaces. This suggests that these interface agents may be particularly effective in reaching diverse non-technical audiences.

One of the limitations of our study was that the majority of our users were a technologically savvy sample of computer scientists working in our research lab. Hence, we plan to further investigate the impact of virtual human interface agents on a more diverse audience by deploying a version of Marve as a virtual receptionist near the main entrance of a frequently visited building on campus. We also plan to investigate factors, in addition to social conversation, that might enhance trust, engagement, and successfully support the development of social relationships between virtual human interface agents and people in a social setting. Psychological research suggests several enhancements, such as a strategy of using self-disclosures from time to time, or laughing at users' jokes, that may increase users' perceptions of friendliness, attraction, and competence, which may result in greater satisfaction and engagement with the virtual human interface.

References

1. Cassell, J.: Embodied conversational interface agents. Communications of ACM 43 (2000) 70-78.
2. Takeuchi, Y. and Katagiri, Y.: Social Character Design for Animated Agents. RO-MAN99 (1999).
3. Reeves, B. and Nass, C.: The media Equation: how people treat computers, televisions and new media like real people and places. Cambridge, Cambridge University Press (1996).
4. Coupland, J., N. Coupland, et al.: "How are you?": Negotiating phatic communion. Language in Society 21: 207-230.
5. Schneider, K. P.: Small Talk: Analysing Phatic Discourse. Marburg, Hetzeroth (1988).
6. Wheeless, L. and Grotz, J.: The Measurement of Trust and Its Relationship to Self-Disclosure. Human Communication Research 3(3): 250-257.
7. Bickmore, T. and Cassell, J.: "How about this weather?" Social Dialog with Embodied Conversational Agents. Proc. Of AAAI Symposium on Socially Intelligent Agents (2000).
8. Rickenberg, R. and Reeves. B.: The effects of animated characters on anxiety, task performance, and evaluations of user interfaces. Letters of CHI 2000 (2000), 49-56.
9. Kramer, N. C., Tietz, B. , Bente, G.: Effects of embodied interface agents and their gestural activity. In: T. Rist et al. (eds.): Intelligent Virtual Agents. Springer (2003) 292-300.
10. Zanbaka, C., Ulinski, A., Goolkasian, P., and Hodges, L. F.: Effects of virtual human presence on task performance. Proceedings of the 14th International Conference on Artificial Reality and Telexistance (ICAT 2004). 174-181.
11. Kramer, N. C., Bente, G., and Piesk, J.: The ghost in the machine. The influence of Embodied Conversational Agents on user expectations and user behavior in a TV/VCR application. IMC Workshop 2003. 121-128.
12. Oviatt, S., Darves, C., and Coulston, R.: Toward adaptive Conversational interfaces: Modeling speech convergence with animated personas. ACM Trans. on CHI, 3 (2004) 300-328.
13. Thorisson, K.: Real-time decision making in multimodal face-to-face communication. Proceedings of the Second International Conference on Autonomous Agents, Minneapolis, MN (1998) 16-23.
14. Cassell, J., Stocky, T., Bickmore, T., Gao, Y., Nakano, Y., Ryokai, K., Tversky, D., Vaucelle, H., and Vilhjalmsson, H.: MACK: Media lab Autonomous Conversational Kiosk. Proc. of Imagina, (2002).
15. http://www.roboceptionist.com
16. Bernsen, N. O., and Dybkjaer, L.: Domain-Oriented Conversation with H. C. Andersen. Affective Dialogue Systems (2004).
17. Kopp, S., Gesellensetter, L., Kramer, N. C., and Wachsmuth, I.: A Conversational Agent as Museum Guide – Design and Evaluation of a Real-World Application, Intelligent Virtual Agents, (2005) 329-343.
18. Babu, S., Schmugge S., Inugala, R., Rao, S., Barnes, T., and Hodges, L. F.: Marve: A Protoype Virtual Human Interface Framework for Studying Human-Virtual Human Interaction. Intelligent Virtual Agents, (2005) 120-133.
19. Isbester, K., and Doyle. P.: Design and Evaluation of Emboided Conversational Agents: A Proposed Taxonomy. AAMAS Workshop: Embodied Conversational Agents (2002).
20. Raij, A., Johnson, K., Dickerson, R., Lok, B., Cohen, M., Stevens, A., Bernard, T., Oxendine, C., Wagner, P., and Lind, D. S.: Interpersonal Scenarios: Virtual ~ Real? Proc. of IEEE Virtual Reality 2006 (VR 2006), Alexandria, USA, (2006) 59-66.

Gesture Expressivity Modulations in an ECA Application

Nicolas Ech Chafai[1,2], Catherine Pelachaud[1],
Danielle Pelé[2], and Gaspard Breton[2]

[1] University of Paris 8
[2] France Télécom R&D
{n.chafai, c.pelachaud}@iut.univ-paris8.fr
{danielle.pele, gaspard.breton}@francetelecom.com

Abstract. In this paper, we propose a study of co-verbal gesture properties that could enhance the animation of an Embodied Conversational Agent and their communicative performances. This work is based on the analysis of gesture expressivity over time that we have study from a corpus of 2D animations. First results point out two types of modulations in gesture expressivity that are evaluated on their communicative performances. A model of these modulations is proposed.

Keywords: Non-verbal and expressive behaviours, annotation, evaluation methodologies, 2D and 3D animations.

1 Introduction

One of the goals of Embodied Conversational Agents (ECA) systems is to determine a model able to generate a communicative and an expressive multimodal behaviour. That is, which factors of gaze, speech, posture, gesture, etc., are meaningful to a user, and how to modelize these factors to generate meaningful animations,

The work we describe in this paper proposes a study of one of these factors: co-verbal gesture expressivity. Our protocol is to follow three main steps of study: first, we process an annotation of a video corpus that provides the data for analysis; then, these data are analysed and provide results; these results are finally evaluated on subjects. Figure 1 gives a more precise overview of the different steps.

We base this study on a corpus of traditional animations that display an expressive behaviour during a conversational interaction. From this corpus, we annotate gesture expressivity (Hartmann et al., 2005), and extract some rules that describe the modulations of these parameters over time. We do not look whether a particular expressivity is displayed, but how this expressivity varies. We performed an evaluation study to measure the effects of these rules on subjects. These rules serve to enrich gestures with expressivity modulations in a conversational animation, described in APML format. Using Greta system (Poggi et al., 2005), ECA animations are generated from these descriptions, and evaluated.

J. Gratch et al. (Eds.): IVA 2006, LNAI 4133, pp. 181 – 192, 2006.

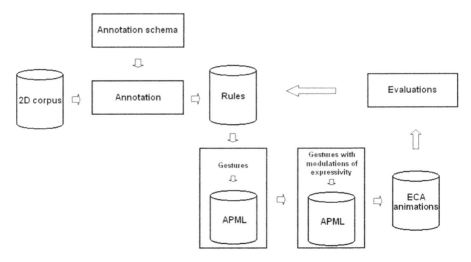

Fig. 1. From 2D animations to ECA animations endow with gesture expressivity modulations

We introduce this work in the two following sections. Part 2 describes the annotation procedure and analysis. In part 3, we detail the evaluation study and propose a model to implement the modulations of gesture expressivity in an ECA system.

1.1 Background

We are currently developing an embodied conversational agent ECA endowed with an expressive and a communicative behaviour (Hartmann *et al.*, 2005; Poggi & Pelachaud, 2000). Our aim is to endow this ECA animation system with the capability to elicit the interest of a user in an ECA animation. At the gesture level we have to set which gestures provide semantic informations (Kendon, 2004), and which gestures attract the gaze of the other interactant: as Cosnier said in preface of Calbris (2003), there is gestures that carry a meaning, and gestures that manage communication and have a pragmatic function.

We focus our study onto gesture expressivity and this expressivity varies over time in the traditional animations. These animations provide an expressive and a relevant corpus for the analysis of movement and in particular for gesture animation. The state of the art gives a first view onto this relevance of traditional animations for the animation of 3D virtual characters. We also investigate how gesture expressivity properties can act as a pragmatic tool during a conversational interaction. Our hypothesis is that gesture expressivity modulations could partly play this role. These modulations could provide, by a sudden change in the perceived behaviour of the speaker, some of her intentions to the listener.

1.2 State of the Art

Some previous works already tried to produce 3D animations based on traditional animations. Several fundamental principles of traditional animation (Thomas &

Johnston, 1981) have been applied to 3D animation: Choi *et al.* (2004) proposed a system able to computationally apply the principle of anticipation onto a 3D animation: through the production of a backward movement over the following movements, this principle leads to direct the spectator's attention towards the place of the action. Lance *et al.* (2004) studied animators' abilities to express emotion and empathy in cartoon characters, and built up a system able to generate an expressive gaze for a virtual character. Bregler *et al.* (2002) captured the animations of 2D objects (deformable or not) by following some feature points; this follow-up allows one to animate in the same way different kinds of 2D or even 3D objects. Not only the movement is identically produced, but it also preserves the same expressivity. But theses works do not resolve the question whether imitating 2D animation in 3D animation is perceptually acceptable by a spectator or not. Lasseter (1987) pointed out how the principles from 2D animation could be successfully applied in 3D animation; however the perception that the spectator has could change if we limit 3D animation to a 2D imitation and if we do not look at finding to which extent the 2D animation principles could be interpreted.

In the domain of human gesture study, there exists some works dealing more specifically with the gesture ability to attract listener's attention. Eye tracking techniques allow the researchers to follow where and when a listener gazes at, and in particular on which gestures he gazes at. This type of disposal was adopted by Gullberg & Holmqvist (1999) to study which are the elements that lead to gaze at a particular gesture; the laterality of a gesture seems to play a preponderant role, as opposed to self centred gestures. With the same kind of disposal, Barrier *et al.* (2005) have determined that through the use of deictic signals, a speaker is able to redirect listener's focal attention toward her gesture, or toward a virtual space built by her gesture. In cartoons (Thomas & Johnston, *op. cit.*) noticed how efficient is an animation that could be understood from its silhouette; this observation complements results from Gullberg & Holmqvist by adding a notion of point of view: a same body gesture can change silhouette type depending from where we are looking at it.

Our work aims at determining new criteria that could enhance the spectator's interest through some kinds of gesture expressivity properties, and to implement these criteria in an ECA. Rather than to measure which are the gestures that attract the gaze of the spectator – that do not imply directly that this gesture has an efficient communicative or expressive impact – we prefer to follow the first approach and to base our study on traditional animations that provide subjective data on the expressive performance of gestures.

2 Corpus Annotation

Our approach is based on the analysis of traditional animations: animators have developed sharp skills over decades in eliciting empathy and in regulating attentional behaviour of the spectators through the character's movements and expressions; we aim at taking into account these skills to develop our application.

To get precise data onto gesture expressivity modulations, we annotate each expressivity parameter defined in Hartmann *et al.* (*op. cit.*), not at a gesture unit or phrase level, but at a gesture *phase* level. We describe our choices for each of the annotated parameters.

2.1 Corpus

We base our corpus on two videos from Tex Avery cartoons (MGM). Each of these videos lasts about ten seconds. Our choice of a low level of analysis (described later) leads to a corpus with little data. In regard of our aim to animate conversational agents, we chose two sequences showing a conversational interaction between characters; the first one serves as basis for our analysis, the second has been used to verify the results from the first one. One of these videos comes from the cartoon Blitz Wolf (1942, Figure 2a): it displays a pig character trying to convince two other pigs to protect their selves against a wolf's threat[1]. The other video comes from Henpecked Hoboes (1946, Figure 2b): in this cartoon, the main two characters are George and Junior[2] who are trying to catch a chicken to feed their selves; in the sequence that we are interested in, George explains to Junior the set of actions they will have to perform to reach their goal. These two sequences exhibit two different discourse goals: in the first one the pig aims to incite and advice; in the second one George aims to communicate some information.

Fig. 2. (a and b) Captions of annotated videos

2.2 Annotation Schemas

To get precise data on the modulations of gesture expressivity, we annotate the expressivity on a gesture phase level. Kendon defines gesture unit, gesture phrase,

---

[1] Produced right in the middle of WW2, this cartoon is a short propaganda film: the animators are displaying Big Bad Wolf under A. Hitler's features and are warning how dangerous he is. The main pig figures the judgement value of the American state. Animators are figuring this pig to display to American people what kind of behaviour they have to adopt towards WW2: they have to support war effort. Obviously, the title of *Blitz Wolf* directly refers to the "Blitz Krieg" practised by Hitler.

[2] Refers to George and Lennie characters from J. Steinbeck's novel "Of Mice and Men" (1937).

and gesture phase, as three different levels in the gesture production (2004, chap. 7). There are different types of gesture phase; Kendon organizes them around the phase of stroke that is recognized as the expressive part of the gesture: preparation, stroke, post-stroke-hold, and recovery. Kita *et al.* (1997) refine these phases and distinguish: preparation, stroke, hold and independent hold, retraction, and partial retraction.

In our analysis, we are using most of the phases described by Kita *et al.* For sake of simplicity we consider 'independent hold' as having the same function as 'hold'; no distinction in both terminologies is made. And we add the phase of anticipation: it refers directly to one of the fundamental principles of animation as described in Thomas & Johnston (1981); from our point of view it seems necessary to add this phase in the analysis. Thus, we consider the following set of gesture phases (Kita *et al.*, *op. cit.*, Kendon, *op. cit.*, Kipp, 2003):

- *anticipation*: preceding a gesture phase, the arm may produce a backward movement. This happens due to motor constraints, but also to get spectator's attention focusing on the following movement;
- *preparation*: the arm moves to the location where the speaker wants to produce his stroke;
- *stroke*: expressive phase of gesture, it is produced synchronously or anticipates the verbal referent;
- *hold*: the stroke may be hold for a while;
- *recoil*: following the stroke, the arm may recoil to emphasize this stroke;
- *retraction*: the arm moves to a rest position;
- *partial retraction*: before the arm finishes moving to a rest position, another gesture starts and thus ends up the retraction.

The expressivity parameters we chose for our annotation are those implemented by Hartmann *et al.* (2005) in their conversational agent GRETA. They correspond to: fluidity is the smoothness and continuity of overall movement (*e.g.* smooth, graceful versus sudden, jerky); power is the dynamic property of the movement (*e.g.* weak/relaxed versus strong/tense); spatial extend is the amplitude of the movement (*e.g.* amount of space taken up by body); repetitivity is the repetition of the stroke.

Three values are available for each parameter: positive, neutral, negative. And we define parameters with a set of criteria:

- *fluidity*: it corresponds either to the level of continuity between successive phases, or to the movement curvature, or even to the presence of an anticipation phase;
- *power*: it stands for the shape opening (opened / closed), or the acceleration of the arm, or even for the continuity in tension at the end of the movement;
- *spatial expansion*: we define it as the gesture space, or the swivel angle, or even as the point of view from which the gesture is seen *i.e.* with a high or a low silhouette (Thomas & Johnston, *op. cit.*);
- *repetitivity*: repetition of the gesture stroke.

Both analysed videos are annotated using the tool Anvil (Kipp, *op. cit.*), which allows us to precise each value of expressivity parameter for each of the gesture phases.

2.3 Hypothesis

We have annotated for each gesture of our corpus the value of each expressivity parameter. When analysing the data we do not consider the annotated value of each parameter as such but we look at the variation over time of these values. On the one hand we try to find some kinds of correlations between these modulations and the production of the corresponding gesture. On the other hand we try to find some correlations between these modulations and the structure of the verbal utterance, in order to observe if there is any regularity in it. This analysis is based on one of the two annotated videos; the second is used to verify the results we obtain. We observe two types of variations that are found over each expressivity parameter. We, now, consider no more the value of each expressivity parameter but these variations which are:

- *irregularities*: it corresponds to a brief period of time (a single gesture phase) in which the annotated modality has a sudden change of value, and then comes back to the original one just after this phase. For example, it happens when a character produces a powerful sequence of movements, except for a single phase that is produced with a low power (Figure 3a);
- *discontinuities*: it corresponds to a sudden change in the annotated modality. For example, it happens when a character of the animation produces a sequence of movements with a low power, succeeding to a sequence with powerful movements (Figure 3b).

That is, each time a sudden variation in gesture expressivity occurs, it is defined as a discontinuity; but if this variation directly precedes another sudden variation we will speak in terms of irregularities. Figure 3 illustrates graphically these concepts.

Each occurrence of these two modulations types has been noticed[3]: (4; 8) for irregularities, and (10; 6) for discontinuities. Some invariance appears to inform on their role in a conversational interaction in a cartoon, as described in the following sections. There are differences in results quantity of the two videos; this is partly due to a difference in the quantity of gesture repetitions for each video and the structure of their utterances.

The functions of irregularities

From the annotation, we observe that irregularities seem to play a role of anticipation by linking similar elements of the enunciative structure as: occurrences of gesture repetitions (2; 7), performatives of a same general class (Poggi & Pelachaud, 2000) (1; 1), gesture phrase (1, 1).

---

[3] In the form (2; 3), we indicate that in the analyzed video there were two occurrences of a modulation type involved in a particular property, and three occurrences in the video used to verified results.

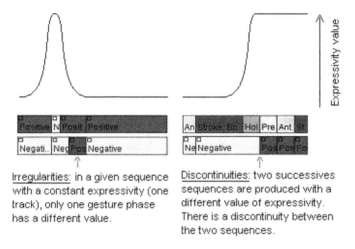

Irregularities: in a given sequence with a constant expressivity (one track), only one gesture phase has a different value.

Discontinuities: two successives sequences are produced with a different value of expressivity. There is a discontinuity between the two sequences.

Fig. 3. (a and b) Irregularity and discontinuity

By linking similar structures, irregularities are able to perform the role of an AND connector that allows the spectator to anticipate the behaviour the character will display. Following the principle of anticipation (Thomas & Johnston, 1981), this property could enhance the visibility of gesture, *i.e.* to enhance our propensity to gaze at this particular gesture.

The functions of discontinuities
We also observe that discontinuities may perform a relation of contrast. This relation may take diverse forms. It could enhance the emphasis on a specific gesture by contrasting it from the others (6; 1): over a whole sequence produced with a low fluidity, only a single gesture phrase (and not phase that would have lead to an irregularity) has been produced with high fluidity. That leads to an isolation effect of this gesture phrase. It could also contrast the action verbs of the utterance when they are gesturally illustrated (3; 2): each occurrence of theses gestures is produced with a specific expressivity. Another form of discontinuity was noticed when the speaker enunciates a new type of general class of performative (1; 2), he changes her expressivity. Thus, discontinuities are a way to oppose different kernels of the enunciative structure.

These different functions of discontinuities seem to be closely linked to a relation of contrast between each of the levels they are referring to. This relation is defined as the speaker's intention that the addressee recognizes, by comparison, similarities and differences of the kernels of the enunciative structure (Mann & Thompson, 1988).

The functions of the modulations
By summarizing the functions performed by the two types of modulations in gesture expressivity, it appears that they act at the different levels of the enunciative structure, and that they do not depend on the type of performative act the speaker enunciates – even if this type of performative can act on the expressive parameter that supports the modulation; but this hypothesis is not supported by the study.

Modulations appear as a pragmatic tool. We noticed that irregularities could affect the spectator's attention through their anticipation properties. Discontinuities perform a relation of contrast that suggests an other attentional effect: as Feyereisen (1997) noticed *"communication supposes to perform contrasts. A signal is perceived with more clarity if it is distinguishable from noise or other signals"* (p. 39).

3 Evaluation and Modelization

The work presented in the last sections lead us to consider some new factors of gesture expressivity. That is, the modulations of gesture expressivity over time. Through their synchronization properties with the different levels of discourse, these modulations could enhance a conversational animation with communicative considerations, as developed previously. Considering a corpus of 2D animations, one of the questions is whether such rules could be applied in 3D animations. Though, we need an evaluation step to validate the hypothesis in a 3D environment during a conversational interaction. This step is processed from an ECA system developed by Pelachaud (Poggi *et al.*, 2005) and able to display a 3D animation of an agent from a high level description of the multimodal behaviour.

We first present this system; then, we only describe our evaluation methodology. This evaluation is currently running, and only ten subjects has completed it; no significant result has been obtained so far. This evaluation will be extended to a much larger population in a near future. A last section proposes a model for the application of gesture expressivity modulations in an ECA.

3.1 An ECA System for the Application of Gesture Expressivity Modulations

The animation system GRETA (Poggi *et al.*, 2005) we are using is able to generate a multimodal behaviour (speech, gaze, gestures, and head movements) from a high level description language called APML. We encode the textual input in this language, enriched with tags consistent with XML format. These tags give us a look on the affects, on which co-occurring gestures, etc., that the ECA should display (Figure 4).

```
<performative type="suggest">
    <rheme affect="sadness">
    Would you just please
        mind your
    <emphasis x-pitchaccent="LstarplusH" adjectival="foreign_to_me">own</emphasis>
    business<boundary type="LH"/>
    </rheme>
</performative>
```

Fig. 4. APML format for the description of the ECA multimodal behavior

Gestures are encoded in a specific file format, describing for each gesture phase the state of this gesture. We add the description of gesture expressivity at this level of encoding to enable the Greta system to run the rules to evaluate. Figure 5 is a description of the different parameters used to describe each gesture phase. "Startframe" specify the relative timing for this phase; "Frametype" is the phase type, and "Arm" and "Hand" are parameter to respectively specify the position of the hand and its shape. For each expressivity parameter (FLT: fluidity, PWR: power, SPC: spatial expansion), '?' specify a global value applied for the all animation; a specific value is given to run different types of modulations on gesture expressivity (in the figure, we introduce a modulation on the stroke phase with the maximum value 1.0 for each expressivity parameter).

```
STARTFRAME 0
FRAMETYPE PREPARATION
EXPR FLT ? PWR ? SPC ?
ARM XC YCC ZMIDDLE
HAND FORM_DEFAULT ADDNOISE
ENDFRAME

STARTFRAME 0.2
FRAMETYPE STROKE
EXPR FLT 1.0 PWR 1.0 SPC 1.0
ARM XP YUPPERP ZMIDDLE
HAND FORM_OPENAPART THUMB_AWAY ADDNOISE
WRIST FBUP PALMAWAY FBUP PALMINWARDS 0.4
ENDFRAME
```

Fig. 5. Description of gesture phases

3.2 Evaluation Methodology

During evaluation process, we aim at measuring whether the modulations of expressivity are a pragmatic tool for the animators. That is, on the one hand, to measure to which extent the modulations of expressivity could emphasize the communicative acts of the speaker, and on the other hand, to measure to which extent they could enhance the interlocutor's memorization of the utterances. We will add another task that does not consist in measuring the pragmatic performance of the modulations, but rather that provide a more general measure of their usefulness in the animation design.

The communicative acts of the speaker
Sperber and Wilson (1986) define the communication as the interlocutor's ability to recognize the speaker's intention to share/convey information. That is, during the perception of an enunciative discourse, the interlocutor does not only record this discourse as a sequence of information, but he recognizes this information as speaker's willingness to express her intentions.

In our experiment, the user task we defined is to identify which utterance from the enunciative discourse represents the main intention of the speaker. For each user test, we "enhance" one proposition of the textual discourse with modulations, to test whether this user identifies the main intention of the speaker as the proposition on which we apply modulations. A list of possible answers is proposed to the user to overcome memorization bias. Three videos are used: a demo with no modulation, a demo with one of the proposition enhanced with modulations, and a demo with another proposition enhanced with modulations.

Memorization of the textual discourse
One of the goals of an ECA application is to convey information to the user. In their application (Pelé *et al.*, 2003), an ECA informs the user on restaurants in Paris; the user should then memorize some of the information the ECA transmitted to her.

The task we propose here is to measure the performance of modulations in enhancing the user capacity to memorize information/utterances. We present a video to the user, and after viewing the video we ask him to transcribe all the sentences he remembers. The videos used in "communicative acts" are re-used, and we add three other videos: in the first one, we apply the full list of irregularities, in the second one we apply the full list of discontinuities, and in the third one we apply all these modulations.

User's preference
In this task, we look at the general preferences of the user. That is, whether he prefers or not a video with modulations. We use the second part of the video used during the memorization task and generate 4 videos: a video with only irregularities, one with only discontinuities, a video with both modulations, and a video with no modulation.

Each user has to undergo two tasks. The first task can be either the evaluation of the speaker's communicative act or the memorization of the textual discourse. The second task is the evaluation of the user's preference. Only ten subjects have processed this evaluation; no valuable statistical analysis, and we plan in a near future to extend this evaluation on a much larger population.

3.3   Modelization in an ECA

In this section we present our model for using gesture expressivity modulations in an ECA.

As previously seen, we can assign affects at the level of textual discourse through specific APML tags (Figure 4). These affects imply a particular expressivity on the gestures, *e.g.* a happy agent may act with more spatial expansion or fluidity than a sad agent (Wallbott, 1998). Another factor that may act on gesture expressivity values is the agent's personality. This factor acts as a global value of the interaction, *i.e.* we consider that the agent's personality does not vary during the whole interaction.

The occurrences of the irregularities and the discontinuities are not constrained by personality factor or affects. To implement expressivity on gestures during a conversational interaction, our algorithm is to work along three steps (Figure 6): first, the personality factor is applied and generate a global value for each expressivity parameter; then, the emotional state of the agent changes this value at different periods of the discourse; depending on which modulation type we want to apply, the final expressivity is generated. A discontinuity changes an expressivity parameter over an undefined period of time, whereas an irregularity changes this parameter for a single gesture phase period.

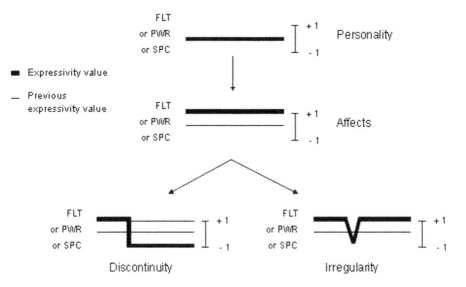

Fig. 6. Three steps to apply expressivity parameters in an animation

4 Conclusion

In this paper we proposed a study of gesture expressivity modulations that occur during a conversational interaction. Two types of modulation in gesture expressivity are considered, that we defined as irregularities and discontinuities. An analysis from an annotation of 2D animations revealed different pragmatic functions for each of these modulation types. These modulations could enhance existing ECA interactions with additional communicative effects expressed in gesture animation, as we described in the paper.

An evaluation study on subjects was proposed to measure the effects of modulations on their communicative performances; some works need to complete this evaluation to obtain significant results. We also proposed a model to apply these modulations into a conversational agent.

References

Barrier, G., Caelen, J. & Meillon, B. (2005). La visibilité des gestes: Paramètres directionnels, intentionnalité du signe et attribution de pertinence. *Workshop Francophone sur les Agents Conversationnels Animés*. Grenoble, France (2005), 113-123.

Bregler, C., Loeb, L., Chuang, E. & Desphande, H. Turning to masters: Motion capturing cartoons. *SIGGRAPH 2002* (2002).

Calbris, G. *L'expression gestuelle de la pensée d'un homme politique*. Paris, CNRS Editions, 2003

Choi, J., Kim, D. & Lee, I. Anticipation for facial animation. *CASA'04*, Geneva, Switzerland, CGS (2004).

Feyereisen, P. La compréhension des gestes référentiels. *Geste, cognition et communication,* PULIM (1997), 20-48.

Gullberg, M. & Holmqvist, K. Keeping an eye on gestures: Visual perception of gestures in face-to-face communication. *Pragmatics and Cognition* 7 (1999), 35-63.

Hartmann, B., Mancini, M. & Pelachaud, C. Implementing expressive gesture synthesis for Embodied Conversational Agents. *Gesture Workshop* (2005)

Kendon, A. *Gesture: Visible action as utterance.* Cambridge University Press, 2004.

Kipp, M. *Gesture generation by imitation: From human behaviour to computer character animation.* Faculties of Natural Sciences and Technology, Boca Raton, Florida (2004).

Kita, S., Van Gijn, I. & Van der Hulst, H. Movement phases in signs and co-speech gestures, and their transcription by human coders. *Gesture Workshop,* Bielefeld, Germany, Springer-Verlag (1997).

Lance, B., Marsella, S. & Koizumi, D. Towards expressive gaze manner in embodied virtual agents. *AAMAS Workshop on Empathic Agents,* New-York (2004).

Lasseter, J. Principles of traditional animation applied to 3D computer animation. *ACM Computer Graphics 21,* 4 (1987).

Mann, W. & Thompson, S. Rhetorical Structure Theory. Toward a functional theory of text organization. *Text 8,* 3 (1988), 243-281.

Pelé, D., Breton, G., Panaget, F. & Loyson, S. Let's find a restaurant with Nestor, a 3D Embodied Conversational Agent on the web". *AAMAS Workshop on Embodied Conversational characters as individuals* (2003).

Poggi, I. & Pelachaud, C. Performative facial expressions in animated faces. *Embodied Conversational Agents.* J. Cassell, S. Prevost, E. Churchill. Cambridge, Mass., MIT Press (2000), 155-188.

Poggi, I., Pelachaud, C., de Rosis, F., Carofiglio, V., De Carolis, B. GRETA. A believable Embodied Conversational Agent, in *Mutimodal Intelligent Information Presentation,* O. Stock and M. Zancarano, eds, Kluwer, to appear, 2005.

Sperber, D. & Wilson, D. *La pertinence, Communication et cognition.* Paris: Editions de Minuit, 1986 (trad.: 1989).

Thomas, F. & Johnston, O. *Disney animation, The illusion of life.* New-York, USA, Abbeville Press, 1981.

Wallbott, G. Bodily expression of emotion. *European Journal of Social Psychology,* 28 (1998), 879-896.

Visual Attention and Eye Gaze During Multiparty Conversations with Distractions

Erdan Gu and Norman I. Badler

Department of Computer and Information Science,
University of Pennsylvania, Philadelphia, PA, 19104-6389
{erdan, badler}@seas.upenn.edu

Abstract. Our objective is to develop a computational model to predict visual attention behavior for an embodied conversational agent. During interpersonal interaction, gaze provides signal feedback and directs conversation flow. Simultaneously, in a dynamic environment, gaze also directs attention to peripheral movements. An embodied conversational agent should therefore employ social gaze not only for interpersonal interaction but also to possess human attention attributes so that its eyes and facial expression portray and convey appropriate distraction and engagement behaviors.

1 Introduction

In order to build a plausible virtual human or embodied conversational agent (ECA), we must understand how it might be given a cognitive ability to perceive, react and interact with the environment [2]. Conventional ECA animation techniques fall short of providing agents with human-like responses to environmental stimuli and internal goals, principally because they endow the agent with perfect cognition. There are, however, many intricate shortcomings to real human perception. Our work seeks to address and rectify these problems by seeking insights from cognitive psychology to model aspects of human vision, memory and attention.

An ECA should also be equipped to perceive and express many non-linguistic social signals to communicate information in a shared environment. Eyes direct attention, expose the actual mood of the subject, and express a wide range of human expressions [14]. For example, the amount of eye opening can reflect various emotional states, the blinking rate decreases when a person is attentive to objects in the environment, and gaze provides an important cue to regulate conversations [15].

People focus on eyes to "read" insights into human behavior. Natural gaze behavior is critical to the realism and believability of an animated character. An ECA should employ social gaze for interpersonal interaction and also possess human attention attributes so that its eyes and facial expression convey appropriate distraction and attending behaviors. Our objective is to develop a computational model of multiple influences on eye gaze behavior for an ECA in a dynamic environment. Eye behaviors should be influenced by human-like imperfect cognitive ability, social aspects of interaction behaviors, as well as some internal cognitive states. Our work here makes

J. Gratch et al. (Eds.): IVA 2006, LNAI 4133, pp. 193 – 204, 2006.
© Springer-Verlag Berlin Heidelberg 2006

two contributions: constructing a social gaze model for multiparty conversation and observing its behavior and consequences under varying environmental distractions, conversation workload, and participant engagement.

The paper is organized as follows. Section 2 describes relevant studies on ECA gaze behavior in order to situate this work within the current state of the art. Section 3 presents a comprehensive eye movement model for conversational and emotive gaze. Section 4 concentrates on the turn-allocation strategy in multiparty conversation and associated gaze behaviors. Section 5 examines an experiment with varying external distractions and internal workload for the agent, who then exhibits appropriate gaze behavior. Section 6 concludes with a discussion and future work.

2 Background

There have been several attempts to model the role of gaze in ECAs. Gaze, combined with gesture, facial expression and body orientation all give information about what we are saying and thinking, and help (perhaps unconsciously) to communicate emotions. Eye movement is heavily related to information processing in the brain. Lee *et al.* [16] exploited an eye saccade statistical model during talking and listening based on empirical eye tracking data. In our work, we explore emotive gaze to expose mood and thought processes. We do not present here specific speech-relevant gaze behaviors which synchronize to verbal communicative acts but rather consider the correlation between eye motor control and general cognitive activity.

Directional gaze cues are frequently present to communicate the nature of the interpersonal relationship in face-to-face interactions [1]. It is estimated that 60% of conversation involves gaze and 30% involves mutual gaze [24]. Garau *et al.* [8] and Colburn *et al.* [7] analyze frequencies of mutual gaze to simulate patterns of eye gaze for the participants. Social gaze serves to regulate conversation flow. Cassell *et al.* [4] use eye gaze as a sign to open and close the communication channel. Novick *et al.* [22] observe two simple gaze patterns (mutual-break and mutual-hold) to account for much of the turn-taking behavior. So far, however, ECA simulations for face-face conversation are mainly dyadic and turn allocation using gaze signals is relatively simple. Multiparty turn-taking behavior is an open challenge and some attempts [28] [29] are based largely on the dyadic situation. Much of this work focuses on user-perceptual issues or has involved mediated communications rather than ECA simulation. Intuitively, a significant difference exists in gaze behaviors between dyadic and multiparty situations: at the minimum the latter must include mechanisms for turn-requests, acknowledgement, and attention capture. We address the role of gaze in turn-taking allocation strategy, appearance of awareness, and expression of the feedback signal.

Ideally, we would like to implement the ECAs such that they interact with their conversational partners and environment in the same way as real people do by having a limited visual resource. Suppressed or inappropriate eye movements damage the experienced effectiveness of an ECA. Gaze behavior should be emergent and responsive to a dynamic environment. Engagement is a key factor that underlies realistic human-like cognitive commitment. Sidner *et al.* [27] define it as "the process by which two or more participants establish, maintain and end their perceived connection during interactions they jointly undertake." We construct a framework to decide engagement due to the demands of simultaneously executing interpersonal tasks and managing exogenous stimuli and, consequently, to predict gaze behavior.

In our recent work [10], we suggested a visual attention model that integrates both bottom-up and top-down filters, and combines 2D snapshots of the scene with 3D structural information. While it is commonly believed that an object requires only reasonable physical (perceivable) properties to be noticed in a scene, recent studies [17] [20] have found that people often miss very visible objects when they are preoccupied with an attentionally demanding task. Green [9] classifies the prominent inadequacies in visual processing into four categories: (sensory and cognitive) conspicuity, mental workload, expectation, and capacity. Based on this descriptive model, we formulated a computational framework that determines successful attention allocation and consequent inattention blindness [11]. In our preliminary investigations, we quantified our model with a computational experiment analogous to other inattention blindness studies [26] and examined the effects of Green's four factors on the subject's awareness level of the unattended object. Here we employ the same model for ECAs and examine some of the most important parameters. The ECA interactions are affected by each other as well as unexpected events in the external environment. The attention model of the ECA decides what should or should not be permitted into consciousness. The ECA may or may not be aware of peripheral movements according to different engagement levels. Our approach attempts to leverage multiple influential accounts from external visual stimuli and social interaction into a computational model that drives consistent ECA gaze animation.

3   Computational Model for Eye Motor Control

The human repertoire of eye motor control can be defined by saccade, fixation, smooth pursuit, squint and blink. There are parameters to describe these ocular movements [16] including gaze direction, magnitude, duration, the degree of eye open, blink, and so on. The magnitude defines the angle the eyeball rotates, while velocity differentiates smooth pursuit and saccade. Duration is the amount of time that the movement takes to execute. Our attention model affects eye motor control by specifying the gaze direction, the degree of eye open, and size of pupil relative to luminance.

There are many eye-related communicative functions. Here we focus on directional gaze patterns such as eye contact, mutual gaze, gaze aversion, line of regard, and fixation. Two participants use mutual gaze to look at each other, usually in the face region. Gaze contact means they look in each other's eyes. In gaze aversion, one participant looks away when others are looking toward her. Head rotation and nod or shake are always linked to eye movement [5]. Head and eyes continuously align with a moving target. Horizontal gaze shifts greater than $25°$ or vertical shifts greater than $10°$ produce combined head and eye movement [6]. Once the head is aligned with the target, the eyes re-center.

In addition, various eye movements accompany a wide range of human expressions. People generally partially close their eyes during unpleasant emotions to reduce vision, but react to happiness by spreading. Table 1 summarizes eye movement patterns in different emotion expressions [14].

Table 1. Emotion state and corresponding eye movement patterns

Type	Face/Eye Behavior Description	Eye Movement
Laughter	Submissive: apprehension around the eyes.	Downcast gaze; decreased eye contacts
	Smile: relaxed, teeth together but lips are barely parted.	Flat gaze
	Laughter: teeth often parted, partially covered by the lips.	Upraised and out-of-focus gaze; eyes wide open
Surprise	Sudden opening of the eyes followed by mixed emotions: pleasant, anger, shock	Fixation and up to mixed emotions
Fear	Similar to surprised	Eye fixation or aversion
Interest	Eyes wide open (object is close) or squint (great distance), fixed on the object	Fixation, scan with longer glances
Anger	Eyes wide open and fixed; face a rigid mask	Fixation
Contempt	Eyes are a little closed, wrinkles under the eyes, but fixed on insignificant object	Eyes looking sideways
Disgust	Upper eyelids may be partially closed, or raised slightly on one side.	Eye aversion

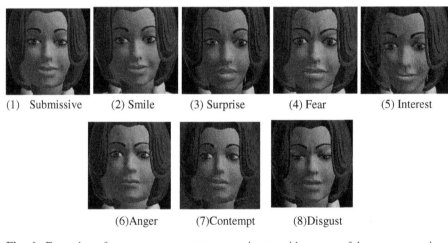

(1) Submissive   (2) Smile   (3) Surprise   (4) Fear   (5) Interest

(6)Anger   (7)Contempt   (8)Disgust

Fig. 1. Examples of eye movements accompanying a wide range of human expressions: (1)Submissive (2)Smile (3)Surprise (4)Fear (5)Interest (6)Anger (7)Contempt (8)Disgust

We are constructing a comprehensive eye model from low level eye motor control to high level gaze patterns exhibited by conversational gaze, emotional state, and visual attention. Conversational gaze as a turn-taking signal is elaborated below.

4   Gaze Roles in Turn-Taking

Gaze behaviors and visual contact signal and monitor the initiation, maintenance and termination of communicative messages [3]. Short mutual gaze (~1s.) is a powerful mechanism that induces arousal in the other participants [1]. Gaze diminishes when disavowing social contact. By avoiding eye gaze in an apparently natural way, an audience expresses an unwillingness to speak.

Conversation proceeds in turns. Two mutually exclusive states are posited for each participant: the speaker who claims the speaking turn and the audience who does not. Gaze provides turn-taking signals to regulate the flow of communication. Table 2 shows how gaze behaviors act to maintain and regulate multiparty conversations.

Table 2. Turn-taking and associated gaze behaviors

State	Signals	Gaze Behavior
Speaker	Turn yielding	Look toward listener
	Turn claiming suppression signal	Avert gaze contact from audience
	Within turn signal	Look toward audience
	No turn signal	Look away
Audiences	Back channel signal	Look toward speaker
	Turn claiming signal	Seek gaze contact from speaker
	Turn suppression signal	Avert gaze contact from speaker
	Turn claiming suppression signal	Look toward other aspiring audiences to prevent them speaking
	No response	Random

In dyadic conversation, at the completion of an utterance or thought unit the speaker gives a lengthy glance to the audience to yield a speaking turn. This gaze cue persists until the audience assumes the speaking role. The multiparty case requires a turn-allocation strategy. Inspired by Miller [19], we address the multi-party issue with two mechanisms: a *transition-space* where the speaker selects the next speaker and a *competition space* where the next turn is allocated by self-selection.

Transition Space (Fig. 2(2))

Speaker

1: She gives a lengthy glance (turn yielding) to one of the audiences.
2.i: Receiving gaze contact (turn claiming) from the audience, the speaker relinquishes the floor.
2.ii: Receiving gaze aversion (turn suppression) from the audience, the speaker decides to keep transition-space to find another audience or go to competition space directly. If no one wants to speak, the speaker has the option of continuing or halting.

Audiences

1: Audience who wants a turn will look toward speaker's eye to signal her desire to speak (turn claiming), and want to draw the attention of the speaker.
2: Audience receiving speaker gaze (turn yielding) uses quick gaze contact (turn claiming) to accept the turn or lengthy gaze aversion (turn suppression) to reject it.

Competition Space (Fig. 2(3))

Speaker
She scans all the audiences, serially sending a turn yielding signal (Fig. 3).

Audiences
They may have eye interactions at that time. The aspiring audience looks towards the speaker to signal a desire to speak (turn claiming). After receiving visual contact from the speaker, she looks at all the other aspiring audiences to signal her taking the floor (turn claiming suppression). Non-aspiring audiences may follow the speaker's gaze direction or use random gaze (no response).

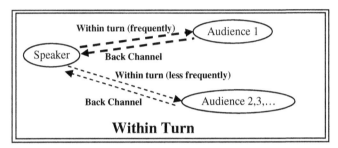

(1) Gaze signals within turn

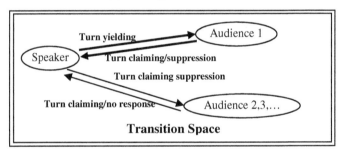

(2) Gaze signals in Transition Space

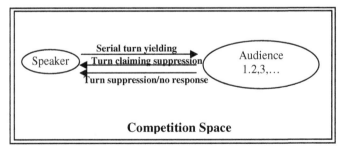

(3) Gaze signals in Competition Space

Fig. 2. Diagram for turn taking allocation and employed conversational gaze signal

Turns begin and end smoothly, with short lapses of time in between. Occasionally an audience's turn-claim in the absence of a speaker's turn signal results in simultaneous turns [14] between audiences, even between audience and speaker. Favorable simultaneous turns will occur that show it is a comfortable and communicative circumstance. The general rule is that the first speaker continues and the others drop out. The dropouts lower gaze or avert gaze to signal giving up.

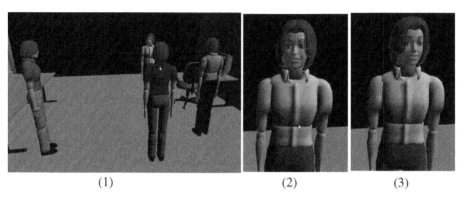

(1)   (2)   (3)

Fig. 3. A four-party conversation. (1) Full view image. (2)(3) Turn yielding gaze signal.

Within a turn, audiences spend more time looking toward the speaker (back channel) to signal attention and interest. They focus on the speaker's face area around the eyes. The speaker generally looks less often at audiences except to monitor their acceptance and understanding (within turn signal). The speaker glances during grammatical breaks, at the end of a thought unit or idea, and at the end of the utterance to obtain feedback. As Fig. 2(1) shows, the speaker usually assigns a longer and more frequent glance to the audience to whom she would like pass the floor.

5 Engagement Level of Conversational Agent

Eye gaze is fundamental in showing interest levels between characters and as a means of anticipating events. When audiences looked at their partner less than normal, the audiences were rated as less attentive [24]. Thus, the duration and frequency of glances directed towards the speaker will be considered indicative of the audience's attentive level. Peters *et al.* [23][24] present an ECA model with the capability of visual perceiving another's level of interest based on direction of the eyes, head, body and locomotion. After being aware of such signals, the speaking agent has the option to continue or stop talking. Both speaker and audience are also influenced by what happens in the external environment. While attending to the conversational partner is the most basic form of signaling understanding by the agent [21], an audience whose eyes never waver from her partner, despite background events, appears lifeless. Therefore, an ECA with a realistic attention system can use perceptual information to project more realistic involvement in conversation.

We discuss two types of engagement behaviors: engagement cues from a conversational partner or herself, and those from the environment. We apply our attention framework to determine attention shifts between these two cues. The speaker determines the arousal or discouragement of talking by perceiving visual contact from the audiences or distractions from any peripheral movements. In the remainder of this section we study these attention effects, particularly the transition from self/partner to the environment. In our system we can experimentally adjust several influence parameters, such as mental workload of participants and conspicuity of distraction.

5.1 Parameterized Experiment

Because human cognitive resources are limited, attention acts as a filter to examine sensory input quickly and limit cognitive processing. We endow the ECA with a human-like perceptual ability to automatically decide to maintain or halt the conversation. Sensory conspicuity refers to the bottom-up properties of an object, while cognitive conspicuity reflects the personal or social relevance it contains [30]. As tasks become more difficult they increase the mental workload of the subject and require more attention, increasing the likelihood of missing an unexpected event. Thus workload and conspicuity are related more to the visual system while expectation and capacity appear closer to other cognitive structures such as memory.

Our attention model relies on the cooperation of internally-driven top-down settings and external bottom-up inputs. The bottom-up input uses the "saliency" (sensory conspicuity features) of objects in the scene to filter perceptual information and compute an objective saliency map. Primary visual features consist of 2D and 3D visual cues relevant to the object, such as its size, depth (distance from the agent to the object), location in the agent's view image (how far from focus center to the object), color and movement speed. Simultaneously, top-down settings, such as expectation and face pop-out, determine the set of items that are contextually important. Known as the attentional set, this is a subjective feature pool of task-prominent properties maintained in memory. At any moment, focused attention only provides a spatiotemporal coherence map for one object [11]. This coherence map highlights the object calculated to be the most important at that moment in the scene, and thus can be used to drive the ECA's gaze.

The appearance and movement of an unexpected object in the scene were varied in order to affect sensory and cognitive conspicuity level. The inherent physical salience value of the unexpected object could be *high*, *medium*, or *low*. We used three objects: one falling red cube outside a window, one big green cube moving on the table, and one man who suddenly appears outside the window. The possible field of vision of the agent is considered. In the third object case, face pop-out detection reveals a man in the agent's visual field; since faces as socially relevant features are meaningful to a person they are more likely to capture attention. As Fig. 4 shows, the speaker exhibits different responses to different peripheral movements.

In the second variation, mental workload could be *high*, *medium*, or *low*, determined by the intensity level of the conversation (Fig. 5). Difficulty increases as parties are added to the interaction. The speaker's mental workload will be high when she wants to maintain an active atmosphere with more than four participants. Simultaneously, more frequent turn exchanges with more participants enhance the arousal

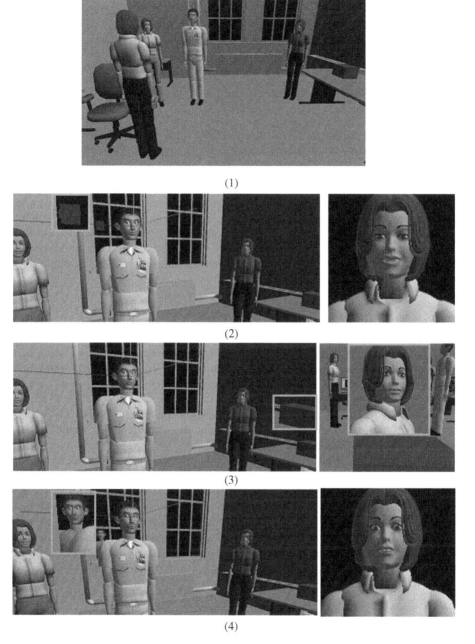

Fig. 4. Adjustment of conspicuity level by varying different distractions. (1) Full view of four party conversation. (2) Red falling cube with low conspicuity level goes unnoticed. (3) Green floating cube grabs attention and causes speaker engagement shift from the partner to the external stimuli; she does smooth pursuit to track the movement. (4) The speaker is surprised since the man's face makes the speaker immediately consciousness of him.

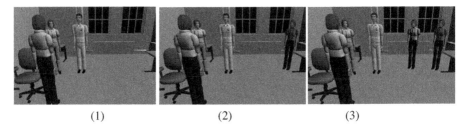

(1)   (2)   (3)

Fig. 5. Adjustment of mental workload level by adding more parties. (1) Conversation with three participants. (2) Conversation with four participants. (1) Conversation with five participants.

of the speaker to maintain the conversation. The interest level of the audience, reflected in the frequency of back channel signals, also augments their involvement. They all occupy considerable attention for the participants and reduce the probability of attention shift. In the highest workload case, we place five participants and four turn exchanges in a 2-minute conversation. The speaker pays no attention to any unexpected objects: not even the human face pop-out although it falls into her line of vision.

6   Conclusion

Our contribution lies in building convincing computational models of human gaze behavior grounded in cognitive psychological principles. To interact with humans in a shared environment, an ECA must posses an analog of human visual attention, visual limitations, and non-linguistic social signals. This model can improve social acceptability and interpersonal interactions between people and animated human agents in diverse applications. These applications include tutoring, teaching, training, web agents, movie special effects, and game characters.

In the future, we aim to further integrate the internal state of the ECA such as emotion, personality and mental states with eye gaze, head motion and facial animation. Appropriate eye movements increase the realism of an agent's engagement behavior. Computational eye gaze models will allow us to explore other inattentional blindness factors, such as expectation and capacity. In addition, experimentally supported quantification and model validation engaging human and synthetic participants in shared spaces is required. Human subjects should be asked to empirically evaluate the naturalness and effectiveness of the animated nonverbal behavior of the ECAs during real-time interactions.

Acknowledgements

This work is partially supported by NSF IIS-0200983 and NASA 03-OBPR-01-0000-0147. Opinions expressed here are those of the authors and not of the sponsoring agencies. Thanks to Catherine Pelachaud for use of the Greta agent and to Jan M. Allbeck for her assistance.

Visual Attention and Eye Gaze During Multiparty Conversations with Distractions   203

References

1. Argyle, M. and Cook, M. (1976) *Gaze and Mutual Gaze*. Cambridge University Press, London.
2. Badler, N., Chi, D. and Chopra S. (1999) Virtual human animation based on movement observation and cognitive behavior models. In *Proc. Computer Animation*, Geneva, Switzerland, IEEE Computer Society Press, pp. 128-137
3. Cassell, J. and Thorisson, K. (2000) The power of a nod and a glance: Envelope vs. emotional feedback in animated conversational agents. *Applied Artificial Intelligence Journal*, 13(4-5):519-538.
4. Cassell, J. and Vilhjalmsson, H. (1999), Fully embodied conversational avatars: Making communicative behaviors autonomous. *Autonomous Agents and Multi-Agent Systems*, 2(1): 45-64. .
5. Chopra-Khullar, S. and Badler, N. (2001) Where to look? Automating attending behaviors of virtual human characters. *Autonomous Agents and Multi-agent Systems* 4, pp. 9-23.
6. Chopra-Khullar, S. (1999) Where to look? Automating certain visual attending behaviors of human characters. Ph.D Dissertation, University of Pennsylvania.
7. Colburn, A., Cohen, M. and Drucker, S. (2000) The role of eye gaze in avatar mediated conversational interfaces.. MSR-TR-2000-81. Microsoft Research, 2000.
8. Garau, M., Slater, M., Bee, S. and Sasse, M. (2001) The impact of eye gaze on communication using humaniod avatars. *Proc. ACM SIGCHI*, pp. 309-316.
9. Green, G. (2004) Inattentional blindness and conspicuity. Retrieved November 10, http://www.visualexpert.com/Resources/inattentionalblindness.html
10. Gu, E., (2005) Multiple Influences on Gaze and Attention Behavior for Embodied Agent, Doctoral Dissertation Proposal, Nov., 2005, Computer and Information Science Department, Univeristy of Pennysylavania.
11. Gu, E., Stocker, C. and Badler, N. (2005) Do you see what eyes see? Implementing inattention blindness. *Proc. Intelligent Virtual Agents* 2005, LNAI 3661, pp 178-190.
12. Gu, E., Wang, J. and Badler, N. (2005). Generating sequence of eye fixations using decision-theoretic bottom-up attention model. 3rd International Workshop on Attention and Performance in Computational Vision, IEEE Computer Society Conference on Computer Vision and Pattern Recognition Workshop, San Diego, pp92.
13. Itti, L. (2003) Visual attention. *The Handbook of Brain Theory and Neural Networks*, Cambridge, Michael A. Arbib (Editor), MIT Press. pp. 1196–1201.
14. Knapp, L. and Hall, A. (1996) The effects of eye behavior on human communication. *Nonverbal communication in human interaction*. Harcourt College Pub., 4th edition, Chapter 10, pp. 369-380.
15. Kendon, A. (1967) Some functions of gaze direction in social interaction. *Acta Psychologica*, 32, pp. 1–25.
16. Lee, S., Badler, J. and Badler, N. (2002) Eyes alive, *ACM Transactions on Graphics* 21(3), pp. 637-644.
17. Mack, A. and Rock, I. (1998) *Inattentional Blindness*. Cambridge, MA, MIT Press.
18. Matsusaka, Y., Fujie, S. and Kobayashi, T. (2001) Modeling of conversational strategy for the robot participating in the group conversation. *Proc. 7th European Conference on Speech Communication and Technology (Eurospeech 2001)*, Aalborg, Denmark, pp. 2173-2176.
19. Miller, E. (1999) Turn-taking and relevance in conversation. For the course, *Ways of Speaking*, at the University of Pennsylvania, May 1999.

20. Most, S., Scholl, B., Clifford, E. and Simons, D. (2005) What you see is what you set: Sustained inattentional blindness and the capture of awareness. *Psychological Review* 112, pp. 217-242.
21. Nakano, Y. and Nishida, T. (2005) Awareness of perceived world and conversational engagement by conversational agents. AISB Symposium: Conversational Informatics for Supporting Social Intelligence & Interaction, England.
22. Novick, D., Hansen, B. and Ward, K. (1996) Coordinating turn-taking with gaze. *Proc. of ICSLP-96*, Philadelphia, PA, pp. 1888-1891.
23. Peters, C. (2005) Direction of attention perception for conversation initiation in virtual environments. *Proc. Intelligent Virtual Agents*, pp. 215-228.
24. Pelachaud, C., Peters, C., Mancini, M., Bevacqua, E. and Poggi, I. (2005) A model of attention and interest using gaze behavior. *Proc. Intelligent Virtual Agents*, pp. 229-240.
25. Slater, M., Pertaub, D. and Steed, A. (1999) Public Speaking in Virtual Reality: Facing and Audience of Avatars, IEEE Computer Graphics and Applications, 19(2), March/April 1999, p6-9
26. Simons, D. and Chabris, C. (1999) Gorillas in our midst: Sustained inattentional blindness for dynamic events. *Perception* 28, pp. 1059-1074.
27. Sidner, C., Lee, C. and Lesh, N. (2003) Engagement rules for human-robot collaborative interactions. *Proc. IEEE International Conference on Systems, Man & Cybernetics (CSMC)*, Vol. 4, pp. 3957-3962.
28. Vertegaal, R., Der Veer, G. and Vons, H. (2000) Effects of gaze on multiparty mediated communication. *Proc. Graphics Interface*. Morgan-Kaufmann Publishers, Montreal, Canada: Canadian Human-Computer Communications Society, pp. 95–102.
29. Vertegaal, R., Slagter, R., Der Veer, G. and Nijholt, A. (2001) Eye gaze patterns in conversations: There is more to conversational agents than meets the eyes. *ACM CHI Conference on Human Factors in Computing Systems*, pp. 301–308.
30. Wolfe J. (1999). "Inattentional amnesia", in Fleeting Memories. In *Cognition of Brief Visual Stimuli*. Cambridge, MA, MIT Press, pp. 71-94.

Towards a Common Framework for Multimodal Generation: The Behavior Markup Language

Stefan Kopp[1], Brigitte Krenn[2], Stacy Marsella[4], Andrew N. Marshall[4],
Catherine Pelachaud[3], Hannes Pirker[2],
Kristinn R. Thórisson[5], and Hannes Vilhjálmsson[4]

[1] Artificial .Intelligence Group, University of Bielefeld, Germany
skopp@techfak.uni-bielefeld.de
[2] Austrian Research Institute for AI (OFAI), Vienna, Austria
{brigitte, hannes}@ofai.at
[3] IUT de Montreuil, University de Paris 8, France
c.pelachaud@iut.univ-paris8.fr
[4] Information Sciences Institute, University of Southern California USA
{marsella, amarshal, hannes}@isi.edu
[5] CADIA, Dept. Of Computer Science, Reykjavik University, Iceland
thorisson@ru.is

Abstract. This paper describes an international effort to unify a multimodal behavior generation framework for Embodied Conversational Agents (ECAs). We propose a three stage model we call SAIBA where the stages represent intent planning, behavior planning and behavior realization. A Function Markup Language (FML), describing intent without referring to physical behavior, mediates between the first two stages and a Behavior Markup Language (BML) describing desired physical realization, mediates between the last two stages. In this paper we will focus on BML. The hope is that this abstraction and modularization will help ECA researchers pool their resources to build more sophisticated virtual humans.

1 Introduction

Human communicative behaviors span a broad set of skills, from natural language generation and production, to coverbal gesture, to eye gaze control and facial expression. People produce such multimodal behavior with ease in real-time in a broad range of circumstances. The simulation of such behaviors with computer-generated characters has, by now, a history of more than ten years [15][1]. A number of approaches have been presented in the field, geared toward specific aspects of generating multimodal behavior, e.g. facial expressions and gesture synthesis. All represent models of a production process in which certain knowledge structures are identified and transformed. Such knowledge structures include representations of communicative intent, lexicons that define available behaviors and their particular overt forms, and rules as to how communicative intent and affective state is mapped onto them.

At the AAMAS 2002 workshop "Embodied conversational agents - let's specify and evaluate them!" it became obvious that most researchers were building their own

J. Gratch et al. (Eds.): IVA 2006, LNAI 4133, pp. 205 – 217, 2006.
© Springer-Verlag Berlin Heidelberg 2006

behavior and functional languages. While diversity is important, another "Gesticon" workshop in 2003 made it clear that a lot of similarities existed among the approaches. To avoid replication of work, as well as to allow for sharing modules, a push was initiated to develop a common specification. In April 2005, a group of researchers in the area of multimodal communication and computer animation came together at Reykjavik University to further the integration and development of multimodal generation skills for artificial humans [18]. Our goals were (1) to frame the problem of multimodal generation in a way that allows us to put it into computational models; (2) to define planning stages of multimodal generation and to identify the knowledge structures that mediate between them; (3) to render these stages and knowledge structures into a framework that lays down modules and interfaces, enabling people to better work together and to use each other's work, that has been directed to different aspects of multimodal behavior, with a minimal amount of custom work. In previous efforts we started by clarifying terminologies such as representation vs. markup vs. scripting languages [9].

In this paper we describe our latest results in this ongoing process. In Section 2, we begin by looking into four existing languages: BEAT, MURML, APML and RRL. Our goal is to bring together our experiences with these languages and to derive a powerful, unifying model of representations for multimodal generation. We present such a model, the SAIBA framework, in Section 3. Two important representation languages emerged as part of this framework. These languages are meant to be application independent, graphics model independent, and to present a clear-cut separation between information types (function versus behavior specification). We will go into one of those languages, the Behavior Markup Language (BML), in more detail in Section 4, and then conclude with remarks on the next steps.

2   Prior Approaches

A number of researchers have construed representation languages for capturing the knowledge structures that were identified as involved in the generation of multimodal behavior. We start here by analyzing four broadly used languages, all being XML compliant. While there are certainly more languages being employed out there (e.g. MPML; [12]), the languages considered here provide a good overview of previous approaches, and allow us to compare the assumptions that underlie their generation models.

One principal commonality among these and related previous systems is the separation of content- and process-related processing. For example, the Ymir architecture used to implement the Gandalf humanoid clearly separated dialog planning and social interaction control [16][17]. The argument behind this was that what an agent chooses to say in a given situation is highly domain-specific, whereas the ability to deliver that content through social interaction is a broad re-usable skill. Consequently, verbal responses related to dialog topic (content) were generated by a separate process, based on the user's interpreted communicative act (the multimodal version of a speech act), using an abstract frame-based representation. The surface form, however, of this content and all necessary process-related responses (turntaking signals, gaze, head movements, gesture, paraverbals), was generated by a realtime, rule-based planner (called Action Scheduler) in incremental chunks of 200-1200 msec duration each, using a library of composite behaviors (called Behavior Lexicon). The whole process was driven by a pervasive representation of time and the high-level abstract communicative goals. The separation of content and process was kept in the architecture of the later Rea system [3]. There, a special generation module was dedicated to verbal and nonverbal behavior generation, taking an abstract representation of communicative intent and giving it surface form according to the rules of social face-to-face interaction. One consequence of these systems' emphasis on modularization has been that formal and re-usable representations that interface between separated stages moved into the focus of research on the automatic generation of multimodal behavior.

2.1 BEAT/Spark

The BEAT "text-to-embodied-speech" toolkit [2] specifically addressed this re-use issue by introducing a plug-in model for nonverbal behavior generators and an XML-based processing pipeline. The pipeline has clear stages that move representations from annotations of communicative intent to behavior suggestions and finally to scheduling and execution. Yet, the behavior generators have access to a variety of information about the text to be spoken, at different levels of abstraction, and therefore don't quite provide a clean interface to communicative intent. The Spark system modified BEAT to work within an avatar-based chat system, using the behavior generators to automatically animate the delivery of text messages between chatting participants[19][20]. The division between communicative intent and behavior was made very clear with Spark's definition of two separate XML tag sets. The text messages are first annotated automatically with tags, describing communica-tive intent or functions (function markup), and then the generators transform those tags into another set of tags (behavior markup), turning communica-tive functions into the behaviors that support them. The XML annotation is all done inline with the spoken text and while that makes temporal co-occurrence easy to process, it does not allow partially overlapping temporal spans.

2.2 MURML

In the MAX system (or, more generally, the *Articulatd Communicator Engine*) [6], a *Multimodal Utterance Representation Markup Language* was designed to describe the results of behavior planning, which are handed to realization [7]. MURML descriptions assume an incremental process model that synthesizes continuous speech and gesture in successive chunks. Each MURML specification contains (1) a textual definition of the verbal part of the utterance, possibly including internal chunk borders marked, and (2) specifications of paraverbal or nonverbal behaviors such as prosodic foci, gestures, or facial animations. MURML also focused on specifying the actual form of body or face behaviors. A communicative hand gesture is represented in terms of the morphological, spatio-temporal features of its meaningful phase (*wrist location* and *trajectory, hand shape, hand orientation*), each of which being described either numerically or symbolically, building upon a notation system for sign languages. The overall structure of a gesture is given by defining *simultaneity, posteriority, repetitions,* or *symmetry* of those components.

With regard to cross-behavioral temporal relations, the occurrence of a coverbal behavior can be defined either in terms of absolute times (start, end, duration) with regard to the start time of the chunk, or by simply stating the affiliation of the behavior with linguistic elements. Using time tags inserted in the text, behavior affiliations can be defined by referring to boundaries of co-expressive words. This way of specifying speech and coverbal behaviors separately allows partially overlapping temporal spans for behavior.

2.3 APML

The *Affective Presentation Markup Language* specifies the agent's behavior at the meaning level [4]. This language is based on Poggi's taxonomy of communicative functions which are defined as a pair (meaning, signal). Four different classes of communicative functions are differentiated depending on the type of information they convey: information about speaker's belief, goal, affective state and meta-cognitive information about speaker's mental state.   A communicative function may be associated with different signals. That is for a given meaning, there may be several ways to communicate it. Another class of languages were designed to describe facial expression and gesture [4][5]. This separation of the languages ensures an independence between the mind module of the agent and the animation player.

2.4 RRL

The *Rich Representation Language* was developed in the NECA project (Net Environment for Emotional Embodied Conversational Agents). It focuses on presentation of simulated multimodal dialogue and was designed for representing the information that is relevant at the interfaces between components of a multimodal dialogue generation system[1] [11] that incrementally script a dialogue between two or more animated agents. The resulting RRL script remains independent of particular player technologies and can be mapped without adding new content to player-specific scripts.

An RRL document represents a dialogue at multiple levels of specification, ranging from an abstract dialogue plan level (scene generation) and an abstract verbal and non-verbal realizations of dialogue acts (multimodal natural language generation) to a concrete behavior specification temporally aligning phoneme-level information, facial expression and gesture. Each RRL document comprises four principal parts: (1) a representation of the initially shared information between the interlocutors (common ground); (2) the participants of the dialogue with name, gender, voice, or personality; (3) the dialogue acts along with their type, speaker, addressees, emotion category, semantic content, what it is a reaction to (adjacency pairs), and realization (prosody, gestures, and sentences out of words, syllables and phonemes); (4) the temporal ordering of the dialogue acts, specified as sequential or overlapping events. Underspecification is particularly useful for the relative timing of dialogue acts, for instance to specify that one multimodal utterance is followed by another, while a back-channel behavior of the listener starts with the first utterance.

---

[1] For the RRL XML Schema see www.ofai.at/research/nlu/NECA/RRL/index.html

3 Towards a Unified Framework: SAIBA

The first step towards a unifying representational framework for multimodal generation is to lay down the general planning stages and knowledge structures that are involved in the creation of multimodal communicative behavior. We do not want to impose a particular micro-architecture here. Yet, as our goal is to define representtation languages that can serve as clear interfaces at separate levels of abstraction—building upon our experiences from the abovementioned previous systems—we need to modularize the problem. We aim for the representation languages to be (1) independent of a particular application or domain, (2) independent of the employed graphics and sound player model, (3) and to represent a clear-cut separation between information types (function-related versus process-related specification of behavior).

The generation of natural multimodal output requires a time-critical production process with high flexibility. To scaffold this production process we introduced the *SAIBA* framework (Situation, Agent, Intention, Behavior, Animation), and specify the macro-scale multimodal generation consisting of processing stages on three different levels: (1) planning of a communicative intent, (2) planning of a multimodal realization of this intent, and (3) realization of the planned behaviors. See Fig. 1 for an illustration of the SAIBA framework.

Fig. 1. SAIBA framework for multimodal generation

The three levels lay down a general structure for every multimodal behavior generation system. While implemented systems have often concentrated on processing steps that pertain to one particular level, and have short-circuited others, we consider these subsequent stages to be in principle involved in the generation of each multimodal behavior an agent is to perform. The stages are bi-directionally linked to one another, with one stage delivering input to the next stage and feedback data running back to previous stages. Ideally, every stage along with its input and output representations is flexible and powerful enough to avoid limiting the expressiveness of the previous stage. We treat the processing within each stage and its internal structure largely as a "black box" or (more appropriately) as open research questions. Instead, we focus on the kind of data that is being processed at these stages, and on specifying the particular type and form of the information that needs to be represented as interfaces bridging the "gaps" between them. The rationale is that a clear-cut definition of information flow at the interfaces allows for a modular architecture and opens the possibility of combining solutions from different researchers without too much code modification.

The interface between stages (1) and (2)—Intent Planning and Behavior Planning—describes communicative and expressive intent without any reference to physical behavior. We call the language that we propose for specifying such information the *Function Markup Language* (FML). It is meant to provide a semantic description that accounts for the aspects that are relevant and influential in the planning of verbal and nonverbal behavior. An FML description must thus fulfill two functions. First, it must define the basic semantic units associated with a communicative event. Secondly, it should allow the annotation of these units with properties that further describe communicative function such as expressive, affective, discursive, epistemic, or pragmatic functions. Previous languages have started to address several of these issues, and a clearer picture of this terrain is forming, but coming up with a unified language is work in progress and beyond the scope of this paper.

The interface between (2) and (3)—Behavior Planning and Behavior Realization—describes multimodal behaviors as they are to be realized by the final stage of the generation pipeline. We propose the *Behavior Markup Language* (BML) for this purpose. In theory, a realization engine can realize every aspect of behavior (verbal, gestural, phonological, etc.) the behavior planner comes up with. In practice, when synthesizing and scheduling speech and animated graphics one often draws from a limited set of predefined animations or sound files. That is, the level of detail of representing behavior between behavior planning and behavior realization depends on the particular realization model. For instance, a realizer that employs a text-to-speech module and is able to produce movements on the fly by means of, e.g., procedural animations could take as input rather flexible descriptions of single words along with prosodic commands or the morphological features of a hand gesture. A behavior realization that rests upon a fixed repository of animations and allows for a low degree of parameterization would need a unique identifier along with a set of appropriate parameters. We aim for BML to stay above such specific process implementations (the boxes in Figure 1), i.e. to provide a general, player-independent description of multimodal behavior that can be used to control an agent. Nevertheless, it needs to provide a sufficient level of detail in describing behavior, from the mere occurrence and the relative timing of the involved actions, to the detailed (yet player-independent) definition of a behavior's form. Behavior Planning will thus be concerned with fleshing out a BML description in necessary detail. In concretizing this specification, the planner could draw upon a lexicon of BML behavior definitions, a *Gesticon* (see Figure 1), that would also provide a basis for attuning to the capabilities of the realizer. Further, it is possible that multiple lexicons like the Gesticon are used by the processes at each stage of planning. This choice is dependent on the particular approach and architectural use of the SAIBA model.

4   Behavior Markup Language: BML

This section describes the proposed communicative behavior markup language, starting with the general features of the language that address fundamental requirements and then goes on to describe some of the behaviors that will be covered. It should be pointed out again that this is work in progress and therefore BML will continue to evolve as our collaboration matures.

4.1 General Structure

The communicative behavior markup language, or BML, is an XML based language that can be embedded in a larger XML message or document simply by starting a `<bml>` block and filling it with behaviors that need to be realized by an agent. The behaviors are listed one after another, at the same level in the XML hierarchy, with no significance given to their order. Generally the behaviors are single elements that contain no text or other elements, but this is not required. Behavior parameters, some of which are general and some of which are behavior specific, are specified as attribute values of the behavior element. A simple behavior block is shown in Fig. 2.

```
<bml>
    <head id="h1" type="nod" amount="0.4"/>
    <face id="f1" type="eyebrows" amount="1.0"/>
</bml>
```

Fig. 2. A simple example of a BML block

Most attributes in a behavior element are optional and the assumption is that reasonable default values will be used when attributes are left out. For example, the behavior `<head type="nod"/>` could be expected to produce a typical nod. If no timing constraints are given, the behaviors are all expected to start immediately and run for their default durations.

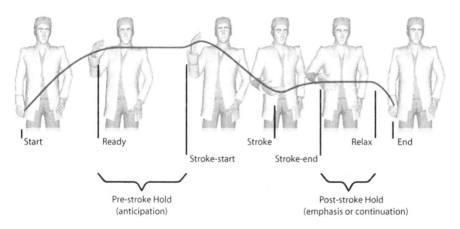

Fig. 3. The synchronization points of a communicative behavior

4.2 Synchronization

While some meaning can be carried by the form of a communicative behavior, it's also the temporal context that shapes its interpretation. For example, the co-occurrence of a pointing gesture and the verbalization of the phrase "that one", allows us to locate a unique referent. Similarly, seeing someone express disgust on their face as they gaze upon their food, gives us a strong clue about what the emotional display describes. In addition to co-occurrence, the order and in-between timing can also demonstrate meaningful relationships. Therefore an important feature of BML is the specification of temporal constraints. When the communication of a particular intent relies on timing, the behavior planner needs to fill in crucial timing constraints while leaving all other timing information unspecified. This gives the realizer maximum flexibility for realizing the behavior while ensuring that meaning does not get lost.

Synchronization Points. Temporal constraints in BML are specified using two important constructs: A behavior ID and a behavior synchronization point. The behavior ID is a unique identifier given to a behavior instance so that it can be referenced from other behaviors. The behavior synchronization points, or sync-points, provide significant points of alignment between behaviors based on the typical movement phases that a behavior goes through during its realization. These phases are illustrated in Fig. 3.

The preparation for or visible anticipation of the behavior occurs between *start* and *ready*, and the retraction back to neutral or previous state occurs between *relax* and *end*. The actual behavior takes place between the *ready* and *relax*, with the most significant or semantically rich motion during the stroke phase, between *stroke-start* and *stroke-end*, with the greatest effort coinciding with the *stroke* point. A behavior does not need to have a stroke phase, so for example looking at something will only involve ready (the time of making eye-contact) and relax (the time of breaking eye-contact). If no preparation or relaxation is needed, then start and ready refer to the same point in time, and relax and end refer to the same point in time.

```
<bml>
  <gesture id="g1" type="beat"/>
  <head type="nod" stroke="g1:stroke"/>
  <gaze target="object1" start="g1:ready" end="g1:relax"/>
</bml>
```

Fig. 4. An example of synchronizing head movement and gaze with a gesture

The sync-points are actual attributes in all BML behavior elements and their value can be a reference to any other sync-point, ensuring temporal alignment. A simple example of a head nod and a targeted gaze co-occurring with various phases of a gesture is given in Fig. 4.

Conditions and Events. In addition to aligning sync-points of behaviors with each other, they can also be aligned with a sync-point that gets triggered based on some condition or by the arrival of an event. This is accomplished by introducing a special <wait> behavior whose duration is either determined by the satisfaction of a condition or the reception of an event. As a fall-back, a time-out duration can also be specified. A couple of different examples of how <wait> can be used are given in Fig. 5. The second example also introduces an <event> behavior that can generate events for synchronization.

4.3 Behavior Elements

The behaviors themselves fall into general behavior categories that can then be further defined through a possible sub-type attribute and several type-specific attributes. The general behavior categorization is meant to be fairly stable, while the set of attributes are expected to evolve with ongoing research (see Table 1). Not all attributes are required, and some attributes may refine the behavior in such detail that only certain animation system can make use of them. The particular decomposition is motivated on the one hand by high-level considerations such as a) physiology (muscular contraction and joint articulation), and b) existing studies on communicative non-verbal behavior. On the other hand there are computational factors. For instance: the same hand configuration can be used with several arm movements. Gaze and head movement are separated in order to provide more flexibility for animation of gaze behavior, in particular allowing head movement while gazing at something. In our formal specification we use <torso> for characterizing spine movement and shoulders. While in the <body> element pelvis and legs are specified as parts of posture. The naming of behavior elements is mostly drawn from the existing set of XML languages discussed earlier in this paper.

Each of these BML elements contains attributes that describe the visual appearance and movement dynamics of the behavior in order to achieve certain expressive effects. In what follows we briefly describe gesture, gaze and face behaviors since they are commonly used during the communicative process and often get special attention in ECAs systems. All of them show different kinds of complexity.

Table 1. The BML behavior elements

BML Element	Description
<head>	Movement of the head independent of eyes. Types include nodding, shaking, tossing and orienting to a given angle.
<torso>	Movement of the orientation and shape of the spine and shoulder.
<face>	Movement of facial muscles to form certain expressions. Types include eyebrow, eyelid and larger expressive mouth movements.
<gaze>	Coordinated movement of the eyes, neck and head direction, indicating where the character is looking.
<body>	Full body movement, generally independent of the other behaviors. Types include overall orientation, position and posture.
<legs>	Movements of the body elements downward from the hip: pelvis, hip, legs including knee, toes and ankle.
<gesture>	Coordinated movement with arms and hands, including pointing, reaching, emphasizing (beating), depicting and signaling.
<speech>	Verbal and paraverbal behavior, including the words to be spoken (for example by a speech synthesizer), prosody information and special paralinguistic behaviors (for example filled pauses).
<lips>	This element is used for controlling lip shapes including the visualization of phonemes.

Gesture Entry. Gestures are complex, usually being composed by one or a sequence of basic gesture elements, each of which describes a basic hand-arm movement trajectory. Adapted from MURML and ASL hand shape configuration description [13], gestures are composed of trajectory, hand shape, a thumb orientation, and fingers shapes. Complex gestures are represented by means of a collection of behavior elements with different type attributes, and which are aligned via synchronization points.

Face Entry. Within behavior specification languages facial expressions are often described by a set of labels such as smile, raise eyebrow, open mouth etc. Such descriptions limit the encoding variability. While FACS allows variability in the specification of surface form, it is not widely used in the graphics community. Facial expression in graphics models is commonly described by sets of low-level parameters, e.g. MPEG-4, or via muscle contraction. Thus to be independent of individual facial models, we propose describing facial expression via sets of face elements, with each set being a placeholder for various model-dependent facial descriptions. Via synchronization points we are able to account for the two major approaches to facial display of emotions: (1) The more static and traditional one, where whole emotional displays are switched on and off instantaneously and (2) the more dynamic approach where emotional displays gradually set in and slowly fade out.

```
<bml>
    <gesture id="g1" type="point" target="object1"/>
    <body id="b1" posture="sit"/>
    <wait id="w1" condition="g1:end AND b1:end"/>
    <gaze target="object2" start="w1:end"/>
</bml>

<bml>
    <speech id="s1" type="text/plain">
        First sentence.
    </speech>
    <event start="s1:end" emit="ACT1_COMPLETE" />
</bml>

<bml>
    <wait id="w1" event="ACT1_COMPLETE" duration="5.0"/>
    <speech type="text/plain" start="w1:end">
        Second sentence.
    </speech>
</bml>
```

Fig. 5. Examples of how <wait> can align a behavior with a condition or an event

Gaze Entry. Gaze is another example of a complex modality, comprising: (1) only eye direction, (2) neck, head and eyes showing one direction or (3) neck, head and eyes showing individual directions. Via the referencing mechanism of BML, gaze direction is specified relative to a target. This is different from FACS and MPEG-4 where gaze direction is absolute (e.g. defined by angle values).

Speech Entry. The speech element is used for specifying the verbal and paraverbal behavior. It typically contains marked-up text to be rendered by a speech synthesizer but also may contain references to plain sound files. The purpose of the mark-up is two-fold. On the one hand it is used for supporting the synthesis process by giving directives on prosody and pronunciation; on the other hand the mark-up is used for identifying elements (e.g. words or prosodic boundaries) within the text. These elements are then to be used as references for the synchronization of speech and non-verbal behavior. In order to keep BML flexible enough to deal with the considerable variety of existing speech synthesizers and speech markup languages (e.g. SSML or VoiceXML) the actual type of mark-up language is left open.

4.4 Gesticon

The design of BML allows for disentangling a behavior *form description* and its *instantiation* in a communicative process. It is therefore easy to create what has been called a Gesticon [9] or Behavior Lexicon [17] – a dictionary of behavior descriptions. A strong property of the BML language is its independence of graphics models, rendering technologies and applications. Creating gesture shape, facial expression, body posture etc. can be very time consuming, so sharing behavior definitions would be a great help to the ECA community.

5 Usage

As we have already mentioned, the Behavior Markup Language presented here is an improvement and extension of prior related languages that have been used extensively in many projects [2, 3, 4, 7, 9, 11, 12, 17, 20]. The authors and their labs have committed to moving towards BML in their work, and several efforts are already underway to build parsers and planning modules that are compatible with it. In the spirit of this effort we are hopeful that software will be made available under relatively open licenses that enables others to adopt the BML in their work without having to replicate a lot of the work that has gone into the language itself as well as the software modules that can use it. Since the processes are intentionally left unspecified as open research questions, we envision there being a selection of approaches to how BML (and later FML) are used and produced – this is where the benefits of a unified approach will become even clearer: By leaving out a reference to the processes that produce and control behavior we intend to reap the benefits of a common foundation without closing the door on new methods of planning and control.

Besides working toward the actual employment of BML and FML in our own system to accelerate the development of software modules, we think it is central to inform and guide the development of the overall framework by working towards differently challenging scenarios. We have thus started to define use cases that describe the kinds of natural multimodal behavior that we ultimately want to be able to specify in BML and FML. Such cases include (1) a speaker waiting until she has finished pointing at an object and has determined that the listener is also attending to the object; (2) two agents shaking hands; (3) a speaker saying "Give me [the cake]", where [the cake] is accompanied by an iconic gesture describing an attribute of the cake; (4) a speaker using indirectness as part of politenss, such as saying "how are we doing for time" to indicate "we need to hurry". Use cases like these pose specific and big challenges for representing and generating multimodal behavior. While implementing and extending our framework, also beyond what we aim to achieve in our current research settings, we consider using these test cases as milestones for actual demos.

6 Conclusion

In this paper we have presented first steps toward a common framework for multimodal generation, enabling people to better work together and to use each other's work with a minimal amount of custom effort. We have proposed BML as a representation language meant as a clear interface between modules of behavior planning and realization. The current focus of this work has been to specify the communicative and expressive behaviors traditionally associated with explicit, verbal communication in face-to-face dialog. We plan to explore extensions to BML and FML that support additional kinds of behavior, including those that may not have any associated communicative intent. Specifying such behaviors may lead us to a more general scripting language that incorporates the BML work described here as a key component. We encourage all researchers and practitioners working on intelligent virtual agents to contribute to this ongoing effort. The more people that join this discussion, the better the chances that we will find a representation that provides the groundwork for many of the employed generation systems, and where people can actively collaborate either by sharing their experiences and knowledge or by directly exchanging system components. The *Mindmakers* website (www.mindmakers.org) provides a forum for discussion and collaboration related to this effort, as well as documentation of the full BML specification.

Acknowledgements

We would like to thank our other collaborators in this effort, in particular Lewis Johnson and Norm Badler. We are grateful to Reykjavik University for supporting our meeting in Iceland. The work on the Gesticon has been partially supported by the EU Network of Excellence HUMAINE (IST-507422) and by the Austrian Funds for Research and Technology Promotion for Industry (FFF 808818/2970 KA/SA). CADIA participation was made possible in part by RANNÍS grant 050013021 and a Marie Curie European Reintegration Grant within the 6th European Community Framework Programme. OFAI is supported by the Austrian Federal Ministry for Education, Science and Culture and by the Austrian Federal Ministry for Transport, Innovation and Technology. This publication reflects only the authors' views. The European Union is not liable for any use that may be made of the information contained herein.

References

1. Cassell, J., Pelachaud, C., Badler, N., Steedman, M., Achorn, B., Becket, T., Douville, B., Prevost, S., and Stone, M., (1994) Animated Conversation: Rule-Based Generation of Facial Expression, Gesture and Spoken Intonation for Multiple Conversational Agents. Siggraph 94 Conference Proceedings, ACM SIGGRAPH, Addison Wesley, 413-420.
2. Cassell, J., Vilhjálmsson, H., and Bickmore T., (2001) BEAT : the Behavior Expression Animation Toolkit, Proc. ACM SIGGRAPH 2001, Los Angeles, August 12-17, 477-486.

3. Cassell, J., Vilhjálmsson, H., Chang, K., Bickmore, T., Campbell, L. and Yan, H., (1999). Requirements for an Architecture for Embodied Conversational Characters, Computer Animation and Simulation '99 (Eurographics Series). Vienna, Austria: Springer Verlag

4. DeCarolis B., Pelachaud C., Poggi I, and Steedman M. (2004). APML, a mark-up language for believable behavior generation. In H. Prendinger and M. Ishizuka, editors, *Life-like Characters. Tools, Affective Functions and Applications*, 65--85. Springer.

5. Hartmann, B., Mancini, M., and Pelachaud, C. (2002). Formational parameters and adaptive prototype instantiation for MPEG-4 compliant gesture synthesis. In *Computer Animation'02*, Geneva, Switzerland. IEEE Computer Society Press.

6. Kopp S.,, B. Jung, N. Lessmann, I. Wachsmuth:, (2003) Max--A Multimodal Assistant in Virtual Reality Construction. KI 4/03: 11-17.

7. Kopp S., Wachsmuth I. (2004): Synthesizing Multimodal Utterances for Conversational Agents. *Computer Animation and Virtual Worlds,* 15(1): 39-52

8. Krenn B. (2005). Representational Lego for ECAs, *Background paper for a presentation held at the FP6 NoE HUMAINE Workshop on Emotion and Interaction. Paris, 10-11 March.*

9. Krenn B., Pirker H. (2004). Defining the Gesticon: Language and Gesture Coordination for Interacting Embodied Agents, in *Proc. of the AISB-2004 Symposium on Language, Speech and Gesture for Expressive Characters*, University of Leeds, UK, 107-115.

10. Martell C. (2002). FORM: An Extensible, Kinematically-based Gesture Annotation Scheme in *Proceedings of the 2002 International Conference on Language Resources and Evaluation*, Las Palmas, Canary Island.

11. Piwek P., Krenn B., Schröder M., Grice M., Baumann S., Pirker H. (2002). RRL: A Rich Representation Language for the Description of Agent Behaviour in NECA, In Proceedings of the Workshop *Embodied conversational agents - let's specify and evaluate them!*, held in conjunction with AAMAS-02, July 16 2002, Bologna, Italy.

12. Prendinger H., Descamps S., Ishizuka M. (2004). MPML: A markup language for controlling the behavior of life-like characters, *Journal of Visual Languages and Computing*,15(2):183-203

13. Stokoe W. C., Casterline D. C. and Croneberg C. G. (1976). *A dictionary of American sign language on linguistic principles.* Linstok Press

14. Searle, J. R. (1969). *Speech acts: An essay in the philosophy of language.* London: Cambridge Univ. Press.

15. Thórisson, K. R. (1993). Dialogue Control in Social Interface Agents. *InterCHI Adjunct Proceedings '93*, Amsterdam, April, 139-140.

16. Thórisson, K. R. (1995). Computational Characteristics of Multimodal Dialogue. *AAAI Fall Symposium on Embodied Language and Action*, Massachusetts Institute of Technology, Cambridge, Massachusetts, November 10-12, 102-108.

17. Thórisson, K. R. (1999). A Mind Model for Multimodal Communicative Creatures and Humanoids. International Journal of Applied Artificial Intelligence, 13(4-5): 449-486.

18. Thórisson, K. R., Vilhjalmsson, H., Kopp, S., Pelachaud, C. (2006). Report on Representations for Multimodal Generation Workshop. *AI Magazine*, 27(1), 108.

19. Vilhjalmsson, H. (2004). Animating Conversation in Online Games. In M. Rauterberg (ed.), *Entertainment Computing ICEC 2004, Lecture Notes in Computer Science 3166*, 139-150, Springer.

20. Vilhjalmsson, H. (2005). Augmenting Online Conversation through Automated Discourse Tagging, 6th annual minitrack on Persistent Conversation at the 38th Hawaii International Conference on System Sciences, January 3-6, Hilton Waikoloa Village, Big Island, Hawaii, IEEE.

MPML3D: A Reactive Framework for the Multimodal Presentation Markup Language

Michael Nischt[1], Helmut Prendinger[2],
Elisabeth André[1], and Mitsuru Ishizuka[3]

[1] Institute of Computer Science, University of Augsburg
Eichleitnerstr. 30, D-86135 Augsburg, Germany
Michael.Rudolf.Anton.Nischt@Student.Uni-Augsburg.De,
Andre@Informatik.Uni-Augsburg.De
[2] National Institute of Informatics
2-1-2 Hitotsubashi, Chiyoda-ku, Tokyo 101-8430, Japan
helmut@nii.ac.jp
[3] Graduate School of Information Science and Technology, University of Tokyo
7-3-1 Hongo, Bunkyo-ku, Tokyo 113-8656, Japan
ishizuka@i.u-tokyo.ac.jp

Abstract. MPML3D is our first candidate of the next generation of authoring languages aimed at supporting digital content creators in providing highly appealing and highly interactive content with little effort. The language is based on our previously developed family of Multimodal Presentation Markup Languages (MPML) that broadly followed the "sequential" and "parallel" tagging structure scheme for generating presynchronized presentations featuring life-like characters and interactions with the user. The new markup language MPML3D deviates from this design framework and proposes a reactive model instead, which is apt to handle interaction-rich scenarios with highly realistic 3D characters. Interaction in previous versions of MPML could be handled only at the cost of considerable scripting effort due to branching. By contrast, MPML3D advocates a reactive model that allows perceptions of other characters or the user interfere with the presentation flow at any time, and thus facilitates natural and unrestricted interaction. MPML3D is designed as a powerful and flexible language that is easy-to-use by non-experts, but it is also extensible as it allows content creators to add functionality such as a narrative model by using popular scripting languages.

1 Introduction

Animated characters were quickly accepted as attractive and engaging mediators for effective human-computer interaction, initially for their mere novelty and entertainment value, but recently more and more for their demonstrated benefit as virtual sales agents, tutors, and social interaction partners, among others [14]. However, when integrated into users' daily life as virtual assistants, users will assume high realism and expressivity of the characters, and more importantly, a high level of interactivity and awareness of their need for high-quality information as well as a natural and enjoyable interaction experience.

J. Gratch et al. (Eds.): IVA 2006, LNAI 4133, pp. 218–229, 2006.
© Springer-Verlag Berlin Heidelberg 2006

The bottleneck for digital content providers typically is the lack of appropriate authoring tools to meet those expectations. For this purpose, we previously designed MPML as a support for non-professionals to create affective multimodal content with life-like characters easily, i.e. without assuming knowledge in a scripting language such as JavaScript or a programming language like Java. Depending on the character system used, including 2D and 3D cartoon-style agents and the Honda humanoid robot ASIMO, different versions of MPML emerged [8]. While the MPML family of markup languages shares a common vision (simple authoring) and some core XML tagging structures, most notably for sequential and parallel character behavior execution, versions with specialized functionality were necessitated by the nature of each character system used and its operating environment (web-based, mobile, real world). In addition, the implementation had to be adapted for each character system, by providing a dedicated parser.

Support for authoring scenarios with frequent interaction among characters and users were not an emphasis of previous versions of MPML, while still possible via (heavily) nested "sequential" and "parallel" tags. In response to the high demand in providing interaction-rich scenarios, we will therefore advocate the next generation of MPML-style markup languages, which is based on a reactive rather than a pre-synchronized behavior model. MPML3D allows content authors to define appropriate verbal and non-verbal responses, which are active during the entire presentation and can therefore suspend the scripted part of the presentation at any time. This paper gives a detailed description of and justification for the re-design of MPML with the overall goal of providing an easy-to-use markup language for highly interactive scenarios.

The rest of the paper is organized as follows. The next section motivates the new language by way of our implemented scenario. Section 3 reports on related work. Section 4 describes the system architecture of our reactive model and its new features. Section 5 is dedicated to an overview of the used tagging structures. Section 6 concludes the paper.

2   Motivating Example

As a show-case for the affordances of a highly interactive scenario, we implemented a virtual sales scenario where a team of two 3D animated agents presents MP3 players to a human user. A professional Japanese character designer for "digital idols" created two highly realistic and expressive 3D agents (female and male), based on the appearance of two famous Japanese actors. Each character can perform body and facial gestures (emotional expressions), speak with proper lip-synchronization and direct its gaze at any specified scene entity as well as the user seated in front of the computer display screen (see Fig. 1).

The story line is that two characters present two MP3 players developed by their enterprise. At the beginning, one character is in favor of a slim, easy to use version and the other one prefers the high-end product with an unparalleled

Fig. 1. Presentation of MP3 players by two Japanese-style 3D characters

feature set. During the presentation they realize, that the gadget presented by the other character would fulfill their particular needs better than what they have presented themselves. Both are startled by that, and try to figure out which player would actually be most attractive to the user. Note that the first part of our presentation is non-interactive and does not put high demands on a markup language. It can in principle be easily dealt with by using available synchronization languages like SMIL [18] and MPML [13,8].

However, in order to increase the level of interactivity and engagement both between characters and between the characters and the user, each character should have the capability to perceive the actions of its counterpart character and the user. This capability is fundamental to lively and engaging human-human communication where participants continuously adapt to the interlocutor's state of attention and emotion, and react accordingly. The new markup language thus provides means for continuously (i) informing each character about the current state of action execution of the other character, and (ii) informing the characters about the state of the user. We handle inter-agent communication and feedback by message-passing, and introduce eye tracking as an input modality to recognize the user's state of attention and interest. Analyzing gaze behavior (or "eye gestures") is a powerful method to detect a user's interest and preference among alternatives [4]. We also allow for simple speech input from the user, following a keyword spotting approach. The second part of the MP3 player presentation thus aims at a high level of interactivity among the participants of the scenario (two characters and one user) and their mutual awareness. This kind of interaction cannot be easily handled by currently available markup languages since it assumes that characters may respond to the other agents (human and virtual) at any time.

3   Related Work

Within the past five years, a range of markup languages and associated technologies were developed in order to direct the verbal and non-verbal behavior of animated agents. The Character Markup Language (CML) puts an emphasis on gesture behavior and its modulation by the agent's emotional state and personality [3]. A similar focus is present in the Parameter Action Representation (PAR), which allows one to specify various action parameters such as purpose, duration, and manner that can be modulated by affect related parameters [1]. While providing effective means to express affect and associated character movement, those languages were designed with professional animators rather than non-expert content authors in mind. The Affective Presentation Markup Language (APML) targets the representation of communicative functions between an agent and a user that may contain the speaker's belief state (certainty of utterance) and intention (request, inform) as parameters [5]. Communicative behavior is also the underlying motivation for the Behavior Expression Animation Toolkit (BEAT) that proposes an elaborate mechanism for the accurate synchronization between speech and conversational gestures of a character [6]. The fine-grained control of parallel and sequential components of gestures was also the motivation behind the development of MURML [9].

All of the above mentioned systems are restricted to synchronizing the behavior of a single character. An interesting approach to authoring multi-character interactions has been suggested in the Inhabited Market Place (IMP) system that creates presentation dialogues automatically by employing a central planner [2]. Character-specific dialogue contributions (e.g. elementary presentation acts) constitute leaf nodes in the decomposed hierarchical plan tree. The IMP system assumes that appropriate STRIPS-style plan operators have been defined, and hence might be an infeasible approach for non-scientists. The system has also been extended to include the user as part of the conversation (and de-centralized planning as a further option), as in the MIAU system [16]. Nevertheless, creating reactive behaviors within MIAU requires basic knowledge of planning formalisms. The Rich Representation Language (RRL) has been developed to specify the interaction between two or more virtual agents [12]. Its use requires less training effort than, for example, the planning mechanism employed in IMP; however, RRL does not deal with anytime user interactions.

There are only a few approaches that explicitly deal with reactive agent behaviors. BEAT accounts for time-line based as well as reactive gesture generation. Nevertheless, reactivity rather refers to events triggered by the speech synthesizer than to user interruptions. Similarly, STEP [17] includes interaction operators to deal with the environment in which the movements and actions take place. ABL (A Behavior Language) is a highly sophisticated language to coordinate multiple characters while being reactive to user input, with the core goal of creating compelling dramatic experiences [10]. Despite its potential for creating highly interactive presentations, generating behaviors with ABL is close to programming in Java, which likely exceeds the skill level of the average content creator. The system most closely related to MPML3D is SceneMaker, a toolkit for composing interactive performances between life-like characters that are adaptive to user actions [7]. The scene flow is realized by a finite state machine, whereby both nodes and transitions can have playable scenes associated with them. A scene is a pre-scripted dialogue (of variable size) between two characters. Like the MPML3D system, SceneMaker targets non-expert content providers. A major distinction between the two systems is that content representation in SceneMaker is scene-based, whereas in MPML3D, each character has its own representation of possible actions (and their conditions), which is a prerequisite for the desired reactive behavior.

4   Multimodal Presentation Markup Language Based on a Reactive Model

In this section, we propose a major re-design of the MPML language based on the following core observation. Multi-character applications with frequent "barge-in interruption" from the user by speech, gesture, or even gaze and physiological activity will become the rule rather than the exception. MPML as currently defined is either not able to handle such situations (e.g. continuous speech) or cumbersome, as in the case of input-dependent branching. In the following sections we will first describe the new system architecture and we will then explain the new features of MPMP3D.

4.1   MPML3D System Architecture

An overview of the MPML3D system architecture is shown in Fig. 2. Its main components are the *user* and *developer layers*, and the *animation engine*, for which accessibility from the developer layer has to be created.

The main modules can be described as follows. The *user layer* is dedicated to creating the content for interactive presentations. It defines the Schema for the

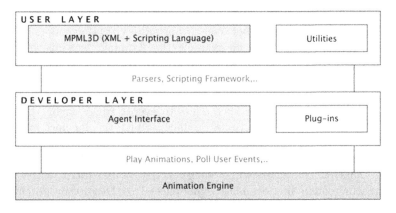

Fig. 2. System architecture

XML-based MPML3D format, to which each instance must conform. In order to maintain a high level of flexibility, statements of a scripting language can be embedded into the markup language. Currently, we only use Javascript (as used in previous MPML versions), but we also envision to support other popular languages like Ruby, Python or Groovy in the near future. Those can be either utilized to access the functionality provided by the developer layer, or to use self-developed Java objects (utilities), e.g. ones that encapsulate emotion or social behavior models.

The *developer layer* can be seen as an intermediate layer, uncoupling the user layer from particular implementations. It is a simple Java API, providing base classes for an agent's actions and its perception capabilities. Although we already provide a basic set of classes, new ones can be easily integrated through the plug-in architecture. By employing annotation and reflection features as offered by languages such as Java or C#, new actions and perceptions can be used in MPML3D without changing the parser. Moreover, this approach allows editors to recognize the plug-ins automatically no matter whether these editors are text based, just provide an auto-completion facility, or are completely graphical editors like the MPML3.0 Visual Editor described in [13].

The *animation engine* itself is not part of the MPML3D system. It is responsible for manipulating a character's internal state and rendering it, and also has to process the user inputs such as gaze behavior or speech. Popular animation engines include game engines, X3D and MPEG4 players, and APIs for mobile phones or physical robots. Currently, we use a self-created system that renders the animated scene using OpenGL and OpenAL. Here, both the environment and the characters are directly transferred from digital content creation tools (Autodesk's 3DS Max or Maya) to the application (see [11] for details).

4.2   New Features of MPML3D

Today's character-based applications demonstrate an increased demand for interactivity and awareness of user input modalities. Although previous versions of MPML were capable of dealing with user input by using conditional statements, the resulting scripts were deeply nested and became cumbersome to extend and read. Specifically, MPML was not designed for anytime interruption of a character's behavior when the user started speaking (or provides other input, e.g. a particular gaze behavior) or when agents interrupt each other.

The issue here is to solve the problem of permanent attendance to react to all possible inputs from the user or another agent. Since previous versions of MPML represent interactive presentations as a branched structure, one had to test all possible user inputs after every action tag and create new character responses for each of those conditional nodes, resulting in an enormous out-degree (if frequent interaction was desirable). In order to overcome this limitation in MPML, the new MPML3D language changes the organization of the presentation to a *reactive model*. In particular, an agent's behavior is determined by its perception that may trigger and interrupt actions, clustered into tasks (i.e. sequences of actions). This not only simplifies the authoring of a scenario, but also allows one to reuse attentive behaviors across different presentations and scenarios. The design of a reactive model deviates from the design of MPML that was derived from markup languages that govern the behavior of multiple processes essentially by sequential and parallel execution, e.g. the popular Synchronized Multimedia Integration Language (SMIL) [18], and thus deserves extra justification. As argued in [15], the similarity of markup languages for characters to "easy to understand" languages such as HTML might not be of primary importance since appropriate easy-to-use editing tools will eventually be available for them, and more importantly, those languages might fail to handle the complexity of interaction among agents (including human agents) as observed in human-human face-to-face communication. While the "parallel" tag used in current markup languages assumes independence of behavior, natural communication demonstrates mutual adaptation between speaker and listener (sometimes called "alignment"). For instance, when noticing undesired effects of their utterance in the listener's facial expression, such as irritation, speakers often take counteractions *while* speaking, by adapting e.g. the politeness level of the utterance. These observations suggest an approach like MPML3D that is based on actions *and* (continuous) perception.

The transition from a pre-synchronized model to a reactive model obviously assumes a revision of other aspects of the language as well, specifically the representation of agent actions. In contrast to former versions, where the script for all characters was defined in a single file, the behavior of each agent is now contained in one dedicated MPML3D file, which is seen as the behavior space of that agent. The advantage of such a distributed architecture combined with a reactive model for executing the agents' tasks regards the greater flexibility in adding additional agents to the presentation. Note that individual actions of the same character, e.g. starting a gesture when a specific word is spoken, are synchronized in its own MPML3D file. This approach is not restrictive since a task, consisting of such an arrangement, can be started, interrupted and resumed upon the perception of actions performed by other agents, as well as user input.

The design principles put forth for the MPML family [13,8] also apply to the new MPML3D language, i.e. *Ease of Use (Intelligibility)*, *Extensibility (Accessibility)*, i.e. provision for embedded scripting statements for accessing e.g. Java classes from code libraries, and *Easy Distribution*.

5   MPML3D Tagging Structures

In this section we will briefly introduce the tags being used in MPML3D. Like in previous versions, the document is divided into a **Head** and **Body** part after the root element noted as **MPML3D**. The **Head** element specifies general information through HTML-like Meta tags that can be used to define the units for the documents. For instance, the preferred distance measure may be either meters or feet and angles could be defined in radians or degrees, depending on what the author is most familiar with. Furthermore, the character's action and perception capabilities must be defined here, no matter whether those are included in the standard set or are new ones available through the plug-in mechanism of the developer layer. This is done using the Extension tag, which also defines the action class, which can be referred in the Body part. Here are two examples:

```
<Extension name="Speak" type="action" class="mpml.Speak"/>
<Extension name="Listen" type="perception" class="mpml.Listen"/>
```

Finally, the Head tag can contain a single Script node, defining the scripting language. It either references an external file or lists the source code directly. Note that in contrast to JavaScript embedded in HTML, the code is never written as a comment. Although MPML3D authors can create presentations entirely without using an embedded scripting language, the potential benefit is significant. The defined functions can be used as event listeners in order to check conditions for execution, but also every defined Task, Action and Perception given an identifier is exposed to the script. This allows the author to access every public property and method defined in the Java objects of the developer layer. An example excerpt for an event-listener deactivating a task with id 'task1' is:

```
<Script language="js">
    function anEventListener() { task1.active = false; }
    .. // other variable, function and object declarations
</Script>
```

The Body part defines the presentation flow. In MPML3D, this is done through a list of Tasks, which are to be performed but can be interrupted by certain Perceptions. A Task, on the other hand, corresponds to a list of Actions along with instructions when and how to execute them. Consequently, these three elements can be seen as the main components of MPML3D. It is important to notice that all of them are temporal constructs, i.e. they have a beginning and ending state. Therefore, the user-code defined in the Script tag can be associated with the optional node attributes onBegin and onEnd.

We now turn to describing properties of these three tags. We begin with describing the Task tag, since it contains the others. Besides the events onInterrupt and onResume, which are fired when the task is interrupted or resumed afterwards, there are a few other attributes as shown below – all being optional.

```
<Task id="task1" priority="100" active="true" once="true" token="token1">
..
</Task>
```

As mentioned before, an id can be assigned to a task to expose it to the script engine. If none is specified, the corresponding Java object is not accessible. The next attribute, called priority, defines how urgent a task is. It is used in the default selection mechanism for the task that could be performed. Only a task of higher priority can interrupt another. The default value is zero. The next two attributes (active, once) are closely related; their specified (default) values cause a task to be active at the beginning and deactivated after a successful execution. Finally, a task can expose a public token while performing. Since this token can be perceived by other characters, it is a convenient way to synchronize the behavior of multiple characters in non-interactive parts of the presentation, which was handled by the "par" tag in previous versions of MPML. By default, a task is not visible to other characters.

Inside the Task element we provide (among others) the two command tags, called Perform and Interrupt, as children. Both can contain perceptions upon which the command is triggered, but before describing those, we will explain their attributes.

```
<Perform interrupt="false" condition="testPerform">
..
</Perform>
<Interrupt resume="false" condition="testInterrupt">
..
</Interrupt>
```

If the interrupt attribute is set to true, the priority of the task is compared to the one of the currently executed task (if there is any) to decide whether it can be interrupted. Without the attribute, or the value set to false, the task will compete for execution with other non-performing tasks depending on their priority only. The resume attribute of the Interrupt node determines whether the task should be resumed after it is interrupted. Finally, the condition attribute can occur within either tag. If present, its value is evaluated along with the perception of the child element by calling script functions. If it evaluates to false, the command is not executed.

As stated above, the commands Perform and Interrupt contain perceptions that may trigger them. A perception belongs to specified class. This is not only used to classify the perception, but also defines a possible list of properties which can be declared to narrow down the potential set of user input. Since the character's action and perception capabilities strongly depend on the underlying animation engine, the MPML3D format does not require any specific classes. However, we hope that there will be a standard set established in the future that allows to reuse of presentation parts across individual applications.

Meanwhile, we have defined a few of them that match the requirements of our application scenario described in Sect. 2.

```
<Perception class="Listen" target="NaomiWatanabe" event="end">
  <Property name="text">*music collection*</Property>
</Perception>
```

In this example, the perception is processed as soon as an utterance containing the phrase "music collection" is spoken, but the enclosed command is triggered only when the sentence is finished ("*...*" refers to a 'wildcard' or 'regex' construct). In order to change this, one simply has to change the event attribute to begin. Furthermore, the speaker must be named 'NaomiWatanabe', which is specified by the target attribute. Note that by not defining this attribute, any speaker would trigger the command.

In case that more than one observation is required to trigger a command –
e.g. in order to have some other character direct its gaze to a specified object, a
character might point to it and also refer to it verbally – multiple Perception
tags can be placed in a node named All. By setting its single attribute order to
true, the observation must be in the specified sequence to trigger the command.
Finally, the related Any tag allows to execute the command if at least one child
element is perceived.

Finally, the MPML3D content author has to define the sequence of actions
to be executed while performing the task. Due to their generic structure Action
nodes and their children have a similar syntax to the Perception tag. As shown
in the example below, all actions are enclosed by the well known Sequential and
Parallel tags. Observe that when considering the behavior of a single character
(rather than the behavior of multiple characters), the meaning of those tags
corresponds exactly to the meaning in previous versions of MPML.

```
<Sequential>
 <Action class="gesture">
    <Property name="type">BowVeryPolite</Property>
 </Action>
   <Parallel>
      <Action class="speak">
      <Property name="text">Hi, my name is Naomi Watanabe.</Property>
      </Action>
      <Action class="focus">
      <Property name="target">User</Property>
        <Property name="angle">-5.0</Property>
      </Action>
   </Parallel>
</Sequential>
```

According to this example, the character first performs a (very polite) bow gesture and then starts introducing itself by the specified sentence. Concurrently to
speaking, the character directs its gaze to the location slightly beside the user
(whose exact position can be determined by the eye tracker).

6   Conclusions

This paper describes and justifies a major re-design of the Multimodal Presentation Markup Language (MPML) [8] that was successful in providing non-expert
digital content creators an easy-to-use tool for authoring multimodal content
with life-like characters. However, MPML was not designed to accept frequent
or continuous input from either other characters or the user. Since interaction-
rich scenarios are of considerable interest for engaging and natural communication with characters, we propose our new MPML3D language that provides
perception (of the behavior of other characters and the user) as a key functionality. The transition from an essentially pre-synchronized model (MPML) to a

reactive model (MPML3D) enables adaptation of character behavior whenever trigger conditions are met throughout the interactive presentation.

The characters in the application scenario described in this paper are able e.g. to attend to the gaze behavior of the user by processing data from a non-contact video based eye tracker. If a relevant gaze pattern is detected, the characters will respond accordingly. For instance, if a user shows (visual) interest in any one of the two MP3 players, the character assigned to promote this product will display happiness about the user's interest, and provide more detailed product information, or even interrupt the other character in its presentation when not currently holding the turn.

MPML3D provides the technology for highly interactive presentations, but currently, resuming a presentation after user interruption is handled in an ad hoc fashion; for instance, incomplete tasks are resumed where they were halted by the interaction. However, it is important to emphasize that typically, interaction (including interruption) between characters is intentionally inserted by the content author to increase the liveliness of the conversation and a resumption strategy is declared. In order to guarantee the overall cohesion and attractiveness of the presentation, a (interactive) narrative model might be added. We also consider adjusting the virtual camera in a gaze-contingent way, e.g. by zooming into the screen area that corresponds to the user's point of interest, or based on some cinematographic principles. MPML3D can be extended by those functionalities in a transparent way while preserving its core purpose as an easy-to-use and powerful authoring language for digital content creators.

Acknowledgments

The first author was supported by an International Internship Grant from NII under a Memorandum of Understanding with the Faculty of Applied Informatics at the Univ. of Augsburg. We would like to thank Dr. Ulrich Apel (NII) for scripting the dialogues and Nikolaus Bee (Univ. of Augsburg, NII) for creating the speech files. The research was supported by the Research Grant (FY1999–FY2003) for the Future Program of the Japan Society for the Promotion of Science (JSPS), by a JSPS Encouragement of Young Scientists Grant (FY2005–FY2007), and an NII Joint Research Grant with the Univ. of Tokyo (FY2005).

References

1. J. Allbeck and N. Badler. Representing and parameterizing agent behaviors. In Prendinger and Ishizuka [14], pages 19–38.
2. E. André, T. Rist, S. van Mulken, M. Klesen, and S. Baldes. The automated design of believable dialogue for animated presentation teams. In J. Cassell, J. Sullivan, S. Prevost, and E. Churchill, editors, *Embodied Conversational Agents*, pages 220–255. The MIT Press, Cambridge, MA, 2000.
3. Y. Arafa, K. Kamyab, and E. Mamdani. Towards a unified scripting language. Lessons learned from developing CML & AML. In Prendinger and Ishizuka [14], pages 39–63.

4. N. Bee, H. Prendinger, A. Nakasone, E. André, and M. Ishizuka. AutoSelect: What You Want Is What You Get. Real-time processing of visual attention and affect. In *Tutorial and Research Workshop on Perception and Interactive Technologies (PIT-06)*. Springer, 2006. In press.
5. B. D. Carolis, C. Pelauchaud, I. Poggi, and M. Steedman. APML: Mark-up language for communicative character expressions. In Prendinger and Ishizuka [14], pages 65–85.
6. J. Cassell, H. Vilhjálmsson, and T. Bickmore. BEAT: the Behavior Expression Animation Toolkit. In *Proceedings of SIGGRAPH-01*, pages 477–486, 2001.
7. P. Gebhard, M. Kipp, M. Klesen, and T. Rist. Authoring scenes for adaptive, interactive performances. In *Proceedings of 2nd International Joint Conference on Autonomous Agents and Multi-Agent Systems (AAMAS-03)*, pages 725–732, New York, 2003. ACM Press.
8. M. Ishizuka and H. Prendinger. Describing and generating multimodal contents featuring affective lifelike agents with MPML. *New Generation Computing*, 24:97–128, 2006.
9. S. Kopp, B. Jung, N. Lessmann, and I. Wachsmuth. Max – a multimodal assistant in virtual reality construction. *KI Zeitschift (German Magazine of Artificial Intelligence), Special Issue on Embodied Conversational Agents*, 4:11–17, 2003.
10. M. Mateas and A. Stern. A Behavior Language: Joint action and behavioral idioms. In Prendinger and Ishizuka [14], pages 19–38.
11. M. Nischt, H. Prendinger, E. André, and M. Ishizuka. Creating three-dimensional animated characters: An experience report and recommendations of good practice. *Upgrade. The European Journal for the Informatics Professional*, VII(2), 2006, pages 36–41.
12. P. Piwek, B. Krenn, M. Schröder, M. Grice, S. Baumann, and H. Pirker. RRL: a rich representation language for the description of agent behavior in NECA. In *Proceedings AAMAS-02 Workshop on Embodied conversational agents—let's specify and evaluate them!*, 2002.
13. H. Prendinger, S. Descamps, and M. Ishizuka. MPML: A markup language for controlling the behavior of life-like characters. *Journal of Visual Languages and Computing*, 15(2):183–203, 2004.
14. H. Prendinger and M. Ishizuka, editors. *Life-Like Characters. Tools, Affective Functions, and Applications*. Cognitive Technologies. Springer Verlag, Berlin Heidelberg, 2004.
15. T. Rist. Issues in the design of scripting and representation languages for life-like characters. In Prendinger and Ishizuka [14], pages 463–468.
16. T. Rist, E. André, S. Baldes, P. Gebhard, M. Klesen, M. Kipp, P. Rist, and M. Schmitt. A review of the development of embodied presentation agents and their appication fields. In Prendinger and Ishizuka [14], pages 377–404.
17. Z. Ruttkay, Z. Huang, and A. Eliens. Reusable gestures for interactive web agents. In *Proceedings of the 4th International Working Conference on Intelligent Virtual Agents (IVA-03)*, pages 80–87. Springer LNAI 2792, 2003.
18. SMIL. Synchronized Multimedia Integration Language. URL: http://www.w3.org/AudioVideo.

Creativity Meets Automation: Combining Nonverbal Action Authoring with Rules and Machine Learning

Michael Kipp

DFKI, Stuhlsatzenhausweg 3, 66123 Saarbrücken, Germany
michael.kipp@dfki.de

Abstract. Providing virtual characters with natural gestures is a complex task. Even if the range of gestures is limited, deciding when to play which gesture may be considered both an engineering or an artistic task. We want to strike a balance by presenting a system where gesture selection and timing can be human authored in a script, leaving full artistic freedom to the author. However, to make authoring faster we offer a rule system that generates gestures on the basis of human authored rules. To push automation further, we show how machine learning can be utilized to suggest further rules on the basis of previously annotated scripts. Our system thus offers different degrees of automation for the author, allowing for creativity and automation to join forces.

1 Introduction

As virtual characters move toward real applications the need for tools becomes more pressing [1] [2]. Authoring tools do not only require intuitive user interfaces with a steep learning curve but also a certain amount of control to allow for rich design decisions on the part of the author.

Gesture generation is an area where automation is interesting because it is so tedious to do by hand. On the other hand, a high level of control is desirable since gestures are an integral part of what you could consider the virtual character's personality and gesture style can add a lot in terms of fun, interest and motivation to an application, even more so if multiple characters are involved. Producing interesting gestures may be more of an art than an engineering task. So, most of the time, authors have to hard-code them into the system. Although there are systems that offer rules to generate gestures [3][4], it often remains unclear how these rules are specified and how intuitive they are to use for non-technical authors. We present a framework which allows direct authoring of actions but also to define rules for automatic generation of actions and, finally, to let the system automatically learn new rules.

The gestures in our system consist of pre-fabricated keyframe animations. It appears that gesture generation calls for sophisticated skeleton-based procedural animation engines where gestural movement can be controlled and situationally adapted to a very fine degree [5] [6]. However, in many applications, even high-end games, procedural control of single bones is not done because it is too

J. Gratch et al. (Eds.): IVA 2006, LNAI 4133, pp. 230–242, 2006.

expensive in terms of development time and performance. Instead, most real-time applications rely on pre-fabricated keyframe animation and sophisticated motion blending techniques [7] [4] [8]. Gesture generation here consists of selecting a motion clip and synchronizing it with speech. Keyframe animation has the further advantage that motion capture can be used which yields a very high degree of authenticity.

This paper deals with a system where gestures can be added and generated on different levels from full authoring control to full automation (Figure 1). The COHIBIT system [12] allows the author to specify actions for two virtual characters in a screenplay-like document (level 1). In a next step, the author can write simple and intuitive gesture generation rules to exploit his or her expert knowledge for automation (level 2). Gestures generated from these rules blend seamlessly with the pre-authored ones, prioritizing the author's direct choices. In COHIBIT, before rules were introduced all actions were hand-coded (level 1) so that a large corpus of scripts with annotated actions existed. We decided to exploit this resource for machine learning. The system can learn new rules based on the annotated scripts and suggests the most appropriate ones to the author (level 3).

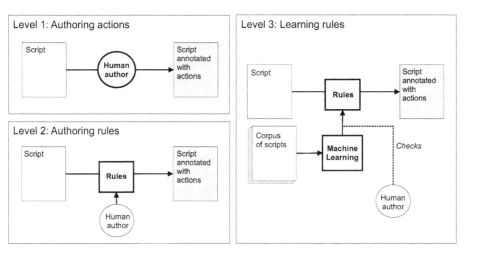

Fig. 1. Three different levels of control and automation when generating actions

So the rules of levels 2+3 automatically generate actions but many scripts already contain hard-coded actions from level 1. As we will show, all these actions can be blended by filtering and resolving conflicts. Thus, all three levels contribute to the final result: the gestural behavior of two virtual characters in the COHIBIT system which is fully implemented and has been running daily in a public exhibition space[1] since April 2006.

---

[1] http://vc.dfki.de

In the following sections the COHIBIT system will be presented first before proceding with how rules can be specified. Then, the automatic rule learning system will be explained. We conclude with a technical evalution and final remarks.

2 Related Work

Automating gesture generation for virtual characters is an interdisciplinary endeavor combining competences from artificial intelligence, computer animation and psychology. Cassell et al. [7] developed a rule-based system that generates audiovisual speech, intonation, facial expression, and gesture. The gesture stroke is synchronized with the accented syllable of the coexpressive word. Noma et al. [4] built the Virtual Presenter where gestures can be added to a text manually or with keyword-triggered rules. Animated gestures are synchronized with the following word. While the number of possible gestures is very small the authors focused on how to extract meaningful rules from the literature on public speaking. A more complex generation system is the Behavior Expression Animation Toolkit (BEAT) [3]. It gets plain text as input and first runs a linguistic analysis on it before generating intonation, facial animation, and gestures. Gestures are overgenerated using a knowledge base with handcrafted mappings and are then reduced by user-defined filters.

Hartmann et al. [5] achieve expressivity in gesture synthesis system by varying gesture frequency, movement amplitude and duration, fluidity, dynamic properties, and repetition. Noot/Ruttkay [9] are also deal with individual gesturing style. A style consists of meaning-to-gesture mappings, motion characteristics, and modality preferences. Combining style dictionaries yields mappings for new cultural groups or individuals.

Kopp et al. [10] [6] present a gesture animation system that makes use of neurophysiological research and generates iconic gestures from object descriptions and site plans when talking about spatial domains, e.g. giving directions. Iconics gestures resemble some semantic feature in the co-occurring speech.

In a different project [11] we have presented a system that generates gestures from statistical models of human speakers' behavior. This approach requires a lot of manual labour but yields character-specific result with the potential of imitating living people.

The approach presented in this paper resembles most closely the rule-based approaches to gesture generation. In this paper, we focus on how generation rules can be specified easily, how generated gestures can be combined with authored ones and how rules can be learned from a corpus of scenes where hand annotated actions are available in large quantities.

3 System Overview

The COHIBIT[2] system is a mixed-reality museum exhibit which features tangible interaction and two conversational virtual characters [12]. The visitor of the

---

[2] COnversational Helpers in an Immersive exhiBIt with a Tangible interface.

exhibit can assemble cars with real car pieces while life-size projected characters assist in the assembly and talk about various topics to convey educational content. The two virtual characters (one male, one female) give context-sensitive hints how to complete the construction, make personalized comments on the visitors' actions, encourage the visitors to continue playing, and provide additional background information about car technology and artificial intelligence. To enhance immersiveness of the exhibit, the characters must be as life-like as possible displaying a varied, yet consistent nonverbal behavior. This is achieved with a hybrid approach of authored actions and rule-based action generation.

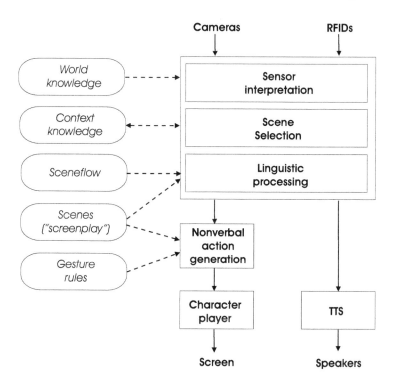

Fig. 2. Overview of the COHIBIT runtime system architecture

The COHIBIT runtime system is depicted in Figure 2. COHIBIT receives input from cameras and RFID tags hidden in the car pieces and the workbench. The signals are interpreted and transformed into events like user arrived, piece X placed on field Y, user departed etc. The scene selection is an extended, hierarchical state machine that uses the state diagram, called sceneflow[3], and the scenes[4] to select, adapt and play an appropriate scene (cf. [13][2]). The linguistic component transforms any generic context components that the author can use

---

[3] In the current system, the sceneflow encompasses 174 nodes, 29 supernodes and 266 transitions.

[4] The current system consists of 752 scenes.

(e.g. name of currently moved car piece, current time or weather conditions) into grammatically correct surface text. This component also generates a stemmed version of the text (e.g. "went" → "go") for later gesture rule application (see Section 4).

The final surface text is sent to the nonverbal action generator that uses rules to add actions to the already existing pre-authored ones and selects the best ones (see Section 4.2). Text and actions are then sent to text-to-speech (TTS) and animation engines which send the final output is to the output devices, i.e. speakers and screen.

The COHIBIT system's basic mechanism is to constantly recombine and select pre-authored scenes. A large corpus of 752 scenes has been written allowing a rich and varied interaction with hardly any repetitions.

3.1 Authoring Scenes and Actions

The corpus of scenes is represented in a single text document that can be written and extended by a naive user in any kind of text processing software.

Scenes are the smallest units to be played by the system. Within each scene, the author writes dialogue like in a screenplay or theatre script, simply by putting the speaker's initial up front and then type text. There are various commands at the speaker's disposal that can trigger nonverbal actions or query context information from the database. See the following example:

```
A: [bow] Welcome [B look@other] to the car construction [B nod] world!
B: [look@visitor] [happy] Could you do us a favor? Please
   take [GET current-piece def acc] from the table.
   [turn2other] What's the time?
A: [look@other] Well, [check_watch] it's around [GET time-fuzzy].
B: [nod] Thank you.
```

Nonverbal actions are specified within square brackets. If the action should not be performed by the current speaker, the speaker initial can be specified in front of the action name (for instance, "[B look@other]" in the above example).

The system has 28 different animations/actions for the two characters, including gestures, facial expressions and body movement. Some actions are only available for one of the characters and some actions are rarely used. Table 1 shows the most frequently used actions. The gesture actions were loosely named after the inventory defined by Kipp [11]. Actions are grouped into four *channels* which facilitates conflict resolution at the filter step (Section 4.2). The groups are: facial expression (F), gaze (Gz), manual gesture (G), and head movement (H).

Our total corpus consists of a script with 752 scenes. These scenes contain 1781 dialogue turns and 2786 single utterances. Within these scenes 1196 actions have already been authored. Using rules, many actions can automatically be generated, although potential conflicts beween these generated actions and the authored ones must then be resolved. How to do this will be shown in the next Section. The huge number of existing actions inspired us to implement automatic rule learning, using the existing scenes as a training corpus. This will be the topic of Section 5.

Table 1. Table of most frequently used actions for the two characters. The leftmost column shows the action channel: facial expression (F), gaze (Gz), manual gesture (G), and head movement (H). The numbers in the right half relate to corpus partitioning and learning evaluation as discussed in Section 5.

	gesture	description	male character				female character			
			pos.	neg.	R_{tr}	R_{te}	pos.	neg.	R_{tr}	R_{te}
G	cup	show palm	29	339	47.1	9.1	43	442	53.8	6.2
F	happy	smile	26	156	62.5	44.4	30	212	38.9	54.5
Gz	look@other	look at other character	132	748	74.7	55.8	127	721	76.3	56.0
Gz	look@visitor	look at user	86	370	94.1	93.9	68	287	97.5	96.2
H	nod	head nod	51	319	38.7	5.3	58	514	41.2	22.7
G	point@panel	point at the display panel behind the characters	12	140	28.6	0.0	—	—	—	—
G	progressive	circular metaphoric gesture	22	263	46.2	50.0	23	282	14.3	0.0
H	shake	head shake	13	195	62.5	0.0	19	313	27.3	14.3
G	so_what	open arms, palm point up	43	402	36.0	12.5	—	—	—	—
Gz	turn2other	rotate torso toward other character	—	—	—	—	20	175	16.7	14.3
Gz	turn2visitor	rotate torso toward user	24	79	78.6	66.7	24	122	64.3	33.3
G	walls	both hands held parallel, palms facing each other	—	—	—	—	25	341	42.1	28.1

4 Using Rules for Automatic Action Generation

To automate the tedious hand annotation of actions we introduced an intuitive rule mechanism based on keyword spotting. The user defines a set of rules that operate on the utterance level. For each utterance, all applicable rules can fire and generate actions which are stored together with any pre-authored actions that were already there for later conflict resolution.

4.1 Rule Syntax and Usage

Action rules are IF-THEN rules with a left hand side (LHS) consisting of conditions and a right hand side (RHS) consisting of effects. All conditions on the left hand side must be true for the rule to fire, i.e. they are connected by AND operators. To implement an OR, you write a new rule with equal effects but different conditions.

In gesture generation, for each utterance every rule is tested. If all conditions are true the rule fires. The author can use the predicates in Table 2 to specify the conditional side, predicates can be negated using "!" as a prefix.

On the right hand side the author specifies what happens if a rule fires. Two commands are at the author's disposal: **gen** and **gen_other**. The first generates a gesture for the character who utters the current utterances, the latter for the other character (our system consists only of two characters). The arguments for these commands specify the action name and the position. Position can be

Table 2. Table of predicates that can be used in the conditional part (LHS) of action generation rules

predicate	description
says(''foo baa'')	True if the string "foo baa" is contained in the utterance.
says([you went])	True if the word stems are found in the (stemmed) utterance. In the case of [you went] the system is looking for "you go".
speaker(X)	True if the utterance is spoken by speaker X.
begin_scene	True if the utterance is the first utterance in the scene.
begin_turn	True if the utterance is the first utterance in the turn.
question	True if the utterance is a question, i.e. it ends with a "?".
command(C, A)	True if the utterance contains the command C with arguments A.

word, begin or end. For word position the system remembers the match position on the conditional side. The action is then inserted before the respective word. This position can be modified by adding an offset like +1 or -2 behind the word keyword. Some sample rules[5] are:

```
says(''of course'')  --> gen(cup, begin)
says([develop])  --> gen(progressive, word - 1)
speaker(Richie) & question  --> gen(cup, begin)
speaker(Tina) & command(picture) &
!command(picture, default.jpg)  --> gen(point@panel, word +1)
```

In our system, we use a set of 57 rules to automatically generate gestures. For the 752 scenes, these rules fire 2688 times.

4.2 Combining Rules and Pre-authored Actions

The rules are interpreted at runtime and are used to generate actions on the fly. However, scripts may also contain pre-authored gestures. The system must decide which actions and how many actions to actually use.

After generation the system has a text utterance annotated with a considerable amount of actions in-between words. Actions are selected by applying a number of constraints. First, at any one spot only *compatible* actions can be executed in parallel which is modelled using four channels: facial expression (F), gaze (Gz), manual gesture (G), and head movement (H). The constraint is that only actions from different channels can be performed in parallel. So a character can look at the user (gaze channel) and make a hand gesture (gesture channel) at the same time, whereas performing two hand gestures at the same time is not possible in our system.

Second, we model that human authored actions are preferred over automatically generated ones by assigning priority values: 2 for human authored actions,

---

[5] The samples are translated from German to English for better readability.

1 for generated ones. To filter out an action, priority is set to -1. We then apply constraints at three different levels to make the distribution of actions across a scene consistent. On the scene level, a constant action rate R must be observed where R can be specified by the developer. Action rate is measured by dividing number of actions by the number of utterances. On the turn level, no gesture or head move is allowed to occur twice in the same turn. On the utterance level, conflicts between simultaneous actions are resolved by selecting the action with the highest priority and actions with priority -1 are filtered out. The result is a sequence of actions, containing both human authored and automatically generated ones, where the amount of activity is controlled and repetitions and conflicts are filtered out.

5   Learning Rules from the Corpus

Our corpus has been extended over time and with the introduction of rules fewer and fewer actions have been manually annotated. We thus have a situation where some scenes are heavily annotated, some sparsely and some not at all. To obtain training and test material for machine learning we must first define criteria for finding suitable material.

5.1   Preparing the Corpus

We first defined a measure to select suitable training material. We did this using the action rate, setting a minimal threshold to 0.3. We obtained a total Corpus C of 334 scenes. In a second step we disjointly divided the corpus into training data C_{train} and test data C_{test}. In C_{train} we had to define positive and negative samples for each action. A positive sample for action A is an utterance where A occurs. Negative samples could theoretically be all utterances where A does not occur but we thought this might be too restrictive. Just because an action is not annotated it does not mean that it *should not* be there. However, we hypothesized that if within one scene the action A occurs, it might be that the user has intentionally put it there and nowhere else in the scene. So we define our negatives as all utterances u belonging to a scene S where A occurs in S but A does not occur in u. There is still doubt of whether these negatives could be too restrictive. However, we tried to balance the importance of positives vs. negatives with weights (Section 6). Table 1 shows the number of positive and negative utterance found for each speaker and action.

5.2   Learning

An important aspect of the learning task is that it is not a pure classification task that could be resolved with standard techniques like SVMs, n-grams, neural networks or ID3/4.5. Instead, we have to learn a set of conditions plus a position (in the simplest version). However, we can re-formulate the problem to map it to a classification problem but with the drawback of having fewer samples. For the sub-case where an action is generated at the very beginning of an utterance we can directly apply a classification based approach (see clustering below). More-over, since we have a hybrid approach where author and machine are supposed to cooperate we pursue the goal of keeping all generated rules human-readable.

We consider rule learning is a two-step process. First, a *rule generator* system-atically generates a number of potentially interesting rules. Then, these rules are tested by the *rule appraisal* module against the positive and negative samples for matches and false positives. The best ones, according to a weighted measure, are selected. So the meat is obviously in the rule generator, whereas the appraisal module allows you to tweak your results using weight parameters. Note that one difficulty in rule learning in our case is that it is not only a question of whether a rule fires or not but also of where the action is placed.

The rule generator runs for one action at a time. For each positive utterance for this action the generator produces different answers to the question "what might have caused this action to be produced here?". We propose two mechanisms for genrating rules: one word based, one cluster based. The word based generation is very easy: each word in the positive utterance is seen as a potential trigger for the action. Let the utterance be $(w_0, ..., w_{i-1}, a_i, w_{i+1}, ..., w_n)$ where w_j are words and a_i is the action at position i. Then, for each w_j we generate a rule of the form:

says(w_j) --> gen(A, word - $(i - j + 1)$)

In the cluster based approach we try to identify patterns of recurring *ordered sequences of words* in the positive samples of one action. This works only for begin and end type rules. In our corpus, we noted that many actions occur specifically at the beginning of utterances so we deemed it worth looking at this special case in detail. A word vector v_1 is an ordered partial vector of v_2 if the words in v_1 are all in v_2 and are ordered in the same way as the corresponding words in v_2. If you have two utterances u_1 and u_2 you can define the ordered word overlap $\hat{w}$ by

$$\hat{w}(u_1, u_2) := \max_{|v|}(\text{vector } v : v \text{ is ordered partial vector of } u_1 \text{ and } u_2)$$

The $\hat{w}$ function gives you an overlap vector v, the number of overlapping words is $|\hat{w}|$ which gives you a distance metric for cluster analysis. Cluster analysis makes it possible to obtain smaller patterns with bigger generality. We applied a simple nearest neighbor clustering algorithm to cluster similar patterns together. The $\hat{w}$ function is trivially expanded to compare an utterance with a set of utterances. We can improve the quality of the rules by using negation. We use the same clustering method for pattern identification to exclude false positives of a rule. The recognized patterns are added to the conditional side as negated conditions.

When learning rules it is important to ignore some words that can be consid-ered "noise". Function words occur often but are also often relatively meaningless in terms of generation. But because of their frequency the learning algorithm of-ten finds patterns in function words. Therefore, we have to ignore them. Which

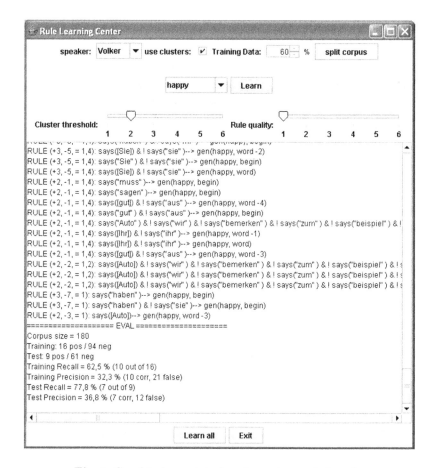

Fig. 3. Graphical user interface for gesture rule learning

words should be ignored is not always clear. Do you take out "and"? It might indicate metaphoric gestures that represent *sequence*. Clearer cases are "of", "by" or "to".

We implemented a graphical user interface (GUI) where the author can experiment with different parameters of rule learning (Figure 3). Our idea is that rule aquisition is not a fully automatic process but rather a source for inspiration for the author who may find some of the generated patterns appealing and illuminating while others might simply be unintuitive.

In the GUI the author can select the partitioning of test/training corpus, the speaker, the action and parameters for rule quality and clustering.

6   Evaluation

To really evaluate generated gestures one would have to set up an experiment where the results of different approaches are judged by independent coders. Then, one can make a comparative analysis and draw final conclusions about each method. While we have not made such an extensive study yet, we did a quantitative analysis of the learning algorithm described above. For this, we partitioned the corpus into training (60%) and test (40%) and then computed recall R and precision P. Recall for an action A is defined as the number of utterances where an action was correctly generated divided by the total number of utterances. Precision is the number of times that rules fired correctly divided by the total number of times that rules fired. Note that we had a very strict measure for precision as every generated action that is at an incorrect position counts as a false positive.

In total, we achieved a recall of 56.9% and precision of 33.7% on the training data, and recall of 33.8%, precision of 13.6% on the test data for the male character. For the female character, we got recall/training of 47.2%, precision/training of 47.1%, recall/test of 32.6% and precision/test of 32.1% for the female character. See Table 1 for detailed results for every speaker and action.

Even though the results may look low one has to reflect what can be expected. Since the placement of actions is a rather arbitrary decision and a large number of different placements may all be correct, we cannot expect our system to predict precisely where an action must be placed. However, if sometimes the placement matches exactly what the human author has done it is an indication that it is a good rule. If it does not match the rule is not necessarily false. So recall/precision values must be looked at sceptically. We were actually quite satisfied with the quality of the output in terms of usability and human readability. The results vary largely across actions, from very good (look@visitor) to zero (nod, shake). These learned rules are meant to extend and complement existing rules, not to replace them altogether.

A more thorough evaluation should look not only at recall and precision but at the actions that the new, learned rules produce. However, judging these produced gestures is a non-trivial task. What are the evaluation criteria? Are we talking about general appropriateness of the gestures or about whether they reflect a certain style of the character? Quality of gestures is hard to grasp. Although first approaches exist (e.g. [5]) more research in terms of evaluation criteria is needed before tackling this difficult task.

7   Conclusions

We presented a system for authoring nonverbal actions in a character based system, for defining generation rules and, finally, for automatically aquiring rules by machine learning. Authoring actions directly is done in a screenplay-like style. Rule definition is done with simple IF-THEN rules. Rule learning relies on systematic rule candidate generation, based on word traversal and clustering, and rule evaluation. Learning was shown to have a very varied quality in terms of recall and precision but these measures are only very tentative indicators of quality. Hence, more qualitative evaluations remain to be done.

All three mechanism are used in a hybrid approach to nonverbal action creation that allows an arbitrary mixture of creative control and economic automation. This technique could also be used for recognizing other kinds of tags in a text, e.g. emotions or emotion eliciting conditions [14], dialogue acts [15], other multimodal actions like displaying pictures, changning light, audio clips.

Future work on this system includes more precise timing capabilities for the generated actions, extending learning to all types of predicates, and integrating more complex gesture types (hold gestures and multiple stroke gestures) to the repertoire.

Acknowledgements

This work is partially funded by the German Ministry for Education and Research (BMBF) as part of the VirtualHuman project under grant 01 IMB 01A.

References

1. Rist, T., André, E., Baldes, S., Gebhard, P., Klesen, M., Kipp, M., Rist, P., Schmitt, M.: A review of the development of embodied presentation agents and their application fields. In Prendinger, H., Ishizuka, M., eds.: Life-Like Characters – Tools, Affective Functions, and Applications. Springer, Heidelberg (2003) 377–404
2. Gebhard, P., Kipp, M., Klesen, M., Rist, T.: Authoring scenes for adaptive, interactive performances. In: Proceedings of the Second International Joint Conference on Autonomous Agents and Multiagent Systems. (2003) 725–732
3. Cassell, J., Vilhjálmsson, H., Bickmore, T.: BEAT: the Behavior Expression Animation Toolkit. In: Proceedings of SIGGRAPH 2001. (2001) 477–486
4. Noma, T., Zhao, L., Badler, N.: Design of a Virtual Human Presenter. IEEE Journal of Computer Graphics and Applications 20 (2000) 79–85
5. Hartmann, B., Mancini, M., Buisine, S., Pelachaud, C.: Design and evaluation of expressive gesture synthesis for embodied conversational agents. In: Proceedings of the fourth international joint conference on Autonomous agents and multiagent systems. ACM Press (2005)
6. Kopp, S., Tepper, P., Cassell, J.: Towards integrated microplanning of language and iconic gesture for multimodal output. In: Proc. Int'l Conf. Multimodal Interfaces 2004. (2004) 97–104
7. Cassell, J., Pelachaud, C., Badler, N., Steedman, M., Achorn, B., Becket, T., Douville, B., Prevost, S., Stone, M.: Animated Conversation: Rule-Based Generation of Facial Expression, Gesture & Spoken Intonation for Multiple Conversational Agents. In: Proceedings of SIGGRAPH '94. (1994) 413–420
8. André, E., Müller, J., Rist, T.: WIP/PPP: Automatic Generation of Personalized Multimedia Presentations. In: Proceedings of Multimedia 96, 4th ACM International Multimedia Conference. ACM Press, Boston, MA (1996) 407–408
9. Noot, H., Ruttkay, Z.: Gesture in style. In: Proc. Gesture Workshop 2003. Volume 2915 of LNAI., Berlin and Heidelberg, Germany, Springer-Verlag (2004) 324–337
10. Kopp, S., Sowa, T., Wachsmuth, I.: Imitation games with an artificial agent: from mimicking to understanding shape-related iconic gestures. In: Proc. Gesture Workshop 2003. Volume 2915 of LNCS., Berlin and Heidelberg, Germany, Springer (2004) 436–447
11. Kipp, M.: Gesture Generation by Imitation: From Human Behavior to Computer Character Animation. Dissertation.com, Boca Raton, Florida (2004)

12. Ndiaye, A., Gebhard, P., Kipp, M., Klesen, M., Schneider, M., Wahlster, W.: Ambient intelligence in edutainment: Tangible interaction with life-like exhibit guides. In: Proceedings of the first Confernce on INtelligent TEchnologies for interactive enterTAINment (INTETAIN), Berlin, Heidelberg, Springer (2005) 104–113

13. Klesen, M., Kipp, M., Gebhard, P., Rist, T.: Staging exhibitions: Methods and tools for modeling narrative structure to produce interactive performances with virtual actors. Virtual Reality. Special Issue on Storytelling in Virtual Environments **7** (2003) 17–29

14. Gebhard, P., Kipp, M., Klesen, M., Rist, T.: Adding the emotional dimension to scripting character dialogues. In: Intelligent Agents, 4th International Workshop, IVA 2003, Kloster Irsee, Germany, September 15-17, 2003, Proceedings. (2003) 48–56

15. Reithinger, N., Klesen, M.: Dialogue act classification using language models. In Kokkinakis, G., Fakotakis, N., Dermatas, E., eds.: Proceedings of the 5th European Conference on Speech Communication and Technology (Eurospeech 97). (1997) 2235–2238

Nonverbal Behavior Generator for Embodied Conversational Agents

Jina Lee and Stacy Marsella

University of Southern California
Information Sciences Institute
4676 Admiralty Way, Suite 1001
Marina Del Rey, CA 90292
{jinal, marsella}@isi.edu

Abstract. Believable nonverbal behaviors for embodied conversational agents (ECA) can create a more immersive experience for users and improve the effectiveness of communication. This paper describes a nonverbal behavior generator that analyzes the syntactic and semantic structure of the surface text as well as the affective state of the ECA and annotates the surface text with appropriate nonverbal behaviors. A number of video clips of people conversing were analyzed to extract the nonverbal behavior generation rules. The system works in real-time and is user-extensible so that users can easily modify or extend the current behavior generation rules.

1 Introduction

Nonverbal behaviors serve to repeat, contradict, substitute, complement, accent, or regulate spoken communication [1]. They can include facial expressions, head movements, body gesture, body posture, or eye gaze. Nonverbal behaviors can also be affected by a range of affective phenomena. For example, an angry person might display lowered eyebrows and tensed lips and more expressive body gestures than one who is not. Such behavior can in turn influence the beliefs, emotions, and behavior of observers.

Embodied conversational agents (ECA) with appropriate nonverbal behaviors can support interaction with users that ideally mirrors face-to-face human interaction. Nonverbal behaviors also can help create a stronger relationship between the ECA and user as well as allow applications to have richer, more expressive characters. Overall, appropriate nonverbal behaviors should provide users with a more immersive experience while interacting with ECAs, whether they are characters in video games, intelligent tutoring systems, or customer service applications [2].

This paper describes our approach for creating a nonverbal behavior generator module for ECAs that assigns behaviors to the ECA's utterances. We are especially interested in an approach that generates nonverbal behaviors provided only the surface text and, when available, the ECA's emotional state, turn-taking strategy, coping strategy, and overall communicative intent. In general, we seek

J. Gratch et al. (Eds.): IVA 2006, LNAI 4133, pp. 243–255, 2006.

Fig. 1. SASO's SmartBody

a robust process that does not make any strong assumptions about markup of communicative intent in the surface text. Often such markup is not available unless entered manually. Even in systems that use natural language generation to create the surface text (e.g., Stabilization and Support Operations system [3]), the natural language generation may not pass down detailed information about how parts of the surface text (a phrase or word, for example) convey specific aspects of the communicative intent or emotional state. As a result, the nonverbal behavior generator often lacks sufficiently detailed information and must rely to varying degrees on analyzing the surface text. Therefore, a key interest here is whether we can extract information from the lexical, syntactic, and semantic structure of the surface text that can support the generation of believable nonverbal behaviors.

Our nonverbal behavior generator has been incorporated into SmartBody, an ECA developed at University of Southern California [1]. SmartBody project is part of the Stabilization and Support Operations (SASO) research prototype, which grew out of the Mission Rehearsal Environment [3] to teach leadership and negotiation skills under high stress situations. In this system, the trainees interact and negotiate with life-size ECA that reside in a virtual environment. Figure 1 shows SmartBody, in this case a doctor, whom the trainee interacts with.

The next section describes related works. Section three describes research on nonverbal behavior and our analysis of video clips to derive the nonverbal behavior generation rules. Section four describes the system architecture of the nonverbal behavior generator and an example that walks through the behavior generation process. We also discuss the extensibility of the nonverbal behavior generator and propose directions for future work.

---

[1] This is a joint work of USC Information Sciences Institute and USC Institute for Creative Technologies.

2 Related Work

Mirroring the studies of nonverbal behavior in human communication, ECA research has shown that there is a significant improvement in the user's level of engagement while interacting with ECA that displayed believable nonverbal behaviors. The work of Fabri et al. [2] suggests that ECA with expressive abilities can increase the sense of togetherness or community feeling. Durlach and Slater [4] observed that ECA with even primitive nonverbal behaviors generate strong emotional responses from the users.

The effort to construct expressive ECA ranges from animating human faces with various facial expressions to generating complex body gestures that convey emotions and communicative intent. Rea [5] engages in a face-to-face interaction with a user and models the intention and communicative intention of the agent to generate appropriate facial expressions and body gestures. Becheiraz and Thalmann [6] developed a behavioral animation system for virtual characters by modeling the emergence conditions for each character's personality and intentions. Striegnitz et al. [7] developed an ECA that autonomously generates hand gestures while giving directions to the user.

There has also been work that emphasizes the reusability of the nonverbal behavior generators by separating the concept of behavior generation and behavior realization. The BEAT [8] system is a plug-in model for nonverbal behavior generation that extracts the linguistic structure of the text and suggests appropriate nonverbal behaviors. It allows users to add new entries to extend the gesture library or modify strategies for generating or filtering out the behaviors.

BEAT's functions and purpose very much informed our work; however, there are several differences. We are crafting our system around the new BML and FML standards [9]. This should provide a clearer, more general and standardized interface for communicative intent and behavior specification. BEAT had a variety of pre-knowledge about the surface text to be delivered at different abstraction levels, which is not the case in our nonverbal behavior generator. We are interested in exploring the degree to which nonverbal behavior generator can work only with the surface text and a minimal set of specification on the communicative intent at a high level of abstraction such as the turn-taking information and the affective state. We are also exploring a different range of expressive phenomena that is complementary to BEAT's work. Specifically, we are analyzing videos of emotional dialogues. Finally, BEAT included a commercial language tagger, while we are planning to maintain our nonverbal behavior generator open-source.

3 Study of Nonverbal Behaviors

3.1 Nonverbal Behaviors and Their Functionalities

There is a large research literature on the functionalities of nonverbal behaviors during face-to-face communication [10] [11] [12] [13] [14]. Heylen [12] summarizes the functions of head movements during conversations. Some included are:

to signal yes or no, enhance communicative attention, anticipate an attempt to capture the floor, signal the intention to continue, mark the contrast with the immediately preceding utterances, and mark uncertain statements and lexical repairs. Kendon [13] describes the different contexts in which the head shake may be used. Head shake is used with or without verbal utterances as a component of negative expression, when a speaker makes a superlative or intensified expression as in 'very very old', when a speaker self-corrects himself, or to express doubt about what he is saying. In [14], lateral sweep or head shakes co-occurs with concepts of inclusivity such as 'everyone' and 'everything' and intensification with lexical choices such as 'very', 'a lot', 'great', 'really'. Side-to-side shakes also correlate with expressions of uncertainty and lexical repairs. During narration, head nods function as signs of affirmation and backchannel requests to the speakers. Speakers also predictably change the head position for alternatives or items in a list. Ekman [10] describes eyebrow movements for emotional expressions and conversational signals. Some examples are eyebrow raise or frowning to accent a particular word or to emphasize a particular conversation point. One of the goals for our nonverbal behavior generator is to find features in the dialogue that convey these attributes and annotate them with appropriate nonverbal behaviors that are consistent with the research literature. Although the above discussion is couched in general terms, nonverbal behaviors vary across cultures and even individuals. We return to this issue later.

3.2 Video Data Analysis

In addition to the existing research literature, we have also studied the uses of nonverbal behaviors in video clips of people conversing. The literature is useful for broadly classifying the behaviors. However, to better assess whether it is feasible to build behavior generation rules that could map from text to behavior, an analysis of actual conversations was needed.

We obtained video clips of users interacting with the Sensitive Artificial Listener system from the Human-Machine Interaction Network on Emotion [15]. Sensitive Artificial Listener (SAL) is a technique to engage users in emotionally colored interactive discourse [16]. SAL is modeled on an ELIZA scenario [17], a computer emulation of a psychotherapist. In SAL, the operator plays the role of one of four characters with different personalities and responds to the user with pre-defined scripts. The main goal is to pull the user's emotion towards the character's emotional state.

video clips were analyzed, each ranging from five to ten minutes in length. The video clips capture only the users' torso and above, and we mainly annotated the facial expressions and head movements exhibited by the users. For each video clip, we annotated the types of nonverbal behaviors portrayed, their frequency, time frame, spoken utterance, and the users' emotional states when the behavior occurred. This was documented in an XML form for easy parsing and processing.

There were a number of different nonverbal behaviors observed in these video clips. These behaviors include:

- Head Movement: nods, shakes, head moved to the side, head tilt, pulled back, pulled down
- Eyebrow Movement: brow raised, brow lowered, brow flashes
- Eye/Gaze Movement: look up, look down, look away, eyes squinted, eyes squeezed, eyes rolled
- Others: shoulder shrug, mouth pulled on one side

To annotate the utterances, we adopted the labels used in the literature and created a few more for the utterances in which we observed a nonverbal behavior but no appropriate labels were used in the literature. The labels used are affirmation, negation, contrast, intensification, inclusivity, obligation, listing, assumption, possibility, response request, and word search. For each utterance accompanying nonverbal behaviors, we attached the labels applicable to the utterance and annotated the behaviors. There were 161 utterances that were annotated using these labels. Table 1 shows the distribution of the number of utterances that includes each label.

Table 1. Breakdown of the number of utterances with corrsponding labels

Label	# of utterances (out of 161)	Label	# of utterances (out of 161)
Affirmation	39	Response Reqeust	9
Negation	62	Inclusivity	7
Intensification	41	Obligation	6
Word Search	25	Assumption	3
Contrast	9		

A number of utterances were annotated with two or more labels, which is why the sum of each component exceeds 161. Besides these 161 utterances, there were 58 utterances that accompanied nonverbal behaviors but could not be labeled appropriately because there was not a clear and consistent pattern between the utterance and the behaviors. The nonverbal behaviors on these utterances were usually observed at the beginning of the sentence or when the user was emphasizing a particular word or context, but the behaviors varied in each case.

In general, we found a close match between the literature and our video analysis on the mappings of nonverbal behaviors to certain utterances. For example, a head shake usually occurred when a word with inclusive meaning such as 'all' and 'everything' was spoken and lowered eyebrow with a head nod or shake occurred when intensifying words like 'really' was spoken. We also analyzed the parse trees of the utterances and found mappings between certain behaviors and syntactic structures. Interjections, which were usually associated with the words

(1) INTERJECTION: Head nod, shake, or tilt co–occurring with these words:
- *Yes, no, well*

(1) NEGATION: Head shakes and brow frown throughout the whole sentence or phrase these words occur:
- *No, not, nothing, can't, cannot*

(2) AFFIRMATION: Head nods and brow raise throughout the whole sentence or phrase these words occur:
- *Yes, yeah, I do, I am, We have, We do, You have, true, OK*

(3) ASSUMPTION / POSSIBILITY: Head nods throughout the sentence or phrase and brow frown when these words occur:
- *I guess, I suppose, I think, maybe, perhaps, could, probably*

(3) OBLIGATION: Head nod once co–occurring with these words:
- *Have to, need to, ought to*

(4) CONTRAST: Head moved to the side (lateral movement) and brow raise co–occurring with these words:
- *But, however*

(4) INCLUSIVITY: Lateral head sweep co–occurring on these words:
- *Everything, all, whole, several, plenty, full*

(4) INTENSIFICATION: Head nod and brow frown co–occurring with these words:
- *Really, very, quite, completely, wonderful, great, absolutely, gorgeous, huge, fantastic, so, amazing, just, quite, important, . . .*

(4) LISTING: Head moved to the side (lateral movement) and to the other before and after the word 'and':
- *X and Y*

(4) RESPONSE REQUEST: Head moved to the side and brow raise co-occurring with these words:
- *You know*

(4) WORD SEARCH: Head tilt, brow raise, gaze away co-occurring with these words:
- *Um, uh, well*

Fig. 2. Nonverbal behavior generation rules. The numbers in the parenthesis indicates the priority or each rule.

'yes', 'no', and 'well' in the video clips accompanied either a head nod, shake, or tilt in most cases.

Based on the study from the literature and our video analysis, we created a list of nonverbal behavior generation rules, which are described in Figure 2. Each rule has associated nonverbal behaviors and a set of words that are usually spoken when the nonverbal behavior is exhibited. We also defined a priority value for each rule based on our analysis to resolve conflicts between rules that could co-occur. For example, in the utterance 'Maybe we shouldn't do that', both the assumption rule and the negation rule could be applied. However, the video analysis tells us that the negation rule overrides the assumption rule in those cases. In general, the nonverbal behavior rules that occur over the whole sentence or phrases overrule those that occur on a single word.

Following are examples on how the rules are applied to given surface texts.

Example 1
Surface Text:
  I do, I do. I'm looking forward to that but I can't rest until I get this work done.
Rules applied:
  Affirmation rule from *I do* and *I'm*
  Negation rule from *can't*
  (Contrast rule applied from *but* is overridden by the negation rule)
Nonverbal Behaviors:
  Head nods on *I do, I do* and *I'm looking forward*
  Head shakes on *I can't rest*

Example 2
Surface Text:
  Yes, Prudence, many times. I actually quite like you.
Rules applied:
  Interjection rule from *yes*
  Intensification rule from *quite*
Nonverbal Behaviors:
  Head nod on *yes*
  Head nod on *quite*

In addition to the nonverbal behaviors associated with certain dialogue elements, we also put small head nods on phrasal boundaries. This is based on our experience that it makes the ECA more life-like, perhaps because the human head is often in constant (small) motion as a person talks.

The next section describes how we use these rules to create execution commands for believable nonverbal behaviors.

4   System Architecture

4.1   Overview

The nonverbal behavior generator is built to be modular and to operate in real time with user-extensible behavior generation rules. The input and output interaction to the system is done by a message pipeline system, and the main data structure for the inputs and outputs is in XML form. More specifically, we are using Function Markup Language (FML) and Behavior Markup Language (BML) as part of the input and output messages (see the next section for more details on FML and BML). The nonverbal behavior generator uses two major tools to select and schedule behaviors: a natural language parser and an XML stylesheet transformation (XSLT) processor. XSL is a language to transform XML documents into other XHTML documents or XML documents. In our case, we will be transforming the input XML string by inserting time markers to the surface utterance and behavior execution codes. The nonverbal behavior generation rules are also represented in XSL format.

Figure 3 illustrates the overview of the system's structure. The nonverbal behavior generator's input XML string contains the surface text of the agent as well as other affective information such as the agent's emotional state, emphasis point, and coping strategy. The NVBGenerator module parses this XML message, registers the agent's affective information, and extracts the surface text. The surface text is then sent to the natural language parser to obtain the syntactic structure of the utterance. Given the parsed result of the utterance and the behavior generation rules, the NVBGenerator selects the appropriate behavior(s). The selected behaviors are then customized and modified by the affective information of the agent. Finally, the execution code for the chosen behavior(s) are generated and sent out to the virtual human controller. The following sections describe parts of the processing steps in greater detail.

4.2   Function Markup Language and Behavior Markup Language

The Social Performance Framework [9] [18] and more recently SAIBA [19] are being developed to modularize the design and research of embodied conversational agents. These frameworks define modules that make clear distinction between the communicative intent and behavior descriptions of the ECA with XML based interfaces. This distinction is defined by two markup languages FML and BML, which consolidate a range of prior work in markup languages (such as the Affective Presentation Markup Language [20] and Multimodal Utterance Representation Markup Language [21]). Function Markup Language (FML) specifies the communicative and expressive intent of the agent and will be part of the input message to our nonverbal behavior generator. The following describes some of the elements defined in FML.

- AFFECT: The affective state of the speaker (e.g. JOY, DISTRESS, RESENTMENT, FEAR, ANGER...).
- COPING: Identification of a coping strategy employed by the speaker.

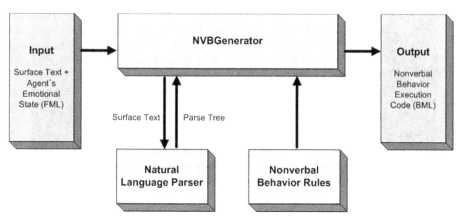

Fig. 3. System architecture of the nonverbal behavior generator

- EMPHASIS: Speaker wants listeners to pay particular attention to this part of the spoken text.
- TURN: Management of speaking turns (TAKE, GIVE, KEEP).

Behavior Markup Language (BML), on the other hand, describes the verbal and nonverbal behaviors an agent will execute. The elements of BML roughly correspond to the parts of human body and the attributes of each element further define the details of specific behavior execution information such as the start and end time and the frequency of the behavior. The set of elements defined in BML includes,

- HEAD: Movement of the head independent of eyes.
- FACE: Movement in the face.
- GAZE: Coordinated movement of the eyes, neck, and torso, indicating where the character is looking.
- BODY: General movement of the body.
- GESTURE: Coordinated movement with arms and hands.
- SPEECH: Spoken delivery.
- LIPS: Movement of the mouth.
- ANIMATION: Plays back a character animation clip.

The selected behaviors from our nonverbal behavior generator are encoded using these BML tags and be included in the output message. Incorporating FML and BML to specify the communicative intent and the nonverbal behaviors of the agent not only gives the structural format to express these information, but allows the developer to easily process the information using any XML processor, which is widely available.

4.3   Nonverbal Behavior Generation Process

Let's have a closer look at how the nonverbal behaviors are selected and generated. Assume the input message to the generator contains the following information.

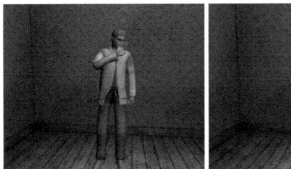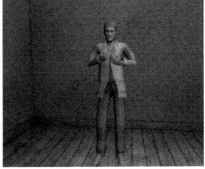

Fig. 4. Nonverbal behaviors animated on SmartBody

- Surface text:
  Yes, I completely agree. I am not interested only in myself, you know.
- Emphasis: Emphasis on *myself*
- Affect: Neutral

The NVBGenerator first parses the input message, extracts the surface string, and sends it to the natural language parser. We are currently using Charniak's parser [22] to process the utterance. The parse tree is sent back and the NVB-Generator inserts time markers between every word of the utterance. Then the NVBGenerator analyzes the semantic and syntactic structure of the utterance to decide which rules could be fired and inserts XML tags for such rules. The XSLT processor looks at these rule tags and matches them to insert the BML codes into the output message. But if there are two rules that overlap with each other, the one with a higher priority will be selected.

In the example above, the rules that apply to the given surface text will be, *interjection rule*, which creates BML codes for a head nod on the word 'Yes', *intensification rule*, which puts a head nod and lowered brow movement on the word 'completely', *negation rule*, which puts head shakes on 'I am not interested', *first noun phrase rule*, which puts a small head nod after 'myself', and the *response request rule*, which puts head nod after 'you know'. Since there is an emphasis on the word 'myself', the NVBGenerator will replace the medium head nod to a big nod and insert lowered brow movement when 'myself' is spoken. The SmartBody system also has a number of pre-animated gesture clips that could be used in place of the BML codes. For example, we have an animation clip where the ECA puts his hand up and shakes his head, which could be used when the *negation rule* is selected instead of outputting a BML code for head shake. Figure 4 shows examples of some nonverbal behaviors animated on SmartBody. Finally, the output message consisting of the surface text with time markers and BML codes are sent to the SmartBody controller [23] that synchronizes and animates the nonverbal behaviors.

4.4   Extensibility and Specialization

The nonverbal behavior generator has been designed for easy extension for the users. As mentioned in section 4.1, the nonverbal behavior generation rules are represented in XSL format. There is one file that stores the behavior descriptions for different nonverbal behaviors and another file that stores the association between the rules and the nonverbal behaviors. More specifically, the behavior description file stores the BML codes for different behaviors such as *big_head_nod, small_head_shake*, and *brow_frown* and the behavior generation rule file stores the information on which behaviors should be generated for each rule. For example, when intensification rule is applied, a small head nod and brow frowning should occur. As described in section 4.2, the whole behavior generation process is done in three steps; first the NVBGenerator analyzes the surface text and inserts an XML tag for the appropriate rule. Then the behavior generation rule file matches this tag to see which behaviors should occur, and finally the appropriate BML codes stored in the behavior description file is inserted to the output message.

The separation between behavior descriptions and nonverbal behavior generation rules allows easy modification and extension without affecting one another. For example, it is simple to add new entries of gesture animations or behavior descriptions into the system. As the animator creates new gesture animations or a programmer creates a new procedural behavior, one can simply extend the behavior description file to add the name of the animations or behavior description for future use. It is also easy to modify the rules that invoke the behavior descriptions. For example, if the current rule for *inclusivity* contains a lateral head movement but one wishes to add a brow raise to it, he or she simply needs to add lines to the file storing the behavior generation rules, which will call the behavior description for brow raise. This separation also supports supports specialization of behavior according to individual or cultural traits. For example, we can have different rules for inclusivity based on culturally-specific gesturing tendencies.

Using XSL to represent the behavior descriptions and behavior generation rules also allows the user to make modifications without knowing the details of the nonverbal behavior generator. There is no need to have other programming language skills or study how the behavior generator is implemented. By learning simple patterns on how to add XSLT templates, one can create, modify or delete behavior descriptions and rules.

5   Conclusion and Future Work

We have developed a framework for text-to-speech nonverbal behavior generation. It analyzes the syntactic and semantic structure of the input text and generates appropriate head movements, facial expressions, and body gestures. We studied a number of video clips to develop rules that map specific words, phrases, or speech acts and constructed our behavior generation rules according to this. The behavior generator is designed to be easy for users to modify or create behavior descriptions and behavior generation rules. The module was successfully incorporated into the SASO and SmartBody system, using the SAIBA markup structure, and works in real time. It has also been fielded in a cultural training application being developed at the Institute for Creative Technology.

Much work still remains to improve the system. Our next step would be to evaluate the system and the behaviors generated. We are particularly interested in the user's responses to the behaviors and what they infer from the behaviors. We expect our current rules are too limited and overly general in their applicability. Thus, we are also seeking ways to use various machine learning techniques to aid us in the process of rule generation. One straightforward approach would be to learn the mapping between bigrams or trigrams of words to gestures. This would require a large gesture corpora; however a suitable corpora for our work is currently not available. In the absence of a large corpora, we rather expect the learning should be informed by higher level features such as syntactic, lexical, and semantic structure of the utterance or the ECA's emotional state, similar to what we used to craft the rules by hand.

Furthermore, we would like to modify the nonverbal behavior generation given the information on ECA's supposed gender, age, culture, or personality. The system also lacks a good knowledge base of the environment in which the ECA resides. A tight connection to the knowledge base of the objects and agents in the virtual world will allow the ECA to have more sophisticated behaviors such as deictic gestures that correctly points at the object referred. Finally, we would like to model the affective state of the user interacting with the ECA and generate appropriate behaviors that respond not only to agent's emotions but also to the user's emotions.

Acknowledgments

This work was sponsored by the U.S. Army Research, Development, and Engineering Command (RDECOM), and the content does not necessarily reflect the position or the policy of the Government, and no official endorsement should be inferred.

References

1. Knapp, M., Hall, J.: Nonverbal Communication in Human Interaction. 4th edn. Harcourt Brace College Publishers (1997)
2. Fabri, M., Moore, D., Hobbs, D.: Expressive agents: Non-verbal communication in collaborative virtual environments. In: Proceedings of Autonomous Agents and Multi-Agent Systems, Bologna, Italy (2002)
3. Swartout, W., Hill, R., Gratch, J., Johnson, W., Kyriakakis, C., Labore, K., Lindheim, R., Marsella, S., Miraglia, D., Moore, B., Morie, J., Rickel, J., Thiebaux, M., Tuch, L., Whitney, R.: Toward the holodeck: Integrating graphics, sound, character and story. In: Proceedings of 5th International Conference on Autonomous Agents, Montreal, Canada (2001)
4. Durlach, N., Slater, M.: Presence in shared virtual environments and virtual togetherness. In: BT Workshop on Presence in Shared Virtual Environments, Ipswich, UK (1998)

5. Cassell, J., Vilhjálmsson, H., Chang, K., Bickmore, T., Campbell, L., Yan, H.: Requirements for an architecture for embodied conversational characters. In Magnenat-Thalmann, N., Thalmann, D., eds.: Computer Animation and Simulation '99. Springer Verlag, Vinna, Austria (1999) 109–120
6. Becheiraz, P., Thalmann, D.: A behavioral animation system for autonomous actors personified by emotions. In: Proceedings of the 1st Workshop on Embodied Conversational Characters (WECC), Lake Tahoe, CA (1998) 57–65
7. Striegnitz, K., Tepper, P., Lovett, A., Cassell, J.: Knowledge representation for generating locating gestures in route directions. In: Proceedings of Workshop on Spatial Language and Dialogue, Delmenhorst, Germany (2005)
8. Cassell, J., Vilhjálmsson, H., Bickmore, T.: BEAT: The behavior expression animation toolkit. In: Proceedings of ACM SIGGRAPH, New York, NY, ACM Press / ACM SIGGRAPH (2001) 477–486
9. Vilhjálmsson, H., Marsella, S.: Social performance framework. In: Workshop on Modular Construction of Human-Like Intelligence at the AAAI 20th National Conference on Artificual Intelligence, Pittsburgh, PA (2005)
10. Ekman, P.: About brows: emotional and conversational signals. In von Cranach, M., Foppa, K., Lepenies, W., Ploog, D., eds.: Human Ethology. Cambridge University Press (1979) 169–248
11. Hadar, U., Steiner, T., Grant, E., Clifford Rose, F.: Kinematics of head movement accompanying speech during conversation. Human Movement Science **2** (1983) 35–46
12. Heylen, D.: Challenges ahead. In: Proceedings of AISB Symposium on Social Virtual Agents. (in press)
13. Kendon, A.: Some uses of head shake. Gesture (2) (2003) 147–182
14. McClave, E.: Linguistic functions of head movements in the context of speech. Journal of Pragmatics (32) (2000) 855–878
15. The HUMAINE Consortium: The HUMAINE portal. Retrieved April 7, 2006, from http://emotion-research.net/ (2006)
16. The HUMAINE Consortium: Multimodal data in action and interaction: a library of recordings and labelling schemes. Retrieved April 14, 2006, from http://emotion-research.net/deliverables/ (2004)
17. Weizenbaum, J.: ELIZA – a computer program for the study of natural language communication between man and machines. Communications of the Association for Computing Machinery **9** (1996) 36–45
18. n.a.: Behavior markup language (BML) specification. Retrieved June 6, 2006, from http://twiki.isi.edu/Public/BMLSpecification/ (2006)
19. Kopp, S., Krenn, B., Marsella, S., Marshall, A., Pelachaud, C., Pirker, H., Thorisson, K., Vilhjálmsson, H.: Towards a common framework for multimodal generation in embodied conversation agents: a behavior markup language. In: International Conference on Virtual Agents, 2006, Marina del Rey, CA (submitted)
20. DeCarolis, B., Pelachaud, C., Poggi, I., Steedman, M.: APML, a mark-up language for believable behavior generation. In Prendinger, H., Ishizuka, M., eds.: Life-like Characters. Tools, Affective Functions and Applications. Springer (2004) 65–85
21. Kopp S., W.I.: Synthesizing multimodal utterances for conversational agents. Computer Animation and Virtual Worlds **15**(1) (2004) 39–52
22. Chariank, E.: A maximum-entropy-inspired parser. In: Proceedings of North American Chapter of the Association for Computational Linguistics. (2000)
23. Kallmann, M., Marsella, S.: Hierarchical motion controllers for real-time autonomous virtual humans. In: Proceedings of the 5th International working conference on Intelligent Virtual Agents (IVA), Kos, Greece (2005) 243–265

[HUGE]: Universal Architecture for Statistically Based HUman GEsturing

Karlo Smid[1], Goranka Zoric[2], and Igor S. Pandzic[2]

[1] Ericsson Nikola Tesla, Krapinska 45, p.p. 93, HR-10 002 Zagreb
karlo.smid@ericsson.com
[2] Faculty of electrical engineering and computing, Zagreb University,
Unska 3, HR-10 000 Zagreb
{Igor.Pandzic, Goranka.Zoric}@fer.hr

Abstract. We introduce a universal architecture for statistically based HUman GEsturing (HUGE) system, for producing and using statistical models for facial gestures based on any kind of inducement. As inducement we consider any kind of signal that occurs in parallel to the production of gestures in human behaviour and that may have a statistical correlation with the occurrence of gestures, e.g. text that is spoken, audio signal of speech, bio signals etc. The correlation between the inducement signal and the gestures is used to first build the statistical model of gestures based on a training corpus consisting of sequences of gestures and corresponding inducement data sequences. In the runtime phase, the raw, previously unknown inducement data is used to trigger (induce) the real time gestures of the agent based on the previously constructed statistical model. We present the general architecture and implementation issues of our system, and further clarify it through two case studies. We believe that this universal architecture is useful for experimenting with various kinds of potential inducement signals and their features and exploring the correlation of such signals or features with the gesturing behaviour.

1 Introduction

Gesturing is integral part of human face-to-face communication. In parallel to the production of gestures in human behaviour other signals may occur, e.g. text that is spoken, audio signal of speech or bio signals. In most cases these signals and gestures happen simultaneously based on common motivation and they supplement, complement or duplicate each other. Those signals may be in a statistical correlation with the occurrence of gestures. We use this fact to build the statistical model of facial gestures based on any kind of such signal. In our system we call such signals *inducement*. Therefore, we think of inducement as any data sequence that happens in parallel with generation of gestures, and that is expected to have some correlation with the gestures. The statistical model is built from a training corpus consisting of gesture sequences and corresponding inducement data sequences. For every state of inducement, a statistical model generator produces

J. Gratch et al. (Eds.): IVA 2006, LNAI 4133, pp. 256–269, 2006.
© Springer-Verlag Berlin Heidelberg 2006

statistical data for every gesture type with probabilities for gesture type, duration and amplitude values. In the runtime phase, the statistical model for gesture generation is used to automatically generate facial gestures from raw inducement data. These gestures are then used to produce real time animation corresponding to the underlying inducement. The idea of our system is to provide a universal architecture for the use with various kinds of potential inducement signals correlated with HUman GEstures (thus the name HUGE). Thus by using our system it is possible to generate facial gestures in real time using statistical model driven by different signals occurring in parallel to the production of gestures with no need of changing the complete system architecture, but only adding modules specific for the used signal. We believe that this universal architecture will ease experimenting with various kinds of potential inducement signals and their features and exploring the correlation of such signals or features with the gesturing behaviour.

The HUGE architecture has its roots in our previous work in the field of Embodied Conversational Agents. In [1] we proposed a system architecture for an Autonomous Speaker Agent that is capable of reading plain English text and rendering it in a form of speech accompanied by the appropriate facial gestures. The statistical model is obtained by analyzing a training data set consisting of several speakers recorded on video and transcriptions of their speech. A lexical analysis of the transcription texts allowed to correlate the lexical characteristics of a text with the corresponding facial gestures and to incorporate this correlation into a statistical model. Lexical structure of input text is the inducement that triggers the obtained statistical model of facial gestures. In [2] we presented a method for automatic Lip Sync of graphically embodied animated agents where parameters of speaker's speech signal are used as inducement.

There are many existing systems that generate facial gestures from the single input (e.g. the text, speech) using statistical models or some other methods driven by rules, semantic data and similar. In [3], Albrect et al. introduce a method for automatic generation of facial gestures from speech: head and eyebrow raising and lowering dependent on pitch, gaze direction, movement of eyelids and eyebrows, and frowning during thinking and word search pauses, eye blinks and lip moistening, or random eye movement during normal speech. Poggi and Pelachaud in [4] focused on the gaze behaviour in simulating automatic generation of face expressions driven by semantic data. The Eyes Alive system [5] reproduces eye movements that are dynamically correct at the level of each movement, and that are also globally statistically correct in terms of the frequency of movements, intervals between them and their amplitudes based on the statistical analysis of eye-tracking video. Cassell et al. [6] automatically generate and animate conversations between multiple human-like agents including intonation, facial expressions, lip motions, eye gaze, head motion and hand gestures from the speaker/listener relationship, the text and the intonation. The BEAT system [7] controls movements of hands, arms and the face and the intonation of the voice from the input text, relying on the rules derived from the extensive research in the human conversational behaviour. Graf et al. in [8] analyze head and facial movements that accompany speech and they relation to the text's prosodic structure, where prosody describes the way speech is intonated with elements such as pauses, pitch, timing effects and loudness. Cao et al. in [9] present a technique for automatically synthesizing speech-driven expressive facial animation from given input utterance. The system is capable of automatic detection of emotional content of arbitrary input utterances by using support vector machine classifier with probabilities with which a given utterance belongs to each of the emotional classes. In addition, lip-synchronization with correct co-articulation is performed. Gutierrez-Osuna et al. in [10] generate animations with realistic dynamics of three-dimensional human faces driven by speech signal represented with perceptually based parameters combined with two prosodic cues (fundamental frequency and frame energy). Similarly in [11], Granström and House use audiovisual representation of prosody to create an animated talking agent capable of displaying realistic communicative behaviour. Brand in [12] generates full facial animation from expressive information in an audio track. An animated agent, in this case called voice puppet, learns a facial control model from computer vision of real behaviour, automatically incorporating vocal and facial dynamics.

As opposed to previously described systems which use a single signal (either text or speech) to produce the animation, our system provides universal architecture that accepts various kinds of potential inducement signals related to facial gestures.

In this section the idea of our proposed architecture is given, as well as the related work. Next section describes in details our universal architecture. Section 3 explains the implementation issues of our system, while it is further clarified through two case studies in Section 4. The paper ends with the conclusion and the discussion of future work.

2 The Architecture

In this section we describe the logical modules and the data flow in the proposed architecture of our HUGE system. The system works in two distinct phases: the statistical model generation phase, and the runtime phase. The statistical model generation phase is typically done offline and may involve some manual steps in analysing the input data. In general, this phase takes the training corpus in form of gesture data and corresponding inducement data and produces the statistical model by correlating the gesture sequence with the inducement sequence. The runtime phase must run in real time and therefore must be fully automatic, without any manual processing of data. This phase takes a new sequence of inducement data and uses it to trigger the statistical model and produce real time animation corresponding to the inducement. We will now describe the two phases in more detail.

Figure 1 describes the statistical model generation and runtime phase. In figure 1 rounded rectangles represent data, plain rectangles represent processes, and arrows represent data flow between processes. The inputs to the statistical model generation are the timed gesture data and timed inducement data. The raw gesture data typically comes in form of recorded video clips of speakers performing natural speech, but it could otherwise come from a feature tracking algorithm or hardware. The raw gesture data is automatically or manually annotated in order to produce timed sequences of gestures. These sequences are represented in the universal gesture data format that is a part of the architecture, and described in detail in the Implementation section.

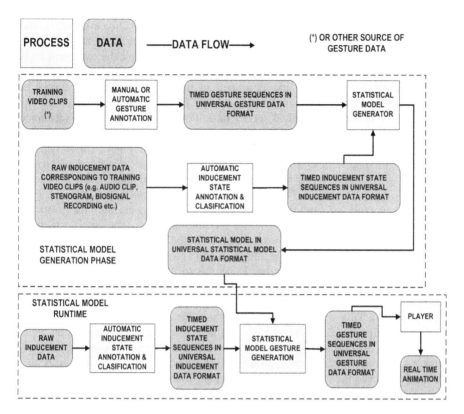

Fig. 1. Universal Architecture for Statistically based HUman GEsturing (HUGE) system

The raw inducement data is the other input to this phase. For example, textual transcript of a video clip can be used as inducement, as it is expected that gestures will be correlated to the text. Another example is the speech recording, since there is also a correlation between certain speech features and the gestures that happen at the same time. Yet another example may be bio signal measurements.

It has to be noted that we use the term inducement because in the runtime phase of this architecture these inducement signals are used to trigger, i.e. induce gestures. The use of this term is strictly system-related, and does not refer to the way these inducement signals relate to the gesture production in real human behaviour - indeed, in most cases the process is quite different, e.g. speech intonation and corresponding gestures happen simultaneously from common motivation, and not by one inducing the other in any way. Still, within this system we find the term appropriate because it describes quite accurately the way the system works.

From the raw inducement data (e.g. text, speech signal, bio signals), an automated feature extraction and classification algorithm produces a timed sequence of inducement states, stored in the universal inducement data format. An inducement state can be any state determined from the inducement that is expected to correlate well with production of gestures. For example, raw text may be lexically analysed to determine when new terms are introduced, and thus create a simple classification of states into theme or rheme. In case of audio signal inducement, a set of audio features may be analysed and classified into a number of states. The choice of states, their number, and the algorithm to extract them is the issue of each implementation.

From the timed sequences of gestures and inducement states, the statistical model generator produces the statistical model in the universal statistical model data format. Facial gesture parameters that are described in universal gesture data format are gesture type, duration and amplitude value. Those parameters represent the components of universal statistical model data. For every state of the inducement, statistical model generator produces the probability of occurrence for every gesture type and for particular type it produces the frequency distribution estimation functions for gesture type duration and amplitude values. Statistical model generator correlates the time-aligned inducement and gesture universal data sequences in order to calculate those parameters. The statistical model describes the probability of occurrence and expected amplitudes and durations of various gestures with respect to the inducement states. This is the basis for the runtime phase. The detail explanation of how statistical model generator works is given in the Implementation section.

The runtime phase generates real time animation based on raw inducement data, in such a way that the overall behaviour is similar to the training corpus in terms of statistics of gesture occurrence and characteristics, as related to the inducement. The input to this phase is the raw inducement data (i.e. plain text, speech recording, bio signal sequence). This input is processed by the same automatic states extraction and classification algorithm that was used in the statistical model generation phase. Therefore it is important that this algorithm can run in real time. Again, a timed sequence of inducement states is produced. The gesture generator now uses these states as a trigger to the statistical model in a semi-random process. This process aims to produce the same global statistics for the frequency of occurrence, amplitude and duration of various gestures as described in the statistical model. These gestures may be output in the gesture data form to the player that can interpret them. The player must synchronize the playing of gestures with the reproduction of the raw inducement data (e.g. the generated gestures must be synchronized with the audio reproduction of speech). The modules are presented here in a way that highlights the logical flow of data. The actual implementation may have to integrate some of the modules of the runtime phase because of different interaction needs. For example, if text is used as inducement, there is no temporal reference in the raw input text - the timing is obtained only when the player synthesizes the speech from the text using a speech synthesizer. Therefore in this case the player and the gesture generator must be closely integrated in order to produce gestures on the fly. These issues will be clearly described in the case studies section.

In this section we explained the architecture of our proposed HUGE system. Processes, data and data flows between processes of two system phases are explained in detail. In the following section a concrete implementation of HUGE system will be presented and explained.

3   Implementation

As we explained the architecture of HUGE system in previous section, in this section our goal is to introduce HUGE system implementation issues. First, we will present the universal data formats for gestures, inducements and statistical models along with technologies that we used in order to realize them. After data elaboration, we introduce the HUGE Application Programming Interface (API) model. Using HUGE API, developers are able to realize and connect processes of HUGE architecture. Furthermore, entry points of HUGE API in HUGE architecture will be presented and explained in detail.

For description of universal data formats that exists in HUGE architecture, we chose Extensible Markup Language (XML[1]).

Table 1 shows the example of XML document snippet that is structured and typed according to our universal data formats for inducements.

Inducement row from table 1 holds valid XML document instance snippet that contains inducement data. Identified inducement has three parameters: starting point in time, ending point in time and inducement type. In order to be in accordance with our universal data format for inducement data, XML document instance has to satisfy following requirements:

File has to be in accordance with the inducement XML schema definition. Schema definition file defines the structure and basic data types (long, decimal). Every inducement end time has to be grater or equal than the start time. All time intervals have to be sorted in accessing order. Interval overlapping is not allowed because we postulate that at the given time interval only one inducement state is possible.

Table 1. Example of XML document snippet for inducements

Inducement	`<Inducement xmlns="http://www.fer.hr/gestures"` `xmlns:xsi="http://www.w3.org/2001/XMLSchema-instance">` `  <IdentifiedInducement>` `    <start>0</start>` `    <end>1</end>` `    <type>STATE00042</type>` `  </IdentifiedInducement>` `</Inducement>`

Every identified gesture has four parameters: starting point in time, ending point in time, gesture type and gesture amplitude value. Gesture universal data has to be in accordance with the following requirements:

File has to be in accordance with the gesture schema definition file for the same reason as the inducement XML document.
Overlapping of gesture time intervals is allowed only for the following gesture groups: head movement group (all nod and swing movements, including reset head movement) can be overlapped with eyebrows raise and eyes blink. Reason for this behavior is simple: at the same time interval humans could blink, move head in various directions and raise their eyebrows.
Time constraint on gesture intervals is that start time must be less or equal than the end time.

---

[1] http://www.w3.org/XML/

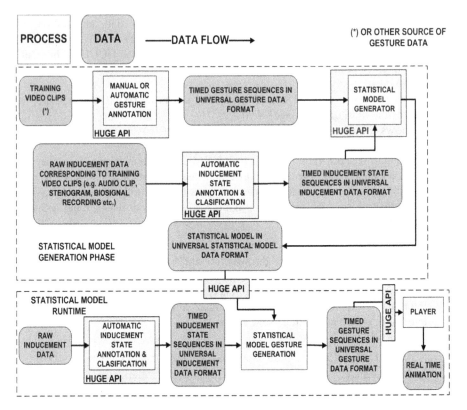

Fig. 2. HUGE API entry points in universal architecture HUGE system

Statistical data are grouped according to identified inducement types. Every inducement statistical data element consists of gesture statistical data elements. Gestures are grouped in four groups: nods, swings, eye blinks and eyebrows raises. It is important to note that we consider head shakes as to consecutive head nods (left nod followed by right nod or vice versa) and that eyebrows frowns are considered as eyebrows raises with negative amplitude. Every sub gesture element has following parameters: type, statistical probability of occurrence value, and cumulative frequency histogram distributions for amplitude and duration parameters. The only exceptions are eyes blink gesture, which does not contain amplitude distribution and overshoot nod, which contains two cumulative histograms of amplitudes. We are using cumulative frequency histogram approximation functions instead of standard frequency histogram because approximation function of cumulative frequency histogram is injection function (one-to-one function). Overshoot nod has two cumulative histograms of amplitude because it consists of two consecutive nods: nod up immediately followed by nod down. Statistical model universal data has to be in accordance with following requirements:

It has to be in accordance with schema definition file.
For every inducement type, total sum of probability occurrences for gesture groups has to be one.

For every inducement type, total sum of probability occurrences for sub gestures also has to be one.

All frequency histograms are cumulative.

After the data formats of HUGE system, we are going to explain the HUGE API. These API is realized using c# programming language of Microsoft .NET[2] platform and its purpose is to provide methods for manipulation with HUGE universal data formats and method for calculation of statistical models. Figure 2 shows how HUGE API fits into the universal architecture of HUGE system. It provides methods for parsing, creating and validating XML document instances of gestures, inducements and statistical models. Those methods are based on functionality for manipulating xml data formats provided in .NET platform libraries. This functionality is extended using c# programming in order to provide features needed by proposed HUGE processes and data formats. Using those API methods, application developers that implement their own instances of HUGE system, are in accordance with our proposed system architecture and they are able to use universal data formats for gestures, inducements and statistical models in object-oriented model. Parsing methods transform universal data from XML format into object model. Creating methods operate in opposite direction, they produce XML data format from the data object model. Validating methods validate the correctness of universal data XML format.

It is important to explain the core process of HUGE architecture. Statistical model generator process (figure 2) first uses validation methods that validate inducement and gesture data formats. Inducement and gesture data formats must have the same starting and ending points in time (have to be aligned in time) so the statistical model generator process is able to produce correct statistical model data. It parses inducement data and counts which gesture types were triggered by the particular inducement state. Only gestures that start in time interval corresponded with inducement state are counted. Probability of occurrence for particular gesture type triggered by the particular inducement is simply calculated by dividing number of particular gesture occurrence (e.g. nod up) with total number of gesture group (e.g. nods) occurrences triggered by the particular inducement state. Gesture type duration and amplitude data are grouped in intervals (interval values for duration and amplitude are specific parameters that depend on the amount of the training corpus, more training data means narrower interval) in order to produce their frequency distributions of occurence. Based on cumulative frequency distribution values, we calculate simple linear approximation of probability functions for duration and amplitude values.

$$f(x)=ax+b \qquad (1)$$

Where x is uniformly distributed random number and represents the probability of occurrence for duration or amplitude value.

Creating methods are used by automatic/manual inducement state and gesture annotation and classification processes (figure 2) and also by statistical model generator process because outputs of those processes are inducement, gesture and statistical model XML data formats. Statistical model gesture generation process uses parsing methods in order to transform statistical model data from XML format into

---

[2] http://www.microsoft.com/net/default.mspx

object model. It also uses validation methods to check the correctness of statistical model XML data format. Player process uses methods for parsing and validating universal gesture data in order to obtain gesture data object model.

Using HUGE API, application development is much easier and quicker and universal data formats databases can be easily shared among developers of HUGE systems.

In this section we discussed the implementation issues of HUGE system: HUGE universal data formats and HUGE API. In the following section we will further elaborate universal HUGE architecture by presenting two case studies, which represent our ongoing work that is based on the universal HUGE system architecture. First, we will present HUGE system where inducement data is lexical structure of spoken text. In second system, inducement data are parameters of speech signal. In the Introduction we also mentioned bio-signals as gestures inducement. Since we have not performed any analysis of inducements based on bio-signals, we will not further discuss them in this paper.

4 Case Studies

4.a Text-Induced Gestures

In this section we will present our HUGE system implementation that uses as inducement lexical structure of uttered text. Figure 3 represents the HUGE system architecture adapted to the lexical structure of uttered text as the system inducement in system real-time part.

In statistical model generation phase, our HUGE system implementation is identical to HUGE system architecture. Using observation of training video clips, and simple Graphical User Interface for HUGE API, we manually created timed gesture sequences in universal gesture data format.

Timed lexical states in universal inducement data format were created semiautomatic. Using automatic lexical analysis of transcriptions corresponded to training video clips, we obtained the lexical states of the particular transcript word groups. Manually correlating transcripts with training video clips and using simple GUI interface for HUGE API, we produced lexical states time information (beginning and ending times).

Input of automatic lexical state annotation and classification HUGE process is plain English text. This process performs linguistic and contextual analysis of a text written in English language. The main goal of this process is to determine if word (or group of words) is new in the utterance context (theme or STATE00001), if extends some previously mentioned word or group of words (rheme or STATE00002) or does not belong to any of these lexical groups (STATE00003). More details about this module can be found in our previous work [1].

Then, using the feedback link to HUGE player process (implemented using Visage SDK API[3] and SAPI 5.0 Microsoft TTS engine[4]), it determines the actual timings and durations of the inducement states. This is possible, because all timing events in

---

[3] Visage Technologies AB http://www.visagetechnologies.com/
[4] Microsoft speech technologies http://www.microsoft.com/speech/

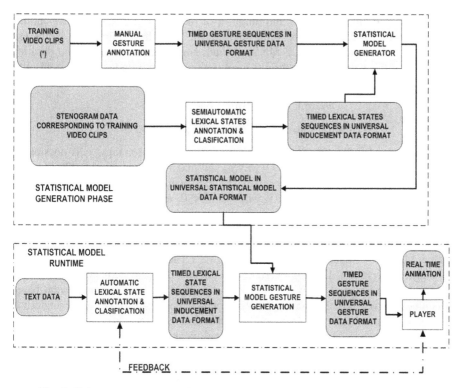

Fig. 3. Universal architecture of HUGE system adapted to text data as inducement

statistical model runtime are driven by the Text To Speech (TTS) HUGE player sub module. Timed lexical state sequences in universal inducement data format are input to statistical model gesture generation which, using the previously calculated statistical model data creates the timed gesture sequence in universal gesture data format. For example, if inducement state is STATE00002, gesture type for this state is determined by first generating a uniformly distributed random number between 0 and 100. Depending on its value and the statistical model for the particular state, gesture type is determined. If that gesture type has duration and amplitude parameters, again two uniformly distributed random numbers are generated and those numbers represent inputs into linear approximation of probability functions for those parameters (equation 1).

HUGE player process, using its TTS sub module, defines the timings of the real time animation. Combining timed gesture data sequence (transformation of the gesture universal data format into Microsoft's SAPI 5.0 TTS event format) and the TTS timing events, player process generates the real time gesture animation supporting all gesture types defined in the universal gesture data format. For example the SAPI5 event bookmark code for rapid left head movement is MARK= 8000000. Those bookmarks with appropriate values are inserted at the starting point of every gesture. Every facial gesture has a corresponding bookmark value. The head and eyebrows movement bookmark values not only define the type of facial gesture, but also contain the amplitude data and duration of the facial movement. For example, bookmark value 8051212 (Bmk_value) defines the rapid head movement to the left (symbol L) of amplitude (A) 1.2 MNS0 (Mouth Nose separation units) and duration (D) of 512 milliseconds. The functions for duration and amplitudes of facial gestures rapid L are:

$$D=(Bmk\_value - Bmk\_code)/100 \qquad (2)$$

$$A=((Bmk\_value - Bmk\_code) - (D \times 100))/10 \qquad (3)$$

In the interval [8000000, 9000000>for bookmark values for rapid L is possible to code maximal amplitude value of 9.9 MNS0 and maximal duration of 9.999 seconds. This limitation is not the problem because the statistical data showed that the maximal amplitude value for facial gesture L was 2.2 MNS0, and duration was never longer than 2 seconds.

TTS/MPEG-4 Playing Module plays in real-time, using the bookmark information, appropriate viseme and gestures model animation. It is based on Visage SDK API[5]. and on Microsoft Speech API SAPI 5.0 engine[6]. The synchronization between the animation subsystem (MPEG-4 Playing) and the speech subsystem (Microsoft's TTS engine) can be realized in two ways: with time-based scheduling and event-based scheduling. Which synchronization method will be used depends on the underling TTS engine implementation. In time-based scheduling, a speech is generated before nonverbal behaviors. Event-based scheduling means that speech and nonverbal behaviors are generated at the same time. In our system we are using the event-based scheduling method. We have implemented simple animation models for eyes blink, simple gaze following and head and eyebrows movement. Our system implementation is open, so every user is able to easily implement its own animation models. The animation model for head movement and eyebrows movement facial gestures is based on the trigonometry sine function. That means that our agent nods his head and raises eyebrows following the sine function trajectory. In gaze following animation model the eyes of our agent are moving in opposite directions of a head movement if a head movement amplitude is smaller than the defined threshold. This gives the impression of eye contact with agent.

4.b   Speech-Induced Gestures

A particular type of signal that frequently accompanies facial gestures is speech signal. In speech-induced gestures an idea is to find a statistical correlation between speech signal and occurrence of gestures and to produce a speech driven facial animation. Such system is a special case of our universal architecture (figure 4). In the statistical model generation phase, audio data is used as raw inducement data to produce statistical model. Similarly, in the statistical model runtime phase, audio data is used as input data. To produce realistic animation, the player needs timed gesture sequences and also correct lip movements.

Implementation of a system that uses speech-induced gestures is still ongoing work. In our previous work we have implemented an automatic Lip Sync system [13].

---

[5] Visage Technologies AB http://www.visagetechnologies.com/
[6] Microsoft speech technologies http://www.microsoft.com/speech/

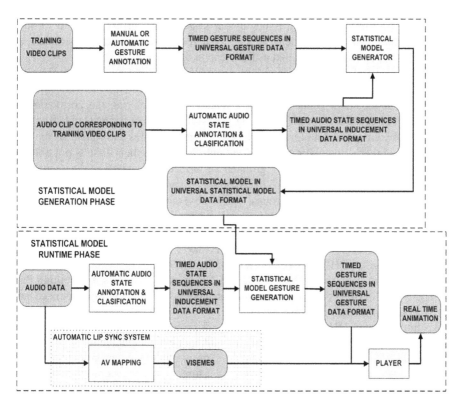

Fig. 4. Universal architecture of HUGE system adapted to audio data as inducement

It takes speech signal as input and performs audio to visual mapping in order to produce the viseme, the visual representative of a phoneme. Next, we need to define audio states using speech representation that takes into consideration speech prosody (e.g. pitch together with fundamental frequency, pauses). Once we have suitable audio states we will create statistical model and use it for gesture generation.

5   Conclusions and Future Work

In this article we presented our universal architecture for statistically based HUman GEsturing (HUGE) system for producing and using statistical models for facial gestures based on any kind of inducement. As inducement we consider any kind of signal that occurs in parallel to the production of gestures in human behaviour and that may have a statistical correlation with the occurrence of gestures, e.g. text that is spoken, audio signal of speech, bio signals etc. The correlation between the inducement signal and the gestures is used to first build the statistical model of gestures based on a training corpus consisting of sequences of gestures and corresponding inducement data sequences. In the runtime phase, the raw, previously unknown inducement data is used to trigger (induce) the real time gestures of the agent based on the previously constructed statistical model. We presented the general architecture and implementation issues of our system, and further clarify it through two case studies which represent HUGE systems adapted to lexical structure of spoken text and audio speech signal as inducement data.

There are several important benefits of using HUGE system architecture. First, we believe that this universal architecture is useful for experimenting with various kinds of potential inducement signals and their features and exploring the correlation of such signals or features with the gesturing behaviour. All data formats and structures are defined by universal data formats for inducements, gestures and statistical models. We postulated that at the given time interval only one inducement state is possible, so inducement parameters have to be grouped in inducement states in the manner to satisfy this time requirement. Also, overlapping of gesture time intervals is allowed only for the following gesture groups: head movement group (all nod and swing movements, including reset head movement) can be overlapped with eyebrows raise and eyes blink. This requirement is based on our observation of training video clips: at the same time interval humans might blink, move head in various directions and raise their eyebrows. HUGE API is defined in order to help developers to easily manipulate those data and to connect the HUGE system processes. Combining data and HUGE API, large database of statistical models could be easily produced and shared among different research teams.

We implemented HUGE API using .NET c# programming language. In order to make HUGE universal architecture easily implemented on other platforms, HUGE API should also be implemented using Java programming language. Furthermore, gesture statistical model should be produced using as the inducement data speech audio signal characteristics.

References

1. Smid, K., Radman, V., Pandzic, I. 2005. Automatic Content Production for an Autonomous Speaker Agent. Conversational Informatics for Supporting Social Intelligence and Interaction: Situational and Environmental Information Enforcing Involvement in Conversation / Nakano, Yukiko I. ; Nishida, Toyoaki (ur.). - Hatfield : AISB, The Society for the Study of Artificial Intelligence and the Simulation of Behaviour, 2005. 103-113

2. Zoric, G., Smid, K., Pandzic, I. 2005. Automatic facial gesturing for conversational agents and avatars. Proceedings of the 2005 International Conference on Active Media Technology (AMT 2005) / Tarumi, Hiroyuki ; Li, Yuefeng ; Yoshida, Tetsuya (ur.). - Piscataway, NJ, USA : IEEE , 2005. 505 - 510.

3. Irene Albrecht, Jorg Haber, and HansPeter Seidel. Automatic Generation of Non-Verbal Facial Expressions from Speech. In Proc. Computer Graphics International 2002 (CGI 2002), pages 283--293, July 2002.

4. I. Poggi and C. Pelachaud. Signals and meanings of gaze in Animated Faces. In P. McKevitt, S. O' Nualláin, Conn Mulvihill, eds.: Language,Vision, and Music,John Benjamins, Amsterdam (2002), 133-144.

5. Lee, S. P., Badler, J. B., and Badler, N. I. 2002. Eyes Alive. In Proceedings of the 29th annual conference on Computer graphics and interactive techniques 2002, San Antonio, Texas, USA, ACM Press New York, NY,USA, 637 – 644

6. J. Cassell, C. Pelachaud, N. Badler, M. Steedman, B. Achorn, T. Becket, B. Douvillle, S. Prevost and M. Stone. Animated Conversation: Rule-based Generation of Facial Expressions, Jesture & Spoken Intonation for Multiple Conversational Agents. In Proceedings of SIGGAPH '94, 1994.

7. Cassell, J., Vilhjálmsson, H., and Bickmore, T., 2001. BEAT: the Behavior Expression Animation Toolkit. In Proceedings of SIGGRAPH 2001, ACM Press / ACM SIGGRAPH, New York, E. Fiume, Ed., Computer Graphics Proceedings, Annual Conference Series, ACM, 477-486.

8. Graf, H. P., Cosatto, E., Strom, V., and Huang, F. J., 2002. Visual Prosody: Facial Movements Accompanying Speech. In Proceedings of AFGR 2002, 381-386.

9. Cao, Y., Tien, W. C., Faloutsos, P., and Pighin, F., Expressive speech-driven facial animation, ACM Trans. Graph. 24, 4 (Oct. 2005), 1283-1302.

10. R. Gutierrez-Osuna, P. Kakumanu, A. Esposito, O.N. Garcia, A. Bojorquez, J. Castillo and I. Rudomin, Speech-driven Facial Animation with Realistic Dynamics, IEEE Trans. on Mutlimedia, Feb. 2005, 7, 1, 33- 42, ISSN: 1520-9210.

11. Granström B and House D., Audiovisual representation of prosody in expressive speech communication. 2005. Speech Communication 46: 473-484.

12. M. Brand, "Voice Puppetry", Proceedings of SIGGRAPH'99, 1999.

13. G. Zorić, I. S. Pandžić, A Real-time Lip Sync System Using a Genetic Algorithm for Automatic Neural Network Configuration, in Proceedings of the IEEE International Conference on Multimedia & Expo ICME, Amsterdam, The Netherlands, July 2005.

A Story About Gesticulation Expression

Celso de Melo and Ana Paiva

IST – Technical University of Lisbon and INESC-ID
Avenida Prof. Cavaco Silva – Taguspark
2780-990 Porto Salvo, Portugal
cmme@mega.ist.utl.pt, ana.paiva@inesc-id.pt

Abstract. Gesticulation is essential for the storytelling experience thus, virtual storytellers should be endowed with gesticulation expression. This work proposes a gesticulation expression model based on psycholinguistics. The model supports: (a) real-time gesticulation animation described as sequences of constraints on static (Portuguese Sign Language hand shapes, orientations and positions) and dynamic (motion profiles) features; (b) multimodal synchronization between gesticulation and speech; (c) automatic reproduction of annotated gesticulation according to GestuRA, a gesture transcription algorithm. To evaluate the model two studies, involving 147 subjects, were conducted. In both cases, the idea consisted of comparing the narration of the Portuguese traditional story "The White Rabbit" by a human storyteller with a version by a virtual storyteller. Results indicate that synthetic gestures fared well when compared to real gestures however, subjects preferred the human storyteller.

1 Introduction

Gesticulation is essential for the storytelling experience. Gesticulation is the kind of gestures humans do in a conversation or narration context [1]. These are idiosyncratic, unconventional and unconscious gestures which reveal the imagery of the story and, thus, support suspension of disbelief. As virtual storytelling systems harness the benefits of traditional storytelling, it is important to endow virtual storytellers with comprehensive models, inspired in humans, for gesticulation expression.

This work proposes a gesticulation expression model which supports:

- Real-time gesticulation animation described as sequences of constraints on static (Portuguese Sign Language hand shapes, orientations and positions) and dynamic (motion profiles) features;
- Multimodal synchronization between gesticulation and speech;
- Automatic reproduction of annotated gesticulation according to GestuRA, a gesture transcription algorithm.

This paper is organized as follows. Section 2 describes relevant research on gesticulation. Section 3 describes the gesticulation expression model. Section 4 describes two studies conducted to evaluate the proposed model in storytelling contexts. Finally, section 5 draws some conclusions and discusses future work.

J. Gratch et al. (Eds.): IVA 2006, LNAI 4133, pp. 270–281, 2006.
© Springer-Verlag Berlin Heidelberg 2006

2   Background and Related Work

Gesticulation is the kind of gestures humans do in a conversation or narration context [1]. They tend to focus on arms and hands, though other body parts may be involved [2]. Gesticulation and speech co-express the same underlying idea unit synchronizing at the semantic and pragmatic levels. According to how it unfolds in time, gesticulation can be structured into phases ([3,4] in [1]): preparation; pre-stroke hold; stroke; post-stroke hold; retraction. The stroke is where actual meaning is conferred and is synchronous with its co-expressive speech 90% of the time [5]. Thus, the proposed gesticulation expression model focuses on arms and hands and supports sub-second gesticulation phase synchronization with speech.

The proposed model is feature-based, i.e., gesticulation is modeled as sequences of static (hand shape, orientation and position) and dynamic (motion profiles) constraints. A feature-based approach is appropriate for several reasons. First, according to McNeill [2] it makes more sense to describe gesticulation according to dimensions and saliency rather than categories and hierarchy. This suggests that meaning distributes across the affordances of the upper limbs and hands and thus, rather than overall form a more granular (or feature-based) description is possible. Second, a feature-based approach is compatible with most speech and gesture production models: the imagistic component in McNeill's growth points [1,2] ultimately materializes into gesture features; de Ruiter's sketch model [6] revolves around the concept of gesture templates (in a gestuary) which correspond to constraints on features; Krauss [7] actually considers knowledge representation as feature-based; finally, Kita & Özyürek [8] even though not detailing gesture morphology, motivate their models with motion gestures described according to features.

Regarding related work, several computational psycholinguistics systems have been proposed. Animated Conversation [9], developed by Cassell and colleagues, is a rule-based system capable of synchronizing gestures of the right type with co-occurring speech. *Real Estate Agent (Rea)* [10,11] presents an embodied conversational agent capable of proper distribution and realization of communicative intent across speech and gesture. In [12] Cassell et al propose the *Behavior Expression Animation Toolkit (BEAT)* which receives as input text and, based on rules, automatically generates appropriate synchronized nonverbal behavior. Kopp and colleagues [13,14] developed a comprehensive model for gesture animation based on research in psycholinguistics and motor control theory. Here, a knowledge base, similar to de Ruiter's gestuary [6], holds gesture templates which consist of hierarchies of constraints on static and dynamic features of the stroke phase. Gesture production instantiates templates and feeds them into a motor planner for execution. Preparation, retraction and co-articulation effects are automatically appended. The model supports sophisticated arm trajectories including velocity profiles. The system also supports speech parameterization through SABLE [15]. Recently, Cassell, Kopp and colleagues brought together the best from the aforementioned systems in *NUMACK* [16], a system capable of synthesizing in real-time co-verbal context-sensitive iconic gestures without relying on a library of predefined gestures. Though the gesture and speech production process is beyond the scope of this work, the underlying gesticulation animation model in these systems shares several aspects with the proposed model, namely: its requisites are strictly based on psycholinguistics research and similar static and dynamic features are explored.

The problem of controlling and integrating gesticulation expression with other modalities is usually solved through markup languages [17]. This work also proposes a control language – *Expression Markup Language (EML)* – which is particularly influenced by: VHML [18], SMIL [19] and MURML [20]. From *Virtual Human Markup Language (VHML)* this work uses the notion of dividing control into subsystems. From *Synchronized Multimedia Integration Language (SMIL)*, which is oriented for audiovisual interactive presentations, this work benefits from the sophisticated modality synchronization mechanism. From *Multimodal Utterance Representation Markup Language (MURML)* this work defines a similar notation for gesture specification and synchronization with co-verbal speech. Finally, in contrast to high-level languages such as GESTYLE [21], which tries to capture an individual's expression style, and APML [22], which represents, among others, communicative intent, emotions, interaction and cultural aspects, the proposed language focuses on low-level body control such as gesticulation animation as sequences of constraints on static and dynamic features and the generation of speech in a text-to-speech system.

Finally, this work supports automatic reproduction from a gesture transcription algorithm. Usually, these algorithms are used to learn aspects from human gesticulation expression and, then, generate databases or explicit rules for virtual humans. However, the added value of being able to automatically reproduce such annotations is flexibility. This idea relates to efforts in automatic gesture recognition [23,24]. Such systems accurately recognize form but, still lag with respect to meaning. In contrast, gesture transcription algorithms rely on knowledge from (human) analysts to interpret meaning and, thus, reproduction from the final annotation, though less accurate in form, is more flexible.

3   The Model

The gesticulation model fits into a broad virtual human real-time multimodal expression model which includes deterministic, non-deterministic, gesticulation, facial, vocal and environment expression [25]. This paper will focus on the first three. The model also supports automatic reproduction of gesticulation annotations according to GestuRA, a gesture transcription algorithm.

The virtual human is structured according to a three-layer architecture [26,27]. The *geometry layer* defines a 54-bone human-based skeleton. The *animation layer* defines deterministic and non-deterministic animation mechanisms. The *behavior layer* defines gesticulation expression and supports a language for integrated synchronized multimodal expression.

3.1   Deterministic Expression

Deterministic expression is about deterministic animation, i.e., sequences of keyframes usually exhaustively conceived by human artists. This modality revolves around *animation players* which animate subsets of the skeleton's bones according to specific animation mechanisms. Several players can be active at the same time and thus, as they may compete for the same bones, an arbitration mechanism based on priorities is defined. Supported animation mechanisms include: (a) *weighted combined animation*, where the resulting animation is the "weighted average" of animations placed on several weighted layers; (b) *body group animation*, where disjoint sets of skeleton's bones – body groups – execute independent animations; (c) *pose animation*, which applies stances to bones, supports combination between two stances and provides a parameter to control interpolation between them.

3.2 Non-deterministic Expression

Non-deterministic expression applies robotics to virtual humans thus, laying the foundations for non-deterministic animation, i.e., human-free procedural animation. In the geometry layer, six revolute joint robotic manipulators are integrated with the skeleton to control the limbs and joint limits are defined according to anthropometry data [28]. In the animation layer, three inverse kinematics and one inverse velocity primitives are defined, namely: (1) *joint interpolation*, which animates the manipulator's target through interpolation in the joint space; (2) *function based interpolation*, which animates the target according to a transformation defined, at each instant, by a mathematical function; (3) *frame interpolation*, which animates the target according to interpolation between the current frame and the intended frame; (4) *Jacobian-based animation*, which applies Jacobian-based inverse velocity algorithms to animate the target according to intended Cartesian and angular velocities.

3.3 Gesticulation Expression

The gesticulation expression model controls arms and hands and is built on top of deterministic expression and non-deterministic expression. In concrete, limb manipulators control the arms, hands' position and orientation while pose animation players control the hands' shape. The model is feature-based, i.e., gesticulation form is modeled as a sequence in time of constraints on static and dynamic features. Features are described on subsection 3.3.1. The model supports multimodal synchronization, in particular, between speech and gesture. Synchronization is described on subsection 3.3.2. Finally, the model supports automatic reproduction of annotated gesticulation according to GestuRA, a gesture transcription algorithm. GestuRA and its integration with the model are described on subsection 3.3.3.

3.3.1 Features

Gesticulation is modeled as a sequence in time of constraints on static and dynamic features. Static features are represented in *gesticulation keyframes* and include: hand shape, position, orientation palm axis, orientation angle, and handedness. Dynamic features define keyframe interpolation motion profiles.

Regarding static features, the *hand shape* feature can assume any Portuguese Sign Language hand shape [32]. Furthermore, any two shapes can be combined and a parameter is provided to define how much each contributes. Implementation relies on pose player ability to combine stances and on a library of stances for Portuguese Sign Language shapes. The *position* feature is defined in Cartesian coordinates in three-dimensional space. Both world and speaker references can be used. Hand shape orientation is defined by two features: *orientation palm axis*, which defines the palm's normal; and *orientation angle* which defines a left handed angle about the normal. Implementation relies on inverse kinematics primitives. The *handedness* feature defines whether the gesticulation keyframe applies to the left, right or both hands. In the last case, remaining features apply to the speaker's dominant hand and *symmetrical* values apply to the non-dominant hand. Symmetry is intuitively understood as the gesticulation which would result if a mirror stood on the sagittal plane.

Regarding dynamic features, the model supports several kinds of (keyframe) interpolators, namely: *linear*, which defines linear interpolation; *cosine*, which defines cosine interpolation; and *parametric cubic curves*, which can represent any kind of velocity profile. Furthermore, interpolators can be structured into hierarchies thus, leading to sophisticated motion profiles. Furthermore, either Cartesian or joint angle velocity can be used. Currently, deceleration near the target position and overshooting effects have been simulated using Bézier and Hermite cubic curves.

3.3.2 Synchronization

To support sub-second synchronization of gesture phases, a control markup language – Expression Markup Language (EML) – supporting phoneme-level synchronization is proposed. The language integrates with SABLE [15] and thus, supports synchronization with speech properties such as intonation contour. Similarly to SMIL [33], modality execution time can be set to absolute or modality relative values. Furthermore, *named timestamps* can be associated with text to be synthesized. The following events can be associated to a named timestamp: (a) start of a word; (b) end of a word; (c) start of a phoneme. EML is further described on subsection 3.4.

As synchronization between speech and gesture is conveniently described at the gesture phase level, the model supports explicit *gesticulation phase keyframes*. The phase keyframe extends regular keyframes as follows: (a) a *duration* feature is added which defines total phase time; (b) sequences of constraints can now be associated to the shape, position and orientation features; (c) constraints within a sequence can be set to start at absolute time offsets relative to phase start time or at percentages of the total phase duration. However, phase keyframes do not add expressiveness to the model in the sense that gesticulation described with phase keyframes could be converted into an equivalent sequence of regular keyframes.

In the current implementation, the Festival [29] text-to-speech system has been used to generate speech, retrieve phoneme information and render SABLE text.

3.3.3 Automatic Reproduction of Gesticulation Annotations

The gesticulation model supports automatic reproduction of *Gesture Recording Algorithm (GestuRA)* annotations. This constitutes an important evaluation tool. As speech and gesture production from communicative intent is not simulated, an alternative to evaluating the model is to compare it to real life situations.

GestuRA, based on [2] and [30], is a linguistically motivated iterative algorithm for gesticulation form and meaning transcription. It is structured in seven passes. First, speech is transcribed from the video-speech record. Second, text is organized into utterances. Third, utterances are classified according to discourse levels – narrative, metanarrative and paranarrative [1]. Fourth, gesticulation is filtered ignoring remaining gestures (such as adaptors, emblems, signs). Fifth, gesticulation phases are annotated. Sixth, gesticulation form is formally annotated. Finally, seventh, gesticulation is classified according to its dimensions and its meaning analyzed. GestuRA integration with the model is achieved through *Anvil* [31], a generic multimodal annotation tool, which exports annotations to a XML format which is, then, converted into EML for immediate execution in virtual humans – Fig. 1.

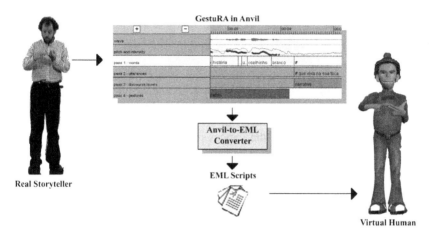

Fig. 1. GestuRA integration with the model

3.4 Multimodal Expression

This work proposes a markup, integrated and synchronized language – Expression Markup Language (EML) – which serves as a control interface for virtual human bodies. The language can be used in two ways, Fig. 2: (1) as an *interface for a mind* which needs to express synchronously, in real-time and multimodaly through the body; (2) as a *script* which describes a story, written by a human or digital author, in real-time or not, where the virtual human expresses multimodaly. In the first case, the mind communicates to the body in real-time, through a socket or API, a set of EML clauses which are immediately executed. In the second case, the script defines a sequence of clauses, temporally ordered, which defines a story which can be played later by different virtual humans. Regarding specification, EML is a markup language

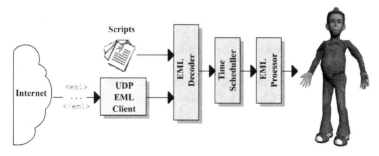

Fig. 2. EML integration with the model

structured into modules: (1) *core*, defines the main elements; (2) *time and synchronization*, defines multimodal synchronization and is characterized as follows: (a) supports execution time definition relative to other clauses; (b) supports execution time definition relative to word or phoneme in vocal expression clauses; (c) supports loops; (d) supports parallel and sequential execution. This module is based on W3C's SMIL 2.0 specification [33]; (3) *body*, controls both deterministic and non-deterministic body expression; (4) *gesture*, controls gesticulation expression.

4 Evaluation

Two studies were conducted to assess the model's expressiveness. In both cases, the idea consisted of comparing the narration of the Portuguese traditional story "The White Rabbit" by a human storyteller with a version by a virtual storyteller. The first study, conducted in the scope of the Papous project at Inesc-ID, aimed at evaluating all forms of expression while the second focused only on gesticulation.

4.1 First Study

The first study was conducted in the scope of the Papous project at Inesc-ID. This project compares a human storyteller with a virtual storyteller with respect to story comprehension, emotion expression, believability and subject satisfaction for each of body, facial and vocal expression. This paper focuses on body expression results. The human storyteller was a non-professional actor which was simply asked to tell the story in an expressive way without imposing any requirements on gesticulation expression. Regarding the virtual storyteller, the voice consisted of synthesized speech audio records. Facial expression was based on a muscular model capable of proper lip-synch and emotion expression. Body expression relied on a GestuRA transcription of the human storyteller video, lasting 7 minutes and 30 seconds. In total, 286 gestures were transcribed of which 95% were automatically reproduced through feature-based gesticulation and 5% through keyframe deterministic animation.

Regarding structure, first the subject visualized the story video and, then, answered to a questionnaire. Each subject was presented one of four video versions: (1) *CRVR* – Human narrator with real voice; (2) *CRVS* – Human narrator with synthetic voice; (3) *CSVR* – Virtual narrator with real voice; (4) *CSVS* – Virtual narrator with synthetic voice. The questionnaire had twelve questions where the subject classified, from 1 (totally disagree) to 7 (totally agree), whether each modality help understand the story, express emotions properly, is believable and is to his liking.

The study was presented to 108 students at the Technical University of Lisbon. Average age was 21 years and 89% of which were males. Most students related to computer science courses. Each video version was presented to 27 students.

Body expression results are summarized in Table 1. In general synthetic gestures are classified lower than real gestures. However, classification differs only in about 0.45 points. Finally, notice that real gesture classification (about 5) was well below 7.

Table 1. Body expression average classifications (scale goes from 1 to 7)

	CRVR	CSVR	CRVS	CSVS
Gestures helped to understand the story	5.19	4.91	5.04	4.82
Gestures expressed the story's emotions	5.15	4.76	5.30	4.82
Gestures were believable	5.07	4.30	5.30	4.61
I liked the gestures	4.89	4.49	5.22	4.82

From these results it is possible to conclude that synthetic gestures fared well when compared to real gestures. Furthermore, in absolute terms, a classification of about 4.6 is reasonably good. However, this study had some limitations. Firstly, subjects were asked to evaluate gestures explicitly when it is known that gesture interpretation is essentially unconscious [1]. Secondly, subject to multiple interpretations, the notion of "believability" is hard to define thus, results related to the question "Gestures were believable" must be interpreted with caution.

4.2 Second Study

So as to further assess the gesticulation model's expressiveness and to correct some of the flaws in the previous study, a second study was conducted. Here, first, subjects are told that the evaluation is about virtual storytelling and "gesticulation expression" is never mentioned throughout. Second, synthetic gestures are indirectly evaluated through story interpretation questions. Third, each subject sees the story alternatively narrated by the human or virtual storyteller thus, allowing for direct storyteller comparison. Finally, as the study focused on gesticulation, the real voice is used for both storytellers and three variations of the virtual storyteller are defined: (1) *ST*, where feature-based and keyframe gesticulation are expressed; (2) *SF*, where only feature-based gesticulation is expressed; (3) *SN*, where no gesticulation is expressed.

The evaluation is structured into three parts. In part 1 – *profile* – the subject profile is assessed. In part 2 – *story interpretation* – the story is presented to the subject in 8 segments. Segments are narrated either by the human or one, randomly selected at the start, of the three kinds of virtual storytellers. In concrete, the third and sixth segments are narrated by a storyteller selected by the subject, while the rest is arbitrarily narrated either by the human or virtual storyteller provided that in the end each gets an equal number of segments. After each segment, multiple choice interpretation questions are posed. In total 32 questions were formulated. Importantly, a subset, named the *highly bodily expressive (HBE)* questions, focused on information specially marked in gestures, i.e., information which was either redundantly or non-redundantly conveyed through complex gestures like iconics or metaphorics. Finally, in part 3 – *story appreciation* – the subject is asked to choose the preferred storyteller and to describe which is the best and worst feature of each storyteller.

The study was presented to 39 subjects, 90% of which were male, average age was 23 years and mostly had higher education. The study was fully automated and average evaluation time was about 20 minutes. Distribution of virtual storyteller kinds across subjects was: 46% for ST; 31% for SF; 23% for SN. Subject recruitment included personal contact mainly at both campuses of Technical University of Lisbon and distribution of the software through the Web.

Regarding story interpretation results, if we define *diff* to be the difference between the percentage of correct answers following the human storyteller and the percentage of correct answers following the virtual storyteller, then *diff* was: for ST, 4.69%; for SF, -0.68%; for SN, -1.62%. However, if we consider only HBE questions, than distribution is as follows: for ST, 4.75%; for SF, 0.00%; for SN, 9.19%. Regarding subject storyteller selection on the third and sixth segments, the human storyteller was selected about 75% of the time (for ST, 75.00%; for SF, 83.30%; for SN, 72.22%). Regarding subject storyteller preference, the human storyteller was preferred about 90% of the time (for ST, 88.89%; for SF, 83.33%; for SN, 100.00%). Finally, some of the worst aspects mentioned for the virtual storyteller were "body expression limited to arms", "static/rigid", "artificial" and "low expressivity". These relate to the best aspects mentioned for the human storyteller, namely "varied postures", "energetic/enthusiastic", "natural" and "high expressivity".

As can be seen by the results, the human storyteller is better than the virtual storyteller. Interpretation with the human storyteller is better, but not that much (*diff* of 4.69% for ST). Furthermore, when given a choice, subjects almost always chose the human storyteller. Analyzing the best and worst aspects selected for each storyteller might give insight into this issue. Surprisingly, if all questions are considered, *diff* actually reduces for SN when compared to ST (-1.63% over 4.69%). The fact that the human storyteller's voice and face were highly expressive and gestures were mostly redundant might help explain this. However, if only HBE questions are considered, *diff* considerably increases for the SN case (from 4.75% to 9.19%). Furthermore, for the SN case, the human storyteller was preferred 100% of the times. This confirms that gesticulation affects interpretation. Finally, comparing ST with SF, *diff* for all questions reduces for the latter case (from 4.69% to -0.68%). This suggests that the lack of feature-based gesticulation support for the small fraction of highly complex gestures does not impede effective interpretation.

5   Conclusions and Future Work

This paper proposed a model for a feature-based real-time gesticulation animation model. Static features include Portuguese Sign Language hand shapes, position, orientation palm axis, orientation angle, and handedness. Dynamic features include motion profiles. For phoneme-level speech-gesture synchronization, a multimodal expression language, which integrates with SABLE, is proposed. Moreover, the model supports automatic reproduction of annotated gesticulation according to GestuRA. Finally, results from two studies indicate that the model's gesticulation expression fares well when compared to real gesticulation in a storytelling context. Still, the human storyteller was consistently preferred to the virtual storyteller hinting that the model can be improved.

Altogether the model seems to be ready to support gesticulation production models thus, moving from automatic reproduction to automatic generation. Regarding de

Ruiter's model [6], the gestuary can mostly be implemented through feature-based and keyframe gesticulation and signal passing synchronization is straightforwardly supported. Krauss' model [7] which is feature-based is also compatible. The language effect on gesture in Kita and Özyürek's model [8] occurs early on the production process and, ultimately, materializes into specific features which this model supports. McNeill's growth point model [1,2] lacks details on morphology generation however, if the dialectic materializes into features and synchronization can be described with respect to a finite number of specific synchronization points, then this model may support it.

Regarding future work, first, gesticulation needs to go beyond arms and hands and explore other body parts. Second, some features' implementation restrict expressiveness. Nothing guarantees that Portuguese Sign Language hand shapes and combinations thereof suffice to model all relevant shapes. Furthermore, lack of redundancy, or elbow control, in the upper limb manipulator limits naturalness. In this sense, seven degrees-of-freedom manipulators should be explored. Third, preparation and retraction motion and co-articulation effects could be automatically generated. Finally, a more anatomically correct hand model with appropriate constraints ([34,35]) would lead to more realistic gesticulation simulation.

Acknowledgments

This research was partially supported by the Papous project at Inesc-ID (Ref.: POSI / SRI / 41071 / 2001).

References

1. McNeill, D.: Hand and Mind: What gestures reveal about thought. University of Chicago Press (1992)
2. McNeill, D.: Gesture and Thought. University of Chicago Press (2005)
3. Kendon, A.: Sign languages of Aboriginal Australia: Cultural, semiotic and communicative perspectives. Cambridge University Press (1988)
4. Kita, S.: The temporal relationship between gesture and speech: A study of Japanese-English bilingual. MhD, Department of Psychology, University of Chicago (1990)
5. Nobe, S.: Where do most spontaneous representational gestures actually occur with respect to speech? in D. McNeill (ed.), Language and Gesture. Cambridge University Press (2000) 186-198
6. de Ruiter, J.: The production of gesture and speech in D. McNeill (ed.), Language and gesture, Cambridge University Press (2000) 284-311
7. Krauss, M., Chen, Y., Gottesman, R.: Lexical gestures and lexical access: A process model in D. McNeill (ed.), Language and gesture. Cambridge University Press (2000) 261-283
8. Kita, S., Özyürek, A.: What does cross-linguistic variation in semantic coordination of speech and gesture reveal? Evidence for an interface representation of spatial thinking and speaking in Journal of Memory and Language 48 (2003) 16-32
9. Cassell, J., Pelachaud, C., Badler, N., Steedman, M., Achorn, B., Becket, T., Douville, B., Prevost, S., Stone, M.: Animated Conversation: Rule-based Generation of Facial Expression, Gesture & Spoken Intonation for Multiple Conversational Agent in Proc. of SIGGRAPH'94 (1994) 413-420

10. Cassell, J., Bickmore, T., Billinghurst, M., Campbell, L., Chang, K., Vilhjálmsson, H., Yan, H.: Embodiment in Conversational Interfaces: Rea in Proc. of the CHI'99 Conference, Pittsburgh, PA (1999) 520-527
11. Cassell, J., Stone, M.: Living Hand to Mouth: Psychological Theories about Speech and Gesture in Interactive Dialogue Systems in Proc. of the AAAI 1999 Fall Symposium on Psychological Models of Communication in Collaborative Systems, North Falmouth, MA (1999) 34-42
12. Cassell, J., Vilhjálmsson, H., Bickmore, T.: BEAT: the Behavior Expression Animation Toolkit in Proc. of SIGGRAPH'01 (2001) 477-486
13. Kopp, S., Wachsmuth, I.: A knowledge-based approach for lifelike gesture animation in Proc. of the 14th European Conf. on Artificial Intelligence, Amsterdam, IOS Press (2000)
14. Wachsmuth, I., Kopp, S.: Lifelike Gesture Synthesis and Timing for Conversational Agents in Wachsmusth, Sowa (eds.), Gesture and Sign Language in Human-Computer Interaction, International Gesture Workshop (GW 2001). Springer-Verlag, (2002) 120-133
15. SABLE: A Synthesis Markup Language (v. 1.0). www.bell-labs.com/project/tts/sable.html
16. Kopp, S., Tepper, P., Cassell, J.: Towards Integrated Microplanning of Language and Iconic Gesture for Multimodal Output in Proc. of the International Conference on Multimodal Interfaces (ICMI'04). ACM Press (2004) 97-104
17. Arafa, Y., Kamyab, K., Mamdani, E.: Character Animation Scripting Languages: A Comparison in Proc. of the 2nd Intl. Conference of Autonomous Agents and Multiagent Systems (2003) 920-921
18. VHML: VHML – Virtual Human Markup Language. www.vhml.org/
19. SMIL: SMIL - Synchronized Multimedia. www.w3.org/AudioVideo/
20. Kranstedt, A., Kopp, S., Wachsmuth, I.: MURML: A Multimodal Utterance Representation Markup Language for Conversational Agents in AAMAS'02 Workshop Embodied conversational agents- let's specify and evaluate them!, Bologna, Italy, (2002)
21. Ruttkay, Z., Noot, H.: Variations in Gesturing and Speech by GESTYLE in International Journal of Human-Computer Studies, Special Issue on 'Subtle Expressivity for Characters and Robots', 62(2), (2005) 211-229
22. de Carolis, B., Pelachaud, C., Poggi, I., Steedman, M.: APML, a Mark-up Language for Believable Behavior Generation in H. Prendinger (ed), Life-like Characters. Tools, Affective Functions and Applications. Springer (2004)
23. Pavlovic, V., Sharma, R., Huang, T.: Visual Interpretation of hand gestures for human computer interaction: A review in IEEE Trans. Pattern Analysis Machine Intelligence, vol.19, July (1997) 677-695
24. Gavrila, D.: The visual analysis of human movement: A survey in Computer Vision and Image Understanding, vol.73, Jan. (1999) 82-98
25. de Melo, C., Paiva, A.: Multimodal Expression in Virtual Humans. Accepted for Computer Animation & Social Agents 2006 (CASA2006) and Journal of Computer Animation and Virtual Worlds (2006)
26. Blumberg, B., Galyean, T.: Multi-Level Direction of Autonomous Creatures for Real-Time Virtual Environments in Proc. of SIGGRAPH '95, 30(3) (1995) 47-54
27. Perlin, K., Goldberg, A.: Improv: A System for Scripting Interactive Actors in Virtual Worlds in Proc. of SIGGRAPH'96 (1996) 205-216
28. NASA Man-Systems Integration Manual (NASA-STD-3000)
29. Black, A.; Taylor, P.; Caley, R.; Clark, R.: Festival. www.cstr.ed.ac.uk/projects/festival/
30. Gut, U., Looks, K., Thies, A., Trippel, T., Gibbon, D.: CoGesT – Conversational Gesture Transcription System. Technical Report, University of Bielefeld (1993)

31. Kipp, M.: ANVIL – A Generic Annotation Tool for Multimodal Dialogue in Proc. of the 7th European Conference on Speech Comm. and Technology, Aalborg, (2001) 1367-1370
32. Secretariado Nacional para a Reabilitação e Integração das Pessoas com Deficiência. Gestuário – Língua Gestual Portuguesa – 5th edition
33. SMIL. "SMIL: Synchronized Multimedia"; www.w3.org/AudioVideo/
34. Thompson, D., Buford, W., Myers, L., Giurintano, D., Brewer III, J.: A Hand Biomechanics Workstation in Computer Graphics, vol.22, no.4 (1988) 335-343
35. Albrecht, I., Haber, J., Siedel, H.: Construction and Animation of Anatomically Based Human Hand Models in SIGGRAPH 2003 (2003) 98-109

Introducing EVG: An Emotion Evoking Game

Ning Wang and Stacy Marsella

Information Science Institute
University of Southern California
4676 Admiralty Way, Marina del Rey, CA 90066 USA
{ning, marsella}@isi.edu

Abstract. A dungeon role playing game intended to induce emotions such as boredom, surprise, joy, anger and disappointment is introduced. From the preliminary study, facial expressions indicating boredom and anger were observed. Individual differences were found on appraisal and facial expression of surprise, joy and disappointment.

Keywords: emotion, game, facial expression.

1 Introduction

This paper introduces the Emotion Evoking Game (EVG), an open-source computer game that can evoke emotions from users. EVG is designed to assist development and evaluation of new techniques for recognizing emotions and generating facial expressions. At a basic level, this tool allows researchers to more systematically explore the factors that elicit emotion and to carry out facial expression study. Specifically, EVG benefits research in embodied virtual agents in several ways. It allows researchers to closely study and capture the features and dynamics of real human emotional expression, a critical precursor to building more expressive virtual human bodies [1]. It also provides a tool that can help evaluate computational models of emotion [10].

EVG is built on the ideas first realized in the Geneva Appraisal Manipulation Environment (GAME) [12] – a Pac-Man like game running under DOS created by Geneva Emotion Research Group from the University of Geneva. In GAME, events representing different values of appraisal dimensions are used to induce emotions in players. Traditionally, researchers have employed a wide range of stimuli to evoke emotions. These include displaying images or videos with emotional impact [13] [15], imagining emotional events [21] [8] [14], interacting with a human confederate [20], etc. The use of computer video games promises several benefits over these traditional approaches. While playing a video game, the subject is involved in a task, so a range of task-related emotions such as frustration can potentially be evoked. Further, there can be other human players or AI-driven characters feigning to be human in the game. Thus a range of social emotions can be evoked such as guilt, or anger due to betrayal of a teammate. In contrast, using the display of static images, the subject is more a passive observer. The social and task contexts are minimal and hard to manipulate freely. As a consequence, certain emotions, such as frustration and guilt, can be hard

J. Gratch et al. (Eds.): IVA 2006, LNAI 4133, pp. 282–291, 2006.
© Springer-Verlag Berlin Heidelberg 2006

to induce. Additionally, the emotions evoked are often indirect, sympathetic of the people and events depicted in the image. Also, computer games, by giving researchers control over the environment in the game, offer a sophisticated and systematic way to manipulate appraisal dimensions through game events.

EVG is built on a modern operating system. It's generally available to the community for use in research on recognition and synthesis of emotions. In this paper, we discuss EVG and an initial, formative evaluation of EVG. For the current study, we set up EVG so that players would experience a sequence of events that aim to induce boredom, followed by surprise, joy, anger and disappointment. Preliminary findings are presented.

2 Related Work

The facial expression of emotion has been one of the more heavily studied topics in emotion research and has become increasingly important in work on intelligent virtual agents. There is a large body of research that addresses questions concerning the structure of facial expressions, the relation of facial expressions to underlying emotions, the role of facial expressions as a signal that mediates social interaction, whether facial expressions are culturally universal, etc. Here, we touch on a small portion of the research relevant to the current discussion.

Research by Ekman [6] shows that facial expression is a pattern of activities across the face. Ekman & Friesen [7] listed action units (AUs) of Facial Action Coding System (FACS) that correspond to different facial expressions. On the other hand, the component-based approach to facial expression argues that certain appraisal checks induce certain facial features, that individual component of facial expressions, such as lowering the eyebrows into a frown, themselves carry meaning [19] [18].

Another research question concerns the degree to which facial expressions are universal or culturally/individually dependent. Ekman's research [6] argues that there are six facial expressions – happiness, surprise, anger, sadness, fear and disgust – that are culturally universal but whose display can be managed by culturally determined display rules. Smith and Scott's summarization [19] of Darwin [4], Frois-Wittmann [9], Izard [11] and Ekman & Friesen [7]'s work on common features of widely recognized expressions shows agreements such as raised lower eyelids, raised lip corners and open mouth are expressions of joy; eyebrow frown and raised upper and lower eyelids are display of anger; eyebrow frown, raised eyebrows and lowering of lip corners are associated with sadness. Surprise, as Darwin pointed out, is a biologically determined facial display consisting of eyebrow raise, widening of the eyes, and opening of the mouth/jaw drop. However, research has shown that facial expressions of emotion are more often partial than complete [2] [16]. Furthermore, strong evidences of stable individual differences in facial expressions in both individual and interpersonal context were found [3]. Further, studies by Reisenzein [17] find that surprise doesn't correspond to the three component display proposed by Darwin. Self-reports and behavioral measures indicated the presence of surprise in most of the subjects' expressions. But surprise expressions were observed only in 4-25%, and most displays consisted of eyebrows raised only. Further frontalis EMG measurement failed to detect notably more brow raisings in the subjects.

EVG, as a platform for conduction facial expression experiments, provides us with the opportunity to study these different theories.

3 Emotion Evoking Game

EVG is adapted from an open source game called Egoboo [5]. Compared to off-the-shelf games, EVG, as an open-source game, gives researchers access to the code that allows precise control over game events. It offers systematic ways to manipulate game events based on appraisal dimensions. With control over timing of events, it provides us with opportunities to study issues such as interactions between emotions. Access to the code also allows us to incorporate hooks into EVG to log the game events and synchronize them with other data sources such as experiment videos, physiological signals, etc.

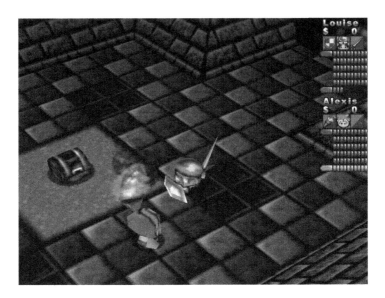

Fig. 1. Screenshot of Emotion Evoking Game

In the present study, EVG is implemented as a role-playing dungeon adventure game, in which the player (subject) completes missions in an underground palace accompanied by a non-player character (NPC) teammate. The current setup includes events targeted to evoke five different emotions: boredom, surprise, joy, anger and disappointment. The events are designed based on the appraisal dimensions described in [10]. Events are timed in certain sequence so that these five emotions are evoked in the same order. The story used in the current study is that the player, accompanied by a teammate, starts out in an underground palace with the goal to collect 2000 units of gold. Towards the end, player defeats the boss enemy and successfully collects 2000 units of gold. Then the teammate betrays the player by killing him and stealing the victory. The five main emotion evoking phrases are discussed below.

Collection: First, the player goes about the dungeon to collect gold by opening up chests placed in separate chambers. Each chamber is connected by hall ways but separated by one-direction shutter doors so that player can't walk back to the previous chamber. The map of the dungeon is also designed in a way that there's only one path through following the direction the shutter opens. This setup reduces the cognitive load for path finding and filters out possible noise in emotions caused by such cognitive load, such as confusion and frustration. We call this stage the Collection Stage. During this stage, there's no enemy presence. There're 10 chests contain a total of 1750 units of gold in the dungeon. We hypothesis that events in this stage have the following characteristics and are intended to evoke boredom.

Table 1. Hypothesis on appraisal dimensions of events during Collection Stage

Appraisal Dimension	Value
Goal contingency	Assist Goal
Coping potential: Controllability	High
Coping potential: Changeability	Low
Causal attribution: Agency	Self/Game Designer
Causal attribution: Blame/credit	Credit
Unexpectedness	Low
Urgency:	Low

Shock-and-Awe: The next stage happens towards the end of the game. The stage starts when player walks into the last chamber and finds the boss enemy accompanied by several other powerful enemies suddenly falling from the ceiling. The relative power of the enemy is controlled by enemy's life points, attack speed, damage per strike, size and appearance. We name this stage the Shock-and-Awe Stage. Player is holding a weapon in hand. The weapon can be operated by pressing a button on the game controller. The weapon is not very powerful judging by the size, appearance and damage per strike. Before this point, player has never faced with any enemy, let alone out-numbered by enemies much more powerful than the player. We hypothesis that events at this stage have the following characteristics and are intended to evoke surprise:

Table 2. Hypothesis on appraisal dimensions of events during Shock-and-Awe Stage

Appraisal Dimension	Value
Goal contingency	Block Goal
Coping potential: Controllability	Low
Coping potential: Changeability	High
Causal attribution: Agency	Others/Game Developer
Causal attribution: Blame/credit	Blame
Unexpectedness	High
Urgency:	High

Victory: After battling with the enemies, player defeats all the enemies and the boss enemy drops 1000 units of gold. Each subject has collected less than 2000 units of gold at this point. The gold left behind by the boss enemy can be collected and help player achieve his goal. In addition, none of the chests placed in the previous chambers has contained more than 500 units of gold. We named the death of the boss enemy the Victory Stage. Events at this stage are hypothesized to have the following characteristics and are intended to evoke joy.

Table 3. Hypothesis on appraisal dimensions of events during Victory Stage

Appraisal Dimension	Value
Goal contingency	Assist Goal
Coping potential: Controllability	High
Coping potential: Changeability	Medium
Causal attribution: Agency	Self
Causal attribution: Blame/credit	Credit
Unexpectedness	High
Urgency:	Low

Betrayal: While player is going around collecting the gold left behind by the boss enemy, the teammate betrays the player by attacking the player. We named this stage the Betrayal Stage. Before this stage, the teammate simply follows the player around the dungeon, watching the player collecting gold along the way. During player's battle with the enemies, the teammate attacks the enemies but doesn't draw out any weapon until this stage, nor is he injured. Our hypothesis is that events at this stage have the following characteristics and are intended to evoke anger.

Table 4. Hypothesis on appraisal dimensions of events during Betrayal Stage

Appraisal Dimension	Value
Goal contingency	Block Goal
Coping potential: Controllability	High
Coping potential: Changeability	High
Causal attribution: Agency	Others/Game designer
Causal attribution: Blame/credit	Blame
Unexpectedness	High
Urgency:	High

Loss: Eventually the teammate kills the player and claims victory. Player loses all the gold collected along the way. We name this stage the Loss Stage. Events at this stage are hypothesized to have the following characteristics and are targeted to evoke disappointment.

Table 5. Hypothesis on appraisal dimensions of events during Loss Stage

Appraisal Dimension	Value
Goal contingency	Block Goal
Coping potential: Controllability	Medium
Coping potential: Changeability	Medium
Causal attribution: Agency	Others/Game designer
Causal attribution: Blame/credit	Blame
Unexpectedness	Low
Urgency:	Low

4 Preliminary Assessment

To investigate whether EVG could be a platform for emotion and facial expression study, a preliminary assessment was carried out to test the effectiveness of EVG.

Subjects
Six volunteers participated in the study. Among them, one subject participated in the pilot study to test the experiment setup. One subject didn't complete the experiment. And one subject experienced technical difficulties at stage five.

Apparatus
The game used in the experiment runs on a Dell Dimension 8400 PC connected to a 19 in LCD. A Logitech Pro 4000 webcam is placed on top of the monitor for facial expression capturing. The webcam also has a microphone built in. Camtasia Studio 3 is running at background on the same machine that runs EVG to do screen capture of the game and recording of the facial expression. A Saitek P2500 Rumble game controller, as well as 2 speakers are connected to the Dell PC.

Material
A questionnaire consists of questions on subject's game experience was used before the test. Another questionnaire, modified from Geneva Appraisal Questionnaire (GAO) was used to report appraisal of emotion evoking events after the test.

Procedure
1. Subject fills out the pre-test questionnaire.
2. Subject sits down in front of the experiment computer.
3. Experimenter explains how to use the game controller.
4. Training level begins. The training level shares the same layout and appearance of the test level. But there're no enemies at this level and there's only one chest to open for training subject how to use the game controller to collect gold. Experimenter also explains to the subject where the number of units of gold collected and the health level are displayed on the screen.
5. Subject acknowledges that he/she understands how to use the controller and displays adequate skills to operate the game controller.
6. Subject reads descriptions of the test level. Test level and recording starts. Experimenter leaves the room.
7. Subject completes the test level. Experimenter re-enters the room and subject fills out the post-test questionnaire.

Result
The screen capture of the game and video of facial expressions are synchronized using Camtasia Studio 3. Facial expressions at stage 1 to 5 are shown from top to bottom in Fig. 2.

   Pictures from the top row are facial expressions from stage 1 – the Collection Stage. During this stage, we observed facial expression with lips closed and eye lids half-closed. We interpret this facial expression as indication of boredom. From the

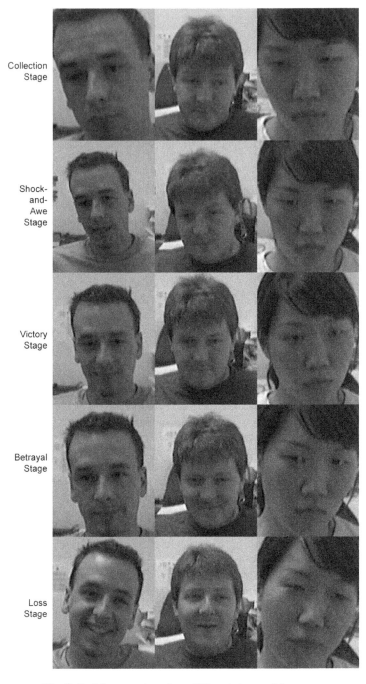

Fig. 2. Facial expressions from different stages of the game

self-reports, all subjects reported that they felt this stage was boring. But nevertheless, subjects still maintained certain level of engagement, trying to keep track of how much gold has been collected.

At stage 2, we designed events to evoke surprise. However no obvious facial muscle movements that correspond to the 3-component theory of surprise expression were observed. Mostly subjects changed their facial expression from boredom to an expression that suggested increased engagement, with their eyes open wider compared to previous stage. But on the post-test questionnaire, subjects reported experiencing surprise at this stage. Contrary to the name of the stage – Shock-and-Awe, some subjects actually reported feeling joy as the secondary emotion accompanying surprise. They also reported that they felt joy because when the enemy appeared, they were happy that after feeling boredom at Collection stage, they finally had something to bash. These subjects have a relatively rich video game experience. Taking the game experience into account, the coping potential of these events should be considered high instead of low. So, it's reasonable that upon seeing the enemy, joy was accompanied with surprise. But some subjects also reported anxiety while actually engaging in battle with the enemy. They reported saying they were afraid that they might die.

At stage 3, the Victory Stage, we didn't observe much facial expression change except with one subject. Other subjects seemed to maintain their facial expression since the battle with the enemies. On the post-questionnaire, there was no self-report on experiencing joy at this stage. Possible explanation is that the events are not strong enough to evoke joy and possibly only significant enough to evoke relief.

At the Betrayal Stage, clear patterns of facial activities, such as tight, pressed lips, were observed as an indication of anger expression. On the post-test questionnaire, all subjects reported feeling anger. During this stage, we also observed that some subjects eventually smiled, perhaps to mask the anger or perhaps as self-directed amusement.

The last stage is the Loss Stage during which a player is defeated by the teammate and newly acquired bounty is stolen. At this stage, we observed diversity in facial expressions. One subject started to laugh possibly due to relief. One subject cried out because of great disappointment. One subject with firmly pressed lips and briefly closed her eyes while head tilted to one side suggesting disappointment mixed with anger.

5   Discussion and Future Work

The ultimate goal of the Emotion Evoking Game is to provide a platform that facilitates research into the design of better algorithms for computationally modeling emotions, recognizing emotions and for generating emotional expressions of embodied conversational agents. The work presented here is a very preliminary study to evaluate EVG. From the study, we successfully evoked boredom and anger, according to the self-report and display of facial expression. We created a sequence of game events to evoke a sequence of emotions. Influence of early emotional experience on later emotional interpretations was observed. For example, boredom could alter the appraisal of stimuli at Shock-and-Awe stage from surprise accompanied by fear to surprise accompanied by joy. We also observed the influence of individual differences on appraisal of emotion evoking events. For example, gaming experience could shift appraisal of supposedly fearsome events from aversive to appetitive. Individual, cultural and gender differences could also have been affecting display of facial expressions. Of course, the current study is a formative evaluation, and any full study of such phenomena would have to address a range of issues. Most notably, a full study using EVG would require multiple coders to encode facial expressions to insure the cross-coder reliability of the classification of the emotional displays.

Going forward, EVG provides an opportunity to study a range of dynamic phenomena. In particular, studies could be carried out to explore emotional trends and sequences such as the impact of prior emotional states on subsequent emotional reactions. Replacing the webcam with a high speed camera will allow us also to explore how expressions evolve. With such a capability, we could evaluate and study the component hypotheses of facial expression [18] [19]. Finally, by using confederates to play against or observing the subject, the game could also allow us to explore the role of social context on emotions and the display of facial expressions.

Acknowledgement

This work was sponsored by the Intelligent System Division (ISD) of Information Science Institute (ISI), University of Southern California (USC) and the content does not necessarily reflect the position or the policy of USC, and no official endorsement should be inferred.

References

1. Bui, T.D., Heylen, D., Nijholt, A., Poel, M: On combining the facial movements of a talking head, in Proceedings Measuring Behavior. In Noldus, L.P.J.J., Grieco, F., Loijens, L.W.S., Zimmerman, P.H. (Eds.). Fifth International Conference on Methods and Techniques in Behavioral Research, 6-9, (2005)
2. Carroll, J. M., Russell, J. A.: Facial expressions in Hollywood's portrayal of emotion. Journal of Personality and Social Psychology, 72, 164-176. (1997)
3. Cohn, J.F., Schmidt, K., Gross, R., Ekman, P.: Individual Differences in Facial Expression: Stability over Time, Relation to Self-Reported Emotion, and Ability to Inform Person Identification. Fourth IEEE International Conference on Multimodal Interfaces, 491-496. (2002).
4. Darwin, C.: The expression of the emotions in man and animals. Chicago: University of Chicago Press. (Original work published in 1872) (1965)
5. Egoboo. http://zippy-egoboo.sourceforge.net/
6. Ekman, P.: Emotion in the human face. New York: Cambridge University Press. (1982)
7. Ekman, P., Friesen, W. V.: Investigator's guide to the Facial Action Coding System. Palo Alto, CA: Consulting Psychologist Press. (1978)
8. Frijda, N.H., Kuipers, P., ter Schure, E.: Relations among emotion, appraisal, and emotional action readiness. Journal of Personality and Social Psychology, 57, 212-228. (1989)

9. Frois-Wittmann, J.: The judgment of facial expression. Journal of Experimental Psychology, 13, 113-151. (1930)
10. Gratch, J., Marsella, S.: Evaluating a computational model of emotion. Journal of Autonomous Agents and Multiagent Systems (Special issue on the best of AAMAS 2004), 11(1), 23-43. (2006)
11. Izard, C.E.: The face of emotion. New York: Appleton-Century-Crofts. (1971)
12. Kaiser, S., Wehrle, T.: Situated emotional problem solving in interactive computer games. In Frijda, N.H., (ed.), Proceedings of the VIXth Conference of the International Society for Research on Emotions, 276--280. ISRE Publications (1996)
13. Lang, P. J., Bradley, M. M., Cuthbert, B. N.: International Affective Picture System (IAPS): Technical manual and affective ratings. Gainsville: Center for Research in Psychophysiology, University of Florida. (1999)
14. Mauro, R., Sato, K., Tucker, J.: The role of appraisal in human emotions: A cross-cultural study. Journal of Personality and Social Psychology, 62, 301-317. (1992)
15. Öhman, A., Flykt, A., Esteves, F.: Emotion Drives Attention: Detecting the Snake in the Grass. Journal of Experimental Psychology; 130, (3), 466-478. (2001)
16. Reisenzein, R.: Exploring the strength of association between the components of emotion syndromes: The case of surprise. Cognition and Emotion, 14, 1-38. (2000)
17. Reisenzein, R., Bördgen, S., Holtbernd, T., Matz, D.: Evidence for strong dissociation between emotion and facial displays: The case of surprise. Journal of Personality and Social Psychology. (in press)
18. Scherer, K. R.: Appraisal considered as a process of multi-level sequential checking. In Scherer, K.R., Schorr, A. & Johnstone, T. (Eds.). Appraisal processes in emotion: Theory, Methods, Research, 92-120. New York and Oxford: Oxford University Press. (2001)
19. Smith, C. A., Scott, H. S.: A componential approach to the meaning of facial expressions. In Russell, J.A., Fernandez-Dols, J.M. (Eds.), The psychology of facial expression. New York: Cambridge University Press. (1997)
20. Stemmler, G., Heldmann, M., Pauls, C. A., Scherer, T.: Constraints for emotion specificity in fear and anger: The context counts. Psychophysiology, 38, 275-291. (2001)
21. Velten, E.: A laboratory task for inductions of mood states. Behavior Therapy and Research, 6, 473-482. (1968)

Towards a Reactive Virtual Trainer

Zsófia Ruttkay, Job Zwiers, Herwin van Welbergen, and Dennis Reidsma

HMI, Dept. of CS, University of Twente,
PObox 217, 7500AE Enschede, The Netherlands
{zsofi, zwiers, welberge, dennisr}@ewi.utwente.nl
http://hmi.ewi.utwente.nl

Abstract. A Reactive Virtual Trainer (RVT) is an Intelligent Virtual Agent (IVA) capable of presenting physical exercises that are to be performed by a human, monitoring the user and providing feedback at different levels. Depending on the motivation and the application context, the exercises may be general ones of fitness to improve the user's physical condition, special exercises to be performed from time to time during work to prevent for example RSI, or physiotherapy exercises with medical indications. In the paper we discuss the functional and technical requirements of a framework which can be used to author specific RVT applications. The focus is on the reactivity of the RVT, manifested in natural language comments on readjusting the tempo, pointing out mistakes or rescheduling the exercises. We outline the components we have implemented so far: our animation engine, the composition of exercises from basic motions and the module for analysis of tempo in acoustic input.

1 Introduction

You have been spending hours working in front of your computer. All of a sudden your friendly Office Trainer – one whom you like the look of – greets you on your screen, suggests that you perform some 5 minutes of exercises right now (or somewhat later, if you do not want to be interrupted instantly) and 'dictates' the exercises for you. To make it less of a routine, you may choose from different pieces of music to give the tempo. Before the session you may indicate if you have specific complaints such as a stiff neck, or ache in the back or in your fingers. The Office Trainer offers appropriately tailored exercises and after a few sessions she asks about your progress.

Another scenario from real life: after a severe illness and several weeks in hospital a patient needs to do regularly special exercises to regain the functioning of certain muscles, to be able to use his hands. However, regular visits to a physiotherapist are not possible due to some forbidding constraint (shortage of experts, distance, lack of money etc.). But there is the Virtual Physiotherapist (VP), programmed by an expert with the sequence of exercises to be done at home. The VP explains each exercise and then coaches the patient, adjusting for example the tempo and the number of repetitions of the exercises, if needed. And she keeps the patient motivated by giving encouragement, feedback, even small talk. The real physiotherapist comes along only occasionally to supervise the progress and to 'instruct' the VP for the next sessions.

J. Gratch et al. (Eds.): IVA 2006, LNAI 4133, pp. 292–303, 2006.

In yet another scenario, a patient needs to do recuperation with the aid of a dedicated device which measures biomedical signals and motion characteristics. The Virtual Trainer gives feedback on whether he is doing well, what he should do in order to improve, or explains another, easier exercise to switch to.

These examples all come from real life. There are more and more people in need of such services due to the growth of the elderly population, the alarming increasing number of people who are overweight [28] and the more and more 'white-collar' jobs done via the computer in Western societies. The application context is a new domain where the usefulness of IVAs for society can be demonstrated.

In general, we will use the terminology Reactive Virtual Trainer (RVT) for IVAs in the previous and similar scenario. The RVT is assumed to be a she, while the real human a he, for sake of simplicity. The practical potential of a RVT is that she is universal: with minor investment she can be applied in any number to suit different users and objectives. Moreover, the RVT shares the most essential characteristics of real trainers such as physiotherapists: she is *reactive*, both on a strictly professional and on a psychological/sociological basis. The latter has proven to be essential to keep the client motivated (not to give up an exercise or drop out) and to make the repetitive exercises more fun [3].

The scientific challenges are related to the three major capabilities of the RVT:

(1) perceiving the user's performance in non-lab environments by using robust and non-intrusive devices;
(2) evaluating the performance of the user and deciding how to react;
(3) generating the reaction of the RVT accordingly and presenting it in a natural, subtle way, where motion, speech and (eventually) music are fine-tuned and coordinated.

For our research group, who have been working on multimodal interaction and human body animation, the application poses the following new challenges in these fields:

* to develop a framework where multiple paradigms (forward/inverse kinematics, motion capture) can be used to define 'building blocks' of pieces of motions, and these different pieces can be parameterised and combined into more complex and/or longer exercises in a uniform way;
* to develop strategies, models and real-time algorithms for smooth adaptation of scheduled motion sequences to observed (re)actions of the user.

This paper reports on our ongoing work towards a RVT. In section 2, we give an overview of related work. In section 3, we articulate the requirements from the point of view of the application and the scientific tasks associated, and describe the modular architecture of the RVT. Section 4 is devoted to already implemented components: the low-level real-time animation engine, the GESTYLE language tailored to author single elements or a complete sequence of exercises, with parameters to be adjusted at run-time, and the acoustic perception module. Finally we outline the issues to be tackled next.

2 Related Work

In *health care applications* where motion is central virtual agents have been used in two roles:

(1) as a *medium* to present certain motions to be mimicked by the patients, and
(2) as an *empathic consultant* to aid and coach the patient with the same empathy and psychological insight as a real expert would do.

For the first type of application, a Tai Chi exercise performer was developed recently [6]. An exercise is generated by finding motion samples in a huge indexed database appropriate for a natural language utterance. The motion samples have been gained by motion capture, and are not altered, in any respect, for example tempo.

There are more examples of medical and psychological consultancy applications, where empathic feedback has turned out to be as a basis for success [4, 16]. Finally, we mention a web-site [7] and two recent workshops devoted to the topic [11, 17]. The possibility of using computer vision for physiotherapy was raised [22]. At one of these workshops [17] the interest was aroused by novel devices to sense physical activity. Such devices, as well as traditional ones providing biomedical signals, may be useful in specific application contexts for a RVT. At the same event there have been industrial proposals to use portable handheld devices during exercises, to keep personalized training instructions downloaded from a web location or a PC and to collect logs of the performance. A physical robot has also been considered as a training companion, but again only as a social coach, without the function of 'making the user move'.

Two industrial projects are the closest to ours. The virtual Fitness Trainer of Philips, projected onto an immersive screen in front of the trainee exercising on a home-trainer, evaluates his performance based on heart rate feedback [9, 10]. Our goals, however, differ substantially, by giving an active, motion-presentation role to the RVT, endowing it with synthetic vision and hearing, empathic multimodal response capabilities and also intelligent motion plan revision. We expect that in our case, where the RVT has more intense and more natural contact with the trainee, the positive effect will be much more significant than what the Philips researchers have reported so far [27].

Sony's new EyeToy: Kinetic 'game' [24] offers personalised as well as ready-made sequences of fitness exercises, commented on by one of two virtual trainers. Though we have not been able to try out the game, on the basis of the descriptions on the web it seems that our project is more challenging just in the two aspects which are the basis for the success of the game: personalization and active feedback from the trainers. Moreover, the EyeToy game is closed; it offers no real authoring tool to customise it.

Finally, we rely on our own earlier work on a dancing ECA which shares many characteristics with a RVT [20]. The virtual dancer times her dance movements to the (external) audio of the music through real-time tempo and beat analysis. She also reacts to the motion of the user - her dancing partner - in front of a camera. The selection of dance moves from a repertoire and the adjustment of the style of these movements reflect global properties of the movement of the user. The dancing movements of the ECA are constructed dynamically, on the fly by selecting from a limited repertoire of basic movements labelled from different aspects.

3 The Framework for an RVT

In this section we discuss the functional requirements and outline a corresponding modular architecture for the RVT. In Figure 1 the components of the RVT are indicated. The major components are *user monitoring*, *action planning* for the RVT and *presentation* of the actions (exercises movements and/or multimodal feedback) by the RVT. Optional modules such as sensors capable of monitoring biosignals are also indicated. A very important non-technological issue is the interaction with the expert who should author the exercises and monitor the global progress of the user, but who may be not very experienced technologically.

3.1 Authoring Exercises

How, when and by whom should the RVT be 'programmed'? Depending on the specific application, the RVT can be pre-programmed for a general, and from a medical point of view not critical, task such as providing morning gymnastic for healthy women around 30. The other extreme is when the RVT acts as a kind of 'assistant' to an expert, who instructs the RVT regularly what exercises to do in the next two weeks with a given patient. The definition of exercises is the task of an authorised person such as an expert physiotherapist. The authorized person should be able to prescribe exercises built up from pieces of basic motions and earlier defined sequences. The authoring should be easy, using high-level scripting language, templates for parametrizing exercises, or restricted natural language. Relative directions and references to body parts should be used, as done e.g. in our earlier work [21]. The tempo of the exercise may be set by acoustic cues (e.g. given by counting, clapping), or in a qualitative or quantitative way. The library of basic motions may be defined in terms of poses and paths, also using some reference points on or around the body. Once some key poses are defined, the motion path and parameters may be chosen from a predefined set. However, it should be possible to define very specific, new motion pieces which cannot be given in the previous frameworks. There should be motion capture means that allow the authoring person to directly 'act out' a sophisticated motion of the repertoire.

3.2 Calibration

The *calibration* of the RVT may have different motivations, affecting different aspects. The *calibration of motion characteristics* to those of the user should assure that the RVT's motion performance remains within the range of the actual, or realistically achievable capabilities of the user. The calibration may take place on a general level, by specifying motion parameters to be used throughout the exercises, as appropriate for the age and physical state of the user. But it may also involve the specification of certain joint parameters (such as stiffness limiting acceleration, or extreme position).

The *calibration of body geometry* similar to the user's *may* have a positive effect on presenting the exercises: a short-legged, bulky person will not be able to mimic the movements of a tall, thin trainer. On the other hand, it is not true per se that a user prefers a RVT with body geometry, weight and age characteristics of his own. Besides the mimicking of exercises, other factors such as aesthetic appeal and a

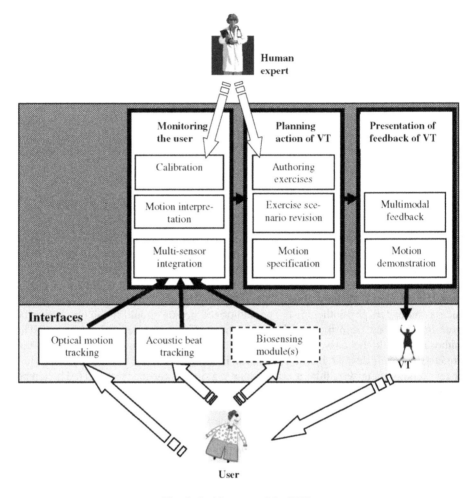

Fig. 1. Architecture of the RVT

preference for matching or different gender or young and good-looking RVTs may override the benefits of letting the RTV mirror the user.

These calibration tasks may involve an expert and in some cases even motion capture, but in less critical cases simple body parameters of the user suffice. An interesting possibility is when the RVT himself is prepared to do an initial self-calibration session by asking the user to perform a few poses and adjusting his own geometry and motion characteristics accordingly. It is also an option to re-calibrate the user from time to time, as his shape and movements improve.

3.3 Motion Demonstration

The most essential capability of the RVT is to act out the exercises prescribed by a script according to the initial body calibration parameters and (maybe dynamically changing) motion parameters. Concatenation of unit motions, automatic transition to start or rest poses and changes in timing parameters as well as 'graceful suspension' of an exercise should be taken care of by the 'motion intelligence', a component of the animation engine.

3.4 Monitoring User Performance

The RVT should monitor the performance of the user in near real time, and in a non-obtrusive way. In the basic scenario this should be achieved by robust synthetic vision getting input from a single, every-day camera connected to the PC hosting the RVT. In the case of some applications biosignals (e.g. heart-rate) are also appropriate. Through these signals, the presence, tempo of motion, the (basic) morphology of the performed movements as well as the physical state of the user should be perceived. By tracking the face too, not only the facial expression, but also coloration and reflection (sweat) may be used as source of information about the physical state.

3.5 Perceiving Acoustic Signals

Besides monitoring the user by synthetic vision, acoustic signals may also be helpful to detect if he is jogging in the right tempo, or if he is out of breath. Another function of the acoustic perception is to define the tempo in the authoring stage, for example by acoustic feedback such as counting or tapping with the feet. Finally, musical beat detection could be useful in assigning pieces of background music to exercises, either stored on the computer in digital form or played for the microphone on some device of the user.

In the first case, detection of tempo in the acoustic cue should be done real-time. The detection of the tempo and the beat of music may be done off-line, if the pieces of music to be used are pre-selected, or on-line, if the user provides new pieces of music from external sources at the time of doing the exercises.

3.6 Reactive Adjustment of Exercises

The RVT observes the user continuously and reacts to the situation by adjusting the current scenario of exercises and accompanying verbal comments. The reaction may involve:

- the adjustment of certain motion parameters of the current exercise;
- the re-scheduling of the exercises to be performed;
- some speech and/or nonverbal feedback to acknowledge performance or to inform about the modifications above (discussed in the next section).

Any single reaction or a subset of the above type of reactions may be triggered. For example, if the RVT notices that the user's rhythm is slower, the reactions may be:

- slowing down the RVT's tempo, to help the user to remain in sync;
- deciding to finish the current exercise and to shorten the number of repetitions still to come, as the user is possibly too tired to be able to keep up with the original schedule;
- warning the user about his delay, giving encouragement, and helping him by counting in a raised voice to get back to the tempo.

Note that in the first case the user drives the RVT indirectly, by his motion. The mechanism to decide when and how to react to the user's performance should be based on expert knowledge, pedagogical goals and a model of the user, reflecting also his physical state. Variations in the style of the RVT may be covered too [12].

3.7 Empathic Multimodal Feedback Generation

The RVT should address the user from time to time, during or in between performing an exercise. As the feedback is a crucial component for success, both from the point of view of the *effect* and *engagement*, it should be believable and subtle, in the following aspects:

- for each type of feedback a set of different natural language utterances should be used to achieve variety, accompanied (or even replaced) by facial expressions and possibly hand-gestures;
- some utterances should be synchronized to the tempo of the exercises (counting, indicating when to finish a sequence);
- addressing the user should be made clear by gaze behavior and head movement, whenever the exercise being performed allows.

4 Reactive Motion Generation

In this section we explain the computational means we have developed so far for the following major tasks: the representation of motion building blocks, the definition of parameterized exercises and driving the RVT by acoustic cues.

4.1 Defining Basic and Compound Motions

Three Kinds of Basic Motions
A *basic motion* is the smallest unit of motion that can be used (possibly in an altered form) to build up compound motions and exercises. A basic motion involves joints of different parts of the body, according to a taxonomy corresponding to the hierarchy of joints (left/right limbs, arms, hands; for a taxonomy see [21]). We use three kinds of basic motions to be explained below. In all cases, a basic motion has at least 2 key postures (the start and end pose), as well as possible in-between poses defining the path through animation space.

In the case of *forward kinematics motion* (FKM), the key poses are defined explicitly by the rotation of the joints involved. Movements are defined as interpolations through key poses. The interpolation determines for a large part the style of execution of movements, and can range from simple linear interpolation between the poses through nonlinear functions giving certain expressivity to a movement to possibly user-specific interpolation functions. A function may assigning the rotation to each time moment of the entire duration, see in Figure 2 the rotation of the wrists.

In the case of *inverse kinematics motion* (IKM), a position is specified on or around the body, and one of the so-called end-effectors - such as the end of a finger or one of the wrists - has to touch or reach for the given position. Similarly, the expert, when authoring an exercise, may specify a motion path by identifying points around the body, to be followed by the right hand, and the IK automatically calculates the rotations of the shoulder and elbow needed to place the hand on this path. The path may be given in terms of Hermite splines. In Figure 2, the path the wrist has to follow is given as a 3D curve parameterized by time.

Basic motions may also be specified in terms of *knowledge-based animation models*, specific for some body parts, as we have used in our earlier work on a virtual presenter [26]. Such models are based on human movement theory, such as Donder's law for head movement [25], detailed analysis of captured motion [1] or more ad-hoc solutions, such as the use of stochastic noise to add expressiveness to a character [19].

Motion Parameters

The motion of the RVT can be modified in real time by adjusting – for the time being – three motion parameters: *tempo*, indicating the timing of the repetitive, rhythmic motions; *amplitude*, indicating the amount of motion performed; and *effort*, indicating the acceleration profile of the motion. Our effort and amplitude parameters are similar to the effort and shape parameters of the Laban Notation, also taken as a starting point in [2] and [8]. In these related works for expressive gesture accompanying speech motion path, hand shape and acceleration profile are taken as dependent variables, and more than one of these are influenced by the higher-level gesture motion parameters. For the motion exercises domain we find it more useful to keep parameters influencing the motion dynamics, the motion path and the morphology separate, as these features are often addressed individually in fitness, and often need to be carefully controlled in physiotherapy exercises. By parameterizing movement, one can put the variants of a movement to different uses: for example tailoring general exercises to specific users (tempo, amplitude, target positions for IKM), accentuating certain movement features (effort) and performing at a slow tempo for a demonstration, and aligning movement in the exercise to the tempo according to music or clapping.

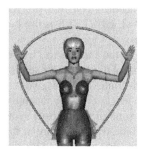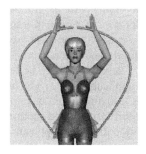

Fig. 2. A clapping exercise in our animation tool, where the movement path shown for the hands and the rotation of the wrists are defined by functions of time t, assigning a 3D point and a triple of Euler angles to each time moment of the entire duration

The position of the left hand:
$X(t) = 0.18 + \sin(t*3.14*1.185)*0.3$
$Y(t) = 0.79 + \sin(t* 3.14 *0.5)*0.9$
$Z(t) = 0.2$

Rotation of the left wrists:
Around-x-axis(t) = 0.5*t
Around-y-axis(t) = 0
Around-z-axis(t) = 0.16* 3.14*t

Combining Motions

Basic motions can be used in their parameterized form to compose more complex ones. This is done by using the GESTYLE scripting language [18]. Gestures may be defined by *motion expressions*, built up from basic motions, by using the *parallel* and *sequential* compositions and *repeat* operators in an embedded way. For example, a clap above the head is defined as the parallel execution of two single-armed movements above the head in the plane of the body, each composed of two basic motions, one for the arm movement, and one for the palm orientation. The definition of this clap in GESTYLE is:

```
<DefGest Name="LeftHand_ClapAboveHead">
  <PAR>    <UseGest Name="LeftHand_Lift" />
           <UseGest Name="LeftWrist_Rot"/></PAR> </DefGest>
<DefGest Name="RightHand_ClapAboveHead">
  <PAR>    <UseGest Name="RightHand_Lift" />
           <UseGest Name="RightWrist_Rot"/></PAR> </DefGest>

<DefGest Name="ClapAboveHead">
  <PAR>    <UseGest Name=" LeftHand_ClapAboveHead" />
           <UseGest Name=" RightHand_ClapAboveHead"/> </PAR> </DefGest>
```

A more sophisticated clapping movement where the wrists are rotated in the last quarter of the entire duration of the motion may be defined by exploiting that GESTYLE which allows delayed start of parallel threads. For the left hand, this looks like:

```
<DefGest Name="LeftHand_ClapAboveHead_1">
  <PAR>    <UseGest Name=" LeftHand_Lift" sub_start_time = "0" />
           <UseGest Name=" LeftWrist_Rot" sub_start_time="0.75"/> </PAR> </DefGest>
```

Compound motions and longer exercises may be given names and have higher-level parameters of their own, which may be used to control the parameters of the building blocks. Timing can be subtly defined by adding 'wait' durations, and thus need not be perfectly parallel for each component. Times are given in terms of abstract units of beats; the actual timing will be computed according to the (maybe changing) specification of the duration of a beat. On this level, GESTYLE is used to author the repertoire which may be used to compose exercises.

Besides the tempo, the amplitude and effort parameters of the motion to be performed as well as the number of repetitions may be left unspecified for an exercise sequence. Moreover, wherever applicable, left, right or both limbs may be given as parameters. Hence GESTYLE also functions as a higher-level scripting language whith parameters referring to specific fine-tuned motions or (one of the half of) symmetric motions or, regarding motion direction, opposite motions. We are aware of the fact that even GESTYLE is too technical for a physiotherapist or a trainer, so ideally there should come a scripting language that is close to natural, as the authoring tool for exercise sequences.

4.2 Performing Motions

All the above types of animations are represented on the lowest level in terms of a function $f(t,a)$, mapping time t and the parameter vector a to a 3D point or a vector of a triple of rotational angles, in order to define animation path for IKM or rotation values for a certain joint for FKM, respectively. The time t ($0\leq t \leq 1$) is relative, and the 1 time duration can be time-warped to real durations. a is a vector of low-level motion parameters that can be modified to allow animation changes in real time. By manipulating t, we can adjust the tempo and the velocity profile of an animation. Key positions given in the definition of basic motion may be used to align their time to external sources, for example to the beat of the music.

4.3 Driving Motion by Acoustic Cues

We use different types of auditory cues for RVT applications with different purposes (see 3.5). For all cases, the audio can be processed for tempo and beat information, which is then used to adapt the movements of the RVT to properly align them to the audio input or to determine whether the user is still performing the exercise in the expected tempo. In all of these situations the beat and tempo tracking can be performed by our improved implementation of Klapuri's beat tracking algorithm, capable of real-time performance. Klapuri's algorithm uses different frequency bands to detect accentuation in the audio signal, then a bank of comb filter resonators to detect the beat [14].

5 Further Work

Our current work follows three lines. First, yet missing modules are being developed. As for synthetic vision, we are going to check how useful the global information is on amplitude and tempo of motion that we can get from our real-time single camera image analysis module used to categorize dance motions [23, 20]. As it is known what motion the user should be performing, the recognition task may be easier. Moreover, the time evolution of basic motions and exercises corresponds to certain patterns in the global characteristics, the timing of which may thus be captured. On the other hand, for subtle visual perception, such as detection of a 'hanging elbow' multiple cameras and special visual markers (e.g. wearing a dress with a color code for different parts of the body) will be necessary. Whether these extensions will be sufficient to gain information detailed enough for interpreting the correctness of physiotherapeutic motions is as yet an open question.

In cooperation with an expert physiotherapist we will develop a knowledge base of standard exercises with feasible default parameters, as well as coaching strategies for a specific application context. Then we will test how likeable and effective the RVT is.

In the second stage, we shall refine the system by extending it with calibration facilities and a choice of different RVTs and with interpretation of the user's state with respect to logged recent performance. Another important extension we are aiming at is the parameterization and re-use of motion-captured samples [13, 15].

Finally, we will continue experimenting with coordination of acoustic cues and motion. In particular, the synchronization of accentuated speech to the predefined motion tempo is an interesting option.

Our ultimate goal is to have different settings for RVTs, as suggested in the introduction, and to collect feedback from real users.

Acknowledgement

The acoustic beat detector has been implemented by P. Bos. We are thankful to the anonymous reviewers for their comments, and to D. Kiss and L. Packwood for proofreading the paper.

References

1. K. Abdel-Malek, J. Yang, Z. Mi, V.C. Patel, K. Nebel: Human Upper Body Motion Prediction, Conference on Applied Simulation and Modeling (ASM) 2004, June 28-30, 2004, Rhodes Greece
2. N. Badler, R. Bindiganavale, J. Allbeck, W. Schuler, L. Zhao, M. Palmer: *Parameterized Action Representation for Virtual Human Agents*, In: [5] pp. 256-284.
3. T. Bickmore, J. Cassell: *Social Dialogue with Embodied Conversational Agents*, In: J. van Kuppevelt, L. Dybkjaer, and N. Bernsen (eds.), Natural, Intelligent and Effective Interaction with Multimodal Dialogue Systems. In press, New York: Kluwer Academic.
4. T. Bickmore, R. Picard: *Towards caring machines*, Proc. of CHI, 2004.
5. J. Cassell, J. Sullivan, S. Prevost and E. Churchill (eds.), *Embodied Conversational Agents*, MIT Press, 2000.
6. S-P.Chao, C-Y Chiu, S-N, Yang, T-G. Lin: *Tai Chi synthesizer: a motion synthesis framework based on key-postures and motion instructions*. Computer Animation and Virtual Worlds, Vol. 15. pp. 259-268, 2004.
7. Cybertherapy URL: http://www.cybertherapy.info/pages/main.htm
8. B. Hartmann, M. Mancini, C. Pelachaud: Implementing Expressive Gesture Synthesis for Embodied Conversational Agents, Gesture Workshop, LNAI, Springer, May 2005.
9. HomeLab Philips, http://www.research.philips.com/technologies/misc/homelab/
10. W. IJsselsteijn, Y. de Kort, J. Westerink, M. De Jager, R. Bonants: *Fun and Sports: Enhancing the Home Fitness Experience*, Proc. of ICEC 2004.
11. International Workshop on Virtual Rehabilitation, http://www.iwvr.org/2005
12. W. Lewis Johnson, P. Rizzo, W.E. Bosma, S. Kole, M. Ghijsen, H. van Welbergen: Generating socially appropriate tutorial dialog, in ISCA Workshop on Affective Dialogue Systems, Kloster Irsee, Germany, ISBN 3-540-22143-3, pp. 254-264, 2004.
13. T. H. Kim, S. I. Park, S. Y. Shin: *Rhythmic-motion synthesis based on motion-beat analysis*, ACM Trans. on Graphics, ACM Press, 22(3), pp. 392-401, 2003.
14. A. Klapuri, A. Eronen, J. Astola: *Analysis of the meter of acoustic musical signals*, in IEEE transactions on Speech and Audio Processing, (2006)
15. M. Mandel, V. Zordan: Beyond Ragdolls: *Generating Versatile Human Behaviors by Combining Motion Capture and Controlled Physical Simulation*, Proceedings of Game Developer's Conference (GDC), 2005.
16. S. Marsella, L. Johnson, and C. LaBore: *Interactive Pedagogical Drama for Health Interventions*, AIED 2003, 11th International Conference on Artificial Intelligence in Education, Australia, 2003.
17. Monitoring, measuring and motivating exercise ubiquitous computing to support fitness, Workshop at Ubicomp 2005, Tokyo, September 11, http://seattleweb.intel-research.net/projects/ubifit/ubicomp05workshop.html
18. H. Noot, Zs. Ruttkay: Style in Gesture, In: A. Camurri, G. Volpe (Eds.), Gesture-Based Communication in Human-Computer Interaction, LNCS 2915, Springer-Verlag, 2004.
19. K. Perlin, Ken: *An Image Synthesizer*. Proceedings of SIGGRAPH '85: 287-296.

20. D. Reidsma, A. Nijholt, R. Poppe, R. Rienks, H. Hondorp: Virtual rap dancer: *Invitation to dance*. In: Proceedings ACM CHI 2006 (Extended Abstracts), Montreal, April 2006, to appear.
21. Zs. Ruttkay, Z. Huang, A. Eliëns: *Reusable Gestures for Interactive Web Agents*, In: R. Aylett, D. Ballin, T. Rist (Eds.), Intelligent Virtual Agents, IVA-2003 Proceedings, LNAI 2792, Springer-Verlag, pp. 80-87.
22. S. Shafaei, M. Rahmati: *Physiotherapy Virtual Training by Computer Vision Approach*, Third International Workshop on Virtual Rehabilitation, 2004. http://www.iwvr.org/2004/
23. S.Takaaki, N. Atsushi and K. Ikeuchi: Rhythmic Motion Analysis using Motion Capture and Musical Information, Proc. of 2003 IEEE International Conference on Multisensor Fusion and Integration for Intelligent Systems 2003, pp. 89-94.
24. Sony: EyeToy: Kinetic, http://www.us.playstation.com/Content/OGS/SCUS-97478/Site/ and http://www.eyetoykinetic.com
25. D. Tweed: A three-dimensional model of the human eye-head saccadic system. J. Neurophysiol. 77, 1997. pp. 654-666.
26. H. van Welbergen, A. Nijholt, D. Reidsma, J. Zwiers: *Presenting in Virtual Worlds: Towards an Architecture for a 3D Presenter explaining 2D-Presented Information*, IEEE transcactions on Intelligent Systems, special issue "Intelligent Technologies for Interactive Entertainment" to appear Sept./Oct. 2006
27. J. Westerink, M. de Jager, M., Y. de Kort, W., IJsselsteijn, R., Bonants, J. Vermeulen, J. van Herk, M. Roersma: Raising Motivation in Home Fitnessing: Effects of a Virtual Landscape and a Virtual Coach with Various Coaching Styles. *ISSP 11th World Congress of Sport Psychology*, 15 - 19 August 2005, Sydney, Australia.
28. The World Health Organization warns of the rising threat of heart disease and stroke as overweight and obesity rapidly increase http://www.who.int/mediacentre/news/releases/2005/pr44/en/

Making It Up as You Go Along - Improvising Stories for Pedagogical Purposes

Ruth Aylett[1], Rui Figueiredo[2], Sandy Louchart[1], João Dias[2], and Ana Paiva[2]

[1] Heriot-Watt University, Edinburgh EH14 4AS, UK
[2] INESC-ID, Avenida Prof. Cavaco Silva - Taguspark,
2780-990 Porto Salvo, Portugal
ruth@macs.hw.ac.uk, rui.figueiredo@tagus.ist.utl.pt,
sandy@macs.hw.ac.uk, joao.assis@tagus.ist.utl.pt,
ana.paiva@inesc-id.pt

Abstract. We consider the issues involved in taking educational role-play into a virtual environment with intelligent graphical characters, who implement a cognitive appraisal system and autonomous action selection. Issues in organizing emergent narratives are discussed with respect to a Story Facilitator as well as the impact on the authoring process.

1 Introduction

A constructivist view of education argues that people are not passive recipients of their experience but active constructors of their own reality through mental activity [19]. In order for this process of active sense-making to take place and transfer outside of the classroom it is also argued [4] that learning must be situated in a rich context, reflective of the real world. Story is a specific mechanism through which the real world can be created in the imagination of learners so as to take on a virtual existence in the classroom.

Educational role-play is one specific use of story in education where social interaction is used as the stimulus for challenging and changing existing beliefs [19] and can result in significant behavioral changes [13] making it highly relevant for social and emotional learning [5,10]. The basic premise of educational role-play is that it is easier to empathise with how another person might feel under certain circumstances if one has experienced something similar, even symbolically as part of a role-play [21].

However role-play is not necessarily an easy option in the classroom - difficult to organize, and sometimes difficult also to sustain given that school students are not experienced actors and through embarrassment or lack of technique may shatter the willing suspension of disbelief required to make it a success. It is for this reason that a number of research groups [9] [8] [14] [15] have explored the use of intelligent synthetic characters as virtual actors in a 3D graphical environment - sometimes an immersive one - with the intention that the sense of presence in the virtual environment, and, much more important, the believability of the characters, will sustain the engagement with the story and thus meet the pedagogical objectives embedded in the experience.

J. Gratch et al. (Eds.): IVA 2006, LNAI 4133, pp. 304–315, 2006.
© Springer-Verlag Berlin Heidelberg 2006

An important characteristic of role-play is that it is improvised rather than scripted so that the story emerges from interaction between the characters involved. It is typically organized around a scenario: the characters are specified in terms of their background, often through past events they are said to have taken part in (their *back-story*), their role, their personality, and their goals. It is not possible to specify a linear plot in the same way as film or standard theatrical drama: educational role-play is often developed as a succession of scenes, in which external events and consequences of actions within scenes may be controlled by the facilitator of the role-play between scenes, and the new back-story and character goals communicated to role-players at the start of each new scene. In some cases the facilitator will themselves play a character with the specific intention of shaping the emerging story in particular ways. It is through these methods that the inevitable tension between the somewhat unpredictable outcomes of role-play and the desired pedagogical objectives is resolved, and the high-level dramatic trajectory of the experience is shaped.

These aspects of role-play have so far had little impact on virtual dramas, which have instead often adopted branching narrative structures, in which a finite number of pre-scripted paths result from a choice made at a specific decision point [8] [15]. In other cases work has tried to cover the whole space of possible options as in the beats of [16], with a correspondingly combinatorial authoring problem. The work discussed in this paper has tried instead to incorporate the role-play approach by developing an emergent narrative [2] in which the story is indeed generated by interaction between autonomous intelligent characters.

This raises a number of interesting challenges. Characters must have a rich repertoire of actions and corresponding graphical animations, and it must be possible to combine these dynamically, both through a character-based action selection mechanism and graphical morphing between animations. Characters must also possess an adequate repertoire of expressive behaviours, since otherwise their motivations and responses may remain opaque. Finally, some at least of the functionality of the facilitator of educational role-play - or the gamemaster of live and table-top role-play - must be incorporated in order to give the experience the desired pedagogic shape.

This paper discusses how the FearNot! demonstrator, initially developed as part of the EU-funded project VICTEC (Virtual ICT with Empathic Characters) and now being further developed in the follow-on project eCIRCUS (Education through Characters with emotional-Intelligence and Role-playing Capabilities that Understand Social interaction), tries to meet these challenges.

2   FearNot!

FearNot! is an Interactive Virtual Environment (IVE) developed for education against bullying behaviour in schools. Bullying behaviour is characterized as "a repeated action that occurs regularly over time, and usually involves an imbalance in strength, either real or perceived" [18] and may involve hitting, kicking or punching (direct bullying), or, in relational bullying, social exclusion or malicious rumour spreading. FearNot! offers a safe environment for individual children where they can witness (from a third-person perspective) bullying situations in virtual 3D scenarios. Each child then acts as an *invisible friend* to the victimised character, discussing the problems that arise and proposing coping strategies, of which there are seven possible ones. This advice influences the actions of the victim in the next episode.

Given the child must be able to see that thier advice influences the victimized character, and given the high branching factor, an emergent approach was a good choice. A scripted system would limit the child's interaction and pose serious scaling problems in authoring. Emergent narrative requires that a story be dynamically generated by the interactions between different characters and the causal relationships between its different elements. Thus episodes are unscripted and result from the actions, interactions and reactions of autonomous agents.

To make such autonomous agents believable and empathic, we focus on two characteristics raised at an early stage by traditional animators and often explored by researchers working in synthetic characters: emotional expressivity and personality. Personality and the character goals associated with it are crucial in achieving pedagogical objectives in emergent narrative because of their role in producing agent behaviour, allowing the facilitator to build an overall narrative by choosing the right set of characters and situations. Mechanisms must be developed supporting models of agent emotions and personality, that can be used within characters to influence their reasoning and actions.

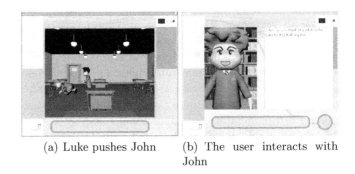

(a) Luke pushes John   (b) The user interacts with John

Fig. 1. FearNot! application

We have developed such agent architecture and applied it successfully to a short physical bullying scenario of two scenes. The first presents an initial bullying situation where Luke (the bully) pushes John's (the victim) books off the table(Fig. 1-a). Afterwards, the child interacts with the victim via free-text keyboard entry, and gives him suggestions on what to do. The *Story Facilitator* (SF) then chooses the next episode in relation to the child's advice (Fig. 1-b). For instance, if the advice is to fight back, the SF confronts John with Luke once more, while if the advice is to tell someone, it puts John and one of his friends together. Due to the number of possible suggestions and the fact that the outcome of an episode is not certain (e.g the victim may succeed or fail in fighting back), this small number of scenes corresponds to a much larger number of distinct stories. It is easy to see the combinatorial explosion if we were to script and foresee each possibility. Because scenes are dynamically generated, scaling up just requires the definition of a much smaller number of additional goals and generic rules in the character's definition.

3   Generating Story Through Character Interaction

The architecture of the characters in FearNot! is of crucial importance given that it through their autonomous action-selection mechanisms that the dramatic content of episodes is generated. Figure 2 shows the main functions of this architecture. The agent mind takes percepts from the virtual world and uses a cognitive appraisal system based on the work of Ortony, Clore and Collins (OCC) [17] discussed in more length in [20] to generate an emotional status. This then affects the agents drives, motivations, priorities and relationships, and produces coping behaviour [12]. FearNot! incorporates two distinct levels in both appraisal and coping mechanisms. The reactive level provides a fast mechanism to appraise and react to a given event, and generates behaviours such as crying, which cannot be considered as planned. The deliberative level takes longer to react but allows a more sequentially complex and rich behaviour, for example a plan by the bully to push the books of a victim off his desk. Thus as improvising actors, characters have substantially more capability than many earlier systems which only included reactive components [9].

Reactive appraisal is handled by a set of emotional reaction rules, based on Elliot's Construal Theory [6]. A rule consists of an event that triggers it and resulting values for OCC appraisal variables (desirability, desirability-for-other, praiseworthiness etc). Reactive coping behaviour is defined by action rules: each contains a set of preconditions that must be true to execute the action together with the eliciting emotion triggering it. The action set is matched against all the emotions present in the character emotional state and the set of rules with positive matches is activated. The rule triggered by the most intense emotion is selected for execution. If more than one action rule is selected (i.e. triggered by the same emotion), the most specific one is preferred.

The deliberative layer appraises events according to the character's goals, thus generating prospect-based emotions like hope and fear. The character's goals result in the generation of plans, using a STRIPS-based partial-order continuous planner, and assessment of both the probability P of success of a given plan and its importance to the character as in [7] generates hope and fear:

$$HopePotential = P(Plan) * ImportanceOfSucess$$
$$FearPotential = (1 - P(Plan)) * ImportanceOfFailure$$

Deliberative appraisal updates all existing plans accordingly to the event being appraised as well as the probability of action effects succeeding. If an action was successfully executed but an expected effect did not occur, the planner updates effect probability accordingly. This process will change the agents' internal plans

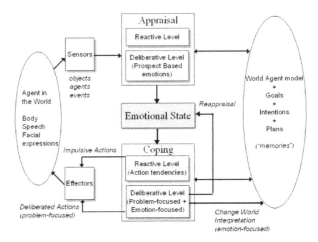

Fig. 2. Architecture Diagram

(and plan probabilities) leading to different emotional appraisals of Hope and Fear. In addition, when an event is appraised, the deliberative level checks if any goal has become active, and if so, an intention to achieve the goals' success conditions is created generating initial hope and fear emotions. The deliberative layer must then choose between existing intentions/goals to continue deliberation (and planning). The idea is that we can use emotions to determine the most relevant intention: the goals generating the strongest emotions are the ones that require the most attention from the agent, and thus are the ones selected by the planner to continue deliberation.

Since the agents in FearNot! are emotionally driven, any significant interaction with a child user or another agent will result in the alteration of the agents' emotional state. Since the agent makes decisions based on that emotional state, this potentially affects its perception of actions and alters the probability of plan success and the resulting feelings of hope and fear. This, in turn, influences the actions selected for execution by the agent and allows for the unfolding of narratives different in form and content (i.e. according to their context) without the need for scripting them.

In role-play, the outcome of physical actions in the world is often decided by facilitator or gamemaster since the real physical world is not usually that of the role-play. The outcome of physical actions in FearNot! is thus decided within the visualized graphical world in which they take place, so that a character who is pushed may or may not fall. The actual outcome of an action like this also has a substantial emotional effect on characters: if the victim pushes the bully and the bully falls, then the victim's level of hope rises and the bully's level of fear rises, impacting their plans. If it fails, the impact runs the other way, and an angry bully may in turn push the victim with a much greater chance of success. These probabilities are taken from analysis of real bullying in which the coping behaviour 'hitting back' is observed to be relatively unsuccessful for real victims.

3.1   Defining a Character

The final intensity of emotions is biased by personality, supporting a greater differentiation of behaviour between different characters. A fearful character has a low threshold and experiences Fear more easily, making this the dominant emotion more often. The character therefore considers goals unachievable (generating strong Fear emotions) earlier, and gives up goals that threaten other interest goals much more easily. A less fearful character is usually driven by Hope, producing a more optimistic and bold behaviour. Characters are defined by their Personality (Table 1), also strongly based on OCC and containing: a set of goals; a set of emotional reaction rules; action tendencies; emotional thresholds and decay rates for each of the OCC 22 emotion types.

Table 1. Structure of the XML file for the characters' Personality

Emotional Thresholds	Thresholds and decay rates for each of the 22 OCC emotion types.
Goals	Set of goals for the character together with importance of success and failure for each one of them.
Emotional Reaction Rules	Set of rules that assess values for the OCC appraisal variables accordingly to the matched event.
Action Tendencies	Set of rules that specify reactive behavior based on an emotion and an event.

Emotional reaction rules represent the character's standards and attitudes and are very dependent on personality. Action tendencies represent character impulsive actions or reactions: when the victim is very sad it will tend to cry while the bully expresses sadness in a completely different way. OCC specifies for each emotion type an emotional threshold and decay rate: emotional thresholds specify a character's resistance towards emotion types, and decay rates, emotional decay over time. A peaceful character has a high threshold and a strong decay for the emotion type of Anger, and its anger emotions will be short and low.

The results obtained from a small evaluation [3], in which the emergent version is compared with a scripted version, suggest that the use of autonomous synthetic characters can lead to believable situations that do evoke empathy in users. However just as in human role-play, the whole burden of the overall narrative cannot be left to the characters especially as their internal complexity is scaled up for multiple episodes and scenarios. Although they possess mechanisms that allow them to select between competing goals, and to perform different coping strategies, these mechanisms are influenced by their always shifting emotional state. Myriads of small things may can change their internal emotional state, ranging from a small event to a bad or good mood. Thus, as the number of goals and character complexity increases, so does their unpredictability and scope of possible behavior. As such, the need for the SF arises once more in order to constrain the character's range of behaviours by setting up their goals at the start of each episode.

4 Scaling Up

In order to produce an application that is usable in the school curriculum, many characters and episodes are required, covering various types of bullying. In addition, as in human role-play, the nature of an episode depends heavily on which characters are involved, what has already happened to them, their goals at the start of the episode and the location and objects around them. Making these initialization choices about an episode should also relate to the advice a child user has given to a victim so that the child feels the story is responding to their intervention.

For all these reasons, a structure that represents an episode was defined,both because bullying has an episodic and repetitive nature, and because human role-play is developed as a succession of scenes. An episode represents a part of the story that can be combined with other episodes, with each combination creating a different overall drama. It contains information that allows contextualization of the part of the story it represents, together with information that allows the system to know at what point each episode should end. An XML file is used, for which the structure is shown in table 2. This is different from the concept of beats [16] because it does not specify character actions within episodes (these are selected by the characters autonomously) and operates at a much coarser level of granularity, corresponding to a scene in a play.

Table 2. The several elements that the author defines in each episode

Name	A unique name that identifies the episode
Set	The set is the location on the virtual environment where the events of this episode will take place.
Characters	The characters of the story that will participate in this episode and a set of properties about them such as their position on the set.
Preconditions	The preconditions are a set of conditions that specify when is the episode eligible for selection.
Goals	Character goals that are communicated to the agents in this particular episode.
Triggers	A trigger is a condition that when satisfied will cause the execution of a set of *narrative actions*.
Finish Conditions	The finish conditions are a set of conditions similar to the preconditions that when satisfied indicate that the episode is finished.
Introduction	This section of the definition of the episode is composed by a set of *narrative actions*.

Sequencing of episodes is handled by a special agent, the already mentioned Story Facilitator (SF), which acts in a similar way to the human facilitator in educational role-play. This agent has special privileges that allow it to keep track of all the events that happen in the virtual environment. An event in this context refers to an action from an agent (or the user) and how and when it was performed. This gives the SF contextual information about the development of the story, and is used to select the most appropriate episode to be played next. For an episode to be selected by the SF, it must have at least one of its preconditions satisfied. A precondition represents a set of tests on events, that when true indicate that this episode fits into the developing story.

Each time a new episode is selected the Narrative Actions contained in its *Introduction* are executed. These actions are inspired by some of the actions a human gamemaster (or facilitator) performs. Table 3 gives the complete list of available narrative actions. During the execution of the narrative actions contained in the introduction section, the minds of the characters are stopped. When all the actions finish the minds continue their normal execution. This section is used to place the characters and objects on the set, and to write some introductory text to the interface. The SF does not however act as a director in the filmic sense, unlike [16] or [22], any more than a human roleplay facilitator does so: the characters must still act autonomously.

Table 3. Narrative actions available to the author

Insert Character	This action inserts a character in the current episode.
Insert Object	Similar to the *Insert Character Action* but applied to objects.
Change Camera	Changes the perspective of the camera.
Narrate	Writes text to the interface
Change Story Mode	Changes the interface.
Remove Object	Removes an object from the set.
Remove Character	Removes a character from the set.

After execution of the narrative actions contained in the introduction, the initial character goals are communicated to the corresponding agents. The SF then monitors execution so as to update its memory with the events of the story. Each time a new event is generated the SF checks the conditions of all triggers contained in the episode. A trigger condition can test the properties of the characters and events that were generated within the current episode. Any trigger that has its condition satisfied is considered for execution, with selection of the one in this set that has the highest priority. The trigger's priority is defined via the authoring of the episode's XML.

Execution of a trigger carries out all the narrative actions contained within it and the minds of the agents are stopped so that there is no interference between agent actions and narrative actions. Triggers can be used to place additional objects and characters in the virtual environment, thus producing events exogenous to the characters like a character entrance, as well as to write narrative text to the visualization interface. The SF also tests for the finish conditions of the current episode - an unscripted episode has no internal way of finishing. When one of the finish conditions is satisfied the episode ends and another is selected. When there are no more episodes that are eligible for selection the story finishes.

5 Authoring for Emergent Narrative

Authoring emergent narrative may sound paradoxical - if the story is to be generated by interaction between characters, then in what sense is it authored?

However emergent narrative is not magic, and just as in human role-play must be carefully organized if it is to reach particular pedagogical objectives. Authoring is not abolished, but it is different from the approach of film and standard theater or written narrative in that it does not involve the design of a linear plot. Rather than working on one particular story and developing the characters for the unfolding of this storyline, the author needs to fully develop characters with respect to a potential 'narrative boundary' or narrative zone. In FearNot! this is currently expressed in the construction of the episode definitions the SF can dynamically invoke.

In FearNot! an author must initially decide, for pedagogical reasons, on the type of bullying that should feature and the number and type of characters that should be involved. Physical bullying involves hitting and pushing, and is much more often carried out by boys; relational bullying involves social exclusion - for example making sure nobody will sit next to the victim in activities - and is much more frequently carried out by girls, especially in the target 8-12 age group of FearNot! The settings required for these types of bullying may be different, and relational bullying usually requires an assistant to the bully, as well as bully and victim, for a plausible story to emerge. Showing the potential role of bystanders and the impact of the victim making a new friend also require relevant settings and characters on stage. The author need not define any rigid sequence for such episodes, but if it is considered important that such types of episodes can be staged by the SF, then the author must specify them at this abstract level along with their conditions and associated narrative events.

A consequence of allowing the characters to select the actions to be played out in a specific episode is that the level of abstraction of authoring is raised [2], and becomes much more declarative in nature, compared to the lower-level procedural requirements of linear or branching story authoring.

The XML character definitions must be considered so that relevant emotional reaction rules and action tendencies are defined for the episodes in which the character may feature. The author must think in terms of interactions between characters and the likely occurrence of actions, interactions and goal conflicts in the episodes being created. This is simple for two characters but more complex as the number of characters in an episode grows. This bottom-up approach can be a relatively complex exercise in finding the right balance between delimiting the boundaries of the episodes with their associated character definitions, and allowing the characters to take charge within episodes. Each character should be thought of as having its own story space, with the existence of multiple narrative threads acting as the boundary of the overall narrative experience. This ability to see multiple stories depending on the character perspective taken is potentially very educationally powerful, and though in FearNot! it is the perspective of the victim that is currently taken, one should not rule out the educational value of seeing the story from the perspective of a bystander, a friend of the victim, or even an assistant to the bully.

The author is required to give up low-level control of the story and instead to develop much more detailed character specifications: the outcome of this process cannot be wholly assessed by inspection but requires simulation runs in order to develop adequate actions and goals or respond to specific needs for a scenario. If characters have been written well enough, then their reactions and decisions should match the role they are asked to play in unfolding the drama within episodes. It may be quite difficult for an author to give up the conventional plot-based approach to story derived from a whole experience of childhood stories, comic strips, TV cartoons, lullabies, folklore and moral tales etc. However the success of role-play and improvisational drama in generating engaging story experiences in our view offers an existence proof for this approach.

This approach to authoring is in fact very similar to that that taken for inter-active theater plays [11]. Here, an event, containing its own sequence of events or sections, is unfolded while characters that would fit the event theme are introduced within the audience and carry out their roles, occasionally reacting or interacting, according to their roles and personalities. This approach still relies on authoring a high-level story, but is very different from creating a plot to which every single character must perfectly relate to in order to generate meaning and sense.

Since this type of interactive storytelling does not conform easily to the clas-sic narrative model of 'beginning, middle and end' [1], it is quite possible that the overall experience ends without all of the character stories having reached a dramatic climax. The existence of multiple stories at various stages of devel-opment, over which the author has only a limited amount of control,raises the issue of how to 'wrap up' the overall experience. As an example, it would be very difficult indeed to engineer an end to a performance such as the ones observed in movies like Bleu, Blanc, Rouge, Traffic or Crash.

Human Role-Playing-Games (RPGs) that share the same issue have addressed the problem by running debriefing sessions where the players can discuss their actions, interventions and motivations for doing so with other involved players. In this way, the players gain a better understanding of the overall picture and can relate to their position within the story world. Often this exercise generates discussion on what could have happened or would have been likely to happen, thus bringing more interaction between participants. FearNot! is aimed at giving each child in a class a somewhat different experience, and rather than funelling the emergent narrative into a contrived generic ending, happy or otherwise, the pedagogical objectives seem much better served by adopting this approach and locating the software within a broader educational process.

6   Conclusions

In this paper we have discussed how the FearNot! demonstrator applies ideas from educational role-play to the development of an emergent narrative. We have described the SF mechanism as a way both of shaping the high-level nar-rative and as a support to a different approach to authoring in which high-level structure, in the form of episode definitions, is fleshed out by the improvisatory abilities of affectively-driven characters alongside the indeterminacy of physical events. Current work is going on to produce a robust and scaled-up version of FeraNot! that can be trialled in schools over a period of months in 2007.

Acknowledgments

This work was partially supported by European Community (EC) under the IST RTD programme, contract IST-2001-33310-VICTEC, and is currently funded by the eCircus project IST-4-027656-STP. The authors are solely responsible for the content of this publication. It does not represent the opinion of the EC, and the EC is not responsible for any use that might be made of data appearing therein.

References

1. Aristotle. 330 B.C. The Poetics of Aristotle, translation and commentary by Stephen Halliwell. Duckworth, 1987.
2. Aylett, R.S. (2000) Emergent Narrative, Social Immersion and "Storification" Proceedings, Narrative Interaction for Learning Environments, Edinburgh, 2000.
3. Aylett, R.S;. Louchart,S; Dias, J; Paiva, A and Vala, M. (2005) FearNot! - an experiment in emergent narrative. Proceedings, IVA 2006, LNAI 3661, Springer, pp305-16
4. Bednar, A.K., Cunningham, D., Duffy, T.M., and Perry, J.D. (1991). Theory into practice: How do we link? In G. Anglin (Ed.), Instructional Technology: Past, Present and Future. Englewood, CO: Libraries Unlimited, Inc.
5. Davison, J.; Arthur, J. (2003). Active Citizenship and the Development of Social Literacy: a case for experiential learning. Canterbury: Citizenship and Teacher Education.
6. Elliot C.: "The Affective Reasoner: A process model of emotions in a multi-agent system". PhD Thesis, Illinois, 92
7. Gratch J. (2000) mile: Marshalling Passions in Training and Education. In 4th International Conference on Autonomous Agents, ACM Press, June 2000
8. Gratch, J. and Marsella, S. (2001). Tears and fears: Modeling emotions and emotional behaviors in synthetic agents. Paper presented at the Fifth International Conference on Autonomous Agents.
9. Hayes-Roth, B. and van Gent, R. Improvisational puppets, actors, and avatars.. In Proceedings of the Computer Game Developers' Conference, Santa Clara, CA, 1996.
10. Henriksen. (2004). On the Transmutation of Educational Role-Play: a critical reframing to the Role-Play to Meet the Educational Demands. In M. Montola & J. Stenros (Eds.), Beyond Role and Play - Tools, Toys and Theory for Harnessing the Imagination (pp. 107-130). Helsinki
11. Izzo, G (1997) The art of Play: New genre of Interactive Theatre. Gary Izzo Greenwood Press Paperback - October 1997
12. Lazarus,R (1991) Emotion and Adaptation. Oxford University Press, 1991.
13. Lewin, K. (1951). Field Theory in Social Science. New York: Harper and Row.
14. Machado, I.,Paiva, A. and Prada, R. (2001, May 28 - June 01). Is the wolf angry or just hungry? Inspecting, modifying and sharing character's minds. Paper presented at the 5th International Conference on Autonomous Agents, Montreal, Canada
15. Marsella, S., Johnson,W.L. and LaBore, C (2003) Interactive Pedagogical Drama for Health Interventions. In 11th International Conference on Artificial Intelligence in Education, Australia, 2003
16. Mateas, M.; Stern,A.: Architecture, authorial idioms and early observations of the interactive drama Façade. Technical report, Carnegie Mellon University, 2002.

17. Ortony,A, G. Clore, A. Collins. (1988) The Cognitive Structure of Emotions. Cambridge University Press
18. Olweus, D. (1991). Bully/victim problems among schoolchildren: basic facts and effects of a school-based intervention programme. In D. Pepler and K. Rubin (Eds.), The Development and Treatment of Childhood Aggression pp411-38. Hillsdale, NJ: Erlbaum
19. Piaget, J. (1972). The Principles of Genetic Epistemology. London: Routledge & Keegan Paul Ltd.
20. Paiva, A., Dias, J., Aylett, R., Woods, S., Hall, L. and Zoll, C (2005). Learning by Feeling: Evoking Empathy with Synthetic Characters. Applied Artificial Intelligence, 19, 235-266.
21. Robertson, J.; Oberlander, J. (2002). Ghostwriter: Educational Drama and Presence in a Virtual Environment. Journal of Computer Mediated Communication, 8(1).
22. Weyhrauch, P. 1997. Guiding Interactive Drama. Ph.D. diss., Dept. of Computer Science, Carnegie Mellon.

A Neurobiologically Inspired Model of Personality in an Intelligent Agent

Stephen Read[1], Lynn Miller[2], Brian Monroe[1],
Aaron Brownstein[1], Wayne Zachary[3],
Jean-Christophe LeMentec[3], and Vassil Iordanov[3]

[1] Department of Psychology, University of Southern California, Los Angeles,
California 90089-1061, USA
{read, monroe, aaronb}@usc.edu
[2] Annenberg School for Communication, University of Southern California,
Los Angeles, CA 90089-0281, USA
lmiller@usc.edu
[3] CHI Systems, Inc., Suite 300, 1035 Virginia Drive,
Ft. Washington, PA 19034, USA
{viordanov, jclementec, wzachary}@chisystems.com

Abstract. We demonstrate how current knowledge about the neurobiology and structure of human personality can be used as the basis for a computational model of personality in intelligent agents (PAC—personality, affect, and culture). The model integrates what is known about the neurobiology of human motivation and personality with knowledge about the psychometric structure of trait language and personality tests. Thus, the current model provides a principled theoretical account that is based on what is currently known about the structure and neurobiology of human personality and tightly integrates it into a computational architecture. The result is a motive-based computational model of personality that provides a psychologically principled basis for intelligent virtual agents with realistic and engaging personality.

1 Introduction

Work on intelligent agents has begun to examine how to create agents with realistic, engaging personalities. However, this work has severe limitations. Much of it takes a fairly shallow approach to human personality and treats it as an add-on, rather than as a fundamental aspect of the human behavior. Other work takes a deeper approach to modeling personality in terms of motivational systems, but does not relate this work to what is currently known about the structure and function of human personality.

Here we examine how what is known about the structure and neurobiology of human personality and motivation can provide the basis for a computational model of personality for intelligent agents. Such a model provides a principled way to integrate human personality into the fundamental architecture of an intelligent agent. Further, it provides a relatively straightforward and comprehensible way to incorporate a broad array of personality traits into agents.

J. Gratch et al. (Eds.): IVA 2006, LNAI 4133, pp. 316–328, 2006.
© Springer-Verlag Berlin Heidelberg 2006

1.1 Previous Work on Personality in Intelligent Agents

One thread of work on personality in agents ([1], [2], [3], [4], [5]) simply represents a small number of broad personality traits (e.g., extroversion, agreeableness, neuroticism) as a variable that modifies the agent's behavior. However, there is little attempt to give a principled account of how the trait influences the agent. Decisions as to how a trait affects an agent's behavior are typically ad hoc.

Another thread tries to capture personality by modeling the motivational structure of the agent. Some of the best examples can be found in the OZ project at CMU ([6], [7], [8], [9]) and in work at MIT by Maes and her students (e.g., [10], [11], [12]). These researchers attempt to capture individual differences by modeling a motivational system composed of an agent's goals and plans. Unfortunately, this work has focused on agents with "animal - like" motivational systems, and largely ignored research on the personality and motivational structures of humans.

The work that is closest conceptually to the current model is Moffat's [13] model of emotion and personality, *Will*. This model is related to Mischel's [14] Cognitive Social Learning Theory Reconceptualization of Personality, which conceptualizes human personality in terms of constructs such as goals, competencies, and expectancies. However, Moffat's model is abstract and it is not related to the structure of human personality. Gratch and Marsella [15] propose an approach similar to Moffat's but, they also do not relate their model to what is known about the structure of human personality.

The current work examines what is known about the neurobiology of human motivation and the structure of human personality, to tie what is known about the structure of human personality to underlying human motives. We first lay out the theoretical basis of our model and then describe its computational implementation.

1.2 Need for Implementable Models of Rich Personality

Personality is defined as enduring tendencies to think, feel, and behave in consistent ways. And traits are the typical units of "personality." But it is not clear how traits can be made part of the planning and control structures of intelligent agents in a principled and transparent way. Our model addresses this serious obstacle to constructing agents with "personality."

In developing our model we drew on various literatures in personality and neuroscience. These literatures converge toward an articulated, general model of personality, providing evidence for a number of potentially important distinctions. This allowed us to develop a model with a core set of processing systems that will simulate the patterning of personality and social behavior, and so capture a number of individual differences in social behavior.

We relied on seven related literatures: (1) Work on the lexical analysis of trait language (e.g., [16], [17], [18]) and work on the structure of a variety of different trait scales (e.g., [19], [20], [21]) provides considerable information on the nature of individual differences as well as the interrelations among them, (2) work on a goal-based model of traits ([22], [23], [24]) provided guidance on how traits could be related to underlying goals and motives, (3) theories of temperament (e.g., [20], [25], [26], [27]) have identified major dimensions of personality (e.g., Neuroticism,

Extroversion, BIS, BAS), as well as providing information about their possible biological bases. (4) Research by Davidson (e.g., [28]) suggests that differences in the activation of the right and left prefrontal cortex (PFC) correspond to chronic individual differences in positive and negative affect. This work and work by Cacioppo, Gardner, and Berntson [29] is consistent with the idea that these higher order brain systems act as integrators of inputs from a variety of relatively independent lower level brain systems, (5) Evolutionary analyses suggest that, given the problems and tasks that all humans must solve, there are likely to be a set of brain systems that have evolved to handle these tasks. Among the systems are those for: mating, nurturance of young, affiliation and bonding with peers, establishing dominance hierarchies, and insuring attachment to caregivers. (6) Recent work in affective neuroscience (e.g., [30]) identifies specific emotional and motivational systems in the brain that have developed to cope with everyday life. (7) Work in affective neuroscience also suggests more general systems that tie together other systems. For example, there are neurotransmitter systems that are widely distributed in the brain and that seem to play a role in almost all systems.

These multiple sources of information allow us to develop a model that can handle a variety of phenomena. At the same time, these converging sources of information provide a strong set of constraints on our ultimate model.

1.3 Theoretical Background

Analysis of Personality Measures and the Lexical Analysis of Trait language.
Work on the development of personality measures and the lexical analysis of trait terms provides a wealth of information about important personality distinctions. There is considerable evidence for what is termed the Big Five: Extroversion, Neuroticism, Agreeableness, Conscientiousness and Openness to Experience.

Further, researchers (e.g., [19], [31]) have proposed that each of the Big Five have a number of subcomponents. For example, Extroversion seems to have separate components for energy level, gregariousness, and dominance. And Neuroticism seems to have separate components corresponding to angry/hostility, anxiety, and fear of social rejection. Digman [16] and Wiggins and Trapnell [21] argue that an important distinction that cuts across the Big Five is that between Agentic (individually focused) and Communal (social or affiliative) goals; thus we might expect Agentic and Communal aspects of Extroversion, Neuroticism, and Conscientiousness.

Traits as Goal-Based, Motive-Based Structures. Other work suggests how traits can be related to human motivational systems. Miller and Read ([22], [23], [24]) have argued that we can effectively capture personality through configurations of chronic goals, plans, resources, and beliefs. For example, the trait helpful can be decomposed into the goal to help others, plans for achieving that goal, resources to do so, and beliefs that one's actions would actually assist the other and that the other desired that assistance.

Traits represented as configurations of goals, plans, resources and beliefs can be translated into the planning and goal structures of an agent. By modifying these configurations, we could create different "personalities" who respond differently to similar input.

Temperament. There is growing agreement (e.g., [25], [26], [27], [32], [33]) on at least three major dimensions of temperament (biologically based individual differences): Extroversion, Neuroticism, and Disinhibition / Constraint. These three dimensions largely map onto three dimensions of the Big Five: Extroversion, Neuroticism, and Conscientiousness.

Researchers, such as Gray [32] and Depue and Collins [34] have argued that underlying Extroversion is a behavioral approach system (BAS) [32] or a behavioral facilitation system [34] and underlying Neuroticism is a behavioral inhibition system (BIS) [32]. The BAS is sensitive to cues signaling rewards and when activated results in active approach, accompanied by feelings of energization. In contrast, the BIS is sensitive to cues of punishment or threat and manages avoidance of threatening situations. Activation of this system is characterized by anxiety or fear. Other authors have similarly argued for such approach and avoidance systems ([25], [29]).

Rothbart and Bates [27] argue that these three dimensions have sub components. Neuroticism may have the three subcomponents: irritable distress or hostility (which may come from blocking the BAS), fearful/anxious distress (may come from activation of BIS), and separation distress. And Extroversion may have both an energy /activity level component and a sociability component. Many temperament researchers (e.g., [25], [27]) also argue for a dimension of Disinhibition / Constraint, which is responsible for the inhibition of or the lack of inhibition of behavior, and which seems to largely operate automatically. In addition, there is probably an affiliativeness component that is independent of Extroversion and may be most closely linked to Agreeableness in the Big Five.

Asymmetries in the Prefrontal Cortex Related to Positive and Negative Emotions. Davidson [28] demonstrated that the left and right prefrontal cortices (PFC) are differentially involved with approach related and withdrawal related emotions and motivations. The left PFC processes positive, approach-related emotions, whereas the right PFC processes withdrawal related emotions, such as fear, disgust, and sadness. Baseline differences in EEG activation were related to dispositional differences in mood. Those with relatively higher right PFC activation showed more negative mood, those with relatively higher left PFC showed more positive mood.

Evolutionary Analysis of Social Tasks. Several researchers (e.g., [35], [36]) have argued that human beings have evolved specific brain systems specialized for handling our most important social tasks. They argue, based on both evolutionary and empirical considerations, that a variety of tasks need to be solved by human beings to survive and reproduce. These include: (1) Status and dominance, (2) Coalition formation, communal sharing, affectional relationships, (3) Reciprocity, (4) Self-protection, (5) Mate choice, (6) Parenting, (7) Attachment, and (8) Play or Exploration.

Affective Neuroscience and Analysis of Emotional/Motivational Systems. Based on a neuroscience analysis, Panksepp [30] has argued for a set of emotional / motivational systems that partially overlap with the evolutionary analysis outlined above, as well as with some of the work on temperament and asymmetries in prefrontal activation. First, in agreement with other researchers' ideas about the BAS, Panksepp argues that all animals have what he terms a SEEKING system, which governs sensitivity to cues of reward and directs approach. Activation of this system leads to a feeling of energization and positive affect, which is distinct from the emotion that arises from the actual satisfaction of a goal. This is a general system that operates in the service of a number of specific goal systems.

There is also considerable evidence for a RAGE system, which is responsible for the anger or rage that an animal feels when frustrated. The strength of the RAGE response is often related to how strongly the SEEKING system was activated.

Unlike many others, Panksepp does not identify a general system for managing avoidance or sensitivity to threat. Instead, he identifies two systems that manage specific types of threat cues. First, there is a FEAR system, which is activated by physical threat. Second, there is the PANIC or separation-distress system, which manages social attachment, such as that between parent and child, or lovers. This system is activated by separation or the loss of a close relationship. Whereas separation leads to feelings of loss and fear, close contact results in the release of brain opioids that cause strong feelings of pleasure.

In humans, there is a separate CARE system that manages a variety of caretaking behaviors and governs bonding with the infant. Neuropeptides, such as prolactin and oxytocin, play a major role in governing it. There is also a LUST system, which manages mating behavior. LUST and the CARE system are tied together in a number of ways. For example, oxytocin seems to play a role in maternal behavior, such as nursing and bonding with the infant, while at the same time playing an important role in sexual behavior. Finally, Panksepp argues that there is a PLAY system, which governs rough and tumble play in juvenile members of a species, and which at various times will recruit a number of other systems so the developing organism can try them out and learn.

Clearly, many of the modules identified by both the evolutionary analysis and Panksepp's affective neuroscience analysis have strong parallels with trait domains. For instance, physical fear, fear of rejection, and hostility are all part of Neuroticism. Dominance, SEEKING, and gregariousness are all part of Extroversion. CARE, cooperation, coalition formation, attachment, and the social bonding component of the PANIC system are related to Agreeableness and Conscientiousness.

General Neurotransmitter Systems. There are also general neurotransmitter systems that have a wide impact on the brain. Individual differences in the levels of those neuro- transmitters would have wide ranging impacts on behavior. For example, serotonin levels influence essentially every function of the brain, typically playing an inhibitory role. Animals with higher levels of serotonin are more agreeable and less socially anxious; those with low levels of serotonin are irritable and prone to impulsive aggression.

Finally, a number of researchers have argued that dopamine plays a central role in the BAS or SEEKING system. Increasing dopamine levels lead to greater activation of that system and to increased exploration and vigor of approach.

2 Architecture of PAC

This work provides the basis for the translation of personality theory into a computational framework (i.e., PAC—Personality, Affect, and Culture). A number of relatively specific brain systems, with specific circuitry and neurotransmitters, manage a variety of different motivational domains and their related behavior. There is also evidence for high level approach and avoidance systems that integrate over the lower level systems [29]. This suggests that a complete model of personality and social behavior needs to have multiple levels. Research reviewed above provides evidence for a set of *level one emotional / motivational systems* that handle the variety of major adaptive challenges that people must incorporate and pursue in everyday life. Among these adaptive challenges are: (1) social bonding, (2) fear of social separation, (3) dominance and the development of authority relations in groups, (4) exploration and play, (5) caring and parenting, (6) mating, and (7) self-preservation and physical safety. Each of these challenges corresponds to a motivational system that organizes a set of more *specific motives*; these motive sets are the basis of specific traits.

At a more general level are *level two overarching motivational systems* -- a Behavioral *Approach* System (BAS), which governs sensitivity to reward and *approach* to rewarding stimuli, and a Behavioral *Inhibition* System (BIS), which governs sensitivity to punishment and *avoidance* of threat ([32], [37]). There is considerable evidence that the *level two motivational systems* provide a biological basis for at least two major dimensions of personality: Extroversion and Neuroticism.

In addition, there is evidence for a third brain system, the Disinhibition / Constraint system (DCS) that provides for a more general level (*level three*) of inhibitory control for the other systems [25]. Inhibition enforces selectivity among activated concepts by enhancing the differences in their activations (see [38]). Higher levels of inhibition result in greater differentiation among concepts, as only the most highly activated concepts will remain active. As a result, variability in strength of inhibition affects the likelihood that various concepts will play a role in cognition, motivation, and behavior. DCS, therefore, may determine the propensity of the system to remain goal-focused (thereby enacting more goal-directed behavior) versus highly reactive to and primarily controlled by changing environmental factors (producing behavior that appears more erratic, impulsive, or inconsistent).

Figure 1 shows the resulting three-level structure in PAC. Individual motives are activated as a result of interactions in and with changing situations. The activations of the motives are a function of:

1. the situation
2. experience (i.e., knowledge and memory), and
3. innate individual differences, represented by:
    a. baseline motive activations, which differ from person to person.

b. individual differences in the overall sensitivities of the BIS and BAS, which affect changing activations of individual motives
c. individual differences in the DCS, which moderate the activity level of the entire system and further focuses (or defocuses) motivations.

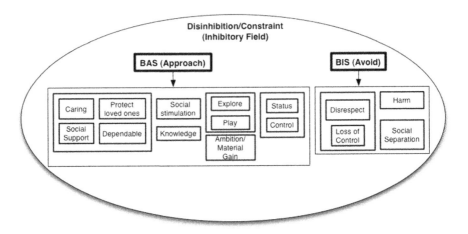

Fig. 1. Motive systems in PAC

2.1 Architecture and Implementation of PAC

The PAC architectural challenge was to integrate the motive framework (Figure 1 above) with a conventional cognitive architecture. This was done by integrating the motive-based processes as a deeper level set of processes. They operate in parallel to the constrained-rationality processes (e.g., the process by which people accomplish work tasks).

The personality-based processes focus on the evolving social situation and on generating and applying strategies to achieve the personal motives that are activated. An on-going social understanding process recognizes situational affordances to pursue specific motivations and activates corresponding motivations depending upon the person's baseline activation for that motive. For example, a person with a low baseline for dominance is less likely to recognize (or react to) situations that could afford increased dominance. Responses to the unfolding social situation can result in short term changes to activations of the motivations, which, in turn, may temporarily change the behavior of the system.

The subsymbolic personality model, which integrates situational understanding with baseline activations of the general motives and the BIS/BAS/DCS sensitivities, provides the central PAC personality subsystem. Its architecture is discussed below, but a prior discussion of how knowledge is organized in PAC is essential.

Knowledge as Story Structures. Knowledge within PAC is represented via an extensible set of generative story structures. These are used both to interpret others' behavior and to generate agents' behaviors. This representation was selected for several reasons. Miller and Read [23] have argued that a simple story is fundamental to the representation of most traits. Also, Read and Miller [24] further argue that a story structure is central to people's understanding of social interaction. And, story structures provide a structured, easily understood way for developers of PAC-based IVAs to represent social knowledge.

Collections of Plot Units (inspired by, but not identical to Lehnert [39]) provide the basis for the representation of a story in PAC: These capture a piece of the story line and the various ways in which it might play out. Each Plot Unit is composed of a series of interconnected Action Structures and Behavioral Options.

At the micro-level, the 'Action Structure' provides a representation of an intended action in the causal-chronological sequence that makes up the Plot Unit. The Action Structure specifies such elements as the agent (WHO), the act (DOES-WHAT), the modality of action (HOW), and the setting (WHERE /WHEN). It also specifies the *opportunities* that different possible evolutions of the story afford for application of the motives in the PAC model. These *motive implications* of the action structure represent the implications that that action structure has for the agent's motives.

The Plot Units (and the stories that they comprise) show the expected changes of the story and are represented from the perspective of a given agent. PAC views story structures as both a model for *understanding behavior* (mapping the perceived action as an instance of one of the Action Structures available at that point in the story) and a model for *generating behavior* (selecting the Behavioral Options from the current Action Structure that are most consistent with that character/agent's motives).

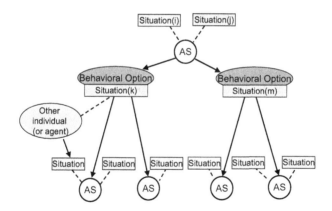

Fig. 2. Plot Units as Inherently Interactive Structures

Each 'next step' in alternative evolutions of the story leads to a different Behavioral Option that is connected to the Action Structure. The Behavioral Option both represents execution of the action and points to the appropriate Action Structure that would occur next. Thus, just as an Action Structure can lead to multiple Behavioral Options, a Behavioral Option can lead to multiple future Action Structures. This gives the story structure a semi-lattice form because two (or more)

Behavioral Options can lead to the same future situation in the external world and thus lead back to a single Action Option. The Plot Units (and the full stories) show all the expected evolutions of the story and are represented from the ego-centric view of the agent. Thus, for interactions to occur, there must be some general mapping of the plot units that are understood by the two actors.

As noted above, PAC views story structures as both a model for generating behavior and a model for understanding behavior as it unfolds. Thus, each agent uses the story structure: (a) to recognize and interpret what each agent/other has done, by mapping the perceived action as an instance of one of the Action Structures available at that point in the story, and (b) to generate new behaviors by selecting the Behavioral Options from the current Action Structures that are most consistent with that agent's motives.

Subsymbolic Personality Model. The story structures afford opportunities for PAC IVAs to exhibit specific personality traits. For example, a part of the story may afford the opportunity for a strongly assertive person to exert leadership, but at the same time may afford opportunity for an insecure person to accept projected authority and be led. The subsymbolic personality mechanism controls the process by which traits of the individual are exhibited in this process. This model is described below. This component is termed the PAC Motive Interpreter (see Figure 3).

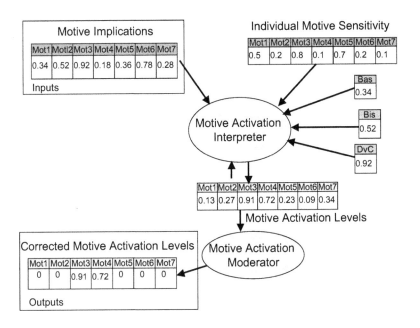

Fig. 3. PAC Motive Interpreter

As the Action Structure is processed, the Motive Interpreter calculates the motive activations for each motive. The next behavior of an agent is selected as a function of the agent's current motive activations and the motive implications of the alternative behaviors. Throughout, the motive interpreter concurrently operates on three types of data:

1. motive implications from the current action structure (values between 0 and 1 corresponding to the relevance of an action structure to a specific motive),
2. a set of predefined individual motive *baseline activations* representing the innate tendency of the individual being simulated to pursue that motive given the opportunity, and
3. three *sensitivity levels* associated with the BIS, BAS, and DCS mechanisms.

The motive interpreter calculates its (new) level of activation R for each motive by using one of two formulas. If an action structure includes a motive implication for this motive, the first formula is used:

$$R = 1 - \frac{1}{1 + \gamma[I + S - DvC]_+} \qquad (1)$$

Where: $[x]_+ = x$ if $x > 0$ and $[x]_+ = 0$ if $x <= 0$; I is the motive implication as provided by the current action structure, S is the individual sensitivity for this motive, *gamma* (γ) is for either the BIS or BAS depending on the type of motive.

Formula (1) adjusts the activations to meet the opportunities afforded in the current Action Structure. If the current Action Structure has no motive implication for a particular motive, a second formula below is used that implements a decay mechanism that progressively returns the activation level to the individual baseline level:

$$R_n = k(S - R_{n-1}) + R_{n-1} \qquad (2)$$

Where: R_n is the resulting level of activation of the motive for the n cycle and, R_{n-1} the activation level at the previous cycle, k is a decay factor, and S is the individual baseline activation for this motive.

2.2 Initial Evaluation and Test

The initial implementation of PAC is presented in Zachary et al. ([40], [41]), along with discussion of IVA simulations of a simple counter-insurgency scenario based on the Iraqi cultural familiarization game VECTOR [42]. In PAC all characters use the same knowledge representation, in the form of a set of shared stories about how interaction should or could unfold, but they vary in their 'role' in those stories and in their underlying personality (as defined above). The simulations reported in Zachary et al. [41] demonstrated that PAC-based IVAs with identical knowledge would generate a broad range of plausible behavior in the same situation simply based on their underlying personalities, expressed as differing motive and motive-control parameters. Further simulations [43] using the same game environment showed the ability of PAC agents to experience and express different emotions, based on varying personality parameters and varying activation thresholds for different emotions. Thus, the PAC architecture 'works' in the sense of creating a general mechanism for personality and emotion that could be used to generate behavioral variability attributable to personality.

3 Discussion

The PAC architecture incorporates neuroscience results and theories through subsymbolic mechanisms such as the motive activation/interpretation process and attendant motive control mechanisms. At the same time, PAC does so in a way that integrates with symbolic level mechanisms. In particular, the story representation and situation understanding are symbolic structures that provide both the stimuli for the motive activation process *and* the links to the (bounded-rationality) symbol processing mechanisms that generate the stream of agent behavior that expresses personality. This tight integration between symbolic and neuroscience-based mechanisms represents a major step forward. Classical neuroscience methods such as neural nets are, in contrast, very difficult to integrate with symbolic architectures for IVA behavioral representation and generation. Similarly, conventional symbolic cognitive architectures have great difficulty integrating with neuroscience representations. A counter example perhaps can be found in John Anderson's ACT-R/PM, system, but even there the integration between symbolic and subsymbolic mechanisms is carefully limited to the representation of memory. In contrast, PAC, and the theory which underlies it, attempts a much greater integration of the broad biological systems which give rise to personality in people, with the fundamentally symbolic processes which are involved in virtually all volitional behavior.

References

1. André, E., Rist, T., van Mulken, S., Klesen, M., & Baldes, S. (2000). The automated design of believable dialogues for animated presentation teams. In Cassell, J., Sullivan, J., Prevost, S., & Churchill, E.. (Eds.). *Embodied conversational agents*. Cambridge, MA: MIT Press.
2. Badler, N. I., Reich, B. D., & Weber, B. L. (1997). Towards personalities for animated agents with reactive and planning behaviors. In R. Trappl & P. Petta (Eds.). *Creating Personalities for Synthetic Actors: Towards Autonomous Personality Agents.* (p. 43-57). Berlin: Springer-Verlag.
3. Ball, G., & Breese, J. (2000). Emotion and Personality in a conversational agent. In Cassell, J., Sullivan, J., Prevost, S., & Churchill, E. (Eds.). *Embodied conversational agents*. (pp. 189-219). Cambridge, MA: MIT Press.
4. Goldberg, A. (1997). IMPROV: A system for real-time animation of behavior-based interactive synthetic actors. In R. Trappl & P. Petta (Eds.). *Creating Personalities for Synthetic Actors: Towards Autonomous Personality Agents.* (p. 58-73). Berlin: Springer-Verlag.
5. Rousseau, D. and Hayes-Roth, B. A Social-Psychological Model for Synthetic Actors. *Proceedings of the Second International Conference on Autonomous Agents.* Minneapolis, MN, May 1998.
6. Bates, J. (1994). The role of emotion in believable characters. *Communications of the ACM, 37, 7.*
7. Bates, J. and A. Loyall, & W. Reilly (1992) Integrating Reactivity, Goals and Emotions in a Broad Agent. *Proceedings of the 14th Annual Conference of the Cognitive Science Society.* Indiana.
8. Loyall, A. B. (1997). Some requirements and approaches for natural language in a believable agent. In R. Trappl & P. Petta (Eds.). *Creating Personalities for Synthetic Actors: Towards Autonomous Personality Agents.* (p. 113-119). Berlin: Springer-Verlag.

9. Reilly, W. S. N. (1996). *Believable Social and Emotional Agents.* Ph.D. Dissertation. Carnegie-Mellon University.
10. Blumberg, B. (1994). Action-Selection in Hamsterdam: Lessons from Ethology. In D. Cliff, P. Husbands, J.A. Meyer, and S.W. Wilson, (Eds) *From Animals To Animats, Proceedings of the Third International Conference on the Simulation of Adaptive Behavior,* MIT Press, Cambridge Ma.
11. Maes, P. (1990a). Situated Agents Can Have Goals. *Journal of Robotics and Autonomous Systems, 6*(1&2).
12. Maes, P. (1990b). How to do the right thing. *Connection Science Journal,* 1(3), 293-325.
13. Moffat, D. (1997). Personality parameters and programs. In R. Trappl & P. Petta (Eds.). *Creating Personalities for Synthetic Actors: Towards Autonomous Personality Agents.* (p. 120-165). Berlin: Springer-Verlag.
14. Mischel, W. (1973). Toward a cognitive social learning reconceptualizaton of personality. *Psychological Review, 80,* 252-283.
15. Gratch, J. & Marsella, S. (2004). A Domain-independent framework for modeling emotion. *Journal of Cognitive Systems Research, 5(4),* 269-306.
16. Digman, J. M. (1997). Higher-order factors of the Big Five. *Journal of Personality and Social Psychology, 73,* 1246-1256.
17. Goldberg, L. R. (1981). Language and individual differences: The search for universals in personality lexicons. In L. Wheeler (Ed.), *Review of personality and social psychology: Vol. 2* (pp. 141-165). Beverly Hills, CA: Sage.
18. John, O. P., & Srivastava, S., (1999). The Big Five Trait taxonomy: History, Measurement, and Theoretical Perspectives. In L. A. Pervin & O. P. John (Eds.). *Handbook of Personality: Theory and Research (2nd edition).* (pp. 102-138). New York: Guilford Press.
19. McCrae, R. R., & Costa, P. T., Jr. (1999). A Five-Factor Theory of Personality. In L. A. Pervin & O. P. John (Eds.). *Handbook of Personality: Theory and Research (2nd edition).* (pp. 139-153). New York: Guilford Press.
20. Tellegen, A., & Waller, N. G. (1997). Exploring personality through test construction: Development of the Multidimensional Personality Questionnaire. In S. R. Briggs, J. M. Cheek, & E. M. Donohue (Eds.), *Handbook of adult personality inventories.* New York: Plenum Press.
21. Wiggins, J. S., & Trapnell, P. D. (1996). A dyadic-interactional perspective on the five-factor model. In J. S. Wiggins (Ed.). *The five-factor model of personality: Theoretical perspectives* (pp. 88-162). New York: Guilford Press.
22. Miller, L. C., & Read, S. J. (1987). Why am I telling you this? Self-disclosure in a goal-based model of personality. In V. Derlega & J. Berg (Eds.). *Self-disclosure: Theory, Research, and Therapy,* (pp. 35-58). New York: Plenum.
23. Miller, L. C., & Read, S. J. (1991). On the coherence of mental models of persons and relationships: A knowledge structure approach. In G. J. O. Fletcher & F. Fincham (Eds.), *Cognition in Close Relationships.* (pp. 69-99). Hillsdale, NJ: Erlbaum.
24. Read, S. J., & Miller, L. C. (1989). Inter-personalism: Toward a goal-based theory of persons in relationships. In L. Pervin (Ed.), *Goal concepts in personality and social psychology* (pp. 413-472). Hillsdale, NJ: Erlbaum.
25. Clark, L. A., & Watson, D. (1999). Temperament: A New Paradigm for Trait Psychology. In L. A. Pervin & O. P. John (Eds.). *Handbook of Personality: Theory and Research (2nd edition).* (pp. 399-423). New York: Guilford Press.
26. Pickering, A. D., & Gray, J. A. (1999). The Neuroscience of Personality. In L. A. Pervin & O. P. John (Eds.). *Handbook of Personality: Theory and Research (2nd edition).* (pp. 277-299). New York: Guilford Press.

27. Rothbart, M. K., & Bates, J. E. (1998). Temperament. In W. Damon (Series Ed.) & N. Eisenberg (Vol. Ed.), *Handbook of Child Psychology: Vol. 3. Social, emotional, and personality development.* (5th ed.) (pp. 105-176). New York: Wiley.

28. Davidson, R. J., Jackson, D. C., & Kalin, N. H. (2000). Emotion, Plasticity, Context, and Regulation: Perspectives from Affective Neuroscience. *Psychological Bulletin, 126,* 890-909.

29. Cacioppo, J. T., Gardner, W. L., & Berntson, G. G. (1999). The affect system has parallel and integrative processing components: Form follows function. *Journal of Personality and Social Psychology, 76,* 839-855.

30. Panksepp, J. (1998). *Affective Neuroscience: The Foundations of Human and Animal Emotions.* New York: Oxford University Press.

31. Hofstee, W. K. B., de Raad, B., & Goldberg, L. R. (1992). Integration of the Big-Five and circumplex approaches to trait structure. *Journal of Personality and Social Psychology, 63,* 146-163.

32. Gray, J. A. (1987). *The Psychology of Fear and Stress.* (2nd Ed). New York: Cambridge..

33. Zuckerman, M. (2005). *Psychobiology of personality* (2nd ed.). Cambridge, England: Cambridge University Press.

34. Depue, R. A., & Collins, P. F. (1999). Neurobiology of the structure of personality: Dopamine, facilitation of incentive motivation and extraversion. *Behavioral and Brain Sciences, 22,* 491-569.

35. Bugental, D. B. (2000). Acquisition of the algorithms of social life: A domain-based approach. *Psychological Bulletin, 126,* 187-219.

36. Fiske, A. P. (1992). The four elementary forms of sociality: Framework for a unified theory of social relations. *Psychological Review, 99,* 689-723.

37. Depue, R. A. (1996). A neurobiological framework for the structure of personality and emotion: Implications for personality disorders. In J. Clarkin & M. Lenzenweger (Eds.) *Major theories of personality disorders* (pp. 347-390). New York: Guilford Press.

38. Nigg, J. T. (2000). On inhibition/disinhibition in developmental psychopathology: Views from cognitive and personality psychology and a working inhibition taxonomy. *Psychological Bulletin, 126,* 220-246.

39. Lehnert, W. G. (1981). Plot units and summarization. *Cognitive Science, 4,* 293-331.

40. Zachary, W., LeMentec, J-C., Miller, L. C., Read, S. J., & Thomas-Meyers, G. (2005a). Steps toward a Personality-based Architecture for Cognition. *Proceedings of the 14th Annual Conference on Behavioral Representation in Modeling and Simulation.* Orlando, FL: IST.

41. Zachary, W., Le Mentec, J.-C., Miller, L.C., Read, S. J., & Thomas-Meyers, G. (2005b). Human behavioral representations with realistic personality and cultural characteristics. *Proceedings of the Tenth International Command and Control Research and Technology Symposium,* McLean, VA.

42. McCollum, C., Deaton, J., Barba, C., Santarelli, T., Singer, M., & Kerr, B. (2004) Developing an immersive, cultural training system. *The Proceedings I/ITSEC 2004.* Arlington , VA : National Training Systems Association.

43. Read, S.J., Miller, L.S., Rosoff, A., Eilbert, J., Iordanov, V., LeMentec, J.-C., and Zachary, W. (2006) Integrating Emotional Dynamics into the PAC Cognitive Architecture. In *Proceedings of the 15th Annual Conference on Behavioral Representation in Modeling and Simulation,* Orlando, FL: Institute for Simulation and Training.

Feeling Ambivalent: A Model of Mixed Emotions for Virtual Agents

Benny Ping-Han Lee[1], Edward Chao-Chun Kao[1], and Von-Wun Soo[1,2]

AI laboratory in
[1] Institute of Information and System Applications
National Tsing Hua University
101 Section 2, Guangfu Road, 300 Hsinchu, Taiwan
[2] Department of Computer Engineering and Information Science,
National University of Kaohsiung
700, Kaohsiung University Road, 811 Kaohsiung, Taiwan
{bennylee, edkao, soo}@cs.nthu.edu.tw

Abstract. Mixed emotions, especially those in conflict, sway agent decisions and result in dramatic changes in social scenarios. However, the emotion models and architectures for virtual agents are not yet advanced enough to be imbued with coexisting emotions. In this paper, an improved emotion model integrated with decision making algorithms is proposed to deal with two topics: the generation of coexisting emotions, and the resolution to ambivalence, in which two emotions conflict. A scenario of ambivalence is provided to illustrate the process of agent's decision-making.

1 Introduction

In addition to rational reasoning, emotions are considered as a central component in architectures of virtual agents to express believability. Emotions affect deliberation of virtual agents by changing their beliefs, resulting in different decisions from rational ones. Each behavior of a virtual agent will be determined by not only its expected utility value, but also the emotion state of the agent. Researches about virtual agents with emotions have been conducted [1][12], and have shown the indispensability of emotions to account for the believability. Current emotion theories [2][7] applied to virtual agents discussed about only the presence of a single emotion state at a time. However, dramatic changes in decisions are often made due to multiple states of mixed emotions that are sometimes in conflict. For example, in the cases of "Plank of Carneades"[1], or the Four Tragedies of Shakespeare, the appraisal of each critical decision is influenced by manifold emotions, rather than only one.

This paper proposes an advanced emotion model to represent states of mixed emotions, which are integrated into a formal decision making mechanism. This model

---

[1] Two people are shipwrecked on the seas and about to drown. One man luckily reaches a wooden plank while another does not. However, the plank is too small to save them both. Saving one's own life means sacrificing the other's.

J. Gratch et al. (Eds.): IVA 2006, LNAI 4133, pp. 329–342, 2006.
© Springer-Verlag Berlin Heidelberg 2006

attempts to clarify types of mixed emotions, and to apply them to simulate the decision making under complex and even conflicted conditions. Nevertheless, due to the limitation of the paper length, only ambivalence, the most important type of mixed emotions, is to be discussed in more details in this paper.

This model of mixed emotion, which is known as Simultaneous Emotion Elicitation Model (SEEM), enables virtual agents to elicit emotions concurrently and take them into account during decision making process. As a result, the decision making processes may lead the agent to pursue an acceptable solution to resolve ambivalence when it is perceived.

The rest of this paper is organized as follows. Section 2 introduces the theoretical foundation of mixed emotions. In section 3, we define the generation process of mixed emotions with SEEM. Section 4 proposes a scenario, in which the virtual actor encounters ambivalence. We conclude in section 5.

2   The Foundation of Mixed Emotions

The idea of emotional agents has been introduced during the last 10 years, but mixed emotions have been an important research topic in other fields such as cognitive science and psychology [8] for a very long period. Section 2.1 describes the related works both in psychology and computer science.

2.1   Related Work

The concept of mixed emotions is defined as having multiple emotions simultaneously. While early psychologists disputed against this concept [8], researchers in computer science have also argued their ideas. In Affective Computing [14], Picard proposed a scenario of mixed emotions, which described a runner's feeling after winning a marathon. The metaphor of "a tub of warm water by mixing hot and cold water" was accounted the medium state of bipolarity emotions. The emotions which arise from different mechanisms can coexist, but there can be only one for those elicited from the same mechanism.

Moreover, recent researches [8][15] have shown more evidences that emotions do occur simultaneously, rather than one at a time. Larsen et al. [8] selected three scenarios which were thought to be able to stimulate mixed emotions effectively to test that if participants could feel both happy and sad at the same time, and positive results were found. Schimmack and Colcombe [15] made a similar experiment with pictures to observe participants' emotional responses, and found the coexistence of pleasure and sadness.

On the other hand, a large portion of emotional agents such as [5][6] were developed based on the OCC model [13] because of its organized structure of emotions. The OCC model classifies emotions into a cognitive structure which divides the events of world into three main aspects, consequences of events, actions of agents, and aspects of objects (including agents). Each aspect runs out the related emotions by more detailed aspects and factors. Affect Reasoner [5] stands as one of the most famous work based on the OCC model. It adopted a method of goal-based appraisal and used a frame named Emotion Eliciting Condition (EEC) to elicit proper emotions. However, the EEC must be written in terms of a fixed, event-specific script. Even though Affective Reasoner mentioned conflicting feelings, it only addressed how to express them in terms of gestures and facial expressions. Émile [6] extended the advantages of Affective Reasoner to build agents based on the plan appraisal rather than the single events. While Affective Reasoner and Émile allowed the coexistence of emotions, the decision making in such circumstances was not further elaborated. Cathexis [16] was implemented with a relevant mechanism that, in the state of mixed emotions, the intensity of one emotion might influence the intensities of others. In FLAME [4], El-Nasr et al. applied fuzzy logic to appraise events, and proposed the idea that both coexisting emotions and emotion conflicts were used to calculate the mood. Carofiglio et al. [3], which is the closest to our model, focused on the generation of mixed emotions by dynamic belief networks, In contrast, our model focus on dealing with the effects of mixed emotions.

Some related works discussed above showed a potential of elaborating the OCC model to incorporate mixed emotions. To extend the OCC model for our use, the modification of emotions toward others is pointed out and is described in section 2.2. After modifying the OCC model, a phenomenon of coexisting emotions is discussed in section 2.3.

2.2 Social Emotions

The first modification to the OCC model is to allow the definition of different emotions with respect to others, which is known as social emotions. Social emotions can be defined as one's emotions projecting on or affected by others. While most of the emotions listed in the OCC model were social and hence implicitly assumed social relations, it did not explain the correspondence between the social emotions and the social relations, and it even lacked for the definition of social emotions about others' future.

In the OCC model, an event related to self can be divided into prospect-relevant and prospect-irrelevant, in order to trigger emotions at current and future status, respectively. However, emotions to others' future status can not be triggered in the OCC model when an event related to others happens. In our extended OCC model, an additional component with emotions "expect" and "worry" are added. As a result, this component in the extended OCC model is enhanced with explicit definitions of social relations and will be discussed in details in section 3.3.

2.3 Ambivalence

The effect of emotion conflicts, or ambivalence, is found to be uncomfortable [10][11]. In our view, ambivalence should not be defined directly from the taxonomy of emotions in the OCC model. The most important reason is that, in specific environments that an agent may be situated, ambivalence may be the consequence of instances from the same kind of emotion. For example, after receiving his salary, the agent's action of buying a dream notebook with all of his salary will cause him to feel ambivalent about it. In the view of emotion bipolarity, mixed emotions may be constituted of emotion instances from not only the opposite sides (positive or negative), but also the identical side, or even the same emotion. However, there is a basic principle to follow before presenting the definitions of ambivalence. The principle is that human beings always tend to desire for pleasure (positive emotions) and avert from pain (negative emotions)[2]. In terms of virtual agents, it implies that they will take some compensation actions to avoid negative emotions and take some reinforced actions to turn towards positive emotions.

Therefore, we adopt a new practical definition on ambivalence in this paper. We propose that, agent's "feeling" of ambivalence can be due to its envision on a future conflict by effects from compensation or reinforcement actions. This is called prospect-based ambivalence. Here we define two situations of prospect-related ambivalence, which are examined throughout this paper. First we define basic notations:

$$e \in E, \ g \in G, \ a \in A,$$

In the assertion above, e is an element of E which denotes an emotion set; a is an element of A which denotes an action set, and g is an element of G which denotes a goal set.

Definition of Situation 1

$$\exists e_1, \ a_1, \ g_1, \ e_1^{a_1} \ Violate(a_1, \ g_1) \Rightarrow \exists e_2^{a_1} \ Ambivalence(e_1^{a_1}, \ e_2^{a_1}) \tag{1}$$

In the assertion of situation 1, e_1 denotes an emotion and a_1 is an action to compensate/reinforce e_1.[3] The emotions which are aroused by executing a_1 denotes $e_1^{a_1}$ and $e_2^{a_1}$. The $e_1^{a_1}$ means the emotion which can be compensated/reinforced by executing a_1 and $e_2^{a_1}$ means the emotion which can be due to the violation or achievement of a goal by executing a_1. The *Violate* predicate asserts that the effect of a_1 violates the precondition of a goal (g_1) and the *Ambivalence* predicate asserts that two emotions are in conflict. Then the situation 1 can be explained as:

Situation 1: if there exists $e_1, \ a_1, \ g_1, \ e_1^{a_1}$ such that a_1 violates g_1 then it implies there exists $e_2^{a_1}$ such that $e_1^{a_1}$ and $e_2^{a_1}$ are ambivalent.

For example, when one pities (e_1) on one's friend being hurt in a car accident and wants to drive friend to hospital (a_1) in order to compensate one's pity ($e_1^{a_1}$), one may feel a fear ($e_2^{a_1}$) that driving to a hospital will cause one's absence from final examination (g_1).

Definition of Situation 2

$$When \ \exists a_1, \ a_2, \ e_1^{a_1}, \ e_2^{a_2}$$

$$Ambivalence(e_1^{a_1}, e_2^{a_2}) \Leftrightarrow Competing(a_1, \ a_2) \tag{2}$$

---

[2] This policy is derived from hedonics.
[3] As in section 3.4, we also assume the principle of hedonics, so an agent will always choose an action to compensate negative emotions, or to reinforce positive emotions.

In the assertion of situation 2, initial emotions, compensating actions, and action-aroused emotions are similar to the assertion of situation 1. The only difference is the binary predicate *COMPETING* that indicates that two actions are competing with each other in the sense that they might compete for a conflicting resource or goal. The situation 2 is then explained as:

Situation 2: When there exists e_1, e_2, a_1, a_2, $e_1^{a_1}$ and $e_2^{a_2}$, $e_1^{a_1}$ and $e_2^{a_2}$ are ambivalent if and only if a_1 and a_2 are competing with each other. We can take the former example, buying a notebook with a whole salary, to elaborate situation 2. When we hope (e_1) to deposit money (a_1) and hope (e_2) to buy a dream notebook (a_2), we will feel ambivalent if and only if deposit money and buy a dream notebook are competing.

3   The Generation of Mixed Emotions

Armed with the concepts of social emotions and ambivalence, the virtual agents are allowed to process events to generate emotions simultaneously.

3.1   Simultaneous Emotion Elicitation Model (SEEM)

SEEM is a network-based model composed of three layers. Its input nodes stand as factors to elicit emotions, and its output nodes represent intensities of various emotions. The total stimulation from all related factors is shown as follows:

$$x_i = \sum W_{j,i} f_j \tag{3}$$

In equation (3), f denotes factors of emotions as the input nodes, and W denotes the weight between input and its linked node which can be a summary factor in the second layer or intensities of emotions, the output nodes. The x_i is the stimulation to emotion i. We adopt the sigmoid function in Affective Computing [14] to calculate the intensity of stimulus x_i:

$$I_i = g /(1 + e^{-(x_i - x_0)/s}) + I_0 \tag{4}$$

In equation (4), e denotes Euler number. Here we take g as the saturation, and minimum, I_0, as the bounds of emotion intensity. The parameter x_i denotes the stimulus of emotion i and the parameter x_0 denotes the inflection point. The shape of curve is controlled by s. The larger the s is, the smoother the curve is, and vice versa. In final, I_i denotes the intensity of emotion i. In this paper, we assume the largest saturated intensity of an emotion is 1 in our theory of ambivalence that will be described later. This assumption will set up g smaller than 1.

Emotion elicitations by enhanced OCC model. To simplify the representations of SEEM, the graphs of components in SEEM is shown in figures below to illustrate the interactions among factors and emotions. All figures of this subsection have four layers from bottom to top, respectively. The first layer is input layer, which consists of basic factors that directly appraise events, actions, and objects. The second layer stands as synthesis layer, including desirability, undesirability, praiseworthiness, and blameworthiness. Any of the factors in the synthesis layer may be affected by social relations when its input factor is related to others. In the third layer, the output layer, emotions receive the value from input layer and second layer and output its intensity. More complex emotions are even subject to emotions in the third layer, and thus form the fourth compound layer. While the categories of emotions are many, in the hedonic point of view, emotions are classified into positive emotions and negative ones, and so are the factors and social relations. At first, it may be intuitive to see that positive emotions can only be aroused by positive factors, and so do the negative emotions. However, when dealing with stimuli from others, social relations must be taken into account to calculate their actual contributions. These factors are inspired by Affect Reasoner [5] and OCC model [13]. However, we make our extension to build a more elaborated and flexible virtual agent. The factors of SEEM are listed in table 1 and the components in our extended OCC model are described as follows.

Table 1. Factors of SEEM

d	desirability	p	praiseworthiness	pr	positive relationship
ds	desirability of self	ps	praiseworthiness of self	n	negative relationship
do	desirability of others	po	praiseworthiness of others	c	chance
ud	undesirability	b	blameworthiness	r	result
uds	undesirability of self	bs	blameworthiness of self	pl	pleasingness
udo	undesirability of others	bo	blameworthiness of others	dpl	displeasingness

Emotions of WELLBEING. This component includes joy and distress, which respectively characterize positive and negative changes about one's own utility, the status of well-being. The factors to emotions in WELLBEING component are: desirability of self, undesirability of self, desirability of others, undesirability of others, pleasingness, and displeasingness.

While the pleasingness may directly come from agent's utility value, the desirability and undesirability depend on both stimuli from self and others. With this extended model, an agent may feel joyful because others inform it that its current status is pretty well. An experiment in The Emotional Brain [9] implies a similar idea.

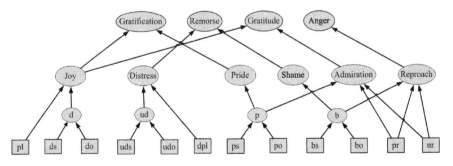

Fig. 1. Component of WELLBEING, ATTRIBUTION, and COMPOUNDS

Emotions of PROSPECT-BASED FOR SELF. This component includes emotions about one's future status, which are hope and fear, and the following emotions after revealing the actual situation, which are satisfaction, fear-confirmed, and their opposites, disappointment and relief, respectively. Factors related to this component are the same as in WELLBEING with two extra ones, which are the probability for the expected status to happen, and achievement rate of this expectation. In the appendix, we use a factor chance (c) to indicate the probability and a factor result (r) to indicate the achievement rate.

Take buying a lottery for example. We may hold the hope of being the biggest winner before running a lottery. When it turns out that we just win a small prize after running a lottery, we may still feel satisfaction that we win a little money and feel disappointment that we did not win the biggest prize. Before the confirmation point – running a lottery, the factor chance influences the intensity of hope; after the confirmation point, the factor result influences the intensity of satisfaction.

The result of achieving a goal can be gradually incremental and it means we may achieve our goal partially. When a goal is partially achieved, it can elicit satisfaction and disappointment at the same time. In the lottery example, if we win 300 dollars and the biggest prize is 1,000 dollars, the achievement rate is 300/1,000 – 30% and this rate can influence the intensity of satisfaction. On the other hand, the non-achievement rate 70% (1-30%) influences the intensity of disappointment. However, if the goal result is binary, the achievement rate is then either 100% or 0%, and the agent can only feel either completely satisfied, or completely disappointed about the final result. For example, if one agent's goal is to join a marathon and become the winner, then this goal is either achieved completely or not at all.

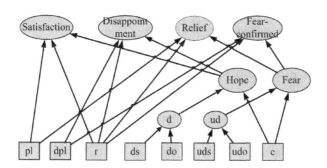

Fig. 2. Component of PROSPECT-BASED FOR SELF

Emotions of FORTUNE OF OTHERS. This component is an analogy to WELLBEING with respect to other agents, which includes happy-for, sorry-for, resentment and gloating. The social relations between self and the subject agent must be considered. According to the original OCC model, we also classify the social relations into two distinct categories, which are positive (friend) and negative (foe).

In brief, the agent will feel happy/sorry for its friend when something desirable/undesirable to its friend happens to its friend (and hence changing its utility). On the other hand, the agent will feel resentment/gloating toward its enemy in the same situation.

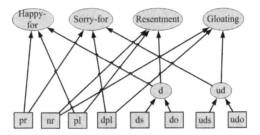

Fig. 3. Component of FORTUNE OF OTHERS

PROSPECT-BASED FOR OTHERS. This component is an analogy to PROSPECT-BASED FOR SELF with respect to other agents. It includes emotions about others' future status, which are expect and worry, and emotions of others' current status, which are those in FORTUNE OF OTHERS. In addition, this component also adds positive relation and negative relation like in FORTUNE OF OTHERS.

After introducing adding positive and negative relation factors, the elicitation of emotions in this component becomes more complex. For example, the factors of worry are desirability, undesirability, positive relationship and negative relationship. These factors can be divided into two pairs, (undesirability, positive relation) and (desirability, negative relation), which both elicit the emotion of worry. The former will elicit worry about a friend's getting undesirable outcome, and the latter will elicit worry about an enemy's getting its desirable outcome. The emotion of expect works in a similar way, just the pairs become (desirability, positive relation) and (undesirability, negative relation).

ATTRIBUTION. The component includes emotions of pride, shame, admiration, and reproach. These emotions arouse only when the agent appraises at the result of an action set by either its own or others'. The factors related to ATTRIBUTION are praiseworthiness of self, blameworthiness of self, praiseworthiness of others, and blameworthiness of others.

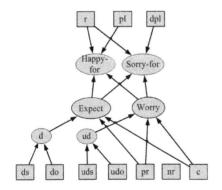

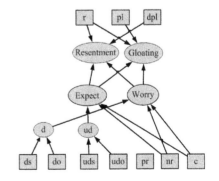

Fig. 4. Component of PROSPECT-BASED FOR OTHERS (for positive relationship)

Fig. 5. Component of PROSPECT-BASED FOR OTHERS (for negative relationship)

Emotions toward others in this component would be further influenced by their social relations with the agent itself. The agent would tend to admire more about its friend's praiseworthy action, and to reproach more for its enemy's blameworthy action.

COMPOUNDS. The COMPOUNDS component includes emotions of gratification, remorse, gratitude, and anger. These emotions are the compounds of WELLBEING and ATTRIBUTION. When a consequence of an event is caused by an action, the compound emotions will be elicited. For example, if an agent is attacked by its enemy, it may feel unhappy about getting hurt, reproach to its enemy's attack and feel angry about this situation. The intensities of emotions in this component are influenced by the intensities of emotions of WELLBEING and ATTRIBUTION.

ATTRACTION. The ATTRACTION component includes emotions of appealingness and disappealingness to objects. The appealingness controls love and the disappealingness controls hate. The weight of links in this component can be seen as how easy of an agent would like something. Agents might also develop both love and hate emotions at the same time based on the different characteristics of the same object.

3.2 Solutions to Ambivalence

According to the definition of ambivalence in Section 2.3, ambivalence sways the decisions of agents. First, the degree of ambivalence stimulus can be derived from this function:

$$x_{ia}=\text{diminish}(\text{difference}(I_1,I_2)) \tag{5}$$

Since there is no exact definition for the intensity of eliciting ambivalence, we assume it to be a function of the difference of intensities between contradictory emotions. The inner function *difference()* calculates how close the intensities of contradictory emotions, I_1 and I_2, are. Later, the outer function *diminish()* reduces the degree of difference through the degree of I_1 and I_2. The reason for using this function is that we assume the intensity of ambivalence will decrease if the intensities of contradictory emotions are weak. So the x_{ia} denotes the degree of ambivalence stimulus and this stimulus will be substituted for x_i in function 4 to get the intensity of ambivalence, I_a. Ambivalence degree stands as an indicator for the agent whether to take a different action set to resolve this ambivalence.

After defining the stimulus of ambivalence, we would like to discuss how people solve their ambivalence in empirical aspect. Take situation 1 as an example. When an action is chosen to be performed with both positive and negative effects on emotion, people would feel ambivalent. The stronger is the intensity of feeling ambivalent, the more likely people would abandon their original action and seek for a new action. On the other hand, while the ambivalence feeling is weak or null, it will be ignored and the original action would be executed. This decision-making process of human would be the basis of our resolving algorithm.

Due to limited computational power, we assume that there is always a time constraint to force agents to make a decision in an ambivalent state. If there is no time constraint and the action sets of an agent are very large, the agent may keep searching or planning a best solution to overcome this ambivalent state for a very long time. So a time constraint is added to the following resolution algorithms to conform the cases in the real world. Within the time constraint, the solving methods of ambivalence are based on a greedy search. One of the reasons for using a greedy search is its time complexity. If we want to find an optimal action set to resolve ambivalence, the best solution is to find all action sets and choose a best one. Let n denotes the number of action sets and m denotes the number of goals, we need a time complexity $\Theta(n*m)$ to evaluate each action set. However, this time complexity is not allowed in virtual environment. If we apply a greedy search whose time complexity is $\Theta(m)$, we can promise to find an acceptable action set in time.

Based on the two ambivalent situations described in section 2.3, the resolutions are provided as follows.

Resolution to Ambivalence in Situation 1. In situation 1, the feeling of ambivalence is emerged form the best compensation/reinforcement action set, a of e_1. So the strategy for resolving situation 1 should be focused on compensating/reinforcing on e_1. While the intensity of ambivalence is calculated by equation (5), its parameters I_1 and I_2 are the intensities of e_1^a and e_2^a.

Step 1: Compare I_a (intensity of ambivalence), I_1 and I_2. If I_1 is not the largest one, the agent should take step 2, otherwise exit to condition 1.

Step 2: Find the next best action set which compensates/reinforces e_1 and assign to a. Update I_1 when a is updated.

Step 3: The action set a should be tested against all current goals of the agent again. If we find a violation again, we should recount I_a and I_2 with a new I_1, and calculate the hedonic value of action set in step 3. The hedonic value, which is a simple addition of emotion intensities to evaluate an action set, will be calculated as I_1 + I_2. After calculating the hedonic value, it returns to step 1 to compare new intensities.

This loop will execute recursively until either of the following two conditions is satisfied:

Condition 1: In step 1, I_1 is the largest emotion then the action set should be executed immediately. This condition includes that there is no violated goal.

Condition 2: Time runs out. The intensity of ambivalence will not longer be considered. The action set with largest hedonic value among those searched before will be chosen and executed only if the hedonic value is larger than zero. Otherwise, the agent just gives up compensating/reinforcing e_1. A detailed pseudo code for solving the ambivalence in situation 1 is shown below.

Resolution to Ambivalence in Situation 2. In situation 2, a conflict is detected between a_1 and a_2. The intensities of $e_1^{a_1}$ and $e_2^{a_2}$ is I_1 and I_2, and these are used calculating I_a.

```
ActionSet Solve_Ambivalence_1(I1, I2, I_a, a) {
  if(time is up) {
    actionSet<-chooseWorthiestAction(consideredAction);
    if(actionSet.worth > 0)
      return actionSet;
    else return null;
  }
  else {
    if(I1 >I2 >I_a || I1 >I_a>I2 )
      return actionSet;
    else {
      actionSets<-pop(actionSet);
      consideredActionSets<-push(actionSet);
      actionSet<-FindBestActionSet(actionSets);
      Recount(I1 , I2 , I_a);
      return Solve_Ambivalence_1(I1 , I2 , I_a);
    }
  }
}
```

Fig. 6. Pseudo code for solving the ambivalence in situation 1

Step 1: Compare I_a, I_1 and I_2. If I_a is the largest one, the agent takes step 2, otherwise exits to condition 1.

Step 2: Find the next best compensation/reinforcement action set for e_1 and assign it to a_1 if I_1 is larger than I_2, otherwise find for e_2 and assign it to a_2 if I_2 is larger than I_1. Update the intensity related to the changed action set.

Step 3: Detect whether a_1 and a_2 are competing again. If it is still competing, I_2 and I_a will be recalculated with new I_1, or I_1 and I_a will be recalculated with new I_2. After calculating the hedonic value of a_1 or a_2, returns to step 1.

This loop will execute recursively until either of the two conditions is satisfied:

Condition 1: In step 1, if I_1 is the largest one, the agent will execute a_1 directly; if I_2 is the largest one, the agent will execute a_2 directly.

Condition 2: Time runs out. The intensity of ambivalence will not longer be considered. The action set with largest hedonic value among those searched before will be chosen and executed only if the hedonic value is larger than zero. However, since a_1 and a_2 are still competing, only one of them will be executed. The agent will execute a_1 and drop a_2 if I_1 is larger than I_2, otherwise it will execute a_2 and drop a_1.

In these two resolving algorithms, the decision-making processes are all based on how much an action can bring positive and negative effects on emotions. The utility and the cost of an action are not taken into consideration. Therefore, the decision-making can be regarded as "reasonable", rather than rational.

4   Scenario: A Traffic Accident

4.1   Preface

Kent is on his way to school to take his final exam. On his way to school, he witnesses a traffic accident, and he sees his friend Mark is hurt and lying down on the ground. Though Kent pities on Mark and wants to drives him to hospital, he knows that the hospital is in the counter direction and is very far away. Driving his friend to school will make him miss the exam and fail that course.

Kent's pity on Mark urges him to take Mark to hospital, which is the best action to remove the fact that Mark is hurt, and hence compensates his pity. However, doing so will violate his goal to arrive school on time, and the possible outcome of failing that course makes him fear.

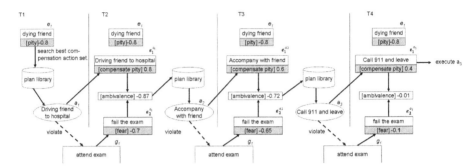

Fig. 7. A decision making flow by Kent in a traffic accident scenario of his friend

4.2 Conflict Resolution

Whenever there is ambivalence, the first step is to calculate the intensity of ambivalence as described in section 3.4. The *difference* function is assumed to be the absolute value of $\min(I_1, I_2)/\max(I_1, I_2)$ and the diminish function is assumed to be multiplying $(I_1+I_2)/2$, whose adjustable parameter alpha is 1. So the stimulus of ambivalence will be $(\min(I_1, I_2)/\max(I_1, I_2))*(\ (I_1+I_2)/2)$. The parameters in function 4, g is 1, x_0 is 0.5, s is 1/12, and I_0 is 0. This sketches a sigmoid function which can be activated as a complete sigmoid curve between 0 and 1. The intensity of pity is set to -0.8 and time constraint is set to 3 ticks in advance. The best action set for compensating pity is listed according to the timeline in table 1.

In table 1, the intensity of ambivalence is the largest one, so Kent will focus on resolving ambivalence by searching a second best action set to compensate the root of conflict, e_1. Before this recursive search of the best action set, the hedonic value of a_1 will be counted as 0.1.

When the new best action set is found in T2, Kent finds a violation of going to school again. The intensity of new fear is -0.65. Because the intensity of compensation for pity and the intensity of fear are totally new, the intensity of ambivalence will be recounted. However, the intensity of the ambivalence is still larger than the other emotions in T3, so Kent keeps searching for an action set after calculating the hedonic value, -0.05, of a_2.

Although Kent still detects a violation when he finds the next best action set in T3, the intensity of ambivalence recounted is smaller than $e_1^{a_3}$ and $e_2^{a_3}$ now. Kent decides to execute a_3. This is the best and acceptable action set to compensate e_1 within the time constraint for Kent. (Call 911 and leave for school)

Were Kent unable to find an acceptable action set within the time constraint, the action set of the largest hedonic value without considering ambivalence, which is a_1 in this scenario, would be carried out. (Drive his friend to hospital)

Table 2. The best action set found in T1, T2 and T3

Action Set Found	Compensation for pity	Fear	Ambivalence	Worth Value
[a_1] Drive friend to hospital	0.8	-0.7	-0.87	0.1
[a_2] Accompany with friend to make him or her comfort	0.6	-0.65	-0.72	-0.05
[a_3] Call 911 and leave for school	0.4	-0.1	-0.01	0.3

5 Conclusion

The fact that dramatic decisions are often made under multiple and coexisting emotions leads us to revise the elicitation process of emotions of virtual agents to allow simultaneous elicitations. SEEM, a network-based model based on the OCC model, is constructed to generate corresponding basic emotions, and ambivalence, one of the most obvious types of mixed emotions, is defined. Two types of ambivalence and corresponding solutions are proposed, and the simulation is done with a scenario similar to the plank of Carneades. Driven by ambivalence, the agent is able to make its decision, which is more human-like and apparently different from rational ones. SEEM has the potential to simulate more types of mixed emotions and hence can add more dramatic elements to the scenarios of games and virtual dramas.

Acknowledgement

This research is supported by National Science Council of ROC under grant number NSC 93-2213-E-007-061.

References

1. Bates, J.: The Role in Emotion of Believable Agents. Communications of the ACM, 37 (1994) 122-125
2. Bazzan, A. L., Bordini, R. H.: A framework for the simulation of agents with emotions. In: Proceedings of AGENT01: the Fifth Inter-national Conference on Autonomous Agents. ACM Press, New York (2001) 292-299
3. Carofiglio, V., De Rosis, F., Grassano, G.: Mixed emotion modeling. In: Canamero, L., Aylett, R. (eds.): Proceedings of the AISB02: Symposium on Animating Expressive Characters for Social Interaction. The Society for the Study of Artificial Intelligence and Simulation of Behaviour. London (2002) 5-10.
4. El-Nasr, M. S., Yen, J., and Ioerger, T. R.: FLAME: Fuzzy Logic Adaptive Model of Emotions. Autonomous Agent and Multi-agent System. 3 (2000) 219-257.
5. Elliot, C.: The Affective Reasoner: A Process Model of Emotions in a Multi-agent System. PhD thesis, Northwestern University. Institute for the Learning Sciences (1992)

6. Gratch, J. Émile: Marshalling passions in training and education. In: Proceedings of Agent00: the Fourth international Conference on Autonomous Agents. ACM Press, New York (2000) 325-332.
7. Gmytrasiewicz, P., Lisetti, C.: Using Decision Theory to Formalize Emotions for Multi-agent System Applications. In Second ICMAS-2000 Workshop on Game Theoretic and Decision Theoretic Agents. Boston (2000)
8. Larsen, J. T., McGraw, A. P., Cacioppo, J. T.: Can People Feel Happy and Sad at the Same Time. Journal of Personality and Social Psychology, 81 (2001) 684-696.
9. LeDoux, J. E.: The Emotional Brain: The Mysterious Underpinnings of Emotional Life. Simon & Schuster (1996)
10. Newby-Clark, I. R., McGregor, I., & Zanna, M. P.: Thinking and Caring about Cognitive Inconsistency: When and for Whom Does Attitudinal Ambivalence Feel Uncomfortable? Journal of Personality and Social Psychology. 82 (2002) 157–166.
11. Nordgren, L. F., van Harreveld, F., van der Pligt, J.: Ambivalence, Discomfort, and Motivated Information Processing. Journal of Experimental Social Psychology. 42 (2006) 252-258
12. Oliveira, E., Sarmento, L.: Emotional Advantage for Adaptability and Autonomy. In: Proceedings of AAMAS03: the Second International Joint Conference of Autonomous Agent and Multi-agent System. ACM Press, New York (2003) 305-312.
13. Ortony, A., Clore, G. L., Collins, A.: The Cognitive Structure of Emotions. Cambridge University Press (1988)
14. Picard, Rosalind W.: Affective Computing. The MIT Press (1997)
15. Schimmack, U., Colcombe, S.: Eliciting mixed feelings with the paired-picture paradigm: A tribute to Kellogg (1915). Cognition and Emotion. (In Press)
16. Velásquez, J.: When Robots Weep: Emotional Memories and Decision-making. In: Proceedings of AAAI98: the Fifteenth National/Tenth Conference on Artificial Intelligence/Innovative Applications of Artificial Intelligence. American Association for Artificial Intelligence (1998)

Are Computer-Generated Emotions and Moods Plausible to Humans?

Patrick Gebhard[1] and Kerstin H. Kipp[2]

[1] German Research Center for Artificial Intelligence,
patrick.gebhard@dfki.de
[2] Experimental Neuropsychology Unit, Saarland University,
Saarbrücken, Germany
k.kipp@mx.uni-saarland.de

Abstract. This paper presents results of the plausibility evaluation of computer-generated emotions and moods. They are generated by ALMA (A Layered Model of Affect), a real-time computational model of affect, designed to serve as a modular extension for virtual humans. By a unique integration of psychological models of affect, it provides three major affect types: emotions, moods and personality that cover short, medium, and long term affect. The evaluation of computer-generated affect is based on textual dialog situations in which at least two characters are interacting with each other. In this setup, elicited emotions or the change of mood are defined as consequences of dialog contributions from the involved characters. The results indicate that ALMA provides authentic believable emotions and moods. They can be used for modules that control cognitive processes and physical behavior of virtual humans in order to improve their lifelikeness and their believable qualities.

1 Introduction and Related Work

The employment of virtual humans as an interface in a human-computer interaction scenarios makes high demands on their believability. This is mainly founded in the sophisticated embodiment of virtual humans that implies human-like conversational abilities and behavior aspects. In general, they can be defined as the embodiment of all internal processes through non-verbal and verbal aspects. Such are the character's gestures, posture, speech characteristics, and facial complexions. On a higher level these internal processes comprise the character's cognitive processes like decision making, subjective appraisal of situations, and dialog strategy selection that are responsible for the conversational behavior in an interaction. In order to increase the believability of a face-to-face virtual conversation partner, researchers have begun to address the modeling and emulation of human-like qualities such as personality and affective behavior. Examples of such systems are COSMO [1], Émile [2], Peedy [3], and the Greta agent [4]. In general, the generation of affective behavior relies on the OCC emotion model that has been defined by Ortony, Clore, and Collins [5]. As a next step, a few research groups have started to address emotion modeling in multi-character scenarios. In the context of a military mission rehearsal application Traum and Rickel [6] address dialog management comprising human-character and

J. Gratch et al. (Eds.): IVA 2006, LNAI 4133, pp. 343–356, 2006.

character-character dialogs in immersive virtual environments. Prendinger et. al. [7] developed a framework for scripting presentations with multiple affective characters in a web-based environment. Part of their work is the SCREAM system that computes affective states based on the OCC-model but also considers aspects of the social context, i.e. role and status of characters.

Another enhancement addresses the emotion based generation of behavior and conversational abilities of virtual characters. Therefore, the used model of emotions has been extended by other affective characteristics that can be exploited for the generation of believable behavior. An important extension consists of the modeling of mood, which represents a diffuse, longer lasting state of affect. Lisetti and Gmytrasiewicz [8] focus on the social expertise of agents. They use a hierarchical model of affect, that consists of emotions, mood, and personality for computing a dynamic emotional state by using probabilistic Markov Models. This should enable the design of autonomous, socially intelligent agents that can predict the emotional state of others. However, they focus on the modeling of emotions that control an agent's actions. The approach from Mehdi et al. [9] uses a one dimensional mood space (good vs. bad) as an affective filter that regulates the intensity of the actual emotion. The Artificial Emotion Engine from Wilson [10] was developed to enhance virtual characters in games and other virtual environments. A one dimensional (good vs. bad) mood model that is driven by punishment or reward signals is used to model a virtual characters motivations. For modeling behavior of synthetic actors, Rousseau and Hayes-Roth [11] rely on a social-psychological model that defines the personality of synthetic actors by moods and attitudes. Moods consist of emotions, triggered by external events and sensations that are event-independent, divided in self-oriented moods and agent-oriented moods. In terms of the OCC model, these moods are rather emotions that represent either the appraisal one's own situation or another one's situation.

Following the motivations of other researchers to enhance conversational abilities and behavior aspects of our virtual characters, our group has started to incorporate personality and affective states to extend a character's conversational and social repertoire. We use affective states to color simulated dialogs through verbal and non-verbal expression of emotions [12]. Focusing on multi-party conversations (rather than performing physical actions), emotions can be used in the dialog generation processes to inform the selection of dialog strategies and linguistic style strategies as proposed by [13]. They also play an important role in the turn-taking behavior (e.g. a spontaneous barge-in may result from an intensive emotion) and in the realization of concrete dialog moves. At some point in our research, we realized that relying solely on emotions might not be sufficient to control behavior aspects like gestures, speech characteristics, or communicative abilities. Inspired by Davidson's thesis that „emotions bias action, whereas moods bias cognition" [14] we enhanced our OCC based computational model of affect by adding „longer-living" moods to „short-living" emotions and personality [15]. We are convinced that mood is a complex affect type, like emotions are. Mood modeled as a one-dimensional value will therefore not be appropriate for a rich exploitation in cognitive processes.

From a technical perspective, we do not rely on a full-fledged affective reasoning process to infer emotions, like the affective reasoner by Elliot [16] or the domain-independent framework for modeling emotion by Gratch and Marsella [17]. Our approach of the generation of affect relies on so-called *appraisal tags* [12, 15] that are used to appraise situational events (e.g. a notification about a prize in a lottery), actions (e.g. someone rescues a child from drowning), objects (e.g. a beautiful butterfly), and on a more abstract level to appraise dialog acts (e.g. to tease, or to praise someone) and affect clues (e.g. blush of shame). In general, appraisal tags can be considered as the final output of a higher-level appraisal reasoning process.

In our opinion, the use of appraisal tags facilitates the generation of affect in both, script-controlled and plan-based virtual character systems. An example for of a script-controlled application using appraisal tags for affect generation is CrossTalk [12]. The VirtualHuman application [15,18] is an example for a more sophisticated system of autonomous virtual humans that use a plan-based higher-level appraisal process to generate appraisal tags (as an intermediate stage) to compute emotions and moods that again influence the virtual humans' behavior.

Before affect-based behavior of virtual characters can be checked for plausibility, the underlying models of the behavior generation process should produce meaningful results. At an abstract-level, a virtual character's behavior should be consistent and believable according to the current situation. First, it must be verified that the generated affect is plausible to the current situation and second that the behavior is consistent with respect to the generated affect. This two step behavior generation is illustrated by figure 1. The relation *has to be consistent with (behavior, situation)* implies for the affect-based behavior generation that affect *has to be consistent with* the situation and behavior *has to be consistent with* affect. In our opinion, this has to be a basic step

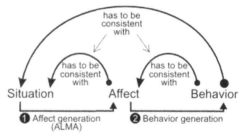

Fig. 1. Consistency relations of affect-based behavior generation

before aspects of a virtual character's behavior can be evaluated according to common evaluation methods collected, for example, by Ruttkay and Pelachaud [19].

2 A Layered Model of Affect

One of the challenges in creating a computational model for the mentioned affect types were the modeling of mood, the „longer-living" affect type. We felt that mood modeled as a one-dimensional value (i.e. good mood vs. bad mood) will not be appropriate for a rich exploitation in cognitive processes. Many interesting behavior aspects might occur, when characters are in a mood out of the good-bad mood dichotomy. Consider, for example, the implications on cognitive processes of the moods anxious or bored. All these requirements raise the question for a model of mood that covers most (or at best all) moods that occur in human beings and that defines how moods can be changed. As a first answer, we have introduced a layered model of affect, which we call ALMA [15] that is based on different psychological models. It comprises three interacting kinds of affect as they occur in human beings:

1. *Emotions* reflect short-term affect. Emotions usually decay and disappear of the individual's focus [18].
2. *Moods* reflect medium-term affect. Moods are longer lasting stable affective states, which have a great influence on human's cognitive functions [21].
3. *Personality* reflects individual differences in mental characteristics (long-term affect). Those can be described by the Big Five model of personality with its traits openness, conscientiousness, extraversion, agreeableness and neuroticism [22].

ALMA is an extension to the computational model of emotions of the EmotionEngine [12,13]. It implements the OCC model of emotions [5] combined with the Big Five factor model of personality [22]. OCC is a cognitive model of emotions, and is essentially based on the concepts of appraisal and intensity. The individual is said to make a cognitive appraisal of the current state of the world. Emotions are defined as valenced reactions to events of concern to an individual, actions of those s/he considers responsible for such actions, and objects/persons. ALMA extends the EmotionEngine by a computational model of mood based on Mehrabian's mood theory [23]. It defines mood as „an average of a person's emotional states across a representative variety of life situations".

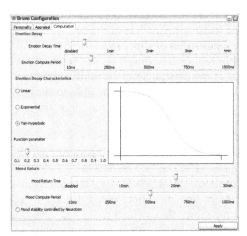

Initially, personality values are used for the computation of the initial emotion intensities. The current ALMA version uses mood values to increase or decrease the intensity of elicited emotions in order to realize a more natural emotion intensity computation. For example, individuals experience stronger joy emotions when

Fig. 2. ALMA affect computation configuration interface

being in an exuberant mood, as when being in a hostile or anxious mood (see also section Mood Change below). In general, the intensity of emotions underlies a natural decay, which is configurable by several decay functions (linear, exponential, and tanhyperbolical). A graphical interface, see figure 2, provides extensive control about almost all parameters that impacts the affect computation.

Mood Model

Mehrabian describes mood with the three traits *pleasure* (P), *arousal* (A), and *dominance* (D). The three nearly independent traits form a 3-dimensional mood space. The implementation of the PAD mood space uses values from -1.0 to 1.0 for each dimension. Mood is described with the following classification for each of the three mood space axes: +P and –P for pleasant and unpleasant, +A and –A for aroused and unaroused, and +D and –D for dominant and submissive. With this classification all mood octants of the PAD mood space are described by Table 1.

While a point in the PDA space represents the mood, a mood octant represents the discrete mood of an individual. For example, a person's (discrete) mood is relaxed, if the value of P is positive, the value of A is negative, and the value of D is positive. We define the strength of a current mood by its distance to the PAD zero point. The maximum distance is √3. This is divided into 3 equidistant sections that describe three discrete mood intensities: slightly,

Table 1. Mood octants of the PAD space

+P+A+D	Exuberant	-P-A-D	Bored
+P+A-D	Dependent	-P-A+D	Disdainful
+P-A+D	Relaxed	-P+A-D	Anxious
+P-A-D	Docile	-P+A+D	Hostile

moderate, and fully. Before mood changes can be computed, it is essential to define an individual's *default mood*. The mapping presented in [24] defines a relationship between the big five personality traits and the PAD space. Relying on this mapping, the EmotionEngine, which uses the big five personality model to define a characters personality, is thereby able to derive a default mood for characters:

P := 0.21•Extraversion + 0.59•Agreeableness + 0.19•Neuroticism
A := 0.15•Openness + 0.30•Agreeableness - 0.57•Neuroticism
D := 0.25•Openness + 0.17•Conscientiousness + 0.60•Extraversion - 0.32•Agreeable.

For example, an individual whose personality is defined with the big five personality traits openness=0.4, conscientiousness=0.8, extraversion=0.6, agreeableness=0.3, and neuroticism=0.4 has the default mood slightly relaxed (P=0.38, A=-0.08, D=0.50).

Table 2. Mapping of OCC emotions into PAD space

Emotion	P	A	D	Mood Octant
Admiration	0.4	0.3	-0.24	+P+A-D Dependent
Anger	-0.51	0.59	0.25	-P+A+D Hostile
Disliking	-0.4	-0.2	0.1	-P-A+D Disdainful
Disappointment	-0.3	-0.4	-0.4	-P-A-D Bored
Distress	-0.4	0.2	0.5	-P+A+D Hostile
Fear	-0.64	0.60	0.43	-P+A+D Hostile
FearsConfirmed	-0.5	0.3	-0.7	-P+A-D Anxious
Gloating	0.3	-0.3	-0.1	+P-A-D Docile
Gratification	0.6	-0.3	0.4	+P-A+D Relaxed
Gratitude	0.2	0.5	-0.3	+P+A-D Dependent
HappyFor	0.4	-0.2	-0.2	+P-A-D Docile
Hate	-0.4	-0.2	0.4	-P-A+D Disdainful
Hope	0.2	0.2	-0.1	+P+A-D Dependent
Joy	0.4	0.2	0.1	+P+A+D Exuberant
Liking	0.40	-0.16	-0.24	+P-A-D Docile
Love	0.3	0.1	0.2	+P+A+D Exuberant
Pity	-0.4	-0.2	-0.5	-P-A-D Bored
Pride	0.4	0.3	0.3	+P+A+D Exuberant
Relief	0.2	-0.3	-0.4	+P-A-D Docile
Remorse	-0.3	0.1	-0.6	-P+A-D Anxious
Reproach	-0.3	-0.1	0.4	-P-A+D Disdainful
Resentment	-0.2	-0.3	-0.2	-P-A-D Bored
Satisfaction	0.3	-0.2	0.4	+P-A+D Relaxed
Shame	-0.3	0.1	-0.6	-P+A-D Anxious

Mood Change

A more challenging task is the simulation of human-like mood changes. Morris [21] has identified four factors that play a role in human mood. All of them are closely related to an emotional experience. To keep the modeling of mood changes as lean as possible, we use emotions as mood changing factors. In order to realize this, emotions must be somehow related to a character's mood. We rely on Mehrabian's mapping of emotions into the PAD space [24]. However, not all 24 emotion types provided by the EmotionEngine are covered by this mapping. For those that lack a mapping, we provide the missing pleasure, arousal, and dominance values by exploiting similarities to comparable emotion types (see Table 2).

For the human-like imitation of mood we rely on a functional approach. We concentrate on how emotions influence the change of the current mood and we consider the aspect that a person's mood gets the more intense the more experiences the person makes that are supporting this mood. For example, if a person's mood can be described as slightly anxious and several events let the person experience the emotion fear, the person's mood might change to moderate or fully anxious.

Our computation of mood changes is based on active emotions generated by the EmotionEngine. Each appraisal of an action, event or object, lets the EmotionEngine generate an active emotion that once generated, is decayed over a short amount of time (i.e. one minute). All active emotions are input for the mood function. The function has two scopes. Based on all currently active emotions the function defines whether the current mood is intensified or changed. It will be intensified if all active emotions are mapped into the mood octant of the current mood. A mood will be changed progressively if all active emotions are mapped into a different mood octant than the current mood. The mood function is visualized by ALMA within the AffectMonitor that is shown in figure 3. It shows the situation, where the current mood will be changed by active emotions. A detailed description of the mood function can be found in [15].

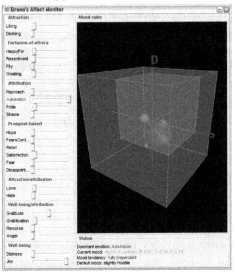

A novelty of the actual version of ALMA is that the current mood influences the intensity of active emotions. The theory is that the current mood is related to personality values that interfere with a character's actual personality values. Technically, this is realized by the reverse use of the (above shown) mapping of big-five personality values on PAD values. Based on the current mood, its temporary virtual personality values will increase or decrease a characters personality values. Those will be used

Fig. 3. ALMA AffectMonitor visualizes ongoing mood changes and elicited emotions

to regulate the intensity of emotions. This increases, for example, the intensity of joy and decreases the intensity of distress, when a character is in an exuberant mood.

Another mentionable aspect is that the current mood has a tendency to slowly move back to the default mood. Generally, the return time depends on how far the current mood is away from the default mood. We take the longest distance of a mood octant ($\sqrt{3}$) for defining the mood return time. Currently this is 20 minutes.

Affect Computation

For the affect computation, ALMA provides a rule based appraisal mechanism. A set of appraisal rules will map affect input to internal values that are used to compute emotions. So called *appraisal tags*, cf. [13], are the symbolical representations of affect input and will be processed by ALMA. We distinguish three types of affect input: 1) *basic appraisal tags*, 2) *act appraisal tags*, and 3) *affect display appraisal tags*. Basic appraisal tags express how a speaking character appraises the event, action or object about which it is talking. Act appraisal tags describe the underlying communicative intent of an utterance, e.g. tease, or congratulate. Affect display appraisal tags are visual cues of an experienced emotion or mood, e.g. a blush of shame or a character that looks nervous for a specific amount of time. Consider the example in which the utterance from Anne is tagged by a human annotator with the act appraisal tag [Admire Anne], which indicates that Anne admires Bruno for something:

Anne: *Bruno, you are dancing like a god. I could dance with you for hours* [Admire Bruno]

Each involved character (Bruno, Anne) appraise the appraisal tag by its own set of appraisal rules. The appraisal tag [Admire Bruno] is appraised by Anne as GoodActOther, a praiseworthy action of another person. Bruno appraises it as GoodActSelf, a praiseworthy action of him self. GoodActOther and GoodActSelf are basic appraisal tags that will resolve into OCC variables for computing emotions. Following the OCC emotion theory a praiseworthy action of oneself will elicit the emotion pride and a praiseworthy action of another person will elicit the emotion admiration. The intensity of the emotions depends on the characters personality values and current mood. For a detailed overview, how we generate emotions by appraisal tags, see [13]. The elicited emotions will impact the mood of each character, according to the mood change function described above. However, more than one (intense) emotion is needed to change a character's current mood.

3 Evaluation

In order to prove that ALMA's computational model of affect is able to produce coherent affect that is comparable to human affect, we ask people how plausible they perceive the generated emotions and moods. To eliminate all (or at least most of the) side-effects that might blur the results, we decided not to evaluate the plausibility of affect through the visualization by a virtual character. The visualization of a specific emotion or mood might be recognized differently from the affect that ALMA has generated. Therefore, we rely on a textual description for generated emotions and moods in the plausibility test. If we could show at this level that the affect generated by ALMA seems plausible, the visualization of them – if done correctly – will be plausible as well.

Methods
We check the plausibility of affect with an offline textual questionnaire that is organized in two sections: one for emotions and one for moods. In the two sections we let the participants judge the plausibility of 24 emotion types and 8 different moods. These are all the affect types that ALMA is able to generate. The sections hold dialog contributions from which we claim that they have an impact on the affect of the involved speaker and addressee.

Participants

In order to investigate relationships regarding affect and participants, we rely on 33 people at different age and gender. The youngest participant was 18 years and the oldest participant was 38 years old. Basically the participants can be divided into two groups: the student group consisting of 17 people between the age of 18 and 19, and the adult group consisting of 16 people between the ages of 25 to 38. Both groups consist of half men and half women.

Material

The materials we use for the evaluation consist of single *dialog contributions*, and *dialog scenes* that can be defined as a set of dialog contributions. Single dialog contributions and dialog scenes have to be annotated with appraisal tags (see section affect computation). Those tags are not shown in the final questionnaire, but used to compute the affect related to the dialog contribution or dialog scene. In addition, we rely on a set of appraisal rules for each involved character, which is needed by ALMA to compute affect.

The basic assumption we made is that emotions will be elicited by dialog contributions. For example, the dialog contribution of Bruno „*Anne, I know you are well prepared for your exam. I am sure you will pass it with a good grade*" elicits the emotion hope on the side of Anne, the addressee. On the side of the speaker (Bruno) the emotion pride is elicited. In general, the elicited emotion type depends on how an individual appraises the dialog contributions. The relationship between characters has a great impact how they appraise actions of each other. We define that all characters like each other, but all dislike the character Clementine. This information is explicitly mentioned in the final questionnaire.

Therefore, they have to be enriched by appraisal tags, which stand for the intentional content (see section Affect Computation). These appraisal tags can be processed by ALMA for generating emotions.

Taking the example above, in which Bruno encourages Anne for her exam, the enriched version of the dialog contribution looks like:

Bruno: *Anne, I know you are well prepared for your exam. I am sure you will pass it with a good grade.* [Encourage Anne]

Only the act tag is used as input for ALMA. As described above, each character has a set of appraisal rules (about 30-50), which appraise the act tag by taking into account the role of the individual. The act tag [Encourage Anne] is appraised by Bruno as GoodActSelf, a praiseworthy action of himself, whereas Anne appraises the act tag as GoodLikelyFutureEvent, a desirable likely future event that Bruno has put into her mind by saying the above line. Following the OCC emotion theory a praiseworthy action of oneself will elicit the emotion pride (Bruno) and a desirable likely future event will elicit the emotion hope (Anne).

Bruno: Anne, it's cool that you're helping grand-mother in cleaning up the garden!

Anne's emotion: *pride*   Bruno's emotion: *admiration*

Fig. 4. Dialog contributions for emotions

According to Morris' theory (see section Mood Change), which is implemented by ALMA, emotions influence the current mood. Emotions elicited by a set of dialog contributions in a specific time interval can change the current mood of an individual to another mood. For the questionnaire, we use short (mostly singular) dialog contributions for the elicitation of emotions and dialog scenes for the change of moods. For the plausibility check of the 24 emotion types, we rely on 24 short dialog contributions that influence both, the speaker's and the addressee's emotions, see figure 4. Therefore, on average, each emotion is rated 2 times. For the plausibility check of the 8 mood types, we rely on 24 dialog situations, see figure 5. Thus, every mood type is rated 3 times.

Because the questionnaire is made for native-speakers, all dialog contributions and dialog situations are originally written in German.

ALMA is used to compute emotions and mood changes based on annotated dialog contributions or dialog situations. The annotation process is part of the evaluation procedure and will be described in the next section. Due to the fact, that ALMA is designed to compute real-time affect comparable to humans, we

Situation: Mark is reorganizing his computer hard drive by letting Microsoft Windows removing unneeded files. Tanja just shows up.

Mark: Crap, Windows has killed all pictures of our last summer holiday at Mallorca.
Tanja: Don't panic, you'll find them surely in the waste bin.
Mark: Are you sure? But what if not, what I'm doing then – they will be lost forever!
Tanja: Well, I've no clue, I'm not the computer expert.
(Mark tries to recover the files by restoring the files of the waste bin)
Mark: No, damn it! All the pictures gone – and there's no way to get them back!
Tanja: Oh no, All our pictures are lost! You are a clean up maniac. I always told you that this will led some days to something bad. Well, and that's just happened. Wonderful!
Mark: Get of my back!

Marks mood after: *hostile*

Fig. 5. Dialog scenes for moods

have to take the duration of a dialog contribution into account. Basically this is only relevant for the dialog scenes. A timer, which is waiting some seconds considering the length of the current contribution, will activate the next dialog contribution as input for ALMA. In the questionnaire, the computed emotions for each individual are noted below a dialog contribution (see figure 4). In case of a dialog situation, the changed mood of the main character is noted below the situation (see figure 5).

Procedure

In a pre evaluation, experts (a computer linguist, a dialog expert, and a psychologist) have reviewed the dialog contributions and the dialog situations for being realistic. All problematic formulations, unrealistic contributions, and unclear situations have been rewritten and modified.

In a next step, the annotated appraisal tags that represent the intentional content are reviewed for being appropriate. All inappropriate tags have been identified and changed. Based on this material emotions and moods are computed by ALMA. The

Table 3. Description of moods

Mood	Description
Exuberant	Extroverted, outgoing, happy, sociable
Bored	Sad, lonely, socially withdrawn, physically inactive
Relaxed	Comfortable, secure, confident, resilient to stress
Anxious	Worried, nervous, insecure, tense, unhappy, illness prone
Dependent	Attached to people, needy of others and their help, interpersonally positive and sociable
Disdainful	Contemptuous of others, loner, withdrawn and calculating, sometimes anti-social
Docile	Pleasant, unemotional, and submissive; likeable; conforming
Hostile	Angry, emotional in negative ways, possibly violent

resulting affect type is displayed below the dialog contributions for the respective dialog situations.

Participants are asked to evaluate during a period about half an hour how plausible emotions and moods are through a discrete ranking scale. The ranking scale was explicitly explained. In the final questionnaire, no more information is given, apart from the list of all possible emotions and moods. Only moods are explained by attributes (translated in German) according to Mehrabian's description of moods (see Table 3).

Data Analysis

In the questionnaire all rankings consisted of a discrete 1-5 scale, 1 denotes the „lowest plausibility", and 5 stands for the „highest plausibility".

Since rating scales can be treated as interval scales [25], we used parametrical tests for the statistical analysis. The *t-test for one sample* is a statistical significance test that proves whether a measured mean value of an observed group differs from an expected value. In our study, ratings were proven to be „positive" if the mean score significantly exceeded the moderate plausible value of 3.

To test the effect of a factor with multiple values (e.g. emotion type) or interactive effects of several factors (e.g. affect type and gender) we calculated *an analysis of variance (ANOVA)*.

Results

Besides the plausibility score and the plausibility significance of computer-generated emotions and moods, we want to know if age or gender has an impact on the rating.

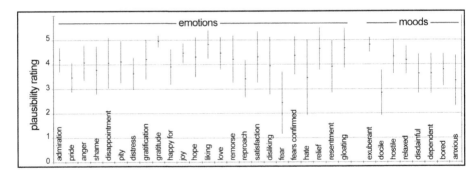

Fig. 4. Plausibility score of emotions and moods

Figure 4 shows the mean plausibility score and the related standard deviation for each emotion and mood. The following subsections present the details of our plausibility evaluation.

Differences in Plausibility Rating Due to Age

To check if differences in the plausibility rating are somehow related to the participants' age a 2 x 2 ANOVA with the factors age group (students, adults) and affect type (emotion, mood) was calculated. Only the factor affect type revealed significance (F(1,31)=23.38; p<.001) which demonstrates that modeled emotions (Mean=4.07) were rated significantly more plausible than modeled moods (Mean=3.81). Neither the factor age (F(1,31)=1.67; p=.21) nor the interaction between affect type and age (F(1,31)=1.57; p=.22) showed a significant effect. Thus, the two age groups did not differ in respect of the rating of emotions and moods and the two age groups were merged for further analysis.

Differences in Plausibility Rating Due to Gender
A 2 x 2 ANOVA with the factors gender (male, female) and affect type (emotion, mood) only revealed the above mentioned significant main effect for affect type (F(1,31)=21.89; p<.001). There was no effect of the factor gender (F(1,31)=.79; p=.38) and no interaction between affect type and gender (F(1,31)=.01; p=.93). This reveals that male and female participants did not rate the plausibility of emotions and moods differently. Therefore, both groups were merged for further analysis.

Emotions and Moods
Analyzing different types of emotions in a one-way ANOVA revealed a main effect of the factor „type of emotion" with 24 levels (F(23,736)=14.29; p<.001). This demonstrates that the different emotions were rated differently plausible with maximum score for gratification (Mean=4.78) and a minimum score for fear (Mean=2,42).

An equal one-way ANOVA for the factor „type of mood" with 8 levels shows a significant main effect (F(7,224)=26.63; p<.001). That is, also modeled moods were rated to be differently plausible. The best score was achieved for exuberant (Mean=4.78) and the worst for dependent (Mean=2.84).

Plausibility of Emotions and Moods
Comparing the mean of the plausibility ratings of all emotions with the neutral score of 3 demonstrates that the modeled emotions are scored significantly above median (t(32)=18.63, p<.001).

The analysis of single emotions shows that except for the two emotions hate and fear all emotions are scored positive (for all: p<.001). The score for fear was significantly lower than 3 (Mean=2.42; t(32)=-2.59; p<.05). Detailed analysis showed that adults scored the plausibility of the modelled fear neutrally (Mean=3.00). However, students' score was negative (Mean=1.81; t(15)=-4.28; p<.001).

The score for hate did not differ from the neutral score of 3 (Mean=3.45; t(32)=1.69; p=.10). This is due to the fact that the adult group's rating was neutral (Mean=3.12; t(16)=.32; p=.76) whereas the student group's rating was clearly positive (Mean=3.81, t(15)=2.14; p<.05).

The mean rating score averaged over all mood types was significantly higher than the neutral score 3 (t(32)=11.32, p<.001). Thus, the plausibility of moods was generally rated positive.

The analysis of single moods revealed positive scores for all mood types (for all: p<.001) except for dependent and anxious. The mood dependent was rated mean (Mean=2.84; t(32)=-1.00; p=.33). The mood anxious shows a tendency to a positive rating (Mean=3.33; t(32)=1.84; p=.08). A separate examination for both age groups demonstrates that adults rate the plausibility positive (Mean=3.88; t(16)=5.08; p<.001), whereas students give a mean rating (Mean=2.75; t(15)=.97; p=.35).

Discussion

A first observation of the results reveals that emotion types are perceived more significantly plausible than mood types in general. We relate this to the fact that emotion types are used for the computation of mood types. The „plausibility weakness" of emotion types will be „transferred" on related mood types according to the mood change functions of ALMA. However, there is no obvious functional description between the plausibility of emotions and related mood.

The bad performance of the emotions fear and hate, which are below neutral and neutral, lacks a well-founded explanation. In case of the emotion fear which is rated better by the adult group, our ad-hoc interpretation was that students have another perception of fear than adults. The related dialog contribution contains a statement in which the addressee's job is about to be recalled if the addressee is not doing its work correctly. Maybe this topic is not (yet) very significant for a student and it is therefore not plausible for them that the addressee experiences fear.

The plausibility rating for the mood dependent was mean. According to our first impression, this might be caused by the German translation of the mood word. In an informal interview this was approved by participants. However, this could also be an effect that is based on the wrong annotation of the dialog contributions of the respective dialog scenes or on the wrong correlation of the elicited emotions to the mood dependent.

4   Conclusion

In this paper we have presented an evaluation of the plausibility of generated emotions and moods by the extended version of ALMA. This version provides a more natural emotion intensity computation because it considers both the personality of an individual as well as its current mood.

We have done a plausibility evaluation of all 24 emotions and 8 moods that can be generated by ALMA. In order not to blur the results, we have explicitly not used virtual characters to visualize emotions and moods. Consequently, the evaluation participants have been confronted with a textual description of the generated emotions and moods.

The overall result of the evaluation is that emotions and moods generated by ALMA are plausible. Considering all participants, the results are independent from age or gender.

Based on these results, we are expecting that the embodiment of ALMA generated emotions and moods through virtual characters will be plausible as well, and will serve well for the generation of behavioral aspects of virtual characters. In addition, the appraisal tag interface allows an easy integration of ALMA's affect computation in script or plan-based virtual character applications.

Acknowledgements

For being a great help in every situation, I would like to thank my colleagues Martin Klesen and Michael Kipp. Also, I would like to thank my brother Gernot Gebhard for coding parts of the ALMA software. The present work is funded by the EU as part of the IST 6th framework network of excellence HUMAINE (Contract no. 507422), and the VirtualHuman project funded by the German Ministry for Education and Research under grants 01 IMB 01A.

References

[1] Lester J., Voerman J. L., Towns S. G., and Callaway C. B. Cosmo: A life-like animated pedagogical agent with deictic believability. In: Proc. of the IJCAI97 Workshop on Animated Interface Agents: Making them Intelligent, Nagoya, 1997

[2] Gratch J. Émile: Marshalling Passions in Training and Education. In: Proc. of Autonomous Agents 2000, 2000, 325–332.

[3] Ball G. and Breese J. Emotion and personality in a conversational agent. In [27], 189–219.

[4] de Carolis B., Pelachaud C., Poggi I., and Steedman M. APML, a Markup Language for Believable Behavior Generation. In [25], 65–85.

[5] Ortony A., Clore G. L., and Collins A. The Cognitive Structure of Emotions. Cambridge University Press, Cambridge, MA, 1988

[6] Traum, D. R. and Rickel, J., Embodied agents for multi-party dialogue in immersive virtual worlds, In: Proc. of the First International Joint conference on Autonomous Agents and Multiagent systems, 2002, 766-773.

[7] Prendinger H., Saeyor S., and Ishizuka M. MPML and SCREAM: Scripting the Bodies and Minds of Life-Like Characters. In [26], 213–242.

[8] Lisetti C. L., Gmytrasiewicz, P., Can Rational Agent Afford To Be Affectless? A Formal Approach, Applied Artificial Intelligence, vol 16. 577-609, 2002

[9] El Jed, M., Pallamin, N., Dugdale, J., Pavard, B. Modelling character emotion in an interactive virtual environment. In: Proc. of AISB 2004 Symposium: Motion, Emotion and Cognition, 2004, Leeds, UK

[10] Wilson, I. The Artificial Emotion Engine, Driving Emotional Behavior, In: AAAI Spring Symposium on Artificial Intelligence and Interactive Entertainment, 2000

[11] Rousseau D., Hayes-Roth B. A Social-Psychological Model for Synthetic Actors, In: Proceedings of the 2nd International Conference on Autonomous Agents, 165-172, 1998

[12] Gebhard P., Kipp M., Klesen M., Rist T. Adding the Emotional Dimension to Scripting Character Dialogues In: Proc. of the 4th International Working Conference on Intelligent Virtual Agents, 2003, 48-56.

[13] Gebhard P., Klesen M., Rist T. Coloring Multi-Character Conversations through the Expression of Emotions. In: Proc. of the Tutorial and Research Workshop on Affective Dialogue Systems, 2004, 128-141.

[14] Davidson, R.J. On emotion, mood, and related affective constructs. In: P. Ekman & R.J. Davidson (Eds.) The Nature of Emotion: Fundamental Questions. New York: Oxford University Press. 1994, 51-55.

[15] Gebhard P. ALMA - A Layered Model of Affect. In: Proceedings of the Fourth International Joint Conference on Autonomous Agents and Multiagent Systems, 2005, 29-36.

[16] Elliot C. Dissertation. The Affective Reasoner: A process model of emotions in a multi-agent system. Northwestern University, Evanston, IL, USA

[17] Gratch J., Marsella S. A Domain-independent Framework for Modeling Emotion. Journal of Cognitve Sytems Research, vol. 5, no. 4, 2004, 269-306.

[18] Ruttkay Z., Pelachaud C, From Brows To Trust, Evaluating Embodied Conversational Agents, Kluwer, Dordrecht, Boston, London, 2004

[19] Markus Löckelt. Action Planning for Virtual Human Performances. In: Proceedings of the International Conference on Virtual Storytelling 2005, Strasbourg, France, 2005

[20] Becker P. Structural and Relational Analyses of Emotion and Personality Traits. Zeitschrift für Differentielle und Diagnostische Psychologie, vol. 22, no. 3, 2001, 155-172.

[21] Morris W. N. Mood: The frame of mind. New York: Springer-Verlag, 1989

[22] McCrae R.R. and John O.P. An introduction to the five-factor model and its implications. Journal of Personality, vol. 60, 1992, 171–215.

[23] Mehrabian A. Pleasure-arousal-dominance: A general framework for describing and measuring individual differences in temperament. Current Psychology, vol. 14, 1996, 261-292.

[24] Mehrabian A. Analysis of the Big-five Personality Factors in Terms of the PAD Temperament Model. Australian Journal of Psychology, vol. 48, no. 2, 1996, 86-92.

[25] Westermann, R. (1985). Empirical tests of scale type for individual ratings. Applied Psychological Measurement, 9, 265-274.

[26] Prendinger H. and Ishizuka, M. Life-Like Characters – Tools, Affective Functions, and Applications, Springer, 2004

[27] Cassell J., Sullivan J., Prevost S., and Churchill E. Embodied Conversational Agents. The MIT Press, Cambridge, Massachusetts, 2000

Creating Adaptive and Individual Personalities in Many Characters Without Hand-Crafting Behaviors

Jennifer Sandercock, Lin Padgham, and Fabio Zambetta

School of Computer Science and Information Technology,
RMIT University, Melbourne, Australia
{jennsand, linpa, fabio}@cs.rmit.edu.au

Abstract. Believable characters significantly increase the immersion of users or players in interactive applications. A key component of believable characters is their personality, which has previously been implemented statically using the time consuming task of hand-crafting individuality for each character. Often personality has been modeled based on theories that assume behavior is the same regardless of situation and environment. This paper presents a simple affective and cognitive framework for interactive entertainment characters that allows adaptation of behavior based on the environment and emotions. Different personalities are reflected in behavior preferences which are generated based on individual experience. An initial version of the framework has been implemented in a simple scenario to explore which parameters have the greatest effect on agent diversity.

1 Introduction

Computer games and interactive applications for entertainment and training are fast growing areas. Today the aim is no longer solely to create good graphics - there are growing demands with regard to the complexity and believability of the virtual characters. Believable characters significantly increase the immersion and the 'fun' that a player has in an interactive application. Typically programmers, designers and animators contribute to hand-crafting the various characters. However this is a time consuming and expensive approach, and not even feasible when large numbers of different characters are needed. Most prior work that aims to create characters with emotions and personality has concentrated on one or two characters (such as [3]) or superficial crowd simulations (such as [2]).

In our work we are investigating models and architectures which allow development of complex and believable characters with minimum effort, using an intelligent agent base, complemented with emotion and personality. Personality has long been seen to be a key aspect of creating believability in virtual characters since it gives them the individuality and quirkiness to make them engaging[12]. Further, personality provides the coherence, or stability that ties together different behavioral choices. We will use the term personality to encompass the individual way that each person reasons and evaluates the world

J. Gratch et al. (Eds.): IVA 2006, LNAI 4133, pp. 357–368, 2006.

based on experience and genetics, which in turn is reflected in behavior and expression. According to Ortony [16] personality can be considered as "a generative engine that contributes to coherence, consistency, and predictability in emotional reactions and responses"[16]. Ideally we want our characters to exhibit individual variability or personality, but for that personality to be coherent, ie similar across situations, rather than chaotic. Further, we would like to achieve all this as simply as possible.

As well as creating diverse characters, we aim to develop characters that are able to adapt their personality over time. Most implementations of personality are static during execution and are based on trait based theories, such as the popular Five Factor Model[14]. This approach does not, however, provide support for ways in which people express different traits, depending on their current situation. For instance, behavior at a football match is usually very different to the behavior of the same person in a cinema. In Ortony's words, behavioral consistency depends on the environmental situation[16]. Using a fixed personality is often justified by the fact that most people believe our adult personalities are relatively static. However, personality does develop over time, particularly during childhood experiences or when the environment itself changes in a substantial and long term manner. For instance, if subjected to a long period of being abused every time someone speaks to a stranger, even an outgoing person eventually becomes introverted to some degree or in certain situations. It is the development phase of personality that we aim to mimic by allowing the characters to adapt quickly to their environment. Characters that are able to adapt to a player would create a significantly more immersive environment compared to characters that are the same no matter how many times they are ignored, for instance. The challenge is to allow the characters to make consistent decisions based on their current state as well as their past experience and environment.

1.1   Our Approach

The approach we take is to use a Belief Desires Intention (BDI) agent platform which supports choices in ways of accomplishing goals and sub-goals, as well as having a robust failure recovery approach. The philosophical foundations of BDI explain rational behavior in terms of concepts such as goals, intentions and commitments, which are modeled explicitly in BDI systems. As discussed in [19] the BDI structure of goals (desires), with multiple plans (intentions) to achieve those goals, which are themselves made up of sub-goal steps, provides enormous possibilities for diversity. We combine this facility for diversity in behavior that can be observed by a player, with a mechanism for modeling emotions and personality, which then influences the choices of each individual agent within this large space of possibilities.

We start with characters that have only minor, and easily achieved, differences. Then, based on the experiences of the characters in the virtual world and their adaptation to that world, we evolve a range of characters with different personalities as expressed in their behavior. Behavior includes anything that the agent is able to do in the environment, for example gestures, actions, conversation, vocal tone.

Characters in interactive entertainment can take two forms: actors and avatars. Actors are characters that can act of their own free will in the virtual environment; whereas avatars are controlled (at times) by a human player. Our work is concerned with the former. In order to avoid confusion between the terms 'character' and 'agent', we will use the term 'agent' to refer to the reasoning part of a 'character'.

Our model is inspired by Ortony's more recent work [16], where he states that in order to create believable agents with individuality they have to be consistent at a global level, "across different kinds of situations, and over quite long time periods" [16]. We call this form of consistency, personality coherence. We believe there are four reasons for differences within and across individuals, the first three are inspired by [16] and are about internal evaluations of emotions, whereas the last is about the way emotions are managed and expressed:

1. Differences in evaluation and construal of the world (e.g. whether you are winning a football match or not depends on which team you are on; and importance placed on winning affects evaluation);
2. Differences in the way that emotions affect us, called *emotionality* (e.g some people are more volatile than others);
3. Current state of the individual and their view of the environment;
4. Differences in how one deals with emotions (e.g. does a person act to try and change the world, or do they adjust their aspirations).

In this paper we describe the simplified representations we use for emotion and personality, inspired by, but simplified from, the work of Lazarus [13] (as implemented by Gratch and Marsella [10]) and the work of Ortony [16] as described above. We also describe a simple interactive environment which we are using to explore and test these models. In our current model we are concentrating on using personality to decide on coping (including action) preferences and to influence evaluation.

We begin by presenting our simplified model of how agent behavior is determined by selection of plans to achieve goals, based on current internal (emotional) and external (environmental) states, combined with personality. We then provide a detailed presentation of our representation of emotions, personality and how they are adapted. Following this we describe the analysis of our test-bed application. We finish with a description of related work and conclusions.

2 Architectural Framework

Our cognitive-behavioral architecture in Figure 1 improves character diversity and personality coherence across situations, and relies on coping processes as a key concept. The term *coping process* refers to any plan that helps the agent deal with its emotions. For instance, coping processes to deal with being scared could be running away, or re-considering the situation to realize that there is nothing to be scared about. Our framework has three core processes (shown as the large diamonds in figure 1): appraisal of coping preferences, selection of coping processes and evaluation or re-appraisal.

Appraisal of coping preferences is a mechanism which can be used at key execution points, and is a process by which the agent ranks the different coping processes available to it. *Selection of coping processes* chooses the actual plan to execute based on preference rankings and plan applicability. This selection process takes into account what plans (or coping processes) are actually viable in the current situation. In the *evaluation process* the agent reviews the success of its chosen approach or evaluates an event from the environment. We begin by giving an overview of our framework and a standard agent execution cycle and then describe the processes and entities in more detail.

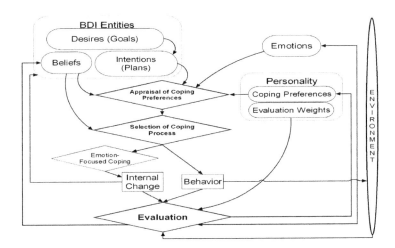

Fig. 1. Cognitive-behavioral Framework

As seen at the top left of our framework diagram in figure 1, an agent's beliefs, desires, intentions, current emotional state and personality feed into appraisal of coping preferences. These preferences, along with beliefs about the world and the BDI plan selection process, allow coping strategies to be chosen. If the first selected plan fails, then the coping preferences guide subsequent choices. Coping processes can affect behavior of the agent in the virtual environment or effect an internal change to its beliefs, desires and intentions. As seen at the bottom of figure 1, evaluation or re-appraisal can be triggered either by: (i) a change to the external environment, (ii) an internal change, or (iii) behavior that the agent has performed. Agent personality and current emotions of the agent itself and of the other agent(s) in the interaction affect evaluation which in turn updates for future emotions, beliefs and coping preferences (which are part of personality). Changes to personality reflect the agent's adaptation to its environment and experience. Our loop of cause and effect means that each aspect of person, environment and behavior can influence any other aspect of the three. This is a core principle of social learning theory [4], although in our model agents adapt behavior based solely on personal experience and not based on observation. The full framework as described above is only used at key execution points which significantly change the agent's behavior. At all other points during execution where the agent is required to make a decision the agent selects its behavior based solely on plan applicability, without the added step of assigning preferences.

The agents begin execution with the same initial emotions, personality, goals and plans, but with different beliefs and emotionality (see section 3 for a description of emotionality). Differences can be specified by the character designer, or randomly ascribed to reduce the designer's workload. In our system we consider there to be two different forms of beliefs: knowledge, perceived 'facts' about the environment and other agents; and opinions, beliefs that are linked to an emotional judgment. Agents are initialized with a small amount of personal knowledge (randomly allocated) and opinions that are independent of the other agents, ie they start with no knowledge or opinions of the other agents. During execution the five aspects of beliefs, desires, intentions, emotions and personality change as the agent interacts with the environment and other agents. It is this that gives the agent its unique identity.

2.1 Example Using Test-Bed Application

We have implemented our framework in a simple virtual world inhabited by young school children who have never met each other before and who can have conversations with each other. The children have one goal: to become happy. How they achieve this goal is entirely based on their diverse personalities and the beliefs and opinions they form about the other agents in the system.

During a full execution cycle the agent begins by finding the plans (intentions) that could achieve its current goals. For example, plans that could help achieve happiness include talking to a friend or re-evaluating who your friends are. The agent's personality, current emotions and current beliefs inform the appraisal process which ranks the preference for each plan, e.g. when the agent is sad and doesn't have many friends it may prefer to find a friend to talk to, or if that doesn't work it's second choice may be to find someone new to talk to. The agent then attempts to execute plans until it finds one that succeeds, e.g. when executing a plan to find a friend to talk to the agent may have no friends, or none that are able to talk to it currently. A selected plan can either change the agent's behavior in the environment or change its internal beliefs, goals and plans, e.g. talking to someone will directly affect the agent's behavior in the environment, and re-evaluating friends or opinions will affect the agent's beliefs. After the plan is completed, the agent evaluates the success of this plan in achieving its goal, e.g did talking to a friend make the agent happier. This evaluation directly affects its own emotions, personality (in the form of allocation of coping preferences) and its opinions of the environment and other agents. For example, if the agent didn't have a 'good' (in its opinion) conversation with its friend then it will decrease its opinion of the other agent, its sadness will increase and if the interaction was very bad, then the agent will be less likely to choose that plan for that situation (ie initial state of the environment and the agent) again. Initial plan preferences are allocated randomly and the evaluation phase has a large random component during initialization. So not all agents who initially try the plan 'be by myself' will enjoy it and therefore not all agents are likely to choose that plan again.

2.2   Implementation of Cognitive Appraisal Model

Our framework is based on the cognitive appraisal model of affect which maintains that emotions can only be updated or triggered after an appraisal of the world and events. There are many variations on cognitive appraisal, but we follow the model proposed by Lazarus [13] which has two main components: coping and appraisal. Coping is we how we deal with emotional encounters. Appraisal is the process of deciding which form of coping to implement and the process of analyzing changes in the internal and external world of the agent. There are two types of coping: *emotion-focused coping* and *problem-focused coping*[13]. Problem-focused coping results in observable behaviors, emotion-focused coping results in changes to beliefs, desires, and intentions. There are also two types of appraisal in our model: *appraisal of coping preferences* and *evaluation* or re-appraisal of changes to the external and internal environment of the agent. Both forms of appraisal are influenced (in our framework) based on the agent's personality.

Although the most obvious way to cope is, perhaps, to act in the world (problem-focused coping), an alternative way is to modify one's internal state (emotion-focused coping). A person (or a agent) who is unhappy because they don't have a car, can work to be able to buy a car, or alternatively they may modify their values so that not having a car is something to be proud of. The emotion-focused coping process in our framework captures this second kind of mechanism and requires an internal reasoning process (rather than simple actions) to occur to change beliefs, desires and intentions. Emotion-focused coping processes include: belief formation and changes; goal formation, adoption, and abandonment; and planning, ie intention modification or generation. Problem-focused coping processes are implemented in our framework as any form of behavior that the agent is able to exhibit in the virtual environment, such as gestures, actions and conversations. Our preliminary implementation uses problem-focused coping only, which can easily be modified to include other coping strategies since the agent adapts based on past experience and not based on hard-coding preferences.

There are two levels to selecting a coping plan, which are represented in figure 1 by the middle two large diamonds. The first is a type of appraisal, *appraisal of coping preferences*, which places preferences for some strategies over others based on personality. The second is *selection of coping processes* which finds applicable plans using beliefs about the environment or the current situation along with the BDI mechanism of context conditions. The plan with the highest preference according to the initial appraisal process is chosen first by the selection process, as long as it is viable in the current situation. However, if the initially chosen plan fails during execution then BDI goal persistence mechanisms ensure that an alternative (less preferred) plan will be tried if it is applicable in the situation.

For example, the agent may prefer to increase its happiness by finding treasure. But if there is no treasure available, and no means to acquire any treasure, a less preferred approach to increasing happiness will be selected, such as finding a job other than treasure hunter.

Our implementation of the two-stage selection process is similar to other models that use an affective phase and then a cognitive phase for the decision-making process. These models are usually based on Damasio's somatic-marker hypothesis [6] which states that before we make every decision our bodies automatically focus attention towards or away from some response options (often this process is subconscious). The appraisal of cognitive preferences process is similar to placing relative somatic-markers on plans in order to guide the cognitive process towards those that have an initial preference based on emotions and personality.

The evaluation phase (which is the second type of appraisal) is triggered by a change to the internal or external world of the agent or by something the agent itself has done. The process analyses changes and determines how these changes affect emotions and beliefs (particularly opinions) and whether personality (coping preferences) needs to be adapted. In this way the agent's personality in the form of preferred ways of coping, does eventually change depending on the agent's experience. Evaluation uses key variables that relate to the process that has triggered the evaluation, as well as the agent and the environment's state. The variables are measured objectively, however they are combined by using weightings to reflect personality differences that result in placing more or less importance on different variables. This aspect of evaluation and personality is described further in section 3.2.

3   Emotion and Personality Representation

Emotions are implemented in line with the OCC method [17], which uses a fixed number of emotions, many of which are paired, e.g. joy and distress. We follow Ortony's [16] suggestion to build an emotional model by beginning with a simple good/bad representation as implemented by, for example, [18]. Each agent has its own *emotionality* [16] or emotion personality which reflects the fact that emotional events affect different people either more or less and that some people express emotions more readily than others.

Emotionality is expressed in the following values for each individual emotion (ie separate values for positive and negative emotions) which are fixed at agent initialization:

– decay - the rate (can be linear, polynomial or exponential function) at which the emotion goes towards its stable value (e.g. zero) at each time tick;
– uptake - the rate at which a relevant evaluation affects the emotion, i.e. a positive evaluation is multiplied by the positive uptake value to determine amount of change in this emotion. High uptake values result in an agent that is easily affected by events;
– threshold - the value above or below which the emotion is expressed, and the value that triggers changes in coping preferences.

In our framework, personality is explicitly present in emotionality, coping preferences, and evaluation weights. The latter two affect the two appraisal processes: appraisal of coping processes and evaluation of changes respectively.

3.1   Personality in Coping Preferences

Coping preferences reflect which plans the agent expects will manage its emotions (or improve its positive emotions) best in a given situation (ie environmental and personal state). An agent's coping preferences, an aspect of its personality, are used by the appraisal of coping strategies process to order which strategies should be tried first. In this case personality reflects the fact that different people use different plans to manage the same emotional event. For instance, when unhappy an introvert may decide to read a book, while an extrovert may decide to go to a party.

The coping preferences of an agent are represented by each input state being one-to-one matched to a list of preference values. The input represents state and emotion variables in a pre-specified order. The list of preference values is ordered so that it is possible to lookup the individual preference value (on a scale of 0-9) for a given plan or coping strategy. The combination of all the input state to preference list pairs make up the agent's coping personality, or more accurately their coping preferences.

As execution progresses the agent encounters new input states, so it randomly allocates initial preferences for these new states. After execution of a coping process the agent performs an evaluation on the process. It may be that, due to environmental or internal changes, the preferred approach no longer produces a desired outcome or produces a much more desirable outcome than expected as determined by the evaluation or re-appraisal process. The coping preference value of the chosen approach is increased or decreased in two stages. In the first stage, preferences are increased or decreased immediately based on whether the last emotion event is above or below (respectively) the threshold set by the agent's emotionality. In the second stage, preferences can only change after repeatedly bad or good experiences, thus allowing for a more stable personality.

Since we include the perceived state of the environment as input to the appraisal of coping preferences process it is possible to get different but consistent behavior across situations. In this case a situation is defined as a specific state of the agent, for example the agent is currently happy and has lots of friends. As a result, if the environment changes and becomes more (or less) adverse the agent changes its coping preferences to match its environment. This process is much easier to implement than tailoring which actions each agent should perform and when. Even though our system is very simple there are already a large amount of diverse experiences available for the agent to encounter. Therefore the agent is able to generate its own coping preferences that are suitably diverse compared to the other agents.

3.2   Personality in Evaluation Weights

Every time we analyze an outcome we weight certain variables more or less highly than others. For instance, depending on the person an event such as obtaining treasure but no friends may or may not be evaluated as successful. We call the weights or importance of different variables, *evaluation weights*.

In some ways many evaluation weights could be decided based on analysis of an agent's goals, and beliefs. However, our aim is to implement a simple system. We do not want to expand goals and beliefs to encompass more than necessary. By including evaluation weights we are assigning these values in a simpler, easier to change manner. If all agents had the same evaluation method their coping preferences would eventually converge since they would all be attempting to reach the same states.

In our system the evaluation weights apply to every variable that is used in evaluation, and the sum of the evaluation weights adds to 100%. An overall result from evaluation is obtained by summing the variable ratings multiplied by their respective weightings. The result or overall success of the triggering event is used to update emotions, opinions (beliefs) about others and the environment and, importantly, to update coping preferences.

In the real world, people continually adapt both coping preferences and evaluation weights at simultaneously relying on feedback from each aspect to make adaptations. It would be awkward to attempt to implement this computationally. So, in our case we decided to fix evaluation weights after an initialization period. Initial weights can be specified for each individual character or can be the same for all characters, usually there is a high weight placed on a random value to ensure further diversity, and to reflect that the agents have not yet determined what is 'good' and 'bad'. Specifying evaluation weights gives a designer more control over the types of character personalities that will be generated. After initialization, experience determines final weighting values and as such their evaluation personality is then fixed for the rest of the execution time.

4   Future Work, Discussion and Conclusion

We are currently testing our application based on school children making friends through conversations, as described in section 2.1. Our main aim in testing this application is to determine which parameters are most important in increasing (or decreasing) agent diversity as defined based on agent behavior. Parameters we will examine include: evaluation weights and method of evaluation, coping preferences, emotionality variables, and initialization variables such as number of agents, amount of initial environmental knowledge and more. Our current goal is to vary parameters one at a time to determine their effect on behavior output of the agent population.

To obtain quantitative results of the effect parameters have on behavior we allow the agents to interact in their virtual world and determine whether we can find groups or clusters of agents based on their personality in the form of behavioral choices. We are searching for clusters that are significantly different to each other, as well as being stable and not skewed undesirably towards certain personalities. This aims to confirm that the agents have believable and distinct personalities that do not change quickly and without reason. We will allow input parameters to range from all agents being initialized with the same values to all agents being randomly or individually ascribed different values. Our future work will concentrate on confirming diverse personalities are obtained and maintained and to determine which parameters are essential to achieve this result. Subsequent work will be to apply the model to a more complex computer game environment using only the essential parameters as found during testing.

There has been increasing use of emotions, personality, and adaptation in virtual characters across a wide-variety of applications. However, prior work does not cover using adaptation for personality development nor apply all these techniques to a game based environment. We will now discuss our work as related to prior work in the field in order to illuminate the gaps that we fill.

Computer game developers are now using emotions and learning to compete with other games beyond graphical improvements. For instance, the game *Romeo and Juliet* [9] allows the player to use a painting canvas to influence the emotions of the two characters, who in turn visualize their emotions with ballet movements. *Façade* [1] is an emotional interactive drama where the player interacts with a couple who are having serious relationship problems. The crowd generating effects that are able to be produced by Massive software [2] have been very successful. Although this work investigates giving personality to the large number of characters that make up crowd scenes, it concentrates on superficial animation effects and is yet to be implemented in an interactive environment. Learning is also an area that is being introduced to games, for example *Black and White* [8], which also implemented BDI techniques. Emotions, personality and learning are not yet widely implemented in games due to perceived high risk and long development times required.

A major method of improving virtual characters in the more academic world is to construct them with emotion and personality models. Our use of coping preferences to guide choice of coping strategies or behaviors is similar to [3,11,22]. However, this past work has relied on emotions only and not personality based on experience to constrain decision-making. One of the most thorough implementations of an emotion model is the work by Gratch and Marsella [10] which also implements beliefs and intentions, however personality and desires are not core concepts. Their model is highly realistic due to their requirement to train military personnel, resulting in more complexity than is required for an entertainment application and their model would be computationally expensive for more than a few characters.

Many implementations of personality are based on trait based approaches from psychology work which do not consider context [15]. That is, it assumes people act in the same manner no matter what the environment and situation. Rousseau and Hayes-Roth [20] attempted to resolve this problem, but then required a substantial amount of set-up time for the designer compared to our adaptation method. Almost all implementations of personality assume that it is static, e.g. [15,20]. This is reasonable, although it assumes that the initial model of personality is sufficiently complex to capture human personality. Our method allows personality to develop according to the environment and become more complex than the initial input values if necessary.

A substantial amount of work into emotions and personality requires programmers to devote long amounts of time writing pre-scripted behaviors or developing character personalities, e.g. [3,5]. Promising work is being done to automate character behavior and the scripting process (e.g. [7]), so that characters do not follow a fixed script like in a play. This later work indicates that users 'prefer' (find more interesting or are more willing to suspend disbelief) non-scripted characters. However, this work often is only suited to a small number of characters where the personality of characters is hand-crafted.

Our work is different to other work such as [21] that uses emotions to assist the learning or adaptation process since we do not assume that there is an optimum solution or personality, nor do we assume that the user is guiding the agent's choice of what is 'good' and 'bad'. We want agents with diverse behaviors where they have their own optimum solution based on a personality that has developed from their unique experience.

In conclusion, emotions and personality are key components of creating believable virtual characters. Current methods of implementing emotions and personality are often too complex or are not freely available to developers of computer games with many virtual characters. In the past personality has usually been implemented in a static, trait-based and hand-crafted manner, leading to long designer development times and characters that are unable to adapt to situation and environment. Our framework applies simplified models of emotions and adaptation to create diverse characters that can develop their personality to suit their environment.

Acknowledgments

We would like to thank Agent Oriented Software and Ralph Rönnquist for their support under the Planning and Learning in BDI Agents Grant, LP0560702.

References

1. Façade website by Procedural Arts. http://www.interactivestory.net/.
2. Massive software website. http://www.massivesoftware.com/.
3. E. André, M. Klesen, P. Gebhard, S. Allen, and T. Rist. Integrating models of personality and emotions into lifelike characters. In *Affective interactions: towards a new generation of computer interfaces*, pages 150–165. Springer-Verlag New York, Inc., New York, NY, USA, 2000.
4. A. Bandura. *Social Learning Theory*. Prentice-Hall, New Jersey, USA, 1977.

5. H. da Silva Corrêa Pinto and L. O. Alvares. Extended behavior networks and agent personality: Investigating the design of character stereotypes in the game unreal tournament. In T. Panayiotopoulos, J. Gratch, R. Aylett, D. Ballin, P. Olivier, and T. Rist, editors, *Intelligent Virtual Agents, 5th International Working Confere nce, IVA 2005, Kos, Greece, September 12-14, 2005, Proceedings*, volume 3661 of *Lecture Notes in Computer Science*, pages 418–429. Springer, 2005.

6. A. Damasio. *Descartes' Error: Emotion, Reason and the Human Brain*. G.P. Putnam, USA, 1994.

7. J. Dias, A. Paiva, and M. Vala. Can users feel sorry for autonomous synthetic characters? In C. Pelachaud, E. André, S. Kopp, and Z. Ruttkay, editors, *Proceedings of the Workshop on Creating Bonds with Embodied Conversational Agents (Humanoids)*, The Fourth International Joint Conference on Autonomous Agents and Multi Agent Systems (AAMAS 2005), July 2005.

8. R. Evans. Varieties of learning. In S. Rabin, editor, *AI Game Programming Wisdom*. Charles River Media Inc, Hingham, MA, USA, 2002.

9. B. Gilman. Student postmortem: 6mSoft's Romeo and Juliet. *Gamasutra*, February 2005. http://www.gamasutra.com/features/20050204/gilman_01.shtml.

10. J. Gratch and S. Marsella. A domain-independent framework for modeling emotion. *Journal of Cognitive Systems Research*, 5:269–306, 2004.

11. S. H. Hemenover and S. Zhang. Anger, personality, and optimistic stress appraisals. *Cognition and Emotion*, 18(3):363–382, 2004.

12. C. Jones. *Chuck Amuck: The Life and Times of an Animated Cartoonist*. Farrar, Straus and Giroux, New York, USA, 4th edition, 1994.

13. R. Lazarus. *Emotion and Adaptation*. Oxford University Press, USA, 1991.

14. R. R. McCrae and O. P. John. An introduction to the five-factor model and its applications. *Journal of Personality*, 60:175–215, 1992.

15. D. Moffat. Personality parameters and programs. In R. Trappl and P. Petta, editors, *Creating Personalities for Synthetic Actors: Towards Autonomous Personality Agents*, volume 1195 of *Lecture Notes in Artificial Intelligence*, pages 120–165. Springer-Verlag, Germany, 1997.

16. A. Ortony. On making believable emotional agents believable. In R. Trappl, P. Petta, and S. Payr, editors, *Emotions in Humans and Artifacts*, pages 189–212. MIT Press, Cambridge, MA, USA, 2002.

17. A. Ortony, G. L. Clore, and A. Collins. *The Cognitive Structure of Emotions*. Cambridge University Press, USA, 1988.

18. L. Padgham and G. Taylor. PAC - personality and cognition: an interactive system for modelling agent scenarios. In *Proceedings of International Joint Conference on Artificial Intelligence IJCAI'97*, Tokyo, Japan, 1997.

19. L. Padgham and M. Winikoff. *Developing Intelligent Agent Systems: A practical guide*. Wiley and Sons, 2004.

20. D. Rousseau and B. Hayes-Roth. A social-psychological model for synthetic actors. In *AGENTS '98: Proceedings of the second international conference on Autonomous agents*, pages 165–172, New York, NY, USA, 1998. ACM Press.

21. M. Seif El-Nasr, T. R. Ioerger, and J. Yen. PETEEI: a PET with evolving emotional intelligence. In *AGENTS '99: Proceedings of the third annual conference on Autonomo us Agents*, pages 9–15, New York, NY, USA, 1999. ACM Press.

22. A. Stern. Creating emotional relationships with virtual characters. In R. Trappl, P. Petta, and S. Payr, editors, *Emotions in Humans and Artifacts*, pages 333–362. MIT Press, Cambridge, MA, USA, 2002.

Thespian: Modeling Socially Normative Behavior in a Decision-Theoretic Framework

Mei Si, Stacy C. Marsella, and David V. Pynadath

Information Sciences Institute
University of Southern California
Marina del Rey, CA 90292
meisi@isi.edu, marsella@isi.edu, pynadath@isi.edu

Abstract. To facilitate *lifelike* conversations with the human players in interactive dramas, virtual characters should follow similar conversational norms as those that govern human-human conversations. In this paper, we present a model of conversational norms in a decision-theoretic framework. This model is employed in the Thespian interactive drama system. In Thespian, characters have explicit goals of following norms, in addition to their other personal goals, and use a unified decision-theoretic framework to reason about conflicts among these goals. Different characters can weigh their goals in different ways and therefore have different behaviors. We discuss the model of conversational norms in Thespian. We also present preliminary experiments on modeling various kinds of characters using this model.

1   Introduction

Interactive dramas allow people to participate actively in a dynamically unfolding story, by playing a character or by exerting directorial control. There has been a growing research interest in computer-based, animated interactive dramas, both for entertainment (e.g., [1,2,3]) and for learning environments (e.g., [4,5]), in part because their design faces a range of research challenges. Ideally, the user's interaction should be facilitated and they should have a sense that they can openly interact with the story. However consistency of story and character becomes harder to maintain in the face of open-ended user interaction. Addressing these challenges can lead to complex designs for interactive dramas, raising an additional challenge of how to facilitate authoring of the drama.

Our approach to these challenges is realized in an interactive drama system called Thespian. Characters in Thespian are realized as goal-driven, decision-theoretic agents that are responsive to the user's interaction while maintaining consistency with their roles in the story (see [6] for a discussion). The decision-theoretic framework allows them to balance multiple competing goals, such as responding sociably to the user but not disclosing sensitive information in a conversation. In prior work, we also demonstrated how the goal-driven agents can be *trained* to perform their roles, based on story scripts provided by authors that are then passed through a semi-automatic fitting process [7]. This process

J. Gratch et al. (Eds.): IVA 2006, LNAI 4133, pp. 369–382, 2006.
© Springer-Verlag Berlin Heidelberg 2006

can reduce authoring effort compared to hand-authoring all possible interactions and ideally transform the authoring process into a more creative (and a more familiar) exercise of writing stories. In this paper, we focus on how Thespian agents model norms in conversations. Much as they do in human-human interaction, norm-following behaviors can facilitate and constrain user interactions in natural/lifelike ways that ideally do not seem restrictive.

In general, social norms are commonly believed rules in social interaction. These rules serve as a guide for human behavior, and as the basis for their beliefs and expectations about others. Without them, communication can break down easily. Though norms are commonly followed, the tendency to follow norms is regulated by other factors, such as more pressing, personal goals. There is a considerable body of work on social norms and norms in conversations in particular, including formalization of norms and obligations [8], how norms emerge, spread and get enforced in a society [9], levels of cooperation in social communications [10], discourse obligations in dialogues [11], maxims in cooperative conversations [12], etc.

Interactive dramas have taken differing approaches to incorporate norm-following in their designs. Norm-following/violating behavior is often not explicitly modeled. Rather, they are modeled conjointly with characters' other behaviors. In FearNot [5], affectively-driven characters are used. Characters' actions are either reactive to their current emotional states or result from the planning process using their internal goals, which are affected by their emotional states. In Façade [13], the story is organized around hand-authored dramatic beats, realized as their pre-conditions, post-conditions, and brief patterns of interactions between characters. Norms are encoded in interactions within beats and the beat selection process which is affected by the pre-conditions and post-conditions of the beats. In Cavazza's storytelling system [3], characters' behaviors are embedded in Hierarchical Task Network (HTN) plans crafted by authors. In SASO [14], there is an extensive dialogue management subsystem that incorporates explicit rules for normative behaviors, specifically conversational norms. The priorities of these rules are adjusted by agent authors to fit the characters' profiles. The modeling of a character's task and conversation are distinct but coupled.

We present a model of conversational norms crafted in Thespian's decision-theoretic framework. Thespian models several basic norms specific to face-to-face communication [15]. Conversational norms enable the characters to behave human-like in terms of three aspects: making relevant responses, following natural turn-taking patterns, and having appropriate conversational flow. Characters (the goal-driven agents) have explicit goals of following norms in addition to their other goals. Thus, we allow characters to reason about the effect of following or violating norms and achieving or sacrificing their other goals using a unified decision-theoretic framework. Moreover, the weights of goals can be automatically tuned using Thespian's fitting process.

In this paper, we discuss Thespian's conversational norms model in detail. We also illustrate its application to the Tactical Language Training System (TLTS) [16] for rapidly teaching students the rudiments of a foreign language and culture.

2   Example Domain

Our conversational norms model is built within the Thespian framework that was used to realize the Mission Environment (Figure 1) of TLTS. The user takes on the role of a male army Sergeant (Sergeant Smith) who is assigned to conduct a civil affairs mission in a foreign town. The TLTS uses a 3D virtual world built on top of the Unreal Tournament Engine. The human user navigates in the virtual world and interacts with virtual characters using spoken language and gestures. An automated speech recognizer identifies the utterance and the mission manager converts them into a dialogue act representation that Thespian takes as input. Output from Thespian consists of similar dialogue acts that instruct virtual characters what to say and how to behave.

Fig. 1. A screen-shot from the Tactical Language Training System

We will use one of the scenes from the Pashto version to illustrate the working of Thespian's conversational norms model. The story begins as the user arrives outside of a Pashto village. Some children are playing nearby and come over to talk to the user as the vehicle arrives. The user's aim in the scene is to establish initial rapport with people in the village through talking to their children in a friendly manner. The children possess different personalities. Some are very shy and some are very curious about the American soldier.

3   Thespian

We developed Thespian as a multi-agent system for controlling virtual characters in an interactive drama. Thespian is built upon PsychSim [17,18], a multi-agent system for social simulation based on Partially Observable Markov Decision Problems (POMDPs) [19].

Thespian's basic architecture uses POMDP based agents to control each character, with the character's personality and motivations encoded as agent goals. Objects (e.g., a town, a house) in the story can also be represented as special Thespian agents that only have state features, but not actions, goals, policy and beliefs about others, to enable characters to reason about the values of their state features in the same way as those of a character. All characters communicate with each other through dialogue acts. A human user can substitute for any of the characters and interact with others.

3.1   Thespian Agent

This section describes the components of a Thespian agent, including its state, beliefs, action dynamics functions, goals, and policies.

State. A character's state is defined by a set of state features, such as the name and age of the character, and the affinity between two characters. Values of state features are represented as a range of real numbers within [-1, 1] (alphabetic values are encoded as real values using a constant convention through out the scene.) For example, an agent's name, Mike, might be encoded as .1. There is usually uncertainty involved in agents' beliefs about other agents' and/or its own state features. The size of the range indicates the character's confidence level about this value. For example, if a character believes another character's name is [-1, 1], it means the character does not know the name. On the other hand [.1, .1] indicates the agent is 100% confident of the value being exactly .1.

Beliefs. The agent's subjective view of the world includes its beliefs about itself and other agents and *their* subjective views of the world, a form of recursive agent modeling [20]. An agent's subjective view about itself or another agent can include every component of that agent, such as state, beliefs, policy, etc.

Dynamics. Dynamics functions define how actions can affect agents' states. For example, greetings among agents set the state feature *conversation status* of all participants to [1.0, 1.0], indicating a conversation among them has started (for more complex examples, see the dynamics defined in the Conversational Norms section.) Dynamics functions in an agent's belief space define how this agent believes an action will affect agents' states. Therefore dynamics functions influence the agent's reasoning about what action to take and hence its behavior.

Goals. We model a character's personality profile as its various goals and their relative importance (weight).

Goals are expressed as a reward function over the various state features an agent seeks to maximize or minimize. For example, Sergeant Smith has a goal of maximizing his *affinity with the children* with initial value set to [.0, .0]; this goal is completely satisfied once the value reaches [1.0, 1.0]. An agent usually has multiple goals with different relative importance (weights). For example, Sergeant Smith may have another goal of knowing the children's names, and this goal may be twice as important to him as the previous goal. The weights of the goals decide what action the agent will choose given the same dynamics.

Policy. In Thespian, all agents use a bounded lookahead policy. Each agent has a set of candidate actions to choose from when making decisions. When an agent selects its next action, it projects into the future to evaluate the effect of each option on the state and beliefs of other entities in the story. The agent considers not just the immediate effect, but also the expected responses of other characters and, in turn, the effects of those responses, and its reaction to those responses and so on. The agent evaluates the overall effect with respect to its goals and then chooses the action that has the highest expected value.

Consider the following simplified example from the story to illustrate the agent's lookahead process. Before the conversation starts, Sergeant Smith considers what he should say first. He can either greet the children or ask the children a question he cares about. Greeting does not affect the value of any of his goals; starting a conversation without greeting will hurt his goal of maintaining a normal conversational flow. In the next step, the responses he expects from the children are "greeting back" and answering the question respectively. Getting the answer from the children will satisfy his goal of obtaining that piece of information, and "greeting back" will not affect his state. What action Sergeant Smith will choose to do depends on the relative importance of maintaining a normal conversational flow versus obtaining that piece of information.

In the above example, only two steps of the interactions are considered by the agent. Theoretically, each agent can perform lookahead for large enough number of steps until there is no gain for itself and other agents. For performance reasons, we limit the lookahead to a finite horizon that we determine to be sufficiently realistic without incurring too much computational overhead (e.g., for the examples in this paper, the horizon is three times the total number of characters in the conversation).

3.2   Fitting Procedure

To craft an interactive experience, the author can either configure the characters' goal weights by hand to ensure they behave appropriately or use the fitting procedure for help. To use the fitting procedure, the author needs to define the characters' roles in the story by creating alternative linear scripts (sequences of dialogue acts) of the desired paths of the story. Using the scripts as constraints on allowable agents' behaviors, the fitting process [21,7] can tune agents' goal weights so that they behave according to the scripts.

Before running the fitting procedure, the author sets the initial conditions including the goal weights for all of the characters. By default these initial values will be used to set the initial beliefs characters have about each other. The goal weights do not necessarily need to be accurate, since the fitting process will automatically adjust them.

In fitting, Thespian proceeds iteratively for each story path, fitting the goals of one agent at a time and holding all other agents' goals as fixed. For each action in the story path, if the action is performed by the agent that is currently being fitted, the fitting process simulates the agent's lookahead process, and calculates constraints on goal weights to ensure that the desired action receives highest utility among all candidate actions. So in the earlier example, Sergeant Smith needs to have a higher weight on maintaining a normal conversational flow than obtaining the information to ensure that he chooses to greet first.

At the end of the fitting process, the constraints resulting from fitting each path can be merged into one common constraint set. Typically, there are multiple candidate goal weight values that are consistent with the preferred story paths. Thespian can pick one of these solutions according to its own heuristics, which is to choose the goal weights as close to the original ones as possible. It also gives the author the option of manually selecting one from the constrained set.

A character's goal weights after fitting are usually different from their initial values set by the author. This difference can lead to discrepancies between a character's actual personality and another character's mental model of it. The author can synchronize the models by repeating the fitting step with the agents' beliefs set to the actual personality. However, characters do not necessarily have to have exact knowledge about other characters or themselves to exhibit the desired behaviors. In fact, it can be dramatically interesting when characters do not have accurate models of each other.

4   Conversational Norms

Thespian's conversational norms model consists of goals that motivate characters to behave socially appropriately, state features that keep track of the status of conversation, affinity among characters and obligations each character has, and dynamics functions for updating these state features. Characters have goals to maximize all of their goal features.

4.1   Adjacency Pairs

Adjacency pairs[22], such as greet and greet back, enquiry and inform are very common in conversations. They are performed by two speakers and follow a fixed pattern. We use an obligation-based approach to model this social phenomenon. Obligations are represented by agents' state features. Figure 2 lists some of the adjacency pairs we model currently and the obligations related to them. The character that performs the first part of an adjacency pair creates an obligation for the addressee to perform the second part. By performing the action desired by the first speaker, the second speaker can satisfy the obligation. For example, if Sergeant Smith opens the conversation by greeting the children, the children have obligations to greet Sergeant Smith back, in which case the values of the corresponding state features are set to [1.0, 1.0]; and once the obligations are satisfied, the values will go back to its default level of [0.0, 0.0], indicating the children do not have such obligations. After creating an obligation for the addressee, the first speaker needs to stop talking to give the addressee a turn to respond. To motivate characters to do so, an obligation of waiting for responses is created by the first speaker for itself. This obligation will be satisfied after getting a response from other characters.

Speaker 1	Speaker 2	Obligation
Greet	Greet back	Greet back to *speaker 1*
Bye	Bye	Say "Bye" to *speaker 1*
Thanks	You are welcome	Say "You are welcome" to *speaker 1*
Offer X	Accept/Reject X	Either accept or reject X to *speaker 1*
Request X	Accept/Reject X	Either accept or reject X to *speaker 1*
Enquiry about X	Inform about X	Inform to *speaker 1* about X
Inform information	Acknowledgement	Acknowledgement to *speaker 1*

Fig. 2. Adjacency Pairs and Corresponding Obligations

To enforce adjacency pairs, we give each character a goal of maximizing its state feature *complete_adjacency_pair_norm*. If the agent's dialogue act satisfies one of its obligations, the value of this state feature will increase. If the dialogue act intends to satisfy an obligation[1], but the agent does not actually have such an obligation (for example, the agent says "you are welcome" when nobody has said "thanks" to it), the value of this state feature will decrease. The specific amounts of increase or decrease only have relative meaning when they are for the same state feature. For example, in Algorithm 1, we believe violating the norm is more serious than following it[2].

Algorithm 1. Dynamics for complete_adjacency_pair_norm

if $self == dialogueact.speaker$ **then**
  if $dialogueact$ intends to satisfy an obligation **then**
    if the agent has such obligation **then**
      return original_value+0.1
    else
      return original_value-0.5
return original_value

4.2 Turn Taking

In addition to motivating characters to complete adjacency pairs, we want their conversation to exhibit natural turn-taking behaviors. Sacks et al. summarized three basic rules on turn-taking behaviors in multiparty conversations [23]:

---

[1] Note that the communicative intent of a dialogue act is explicit in Thespian at this level. So we are always able to tell if the character is trying to create or satisfy an obligation.

[2] It is meaningless to compare the amounts of changes on different state features, since the fitting process will scale the agent's goal weights and therefore counter this difference.

1. If a party is addressed in the last turn, this party and no one else must speak next.
2. If the current speaker does not select the next speaker, any other speaker may take the next turn.
3. If no one else takes the next turn, the current speaker may take the next turn.

In Thespian, we use the goal state feature *initiate_adjacency_pair_norm* to keep track of how appropriate it is for a character to create obligations for others. The character's degree of achieving this goal will reduce if it creates new obligations for others when somebody in the conversation still has obligations. Hence, under this circumstance, only the characters that have obligations will not get punished for seizing the turn to act. If the dialogue act performed in the current turn is aimed at satisfying an existing obligation, we count it as a case of the current speaker not selecting the next speaker.

Algorithm 2. Dynamics for initiate_adjacency_pair_norm

> **if** $self == dialogueact.speaker$ **then**
>   **if** $dialogueact$ does not intend to satisfy an obligation **then**
>   **for** $character$ in $conversation$ **do**
>   **if** $character$ has unsatisfied obligations **then**
>   **return** original_value-0.1
> **return** original_value

To make face-to-face conversation different from lecturing, we give agents a goal of maximizing their *keep_turn_norm* to prevent them from dominating the conversation. If a character keeps talking after reaching the maximum number (currently set to 2) of dialogue acts it can perform within a conversational turn, its degree of achieving this goal decreases. The counter of dialogue acts will reset to zero only after another character starts speaking. In the case when the turn is free to be taken by anybody and the previous speaker has reached its maximum number of dialogue acts in its turn, this goal prevents the previous speaker from taking the turn again. This is consistent with what is described in Sacks' second and third rules.

Algorithm 3. Dynamics for keep_turn_norm

> **if** $self == dialogueact.speaker$ **then**
>   **if** $self.sentences\_in\_current\_turn > 2$ **then**
>   **return** original_value-0.1
> **return** original_value

4.3   Conversational Flow

We want conversations to exhibit the right structure. Conversations normally have an opening section, body and closing section [22]. In Thespian, we use a state feature *conversation status* to keep track of what a character thinks the current status of the conversation is. Initially the value for *conversation status* is "not opened". Once a character starts talking to another, the value changes to "opened". After the conversation finishes (judged by characters walking away from each other, or no eye contact for a long time), the value of *conversation status* is changed back to "not opened". We use the goal of maximizing *conversational_flow_norm* to enforce an appropriate conversational flow. The character that opens the conversation should open with proper greeting, and if a character ends a conversation, it needs to have said *bye* to other characters. Otherwise, the value of this goal feature will get reduced.

Algorithm 4. Dynamics for conversational_flow_norm

---

  if *self* == *dialogueact.speaker* **then**
    if *self.conversation* == 'not opened' **then**
      if *dialogueact.type* != 'initiate greeting' **then**
        return original_value-0.1
    else if *dialogueact.type* == 'end conversation' **then**
      if characters have not said bye to each other **then**
        return original_value-0.1
  return original_value

4.4   Affinity

Finally, we want to consider the effect of affinity. In order to take place, most social interactions require the affinity between the two characters involved to be within a certain range. Some social interactions require closer affinities than others. For example, greeting, saying "thanks", and asking about time can happen between almost any two characters. While asking private or potentially sensitive questions, e.g. who is the leader of the town, closer affinity is required.

To enable characters to anticipate that their actions may not trigger desired responses, we augmented *initiate_adjacency_pair_norm* with *affinity*. If satisfying an obligation requires closer affinity between the two characters than what it is currently, ignoring this obligation will result in much less punishment than if the affinity between the two characters is appropriate. The augmented rule will allow characters to ignore unreasonable requests, such as an enquiry of personal information from a stranger. And because characters have models of each other, the enquirer will know his/her enquiry is unreasonable and may be ignored.

Affinity is affected by many factors. First, it is affected by whether the characters act following norms. In Thespian, characters are closer to each other after having successful social interactions; and if a character constantly violates norms, its affinity with other characters will decrease. Affinity is also affected by the attitude associated with a dialogue act. Currently, we use a simple model that only takes one rule into account. If the dialogue act is performed in an impolite manner, it will decrease the affinity between the speaker and the addressee. Finally, the main effect of many types of dialogue acts is to change affinity. For example, the following dialogue acts, when not violating norms, can always increase affinity between two characters: compliments, small talk such as asking "how are you", "how is your family", and giving offers. And some other dialogue acts, such as accusations, once performed will usually reduce the affinity between two characters.

5 Example Dialogues

There are four main characters in the story, three children and Sergeant Smith. The children's names are Hamed, Xaled, and Kamela. The possible actions for the characters are greeting each other, asking each other various questions, answering questions, saying good-bye to each other, small talk, and introducing information about oneself to others. The last action can increase the affinity between Sergeant Smith and the children and does not create any obligations for replying.

Each of these four characters has the goals of following norms, and several other goals including collecting information from each other. Sergeant Smith wants to have a close affinity with the children, and wants to know the children's names, the names of the adults close by, etc. The children on the other hand are curious about what Sergeant Smith's nationality is, and how much Pashto he understands, etc. These goals on information collection can be fully achieved once the character gets the corresponding piece of information. In addition, the children need their affinity with Sergeant Smith to be close enough to feel comfortable telling their parents' names, but can answer other questions without considering affinity. In the following examples, to demonstrate the effect of varying goal weights on agents' behaviors, Sergeant Smith is controlled by an agent. However, normally a human learner would play Sergeant Smith, in which case the agent could be used to provide hints to the learner about what to do next. Even though in the actual authoring process, characters' goal weights are often fitted to their desired behaviors defined by the author, in the following examples, we will directly manipulate characters' goal weights to show the possible range of behaviors our model can create.

Example 1 is a sample dialogue in which obeying norms dominates all other goals for all the characters. In line 1 of example 1, Sergeant Smith chooses to greet the children first because performing any other action will result in opening the conversation inappropriately (hurting his goal of *conversational_flow_norm*). Then Sergeant Smith chooses to give up the turn, because of his goal of maximizing *initiate_adjacency_pair_norm*. The action he just performed has created obligations for the children to reply, as well as an obligation for him to wait for replies. Each child greets back in his/her turn because of their *complete_adjacency_pair_norm* goals. Xaled and Hamed stop talking after greeting because they know Kamela has not greeted back yet; if they create obligations for others, their *initiate_adjacency_pair_norm* goals will be hurt. In line 7, Xaled has satisfied his obligation and knows that nobody in the conversation has obligations. Xaled is then free to ask Sergeant Smith questions to satisfy his goal of curiosity. Lines 6-7, 8-9, 10-11, and 12-13 demonstrate the effect of the

Example 1:
1. Sergeant Smith to Kids: Hello!
2. Xaled to Sergeant Smith: Hello!
3. Hamed to Sergeant Smith: Hello!
4. Kamela to Sergeant Smith: Hello!
5. Sergeant Smith to Xaled: What is your name?
6. Xaled to Sergeant Smith: My name is Xaled.
7. Xaled to Sergeant Smith: What is your name?
8. Sergeant Smith to Xaled: My name is Mike.
9. Sergeant Smith to Xaled: How are you?
10. Xaled to Sergeant Smith: I am fine.
11. Xaled to Sergeant Smith: Are you an American?
12. Sergeant Smith to Xaled: Yes, I am an American.
13. Sergeant Smith to Xaled: I am learning Pashto.
. . .

keep_turn_norm goal. Especially in lines 12-13, even though introducing himself more will further increase affinity, Sergeant Smith chooses to follow norms by not holding the turn too long. Lines 8-13 also show the effect of affinity. Sergeant Smith does not ask the names of the children's parents directly, but chooses to talk about other topics to increase the affinity between them first.

We can create various character personalities by varying the pattern of norm weights. For example, we can create a character that seems either rude or in a hurry by letting it not respect *conversational_flow_norm*; a character who does not like to respond to others by letting it not respect *complete_adjacency_pair_norm*. As we will see, the Sergeant Smith character in Example 3 can be viewed as a combination of these two types. In addition, we can create a talkative character by giving a low weight on *keep_turn_norm*, a character who likes to interrupt other people's conversation by lowering the weight of *initiate_adjacency_pair_norm*. The above examples show varying the weights of different norms gives us a large space for creating different characters. The author does not need to worry about the correspondence between goal weights patterns and characters' personalities, because the fitting process can automatically configure characters' goal weights given scripts describing their behaviors.

Example 2 :
1. Sergeant Smith to Xaled: What is your name?
2. Xaled to Sergeant Smith: My name is Xaled.
3. Xaled to Sergeant Smith: What is your name?
4. Sergeant Smith to Xaled: What is the name of this town?
. . .

Next, we want to show how the goals of following norms interact with other goals to decide a character's behavior. Because the agents are decision-theoretic, we can get this effect easily. In Example 2, we make Sergeant Smith's information gathering goals his most important goals. As a consequence, Sergeant Smith does not respect having proper conversational flow and ignores his obligation to answer question. All his actions are aimed at gathering the information.

Example 3 :
1. Sergeant Smith to Xaled: What is your name?
2. Xaled to Sergeant Smith: What is your name?
3. Hamed to Sergeant Smith: Who is that man?
4. Kamela to Sergeant Smith: Do you have children?
5. Sergeant Smith to Xaled: What is your name?
. . .

Example 3 shows an extreme case in which none of the characters respect norms. However, they believe others will follow norms. The important goals for them are to get the information they are interested in. The characters are not able to conduct a meaningful interaction. Since none of them answer questions, they keep on asking for the information they are interested in.

What would happen if the characters did not even expect others to follow norms? In this case, the conversation would totally break down. The characters would choose an action that can bring them maximum immediate benefit. But, in this story all of their non norms goals require getting responses from others to get benefit; hence the characters will just choose actions randomly.

6 Discussion and Future Work

The examples we presented in Section 5 have shown that our conversational norms model is capable of modeling various kinds of characters in social communication. This model has been applied to 11 characters in three TLTS scenes, which consists of 65 lines on an average.

As the norms we included are the most basic ones, we will be working on enriching our model. As part of future work, we want to extend our model to better support subgroups in conversations. We want to support modeling situations that characters have shared obligations, e.g. characters can answer questions for their friends, and a character can impose obligations onto a group of characters.

On the other hand, we are also interested to study how the norms (or action dynamics in general) modeled with different degrees of details affect user experiences in the interactive drama, both in terms of believability of the characters and immersive nature of the interaction.

In addition, the evaluation of this work is currently primitive. As future work, we would like to develop more formal methodology for evaluating the system.

7 Conclusion

We discussed a model of basic conversational norms for face to face communication. These norms are implemented inside Thespian as goals and dynamics functions for decision-theoretic goal-driven agents. We have demonstrated that Thespian's conversational norms model is capable of modeling various kinds of characters in social interactions.

The benefit of building our model within Thespian's framework is three-fold. First, because of the underlying POMDP model each character has, we can easily create the effect of norms interacting with a character's other goals in deciding the character's behavior. Secondly, since the dynamics functions are independent of the characters (their goals, beliefs), this same model can be applied to any character. Finally, the approach is consistent with the automated authoring in Thespian, which enables characters to be tuned to behave according to dialogue act sequences specified by authors via automated tuning of goal parameters.

Our future work involves enriching our model and developing evaluation methodologies. For enriching the model, we are particularly interested in supporting subgroups in multiparty conversations, and studying how the levels of complexity embedded in the norms affect users' experiences in the interaction.

Acknowledgments

We thank our colleagues, especially Lewis Johnson, Hannes Vilhjálmsson and David Traum for their support and thoughtful discussions. This project is part of the DARWARS initiative sponsored by the US Defense Advanced Research Projects Agency (DARPA).

References

1. Kelso, M.T., Weyhrauch, P., Bates, J.: Dramatic presence. PRESENCE: Teleoperators and Virtual Environments **2(1)** (1993) 1–15
2. Riedl, M., Saretto, C.J., Young, R.M.: Managing interaction between users and agents in a multi-agent storytelling environment. In: AAMAS. (2003) 741–748
3. Cavazza, M., Charles, F., Mead, S.J.: Emergent situations in interactive storytelling. In: Proc. of ACM Symposium on Applied Computing (ACM-SAC). (2002)
4. Marsella, S.C., Johnson, W.L., Labore, C.: Interactive pedagogical drama for health interventions. In: AIED. (2003)
5. Paiva, A., Dias, J., Sobral, D., Aylett, R.: Caring for agents and agents that care: Building empathic relations with. In: AAMAS. (2004) 194–201
6. Si, M., Marsella, S.C., Pynadath, D.V.: Thespian: An architecture for interactive pedagogical drama. In: AIED. (2005)
7. Si, M., Marsella, S.C., Pynadath, D.V.: Thespian: Using multi-agent fitting to craft interactive drama. In: AAMAS. (2005) 21–28
8. Boella, G., Torre, L.v.d.: Obligations as social constructs. In: Proc. of the Italian Conf. on Artificial Intelligence (AI*IA'03). (2003) 27–38
9. Castelfranchi, C.: Commitments: From individual intentions to groups and organizations. In: ICMAS. (1995) 41–48
10. Airenti, G., Bara, B.G., Colombetti, M.: Conversation and bahavior games in the pragmatics of dialogue. In: Cognitive Science. Volume 17(2). (1993) 197–256–48
11. Traum, D.R., Allen, J.F.: Discourse obligations in dialogue processing. In: ACL. (1994) 1–8

12. Grice, H.P.: Logic and conversation. In Cole, P., Morgan, J., eds.: Syntax and Semantics: Vol. 3: Speech Acts. Academic Press (1975) 41–58

13. Mateas, M., Stern, A.: Integrating plot, character and natural language processing in the interactive drama façade. In: Proc. of the Internat'l Conf. on Tech. for Interactive Digital Storytelling and Entertainment. (2003)

14. Traum, D.R., Swartout, W., Marsella, S.C., Gratch, J.: Fight, flight, or negotiate: Believable strategies for conversing under crisis. In: IVA. (2005)

15. Clark, H., ed.: Using Language. Cambridge University Press, New York, NY (1996)

16. Johnson, W.L., Beal, C., Fowles-Winkler, A., Lauper, U., Marsella, S.C., Narayanan, S., Papachristou, D., Vilhjálmsson, H.H.: Tactical Language Training System: An interim report. In: Proc. of the Internat'l Conf. on Intelligent Tutoring Sys. (2004) 336–345

17. Marsella, S.C., Pynadath, D.V., Read, S.J.: PsychSim: Agent-based modeling of social interactions and influence. In: Proc. of the Internat'l Conf. on Cognitive Modeling. (2004) 243–248

18. Pynadath, D.V., Marsella, S.C.: Psychsim: Modeling theory of mind with decision-theoretic agents. In: IJCAI. (2005) 1181–1186

19. Smallwood, R.D., Sondik, E.J.: The optimal control of partially observable Markov processes over a finite horizon. Operations Research 21 (1973) 1071–1088

20. Gmytrasiewicz, P., Durfee, E.: A rigorous, operational formalization of recursive modeling. In: ICMAS. (1995) 125–132

21. Pynadath, D.V., Marsella, S.C.: Fitting and compilation of multiagent models through piecewise linear functions. In: AAMAS. (2004) 1197–1204

22. Schegloff, E.A., Sacks, H.: Opening up closings. Semiotica 7 (1973) 289–327

23. Sacks, H., Schegloff, E.A., Jefferson, G.: A simplest systematics for the organization of turn-taking for conversation. Language 50 (1974) 696–735

Autobiographic Knowledge for Believable Virtual Characters

Wan Ching Ho and Scott Watson

Adaptive Systems Research Group
School of Computer Science, University of Hertfordshire
College Lane, Hatfield, Hertfordshire, AL10 9AB, UK
{W.C.Ho, S.E.J.Watson}@herts.ac.uk

Abstract. It has been widely acknowledged in the areas of human memory and cognition that behaviour and emotion are essentially grounded by autobiographic knowledge. In this paper we propose an overall framework of human autobiographic memory for modelling believable virtual characters in narrative story-telling systems and role-playing computer games. We first lay out the background research of autobiographic memory in Psychology, Cognitive Science and Artificial Intelligence. Our autobiographic agent framework is then detailed with features supporting other cognitive processes which have been extensively modelled in the design of believable virtual characters (e.g. goal structure, emotion, attention, memory schema and reactive behaviour-based control at a lower level). Finally we list directions for future research at the end of the paper.

1 Introduction

It is widely held that a human's personality and problem-solving abilities are strongly influenced by his/her past experience. Inspired by psychological research in human memory, which states that autobiographic memory is a specific kind of episodic memory that may develop in childhood [1], Dautenhahn introduced autobiographic agents; agents which are embodied and situated in a particular environment (including other agents), and which dynamically reconstruct their individual history (autobiography) during their lifetimes [2]. Since autobiographic memory particularly focuses on meaningful and significant events for intelligent agents, it can also be used for 1) synthesising agents that can behave adaptively [3] and in socially intelligent ways [4] and 2) designing agents that appear believable and acceptable to humans.

Research in believable virtual agents has also utilised the human cognitive memory model [5] from the field of cognitive science and psychology, such as the study in synthetic vision for autonomous virtual humans [6]. Strategies for memory storage are usually divided into Sensory, Short-term and Long-term memories according to the rehearsal process and the retaining length of time for an item to be remembered. However, imposing a human memory model on virtual agents without taking its real cognitive abilities into account would meet various limitations. For example, only simple items can be remembered, agents are not able to decide which item is more

J. Gratch et al. (Eds.): IVA 2006, LNAI 4133, pp. 383–394, 2006.
© Springer-Verlag Berlin Heidelberg 2006

important to itself or to other agents, and the difficulty in creating temporal sequences of items in memory.

In addition to memory models, modelling other human cognitive processes has also been a popular research direction in developing architectures for IVAs (intelligent virtual agents) in recent years. For example, general computational models of human emotion for IVAs have attracted a lot of attention. Marsella and Gratch [7] utilised appraisal theory from psychology to model emotion for believable characters that perform in various applications. Their approach has also been used and enhanced by the VICTEC project team [8] to create believable synthetic characters acting in anti-bullying dramas.

Marsella and Gratch stated that appraisal variables enable agents to characterize the significance of events from the individual's perspective as the interpretation of each event is altered by an agent's own beliefs, desires and intentions, and *past events*. Here we are interested in establishing links between agents' current cognitive processes (e.g. goal formulation and emotion) and their past experiences – autobiographic memory.

Furthermore, research findings from psychologists Conway [9, 10 and 13] and Healy and Williams [11] provide rich evidence to show how autobiographic memory grounds other cognitive processes which operate in everyday human life. These findings have inspired us to develop an overall framework for an agent architecture supported by autobiographic knowledge.

2   Autobiographic Memory Research in Psychology, Cognitive Science and AI

"In the past, it (autobiographic memory) has usually been conceived of in terms of childhood (or infantile) amnesia, the phenomenon, first identified by Freud and familiar to all who reflect on it, that memories for events from the early years of our lives – before about 3 to 4 years – are not available to adult consciousness, although many memories from later childhood usually are easily called up." [1, page 8]

2.1   Autobiographic Memory Research in Psychology and Cognitive Science

Autobiographic memory is a specific kind of episodic memory that contains personally significant and meaningful experiences. Two features of autobiographic memory are generally defined and accepted by researchers in psychology, as pointed out by [12]:

- Autobiographic memories are mental constructions of the self.
- They very often feature imagery whilst simultaneously containing abstract personal knowledge.

Figure 1.1 extracted from [13] shows the hierarchical knowledge structures in the autobiographic knowledge-base in which Conway indicates that lifetime periods may themselves be thematically linked together (he uses work and relationship themes from his own past as examples in this figure). Conway shows that the conceptual self

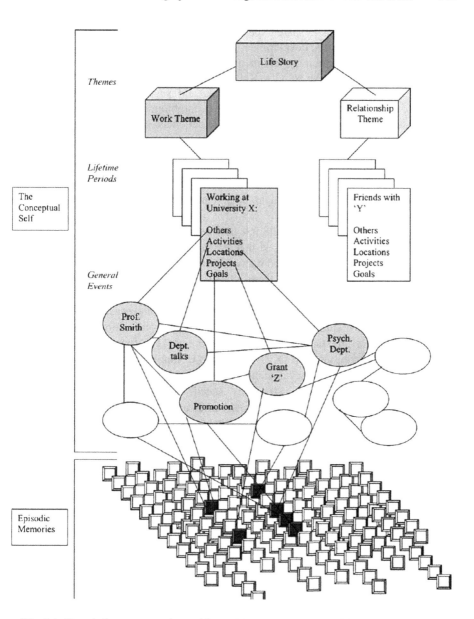

Fig. 1.1. Knowledge structures in autobiographic memory. Extracted from [13, page 609].

of a human being is composed and shaped by frequently reconstructing general events from retrieved episodic memories - these general events eventually form different life periods and themes in someone's life story.

From the perspective of considering humans as social beings, Nelson (a developmental psychologist) carried out her investigations into how children develop their own autobiographic memory, and suggests that the primary function of autobiographic memory is to share experiences with other people [1]. Other studies in psychological and cognitive development have also pointed out the cognitive, as well as social, functions of autobiographic memory as underlying all of human story telling and history-making narrative activity. Kelly and Dickinson studied the autobiographic accounts of the experience of chronic illness and suggested that "self is not a biologistic or psychologistic thing, rather self is autobiographic narrative." [14, page 224]. Neisser [15] suggests that recalling an experienced event from autobiographic memory is not a matter of reviving a single record but of moving appropriately among nested levels of structure. As the rehearsal process takes place, the memory structure is fundamentally changed by this recall. Moreover, a recall is always reconstructing an event by some other similar events of experience: Specifically, goals and current situations of the recall affect how much detail can be obtained from the event which is being remembered [15].

Self-schemata for maintaining the integrity and gist of past life events have been discussed by Barclay [16]. He argued that events in autobiographic memories change over time since new events occur and many life experiences become repetitious, making any single event indistinguishable from related happenings. Thus inaccurate remembering and forgetting take place because of the merging of episodic memories into more generic event categories representing the semantic features of everyday activities.

The importance of autobiographic memory to everyday life is further supported by findings from clinical studies. Healy and Williams [11] found that PTSD (Post Traumatic Stress Disorder) and OCD (Obsessive-Compulsive Disorder) patients tend to retrieve over-general memory contents in order to avoid emotional depression when remembering any specific episode. They stated, however, that this phenomenon influences patients' memory encoding and retrieval in their autobiographic memory over a long period of time. As a result, patients' working memories are decayed by the frequent and active forgetting of details of depressing episodes - thus also leading to a reduction in their general problem solving skills. This is significant as it demonstrates the negative effects which can occur when autobiographical memory goes wrong.

Applying Autobiographic Memory in Agent Research

Dautenhahn and Coles [17] carried out the first set of pioneering experiments on autobiographic agents, in which Situation-Action-Situation triplets were used as the core of the agents' autobiography. This work compared trajectories and lifetimes of purely reactive (sensory-driven) and post-reactive (memory-driven) control agents. Results from the experiments show that autobiographic memory, when embedded in the control architecture, can effectively extend an agent's lifetime.

Studies from [18] and [19] implemented finite-state autobiographic memory into the basic control architecture for a Purely Reactive agent to study autobiographic agents from the bottom-up approach and Artificial Life perspective. Different static virtual environments with resource allocations are created for either single or multiple agents to 'survive' in. In order to find out the location of resources by using local information from sensory data, autobiographic agents are able to remember their previous action sequences for going back to the particular resources. Taken together, these studies show that autobiographic agents and agents that share experiences outperform purely reactive agents in surviving in the static environments (this is true for both single agent and multi-agent experiments). After these early studies on basic memory architectures for narrative autobiographic agents, recent studies from [20] and [21] with enhanced computational autobiographic memory architectures and a complex and dynamic environment again show that autobiographic memory can prove beneficial – as indicated by the increased lifespan of autonomous, autobiographic, minimal agents. Furthermore, higher communication frequency brings better group performance for Long-term Autobiographic Memory agents in multi-agent experiments. It is evident that embedding narrative story-telling in LTM control architecture as an additional communication feature helps agents to be more adaptive in coping with different environmental dynamics.

Agent architectures with Categorical Long-term Autobiographic Memory which remember both positive and negative events are developed and investigated in [22]. Experimental results from the study show that it is advantageous for agents to 1) categorise the remembered events for efficient memory retrieval, and 2) remember various negative events so that they can avoid making same mistakes again.

3 Computational Framework for Autobiographic Agents

Figure 2.1 illustrates our overall framework of autobiographic agents. Although many human cognitive processes we propose in this framework have been modelled by

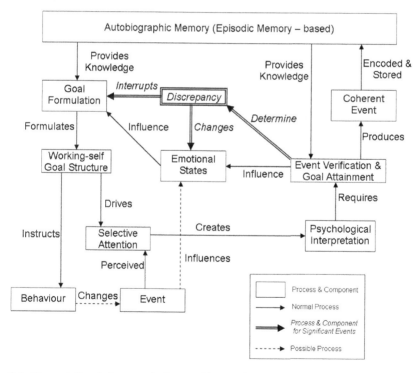

Fig. 2.1. Computational framework for autobiographic agents showing how autobiographic knowledge supports other cognitive processes

researchers working on believable virtual characters, such as attention, emotion and goal structure; many links between these cognitive processes and agents' knowledge base which contains agents' past experiences are still missing.

In this section we first focus on features of autobiographic knowledge and the components which are associating with it, as follows:

- Knowledge representation in autobiographic memory, based on episodic memory.
- Goal structure, emotion, and attention processes, in supporting or being influenced by, other cognitive processes.

Furthermore, we are also interested in exploring the potential of autobiographic agents for character-based narrative story-telling systems. How autobiographic narrative is generated from our agent framework is discussed at the end of this section.

Knowledge Representation in Autobiographic Memory

Information remembered in human autobiographic memory is based on event reconstructions on top of episodic memory. This process of event reconstruction provides memory rehearsal to consolidate frequently remembered information and elaborates cues for memory retrieval dealing with the current situation [10]. Computational autobiographic memory architectures supporting real-time event reconstructions for Artificial Life agents have been implemented in [20] and [21]. Experimental results from both papers show agents with Long-term Autobiographic Memory architectures have higher adaptivity when surviving in a complex and dynamic environment, compared to Reactive and Short-term Memory architectures.

As described in the previous section, literature from Psychology and Cognitive Science indicate that human autobiographic memory contains meaningful personal experiences – information that constructs the 'self' and shapes someone's 'personality'. The significance of each event remembered in agents' autobiographic memory plays an important role during processes of memory encoding and retrieval. Previous studies have shown that, having recognised the event significance, agents are able to re-experience a typical action sequence of the most meaningful event in their memory; therefore they outperform other types of agents, as shown in studies [20-23].

Autobiographic memory contains coherent personal events. New experiences must therefore be encoded into autobiographic memory in a similarly coherent way. In this way, experiences are verified with existing knowledge, maintaining the agent's autobiographic 'self'. In the case that a novel situation is experienced, the agent may lack relevant autobiographic knowledge, and will have to fall back on more instinctive behaviours.

It is worth pointing out here the difference in roles played by semantic knowledge in contrast with autobiographic knowledge. Semantic knowledge provides objective information about the world and is entirely passive; whereas autobiographic knowledge includes subjective representations of events that are actively encoded into memory [37].

Goal Structure, Emotion, and Attention Processes

The goal structure in our model follows that of Conway [13], in that it is designed to form an iterative loop whose purpose is to reduce the discrepancy between desired and actual goal states. In performing this discrepancy reduction, behaviour is regulated. Goals (and their respective sub-goals) emerge from autobiographic knowledge and guide selective attention and the behavioural processes necessary to perpetuate the current goal structure. In order to ensure this structure is maintained, the autobiographic knowledge base also continuously monitors events and verifies the current goal attainment. In this way, the goal structure directs behaviour in a manner which compliments the agent's previous understanding of the situation. In turn, this verification process will lead to the encoding and further consolidation of a generic schema-based memory (e.g. Barclay [16]) – presumably in order to reduce the quantity of information that actually has to be stored and to facilitate a more cohesive 'self'. In summary, the autobiographic knowledge-base is instrumental in the generation and maintenance of a goal structure, thus providing a cohesive narrative for the agent to follow.

This perpetual goal structure may be interrupted, however, most likely by causes outside of the agent's control. In the case that the desired goal is not attained, or the current situation cannot be verified, a large discrepancy (between desired and actual goal states) can occur. This discrepancy will interrupt the normal goal-formulation process and will also negatively affect the agent's emotion.

A new set of goals will need to be formed in order to cope with the current situation and to reduce this discrepancy as quickly as possible – again drawing upon information contained in the autobiographic knowledge-base. If the discrepancy is so large that the autobiographic knowledge-base contains no information relevant to the formulation of appropriate goals, the agent will be forced to fall back on emotion-based coping strategies and (in extreme cases) instinctive behaviours.

For this reason it is also necessary to model the role that emotion plays on the goal formulation process. Recent evidence from psychophysiological studies is consistent in the finding that events may generate emotions quickly (within 100-300ms of stimuli) and without conscious processing – a pattern which suggests 'pre-attentive' processing of emotional valence (see Compton [24] for a recent review). Furthermore, it is becoming apparent (under a number of methodological paradigms) that this pre-attentive activation of emotions can guide selective attention via both high-level cortical pathways as well as low-level routes through the amygdala. Taken together, this pattern of results suggests that emotion influences the normal goal formulation process (by shaping sub-goals which govern selective attention), but can also generate coping strategies when the autobiographic knowledge-base is found lacking. Whether successful or unsuccessful, these novel coping strategies are themselves encoded into the autobiographic knowledge-base thus creating new schemas which can be used to inform future goal formulation.

A major advantage of this model over previous appraisal models, such as those based on the OCC (Ortony, Clore and Collins) model, is that it conceives a perpetual schema-based, autobiographically-driven narrative 'self' which also allows the agent to learn from the experience of novel situations. Without autobiographic memory an agent may be doomed to repeat actions that have previously been unsuccessful. However, with autobiographic memory implemented an agent is free to learn from its mistakes and generate new coping strategies. Therefore the OCC model would benefit from the inclusion of the history function afforded by autobiographic memory [38].

Supporting Narrative Story-Telling

Research in narrative intelligence aims to develop agents which can have the capacities of story-awareness, story-telling and historical grounding. Concerned with building this kind of narrative agent, the area has investigated various directions such as interactive drama or story-telling [29-32], social understanding [33-35] and narrative in virtual environments [36]. Researchers have generated fruitful ideas that enhance both story-telling abilities and believability of narrative agents which interact with human users.

Narrative agents are usually pre-programmed either with temporal and structured stories or with simultaneously selecting story sequences from a large story database when they are interacting with human users in story-telling systems. Therefore they can take advantage of mechanisms used in natural historically grounded systems (Nehaniv [27]) and enhance the friendliness of these systems. While appreciating the success narrative agents bring to story-telling systems or software interfaces, the investigation of how agents themselves can benefit from autobiographic narrative – using their existing experiences to interpret a new story – is missing in the Narrative Intelligence research field. A new story is defined here as an agent perceiving a new event itself or receiving a story from other another agent through communication. An agent should then be able to form a unique psychological interpretation of this story by drawing upon their own existing autobiographic knowledge.

Humans are naturally expert in both understanding and producing narrative as we can express almost anything without necessarily using natural language but simply by showing appropriate gestures or facial expressions. In contrast, it is very difficult for virtual agents to have the same quality of result. This leads to the problem of behavioural incoherence – human observers often cannot understand why agents behave as they do. This phenomenon is described by Sengers as 'schizophrenia' [25]. She argues that architecture for narrative agents should be able to structure behaviour to be comprehensible as narrative. This behavioural coherence which originated with the life story of human beings [28] is particularly important for believable agents in narrative story-telling environments. Therefore, except system interfaces which show the agents' 'intentions' to the user [23], behavioural patterns expressed by narrative virtual agents have to be generated from 1) reconstructing their past experiences in autobiographic memory and 2) existing knowledge of the surrounding agents and the environment.

Another main research issue in character-based narrative story-telling system, i.e. role-play dramas or games, is how to provide good 'actors' – agents that react to different situations in stories with appropriate emotional expression [23]. We argue that taking a long-term character development approach, rather than setting a fixed group of parameters for instructing agents to 'act' in a particular situation, is more realistic and flexible to shape agents' 'personality' in a story and to determine their emotion in a given situation by allowing them to have their own autobiographic knowledge. This approach thus 1) allows for the creation of agents which are 'born with' certain types of personality for role-play stories, and 2) supports long-term development and learning of virtual actors as they gain new experience from acting in each new situation.

Furthermore, the potential of autobiographic agents to create stories from their own experiences and understand stories from others enhances the endurance of events remembered in their autobiographic memory. Nelson [1] pointed out that in addition to the function of language, humans sharing memories with other people can be seen as narrative story-telling that performs a significant social-cultural function, and both these two functions explain why personal autobiographic memories continue to persist during their lifetime.

4 Conclusion and Future Work

In this paper, we propose a framework to model human autobiographic memory for believable virtual characters. From research findings in Psychology and Cognitive Science, we argued that autobiographic knowledge is necessary for virtual agents in terms of learning from past experiences and long-term developments. We have also discussed our previous studies in Artificial Life autobiographic agents. On a behavioural level, they can be perceived as a foundation for investigating how autobiographic memory enhances agents' adaptivity and believability. Similarly, other important cognitive processes, such as goal formulation and emotion lead agents to perform appropriate behaviours in a given situation, should also be grounded by autobiographic knowledge.

Further development for the currently proposed autobiographic knowledge framework is to implement it into an agent-based emergent narrative system, which will be developed in the EU Framework 6 funded project 'eCIRCUS' (Education through Characters with emotional-Intelligence and Role-playing Capabilities that Understand Social interaction).

The first step is to specify the knowledge representation in episodic memory in order to reconstruct general events, themes and possibly life periods for forming agents' autobiographic 'self', based on the prototype created for Artificial Life agents in [22] and [23]. Memory encoding and retrieval mechanisms also need to be developed and validated for guiding agents' behaviour, planning, and changes in emotion. The second step would be to create semantic memory from accumulated repetitive episodic events. Semantic memory, as utilized in many conventional AI learning approaches, may allow agents to take advantage of prior knowledge in perceiving and organizing both the physical can social world around them.

Human memory is fallible. False memories can constructed, while true memories may be incorrectly recalled or even forgotten. While these negative characteristics of human autobiographic memory are important (and could be modelled for academic purposes), we do not believe that users currently interact with agents for long enough periods of time to require this be included.

In addition to the implementation of the whole autobiographic memory framework for creating believable characters, the component of autobiographic memory can be separately integrated into other agent cognitive architectures, such as [7] and [8]. In this case, links between agents' autobiographic memory and other cognitive processes are critical in establishing 1) the generation of believable behaviour and 2) agents' learning ability and long-term development.

Acknowledgements

This paper is supported by the eCIRCUS project carried out with the provision of the European Community in the Framework VI Programme.

References

1. Nelson, K. (1993) The Psychological and social origins of autobiographical memory. Psychological Science, 4:7-14.
2. Dautenhahn, K. (1996) Embodiment in animals and artefacts, Proc. AAAI FS Embodied Cognition and Action, AAAI Press, Technical report FS-96-02, 27-32.
3. Nehaniv, C. L. and Dautenhahn, K. (1998) Embodiment and memories - algebras of time and history for autobiographic agents, 14th European Meeting on Cybernetics and Systems Research, Embodied Cognition and AI symposium, pp. 651–656.
4. Dautenhahn, K. (1999), Embodiment and interaction in socially intelligent lifelike agents, in C. L. Nehaniv (ed.), Computation for Metaphors, Analogy and Agent, Vol. 1562 of Springer Lecture Notes in Artificial Intelligence, Springer, pp. 102–142.
5. Norman, D. A. and Bobrow, D. G. (1975) On the role of active memory processes in perception and cognition, in C. N. Cofer (ed.), The Structure of Human Memory, W. H. Freeman and Company, pp. 114–132.
6. Peters, C. and O'Sullivan, C. (2002) Synthetic vision and memory for autonomous virtual humans, Computer Graphics Forum 21(4), 743–753.
7. Marsella, S., Gratch, J. (2003) Modelling coping behaviour in virtual humans: Don't worry, be happy, Proceedings of Second International Joint Conference on Autonomous Agents and Multiagent Systems, ACM Press, 2003.
8. VICTEC (2005) Virtual ICT with empathic characters, http://www.victec.net/. Last accessed 29-03-2006.
9. Conway, M. A. (1996) Autobiographical memories and autobiographical knowledge, in D. C. Rubin (ed.), Remembering our past: Studies in autobiographical memory, Cambridge Univ. Press, Cam0bridge, UK, pp. 67–93.
10. Conway, M. A. and Pleydell-Pearce, C. W. (2000) The construction of autobiographical memories in the self memory system, Psychological Review 107, 261–288.
11. Healy, H., Williams, J. M. G. (1999) Autobiographic Memory, Handbook of Cognition and Emotion, pp. 229–242.
12. Conway, M. A., Pleydell-Pearce, C. W. and Whitecross, S. E. (2001) The neuroanatomy of autobiographical memory: A slow cortical potential study (SCP) of autobiographical memory retrieval, Memory and Language, 45, pp. 493–524.
13. Conway, M. A. (2005), Memory and the self, Journal of Memory and Language 53, pp. 594–628.
14. Kelly, M. P. and Dickinson, H. (1997) The narrative self in autobiographical accounts of illness, The Sociological Review, 45(2), pp. 254–278.
15. Neisser, U. (1986) Nested structure in autobiographical memory, in D. C. Rubin (ed.), Autobiographical Memory, Cambridge University Press, Cambridge, UK, pp. 71–88.
16. Barclay, C. R. (1986) Schematization of autobiographical memory, in D. C. Rubin (ed.), Autobiographical Memory, Cambridge University Press, Cambridge, USA, pp. 82–99.
17. Dautenhahn, K. and Coles, S. (2001) Narrative intelligence from the bottom up: A computational framework for the study of story-telling in autonomous agents, The Journal of Artificial Societies and Social Simulation (JASSS), 4(1), pp. 1–15. http://jasss.soc.surrey.ac.uk/4/1/1.html (Last accessed 16-09-2005).

18. Ho, W. C., Dautenhahn, K. and Nehaniv, C. L. (2003) Comparing different control architectures for autobiographic agents in static virtual environments, Intelligent Virtual Agents 2003 (IVA 2003), Springer LNAI, pp. 182–191.
19. Ho, W. C., Dautenhahn, K., Nehaniv, C. L. and te Boekhorst, R. (2004) Sharing memories: An experimental investigation with multiple autonomous autobiographic agents, IAS-8, 8th Conference on Intelligent Autonomous Systems, IOS Press, Amsterdam, NL, pp. 361–370.
20. Ho, W. C., Dautenhahn, K. and Nehaniv, C. L. (2005) Autobiographic agents in dynamic virtual environments - performance comparison for different memory control architectures, Proceedings of IEEE Congress on Evolutionary Computation - Special Session: Artificial Life, pp. 573–580.
21. Ho, W. C., Dautenhahn, K. and Nehaniv, C. L. (submitted) A bottom-up study in autonomous agents with autonomous memory and narrative storytelling in a dynamic virtual environment, Cognitive Systems Research.
22. Ho, W. C., Dautenhahn, K. and Nehaniv, C. L. (2006) A study of episodic memory-based learning and narrative structure for autobiographic agents, Proceedings of Adaptation in Artificial and Biological Systems, 3, AISB 2006 conference, pp. 26–29.
23. Ho, W. C., (2005) Computational memory architectures for autobiographic and narrative virtual agents, Unpublished PhD Thesis, University of Hertfordshire.
24. Compton, R.J. (2003) The interface between emotion and attention: A review of evidence from psychology and neuroscience, Behavioural and Cognitive Neuroscience Reviews, 2(2), pp. 115-129.
25. Sengers, P. (2003) Narrative and schizophrenia in artificial agents, in M. Mateas and P. Sengers (eds), Narrative Intelligence, Amsterdam: John Benjamins, pp. 259–278.
26. Louchart, S., Aylett, R., Enz, S. and Dias J. (2006) Understanding emotions in drama, a step towards interactive narrative, Proceedings of Adaptation in Artificial and Biological Systems, 3, AISB 2006 conference, pp. 38-44.
27. Nehaniv C. L. (1999) Story-telling and emotion: Cognitive technology considerations in networking temporally and affectively grounded minds, Third International Conference on Cognitive Technology: Networked Minds (CT'99), Aug. 11-14, 1999 San Francisco/Silicon Valley, USA, pp. 313-322.
28. Linde, C. (1993) Life Stories: The Creation of Coherence, Oxford University Press.
29. Mateas, M. (1999) An Oz-centric review of interactive drama and believable agents, Artificial Intelligence Today pp. 297–328.
30. Mateas, M. and Stern, A. (2002) Architecture, authorial idioms and early observations of the interactive drama facade, Technical report, School of Computer Science, Carnegie Mellon University. CMU-CS-02-198.
31. Stern, A. (2003) Virtual babyz: Believable agents with narrative intelligence, in M. Mateas and P. Sengers (eds), Narrative Intelligence, John Benjamins Publishing, pp. 215–227.
32. Cavazza, M., Martin, O., Charles, F., Mead, S. J. and Marichal, X. (2003) Interacting with virtual agents in mixed reality interactive storytelling, Intelligent Virtual Agents 2003 (IVA 2003), Springer LNAI, pp. 231–235.
33. Dautenhahn, K. and Nehaniv, C. L.: 1998, Artificial life and natural stories, International Symposium on Artificial Life and Robotics (AROB III), Vol. 2, Beppu, Oita, Japan, pp. 435–439.
34. Dautenhahn, K. (2002) The origins of narrative in search for the transactional format of narratives in humans and other social animals, Cognition and Technology: Co-existence, Convergence, Co-evolution (IJCT) pp. 97–123. John Benjamins Publishing Company.

35. Dautenhahn, K. (2003) Stories of lemurs and robots - the social origin of storytelling, in M. Mateas and P. Sengers (eds), Narrative Intelligence, John Benjamins Publishing, pp. 63–90.

36. Aylett, R. (1999) Narrative in virtual environments: Towards emergent narrative, Proc. Narrative Intelligence, AAAI Fall Symposium 1999, AAAI Press, pp. 83–86.

37. Fentress, J. & Wickham, C. (1992) Social memory – new perspectives on the past. Blackwell.

38. Bartneck, C. (2002). Integrating the OCC model of emotions in embodied characters. Proceedings of the workshop on virtual conversational characters: applications, methods, and research challenges, Melbourne.

Teachable Characters: User Studies, Design Principles, and Learning Performance

Andrea L. Thomaz and Cynthia Breazeal

MIT Media Lab, Cambridge, MA 02139, USA
alockerd@media.mit.edu

Abstract. Teachable characters can enhance entertainment technology by providing new interactions, becoming more competent at game play, and simply being fun to teach. It is important to understand how human players try to teach virtual agents in order to design agents that learn effectively from this instruction. We present results of a user study where people teach a virtual agent a novel task within a reinforcement-based learning framework. Analysis yields lessons of how human players approach the task of teaching a virtual agent: 1) they want to direct the agent's attention; 2) they communicate both instrumental and motivational intentions; 3) they tailor their instruction to their understanding of the agent; and 4) they use negative communication as both feedback and as a suggestion for the next action. Based on these findings we modify the agent's learning algorithm and show improvements to the learning interaction in follow-up studies. This work informs the design of real-time learning agents that better match human teaching behavior to learn more effectively and be more enjoyable to teach.

1 Introduction

The development of interactive characters that learn from experience continues to be an exciting area of research. In particular, teachable characters, where the human player can shape their behavior, have been successfully incorporated into a number of computer games. In *Black & White*, for instance, human players shape their characters by leading them with different leashes to be "nice" or "naughty" [1]. In *NERO*, virtual armies can be incrementally taught new battle skills from human crafted training exercises [2]. Animal training paradigms are also popular. In *Dogz*, for instance, people can teach their virtual canines new tricks through reward (i.e., treats) or punishment (i.e., spray bottle) [3], whereas Blumberg *et al.* present a learning architecture for a virtual dog that can be taught via clicker training [4]. In sum, teachable characters can enhance game play by either introducing the opportunity for new interactions, becoming more competent at a game, or by simply being fun to teach.

Most of the above examples are Reinforcement Learning (RL) based approaches. RL has certain desirable qualities, in particular the general strategy of exploring and learning from experience. Although the theory of reinforcement learning was originally formulated for systems to learn on-line, independent of human participation, a number of prior works have explored having a human contribute in a supervisory role [4,5,6,7]. This models the human input as indistinguishable from any other feedback coming from the environment. *But is this a good assumption?* We posit that the human is a

J. Gratch et al. (Eds.): IVA 2006, LNAI 4133, pp. 395–406, 2006.
ⓒ Springer-Verlag Berlin Heidelberg 2006

Fig. 1. *Sophie's Kitchen*: oven, table, shelf, and five baking objects

special part of the environment that needs to be more fully understood, supported, and leveraged in the learning process. To do this properly, we must understand the human's contribution: *how* do they teach, *what* are they trying to communicate to the learner?

The contribution of this paper is two-fold. First, we present a systematic study and analysis of human behavior when teaching a virtual robot agent within a reinforcement-based learning framework. Our system, *Sophie's Kitchen*, is a computer game that allows an agent to be trained interactively to bake a cake through sending the agent feedback messages. We use this platform to study people's interactions, and we report four characteristics of how humans approach explicitly teaching a game agent. 1) People want to direct the agent's attention and guide the exploration. 2) Players communicate both instrumental and motivational intents. 3) Transparency behaviors that reveal the internal state of the agent can improve the human's teaching. 4) The human's negative feedback is both feedback and a suggestion to reverse the action if possible.

Second, we incorporated these findings into specific modifications of the agent's interface and learning algorithm. Over 200 people played the *Sophie's Kitchen* game in a second set of experiments, showing that our modifications significantly improve the agent's learning performance. This work contributes to the design of real-time learning agents that are better matched to human teaching behavior.

2   Experimental Platform: Sophie's Kitchen

We implemented a Java-based simulation platform, *Sophie's Kitchen*. The scenario is a kitchen (Fig. 1), where the agent (Sophie) learns to bake a cake. In all of the experiments described in this paper the agent uses Q-learning [8] to learn the value of various state-action pairs toward arriving in a state with a baked cake in the oven. The kitchen creates a sufficiently complex domain with on the order of 10,000 states, and 2-7 actions available from each state. The task is hierarchical with subgoals that can be completed out of order. A successful task completion requires 30-35 actions.

We use RL to investigate how people interactively teach an agent. Importantly, we believe these lessons and modifications can be applied to the general class of reinforcement-based learning approaches, and not just Q-learning in particular. In a straightforward task such as this, it may in fact be easier to just teach the agent with declarative knowledge or procedural rules—i.e., programming; however, the drawback of such an approach is that agent is completely dependent on the human in order to learn anything and the human must know the steps of the task exactly. Our research aims to build agents that can learn on their own but also take full advantage of human teaching or guidance in a way that is natural and intuitive for the human partner.

The kitchen has Flour, Eggs, and a Spoon each with a single object state. The Bowl has five states: empty, flour, eggs, unstirred, stirred, and the Tray has three states: empty, batter, baked. There are four locations: Shelf, Table, Oven, Agent. The locations are arranged in a ring, thus the agent can GO left or right. She can PICK-UP any object in her current location; she can PUT-DOWN any object in her possession; and she can USE any object in her possession on any object in her current location. Each action advances the world state (e.g., executing PICK-UP <Flour> changes the state such that the Flour is in location Agent). The agent can hold one object at a time. USEing an ingredient on the Bowl puts that ingredient in it; using the Spoon on the unstirred Bowl transitions its state to stirred, and so on.

In the initial state, the agent faces all the objects on the Shelf. A successful task completion includes putting flour and eggs in the bowl, stirring the ingredients using the spoon, putting the batter into the tray, and putting the tray in the oven. The goal state has a positive reward ($r = 1$), and some end states are so-called *disaster* states since they are unrecoverable (e.g., putting the eggs in the oven). These result in a negative reward ($r = -1$), the termination of the current trial, and a transition to the initial state.

A central feature of *Sophie's Kitchen* is the interactive reward interface. Using the mouse, a human trainer can—at any point—award a scalar reward signal, $r \in [-1, 1]$. The user receives visual feedback enabling them to tune the reward before sending it, and choosing and sending the reward does not halt the progress of the agent, which runs asynchronously to the reward interface. After the initial experiment, additional elements (guidance, motivation) were added to the interaction, these are detailed in Section 4.

3 Experiments

We conducted two experiments with *Sophie's Kitchen* where participants played a computer game. Their goal was to get the virtual robot, Sophie, to learn how to bake a cake. Participants were told they could not tell Sophie what actions to do, nor could they do any actions directly. They were only able to send messages with the mouse to help Sophie learn the task. The experiments differed in messages available and in the behavior of the agent. The experiments are introduced briefly and detailed in Section 4.

Experiment 1: The purpose of the first experiment was to understand, when given a single reward channel, how do people use it to teach the agent? We solicited participation from the campus community and obtained 18 volunteers. In this experiment, people have direct control of the reward signal that the agent uses in the Q-Learning algorithm. The system maintains an activity log of each of the following: state transitions, actions, human rewards, reward aboutness (described in section 4.1), disasters, and goals. Players were only able to give Sophie feedback messages with the mouse and were given the following explanation of the messages: Drag the mouse up for a green box, a positive message; and down for red/negative (Figure 2(a) shows a positive feedback message). Lift the mouse button to send the message, and Sohpie sees the message color and size.

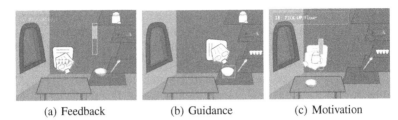

(a) Feedback   (b) Guidance   (c) Motivation

Fig. 2. The embellished communication channel. 2(a): feedback is given by left-clicking and dragging the mouse up to make a green box (positive) and down for red (negative). 2(b): guidance is given by right-clicking on an object, selecting it with the yellow square. 2(c): a motivation message is given by doing a feedback message on top of Sophie.

Experiment 2: After the first experiment, we made four algorithm and interface modifications (Guidance, Gaze, Motivation, and Undo), making the exploration process more accessible and guidable to the human partner, as well as making the behavior of the character more expressive, natural and understandable (transparent) to the human. To evaluate the benefits of these modifications, we deployed *Sophie's Kitchen* on the World Wide Web, and collected data from over 200 players.

4   Results

We present four sets of results. In each case a finding in the first experiment led to one of the modifications mentioned above. This modification is explained in detail, and then the second experiment sheds light on its effect on the learning interaction.

4.1   Teaching Is More Than Simple Feedback

One of the major findings of the first experiment was that, perhaps not surprisingly, people have multiple communication intentions beyond the simple feedback that the Q-Learning algorithm expects. In particular, people want to guide the agent and they want a generic encouragement/discouragement channel of communication.

Guidance. Finding from Experiment 1: In the first experiment the interface let the user assign their feedback to a particular object (object specific rewards). The hypothesis was that people would prefer to indicate what their feedback was 'about'. Object specific rewards are used only to learn about the human trainer's communicative intent; the learning algorithm treats all rewards *equally* and in the traditional sense of pertaining to the whole state. Even though the instructions clearly stated that all communication and rewards were *feedback* messages, we saw that many people assumed that object specific rewards were future-directed messages or guidance for the agent. This is evident from both interviews with participants and from the correlation of object/action pertinence and rewards given.

  If people were using the object rewards in a traditional RL sense, they should be feedback and pertain to the agent's last action. In Figure 3(a), there is a mark for each

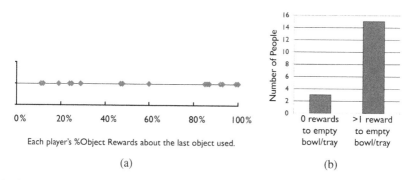

Each player's %Object Rewards about the last object used.

(a)

(b)

Fig. 3. Fig. 3(a) shows each player's percentage of object rewards that were about the most recent object used; many were rarely feedback oriented. Fig 3(b), shows the number of people that gave (0 vs. 1 or more) rewards to the bowl or tray empty on the shelf, which is assumed to be guidance.

player indicating their percentage of object rewards that were about the last object used. A substantial number of people had object rewards that were rarely correlated to the last object of attention, thus not feedback oriented.

We suspect these people's rewards actually pertain to the future, indicating what they want (or do not want) the agent to use next. To test how many people were using the object rewards as guidance, we consider an example case. When the agent is facing the shelf, a guidance reward could be administered (about what object to pick up). A reward given to either the empty bowl or empty tray on the shelf should *only* be a guidance reward since these are not be part of any desired sequence in the cake baking task. In Fig.3(b), we see that 15 of the 18 people had a non-zero number of rewards to the empty bowl or tray on the shelf. Thus we conclude that many participants tried using the reward channel to guide the agent's behavior to particular objects, giving rewards for actions the agent was *about to do* in addition to traditional feedback. While delayed rewards have been discussed in the RL literature [9], these *anticipatory* rewards observed from everyday human trainers will require new tools and attention in learning algorithms in order for the agent to use them as the human partner intended.

Modifications to the Learning Agent to add Guidance: This behavior suggests that people want to speak to the action selection of the algorithm to influence the exploration. To accomplish this, we added a guidance communication channel. Clicking the right mouse button draws a yellow square. When the yellow square is administered on an object, this is a guidance message to the agent, the content of which is the object. Figure 2(b) shows the player guiding Sophie to the bowl. Note, the left mouse button allows the player to give feedback in the same way as the first experiment.

An RL algorithm can be described as continually looping through the following: `select-action`, `take-action`, `sense-reward`, `update-values`. Our modified Q-Learning algorithm adds a phase where the agent registers guidance communication to bias action selection. Thus, the process becomes: `sense-guidance`, `select-action`, `take-action`, `sense-reward`, `update-values`. The agent waits for guidance messages during the `sense-guidance` step (a short delay allows the teacher time to administer guidance). Upon receiving a guidance mes-

Table 1. 1-tailed t-test, effects of guidance on learning performance. (F: failures, G: first success)

Measure	Mean no guide	Mean guide	chg	t(26)	p
# trials	28.52	14.6	49%	2.68	<.01
# actions	816.44	368	55%	2.91	<.01
# F	18.89	11.8	38%	2.61	<.01
# F before G	18.7	11	41%	2.82	<.01
# states	124.44	62.7	50%	5.64	<.001

sage the agent saves the object as the `guidance-object`. In the `select-action` step, the default behavior (a standard approach) chooses randomly between the set of actions with the highest Q-values, within a bound β. If any guidance was received, the agent will *instead* choose randomly between the set of actions that have the `guidance-object` as their object.

Evaluation of Guidance: In the second experiment we evaluate the effects of this guidance feature by analyzing training sessions with human subjects in two conditions: the `no guidance` condition has feedback only; the `guidance` condition has both guidance and feedback available. The comparison is summarized in Table 1. The `guidance` condition shows improvements in how long it takes to learn the task. The number of training trials needed to learn the task was 49% less; and the number actions needed to learn the task was 55% less. In the `guidance` condition the number of unique states visited was 50% less, thus the task was learned more efficiently and presumably without visiting as many non-useful states. And finally the `guidance` condition provided a more successful training experience. The number of trials ending in failure was 38% less, and the number of failed trials before the first successful trial was 41% less.

Motivation. Findings from Experiment 1: For many people, a large majority of rewards given were positive, the mean percentage of positive rewards for all the players was 69.8%. We thought this may be due to the agent improving and behaving more correctly over time (soliciting more positive rewards); however, data from the first quarter of training shows that well before the agent is behaving correctly, the majority of participants show a positive bias. Fig. 4 shows reward histograms for each participant's first quarter of training; the number of negative rewards on the left and positive rewards on the right. Most participants have a much larger bar on the right. A plausible hypothesis is that people are falling into a natural teaching interaction with the agent, treating it as a social entity that needs encouragement. Some people specifically mentioned in the interview that they felt positive feedback would be better for learning.

Modification to the Learning Agent to add Motivation: Due to this bias, a second embellishment to the communication channel adds a dedicated motivational input. This is done by considering a reward motivational if it is administered *on* Sophie. For visual feedback the agent is shaded yellow to let the user know that a subsequent reward will be motivational. Figure 2(c) shows a positive motivational message to Sophie. Instructions indicate this communication channel is for general feedback about the task (e.g. "Doing good Sophie!" or "Doing bad!") as opposed to feedback about a particular action.

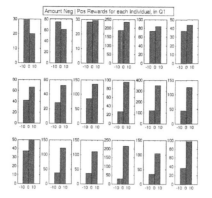

Fig. 4. Histograms of rewards for each individual in the first quarter of their session. The left column is negative rewards and the right is positive rewards.

Evaluation of Motivation: In the second experiment, players that had the motivation signal had a significantly more balanced feedback valance than the players that did not have it. Players that did not have a motivational channel had a mean ratio (#*positive*/#*negative*) of 2.07; whereas those with the motivational channel had a mean ratio of 1.688. This is a significant effect, $t(96) = -2.02, p = .022$. Thus, we conclude that motivation is a separate intention that was folded into the positive feedback in the initial study. Future work is to understand how an agent can utilize this signal in a different way to improve the learning interaction.

4.2 The Human Tries to Maximize Their Impact

In human learning, teachers direct a learner's attention, structure experiences, support attempts, and regulate complexity. The learner contributes by revealing their internal state to help guide the teaching process. This *collaborative* aspect of teaching and learning has been stressed in prior work [10], and the findings in this study support this notion of *partnership*. When everyday users train a machine learning agent, we see them adjust their training as the interaction proceeds, reacting to the behavior of the learner.

Findings from Experiment 1: We expected people would habituate to the activity and that feedback would decrease over the training, informed by related work [6]. However, we see an increasing trend in the rewards-to-actions ratio over the first three quarters of training. Fig. 5 shows data for the first three quarters of training, each graph has one bar for each player indicating the ratio of rewards to actions. By the third graph more bars are approaching or surpassing a ratio of 1. One explanation for this trend is a shift in mental model; as people realize the impact of their feedback they adjusted their training to fit this model of the learner. This finds anecdotal support in the interview responses. Many users reported that once they concluded that their feedback was helping they subsequently gave more rewards.

Additionally, we had a second hypothesis about the unbalanced use of feedback (Fig. 4), namely that the agent did not have enough of a behavioral response to

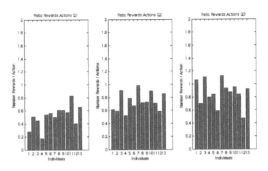

Fig. 5. The rewards to actions ratio has an increasing trend over the first three quarters of training

negative rewards. A typical RL agent does not have an instantaneous reaction to either positive or negative rewards, but particularly in the case of negative rewards, this could be interpreted as the agent 'ignoring' the feedback. The user may stop using them when they feel the agent is not paying attention to them.

These are concrete examples of the human trainer's propensity to learn from the agent how to best impact the process. This presents a huge opportunity for an interactive learning agent to *improve its own learning environment* by communicating more of its internal state to the teacher, making the learning process more transparent. This led us to make the following two modifications: 1) adding a gaze behavior to increase the transparency and foster more timely and relevant guidance, and 2) adding an UNDO behavior to create a more immediate response to negative feedback.

Gaze Behavior. Modification to the Learning Agent: We explored gaze as a means of making the learning process more transparent to the human. Gaze requires that the agent have a physical/graphical embodiment that can be understood by the human as having a forward heading. In general, gaze precedes an action and communicates something about the action that is going to follow.

We extended *Sophie's Kitchen* to add gaze. Recall our interactive Q-Learning loop: `sense-guidance`, `select-action`, `take-action`, `sense-reward`, `update-values`. In the `sense-guidance` phase, the learning agent now finds the set of actions, A, with the highest Q-values, within a bound β. For every action, a, in A, the agent gazes for 1 second at the `object` of a (if it has one). For example, in Fig. 1 Sophie is gazing at the tray, and at the bowl in Fig. 2(b). This communicates a level of uncertainty through the amount of gazing that precedes an action. It introduces an additional delay (proportional to uncertainty) prior to `select-action`, soliciting and providing the opportunity for guidance. We expect this transparency to improve the teacher's model of the learner, creating a more understandable interaction for the human and a better learning environment for the agent.

Evaluation of Gaze Behavior: Our hypothesis is that the gazing behavior helps the human understand when the agent did (and did not) need their guidance instruction. We evaluate this in the second experiment, studying players that used the feedback and guidance *without gaze* versus those that had the feedback and guidance *with gaze*

Table 2. 1-tailed t-test. Gaze helped players give more guidance if needed and less if not. (uncertainty low: ≤ 3 choices; uncertainty high: ≥ 3 choices.

Measure	Gaze	No Gaze	t(51)	p
% guidance when uncertainty low	79	85	-2.22	< .05
% guidance when uncertainty high	48	36	1.96	< .05

(summarized in Table 2). Note that players without the gaze behavior had ample opportunity to administer guidance messages; however, the time that the agent waits is uniform throughout the interaction. We found that the players in the gaze condition gave less guidance than the no gaze condition when the agent had three or less action choices (uncertainty low), $t(51) = -2.22, p = .015$. And conversely they gave more guidance then the no gaze condition when the agent had three or more action choices (uncertainty high), $t(51) = 1.96, p = .027$. Thus, when the agent uses the gaze behavior to indicate which actions it is considering, the human trainers do a better job matching their instruction to the needs of the agent throughout the training session.

Undo Behavior. Modification to the Learning Agent: In the standard Q-Learning framework, the effects of feedback on the policy are not seen until the state from which the action was made is revisited (which can take a long time). In many cases being too responsive to any one reward would be detrimental to the exploration needed to learn; however, we argue that when this signal is from a benevolent human teacher the agent should be more responsive to negative feedback. We expect just-in-time error correction more closely resembles a natural human teaching interaction and will be more understandable for the human.

We modified the Sophie agent to respond to negative feedback with an UNDO behavior (a natural correlate or opposite action) when possible. A negative reward is handled in both the `update-values` step and the subsequent `select-action` step. In the `select-action` step immediately following negative feedback, the action selection mechanism chooses the action that reverses the last action if possible. The proper UNDO behavior is represented within each primitive action (e.g. GO <direction> returns GO <-direction>; PICK-UP <object> returns PUT-DOWN <object>; etc.).

Evaluation of Undo Behavior: We found the UNDO response to negative feedback from the human trainer significantly improves the learning performance of the agent in a number of ways. In the second experiment, we compare players that had the UNDO

Table 3. 1-tailed t-test, effects of UNDO on learning performance. (F = failures, G = first success)

Measure	Mean without undo	Mean with undo	chg	t(96)	p
# states	48.3	42	13%	-2.26	=.01
# F	6.94	4.37	37%	-3.76	<.001
# F before G	6.4	3.87	40%	-3.7	<.001
# actions to G	208.86	164.93	21%	-2.25	=.01
# actions	255.68	224.2	12%	-1.32	=.095

behavior to those that did not. Table 3 summarizes these results. The agent visits 13% fewer states using 12% fewer action with the UNDO behavior, thus the learning process is more efficient. The agent takes 21% fewer actions before its first success. The UNDO behavior helps the agent avoid failures: The total number of failed trials was 37% less, and the number of failed trials before the first successful trial was 40% less.

5 Discussion

This work emphasizes the *interactive* elements in teaching. There are inherently two sides to an interaction, in this case the human teacher and the machine learner. Our approach aims to enhance machine learning from both perspectives: modifying the algorithm to build a better learning agent, and modifying the interaction techniques to provide a better experience for the human teacher. Understanding how humans want to teach is an important part of this process.

Our studies show that *people want to guide the agent*. This makes intuitive sense, and techniques like 'luring' the agent into particular behaviors have been explored [4,1]. In the past this choice has been inspired by animal learning, but our work formalizes this inspiration, grounding it in human behavior with a game character. In *Sophie's Kitchen* we observed people's desire to guide the character to an object of attention, even when explicitly told that only feedback messages were supported. In doing this people meant to bias the action selection mechanism of the RL algorithm. When we allow this, introducing a separate interaction channel for attention direction and modifying the action selection mechanism of the algorithm, we see a significant improvement in the agent's learning performance.

We also see that players treat the agent as a social entity and want a *motivational channel of communication* to encourage it. This is seen despite the fact that the learning agent is not particularly human-like. One can assume this effect will only be more prominent with agents designed to be socially and emotionally appealing. We argue that to build successful agents that learn from people, attention of the research community should focus on understanding and supporting the psychology and social expectations of the human teacher. It remains future work to explore how this motivational channel of communication should influence the learning algorithm in a different way than ordinary feedback. Our hypothesis is that this communication is intended to influence the internal motivations, drives and goals of the agent.

Another important question of this research is how the learning agent's behavior can shape the behavior of the teacher. In a social learning interaction both learner and teacher influence the performance of the tutorial dyad. While this observation seems straightforward in the human literature, little attention has been paid to the communication between human teacher and artificial agent in the machine learning literature. Particularly, we believe that the transparency of the learner's internal process is paramount to the success of the tutorial dialog. However, a fine balance must be struck between engulfing the human teacher with all pertinent information, and leaving them in the dark. This work offers a concrete example that *transparent behavior can improve the agent's learning environment*. Specifically, when the learning agent uses gaze to reveal its potential next actions, people were significantly better at providing more guidance when it was needed and less when it was not. Thus the agent, through its own behavior, was able to shape the human's input to be more appropriate.

Additionally these transparency behaviors boost the realism and believability of the character, thereby making it more engaging for the human. The creation of believable characters that people find emotionally appealing and engaging has long been a challenge [11,12]. Autonomy complicates this goal further, since the agent has to continually make action choices that are useful as well as believable. Blumberg *et al.* have some of the most extensive work in this domain [13,14] within a dog learning context. Thus another challenge for teachable characters is to be appropriately responsive to the human's instruction. In this work we have studied one aspect of such responsiveness, informed by our initial study. Negative feedback from a human teacher can be treated as both feedback and suggestion to *reverse the action if possible*. With this strategy the agent's learning is improved in both speed and efficiency.

We chose to use Q-Learning for this work because it is widely understood. Thus affording the transfer of these lessons and modifications to any reinforcement-based approach. We have shown significant improvements in an RL domain showing that learning in a situated interaction with a human partner can help overcome some well recognized problems of RL. Furthermore, these improvements in performance will contribute to higher quality interactive characters and more fun and enjoyable game play.

In sum, our empirically informed modifications indicate ways that an interactive game agent can be designed to learn better and faster from a human teacher across several dimensions. Our studies show the modified agent is able to learn tasks using fewer executed actions over fewer trials. Our modifications also led to a more efficient exploration strategy with less time in irrelevant states. A learning process, as such, that is seen as less random and more sensible will lead to more understandable and more believable game characters. The guidance and undo modifications illustrate avenues to a more responsive and natural interactive character. Our modifications also led to fewer failed trials and less time to the first successful trial. This is a particularly important improvement for interactive characters in that it implies a less frustrating experience, which in turn creates a more fun and engaging interaction.

6   Conclusion

Dynamic and engaging teachable characters that learn from human players would usher a new genre of entertainment technology, and we posit that such agents should support how people naturally approach teaching. Accordingly, this paper describes an experimental platform and a series of studies that reveal lessons about how people interactively teach graphical AI characters via reward and punishment.

Given these findings, we made modifications to our learning agent and interface to improve the interaction. Our modifications include: an embellished communication channel that distinguishes guidance, feedback, and motivational intents; transparency behaviors that reveal aspects of the learning process to the human; and a more natural reaction to negative feedback. A second set of studies show that these empirically informed modifications improve several learning dimensions including the speed of learning, the efficiency of exploration, the human's ability to understand the agent's learning process, and a significant drop in the number of failed trials.

These empirical results inform and ground the design of teachable characters. We believe these lessons and modifications are not specific only to the particular algorithm and agent used in these studies, and that this work broadly contributes to the creation of fun and engaging teachable characters that learn in real-time from human players.

References

1. Evans, R.: Varieties of learning. In Rabin, S., ed.: AI Game Programming Wisdom. Charles River Media, Hingham, MA (2002) 567–578
2. Stanley, K.O., Bryant, B.D., Miikkulainen, R.: Evolving neural network agents in the nero video game. In: Proceedings of IEEE 2005 Symposium on Computational Intelligence and Games (CIG'05). (2005)
3. Stern, A., Frank, A., Resner, B.: Virtual petz (video session): a hybrid approach to creating autonomous, lifelike dogz and catz. In: AGENTS '98: Proceedings of the second international conference on Autonomous agents, New York, NY, USA, ACM Press (1998) 334–335
4. Blumberg, B., Downie, M., Ivanov, Y., Berlin, M., Johnson, M., Tomlinson, B.: Integrated learning for interactive synthetic characters. In: Proceedings of the ACM SIGGRAPH. (2002)
5. Kaplan, F., Oudeyer, P.Y., Kubinyi, E., Miklosi, A.: Robotic clicker training. Robotics and Autonomous Systems 38(3-4) (2002) 197–206
6. Isbell, C., Shelton, C., Kearns, M., Singh, S., Stone, P.: Cobot: A social reinforcement learning agent. 5th Intern. Conf. on Autonomous Agents (2001)
7. Kuhlmann, G., Stone, P., Mooney, R.J., Shavlik, J.W.: Guiding a reinforcement learner with natural language advice: Initial results in robocup soccer. In: Proceedings of the AAAI-2004 Workshop on Supervisory Control of Learning and Adaptive Systems, San Jose, CA (2004)
8. Watkins, C., Dayan, P.: Q-learning. Machine Learning 8(3) (1992) 279–292
9. Kaelbling, L.P., Littman, M.L., Moore, A.P.: Reinforcement learning: A survey. Journal of Artificial Intelligence Research 4 (1996) 237–285
10. Breazeal, C., Brooks, A., Gray, J., Hoffman, G., Lieberman, J., Lee, H., Lockerd, A., Mulanda, D.: Tutelage and collaboration for humanoid robots. International Journal of Humanoid Robotics 1(2) (2004)
11. Thomas, F., Johnson, O.: Disney Animation: The Illusion of Life. Abbeville Press, New York (1981)
12. Bates, J.: The role of emotion in believable agents. Communications of the ACM 37(7) (1997) 122–125
13. Blumberg, B.: Old tricks, new dogs: ethology and interactive creatures. PhD thesis, Massachusetts Institute of Technology (1997)
14. Tomlinson, B., Blumberg, B.: Social synthetic characters. Computer Graphics 26(2) (2002)

FearNot's Appearance: Reflecting Children's Expectations and Perspectives

Lynne Hall[1], Marco Vala[5], Marc Hall[1], Marc Webster[1], Sarah Woods[2],
Adrian Gordon[3], and Ruth Aylett[4]

[1] School of Computing and Technology, University of Sunderland,
Sunderland, SR6 0DD, UK
{lynne.hall, marc.hall, marc.webster}@sunderland.ac.uk
[2] Psychology Department, University of Hertfordshire,
Hatfield, Herts, AL10 9AB, UK
s.n.woods@herts.ac.uk
[3] Mimosa Wireless Ltd., 63 Galen House, Low Friar Street,
Newcastle, NE15UE, UK
adriangordon@mimosa-wireless.co.uk
[4] Mathematics and Computer Science, Heriot-Watt University, Edinburgh,
EH14 4AS, UK
ruth@macs.hw.ac.uk
[5] INESC-ID, TagusPark, Av. Prof. Dr. Cavaco Silva, 2780-990 Porto Salvo, Portugal
marco.vala@tagus.ist.utl.pt

Abstract. This paper discusses FearNot, a virtual learning environment populated by synthetic characters aimed at the 8-12 year old age group for the exploration of bullying and coping strategies. Currently, FearNot is being redesigned from a lab-based prototype into a classroom tool. In this paper we focus on informing the design of the characters and of the virtual learning environment through our interpretation of qualitative data gathered about interaction with FearNot by 345 children. The paper focuses on qualitative data collected using the Classroom Discussion Forum technique and discusses its implications for the redesign of the media used for FearNot. The interpretation of the data identifies that the use of fairly naïve synthetic characters for achieving empathic engagement appears to be an appropriate approach. Results do indicate a focus for redesign, with a clear need for improved transitions for animations; identification and repair of inconsistent graphical elements; and for a greater cast of characters and range of sets to achieve optimal engagement levels.

1 Introduction

A wide range of virtual environments populated by synthetic characters have been developed for children. The most common examples of these are in the home, where many games involve interaction both with synthetic characters and other users in the form of avatars, such as The Sims and World of Warcraft. There has been increasing use of synthetic characters for educational purposes [10], particularly for educational drama and story telling applications [13] and Personal, Health and Social Education [9].

J. Gratch et al. (Eds.): IVA 2006, LNAI 4133, pp. 407–419, 2006.
© Springer-Verlag Berlin Heidelberg 2006

Where children are the intended users of the application, research clearly shows the need to incorporate their views, expectations and perspectives within the design process. Although this is important for all applications involving child users, where the interaction approach requires the child to interact with synthetic characters within the virtual world this is crucial. If the appearance of the world and the behaviours of the objects and characters within it are not appropriate, then it is highly likely that the child will reject it. Even when the technical aspects of such an experience are perfect; *inconsistency*, lack of realism, or poor design of the behavioral aspects of the virtual elements could cause breaks in conviction [8]. Such rejection is not uncommon with children having unprecedented choice of competitive traditional and technology oriented products.

Wages et al (2004) point out that more than 99% of the information taken in everyday reality is non-essential in the sense that it is not used to create a person's internal representation of the world [14]. In addition, where children are the end-users, the developers may not be able to predict where this 1% of essential information lies, without in-depth user involvement. Children's feedback can identify those characteristics of a VLE that are immediately noticed by the users as inconsistent, inadequate or wrong. This would help identify what aspects need improvement and what aspects are best left relatively untouched. For example, there may be aspects that, although unrealistic, might not have been noticed as such or may derive a pedagogical benefit from being this way.

There are many issues and factors to ensure that a virtual learning environment populated by synthetic characters will provide a valuable, engaging and enjoyable experience for the child. A significant factor impacting upon this experience relates to the design of the graphics, the animation of objects and characters, and the character interactions with the child and additionally the design of AI responses.

In this paper we discuss our approach to FearNot (Fun with Empathic Agents to Achieve Novel Outcomes in Teaching). This application was initially developed within the VICTEC (Virtual ICT with Empathic Characters) project. FearNot provides a school-based Virtual Learning Environment populated by synthetic characters representing the various characters in a number of bullying scenarios using 3D self-animating characters to create improvised dramas [1]. Currently, FearNot is undergoing an extensive redesign in the European Framework 6 project eCIRCUS.

A learner-centred approach is taken to elicit children's reactions to interactions with FearNot [3] and here, we focus on our approach to gaining children's views and perspectives on the graphical, visual and interactive issues related to their use of FearNot, and their impact on our redesign. Section 2 briefly outlines FearNot. In section 3 our approach to designing media for FearNot is discussed. In section 4 we discuss our approach to qualitative data collection, Classroom Discussion Forums (CDF). A large scale evaluation of FearNot with primary school children is presented in section 5. In section 6 we present the main results and their implications for the redesign of FearNot are discussed in section 7. Finally, potential future steps are outlined.

2 FearNot

FearNot (see figure 1) depicts bullying incidents in the form of an episodic virtual drama. The child user views the bullying incidents that take place between autonomous agents in a virtual school and acts from the perspective of the 'invisible friend' of the victimised character or (initially) impartial 3rd person in between episodes, providing help and advice. Each episode is framed by an introduction segment at the start of the episode, and a reflective interactive segment at the end.

FearNot aims to enable children to explore physical and relational bullying issues, and coping strategies, through empathic interaction with the synthetic characters who populate the virtual school. This is achieved through providing scenarios in which the main purpose of the communication was to engage in social interaction as opposed to accomplishing a task as efficiently as possible.

Fig. 1. Screenshots from FearNot

A preliminary version of FearNot with scripted rather than emergent scenarios was developed for evaluation purposes. Although this scripted version did not feature autonomous agents, emergent narrative or a language system, it permitted a high-fidelity mock-up that enabled user testing and evaluation. Whilst characters behaved in a similar manner as they would in the final FearNot, their behaviour was pre-scripted and not a result of the character's autonomous reactions to each other or the user.

3 Designing FearNot's Media

Our goal in eCIRCUS is to create synthetic characters that by their appearance, behaviours and features allow the user to build an empathic relationship with them. Our domain with FearNot is of bullying and our pedagogical goal is to enhance children's ability to empathise with the protagonists in the bullying scenario. The aim is to provide children with the strategies that will enable them to help identify and defuse a potential or actual bullying situation.

For the child to have the potential to develop empathic relationship with the characters, they must believe in the characters and their experiences, or rather the child must be prepared to suspend disbelief. The dramas within FearNot were written by experienced scriptwriters and extensively evaluated with children and teachers prior to their virtual representation, including extensive evaluation of mid-tech prototypes in the form of electronic storyboards. These evaluations highlighted that the stories and characters were believable and that the script was appropriate and highly understandable.

Taking a believable script and using it to create a believable virtual world poses considerable difficulties. Not least, that there are two paradoxes associated with attaining believable virtual environments [14]. Firstly, that decreasing the discrepancy between the real and the virtual causes the user to become more analytical of smaller discrepancies. Secondly, that the realism of different aspects of the virtual world are interdependent, so making one aspect of the virtual world more realistic can highlight the non-realism of a different aspect of the virtual world. Thus, aiming to increase the realism of the virtual environment may degrade the user's sum conviction therein.

This is particularly pertinent for the design of characters. Whilst it is relatively simple to create near-realistic graphical environments and objects, creating near-realistic characters offers considerable problems. Further, the "uncanny valley" has highlighted that if a character is too realistic, but not quite humanistic, this can result in discomfort. Continuing work with Embodied Conversational Agents highlights the ongoing difficulty of creating realistic animations of emotion. If the characters themselves are relatively limited in terms of actions and behaviours, then the world itself must also reflect that limitation.

Fig. 2. Screenshots of the virtual environment provided in FearNot

The virtual world of FearNot, see figure 2 has a cartoon style which is fairly simplistic and fun. Not only were children most in favour of cartoon characters [3], but additionally this offers a technical safety net in that highly naturalistic behaviour is not expected in cartoons making the element of jerkiness natural to experimental software less of an issue for children. Furthermore, the cartoon metaphor already provides design decisions that most cartoon-viewing children accept naturally. The design of the virtual world and characters were developed in collaboration with a media company that had created highly successful on-line resources for children. The design was derived from characters and environments that had been used successfully with children in the 8-12 age group. The characters and the environment were successfully evaluated with children at an early stage of the development.

There are essentially two types of animation in FearNot, the movement associated with geometry and the facial animations. FearNot used a set of animations representing individual actions and states associated with the characters geometry. One approach taken to provide the appearance of emotion in FearNot was through the use of a number of images, representing fixed expressional states, which were changed to suggest facial motion. This approach was successfully evaluated in small-scale evaluation with children using a mid-tech prototype [6]. However, this evaluation involved children watching the researcher interacting with a trailer version of FearNot for only 2 minutes. Here, we report on a large scale evaluation of a 20 minute individual interaction with FearNot.

Knowing that separately and even in a mid-tech form that the script, cast and set are believable, understandable and appear to appeal to the user group still does not necessarily result in a successful product. It is the whole interactive experience that determines acceptance and positive effect. We have to know what specific aspects of the aesthetics of the software and the animations of the characters should be improved in order give the user the right cues for believability, ensure comprehensibility and promote empathic engagement. The only way to be really certain about these aspects is to ask the children.

4   Classroom Discussion Forums

Classroom Discussion Forums (CDFs) [6] assist children in verbalising opinions about novel, innovative software, such as FearNot. CDFs allow children to partici-pate and to inform the design process. CDFs form a significant method within the classroom-based curriculum-focused learner-centred approach to be developed for eCIRCUS. Their use helps to ensure that FearNot is created from a child-centred perspective, rather than relying on adult aspirations and goals.

With our over-arching aim of producing methods and techniques to permit in-classroom design and evaluation, our intention in the development of CDFs was to create a method that worked effectively in a classroom context. Thus, CDFs differ significantly from other approaches through the incorporation of classroom culture and organization into a data collection method.

Following the format preferred by teachers, CDFs follow the normal classroom ap-proach of "Table Time" (small group discussion) followed by "Circle Time" or "on the carpet" (whole class discussion). Classroom culture strongly impacts on the dis-cussion activity, requiring it to be structured with clear goals and steps. Thus al-though, CDFs clearly have some similarities with focus groups, where they differ most strongly is in their staccato pace, something that strongly reflects the classroom situation.

Rather than a facilitated discussion, a CDF involves a question and answer session, involving many small, related questions from the researchers and rapidly raised hands and responses from the children. Even when a child responds to another child, our fieldwork has identified that rather than a free-flowing discussion, children in this age group typically turn-take via the researcher who nominates whoever has a raised hand to respond.

CDFs have been extensively used in the VICTEC project with a range of different prototypes, including mid-tech such as electronic storyboards and trailers [3]. For instance, small-scale pilot evaluations were carried out with approximately 90 primary school children from schools in Hertfordshire and Worsley, using a scripted trailer of FearNot!

After children had finished interacting with the scripted trailer, they participated in a CDF session in groups of between 8-10 children for a period of 15-20 minutes. These initial evaluation sessions were invaluable as they provided important information about necessary improvements required for the FearNot! software before a large scale evaluation event was carried out. For example, it was clear from the CDF sessions that overall children wanted FearNot! to contain spoken language that they could hear through the use of earphones, as opposed to having to read the story content off a screen. Reading from the screen was difficult from some children with dyslexia or below average reading abilities. Furthermore, it was difficult to find the right speed to present the storyline text due to such wide variations in children's reading speed.

Other important outcomes from these preliminary CDF evaluations revealed that although the children found some of the graphics amusing, simplistic and unreal, this did not adversely affect the level of storyline believability, engagement and empathy with the characters, and overall enjoyment with FearNot! A further crucial observation was that children were extremely positive towards the idea of being able to interact with an educational piece of software in a private and safe environment, where the fear of being ridiculed by peers is eradicated. Children expressed that this enabled them to explore different issues surrounding the sensitive subject of bullying behaviour that they might not feel comfortable doing in a classroom circle time session.

Here the results from CDFs with 345 children at the 'Virtually Friends' FearNot evaluation event are discussed.

5   Method

The evaluation of the Scripted FearNot was achieved through a large scale study, further discussed in [5]. This large scale evaluation event called "Virtually Friends" was held at the University of Hertfordshire, UK, in June 2004, and involved 345 children aged 9-11 years. Two classes from different schools participated each day in the evaluation event. These full day events involved a number of sessions including interactions with robots, virtual learning environments and storyboarding software in addition to FearNot.

Children completed several questionnaires before their interaction with FearNot to assess empathy, bullying behaviour and emotion recognition [12]. Each child then individually interacted with FearNot on standard PCs for approximately 30 minutes. After the interaction with FearNot children completed a theory of mind questionnaire [4] and a Character Evaluation Questionnaire [5].

The majority of the assessment instruments used in the Virtually Friends event were highly structured and collected quantitative scaled data. Recognising the need to also collect qualitative data relating to user reactions, perspectives and views of FearNot, we concluded each day with a Classroom Discussion Forum.

5.1   Interaction with FearNot

In the scripted version of FearNot, the child user views one direct physical bullying scenario and one relational scenario. Physical bullying includes acts such as hitting, kicking, punching, and taking others' belongings and relational bullying is the purposeful damage and manipulation of peer relationships and feelings of social exclusion.

Fig. 3. Interaction with victim

After the introduction of the characters, school and situation, users view the first bullying episode, followed by the victimised character seeking rescue in the school library, where it starts to communicate with the user. Within the initiated dialogue the user selects an advice from a list of coping strategies (shown as a drop down menu). The user also explains his/her selection and what he/she thinks will happen after having implemented the selected strategy, by typing it in (see figure 3).

The next episode then starts. The content of the final episode depends to some extent on the choices made by the user concerning the coping strategies: Paul, the bystander in the physical bullying scenario, might act as a defender for John (the victim), in case the user has selected a successful strategy, i.e. "telling someone"; or Martina (the bystander) might offer Frances (the victim) help. If the user has selected an unsuccessful strategy, i.e. "run away", the victim rejects the help in the final episode. However, even if the advice is appropriate the victim does not always follow this and may pursue a strategy counter to that suggested by the user. At the end of the scenario, a universal educational message is displayed pointing out that "telling someone" is always a good choice. This universal message had to be incorporated as all teachers had strong preferences for children to finish the interaction with a positive feedback message.

5.2   Classroom Discussion Forums at Virtually Friends

The CDFs allowed children to discuss the Virtually Friends event, with general discussion and a number of topics specifically about FearNot. The CDFs took place at the end of the day, with groups of approximately 10 children, led by a trained researcher, and lasted around 10-15 minutes. In addition to questions about FearNot children were also asked about their other experiences during Virtually Friends. In relation to FearNot, the main topics discussed were the children's views and perspectives of the best and worst aspects of FearNot; what, if anything, they had learned from using FearNot and had this changed their perspective of bullying; and was FearNot easy to use, interesting and would they use it again. Typically many groups mentioned the same points, and a number of relevant quotes from a range of the CDFs are included in the results.

6 Results and Interpretation

The results reported here focus primarily on aspects of FearNot that are relevant for the graphical redesign of the interaction. The results along with a range of quotes from the participating children are summarised in the following sections.

6.1 What Children Felt That They Learned from Interactions with FearNot and Changes in Perspective of Bullying

In all of the CDFs children highlighted that their interaction with FearNot had changed their perspective of bullying: "*I hadn't realised how bad it was for the victim*" or extended their knowledge / awareness of coping strategies and reasons for being bullied "*...don't know why they picked on her, there didn't seem to be a good reason. The other girls should have helped her*".

Where children were less effusive about the increase in knowledge this was typically due to their already having studied coping strategies in some depth and already having reasonable levels of knowledge. Typically, boys were more likely than girls to identify that they had increased their awareness and knowledge "*I would probably try to do something like ask him to join in,*" whilst girls frequently expressed already existing knowledge "*the only way to deal with them is to make friends.*"

6.2 Communication and Interaction with the Characters

Many children highlighted that communication with the victim "*When they ask you questions and you answer them*" and "*being able to provide advice,*" were the best aspects of FearNot. Children enjoyed the interaction with the characters "*It really involved us*" viewing this as one of the most positive aspects of FearNot. Not all children had such positive interactive experiences, particularly in those cases where the character did not act upon the children's advice: "*he didn't do what I said, if he had it would have stopped and I told him the same thing more than once.*"

Even though the children liked "*telling John and Frances what to do,*" most children did not like the interactive menu that enabled them to select their response "*I wanted to tell her to do something that wasn't there and it wouldn't let me,*" and "*It would be more fun to make up your own answer.*" Other children were blunter: "*It looked really old fashioned*" and "*using that menu thing made it hard to concentrate on John's problems.*"

6.3 Story Realism and Believability

Many girls commented on the storyline and identified that the relational scenario was more realistic than the physical bullying scenario. Children reported on the story realism represented through the character's actions, finding the *"bullying behaviour really like what happens at school."* However, in general children did not find that the characters exhibited physically realistic behaviours or rather, or they found specific aspects of the characters appearance and actions unbelievable: *"3D stuff looks really good, but the characters don't move right."*

6.4 Graphics and Animations

A number of children commented on the graphics in a positive way saying that there were *"cool looking streets"* and that the graphics were *"funny and made you smile."* However, when children highlighted that they approved of the graphics, this was often with a qualifying statement identifying graphical issues that need addressing: *"Graphics were good except for some weird faces when they cry."* Boys were particularly keen on the football episode *"even though the way the ball moved was wrong,"* identifying the need to increase the realism of the ball's movement to improve believability. Girls identified that they would want more variety with *"a whole class of kids not just a couple"* and *"more places, like where we go... swings or something like that."* No one noted that the scenarios were adult free or suggested that adults should be included within the scenarios.

Several groups commented on the clothes of the characters: *"The girls looked wrong, the skirts didn't move"* and *"the clothes need patterns and stuff or they don't look real."* The criticisms of characters were typically related to their appearance, but this related to factors such as hair styles and clothes.

In general, children were of the opinion that the animations were poor and this was often seen as being one of the weakest aspects of FearNot. The facial expressions of the characters were criticized in several groups: *"faces need to be made more real."* The movement was criticized in all groups *"he kept waving his hands about,"* *"he looked like he'd killed him"* *"she jerked about, no one moves like that"* and *"it jumped about except for the ball, that went straight."*

6.5 Sound

Many children commented on the lack of sound: *"The worst thing about FearNot was that it didn't have enough sound. It was annoying having to read the text and would have been much better with sound all the way through."* Most children suggested that sound should be added and that this would improve FearNot: *"There needs to be sound all the way through rather than having to read from the screen as this made it not very believable."*

6.6 User Experience

Children found FearNot interesting and useful, *"because you get to meet the virtual people and you learn about bullying and how to react in situations in the playground."* Most children identified that they would definitely prefer to use the software compared to a classroom session such as circle time "*to find out stuff and discuss things to do with bullying problems.*" Children could see the benefits of using FearNot for exploring bullying and coping strategies: "*I liked the fact that it was just me trying stuff out, you could try different things and then see what happened to the bullying.*" Children were asked what they had enjoyed most and least in general at the Virtually Friends event. However, the interaction with FearNot rarely appeared in either of these categories, typically losing out to the robots (best bit of the day) and the filling in of questionnaires (worst bit of the day). So, even though our evaluation of FearNot was positive it still was not the most interesting of the opportunities on offer.

7 Design Implications for FearNot

This study focused on a scripted version of FearNot which was used to evaluate children's reactions to empathic engagement with synthetic characters. Some of the design implications resulting from this study have already significantly impacted upon FearNot and are discussed in the context of the emergent version of FearNot already developed. A number of other design implications are still under consideration as we prepare FearNot for the classroom within the European Framework 6 eCIRCUS project.

CDFs clearly indicate that children believe that they are increasing their knowledge of exploring bullying and coping strategies and that FearNot is achieving at least to some degree its pedagogical objectives. Most of the children appeared to have changed their perspective of bullying to some degree, many expressing that the interaction had increased their understanding of the victim. Most of the children clearly empathized with the victim, feeling sorry for them and wishing to assist them in improving the situation. This supports the approach that we have taken with FearNot, highlighting that this virtual learning environment provides an interactive experience that helps children learn about bullying and strategies to cope with it.

Children clearly enjoyed interacting directly with the victim to provide advice. Although the character's behaviour was not actually tailored to the children's responses, where the character did appear to followed the child's advice, this tended to make the child more empathic towards the character. This result has also been supported by quantitative analysis [5]. This was reflected in the design of emergent FearNot and is being further extended, with particular attention given to ensuring that the characters typically appear to act on the advice of the child, or at least explain why they will not.

Although this is not realistic, in that frequently children being bullied agree to strategies proposed by others, but will not actually enact them, it appears to be an important aspect in the child's development of an empathic relationship with the character.

Children indicated that they would prefer to interact with free text [7]. Language actions had already been used to allow the agent action-selection system to select language as well as physical actions, and a shallow template-based system is used to turn these into utterances. The child user is treated as just another agent, with the additional requirement to infer the language action they are using rather than be told via the internal event system.

Of course this approach is potentially fragile, but tests so far suggest it is nevertheless adequate in this case. This is because the interaction with the victim is short and directed, with the conversational initiative kept on the victim side, the child users are slow typers who do not imput complex language, and there are only a limited number (seven) of possible coping responses that can be suggested. This change has already been implemented into the current version of FearNot, with children now able to enter free text. Current work focuses on improving and extending this language system to ensure that a wide range of inputs can be understood.

Due to constraints on time and resource, FearNot includes very little sound, with some speech at the beginning of one scenario and background music. The amount of foreknowledge the children possessed regarding real-time 3D multimedia lead to some surprisingly technical and sophisticated analysis of the experience and in turn suggestions on improving the same.

Supporting the earlier evaluations, children found the story realistic and believable, and in general, the look of FearNot was viewed positively. Children did identify that they would expect a far wider range of settings, characters and stories if FearNot was to be used in the classroom. Although there were a number of issues related to the graphics and animations these were largely resolved in the development of a fully emergent version of FearNot and now the focus is content development to support this emergence.

The facial textures used in FearNot provide a very basic level of graphic realism compared with what the children are likely to be familiar with. Some children did identify that they found the facial expressions unrealistic, which could lead to the implication of a need to improve the visual quality of the environment and characters. However, as noted by Cheng & Cairns (2005) the user's expectations of a game world's behavioural characteristics are based on the characteristics of the game itself [2]. This means that, for example, they might expect a character that looks cartoon-like to behave in a way that is different than a character that looks more realistic. Users seem less critical of characters (and indeed environments) that are not overly realistic. This leads to the problem that increasing the graphical realism of the characters could result in higher expectations that cannot be fulfilled by other aspects of FearNot. This was one of the major reasons that we decided to use textures for facial expressions and not a complex facial model. However, current experimentation identifies that we may need to increase and enhance the transitions between textures.

Although the animations used in FearNot were adequate, many children identified that the graphical poverty of the animations reduced the realism for them, identifying that this is a key issue for the redesign of FearNot. Wages et al (2004) suggest that that increasing realism causes an increase in the user's critical analysis of the game and that realism of different components of the game are interdependent, meaning that in order to cultivate believability the designer must choose carefully what aspects of realism to improve. Although scripted FearNot does not offer a way to transition smoothly from one animation to another (for either type of animation), a significant issue for many children, this issue had been resolved for the emergent version. Through using an underlying state machine to define stances, pre-conditions and neutral positions we have been able to ensure smooth transitions between all pairs of animations.

In emergent FearNot each animated character is under the control of an agent 'mind' (an autonomous intelligent agent whose behaviour is determined by a set of goals and a set of personality traits, such as a propensity for bully or victim behaviours, for example). The behaviours of each of these agents during a learning episode cannot be predetermined (unlike in the earlier scripted prototype). Any of the range of possible actions permissible for the characters could possibly be followed by any other possible action.

Thus, an extensive library of animations is needed to represent the range of possible actions permissible by the characters. Many of these animations also needed to represent similar actions performed in differing moods (for example an angry walk, a sad walk etc.). The sheer number of these animations creates a problem when trying to transition from the end of one animation to the beginning of another. In the prototype reported here, this problem was not solved. In emergent FearNot the use of a state machine with neutral positioning has largely resolved this issue, although refinements continue, particularly focusing on increasing flexibility.

Interactively transitioning between geometric animation data is possible but transitioning between images (i.e. image morphing) is very problematic with a better solution being one that allows the game engine to interactively merge animations together. This would allow a kind of cross-fade from one animation to another. This system would still require some rules be put in place to stop animations from being put together that shouldn't, As noted in [11] "if a character animation transitions from one pose to the next, bringing all parts of the body into the pose at the same time and in a linear fashion as commonly happens in physical and kinematic control solutions, the result will not only have a very robotic appearance"… but can give rise to unnaturally interpenetrating geometry. For example if animation A ends with the character's hand in front of the character and animation B begins with the character's hands behind the characters, the resulting transition AB could cause the characters hands to intersect it's own body. These rules would probably manifest themselves as a flowchart in which each node represents an animation and each connection represents a permissible transition.

8   Conclusions and Next Steps

FearNot is now undergoing redesign and development, prior to its use as a classroom tool in a longitudinal classroom study of over 1800 children in the UK and Germany, beginning in January 2007. This redesign is based on the results of the evaluations and in this paper results from Classroom Discussion Forums with 345 children were summarised and interpreted, identifying a number of key issues that require further design and development. In general, children approved of the graphical style and we are currently focusing on those elements that children have identified as being unrealistic or inconsistent with the other aspects of interaction with FearNot. We are also extending the world of FearNot with a greater cast of characters and settings to offer more variety within a longer classroom-based interaction. Current work focuses on achieving a believable emergent narrative with more and better content.

References

[1] Aylett, R. S., Paiva, A., Woods, S., Hall, L., and Zoll, C., "Expressive Characters in Anti-Bullying Education," in *Animating Expressive Characters for Social Interaction*, L. Canamero and R. Aylett, Eds.: John Benjamins, 2005.

[2] Cheng, K. and Cairns, P. A., "Behaviour, realism and Immersion in games," presented at ACM Conf. on Human Factors in Computing Systems, CHI 2005, 2005.

[3] Hall, L., Woods, S., and Aylett, R., "FearNot! Involving children in the design of a Virtual Learning Environment," *Artificial Intelligence & Education*, in print.

[4] Hall, L., Woods, S., Aylett, R., and Paiva, A., "Using Theory of Mind methods to investigate empathic engagement with synthetic characters," *International Journal of Virtual Humanoids*, in print.

[5] Hall, L., Woods, S., Aylett, R., Paiva, A., and Newall, L., "Achieving empathic engagement through affective interaction with synthetic characters," presented at 1st International Conference on Affective Computing & Intelligent Interaction (ACII 05), Beijing, China, 2005.

[6] Hall, L., Woods, S., and Dautenhahn, K., "FearNot! Designing in the Classroom," presented at British HCI, Leeds, UK, 2004.

[7] Louchart, S., Romano, D., and Aylett, R., "Speaking and acting -Interacting language and action for an expressive character," presented at Workshops on Intelligent Computing, MICAI 2004, 2004.

[8] MacIntyre, B., Bolter, J. D., and Gandy, M., "Presence and the Aura of Meaningful Places," presented at 7th Annual International Workshop on Presence (PRESENCE 2004), Valencia, Spain, 2004.

[9] Marsella, S., Johnson, W. L., and LaBore, C., "Interactive Pedagogical Drama for Health Interventions," presented at 11th International Conference on Artificial Intelligence in Education, Sydney, Australia, 2003.

[10] McFarlane, A., Sparrowhawk, A., and Heald, Y., "Report on the Educational use of Games," Available at http://www.teem.org.uk/publications 2005.

[11] Neff, M. and Fiume, E., "Aesthetic Edits for Character Animation," presented at ACM SIGGRAPH/Eurographics Symposium on Computer Animation, 2003.

[12] Nowicki, S. and Duke, M. P., "Individual differences in nonverbal communication of effect: The diagnostic analysis of nonverbal accuracy scale," *Journal of Nonverbal Behavior*, vol. 18, pp. 9-35, 1994.

[13] Robertson, J. and Oberlander, J., "Ghostwriter: Educational Drama and Presence in a Virtual Environment," *Journal of Computer Mediated Communication*, vol. 8, 2002.

[14] Wages, R., Grunvogel, S. M., and Grutzmacher, B., "How Realistic is Realism? Considerations on the Aesthetics of Computer Games," presented at ICEC 2004, 3rd international conference on Entertainment Computing, Eindhoven, The Netherlands, 2004.

Populating Reconstructed Archaeological Sites with Autonomous Virtual Humans

Wei Shao[1] and Demetri Terzopoulos[2]

[1] Media Research Lab, New York University, New York NY, USA
[2] Computer Science Department, University of California, Los Angeles CA, USA

Abstract. Significant multidisciplinary efforts combining archaeology and computer science have yielded virtual reconstructions of archaeological sites for visualization. Yet comparatively little attention has been paid to the difficult problem of populating these models, not only to enhance the quality of the visualization, but also to arrive at quantitative computer simulations of the human inhabitants that can help test hypotheses about the possible uses of these sites in ancient times. We introduce an artificial life approach to populating large-scale reconstructions of archaeological sites with virtual humans. Unlike conventional "crowd" models, our comprehensive, detailed models of individual autonomous pedestrians span several modeling levels, including appearance, locomotion, perception, behavior, and cognition. We review our human simulation system and its application to a "modern archaeological" recreation of activity in New York City's original Pennsylvania Station. We also describe an extension of our system and present its novel application to the visualization of possible human activity in a reconstruction of the Great Temple of ancient Petra in Jordan.

1 Introduction

Significant multidisciplinary efforts combining archaeology and computer science have yielded virtual reconstructions of archaeological sites for visualization. State-of-the-art computer graphics enables architectural reconstructions that exhibit impressive geometric and photometric detail. Yet comparatively little attention has been paid to the difficult problem of populating reconstructed models with virtual humans, not only to enhance the quality of the visualization, but also to arrive at quantitative computer simulations of the human inhabitants that can help test hypotheses about the possible uses of these sites in ancient times.

Human simulation has become an increasingly "hot" topic in advanced computer animation. Its application to creating amazing background crowd scenes in feature films has proved its commercial value and this continuously pushes the technology forward. To date, however, the individual characters in such simulated crowds do not have much intelligence and can only serve as background "extras". By contrast, our artificial life approach [1] to modeling humans spans the modeling of human appearance, locomotion, perception, behavior, and cognition. While our work is innovative in the context of behavioral animation, it

J. Gratch et al. (Eds.): IVA 2006, LNAI 4133, pp. 420–433, 2006.

is very different from conventional crowd animation, where one character algorithmically follows another in a manner that is relatively easy to program with a few simple behavioral rules. We are uninterested in crowds *per se*. Rather, the goal of our work has been to contribute a comprehensive, self-animated model of individual human beings that incorporates nontrivial human-like abilities. In particular, we have paid serious attention to deliberative human activities over and above the underlying reactive behavior level.

In particular, we have been developing a decentralized, comprehensive model of pedestrians as autonomous *individuals* capable of a broad variety of activities in large-scale synthetic urban spaces. The pedestrian simulation system that we have implemented enables us to create lengthy animations of numerous pedestrians in large urban environments without manual intervention. We review our pedestrian simulation system in the context of a "modern archaeological" recreation of activity in New York City's original Pennsylvania Station, which was tragically demolished in 1963. The contribution of this paper, however, is to develop our pedestrian simulator further through the introduction of new behavioral routines, and to report on its novel application to the visualization of possible human activity in a reconstruction of the Great Temple in the ancient Nabataean city of Petra.

The remainder of the paper is organized as follows: We briefly discuss related work in Section 2. Section 3 reviews our simulation system, which comprises an environment model and an autonomous pedestrian model. Section 4 describes a novel application of our simulator in the domain of archaeology. Finally, Section 5 presents our conclusions.

2   Related Work

State-of-the-art computer graphics modeling and rendering techniques enable artists, architects, and archaeologists to create or recreate static ancient scenes with high fidelity. There are many practitioners in this field, now called "Virtual Heritage," which was pioneered in the early 1990s (e.g., [2,3,4]). As these reconstructed virtual sites become increasingly realistic, the lack of mobile human occupants becomes increasingly conspicuous and detracts from the overall realism. Only recently have researchers begun to populate various reconstructed models, especially ancient archaeological sites, with reactive human agents [5,6].[1] Although these characters do not have much intelligence and hardly locomote within their virtual environment, they offer new opportunities for scientific research. Recently, researchers have started to apply computer simulation

---

[1] Note, however, that there are several reasons why virtual humans have not commonly populated virtual models in archaeology, and they do not necessarily have to do with technical issues; for example, archaeologists are generally reluctant to show what they do not have sufficient evidence for, such as humans in action or their clothing (which does not generally survive), and archaeologists generally know very little about spatial behavior, and often not enough about spatial reconstruction (D. Sanders, personal communication).

Fig. 1. Original Pennsylvania Station in New York City

Fig. 2. Large-scale simulation of human activity in the reconstructed Penn Station

to visualize, test, and refine hypotheses about the usage of architectural structures in ancient times, such as the Colosseum in Rome [7].

Emulating human characters is a highly challenging problem in computer graphics [8]. Prompted by the seminal work of Reynolds [9], behavioral animation has been further developed to simulate artificial animals [10,11,12] and it has given impetus to an entire industry of applications for distributed (multiagent) behavioral systems that are capable of synthesizing flocking, schooling, herding, and other behaviors for lower animals, or in the case of human characters, crowd behavior. Numerous crowd interaction models have been developed [13,14,15,16] and work in this area continues.

Rather than "crowd simulation", our work focuses on the modeling of intelligent virtual *individuals* that have non-trivial humanlike abilities suitable for urban environments. Our approach is inspired most heavily by the work of Tu and Terzopoulos [10] on artificial animals and by Funge *et al.* [17] on cognitive modeling for intelligent characters that can reason and plan their actions. Recently, we have further developed this comprehensive, artificial life approach and have adopted it for the first time to the case of virtual humans occupying large-scale urban environments [18].

3   Autonomous Pedestrian Simulation System

We have developed a realistic simulator of autonomous pedestrians in reconstructed environments. Our initial application of this model was to populate a "modern archaeological" reconstruction of the original Pennsylvania Train Station in New York City (Fig. 1) with hundreds of virtual pedestrians, demonstrating realistic human activity (Fig. 2). This section reviews our simulation system, whose details are presented in [18].

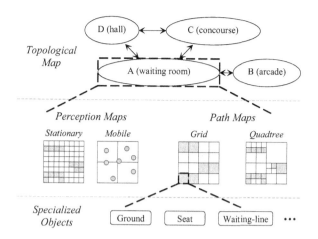

Fig. 3. Hierarchical environment model

3.1   Virtual Environment Model

As detailed in [19], we represent the virtual environment by a hierarchical collection of maps. Fig. 3 illustrates the environment model, which comprises (i) a topological map that represents the topological structure between different parts of the virtual world. Linked within this map are (ii) perception maps, which provide relevant information to perceptual queries, and (iii) path maps, which enable online path-planning for navigation. Finally, on the lowest level, are (iv) specialized objects that support quick and powerful perceptual queries.

In the *topological map*, nodes correspond to environmental regions and edges represent accessibility between regions. A walkable surface within a region is mapped onto a horizontal plane to enhance the simplicity and efficiency of environmental queries.

The *perception maps* are two types of grid maps that represent stationary environmental objects and mobile objects (usually virtual pedestrians), respectively. On the first type of perception map, a pedestrian emits rasterized "eye rays" to detect nearby static obstacles. On the second type, a sensing fan containing a constant number of neighbor cells are examined by the character to identify nearby pedestrians. Both perceptual algorithms are localized and are independent of the size of the world or the number of contained objects or pedestrians.

The *path maps* of each region consist of a quadtree map and a grid map. Quadtree maps support the execution of several variants of the A^* graph search algorithm, which are employed to compute quasi-optimal paths to desired goals. The efficient quadtree search algorithm enables pedestrians to do global, long-range path planning in an online fashion. On the other hand, grid maps are employed when detailed, short-range paths are needed. A typical example of their use is when a pedestrian is behind a chair or bench and must navigate around it in order to sit down.

The *specialized objects* at the lowest level of the environment hierarchy are able to provide answers to queries that cannot be handled directly by perception maps. For instance, a bench object keeps track of how many people are seated and where they sit. By querying nearby bench objects, weary virtual pedestrians are able to determine the available seat positions and decide where to sit without further reference to the perception maps. Other types of specialized objects include queues where pedestrians wait in line, purchase points where pedestrians can make a purchase, portals through which pedestrians can enter and exit, etc. These specialized objects make it easy for pedestrians to acquire higher level perceptual information from the virtual world.

3.2   Autonomous Pedestrian Model

Analogous to real humans, our synthetic pedestrians are fully autonomous. They perceive the virtual environment around them, analyze environmental situations, behave naturally, and plan their actions over global spatiotemporal scales. To this end, our autonomous human model incorporates appearance, motor, perception, behavior, and cognition sub-models, each of which we will review next.

Appearance and Locomotion. As an implementation of the appearance and motor levels of the character, we employ a human animation package called *DI-Guy*, which is commercially available from Boston Dynamics Inc. DI-Guy provides a variety of textured geometric human models together with a set of basic motor skills, such as strolling, walking, jogging, sitting, etc. Emulating the natural appearance and movement of human beings is a highly challenging problem and, not surprisingly, DI-Guy suffers from several limitations, mostly in their kinematic control of human motions. To ameliorate the visual defects, we have customized the motions of DI-Guy characters and have implemented a motor control interface to hide the details of the underlying kinematic layer of DI-Guy from our higher-level behavior modules, enabling the latter to be developed more or less independently.

Perception. In a highly dynamic virtual world, an autonomous intelligent character must have a keenly perceptive regard for the external world in order to interact with it effectively. The hierarchical world model is used extensively by pedestrians to perceive their environment, providing not only the raw sensed data (such as those obtained from perception maps), but also higher-level interpretations of perceived situations (such as those obtained from specialized objects) that are at least as important and useful to a pedestrian.

Behavior. The purpose of realistic behavioral modeling is to link perception to appropriate actions. We adopt a bottom-up strategy similar to [10], which uses primitive reactive behaviors as building blocks that in turn support more complex motivational behaviors, all controlled by an action selection mechanism.

   At the lowest level, we developed six key reactive behavior routines that cover almost all of the obstacle avoidance situations that a pedestrian can encounter.

The first two are for static obstacle avoidance, the next three are for avoiding mobile objects (mostly other pedestrians), and the last one is for avoiding both. Given that a pedestrian possesses a set of motor skills, such as standing still, moving forward, turning in several directions, speeding up and slowing down, etc., these routines are responsible for initiating, terminating, and sequencing the motor skills on a short time scale guided by sensory stimuli and internal percepts. The routines are activated in an optimized sequential manner, giving each the opportunity to alter the currently active motor control command (speed, turning angle, etc.).

While the reactive behaviors enable pedestrians to move around freely, almost always avoiding collisions, navigational behaviors enable them to go where they desire. We developed several such routines—*passageway selection, passageway navigation, perception guided navigation, arrival-at-a-target navigation*, etc.—to address issues, such as the speed and scale of online path planning, the realism of actual paths taken, and pedestrian flow control through and around bottlenecks. Furthermore, to make our pedestrians more interesting, we have augmented their behavior repertoires with a set of non-navigational, motivational routines such as *select an unoccupied seat and sit, approach a performance and watch, queue at ticketing areas and purchase a ticket*, etc.

An action selection mechanism triggers appropriate behaviors in response to perceived combinations of external situations and internal affective needs represented by the mental state. For example, in a pedestrian whose thirst exceeds a predetermined threshold, behaviors will be triggered, usually through online planning, to locate a vending machine, approach it, queue if necessary, and finally purchase a drink. In case more than one need awaits fulfillment, the most important need ranked by the action selection mechanism receives the highest priority. Once a need is fulfilled, the value of the associated mental state variable decreases asymptotically back to its nominal value. We instantiate different classes of pedestrians suitable for a train station environment, each class having a specialized action selection mechanism, including commuters, tourists, law enforcement officers, and street performers.

Cognition. At the highest level of autonomous control, a cognitive model [17] yields a deliberative autonomous human agent capable of applying knowledge to conceive and execute intermediate and long-term plans. A stack memory model enables a pedestrian to "memorize", "update", and "forget" chains of goals. The stack couples the deliberative intelligence with the reactive behaviors, enabling a pedestrian to achieve its goals. For example, a commuter can enter the station, with the long-term goal of catching a particular train at a specific time. The cognitive model divides this complex goal into simpler intermediate goals, which may involve navigating to the ticket purchase areas to buy a ticket (which may involve waiting in line), navigating to the concourse area, possibly purchasing a drink if thirsty, sitting down to take a rest if tired, watching a street performance if interested, meeting a friend, and/or navigating to the correct stairs and descending to the proper train platform when the time comes.

(a)   (b)

Fig. 4. Original Petra site (a) and reconstructed 3D model of Petra Great Temple (b)

4   Application to Archaeology

As we have discussed, archaeology is a domain that can benefit from the application of autonomous virtual pedestrians, particularly for the purposes of visualizing human activity in computer reconstructions of archaeological sites and, potentially, for the testing and refinement of archaeological theories of site usage in ancient times.

Petra (from the Greek word for "rock") lies in a great rift valley east of Wadi Araba in Jordan about 80 kilometers south of the Dead Sea. As the principal city of ancient Nabataea in its heyday, Petra has a history that can be traced back over 3,000 years. The Great Temple of Petra is a major archaeological and architectural component of central Petra. It is now recognized by archaeologists to have been one of the main buildings of ancient Petra and it is thought to have been dedicated to the most important cult deity of the city. Unfortunately, earthquakes in ancient times demolished the temple and buried it under debris.

4.1   Petra Great Temple

The temple site has been explored since the 1890s. A major excavation recently carried out by an archaeological team from Brown University has unearthed many amazing structures and sculptures [20]. With the new findings, archaeologists, computer scientists, and artists have been collaborating to reconstruct the original appearance of the temple in a virtual 3D model [21]. Fig. 4(a) shows a photo of the temple site under excavation and Fig. 4(b) shows a rendered image of the reconstructed 3D model.

As the Temple has sustained severe damage and most of its parts have not yet been found. Many aspects of the Temple, from the layout of the missing structures to details of the sculptures to the purpose and use of the Temple and the theater inside, remain unclear. Archaeologists engage in scholarly speculation while studying the site.

Assimilating the reconstructed temple model within our autonomous pedestrian simulation system, we are able to visualize possible interactions between the

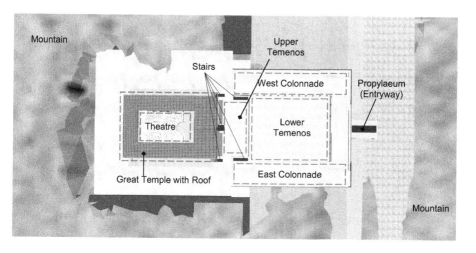

Fig. 5. Layout of the Petra Great Temple precinct

temple and its human occupants, thus potentially providing a simulation/visualization tool to archaeologists for use in their speculations about various functional aspects of the Temple.

4.2   Temple Precinct Environmental Model

Fig. 5 shows the configuration of the various parts of the Temple Precinct. Located on the southern citadel hill of Petra, the Temple Precinct covers about 7560 square meters. We divide the entire space into 20 regions, including the Propylaeum (monumental entryway), the Lower Temenos (lower square with two colonnades on the east and west sides), the Upper Temenos (upper square), the Great Temple itself (measuring 28m×42m), the theater inside the temple, and the stairs connecting different regions, including those beneath the theater that lead to its auditorium. Objects such as columns and walls are automatically loaded during map initialization. This large model consists of over 410,000 triangles and consumes about 22 MB of memory for its geometry and textures. To prepare the model for use by our autonomous pedestrians, our environmental data structures consume an additional 65 MB of memory.

An issue of interest from the archaeological perspective is to determine how many people can sit in the theater and how efficiently they can enter and exit it. To this end, we developed a new specialized environment object to model the theater inside the temple. According to several user-specified parameters loaded upon initialization, the theater object defines the locations of the stage and the auditorium, including the arrangement of the seats. During simulation, the environment object keeps track of the size of the audience and where each member of the audience is sitting.

In our simulations, we set the theater parameters such that isle space is reserved for people to reach their seats, even when the auditorium is almost full.

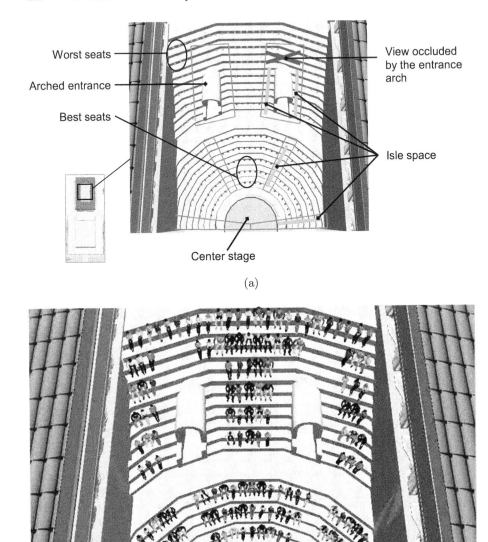

Fig. 6. (a) Layout of the theater. Seats are color-coded from red (best seats) to green (worst seats). The spacing between neighboring seats is defined as 0.6m laterally and 1.0m in the anterior-posterior direction. The setting shown includes 201 seats. (b) Theater filled with 201 seated spectators.

Fig. 7. Autonomous pedestrians fill the Petra Great Temple theater. (a) Hundreds of pedestrians enter the Temple Complex through the Propylaeum. (b) On the lower Temenos, the stream of pedestrians bifurcates towards the east and west stairways. (c) Through two arched gates, each pedestrian enters the auditorium, selects a seating area, makes their way to their selected seat and sits down. (d) Spectators seated and attending to a speaker on stage.

Regions from which the stage area is largely occluded are excluded as possible seating areas. Fig. 6(a) illustrates the theater layout in our simulation tests.

4.3   New Behavior Routines

To function properly within the theater environment, our autonomous pedestrians required several new navigational and motivational behavior routines designed particularly for an auditorium-like environment; in particular,

1. a seat selection behavior to pick a seat in the auditorium,
2. a navigation behavior to reach the selected seat to sit down, and
3. an exit behavior to leave the auditorium.

The first routine belongs to a category of selection behaviors suitable for pedestrians. These behaviors address the resolution of inter-personal conflicts among pedestrians for available resources. A pedestrian employs these behaviors to make a selection in order to mitigate the conflict while maximizing its own benefit. More specifically, the pedestrian will autonomously pick a seat based on availability, proximity, and stage-view quality. Fig. 6(a) shows seats color-coded according to their stage-view qualities. In the second routine, a pedestrian will regard other seated pedestrians as static obstacles and will appropriately apply detailed path planning and static obstacle avoidance routines to reach the selected seat. Finally, in the third routine, a pedestrian will simply follow pedestrians ahead in order to exit the auditorium.

4.4   Simulation Example

An animation example that is typical of our simulation tests within the Petra Great Temple environment unfolds as follows: In the beginning, the simulation instantiates hundreds of pedestrians that enter the Temple Complex through the Propylaeum—its grand entryway. On the Lower Temenos, the stream of pedestrians bifurcates to approach the two stairways at the east and west sides. Proceeding to the Upper Temenos, the pedestrians enter the Great Temple via the three small staircases. Once inside the Temple, pedestrians approach the theater entrance stairs located on the east and west sides beneath the theater. Through two arched gates, each pedestrian autonomously enters the auditorium, selects a seating area and navigates to it, selects an empty seat, makes their way to it, and sits down. After all the spectators are seated, a "tour guide" comes to the center stage to enact the delivery of a short lecture about the Great Temple. At its conclusion, the spectators rise and start to evacuate the theater through the two narrow arched gates, which are hardly wide enough to accommodate two pedestrians side by side. Exiting the same way they entered, the pedestrians leave the Temple through the Propylaeum. Sample frames from the animation are shown in Fig. 7.

4.5   Experimental Results

Our simulation experiments reveal that, given the structure of the theater, the fact that each row seems too narrow for the feet of someone seated in a row immediately above to fit comfortably behind the derriere of a person seated in the row below, and with an inter-personal distance (i.e., the distance between the centers of two spectators seated side by side) set to 0.6m laterally and 1.0m in the anterior-posterior direction, the theater can comfortably accommodate 201 spectators in the alternating-row seating arrangement shown in Fig. 6(b).

Given the alternating-row seating arrangement, it requires approximately 7–8 minutes for the audience of 201 to enter and fill the theater and approximately 5 minutes to exit and evacuate the theater. Note that the two arched stairways leading from underneath the theater to its auditorium are the only portals for people to enter and exit; thus, as expected, they become bottlenecks to pedestrian traffic.

5   Conclusion

We described a simulation system that incorporates a comprehensive decentralized, autonomous pedestrian model and a hierarchical environmental model. This simulator enables us to deploy a multitude of self-animated virtual pedestrians within large urban environments. We reviewed a virtual reconstruction of the original Pennsylvania Train Station in New York City, and reported on a large ancient outdoor environment, the archaeologically-reconstructed Petra Great Temple in Jordan. In the latter application, which was the novel contribution of this paper, we augmented our autonomous pedestrian model with new behavioral routines specialized for the theater environment within the Temple.

Our simulations suggest that the theater capacity is approximately 200 spectators, who can enter and be seated in approximately 7–8 minutes and exit in approximately 5 minutes. Interestingly, the archaeologist authorities on Petra with whom we have consulted in this project had estimated the theater capacity to be up to three times as many spectators. Our simulations have compelled them to reconsider their estimates. We are also considering seating arrangements alternative to the one shown in Fig. 6, which may require additional behavioral routines to implement more intricate social protocols.

Our simulation system has the ability to produce prodigious quantities of elaborate animation of pedestrians carrying out various individual and group activities suitable to their environment. Applying clever rendering techniques, such as those used in [22], we should be able to improve rendering performance eventually to achieve real-time animation rates. The pedestrian model promises to be of value in the visualization of and speculation about urban social life in the Great Temple precinct of ancient Petra. With this in mind, it will be necessary for us to further augment the behavioral repertoires of the autonomous pedestrians. We also intend to develop a satisfactory set of subconscious, reactive and deliberative head and eye motion behaviors for our virtual pedestrian model in order to make their upper bodies look less rigid during navigation. We will also augment the ability of pedestrians to interact with one another in small groups. This will require better modeling of personal space, territoriality, and familial behaviors.

Acknowledgements

The research reported herein was supported in part by grants from the Defense Advanced Research Projects Agency (DARPA) of the Department of Defense and from the National Science Foundation (NSF) under Grant No. 0205477. The research has benefitted from collaboration with Brown University, in particular with Dr. Eileen Vote who created the reconstructed model of the Petra Great Temple (Daniel Feliz provided a recent version of the model) and with Professor David Cooper. We appreciate the extensive discussions about the Petra Great Temple and the occupancy of its theater with Dr. Paul C. Zimmerman and Professor Martha Joukowsky. Our thanks also go to Dr. Donald Sanders of the Institute for the Visualization of History for his advice and feedback on the application of our pedestrian simulator to archaeology and for his comments on a draft. The majority of the research reported herein was done while the authors were at the Media Research Lab of the Courant Institute of Mathematical Sciences at New York University.

References

1. Terzopoulos, D.: Artificial life for computer graphics. Communications of the ACM **42**(8) (1999) 32–42
2. Learning Sites: (2006) www.learningsites.com.
3. Digital Archaeology: (2006) www.digital-archaeology.com.
4. The Institute for the Visualization of History: (2006) www.vizin.com.
5. Ciechomski, P., Ulicny, B., Cetre, R., Thalmann, D.: A case study of a virtual audience in a reconstruction of an ancient Roman odeon in Aphrodisias. In: Proc. 5th International Symposium on Virtual Reality (VAST 2004), Archaeology and Intelligent Cultural Heritage, Eurographics Association (2004) 9–17
6. Papagiannakis, G., Foni, A., Magnenat-Thalmann, N.: Real-time recreated ceremonies in VR restituted cultural heritage sites. In: Proc. CIPA 2003 XIXth International Symposium. (2003)
7. Gutierrez, D., Seron, F., Frischer, B., Abernathy, D.: The Flavian Amphitheater (Colosseum) in Rome: An excellent people-mover? In: Proc. Computer Applications and Quantitative Methods in Archaeology Conference. (2005)
8. Badler, N., Phillips, C., Webber, B.: Simulating Humans: Computer Graphics, Animation, and Control. Oxford University Press (1993)
9. Reynolds, C.W.: Flocks, herds, and schools: A distributed behavioral model. Computer Graphics **21**(4) (1987) 25–34 (Proc. ACM SIGGRAPH 87 Conf.).
10. Terzopoulos, D., Tu, X., Grzeszczuk, R.: Artificial fishes: Autonomous locomotion, perception, behavior, and learning in a simulated physical world. Artificial Life **1**(4) (1994) 327–351
11. Tomlinson, B., Downie, M., Berlin, M., Gray, J., Lyons, D., Cochran, J., Blumberg, B.: Leashing the alphawolves: Mixing user direction with autonomous emotion in a pack of semi-autonomous virtual characters. In: Proc. ACM SIGGRAPH / Eurographics Symposium on Computer Animation (SCA'02), ACM Press (2002) 7–14
12. Loyall, A.B., Reilly, W.S.N., Bates, J., Weyhrauch, P.: System for authoring highly interactive, personality-rich interactive characters. In: Proc. ACM SIGGRAPH / Eurographics Symposium on Computer Animation (SCA'04), ACM Press (2004) 59–68
13. Loscos, C., Marchal, D., Meyer, A.: Intuitive crowd behaviour in dense urban environments using local laws. In: Theory and Practice of Computer Graphics, IEEE Computer Society (2003) 122–129
14. Sung, M., Gleicher, M., Chenney, S.: Scalable behaviors for crowd simulation. Comput. Graph. Forum **23**(3) (2004) 519–528
15. Ulicny, B., de Heras Ciechomski, P., Thalmann, D.: Crowdbrush: Interactive authoring of real-time crowd scenes. In: Proc. ACM SIGGRAPH / Eurographics Symposium on Computer Animation (SCA'04), ACM Press (2004) 243–252
16. Lamarche, F., Donikian, S.: Crowd of virtual humans: A new approach for real time navigation in complex and structured environments. Comput. Graph. Forum **23**(3) (2004) 509–518

17. Funge, J., Tu, X., Terzopoulos, D.: Cognitive modeling: Knowledge, reasoning and planning for intelligent characters. In: Proc. ACM SIGGRAPH 99 Conf. *Computer Graphics* Proceedings, Annual Conference Series, Los Angeles, CA (1999) 29–38

18. Shao, W., Terzopoulos, D.:   Autonomous pedestrians.   In: Proc. ACM SIG-GRAPH / Eurographics Symposium on Computer Animation (SCA'05), New York, NY, ACM Press (2005) 19–28

19. Shao, W., Terzopoulos, D.: Environmental modeling for autonomous virtual pedestrians. SAE Symposium on Digital Human Modeling for Design and Engineering. (2005) 1–8 (SAE Technical Paper 2005-01-2699).

20. Joukowsky, M.S.: Petra Great Temple Volume I: Brown University Excavations 1993-1997. E.A. Johnson Company, Providence, RI (1998)

21. Vote, E., Acevedo, D., Laidlaw, D.H., Joukowsky, M.: Discovering Petra: Archaeological analysis in VR. IEEE Computer Graphics and Applications **22**(5) (2002) 38–50

22. Dobbyn, S., Hamill, J., O'Conor, K., O'Sullivan, C.:   Geopostors: A real-time geometry/impostor crowd rendering system. In: Proc. Symposium on Interactive 3D Graphics and Games (SI3D'05), Washington, DC, ACM Press (2005) 95–102

Evaluating the Tangible Interface and Virtual Characters in the Interactive COHIBIT Exhibit

Michael Kipp[1], Kerstin H. Kipp[2], Alassane Ndiaye[1], and Patrick Gebhard[1]

[1] DFKI, Stuhlsatzenhausweg 3, 66123 Saarbrücken, Germany
{kipp, ndiaye, gebhard}@dfki.de
[2] University of the Saarland, Experimental Neuropsychology Unit,
66123 Saarbruecken, Germany
k.kipp@mx.uni-saarland.de

Abstract. When using virtual characters in the human-computer interface the question arises of how useful this kind of interface is: whether the human user accepts, enjoys and profits from this form of interaction. Thorough system evaluations, however, are rarely done. We propose a post-questionnaire evaluation for a virtual character system that we apply to COHIBIT, an interactive museum exhibit with virtual characters. The evaluation study investigates the subjects' experiences with the exhibit with regard to informativeness, entertainment and virtual character perception. Our subjects rated the exhibit both entertaining and informative and gave it a good overall mark. We discuss the detailed results and identify useful factors to consider when building and evaluating virtual character applications.

1 Introduction

Virtual characters are a versatile tool for conveying information or educational content in a playful and entertaining fashion [1]. The interactive edutainment system COHIBIT[1] is a good example for a system that pursues both entertainment and education with the help of virtual characters [2]. In this system, we have an unusual condition because the user interacts with the system only by manipulating tangible bits: moving around physical building blocks from a car the user elicits reactions from the two virtual characters who, through speech, give comments, helpful advise and educational background information. Hence, there is an asymmetrical distribution of communication channels. The characters can talk but not act, the user can act but not talk (or at least talk has no effect on the characters). Various questions arise in such a scenario: Can the characters capture the user's attention at all? Is the exhibit entertaining? Does the user find the information interesting? And how are the characters perceived?

These questions are interesting for most virtual character systems, no matter what modalities are employed. However, evaluations have rarely been done in the past, all too often they were only worth a side remark in the "Future Work" section. This is unfortunate because evaluations are a good way to find

---

[1] COnversational Helpers in an Immersive exhiBIt with a Tangible interface.

J. Gratch et al. (Eds.): IVA 2006, LNAI 4133, pp. 434–444, 2006.

out whether your objectives were achieved or not, and to discover some of the reasons for success and failure. In iterative development, evaluation is the key factor in the development cycle. We present such an evaluation for the COHIBIT system. Subjects performed an interaction session and filled in a subsequent questionnaire that addresses all of the mentioned issues. We show how we designed and analyzed the questionaire. We try to address some issues of general interest, e.g. how do you capture a virtual character's personality? We propose 5 personality dimensions and discuss why they might be useful. We look at the structure of the questionnaire and the role that question order plays. We illuminate the role of speech synthesis, confirming findings by [3] that speech plays a major role in how well the system is perceived. We propose to analyze dialogue diversity, a core quality for Eliza-type systems, which we assume might compensate for the users' impression that a system is too talkative.

Although this paper is far from being a cookbook for systems evaluation it might give researchers who just completed their own virtual character system a starting point for their own evaluation.

2   Related Work

The topic of evaluation, especially for virtual character systems, has been of growing interest in the community [4]. In this section, we focus on three relevant evaluation studies.

McBreen et al. [3] conducted a study to measure the effectiveness and user acceptibility of animated agents. The domain was a multimodal e-retail application. The 36 subjects only passively watched an interaction with different set-ups (voice only, 2D/3D talking head, 2D/3D full body agent) and did not participate themselves. Questionnaires were to capture the subjects impressions. Results for voice indicated that the voice of the agent may effect the participants' attitudes towards the appearance of the agent. A finding that our results support. For capturing agent personality the authors used four dimensions: politeness, friendliness, competence, and forcefulness. There were indications that gesturing may play a role in subjects' perceptions of politeness because embodied versions were found to be more polite. Gestures also contributed to perceived friendliness. They found that forcefulness can be off-putting for the participant. They suggested to design systems where the agent can make suggestions without being too forceful. We picked up these suggestions, and found that our agents were perceived helpful, polite and friendly. As opposed to McBreen et al. we found no gender differences. Some findings correspond to our design decisions: 3D agents (as well as 3D talking heads) were found to be preferred by subjects. Also, we tried to carefully select nonverbal behaviors to maximize believability but the somewhat indifferent results in this area indicate that further research is needed to pinpoint the factors of "good" and "appropriate" gesturing.

Hartmann et al. [5] presented a system that produces expressive gestures for embodied conversational agents. They identified six attributes from psychological literature to model expressivity. In their user studies they asked 54 subjects to rank three different animations for preference (most appropriate to least appropriate with respect to the expressive intent). The three clips were: neutral, coherent (as generated by their system) and inconsistent. The results showed that participants preferred the coherent performance above neutral and inconsistent actions. This shows that principled coherent generation of gestures is perceivable and preferred by human observers.

Van Mulken et al. [6] pointed out that many virtual character systems do not exploit the affordances of the human bodies. In our system the presence of the embodied characters is an integral part of the experience. As the set-up in Figure 1 shows, the two life-size virtual characters can be seen as performers who react to user actions, act pro-actively if the user idles and even live on and talk with each other after the user has left the exhibit in order to attract new visitors. The attention the user gives to the agents while interacting but also when watching from a distance is largely due to their quality as life-like embodied beings.

3   COHIBIT System and Research Questions

COHIBIT is a mixed-reality museum exhibit which features tangible interaction and conversational virtual characters [2]. Figure 1 shows the spatial arrangement: The exhibit consists of a life-size projection of two virtual characters (VCs), a table in front of it and a large shelf on the side which houses 10 real car pieces (front piece, middle piece, various rear pieces). Museum visitors entering the exhibit are detected by cameras and welcomed by the two VCs. They point out the possibility of assembling a car using the real car pieces in the shelf and offer their (verbal) assistance. If the visitor starts putting pieces on the table the VCs engage in a dialogue to motivate, guide and inform the visitor: for instance, they comment on recognized actions ("you shifted the front piece to the left"), give corrections ("you have to turn the cockpit") or suggest further action ("if you place a middle piece between cockpit and rear, you're done"). Once a car is finished the VCs congratulate the visitor and tell him/her about the model just built. As the interaction unfolds, i.e. the user builds more and different models, the system shifts focus from assisting to conveying more and deeper information about cars (security systems, environmental aspects, technical data), reflect their own technology by talking about virtual character technology (speech synthesis, computer graphics, behavior control etc.), and weave in current context knowledge like daytime, number of finished cars and even the weather. If the visitor leaves, the VCs continue living and engage in smalltalk with each other to attract further potential visitors. The complex, varied and context-aware behavior is modeled by a 70-page "screenplay" of text chunks which is traversed using a so-called sceneflow. The sceneflow is a hierarchical state-based tool for modelling complex context-aware behavior [7][8].

The mixed-reality installation provides a tangible, multimodal, and immersive experience for a single visitor or a group of visitors. The ten tangible objects

Fig. 1. Overview of the COHIBIT system. Left is a frontal view that shows the projection of the VCs, the car pieces and the table (workbench). Right is a top view showing projection, table, car pieces, visitors and the cameras for detecting visitor presence.

are instrumented with passive RFID tags and represent car-model pieces on the scale 1:5, the table (workbench) has five adjacent areas with RFID readers where car pieces can be placed. The back projection for the two virtual characters measures 3x3 meters. For speech output we use the commercial hi-end text-to-speech (TTS) synthesis system rVoice (Rhetorical) by Nuance. The VCs are animated with a real-time animation engine by Charamel[2] featuring 3D based keyframe animation and motion blending. The nonverbal behavior of our agents consists of a total repertoire of 28 actions (including idle-time behaviors) for each character. The gestures are in part authored and in part automatically generated from a set of rules [9].

4   Method

4.1   Participants

16 subjects (9 female) participated in the evaluation. Nine of them were 19-30 years old and the other seven 31-45 years old. All subjects were German native speakers and each subject was tested individually.

4.2   Procedure

The experiment consisted of letting each subject interact alone with the system for a duration of 15 minutes. Since our system also "lives on" during times when no user is present it was important to let the subject observe system behavior for some time before and after the interaction (4 minutes total).

All subjects were instructed that they would be watching the exhibit passively for some minutes before, upon a sign by the supervisor, they could "enter" the

---

[2] http://www.charamel.com

exhibit to interact for 15 minutes until, upon a second sign, they would watch the characters' final remarks, again passively. For the time of the interaction the subject was left alone with the system. Pre-evaluation studies showed that subjects often become nervous and self-conscious if a supervisor is present or a camera is visibly installed. Leaving subjects alone helped eliminating any kind of "examination fear" that they might have felt if being observed. We also told all subjects during instruction that it is the *system* that is being tested and not them, that they cannot make any mistakes and that they should feel free to experiment with the system.

After the experiment each subject filled in an anonymous, 2-page post-questionnaire.

4.3   Questionnaire

The post-questionnaire used 34 attitude statements with a 5-ary rating scale to capture how the subjects experienced the system (see Table 1 for an excerpt). The questionnaire had four major aspects: (1) general impression, (2) virtual characters, (3) dialogue, and (4) target age groups.

The questionnaire's first question was "Did you find the interaction entertaining?" aiming at a spontaneous reaction. In contrast, the questionnaire's final question asked for an overall school mark for the exhibit. The placement of the final question is meant to profit from the many previous questions that allowed the user to gain a differentiated view on her/his opinions of the system. As can be seen in Table 1, the rating for the first question (spontaneous impression) is very similar to the rating in the last question (differentiated judgment).

The "personality" of the characters was inquired using five dimensions: likability, competence, politeness, humanlikeness, talkativeness. We decided against

Table 1. Sample questions from the questionnaire (but in original order) with the 5-point scale and mean value over all subjects

question	*scale*	*mean*
Did you find the interaction entertaining?	*not at all* – 1 2 3 4 5 – *very much*	4.3
Did the characters manage to get your attention?	*not at all* – 1 2 3 4 5 – *very much*	3.9
Did you find the system informative wrt. cars	*not at all* – 1 2 3 4 5 – *very much*	3.8
How did you find the dialogue variation?	*predictable* – 1 2 3 4 5 – *predictable*	4.1
The characters talked...	*too little* – 1 2 3 4 5 – *too much*	3.4
For the task the characters' comments were...	*distracting* – 1 2 3 4 5 – *helpful*	3.9
What overall mark would you give the system?	*very bad* – 1 2 3 4 5 – *very good*	4.2

using the "Big Five" (openness, conscientiousness, extraversion, agreableness, and neuroticism) for two reasons. First, the range of human attributes in our system is limited. One could call our scenario a "service oriented" interaction, like a sales talk, a professional consulting session or a university lecture. In such interactions only a limited range of human behaviors occur. Extreme behaviors like screaming, crying or sulking silently are unlikely because the topics (car assembly, artificial intelligence, car research etc.) are relatively neutral and unemotional, plus the interaction protocol makes extreme behaviors a taboo. We therefore focused on those dimensions where we expect variations, "zooming in" on some of the Big Five. Thus, likability is an aspect of agreeableness, politeness may be considered a cross-product of agreeableness and conscientiousness, talkativeness is an aspect of extraversion and competence a cross-product of openness and conscientiousness. Also, for the questionaire, the notions we used should be very specific in how they are understood by the subjects. The Big Five notions might be somewhat unfamiliar to naive users. Finally, our characters are simply not human beings but artificial characters whose behavior is "designed". Therefore, we introduced the personality trait "humanlikeness" that you would not ask when rating humans.

5   Results

Most items of the questionnaire were unidirectional on a 5-ary scale (very bad to very good). For statistical analysis the data was transformed so that for all items the negative end of the scale was assigned "1" (e.g. not entertaining, very disturbing) and the positive end to "5" (e.g. very entertaining, not disturbing). Since rating scales can be treated as interval scales [10] we used parametrical tests for the statistical analysis. The *t-test for one sample* is a statistical significance test that proves whether a measured mean value of an observed group differs from an expected value. In our study, ratings were proven to be positive if the mean score significantly exceeded the neutral value of "3". Interaction between two factors (e.g. gender and questionnaire statement) were proved by an *analysis of variance* (ANOVA).

Some items were bi-polar (for instance, a 5-point scale ranging from "characters talk too much" to "talk too little"). In this case, both ends of the scale represent negative extremes. Therefore, the ideal value is "3". Tendencies to one of the negative sides were proved by *t-tests for one sample*.

5.1   Role of Gender and Age

Nine women and seven men participated in the evaluation. A 2 x 34 ANOVA with the factors gender and questionnaire statement revealed a significant effect of the factor questionnaire statement ($F(33, 462) = 5.80; p < .001$) which simply means that different questions were answered differently by the subjects. However, did gender display any visible answering pattern? The factor gender ($F(1, 14) = 1.34; p = .27$) as well as the interaction between gender and questionnaire statement ($F(33, 462) = 1.02; p = .45$) were not significant. This pattern of effects does not change when analysing the four main issues of the questionnaire separately. There are no significant gender differences, men and women perceive the system in a similar way.

Since our subjects could be split into two age groups of similar size (9 subjects 19-30 years, 8 subjects 31-45 years) we could also compare age groups differences using analoguous means as for gender. However, we did not find any significant effect. Subject of age groups 19-30 and 31-45 perceived the system in a similar way.

5.2 General Impression

The subjects found the interaction entertaining $(t(15) = 7.46; p < .001)$. At the same time, the interaction was informative in terms of cars $(t(15) = 3.00; p < .01)$ but middle informative in terms of computer technology $(t(15) = .75; p = .47)$.

The car construction task demanded the participants' attention $(t(15) = 3.16; p < .01)$ and the characters' comments to the car construction task were perceived as helpful $(t(15) = 4.34; p < .001)$. The participants rated the reactions of the characters towards their actions to be appropriate and neither very fast nor too slow $(t(15) = -1.25; p = .23)$.

All in all, the participants marked the exhibit with 4.2 which is highly significantly above average $(t(15) = 8.73; p < .001)$.

5.3 Characters

Despite the demands of the car construction task the virtual characters were able to catch participants' attention $(t(15) = 4.87; p < .001)$.

Both characters were rated above mean in regard to liking $(t(15) = 5.66; p < .001)$, competence $(t(15) = 3.81; p < .01)$ and politeness $(t(15) = 12.85; p < .001)$. Only concerning the impression of human-likeness the characters received mean rating $(t(15) = .99; p = .34)$. Regarding talkativeness, the characters were rated to be rather too talkative $(t(15) = 2.35; p < .05)$. See Figure 2 for a direct comparison of mean values for both characters.

A comparison of the personality profile of both characters calculating a 2 x 5 ANOVA with the factors character (male and female) and personality attribute (likable, competent, polite, human-like, talkative) did not reveal a main effect of the character $(F(1, 16) = 3.10; p = .10)$. Overall, both characters received the same degree of positive perception. The factor personality attribute showed a significant effect $(F(4, 64) = 8.14; p < .001)$. Moreover, the interaction between character and personality attribute was highly significant $(F(4, 64) = 5.52; p < .001)$. This demonstrates that both characters are perceived as virtual agents with different personality profiles. Post-hoc comparisons using LSD-tests showed that the female character was rated as more likable $(p < .001)$, more competent $(p < .01)$ and more human-like $(p < .05)$. With regard to politeness and talkativeness the characters did not differ.

A direct comparison between the male and female character was requested by two questions in the questionnaire concerning dominance and sympathy. A

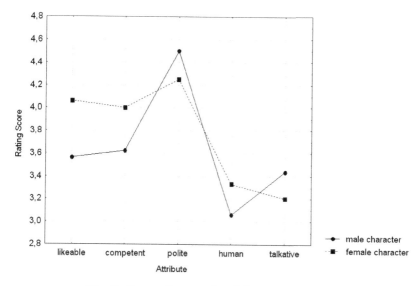

Fig. 2. Personality graphs of the two characters

value below 3 indicates an advantage for the male character and a value above 3 favours the female character. The female character was rated to be more dominant $(t(15) = 3.22; p < .01)$ but in terms of sympathy the characters did not differ $(t(15) = 1.29; p = .22)$.

5.4   Dialogue, Speech and Nonverbal Behavior

Subjects found the system too talkative $(t(15) = 3.42; p < .01)$. However, at the same time the dialogue were perceived as being rich in variety $(t(15) = 5.51; p < .001)$.

The intelligibility of speech was rated above average $(t(15) = 4.86; p < .001)$ and the synthetic speech did not annoy the participants $(t(15) = 9.41; p < .001)$. The coordination between speech and movements was rated average $(t(15) = 1.17; p = .26)$.

5.5   Potential Target Age Groups

We asked the participants to estimate how enjoyable our exhibit would be for various age groups. Five disjoint age groups were presented. Except for the group "infants up to 6 years" $(t(15) = -.45; p = .66)$ all age groups were expected to enjoy the exhibit (for all: $p < .01$). This is of course only an indicator for "appeal to different age groups". However, it is one way of approximation if time and/or budget do not allow to test a sufficient amount of subjects from the full range of age groups.

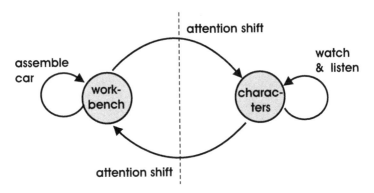

Fig. 3. The attention of the user repeatedly switches from assembling the car (active/play) and listening to the characters (passive/listen) and vice versa. The challenge is to find a good balance between entertainment (play) and education (listen).

6   Discussion

We presented an evaluation of a virtual character system that addressed important questions about the quality of the COHIBIT system in particular and about edutainment systems with virtual characters in general.

The major challenge when modeling VC behavior is to find a good balance between letting the user "play" with the car pieces and talking to him/her to convey some (possibly educating) information. This is a core problem in edutainment systems: you use entertainment to motivate, energize and get attention but you also need to get the educational content across – how do you balance the two? This pricipal dichotomy is even more pronounced in our system since the user cannot talk to the system, making the user either very active but unattentive (play) or very attentive but passive (listen) as depicted in Figure 3. Our questionaire focuses on this general problem. Since our tools allow to efficiently build behavior models, the flow of the conversion can be adapted very quickly after a number of exploratory tests. Thus, our iterative development has short and frequent test-adapt-compile loops. We used our questionaire to guide our development and, hopefully, our researchers can profit from it.

How entertaining the exhibit was found by the subjects was significantly correlated with the perception of the speech synthesis. The less annoying subjects found the virtual characters' speech, the more entertaining the whole exhibit was rated (Pearson Product-Moment Correlation: $r = .57; p < .05$). This confirms the finding by [3] that the quality of speech synthesis has a significant impact of how the system is perceived.

The fact that gender did not have an effect on perception is interesting, especially because the domain of cars would make you expect a slight bias towards male subjects. The number of subjects was too low to draw any hard conclusions but it appears as if a virtual character driven system does appeal to male and female subjects in similar ways which is equally true for subjects differing in age, however restricted to two age groups of 19-30 and 31-45.

Concerning the characters' profiles we have carefully selected the personality traits to examine (Figure 2). We focused on those aspects that we wanted to design. They can be considered "quality criteria" of the characters' personality design. We wanted the characters to be likable, competent, polite, not too talkative and very human-like. We succeeded in most of these aspects. However, humanlikeness appears to be an important avenue for future improvement. The characters were also perceived as too talkative which might also be due to the quality of the speech synthesis. This result is balanced by the fact that subjects found the dialogue varied and informative. In terms of personality, we wanted the characters to differ so that they are perceived as distinct. The graph in Figure 2 shows that this was the case, especially with respect to liking and competence. Since there remains work to be done with respect to human-likeness, further evaluations should identify the factors that govern human-likeness. Synchrony of nonverbal behavior with speech was only rated average which might indicate that improvement might be necessary here to increase human-likeness, although again speech synthesis quality might have influenced this judgment negatively.

Our evaluation showed that our system was both informative and entertaining. The characters were able to catch the attention of the user without distracting him/her from the assembly task (Figure 3). On the contrary, the characters' comments were perceived as helpful in the task. Moreover, subjects thought that the exhibit would be enjoyed by people in a wide age range (everyone older than 6). Thus, the evaluation was helpful in confirming that our system was perceived as intended, potentially enjoyable to a wide range of people, and in identifying hotspots for future work.

Acknowledgements

Thanks to our colleague Martin Rumpler and our students Gernot Gebhard and Thomas Schleiff for their excellent work on the COHIBIT system. This work is partially funded by the German Ministry for Education and Research (BMBF) as part of the VirtualHuman project under grant 01 IMB 01A.

References

1. Rist, T., André, E., Baldes, S., Gebhard, P., Klesen, M., Kipp, M., Rist, P., Schmitt, M.: A review of the development of embodied presentation agents and their application fields. In Prendinger, H., Ishizuka, M., eds.: Life-Like Characters – Tools, Affective Functions, and Applications. Springer, Heidelberg (2003) 377–404
2. Ndiaye, A., Gebhard, P., Kipp, M., Klesen, M., Schneider, M., Wahlster, W.: Ambient intelligence in edutainment: Tangible interaction with life-like exhibit guides. In: Proceedings of the first Confernce on INtelligent TEchnologies for interactive enterTAINment (INTETAIN), Berlin, Heidelberg, Springer (2005) 104–113

3. McBreen, H., Anderson, J., Jack, M.: Evaluating 3D embodied conversational agents in contrasting VRML retail applications. In: Proceedings of the Workshop on "Multimodal Communication and Context in Embodied Agents" held in conjunction with the Fifth International Conference on Autonomous Agents (AGENTS), Montréal (2001) 83–87

4. Ruttkay, Z., Pelachaud, C., eds.: From Brows to Trust: Evaluating Embodied Conversational Agents. Kluwer (2004)

5. Hartmann, B., Mancini, M., Buisine, S., Pelachaud, C.: Design and evaluation of expressive gesture synthesis for embodied conversational agents. In: Proceedings of the fourth international joint conference on Autonomous agents and multiagent systems. ACM Press (2005)

6. van Mulken, S., André, E., Müller, J.: The Persona Effect: How Substantial is it? In: Proceedings of the British Computer Society Conference on Human Computer Interaction (HCI 98). (1998) 53–66

7. Klesen, M., Kipp, M., Gebhard, P., Rist, T.: Staging exhibitions: Methods and tools for modeling narrative structure to produce interactive performances with virtual actors. Virtual Reality. Special Issue on Storytelling in Virtual Environments 7(1) (2003) 17–29

8. Gebhard, P., Kipp, M., Klesen, M., Rist, T.: Authoring scenes for adaptive, interactive performances. In: Proceedings of the Second International Joint Conference on Autonomous Agents and Multiagent Systems. (2003) 725–732

9. Kipp, M.: Creativity meets Automation: Combining Nonverbal Action Authoring with Rules and Machine Learning. In: Proceedings of the 6th International Conference on Intelligent Virtual Agents (IVA 2006), Springer (2006)

10. Westermann, R.: Empirical tests of scale type for individual ratings. Applied Psychological Measurement 9 (1985) 265–274

Invited Talk:
Rule Systems and Video Games

Rod Humble

Vice President, Head of *The Sims Studio*
Electronic Arts

In this talk I will examine the different kinds of rule systems which have been used historically within games. I will then explore the emerging field of self modifying rule systems within computer games. In conclusion I will cover various techniques which maybe applied and how games relating to everyday life such as The Sims can benefit from such systems.

Rod Humble has been in the games industry for over 16 years. His first original game design The Humans was released by GameTek in 1991. Since then he has worked on and released well over a hundred games as designer, producer and executive producer. Before coming to Electronic Arts in 2004 he was Vice President of Product Development heading up the EverQuest studio for Sony Online Entertainment.

J. Gratch et al. (Eds.): IVA 2006, LNAI 4133, p. 445, 2006.
© Springer-Verlag Berlin Heidelberg 2006

Invited Talk:
Façade: Architecture and Authorial Idioms for Believable Agents in Interactive Drama

Michael Mateas[1,2] and Andrew Stern[2]

[1] Computer Science Department
University of California at Santa Cruz
Santa Cruz, CA
[2] Procedural Arts, LLC
Portland, OR

Façade is a first person, real-time interactive drama that integrates autonomous characters, an interactive plot that goes beyond simple story graphs, and natural language understanding, into a first-person, real-time interactive drama experience. Since its release in July 2005 as freeware, *Façade* has been downloaded over 350,000 times and received widespread critical acclaim among players, game developers and mainstream press.

In *Façade* you, the player, using your own name and gender, play the character of a longtime friend of Grace and Trip, an attractive and materially successful couple in their early thirties. During an evening get-together at their apartment that quickly turns ugly, you become entangled in the high-conflict dissolution of Grace and Trip's marriage. No one is safe as the accusations fly, sides are taken and irreversible decisions are forced to be made. By the end of this intense one-act play you will have changed the course of Grace and Trip's lives - motivating you to re-play the drama to find out how your interaction could make things turn out differently the next time.

The *Façade* architecture includes ABL (A Behavior Language), a new reactive planning language for authoring believable agents that includes language support for joint action; a probabilistic agenda-based drama manager that sequences story units, motivated by the theory of dramatic beats; and a semantic parser and simple discourse management system. The architecture co-evolved with a collection of authorial idioms for structuring story-based character goals (beat goals) and global mix-in reactions.

Our presentation will describe the *Façade* architecture, the authorial idioms used to construct our story within this architecture, and our lessons learned during this five year research effort. The process of building *Façade* has involved three major research efforts: designing ways to deconstruct a dramatic narrative into a hierarchy of story and behavior pieces; engineering an AI system that responds to and integrates the player's moment-by-moment interactions to reconstruct a real-time dramatic performance from those pieces; and understanding how to write an engaging, compelling story within this new organizational framework.

J. Gratch et al. (Eds.): IVA 2006, LNAI 4133, pp. 446–448, 2006.
© Springer-Verlag Berlin Heidelberg 2006

The talk will also provide an overview of the process of bringing our interactive drama to life as a coherent, engaging, high agency experience, including the design and programming of thousands of joint dialog behaviors in the reactive planning language ABL, and their total organization into a collection of story beats sequenced by a drama manager. The process of iteratively developing the architecture, its languages, authorial idioms, and varieties of story content structures will be discussed. These content structures are designed to intermix to offer players a high degree of responsiveness and narrative agency. We conclude with design and implementation lessons learned and future directions for creating more generative architectures.

Andrew Stern is a designer, writer and engineer of personality-rich, AI-based interactive characters and stories. With Michael Mateas he recently completed the interactive drama *Façade*, a 5-year art/research project that has been downloaded over 350,000 times, recently won the Grand Jury Prize at the 2006 Slamdance Independent Game Festival, and has been critically acclaimed by the press and gaming community. Previously Andrew was a lead designer and software engineer at PF.Magic, developing *Virtual Babyz*, *Dogz* and *Catz*, which sold over 2 million units worldwide. He and Michael recently founded the game studio Procedural Arts, and regularly blog at grandtextauto.org. Andrew has presented and exhibited work at the Game Developers Conference, Independent Games Festival, SIGGRAPH, ISEA, Digital Arts and Culture, DiGRA, TIDSE, AAAI symposia, Autonomous Agents, and Intelligent User Interfaces. Awards include a Silver Invision 2000 award for Best Overall Design for CDRom, for *Babyz*; *Catz* received a Design Distinction in the first annual I.D. Magazine Interactive Media Review, and along with *Dogz* and *Babyz* was part of the American Museum of Moving Image's Computer Space exhibit in New York. The projects have been written about in The New York Times, Time Magazine, Wired and AI Magazine. Andrew holds a B.S. in Computer Engineering from Carnegie Mellon University and a Masters degree in Computer Science from the University of Southern California.

Michael Mateas' work explores the intersection between art and artificial intelligence, forging a new art practice and research discipline called Expressive AI. He is currently a faculty member at the Georgia Institute of Technology, where he holds a joint appointment in the College of Computing and the school of Literature, Communication and Culture. At Georgia Tech, Michael is the founder of the Experimental Game Lab, whose mission is to push the technological and cultural frontiers of computer-based games. With Andrew Stern he developed the interactive drama *Façade*, which uses AI techniques to combine rich autonomous characters with interactive plot control to create a first-person, real-time, interactive story. Michael has presented papers and exhibited artwork internationally including SIGGRAPH, the New York Digital Salon, AAAI, the Game Developers Conference, TIDSE, DiGRA, Digital Arts and Culture, ISEA, the Carnegie Museum, the Warhol Museum, and Te PaPa, the national museum of New Zealand. Michael received his BS in Engineering Physics from the University of the Pacific, his MS in Computer Science from Portland State

University, and his Ph.D. in Computer Science from Carnegie Mellon University. Prior to CMU, Michael worked at Intel Laboratories, where he helped introduce ethnographic techniques into the Intel research culture, and Tektronix Laboratories, where he developed qualitative design methodologies and built advanced interface prototypes.

Invited Talk:
Social Effects of Emotion: Two Modes of Relation Alignment

Brian Parkinson

Department of Social Psychology
University of Oxford
South Parks Road
Oxford OX1 3UD, England

This talk proposes that a central function of many emotions is to configure and reconfigure the relational positions of two or more social agents with respect to some intentional object. This process of relation alignment can proceed at two levels (often in parallel). At one level, there is implicit adjustment to the unfolding transaction on a moment-by-moment basis. At the second level, there is a more strategic presentation of a relational stance oriented to anticipated reactions from the other (and from the material environment). I contrast this relational approach to emotion with the appraisal account which sees emotions simply as reactions to apprehended relational meaning. In my view, appraisal often emerges as a consequence of the adoption of a relational stance rather than as its original cause. This distinction is illustrated with apparently anomalous examples of emotions such as embarrassment and guilt.

Brian Parkinson lectures in social psychology at Oxford University, UK. His research focuses on how other people affect our emotions and on how our emotions affect other people. Current projects include investigations of relations and dissociations between explicit and implicit registration of emotion information (as part of the EC sponsored HUMAINE network of excellence), and of the role of social referencing in adult risk perceptions (funded by the Economic and Social Research Council, UK). His books include Ideas and Realties of Emotion (1995), Changing Moods (1996) and Emotion in Social Relations (2005). He has served as Associate Editor for the journal Cognition and Emotion and is currently chief editor of the British Journal of Social Psychology.

J. Gratch et al. (Eds.): IVA 2006, LNAI 4133, p. 449, 2006.
© Springer-Verlag Berlin Heidelberg 2006

Computer Model of Emotional Agents

Dilyana Budakova[1] and Lyudmil Dakovski[2]

[1] Technical University-Plovdiv,
Sankt Peterburg Blvd. N:61,Plovdiv, Bulgaria
[2] Center of Biomedical Engineering Bulgarian Academy of Sciences,
Acad. G. Bonchev Str.,bl.105, 1113 Sofia, Bulgaria
dilyana_budakova@yahoo.com, seven_in@cablebg.net

Abstract. This article presents a computer model of intelligent agents inhabiting a virtual world. The software model we developed, the agent parameters are stored in relational tables. The agents based on this architecture can be visualized graphically.

The agent's architecture includes the following components: needs, emotions, actions, self-knowledge, knowledge of places and events, rules, meta-rules and characteristics. Every component can influence over every another component.

The agent's characteristics are energy, work, adaptation, and inertia. The agent performs work to gather features and to evaluate and use them. Then, its potential energy will be equal to the work on collecting features from the world. Inertia is the inflexibility of the intelligent agents towards the alteration of their state.

A behavior rule is each statement that has one or more antecedents and conclusion. When the agent acquires some new information, it is able to change its behavior rule considering its own "principles".

The meta-rule conceives as abstract "principle" or "consciousness" of the agent. It has attitude to concrete behavior rules in situations, which requires behavior choice or reconsideration. They are fewer than the behavior rules and require more time and knowledge. The rules and meta-rules for agent's behavior are dynamically content of relational tables and the program interprets them as a data. Thus, any modification is only the table content change.

The explorer always knows the agent's state and the reasons for this state. Every place, action, state, event or rule is a function of its features. Its value is a sum of the values of the features divided by their count. Every feature or a rule antecedent is a function of its emotions, emotions values, values and weights of the needs, and inertia. Every feature interacts with all other features.

Relations between the components are shown and the possibilities for their quantitative representation are suggested. Expressions for calculating various parameters of the model including basic agent need weights and features of the places, actions, states, generalized agent states are presented and summarized. A coefficient used for reordering the basic needs is introduced.

For the purposes of the experiment, the simple scenario is suggested.

J. Gratch et al. (Eds.): IVA 2006, LNAI 4133, p. 450, 2006.
© Springer-Verlag Berlin Heidelberg 2006

Affective Robots as Mediators in Smart Environments

Gianni Cozzolongo and Berardina De Carolis

Dipartimento di Informatica – Università di Bari (Italy)
{decarolis, cozzolongo}@di.uniba.it

Following the Ambient Intelligence vision, a Smart Environment (SE) has the main aim of facilitating the user in interacting with its services by making their fruition easy, natural and adapted to the user needs. In this abstract we propose, as counterpart of the interaction, an "affective robot" that acts as mediator between the user and the environment. On one hand, the robot can be thought as a mobile and intelligent interface to the environment system. On the other hand, users establish an affective and familiar relation with it. Since this kind of interaction involves socio-emotional content it is important to take social-affective factors into account. In this case robots lose their connotation of technological tools and embody the one of friendly companion [3]. According to this metaphor, the robot has a role, a personality and coherent behaviours that allow it to follow social dynamics, to create relationships with humans and to invoke social responses. Then, as a consequence, **user modelling** becomes a key issue for developing such a successful proactive robot: it has to be able to consider and combine rational factors (i.e. interests, beliefs, abilities, preferences) and extra-rational ones (i.e. attitude, affective and social factors) considering the dependencies and influences between them.

The purpose of this research is to make a first step toward the recognition of the user attitude in interacting with a robot that acts as a mediator between the user and the environment. To this aim, we have developed a Wizard of Oz study for collecting a corpus of human-robot dialogs which is enough articulate to offer examples of a variety of user attitudes and reactions. As "affective robot" we used Sony AIBO (www.aibo.com). From the performed experiment we collected two types of results, one concerning the use of the annotated corpus to structure the model for recognizing the user attitude towards the robot, the other regarding the subjective evaluation of the interaction with AIBO obtained from the questionnaire results. As far as the model of the user attitude is concerned, we need to evaluate its effectiveness in real context of use. In fact, we plan to partially overwrite the AIBO mind in order to give it the capability to use this model and to plan the interaction accordingly. The overall response of the users to the experiments seems to confirm that the idea of using an affective robot as a mediator is a good way to overcome barriers that people may find in using smart environments.

References

1. Kerstin Dautenhahn. Robots as social actors: Aurora and the case of autism. In Proc. CT99, The Third International Cognitive Technology Conference, August, San Francisco, pages 359--374, 1999.

J. Gratch et al. (Eds.): IVA 2006, LNAI 4133, p. 451, 2006.
© Springer-Verlag Berlin Heidelberg 2006

Expression of Emotion in Body and Face

Elizabeth A. Crane[1], M. Melissa Gross[1], and Barbara L. Fredrickson[2]

[1] Department of Movement Science, University of Michigan
[2] Department of Psychology, University of North Carolina at Chapel Hill
{bcrane, mgross}@umich.edu

Abstract. Intelligent interaction with an environment, other IVAs, and human users requires a system that identifies subtle expressive cues and behaves naturally using modalities such as body, face, and voice to communicate. Although research on individual affective channels has increased, little is known about expressive qualities in whole body movement. This study has three goals: (1) to determine rates of observer recognition of emotion in walking, (2) to use kinematic analysis to quantify how emotions change gait patterns in characteristic ways, and (3) to describe the concurrence of facial and bodily expression of emotion.

Twenty-six undergraduate students recalled an experience from their own lives in which they felt angry, sad, content, joy, or no emotion at all (neutral). After recalling a target emotion, participants walked across the lab. Whole body motion capture data were acquired using a video-based, 6-camera system. Side view video was also recorded. Ten participants wore a special head mounted camera designed to record video of facial expression. After each trial, participants rated the intensity of eight emotions (4 target and 4 non-target). After blurring the faces in the side view video so that facial expressions were not observable, randomized composite videos were shown to untrained observers. After viewing each video clip, observers selected one of ten responses corresponding to the emotion that they thought the walker felt during the trial. FACS coding was used to evaluate the face video for evidence of emotion and timing of facial expressions with respect to the gait cycle.

Self-report data indicated that the walkers felt the target emotions at levels corresponding to "moderately" or above in all trials. Validation data were collected from five observers on gait trials from a subset of subjects (n=16). Recognition rates for sad, anger, neutral and content were 45%, 25%, 20% and 16%, respectively. Joy was recognized at chance levels (10%). Normalized velocity, normalized stride length, cycle duration and velocity were significantly affected by emotion.

This study is unique in describing the effects of specific emotions on gait. The preliminary results indicate that gait kinematics change with emotion. Although temporal-spatial kinematics were related to arousal levels, angular kinematics are needed to distinguish emotions with similar levels of arousal.

J. Gratch et al. (Eds.): IVA 2006, LNAI 4133, p. 452, 2006.
© Springer-Verlag Berlin Heidelberg 2006

Towards Primate-Like Synthetic Sociability

Pablo Lucas dos Anjos and Ruth Aylett

Heriot-Watt University, School of Mathematical and Computer Sciences
Edinburgh, EH14 4AS, United Kingdom
{anjos, ruth}@macs.hw.ac.uk

This research addresses synthetic agents as autonomous software entities, capable of managing social relationships in small scale societies. An individual architecture is structurally designed as enabling primate-like social organization, which is in turn individually modulated by an affective action-selection mechanism. The aim is to improve agent social reactive, and social cognitive capabilities, by implementing plain communication conveying behavioral rewards or sanctions. This artificial society simulation is being developed as an experimental model aimed at exploring the nature of (1) the adaptation of inter-agent social norms, (2) individual behavioral arbitration, and the (3) interplay of reaction and deliberation. This computational outlook on social cognition offers a contrast with traditional socio-unaware action-selection systems, frequently based on function optimization of decision-making processes [1]. To anthropomorphize the model, social networks are analyzed in terms of situated agents and their internal states. Individuals are able to recognize current counterparts and have their community size dependent on accumulated experiences [2]; thus food and relationship management become crucial individual tasks. However, this work does not seek an ethologically realistic approach like [3] - nor does it aim at a complete account of animal or human language interaction. It rather argues for a simpler alternative to represent synthetic social intelligence. By interleaving processes of reaction and planning, agents are expected to act following their individual modulation of pre-configured abilities - dealing both with passive objects (resources) and other active characters (agents). Finally, to interpret interactions and the operation of affective feedback, essential observations and analysis are required on the (1) administration of basic social constraints and (2) processes producing social change, relating invidual behavior choices to group dynamics [4].

References

1. Cristiano Castelfranchi. Formalising the informal: Dynamic social order, bottom-up social control, and normative relations. Journal of Applied Logic, 2003.
2. Robin. Dunbar. Coevolution of neocortical size, group size and language in humans. Behavioral and Brain Sciences, Volume 16, Number 4, Pages 681–735, 1993.
3. Charlotte K. Hemelrijk. Towards the integration of social dominance and spatial structure. The Association for the Study of Animal Behaviour. Journal of Animal Behavior, 9, 1035–1048, 2000.
4. Robert B. Cialdini, Melanie R. Trost. Social influence: Social norms, conformity and compliance. in The Handbook of Social Psychology, 151, 151, Edition 4 Daniel T. Gilbert et al, 2006.

J. Gratch et al. (Eds.): IVA 2006, LNAI 4133, p. 453, 2006.
© Springer-Verlag Berlin Heidelberg 2006

Here Be Dragons: Integrating Agent Behaviors with Procedural Emergent Landscapes and Structures

Todd Furmanski

University of Southern California, Lucas 310
850 W 34th St, Los Angeles, CA 90089
tfurmanski@gmail.com

Abstract. Here Be Dragons is a virtual environment containing creatures and cities that have no direct human designer. Digital genes, defining a structure similar to a Lindenmeyer system, form both the agents and structures within the space. Each component of these genes contains behavioral as well as structural content, and their format allows alterations like genetic crossbreeding and mutation. Protocol exists for communication between the cities and inhabitants, allowing more intricate interactions.

The name "Here Be Dragons" refers to the unexplored regions found past the borders of old maps. The virtual space invites exploration, and to that end creature and city structures form novel shapes and behaviors as the user navigates the terrain. Explicitly authored spaces can only be as large as someone makes them, while traditional procedural spaces either become too predictable or too chaotic. Using algorithms traditionally reserved for virtual agents, as well as a mixture of techniques found in Artificial Life and other emergent schools of thought, the virtual space attempts to balance coherency with novelty. This approach has turned the typical production pipeline on its head. Traditional asset creation has been replaced with designing ways to generate and interpret pliable data. Upon completion of this design phase, a world can be generated in seconds.

The creatures have an enforced symmetry, and are rendered in silhouette, inviting analogies to birds, bats, viruses, and dragons. Each segment within a creature acts as its own state machine, its own actions rippling through the entire body, generation the illusion of animism. The cities take information similar to those of the creatures but instead use it to build walls, spires, and buttresses. While the underlying code can inform very concrete visuals, Here Be Dragons intentionally abstracts the forms, invoking an effect similar to a Rorschach inkblot.

As the line between agents and environment blurs, the potential for coherent interaction and visualization increases. A universal gene could potentially define 3D models, music, decision trees, and story flow within the same virtual space.

J. Gratch et al. (Eds.): IVA 2006, LNAI 4133, p. 454, 2006.
© Springer-Verlag Berlin Heidelberg 2006

Virtual Pedagogical Agents: Naturalism vs. Stylization

Agneta Gulz and Magnus Haake

Div. of Cognitive Science & Dept. of Design Sciences, Lund University, Sweden
agneta.gulz@lucs.lu.se, magnus.haake@design.lth.se

In discussions on naturalism vs. stylization in the design of virtual pedagogical agents (VPAs), the *smooth communication argument* is one of the most central in favour of visual naturalism. Yet, this argument dissolves if we separate design into the levels of: (1) *linguistic performance*, where the support for naturalism is strong; (2) *dynamic visual appearance,* in the sense of bodily behaviour, with increasing design freedom still matching positive user responses; and (3) *static visual appearance*, as the underlying, inanimate, visual model, with naturalism a well defined state, but stylization spanning a complex, multidimensional design space. A comparison with cartoons and animated movies here suggest a potential for stylized designs.

A consequence of not recognizing these different levels of design, is that a (reasonable) strive for naturalism in some aspects ends up in a non-reflected strive for overall naturalism – not realising that a certain degree of naturalism in visual dynamic appearance does not require the same degree of naturalism in visual static appearance, and that, in particular, naturalism in linguistic behaviour is practically independent of naturalism in visual static appearance.

The identification argument in favour of naturalism regards VPAs' potential to take advantage of human social affordances. Close emulating of human beings will enable us to recreate phenomena that are pedagogically valuable in the human–human context, such as emotional support, identification and role modelling. When a student experiences similarity with a role model, the efficiency of the role model increases – therefore preconditions for role modelling will be superior if a character looks really like a human being. This line of reasoning may have intuitive appeal, but is not supported by empirical evidence. On the contrary, it seems even easier for people to experience social relationships, and identify themselves, with stylized characters.[1]

Behind conflicting arguments on visual naturalism we find different *motives* for research and development of VPAs. One is to obtain smooth and beneficial interaction between human and computer in pedagogical contexts. Another is to model and understand human behaviour: human dialogues, gestures, facial expressions, etc. With respect to the latter motive, but not the former, naturalism is a self-evident ultimate goal. Therefore, when researching naturalism–stylization in VPAs, the scientific modelling of naturalistic human behaviour and the pragmatic approach focusing on the development of a usable tool, must be distinguished. Only this way will we be able to benefit fully both from the pedagogical potentials of VPAs – for role modelling, identification, the use of stereotypes, etc. – and from their potentials as powerful test-beds for theoretical modelling.

---

[1] E.g: Gulz, A., and Haake, M. Design of animated pedagogical agents – a look at their look. Int. J. of Human-Computer Studies, 64, 6 (2006), 322-339.

J. Gratch et al. (Eds.): IVA 2006, LNAI 4133, p. 455, 2006.

The Role of Social Norm in User-Engagement and Appreciation of the Web Interface Agent Bonzi Buddy

Johan F. Hoorn and Henriette C. van Vugt

Free University, Amsterdam

Whether or not an agent application is accepted or rejected is not only the effect of its empathic qualities but also of the assessment of empathy by the user as influenced by peer group norms. If a Computer Science student visits, for example, a Web site that advertises the Bonzi Buddy Web agent, he or she will be prejudiced against the agent before even interacting with it and despite the empathic qualities it advertises. One of the factors causing these effects is that Computer Science students reckon with the group norms of their peers, who forbid appreciating Microsoft applications in the first place, particularly user applications that may be judged childish. This study focused on the effects of peer-group norms on individual judgments of Bonzi Buddy. Hypotheses and other details on the experiment can be found in Hoorn and Van Vugt (2004).[1]

University master students (N=14, age 21-27) were seated in a dimly lit classroom opposite of a projection screen, on which a coloured screenshot of the Bonzi Buddy homepage was projected. A black and white screenshot was printed on the two versions of the questionnaire (Likert-type items). One focused on the respondent's subjective norms and one on estimations of the group norms (of the other 13 respondents). Respondents completed the group version prior to the subjective version or v.v. The dependent variables were engagement (involvement-distance, e.g., 'I have friendly feelings for Bonzi Buddy', 2x20 items), and appreciation (e.g., 'Bonzi Buddy is fun', 2x12 items).

Results showed that involvement estimated for the group was higher than personal involvement, while distance estimated for the group was lower than the personally experienced distance. Conscious activation of the peer-group norms thereafter positively impacted the subjectively experienced level of involvement as well as of distance. Given the initial low personal involvement, this may be interpreted as a result of group conformity and regression to the average, but in view of the moderate level of estimated group distance, unexpectedly, as rebellion against such group restraints as well. The most interesting finding, however, is perhaps that appreciation remained unaffected. Probably, the mild appreciation of Bonzi Buddy expressed a harmless judgment that hid what was actually felt inside (i.e. less involvement and more distance than probably allowed); so to 'keep your nose clean' as it were. If one looks at appreciation alone, one could think that the social group is so homogeneous that no differences can be detected between group norm and subjective norm in parasocial behavior with fictitious others. However, in the light of the observed interactions between subjectively experienced engagement and social norm, this was not the case. Social Norm as a factor in engaging with fictional characters and mediated people seems to have a complex socio-emotional impact on parasocial behavior.

---

[1] Hoorn, J.F., Van Vugt, H.C.: The role of social norm in user-engagement and appreciation of the web interface agent Bonzi Buddy (2004). AAMAS, workshop on Empathic Agents.

J. Gratch et al. (Eds.): IVA 2006, LNAI 4133, p. 456, 2006.
© Springer-Verlag Berlin Heidelberg 2006

Countering Adversarial Strategies in Multi-agent Virtual Scenarios

Yu-Cheng Hsu[1], Paul Hsueh-Min Chang[1], and Von-Wun Soo[1, 2]

[1] Department of Computer Science, National Tsing Hua University
101, Section 2, Guangfu Road, Hsinchu 300, Taiwan
[2] Department of Computer Science, National University of Kaohsiung
700, Kaohsiung University Road, Kaohsiung 811, Taiwan
{mr936334, pchang, soo}@cs.nthu.edu.tw

Mutual modeling and plotting between virtual characters is an important issue in scenarios with an interactive multi-agent drama and games. This paper provides a framework for agents to model the intentions of others and to select the optimal strategy by simulating multi-level mutual modeling. The resulting plan considers multiple rounds of counter-strategy and possible adversarial reactions, creating deeper strategic interaction.

The framework use a hierarchical tree similar to an AND-OR tree in structure to represent both the plans of self and of the adversary, allowing agents to reason about multi-level countering strategies and decide whether a strategy is optimal or worth taking. The method for countering one-level strategy may work if an agent's opponent is completely unaware of my intention to counter it. If the opponent is clever, however, it will predict the agent's intention to counter his plan and will try to devise schemes to obstruct it. Then the agent will take action to prevent its counterplan from being countered. It is evident that a "clever" agent should be capable of simulating multi-level mutual modeling in mind. Finally, the framework for multilevel modeling should be incorporated in the architecture of the virtual agent, who has a sensor to receive events in the virtual world and an actuator to impose actions. These action results cause the structure of and probabilities in the intention trees to be updated. A counterplanning agent should dynamically adjust its strategies as a response to the adversarial actions.

There are still some issues to be dealt with. Since an action could fail disastrously rather than "just fails", the agent should expect the possibility of failure and prepare remedies. Time control in executing countering actions is also an important issue. Still, we hope this work brings a step closer to automatic scenario performance.

References

1. Carbonell, J. G.: Counterplanning: A Strategy-Based Model of Adversary Planning in Real-World Situations. Artificial Intelligence **16** (1981) 295-329
2. Cavazza, M., Charles, F., Mead, S. J.: Interacting with Virtual Characters In Interactive Storytelling. Proceedings of the First International Joint Conference on Autonomous Agents and Multiagent Systems. ACM Press, New York (2002) 318-325

J. Gratch et al. (Eds.): IVA 2006, LNAI 4133, p. 457, 2006.
© Springer-Verlag Berlin Heidelberg 2006

Avatar's Gaze Control to Facilitate Conversational Turn-Taking in Virtual-Space Multi-user Voice Chat System

Ryo Ishii, Toshimitsu Miyajima, Kinya Fujita, and Yukiko Nakano

Graduate School of Tokyo University of Agriculture and Technology,
Koganei, 184-8588 Tokyo, Japan
ryo@reality.ei.tuat.ac.jp,
{tomiyaji, kfujita, nakano}@cc.tuat.ac.jp

Abstract. Aiming at facilitating multi-party conversations in a shared-virtual-space voice chat environment, we propose an avatar's gaze behavior model for turn-taking in multi-party conversations, and a shared-virtual-space voice chat system with automatic avatar gaze direction control function using user utterance information. The use of the utterance information attained easy-to-use automatic gaze control without eye-tracking camera or manual operation. In our gaze behavior model, a conversation was divided into three states: during-utterance, right-after-utterance, and silence. For each state, avatar's gaze behaviors are controlled based on a probabilistic state transition model. Previous studies reveled that gaze has a power of selecting the next speaker and urge her/him to speak, and continuous gaze has a risk of giving intimidating impression to the listener. Although explicit look-away from the conversational partner generally means interest to others, such gaze behaviors seem to help the speaker avoid threatening the listener's face. In order to express less-face-threatening eye-gaze in virtual space avatars, our model introduces vague-gaze: the avatar looks at five degrees lower than the user's eye position. Thus, in during-utterance state, the avatars were controlled using a probabilistic state transition model that transits among three states: eye contact, vague-gaze and look-away. It is expected that the vague-gaze reduces intimidating impression as well as facilitates conversational turn-taking. In right-after-utterance state, the speaker avatar keeps an eye contact for a few seconds to urge the next speaker to start a new turn. This is based on an observation of real face-to-face conversation. Finally, in silent state, avatar's gaze direction is randomly changed to avoid giving intimidating impression. In our evaluation experiment, twelve subjects were divided into four groups, and requested to chat with the avatars and answer impressions for them using Likert scale. As for the during-utterance state, in terms of naturalness, intimidating impression reduction and turn-taking facilitation, a transition model consisting of vague-gaze and look-away was significantly effective, compared to the vague-gaze alone, the look-away alone and the fixed-gaze alone models . In the right-after-utterance state, any of the gaze control methods were significantly effective in facilitating turn-taking, compared to the fixed-gaze method. The evaluation experiment demonstrated the effectiveness of our avatar's gaze control mechanism, and suggested that the gaze control based on the user utterance facilitates multi-party conversations in a virtual-space voice chat system.

Keywords: gaze, avatar, multi-party conversation, voice chat, utterance.

J. Gratch et al. (Eds.): IVA 2006, LNAI 4133, p. 458, 2006.
© Springer-Verlag Berlin Heidelberg 2006

The Role of Discourse Structure and Response Time in Multimodal Communication

Patrick Jeuniaux, Max M. Louwerse, and Xiangen Hu

Department of Psychology / Institute for Intelligent Systems
38152 Memphis, Tennessee, USA
{pjeuniau, mlouwers, xhu}@memphis.edu

In an ongoing project on multimodal communication in humans and agents [1], we investigate the interaction between two linguistic modalities (prosody and dialog structure) and two non-linguistic modalities (eye gaze and facial expressions). The goal is to gain a better understanding of the use of communicative channels in discourse and can subsequently aid the development of more effective animated conversational agents. We studied conversations between humans involved in the Map Task scenario whereby an Instruction Giver (IG) navigates an Instruction Follower (IF) from a starting point to an end point on a map [2].

In the development of animated conversational agents it is often assumed that the agent should respond promptly to the content of the utterance. The present poster presents preliminary results on the frequency distributions of multimodal events occurring during four dialogs, across three time comparison frames (0, 1 and 2 second intervals). For example, we want to determine if P (IG blinks, at time $t + 1s$ | IF asks a Yes-No question, at time $t) \neq$ P (IG blinks, at time $t)$. Knowing that the former is smaller or greater than the later can be used in an agent, to modify the probability of its behavior.

Our study focuses on how fast IGs tend to respond to dialog moves of the IFs in terms of (1) facial expressions conveying negative, neutral or positive emotions; (2) eye gaze at the map, at the IF and (3) eye blinks. Results suggest that some valuable information resides in the dialog moves and that the time at which the behavior of the IF occurs matters.

For instance, we found that when the IF is clarifying a point of the conversation, the IG more likely shows a negative face ($F(1, 12) = 54.89$, $p < .01$) but this significantly decreases after two seconds ($F(2, 12) = 6.88$, $p = .01$). On the other hand, the IG is likely to show a positive facial expression in case the IF checks the attention or agreement of the dialogue partner ($F(1, 15) = 2.959$, $p < .01$), after one or two seconds. For the modality of eye gaze we found that the IG more likely looks at the map as soon as the IF clarifies an aspect of the conversation ($F (1, 12) = 1.91$, $p = .19$). The IG more likely watches the map one or two seconds after the IF asked for the confirmation of some information ($F(1, 15) = 3$, $p < .1$).

The small data set does not allow yet designing strong guidelines about what the agent's behaviour should be, but shows that dependencies exist, and that the time frame should be taken into account in these dependencies.

J. Gratch et al. (Eds.): IVA 2006, LNAI 4133, pp. 459–460, 2006.
© Springer-Verlag Berlin Heidelberg 2006

References

1. M. Louwerse, P. Jeuniaux, M. Hoque, J. Wu, and G. Lewis, "Multimodal Communication in Computer-Mediated Map Task Scenarios," presented at The 28th Annual Conference of the Cognitive Science Society, Vancouver, Canada, 3 July 2006.
2. A. Anderson, M. Bader, E. Bard, E. Boyle, G. M. Doherty, S. Garrod, S. Isard, J. Kowtko, J. McAllister, J. Miller, C. Sotillo, H. S. Thompson, and R. Weinert, "The HCRC Map Task Corpus," *Language and Speech*, vol. 34, pp. 351-366, 1991.

The PAC Cognitive Architecture

Lynn C. Miller[1], Stephen J. Read[2], Wayne Zachary[3],
Jean-Christophe LeMentec[3], Vassil Iordanov[3],
Andrew Rosoff[3], and James Eilbert[3]

[1] Annenberg School for Communication, University of Southern California,
Los Angeles, CA 90089-0281, USA
lmiller@usc.edu
[2] Dept. of Psychology, University of Southern California, Los Angeles,
California 90089, USA
read@usc.edu
[3] CHI Systems, Inc., Suite 300, 1035 Virginia Drive, Ft. Washington,
PA 19034, USA
{wzachary, jclementec, viordanov, arosoff,
jeilbert}@chisystems.com

The **PAC** (personality, affect, and cognition) Architecture is a new modeling architecture designed to create Intelligent Virtual Agents with specific personality traits, emotions, and cultural characteristics. PAC integrates theory and data from personality and social psychology, cognitive science, and neuroscience to build a model of personality, emotion, and culture based on fundamental underlying human motivational systems (e.g., dominance, coalition formation, affectional relationships, self-protection, mate choice, parenting, and attachment). These motives are activated by situational cues, but individual agents can have differing baseline activations for different motives. Motives are controlled through a hierarchy of control processes (e.g., Approach and Avoidance systems, Disinhibition/Constraint system) that can be differentially set to capture individual differences. In PAC, the activation dynamics of underlying motives influence both the way in which another agent's behavior is interpreted and the target agent's choice of actions. Thus, the motive dynamics give rise to persistent individual behavioral tendencies, that is, differences in personality.

Emotions are activated both via situational features and through appraisal of what is happening to the agent's currently activated motives. Thus, emotional responses are influenced by individual differences in the agents' motives (their personalities).

Further, the activation of motives and emotions and the enactment of behavior depend on the application of social knowledge, which, in PAC, is encoded in narrative (story-like) structures. These narrative structures are used to make sense of other agent's behavior, as well as generating the agent's possible behaviors. Thus, these story structures convey many aspects of the shared social knowledge that is a key component of culture and can be used to capture cultural differences.

Unlike existing models that attempt to build affective and personality factors as customizations or additions to an underlying formally rational symbolic architecture, in PAC, personality, emotion, and culture directly arise from fundamental motivational systems that are integral to the agent. The structure of PAC allows it to function either as a personality/emotional layer that can be used stand-alone or else integrated with existing constrained-rationality cognitive architectures.

J. Gratch et al. (Eds.): IVA 2006, LNAI 4133, p. 461, 2006.
© Springer-Verlag Berlin Heidelberg 2006

Control of Avatar's Facial Expression Using Fundamental Frequency in Multi-user Voice Chat System

Toshimitsu Miyajima and Kinya Fujita

Graduate School of Tokyo University of Agriculture and Technology,
Koganei, 184-8588 Tokyo, Japan
{tomiyaji, kfujita}@cc.tuat.ac.jp

Abstract. An automatic facial expression control algorithm of CG avatar based on the fundamental frequency of the user's utterance is proposed, in order to facilitate the multi-party casual chat in a multi-user virtual-space voice chat system. The proposed method utilizes the common tendency of the voice fundamental frequency that reflects the emotional activity, especially the strength of the delight. This study simplified the facial expression control problem by limiting the expression in the strength of the delight, because it appears the expression of the delight is the most important to facilitate the casual chat. The problem of using the fundamental frequency is that fundamental frequency varies with intonation as well as emotion; hence the use of the raw fundamental frequency changes the expression of the avatar passionately. Therefore, Emotional Point by emotional Activity (EPa) was defined as the moving-average of the normalized fundamental frequency, to suppress the influence of the intonation. The strength of the delight of the avatar facial expression was linearly controlled using EPa, based on the Facial Action Coding System (FACS). The duration of the moving average was chosen as five seconds experimentally. However, the moving average delays the avatar behavior, and the delay is more serious especially in the response utterance. Therefore, to compensate the delay of the response, the Emotional Point by Response (EPr), was defined using the initial voice volume of the response utterance. EPr was calculated for only the response utterance, which means the utterance just after another user's utterance. The ratio of EPr to EPa was decided experimentally as one to one. The proposed automatic avatar facial expression control algorithm was implemented on the previously developed virtual-space multi-user voice chat system. The subjective evaluation was performed in ten subjects. The each subject in separate room was required to chat with an experimental partner using the system for four minutes and to answer four questions using Likert scale. Throughout the experiments, the subjects reported better impression of the automatic control of facial expression according to the utterances. The facial control using both EPa and EPr demonstrated better performance in terms of naturalness, favorability, familiarity and interactivity, compared to the fixed facial expression, the automatic control using EPa alone and the EPr alone conditions.

Keywords: facial expression, avatar, communication, voice chat.

J. Gratch et al. (Eds.): IVA 2006, LNAI 4133, p. 462, 2006.

Modeling Cognition with a Human Memory Inspired Advanced Neural Controller

D. Panzoli, H. Luga, and Y. Duthen

Toulouse Research Institute for Informatics (IRIT)
Université Toulouse 1, 31042 Toulouse Cedex, France
{panzoli, luga, duthen}@irit.fr

In this paper is studied how the imitation of the structures and the processes of memory can possibly makes cognition arise in a computational model. More precisely, the combination of a perceptron and an associative memory leads to build a scalable behavioral controller expected to reveal *intelligent* behaviors. This approach differs from traditional behavioral animation hybrid architectures[1], in which the agent knowledge is a collection of modeller-defined symbolic objects or frames[2] and its behavior a set of scripts or automatons[3]. To our concern, this prevents the agent from adaptiveness in dynamic environments.

The advanced neural network proposed below is the association of two networks. The vertical "procedural" network is a traditional perceptron that binds perception to action for achieving the agent's *action selection*. Classical gradient methods such as the delta rule can be used to train this network. The horizontal "semantic" layer is an associative network that builds inner representations from assembling perceptions together into patterns. The unsupervised Hebbian rule[4] is used for that purpose.

Simple examples can reveal how the network takes advantage of inner representations to outperform the behaviors traditionally obtained with classical perceptrons.

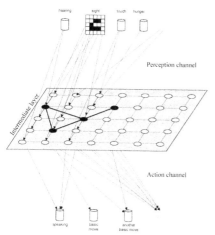

Fig. 1. On the intermediate layer, patterns of perceptions are stored and used

References

1. Toni Conde and Daniel Thalmann. An artificial life environment for autonomous virtual agents with multi-sensorial and multi-perceptive features. *Computer Animation and Virtual Worlds*, 15:311–318, 2004.
2. Marvin Minsky. A framework for representing knowledge. *The psychology of computer vision*, pages 211–277, 1975.
3. Rodney A. Brooks. A robust layered control system for a mobile robot. *IEEE Journal of Robotics and Automation*, pages 14–23, 1986.
4. Donald Hebb. *The Organisation Of Behavior*. Wiley, 1949.

J. Gratch et al. (Eds.): IVA 2006, LNAI 4133, p. 463, 2006.
© Springer-Verlag Berlin Heidelberg 2006

Storytelling – The Difference Between Fantasy and Reality

Guilherme Raimundo, João Cabral, Celso Melo,
Luís C. Oliveira, and Ana Paiva

INESC-ID
Avenida Prof. Cavaco Silva - Taguspark
2780-990 Porto Salvo, Portugal
guilherme.raimundo@tagus.ist.utl.pt, ana.paiva@inesc-id.pt

Abstract. Can we create virtual storytellers that have enough expressive power to convey a story? This paper presents a study comparing the storytelling ability between a virtual and a human storyteller. In order to evaluate it, three means of communication were taken into account: voice, facial expression and gestures. One hundred and eight students from computer engineering watched a video where a storyteller narrated the traditional Portuguese story entitled "O Coelhinho Branco" (The little white rabbit). The students were divided into four groups. Each of these groups saw one video where the storyteller was portrayed either by a synthetic character or a human. The storyteller's voice, no matter the nature of the character, could also be real or synthetic. After the video display, the participants filled a questionnaire where they rated the storyteller performance.

For all dependent variables in Facial Expression, the synthesized version has a significant lower rating than the real one. Of particular interest is that the rating of this communication means is strongly affected not only by the visual expression but also by the voice. In fact, the use of synthesized voice has a significant negative effect when rating the facial expression.

Regarding gestures, only one significant difference was found in the rating of its believability. In this case the synthetic storyteller presents worse performance than the human actor. In the remaining ratings the data suggests that the synthetic gestures have a close performance to the real ones. It is also worthy of notice that gestures rating have always a majority of positive ratings. Similarly to what happens in the facial expression, gestures also seem to be affected by the nature of the used voice, but this time in an inverse manner. Positive gestures ratings percentages have an increase or stay on the same value when the synthesized voice is taken into account.

The voice was the medium that had a clearer significant difference between the real and the synthetic versions , having the real voice higher ratings than its counterpart. Nevertheless, only the satisfaction regarding the synthetic voice obtained a majority of negative ratings. Both the emotion and believability aspect of the synthetic voice gathered a majority of positive ratings.

J. Gratch et al. (Eds.): IVA 2006, LNAI 4133, p. 464, 2006.
© Springer-Verlag Berlin Heidelberg 2006

A Plug-and-Play Framework for Theories of Social Group Dynamics

Matthias Rehm, Birgit Endraß, and Elisabeth André

Augsburg University, Institute of Computer Science
86159 Augsburg, Germany
{rehm, andre}@informatik.uni-augsburg.de
http://mm-werkstatt.informatik.uni-augsburg.de

We present an extensible framework for behavior control of social agents in a multi-agent system that has the following features. It implements a basic repertoire of socio-psychological models of behavior and interpersonal interactions that can be plugged and unplugged at will depending on the specific context of the application. This enables us to test several theories in isolation or combination to increase the transparency of the system and to investigate how the inclusion of a certain theory influences the behavior of the agents. Unlike earlier approaches, our approach is not bound to a specific theory. Thus, it becomes possible to run a simulation with the same set of agents using different theories to compare their effect.

Agent profiles are given in XML, including aspects like name, age, or personality, relationships to other agents in terms of liking, familiarity, trust, and commitment, and attitudes towards objects8 in the environment. The framework was realized in JAVA and can be used either as a stand-alone application to simulate the interactions of sets of pre-defined agents (see Fig. 1 left) or as a control layer for a multi-agent application (see Fig. 1 right). So far, the framework has been tested with the virtual beergarden where agents wander around to meet friends or to build up new relationships. The users are involved as active

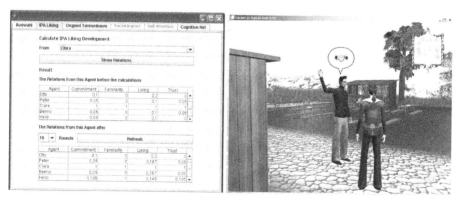

Fig. 1. Left: GUI to select and deselect supported theories. Right: The Beergarden. Agents interactions are controlled by the framework.

J. Gratch et al. (Eds.): IVA 2006, LNAI 4133, pp. 465–466, 2006.
© Springer-Verlag Berlin Heidelberg 2006

participants in the beergarden scenario, freely navigating with a first person view through the scenario, joining or leaving groups of other agents.

In our future work, we will employ the virtual beergarden to perform controlled experiments that investigate (i) whether human observers perceive agents following the framework as socially believable individuals and (ii) how humans respond to encounters with virtual agents opposed to encounters with real humans.

Learning Classifier Systems and Behavioural Animation of Virtual Characters

S. Sanchez, H. Luga, and Y. Duthen

Toulouse Research Institute for Informatics (IRIT)
Université Toulouse 1, 31042 Toulouse Cedex, France
{sanchez, luga, duthen}@irit.fr

Producing intuitive systems for the directing of virtual actors is one of the major objectives of research in virtual animation. So, it is often interesting to conceive systems that enable behavioral animation of autonomous characters, able to correctly fulfill directives from a human user considering their goal and their perception of the virtual environment. Common ways to generate behaviors of such virtual characters use usually determinist algorithm (scripts or automatons [1]). Thus the autonomy of the characters is a fixed routine that cannot adapt to novelty or any situation not previously considered. To make these virtual actors able of adaptation, we propose to combine a behavioral framework (ViBes [2]) and an evolutionist learning system, the Learning Classifier Systems [3]. Using classifiers systems we managed to make a virtual human to learn to select and to cook an aliment in order to eat something. The association of ViBes framework and two trained classifiers systems produced the following real time animation (fig. 1) in a dynamic virtual environment.

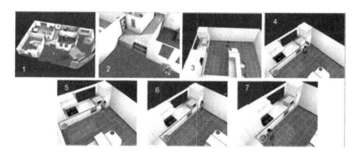

Fig. 1. 1- The virtual character on the left is hungry and it is going towards the kitchen. 2-It handles the closed door of the kitchen. 3- The character grabs a raw apple. 4- It decides to cook it in the oven. 5- It waits the end of the cooking. 6- The character eats the cooked apple. 7- The character trashes the remains of the apple.

References

1. S. Donikian. Hpts : a behaviour modelling language for autonomous agents. In *Fifth International Conference on Autonomous Agents*, pages 401–408, may 2001.
2. Sanchez S., Luga H., Duthen Y., and Balet O. Bringing autonomy to virtual characters. In *ISSADS*, pages 401–408, 2004.
3. Wilson S.W. Classifier fitness based on accuracy. *Evolutionary Computation, 3(2)*, pages 149–175, 1995.

J. Gratch et al. (Eds.): IVA 2006, LNAI 4133, p. 467, 2006.

Using Intelligent Agents to Facilitate Game Based Cultural Familiarization Training

Thomas Santarelli, Charles Barba, Floyd A. Glenn, and Daphne Bogert

CHI Systems, Inc, 1035 Virginia Drive, Suite 300, Fort Washington, PA,
19034 Philadelphia, USA
{tsantarelli, cbarba, fglenn, dbogert}@chisystems.com

Abstract. CHI Systems, under contract to the U. S. Army Research Institute, developed an immersive training system, called Virtual Environment Composable Training for Operational Readiness Training Delivery (VECTOR-TD), which provides scenario-based virtual environments for cultural familiarization. VECTOR-TD was designed to provide a new technology for game-based training in cultural familiarization through the application of scenario-based training. VECTOR-TD integrates the Lithtech Jupiter game engine for the virtual environment and CHI System's iGEN® cognitive agent development toolkit to implement intelligent game characters and integrated performance monitoring. In order for VECTOR-TD to have true long term value to the Army, it was determined that it would be necessary to develop content management tools which would allow Army training personnel to edit and author VECTOR-TD scenarios. To address this, VECTOR-Scenario Editor (VECTOR-SE) was developed based on VECTOR-TD XML-based scripting language to externalize the representation of the training scenario, the behavior of non-player characters (NPCs) within the scenario, and the behavior of the instructor NPC responsible for performance evaluation and After Action Review (AAR). The XML-based language provides direct control of the behavior, dialog, emotional state, and predispositions of NPCs within the scenario. VECTOR-SE was successfully developed to provide content development and management tools that allow non-programmers to author scenarios and manipulate training parameters. VECTOR-SE is based on an instructional design process model and involves the specification of learning objectives, the creation of scenario segments (i.e., vignettes), the authoring of character/trainee dialog, the designation of dialog branching, the placement of characters at game locations, and the designation of when training assistance/remediation will be delivered. The significance of VECTOR-SE is twofold. First, it drastically reduces the time and skill required to develop VECTOR scenarios. Within the original VECTOR project, a 15-minute cultural training scenario was developed which required 2 months of programming and cognitive modeling effort. The same scenario was later implemented in VECTOR-SE in under 3 days. Additional scenarios with comparable complexity have also been implemented using VECTOR-SE and similar significant reductions in development time have been observed. Second, VECTOR-SE makes scenario development or modification accessible to a wider audience of professionals. VECTOR-TD and SE are currently being evaluated at the U.S. Military Academy at West Point.

J. Gratch et al. (Eds.): IVA 2006, LNAI 4133, pp. 468 , 2006.
© Springer-Verlag Berlin Heidelberg 2006

Mind the Body
Filling the Gap Between Minds and Bodies in Synthetic Characters

Marco Vala, João Dias, and Ana Paiva

INESC-ID and IST – TagusPark, Av. Prof. Dr. Cavaco Silva
2780-990 Porto Salvo, Portugal
{marco.vala, joao.assis}@tagus.ist.utl.pt
ana.paiva@inesc-id.pt

Abstract. Interactive virtual environments (IVEs) are inhabited by synthetic characters that guide and engage children in a wide variety of activities, like playing games or learning new things. To build those environments, we need believable autonomous synthetic characters that are able to think and act in very dynamic environments. These characters have often able minds that are limited by the actions that the body can do. In one hand, we have minds capable of creating interesting non-linear behaviour; on the other hand, we have bodies that are limited by the number of animations they can perform. This usually leads to a large planning effort to anticipate possible situations and define which animations are necessary. When we aim at non-linear narrative and non-deterministic plots, there is an obvious gap between what minds can think and what bodies can do. We propose smart bodies as way to fill this gap between minds and bodies. A smart body extends the notion of standard body since it is enriched with semantic information and can do things on its own. The mind still decides what the character should do, but the body chooses how it is done. Smart bodies, like standard bodies, have a model and a collection of animations which are provided by a graphics engine. But they also have access to knowledge about other elements in the world like locations, interaction information and particular attributes. At this point, the notions of interaction spot and action trigger come into play. Interaction spots are specific positions around smart bodies or items where other smart bodies can do particular interactions. Action triggers define automatic reactions which are triggered by smart bodies when certain actions or interactions occur. We use both these constructs to create abstract references for physical elements, to act as a resource and precondition mechanisms, and to simulate physics using rule-based reactions. Smart bodies use all this information to create high-level actions which are used by the minds. Thus, minds operate at a higher level and do not have to deal with low-level body geometry or physics. Smart bodies were used in FearNot!, an antibullying application. In FearNot! children experience virtual stories generated in real-time where they can witness (from a third-person perspective) a series of bullying situations towards a character. Clearly, in such an emergent narrative scenario, minds need to work at a higher-level of abstraction without worrying with bodies and how a particular action is carried out at low-level. Smart bodies provided this abstraction layer. We performed a small study to validate our work in FearNot! with positive results. We believe there may be other applications where smart bodies have much to offer, particularly when using unscripted and non-linear narrative approaches.

J. Gratch et al. (Eds.): IVA 2006, LNAI 4133, p. 469 , 2006.
© Springer-Verlag Berlin Heidelberg 2006

CAB: A Tool for Interoperation Among Cognitive Architectures

Jean-Christophe LeMentec[1] and Wayne Zachary[2]

[1] Caterpillar, Inc., Technical Center, Bldg. E., P.O. Box 1875, Peoria,
IL 61656-1875, USA
Le_Mentec_JC@cat.com
[2] CHI Systems, Inc., Suite 300, 1035 Virginia Drive, Ft. Washington,
PA 19034, USA
wzachary@chisystems.com

The rapid technology development for modeling and simulating human behavior and cognition as Intelligent Virtual Agents (IVAs) has resulted in broad incompatibilities among underlying architectures and specific models. At the same time, the growing interest in practical application of IVAs in defense/aerospace, healthcare, and training systems is bringing demands of easier and cheaper IVA development, and increased re-usability of agent features and components. The Cognitive Architecture Bridge (CAB) is being developed as a new 'middleware' approach to providing multiple levels of interoperability and composibility between and among IVA models and model-components. CAB is designed to allow capabilities from different IVA models and modeling architectures to be integrated into a single 'virtual' IVA model, through four general classes of mechanisms and a common run-time infrastructure.

A procedure call mechanism allows one IVA model to call a procedure from another model, e.g., to perform a specific cognitive task, or to perform an action on the external world. This is a synchronous form of interoperation, where the calling model thread waits for the completion of the function before continuing its own thread of execution. A message passing mechanism allows information to be sent explicitly from one model to another, in the form of a message which may contain any type of data, not only textual information. Unlike procedure calling, this is an asynchronous interoperation mechanism, in which the sending model thread continues its execution without waiting for feedback from the model receiving the message. A distributed memory mechanism enables parts of the memory content of one model to become visible to other models or components of other models. Unlike the procedure call and message passing interaction modes, the distributed memory mode does not require any explicit invocation, but instead allows a model to react to changes in the memory state of another model just as it would react to changes that occur in its own memory contents. Finally, a resource sharing mechanism allows an architectural construct or component to be used by many other components or models, but only by one entity at a time. For example, an eye resource could be used by several partial IVA models to provide vision, but could only be controlled by one of them at a time. A preemption capability is included to reassign the resource to a model having a suddenly higher- priority need for the resource. Existing IVA engines and architectures can be made CAB-compliant through a one-time adaptation to support the CAB application program interfaces.

J. Gratch et al. (Eds.): IVA 2006, LNAI 4133, p. 470, 2006.
© Springer-Verlag Berlin Heidelberg 2006

Author Index

Lecture Notes in Artificial Intelligence (LNAI)